PRAISE FOR
HOLLYWOOD: THE ORAL HISTORY

"Hollywood's ultimate oral history . . . a hard book to put down. The special virtue of Basinger and Wasson's work is its seamlessly sequential organization. . . . With a net cast this wide, many glimmering fish are drawn up." —Adam Gopnik, *The New Yorker*

"A fat, showbiz-nerd-satisfying tome with something for every showbiz-nerd taste. . . . A trove of direct, unselfconscious observations about the times and ways in which these pros worked." —*New York Times*

"Something fresh, revealing, and frequently amusing on nearly every page. . . . *Hollywood* will surely bring joy to any cinephile." —*Wall Street Journal*

"The secrets of Tinseltown burn bright in this collection of interviews culled from the American Film Institute's archives and assembled by film scholar Basinger and author Wasson. . . . The commentary crackles with humorous anecdotes and acerbic insights. . . . The result is a fascinating conversation about Hollywood's magical blending of art and commerce." —*Publishers Weekly* (starred review)

"Surely the most comprehensive portrait of America's dream factory ever committed to paper." —*The Guardian* (London)

"As close to a comprehensive Who's Who of American film as we're likely to see, and as close to a definitive history of American cinema as we've seen so far. An absolute must-read for industry pros and fans alike." —*Booklist* (starred review)

"This book is a movie buff's dream (especially if you love gossip). Even if you think you know a lot about Hollywood and its leading players, I guarantee you'll gain new insight from this book. It's a perfect one to keep in mind when you need gifts for the cinephiles in your life this holiday season."
—*BuzzFeed News*

"Unparalleled in its scope and vision . . . Jeanine Basinger and Sam Wasson are two of our best chroniclers of Hollywood's past, but this collaboration marks their most ambitious work yet. . . . Offers a unique firsthand account of the industry's founding and ever-evolving approaches."
—*Entertainment Weekly*

"Recommended for the large audience of popular culture enthusiasts for whom knowledge of the Hollywood past will enable them better to appreciate occurring and anticipated industry changes."
—*Library Journal* (starred)

"There is something majestic about this book. . . . A must-have for any fan of Hollywood history. . . . Will remain a standard work of reference for many years to come."
—*Los Angeles Review of Books*

"This book is enjoyably absorbing and genuinely unputdownable. . . . Resounding with the multitudinous voices of Hollywood's first century, it delivers a narrative sweep as embracing as any Cinemascope historical drama. . . . These are stories you have never heard before . . . reflections of the famous and the not-so-famous directors and stage hands, major and minor performers, script girls and sound engineers, set and clothing designers, agents and critics—all seamlessly spliced together without a narrative glitch in sight."
—*The Spectator* (London)

"An incredible look inside one of the world's most storied industries . . . honest, surprising, and delightful details about what life is like on and off camera."
—*Town & Country*

"This volume is a gold mine of production details, backroom deals, and inside gossip. There are surprising revelations—e.g., Joan Crawford was more beloved than her reputation for derangement would have one believe—and memorably graphic stories, as when Billy Wilder noted that during the filming of *Greed* (1924), Erich von Stroheim 'stopped shooting for three days because there wasn't enough horseshit in the streets' and forced staff to collect more for him 'because that's what he wanted. Plenty of good horseshit.' . . . Fun firsthand accounts from one hundred years of Hollywood history."　　　　　—*Kirkus Reviews*

"These Hollywood scholars have assembled what is arguably the most comprehensive, gossipy and insightful oral history of Tinseltown ever made."　　　　　—*Globe and Mail* (Toronto)

"A delightful and illuminating account of moviemaking."
　　　　　—*Christian Science Monitor*

"Hollywood aficionados, especially Tinseltown's queer fans, will find it hard to resist this book."　　　　　—*Washington Blade*

HOLLYWOOD

THE ORAL HISTORY

ALSO BY THE AUTHORS

BY JEANINE BASINGER

Shirley Temple

Gene Kelly

Lana Turner

The World War II Combat Film: Anatomy of a Genre

Anthony Mann

The *It's a Wonderful Life* Book

A Woman's View: How Hollywood Spoke to Women, 1930–1960

American Cinema: 100 Years of Filmmaking

Silent Stars

The Star Machine

I Do and I Don't: A History of Marriage in the Movies

The Movie Musical!

BY SAM WASSON

A Splurch in the Kisser: The Movies of Blake Edwards

Fifth Avenue, 5 A.M.: Audrey Hepburn, *Breakfast at Tiffany's*, and the Dawn of the Modern Woman

Paul on Mazursky

Fosse

Improv Nation: How We Made a Great American Art

The Big Goodbye: *Chinatown* and the Last Years of Hollywood

The Path to Paradise: A Francis Ford Coppola Story

HOLLY WOOD

THE ORAL HISTORY

JEANINE BASINGER
and SAM WASSON

HARPER

NEW YORK • LONDON • TORONTO • SYDNEY

HARPER

A hardcover edition of this book was published
in 2022 by HarperCollins Publishers.

HOLLYWOOD: THE ORAL HISTORY. Copyright © 2022 by Jeanine
Basinger and Sam Wasson. All rights reserved. Printed in the
United States of America. No part of this book may be used
or reproduced in any manner whatsoever without written
permission except in the case of brief quotations embodied
in critical articles and reviews. For information, address
HarperCollins Publishers, 195 Broadway, New York, NY 10007.

HarperCollins books may be purchased for educational, business,
or sales promotional use. For information, please email the
Special Markets Department at SPsales@harpercollins.com.

FIRST HARPER PAPERBACKS EDITION PUBLISHED 2023.

Designed by Nancy Singer

Library of Congress Cataloging-in-Publication Data has been applied for.

ISBN 978-0-06-305695-4 (pbk.)

23 24 25 26 27 LBC 5 4 3 2 1

To George Stevens, Jr., Jean Firstenberg, and Bob Gazzale,

and John Basinger—one author's husband, one author's friend.

CONTENTS

INTRODUCTION

In 1969, the American Film Institute held the first of what would be an on-going series of intimate conversations between Hollywood professionals and AFI conservatory students. These became the Harold Lloyd Master Seminars, named in honor of their very first guest.

As Hollywood's day-to-day working insiders, the men and women who have participated in the seminars represent the complete life of Hollywood throughout its history. All are experts in their fields. They are the artists, the craftspeople, the producers, the salesmen. Some are famous, others obscure. They speak with the attitudes of their own time, but they speak with authority.

There have been many attempts to tell the story of Hollywood, but there is simply no other spoken accounting of Hollywood as extensive as AFI's. There never will be.

We were granted total and unprecedented access to the AFI's Harold Lloyd seminars, oral histories, and complete archives, which feature more than three thousand guest speakers and total nearly ten thousand hours of conversation. To our knowledge this represents the only comprehensive firsthand history of Hollywood, which is to say, the true story of Hollywood, told not by outsiders, academics, historians, revisionists, or fantasists prone to legend, but by those who are singularly qualified to understand it, the filmmakers themselves.

THE SPEAKERS

JJ Abrams, *director, producer, writer*

Ken Adam, *art director*

Robert Aldrich, *director, producer*

Scott Alexander, *writer, producer*

Dede Allen, *editor*

Robert Altman, *director, producer, writer*

Preston Ames, *art director*

Paul Thomas Anderson, *director, producer, writer*

Julie Andrews, *actress*

David Ansen, *critic*

Sam Arkoff, *producer*

Hal Ashby, *director, editor*

Gertrude Astor, *actress*

Sean Baker, *director, producer, writer, editor*

Lucille Ball, *actress*

Nira Barab, *actress, director*

Warren Beatty, *actor, producer, director, writer*

William Beaudine, *director*

Rudy Behlmer, *film historian*

Lawrence Bender, *producer*

Ben Benjamin, *agent*

Jack Benny, *actor*

Pandro Berman, *producer, studio executive*

Elmer Bernstein, *composer*

Bernardo Bertolucci, *director, writer, producer*

Kathryn Bigelow, *director, producer, writer*

Henry Blanke, *producer*

Jason Blum, *producer*

Budd Boetticher, *director, writer*

Peter Bogdanovich, *director, writer, producer, film historian*

Margaret Booth, *editor*

Robert Boyle, *art director*

John Brahm, *director*

Mel Brooks, *director, producer, writer*

Richard Brooks, *director, producer, writer*

David Brown, *producer*

Jerry Bruckheimer, *producer*

Charles Burnett, *director, producer, writer*

Michael Caine, *actor*

Ridgeway Callow, *assistant director*

Donn Cambern, *editor*

James Cameron, *director, producer, writer*

Dyan Cannon, *actress*

Marie Cantin, *executive producer*

Mark Canton, *producer, studio executive*

Frank Capra, *director, producer, writer*

Teete Carle, *publicist*

Leslie Caron, *actress*

Diahann Carroll, *actress*

John Cassavetes, *director, producer, writer, actor*

Charles Champlin, *journalist, critic*

David Chasman, *studio executive*

David Chierichetti, *costume designer, film historian*

Caldecot Chubb, *producer*

Michael Cimino, *director, producer, writer*

Shirley Clarke, *director*

George Clooney, *director, actor, producer, writer*

Anne V. Coates, *editor*

Merian C. Cooper, *producer, director*

Roger Corman, *producer, director, writer*

Stanley Cortez, *director of photography*

Sherrill Corwin, *exhibitor*

Joel Cox, *editor*

John Cromwell, *director*

Floyd Crosby, *director of photography*

Cameron Crowe, *director, producer, writer*

George Cukor, *director, producer*

Frank Darabont, *director, producer, writer*

Bette Davis, *actress*

Olivia de Havilland, *actress*

Bruce Dern, *actor*

I. A. L. Diamond, *writer*

Denise Di Novi, *producer*

Edward Dmytryk, *director*

Stanley Donen, *director, producer*

Gordon Douglas, *director*

Melvyn Douglas, *actor*

Philip Dunne, *writer, producer*

Minta Durfee, *actress*

Allan Dwan, *director*

Clint Eastwood, *director, actor, producer, composer*

Blake Edwards, *director, producer, writer*

Harlan Ellison, *writer*

Robert Evans, *studio executive, producer*

Peter Falk, *actor*

Jon Favreau, *director, producer, writer, actor*

Paul Feig, *actor, director, producer, writer*

Verna Fields, *editor*

Lucy Fisher, *studio executive, producer*

George Folsey, *director of photography*

Henry Fonda, *actor*

Jane Fonda, *actress*

Carl Foreman, *writer*

Sidney Franklin, *director, producer*

Mike Frankovich, *studio executive, producer*

Arthur Freed, *producer, songwriter*

Morgan Freeman, *actor*

Friz Freleng, *cartoonist*

William Friedkin, *director, producer, writer*

Sam Fuller, *director, producer, writer*

Lee Garmes, *director of photography*

Tay Garnett, *director*

Bob Gazzale, *American Film Institute president*

Larry Gelbart, *writer*

Hoot Gibson, *actor*

Lillian Gish, *actress*

Richard Gladstein, *producer*

Jeff Goldblum, *actor*

Lawrence Gordon, *producer*

Lee Grant, *actress, director*

Brian Grazer, *producer*

Johnny Green, *composer, conductor, music director*

Peter Guber, *studio executive, producer*

Conrad Hall, *director of photography*

Tom Hanks, *actor, producer, director, writer*

Aljean Harmetz, *journalist*

Curtis Harrington, *director*

Henry Hathaway, *director*

Howard Hawks, *director, producer*

Edith Head, *costume designer*

Amy Heckerling, *director, producer, writer*

Jerome Hellman, *producer*

Buck Henry, *writer, actor, director*

Jim Henson, *director, producer, writer, puppeteer*

Katharine Hepburn, *actress*

Charlton Heston, *actor*

Charles Higham, *film historian*

George Roy Hill, *director*

Arthur Hiller, *director*

Alfred Hitchcock, *director, producer, writer*

Dustin Hoffman, *actor*

Dennis Hopper, *actor, director, writer*

Harry Horner, *art director*

Ron Howard, *director, actor, producer*

James Wong Howe, *director of photography*

Gale Ann Hurd, *producer*

John Huston, *director, producer, actor, writer*

Nessa Hyams, *casting director*

Rick Ingersoll, *office boy, publicist*

Paul Ivano, *director of photography*

James Ivory, *director, writer, producer*

Honore Janney, *script timer*

Nunnally Johnson, *writer, producer, director*

Neil Jordan, *director, producer, writer*

Stan Kamen, *agent*

Fay Kanin, *writer*

Bronislau Kaper, *composer*

Larry Karaszewski, *writer, producer*

Jeffrey Katzenberg, *studio executive*

Elia Kazan, *director, producer, writer, actor*

Diane Keaton, *actress*

Harvey Keitel, *actor*

Gene Kelly, *actor, choreographer, director*

Kathleen Kennedy, *producer, studio executive*

Henry King, *director*

Arthur Knight, *film historian*

Don Knox, *film historian*

Howard W. Koch, *producer, studio executive*

Arnold Kopelson, *producer*

László Kovács, *director of photography*

Stanley Kramer, *producer, director, writer*

Milton Krasner, *director of photography*

Richard LaGravenese, *writer, director*

Gavin Lambert, *writer, critic*

Jon Landau, *producer*

John Landis, *director, producer, writer*

Fritz Lang, *director, producer*

Sherry Lansing, *studio executive, producer*

Alex Lasker, *writer*

John Lasseter, *director, producer, writer, studio executive*

David Lean, *director, producer, writer*

Alfred Lebovitz, *camera operator*

Spike Lee, *director, producer, writer, actor*

Mitchell Leisen, *director, producer, costume designer*

Charles LeMaire, *costume designer*

Jack Lemmon, *actor*

Mervyn LeRoy, *director, producer*

Joseph E. Levine, *producer*

Barry Levinson, *director, producer, writer*

Jerry Lewis, *director, producer, writer, actor*

Lynne Littman, *director*

Harold Lloyd, *actor*

Norman Lloyd, *actor*

Joseph Losey, *director, producer, writer*

Jean Louis, *costume designer*

David Lynch, *director, producer, writer*

Barré Lyndon, *writer*

Adrian Lyne, *director*

Ranald MacDougall, *writer*

Shirley MacLaine, *actress*

Rouben Mamoulian, *director, producer*

Abby Mann, *writer*

Daniel Mann, *director*

Michael Mann, *director, producer, writer*

Frank Marshall, *producer, director*

Garry Marshall, *director, producer, writer, actor*

Penny Marshall, *director, producer, writer, actress*

Mardik Martin, *writer*

Sam Marx, *writer*

Paul Mazursky, *director, producer, writer, actor*

Leo McCarey, *director, producer, writer*

John McTiernan, *director, producer*

Mike Medavoy, *studio executive, producer, agent*

Daniel Melnick, *studio executive, producer*

Sue Mengers, *agent*

Ismail Merchant, *producer*

Lewis Milestone, *director, producer*

Anthony Minghella, *director, producer, writer*

Vincente Minnelli, *director, producer*

Hal Mohr, *director of photography*

A. D. Murphy, *journalist*

Marcia Nasatir, *studio executive, producer*

David Newman, *writer*

Mike Nichols, *director, producer, actor*

Jack Nicholson, *actor, director, writer*

Alex North, *composer*

Lynda Obst, *producer*

Barrie Osborne, *producer*

Michael Ovitz, *agent*

Al Pacino, *actor*

Alan Pakula, *director, producer, writer*

Alexander Payne, *director, producer, writer*

Gregory Peck, *actor*

Jordan Peele, *director, producer, writer, actor*

Oren Peli, *producer, writer, director*

Arthur Penn, *director, producer*

Eleanor Perry, *writer*

Jon Peters, *producer, studio executive*

Julia Phillips, *producer*

Michael Phillips, *producer*

David Picker, *studio executive, producer*

Frank Pierson, *writer, director*

Eric Pleskow, *studio executive*

Walter Plunkett, *costume designer*

Sidney Poitier, *actor, director*

Roman Polanski, *director, writer, producer, actor*

Sydney Pollack, *director, producer, actor*

Tom Pollock, *studio executive, lawyer*

Abraham Polonsky, *director, writer*

István Poór, *director*

Edward Pressman, *producer*

John Ptak, *agent*

David Puttnam, *producer, studio executive*

Mario Puzo, *writer*

Anthony Quinn, *actor*

Bob Rafelson, *director, producer, writer*

David Raksin, *composer*

Irving Rapper, *director*

Rob Reiner, *director, producer, writer, actor*

Walter Reisch, *writer*

Ray Rennahan, *director of photography*

Thomas Rickman, *writer*

Owen Roizman, *director of photography*

Robert Rosen, *educator, film historian*

Lee Rosenberg, *film agent*

Leonard Rosenman, *composer*

Hal Rosson, *director of photography*

Al Ruddy, *producer*

Alan Rudolph, *director, producer, writer*

Richard Rush, *director, producer, writer*

David O. Russell, *director, producer, writer*

Ann Rutherford, *actress*

Joseph Ruttenberg, *director of photography*

Gary Rydstrom, *rerecording mixer, sound designer*

Adela Rogers St. Johns, *writer*

Waldo Salt, *writer*

Andrew Sarris, *critic*

Dore Schary, *producer, studio executive, writer*

Maximilian Schell, *actor*

Richard Schickel, *critic, director, producer, film historian*

John Schlesinger, *director*

Paul Schrader, *director, producer, writer, critic*

Budd Schulberg, *writer*

Howard Schwartz, *director of photography*

Martin Scorsese, *director, producer, writer, film historian*

George Seaton, *director, producer, writer*

John Seitz, *director of photography*

Irene Mayer Selznick, *daughter of Louis B. Mayer, Broadway producer*

Joyce Selznick, *casting director*

Irene Sharaff, *costume designer*

Hannah Sheeld, *script girl*

Sidney Sheldon, *writer*

Vincent Sherman, *director*

Geoffrey Shurlock, *Production Code director*

Joel Silver, *producer*

Don Simpson, *producer*

John Singleton, *director, producer, writer*

Stacey Snider, *studio executive*

Steven Soderbergh, *director, producer, writer, director of photography, editor*

Steven Spielberg, *director, producer, writer*

Lynn Stalmaster, *casting director*

Donald Ogden Stewart, *writer*

Vittorio Storaro, *director of photography*

Meryl Streep, *actress*

Barbra Streisand, *actress, director, producer, writer, composer, songwriter*

Howard Strickling, *publicist*

Karl Struss, *director of photography*

Gordon Stulberg, *studio executive, lawyer*

H. N. Swanson, *agent*

Anthea Sylbert, *costume designer*

Richard Sylbert, *art director*

Ned Tanen, *studio executive, producer*

Quentin Tarantino, *director, writer, producer*

Norman Taurog, *director*

Ella Taylor, *journalist*

Joan Tewkesbury, *writer, director*

Richard Thorpe, *director*

Emily Torchia, *publicist*

Robert Towne, *writer, director, producer*

François Truffaut, *director, writer, producer*

Dalton Trumbo, *writer*

Camille Tucker, *writer*

Kenneth Turan, *critic*

Larry Turman, *producer*

William Tuttle, *makeup artist*

Harry Ufland, *agent, producer*

Jack Valenti, *Motion Picture Association of America president*

Toni Vellani, *producer, AFI conservatory director*

Gore Vidal, *writer*

King Vidor, *director, producer*

Paula Wagner, *studio executive, producer, agent*

Robert Wagner, *actor*

Hal Wallis, *producer, studio executive*

Raoul Walsh, *director, producer*

Harry Warren, *songwriter*

Michael Wayne, *son of John Wayne, producer*

Lawrence Weingarten, *producer*

Eric Weissmann, *lawyer*

Gareth Wigan, *studio executive, producer, agent*

Crane Wilbur, *actor, writer*

Billy Wilder, *director, writer, producer*

John Williams, *composer*

Irwin Winkler, *producer*

Robert Wise, *director, producer, editor*

Natalie Wood, *actress*

Stephen Woolley, *producer*

Fay Wray, *actress*

William Wyler, *director, producer*

Frank Yablans, *studio executive, producer*

Saul Zaentz, *producer*

Steven Zaillian, *writer, director, producer*

Richard Zanuck, *studio executive, producer*

Robert Zemeckis, *director, producer, writer*

Fred Zinnemann, *director, producer*

Laura Ziskin, *producer, studio executive*

HOLLYWOOD

THE ORAL HISTORY

CHAPTER 1

BEGINNINGS

RIDGEWAY CALLOW: This is the true story of Hollywood. The most cruel, most despicable town in the world. Ruthless. Completely heartless.

RICHARD SCHICKEL: . . . or at least that's the way people like to picture it . . .

STANLEY DONEN: . . . but it's a myth . . .

GEORGE CUKOR: . . . there are all sorts of stories . . . usually untrue . . .

STANLEY DONEN: . . . because it was simply a group of people who kept working there in those pictures, going from one job to another . . .

HOWARD STRICKLING: . . . everything done carefully, thoughtfully, and in real detail. Everybody working together. We got on the same page, film by film. It was a business made up of creative, intelligent, hardworking people all united around our product. Our films. Our mutual interests.

RAOUL WALSH: Work. That's the true story of Hollywood. But who wants to hear it? They're looking for something else. Who took off whose panties behind the piano while the director shot the producer in the head? People want to know stuff like that, even if it isn't true.

BRONISLAU KAPER: Hollywood drew envy. All that money and power. People liked to ridicule Hollywood. "Oh, that's Hollywood." Everything is "typical Hollywood." "Oh, he's going Hollywood." Nobody says "He's going San Francisco." No. "He's going Hollywood," where everyone really secretly wanted to go.

GEORGE CUKOR: Hollywood throughout the years was always a real stop on the bus. People were very interested in everything that went on in Hollywood. It was rich. It was exciting. It had all the glamorous people. Everybody wanted to come to Hollywood. But when they got here, they found these glamorous people had to get up at six in the morning and work until seven at night. From that point of view, it was a little disappointing.

FRANK CAPRA: Hollywood! What the hell good could come out of a Hollywood? Three thousand miles west of the Hudson River, where nothing west of the Hudson was any good anyhow? A little town way out in the west, a little bit of a dusty burg called Hollywood? Ah, but here film was being made, being sold, being canned, being shipped. We invented it. We created it . . . this enormous thing that has the tremendous power to move and influence. An art form and a business. Hollywood!

VINCENT SHERMAN: What started out as a nickel-and-dime, honky-tonk business grew to be a great industry. It gave employment to many people doing all kinds of jobs, all of which had to be coordinated and put together. Some great films were turned out during this period. A town was created as a result of the picture business: Hollywood. I would say that the films that Hollywood made stood at the forefront of the entire world. Hollywood became a legend.

ALLAN DWAN: In the beginning, of course, it wasn't Hollywood. Films were being made all over the country: New York City, New Jersey, Florida, Chicago, St. Louis, Arizona and New Mexico, Oregon, San Francisco, and San Diego. Everywhere. And nobody knew they were going to work in the movies because there was no such thing, really, when they were born. Everybody originally planned to do some other thing to make a living.

HAL MOHR: You couldn't dream about being in a business that didn't exist yet.

TAY GARNETT: As a matter of fact, I don't think it ever occurred to anybody that the movies would ever *be* a business.

LEO MCCAREY: I planned to be a lawyer. I even practiced. I started out very young, and they mistook me for the office boy. I was a very poor lawyer. A discouraging factor in my legal career is that I lost every case. One day a client was chasing me down the street. I saw a friend of mine who called out, "What are you doing, Leo?" And I said, still running, "Practicing law."

RAOUL WALSH: I was an actor. I was terrible. Just terrible. It's a wonder I wasn't shot.

CHARLES LEMAIRE: I was a song plugger. I was a soda jerk. I did all kinds of things.

GERTRUDE ASTOR: I was kind of silly when I was young. I learned to play the trombone, first on a valve trombone and then on a slide trombone. And then I was told by everyone that ladies didn't do that. Ladies didn't play, you know, wind instruments, or they weren't ladies.

FRITZ LANG: I ran away from home when I was eighteen or nineteen. Anybody who wants to be somebody should run away from home. I wanted to be a painter, so I ran to Paris. I made a little money doing a stupid comedy act in a cabaret.

HOOT GIBSON: I never had plans to be anything. I was born August 6, 1892, in a small town called Tekamah, Nebraska, on the eastern side of the Rosebud reservation. I was raised there. I went to school there through the seventh grade. I started riding my first horse when I was two and a half years old—well, my first pony. The country around Tekamah was made up of horses, cattle, and farming. I never took to farming very well, and cattle weren't anything to me, but I was crazy about horses. I was always with the horses. That was my life. I just planned to live with horses and ride horses.

FRED ZINNEMANN: Actually, I'm a disappointed musician.

HOWARD HAWKS: I studied engineering in college . . . well, I didn't *like* engineering. In my vacation from school time I drove race cars and I did a lot of flying.

EDITH HEAD: Very simply, I lived in mining camps until I was ready to go to high school. I never went to grade school. I do not know the multiplication tables. I do not know the names of the capitals of the states. I know nothing that I should know. I had to tutor to get into high school, and then I went to California at Berkeley for four years and took my Master's at Stanford. I majored in Romance languages, French and Spanish. I planned to be a language teacher.

FRANK CAPRA: I went to Caltech to become an engineer. That was what I planned to be. It seemed to be dream enough.

TAY GARNETT: I was a cartoonist.

HARRY WARREN: I was always crazy about show business. I was a candy boy in the theater. I was an usher. I always wanted to be in show business. I don't know why. Show business meant the theater, of course, not movies.

ALLAN DWAN: I planned to be an electrical engineer. I'd studied for it, and graduated from the university and was busy at it long before I thought of moving pictures.

HAL MOHR: You may wonder how I got into the picture business. Or how anyone got into the picture business. Well, there was no way of getting in. There was no American Film Institute or university courses or anything of that nature . . . even any literature of any kind that had information in it. It was a case of finding the business. Stumbling into it if you weren't looking to be in it. Forcing your way in if you did. That was it.

HENRY HATHAWAY: To think about being in movies, first you had to see a movie. My mother sang for illustrated slides in Sid Grauman's first theater in San Francisco. If they had slides with river scenes and riverboats, for instance, she'd sing "Down upon the Swanee River." Sometimes she went out on the road, and once she was in San Diego with some company and they went broke and she was on her own with no way to get home. That was in about 1908. She looked in the want ads and saw an ad for a motion picture company that was forming. She applied for the job and got it. It was working with Broncho Billy [Anderson] . . . he was making those westerns, so my mother was suddenly in the movies, and the first motion picture that I ever saw was down on what they called the Promenade in Long Beach. They had two theaters there. There was a concession on that you paid a nickel or a dime to go into, and there was a little platform that resembled the observation car on a train. And it had a fence, and you're sitting on the chairs like on the rear end of a train . . . you know, on the back end they had an observation car where you could sit and look at the scenery. There were eight chairs, and you went into the little theater and sat in those chairs. You were facing a screen in front of you, about eight feet across. You kind of sat up close to it. From behind you they projected on the screen a train trip. So you're sitting there on the observation train, and you're seeing a shot they took of going through woods and going through trees and going through gullies and going through gaps. You're sitting on the train watching what's going away from you as you pass by. And they had the sound of *clickety-clack*. I don't know how they got it, 'cause they didn't have sound in those days, of course. That was the first motion picture I ever saw.

HAL MOHR: The first movie I ever saw was a shot of a railroad train coming towards the camera and passing the camera. Now, I was twelve years old, and I'd had magic lanterns and all that sort of thing, and I was an inquisitive kid. I wanted to know how everything worked. So when I saw this magic lantern on the screen and saw the train actually coming by with smoke coming out of the smokestack and everything, that was a miracle to me. I had no idea how it was done. So that became the aim of my life, to find out how that picture was made to move. It's been the aim of my life ever since. . . .

So I got a part-time job, and the first man I ever worked for in San Francisco was [producer] Sol Lesser. Sol had a little junk film exchange, and I went to work for him. I wanted to find out what made these pictures move, so it was a natural course to go to the source. I got a job as a film inspector. When the film would come back from the theaters, we would rewind the reels by hand on rewinds and run the film through our fingers, feeling the sprocket holes on the edges, and if there was a crack in the sprocket hole, we'd stop and cement a little piece of celluloid on the sprocket hole so the film wouldn't tear. I would go through fifty or sixty reels of film in the course of a day, winding this through my fingers and making splices.

I worked as an editor—we called them film cutters. I did that for about a year, and I was still just a kid. I did a lot of photography whenever I could. I started learning all aspects of filmmaking. When a guy I worked for came down here to Los Angeles and went to work for Universal, I wandered down here, too. It was just about that time that the company was moving from Gower Street in Hollywood out to what is now Universal City. Universal became my home studio for many, many years. I was here for the opening of Universal Studios, which was in the winter of 1914–1915. No, maybe 1915–1916. No, it was 1914–1915.

LEO MCCAREY: A friend of mine was an actor in pictures early on. I'd met him playing golf. I asked him how you could break into the movies. I'd take any kind of a job, I told him. So he got me a job keeping the script. I was a script girl and didn't even know it! At the end of the picture, they were measuring me for jodhpurs!

MARGARET BOOTH: Well, my brother was an actor on the Broadway stage, and he came out here to be in pictures and he was only here three months when he was killed. My mother and I were left alone. I was just sixteen years old. They said at the studio that they would help us out during the summer by giving me a job in their lab. I went there to work because I had to. It was Griffith Studio on Sunset and Franklin. [D. W.] Griffith worked there, Mary Pickford worked there, Douglas Fairbanks, Sr., worked there. I was learning to cut negative, and I used to look out and see all these people. I loved it so much that I never wanted to go to college or anything.

RAOUL WALSH: I was trying to make a living as an actor. I dropped into an agency one time run by a fellow by the name of Bill Gregory. He wasn't there, but his secretary was, and she said, rather hesitant, "Mr. Walsh, would you consider a job in moving pictures?" You see, in those days, stage actors never went near moving pictures. They wanted no part of it. But I had nothing else going on, so I said yes. "Can you ride a horse?" she asked. I said, "That's my middle name."

GERTRUDE ASTOR: I was from Ohio. That was my home. I came out here because of sort of a bad left lung. I was sent here to get well, and it was so wonderful, so warm and nice out here all the time, you know, that I got slowly better and beat all that and everything, and then I didn't want to go back. I wanted to stay here. In those days, Los Angeles—the whole area—was so beautiful, like a garden. So somebody took me for the first time to a picture studio, and it was in an old barn off Vine Street there in Hollywood. It was Universal. And it just looked like an old horse shed or something. The way you opened the door—there was a piece of old rope hanging there, and you pulled on that rope and stepped into the place, and then you went down into where they were shooting. They were making silent pictures, but boy, was it noisy in there! I thought it looked like a great lot of fun. I just figured the thing for me to do was stay here and do that myself, you know? Have all that fun. I didn't know if there was a future in it or anything, but I was young enough that I could handle myself and do what I had to do. I got in with people who knew the works already, and I started to work extra. I worked with Griffith's group in *The Scarlet Letter.* . . . I worked a day on that, and I got five dollars. Gee, for five dollars you could live swell out here then.

PANDRO BERMAN: My father was sent to Kansas City, Missouri, as the branch manager of the old Metro Film Corporation long before MGM was ever heard of. I used to go around with my father to visit small neighborhood theaters at night when he used to sell film. Then he went to work for the World Film Corporation in 1916 as manager of the New York office, but before very long he was promoted to be general manager of sales for the entire United States, and that was when his career actually got underway.

I remember quite clearly that my father organized and conducted the first junket that I think ever happened in the film business. He brought the censors from the various film-censoring departments of the various states, which at the time were numerous, to California at the expense of Universal to see one of those Erich von Stroheim pictures, which was considered at that time to be slightly dangerous censorwise. Somehow or other, he got them, as the result of this junket, to be more lenient in their attitude in the various states. He was a great salesman—a quality, incidentally, which I inherited none of. All of my relatives in the business used to sing the same song to me: "Never become a film salesman. If you ever want to work in this business, learn to *make* pictures, because that is the only place you will ever get any money." So naturally I had my eyes set on that. I immediately persuaded my father to forgo any college plans that he had for me, which included the Wharton School of Business at the University of Pennsylvania, and permit me to come to California at the age of eighteen in 1923, where he arranged for me to get a job at $25 a week as a flunky or third assistant director. And the first job I ever had, I worked for a director called Mal St. Clair.

LEWIS MILESTONE: It was the war—World War I, that is—that brought me into the army, and I worked with the Signal Corps, and we had a motion picture lab there, and that's where I started, really. By accident. That's where I was introduced to films. Because we were making all sorts of pictures, you know, for the soldiers. On how to keep your teeth clean and all that business that the army gives you. . . . I assisted a great cameraman by the name of Lucien Andriot. Everybody in our outfit was from California. . . . I came out of the war in 1919 and went to California, and I got into this business. . . . It was a new business: the motion picture industry.

FRANK CAPRA: I fulfilled my dream and graduated from Caltech as a chemical engineer, but when I came back to California after World War I, I couldn't get a job in my field. I just couldn't get a job anyplace, but I needed to work, so I got a job in show business as a gagman. For three years I had to write funny stuff for stand-up comics. A gag was something you had to think up, and in many cases you had to think up stuff to pantomime. That was harder than being funny with words, you see, because you didn't have the words to help you. So I was thinking in humorous ways before I got to silent films. I was saving the money they paid me because I had in mind going back to Caltech and getting my doctorate in physics. Then I was offered an opportunity in the movies, and the money was better, and I thought, Well, if they wanted to pay me for those silly little things I was going to do . . . well, fine. I said to myself, "This is crazy. A graduate of Caltech who's never seen the inside of a studio, who's never been backstage, is making films for people? That's crazy. It doesn't make sense. Science, yes. But films?" It was one of the reasons I got what I wanted, because I could be arrogant. This wasn't to be my career. I didn't have to kiss anybody's ass. I didn't care. If they wanted to pay me for the crap I was doing, they must be nuts, but I didn't care.

GEORGE FOLSEY: Like most people in those days, I got into the picture business quite by accident. I was an office boy in a magazine company housed in the Flatiron Building in New York . . . 23rd Street and Fifth Avenue. There was a number of boys there who had jobs similar to mine, and I looked around and figured that I didn't have the education to compete with them and I didn't know how I was going to get it. I thought I'd better get out of there, because I had to get a better job. So I quit and went to an agency that sent me up to a place called the Famous Players Film Company. I had no idea what it was. The man said I could go to work, but I had to start that afternoon. Being a kid, I had wanted the afternoon off, but I said I'd stay. I worked until six o'clock and then went home. The next morning I got to work at a quarter to eight. The office, which had been absolutely devoid of people yesterday, was now getting rapidly filled with lots of people. In among them came Mary Pickford, Marguerite Clark, Harold Lockwood, Pauline Frederick, Hazel Dawn. These were all people

I recognized, and I was enthralled. I always remember Justine Johnstone. She was a Follies girl and is now a biochemist . . . which is a hell of a switch.

After a while, I started looking around to see which way I might be able to make steps. At that time, there were no assistant cameramen, at least not in New York. Ed Porter, who photographed *The Great Train Robbery*, was there. He was also part owner of the Famous Players Film Company, and he was a pretty busy guy. He had to load his own magazines, and he'd have to cut the film and sometimes develop it, and that plus all his administrative duties . . . he needed help to load the magazines and bring them out to him and unload the other ones and put them in cans. I saw a great opportunity in that.

WALTER PLUNKETT: After I graduated from the University of California at Berkeley and I had told my dad being a lawyer was not for me, he nicely gave me a ticket to New York and sent me there. During college I was part of a little theater group. I acted, but I wasn't a very good actor. In New York, I played a couple of small parts. In college, I had an interest in artwork, so I had become the "art director" for my little theater group, doing scenery and costumes. So I eked out a living by doing some costume designs for dancers and singers that I had met. Since things weren't working out in New York, I came back to Hollywood in 1925. I worked extra in quite a few pictures, and I again added to that by doing some commercial art, little brochures and things for shops that were around in Hollywood, and a few costumes again for dancers and whoever might want something.

Then in 1926, a designer I knew socially called me and said they had asked him to come over and possibly to organize a wardrobe department at the FBO [the film booking and distribution company that was acquired by Joseph P. Kennedy, Sr., in 1926], but they didn't want to pay anything like his money. He suggested that they talk to me, so they called me and I made the appointment and went over, and they gave me the job. I think it was $75 a week, and I thought it was a tremendous amount of money at that time. It was so great to be working every day and guaranteed months ahead of time. In college, I had taken a course in the history of costume because I thought it might be of interest to me as an actor. If I should ever develop into a director or producer, it would be nice to know. So I felt I could do the job.

PAUL IVANO: After I got gassed on the front in World War I in 1918 and I came out of the hospital, they wanted to give me an honorable discharge. I said, "Why? The war isn't over. Isn't there something else I could do?" They said, "Do you know anything about photography?" I said, "Well, I've taken pictures since I was eight years old. My father was a surgeon and a doctor and a very good amateur photographer, and I used to play around with him." And so they put me in the photographic service of the American Signal Corps in Paris, where I met a lot of Hollywood people. I wound up with a guy who was supposed to be a motion picture cameraman, but he didn't know anything about it. So I asked him, "Where did you shoot pictures?" And he said, "Don't tell anybody. I wasn't a cameraman. I was a projectionist in Chicago." I said, "Well, this is different. Go sit down, and I'll shoot the stuff." I had never shot any motion pictures in my life, but I shot them. After all, it's just photography. The next day the developing sergeant, who was in charge of the lab, said, "Who shot this stuff?" I told him the other guy, but he said, "No, this stuff is too good." When I admitted I did it, he just said, "From now on, you're the motion picture cameraman." That's how I started.

HENRY BLANKE: My father was a very famous German painter, Wilhelm Blanke, and one day, Paul Davidson, the president of the UFA [the German film production company], called up our secretary and says, "We want Mr. Blanke to do a poster." My mother said, "My husband doesn't do posters," but they kept on calling, calling, calling and Davidson says, "I would like to come out and see Mr. Blanke. I own forty paintings by him myself. We are doing a religious subject which he would be marvelous for." So they came out. They had coffee. And my father said he would make a little poster sketch, and Davidson felt obliged to say to me, "If you ever want to work in motion pictures, please come and see me." That was the end of it.

After half a year—I was studying music and art right after the war, which Germany had lost—I went to Davidson, and I said, "You told me that if I want a job, I can have it," and I got the job. Then he said, "What do you want to do?" I said, "I only want to work with one man, Ernst Lubitsch." He says, "Lubitsch is now making *The Mountain Cat* in Bavaria. When he comes back, I'll get you together. In the meantime, you can work here with So-and-So and So-and-So." So this was the very beginning. I worked myself up the ladder. I carried coffee and did everything for everybody.

Then I read in the paper that Paul Davidson and Ernst Lubitsch had left UFA and had joined the European Film Alliance to make pictures. So I went to the EFA studio, where Lubitsch was now starting *The Wife of Pharaoh*, and I went to Davidson. He says, "What are you doing here? You are under contract with the other studio." I said, "I quit." And he took me by the arm, took me downstairs into the studio where Lubitsch was working, and he told Lubitsch the whole story. And Lubitsch says, "Come with me." And I was with him there from that day on. And after a few pictures, *The Wife of Pharaoh* and *The Flame*, Lubitsch asked me, "Would you like to go to America?" And I said, "Yes." And I had to ask my parents because I was underage, and they said, "Go ahead. God bless you." And that's how I arrived in 1922, in December, in America, when I had just turned twenty-one years old.

HOOT GIBSON: I got a job at the Owl Drug Company. I delivered things, riding a bicycle. That is where I got the name of "Hoot." It came from "Owl." The boys started calling me Hoot Owl, and then it got down to Hoot, and Hoot has been with me ever since.

I enlisted in the Tank Corps in World War I. I decided I wanted to do anything but walk, so I wanted to ride one of those iron horses. So I enlisted in the Tank Corps, and I never walked so many miles in my life. I came out of the Tank Corps as a sergeant in 1919.

I went right out to Universal, where I had done stunt riding before the war. I got a part in a picture—a two-reeler—with Breezy Eason directing. I had a juvenile part in this picture, and it was bigger than the lead. Carl Laemmle [founder of Universal Pictures] saw the picture, and he wanted to know who that guy was. Somebody told him that I had been there with Harry Carey before and played a couple of parts that Harry Carey had given me—first man that had ever given me a part—and Laemmle said, "Well, give him a lead."

That's the way I got started in two-reel westerns at Universal in 1919. I made over forty westerns in 1919 and part of 1920—altogether they ran about sixty westerns, and I directed and played in the lead in about thirty of them. Then I was graduated into full-length features, with Jack Ford—who is now John Ford, but we always called him Jack—as my first director. From then on I made eight pictures a year at Universal, up through and including 1930.

HOWARD HAWKS: I got a job as a propman during the summers. I kept hanging around. I wrote titles for pictures over at Famous Players. They wanted to make forty pictures, and they asked me to find forty stories. I said, "If you've got some money, I can find forty stories." So I bought two Zane Greys, two Rex Beaches, two Jack Londons, two Joseph Conrads. It was easy. You had the choice of everything. And I bought forty stories, and we made them, and they made more money than that company had ever made before. Then I went over to Metro, and I had charge of seventy writers. Then I got bored with that. Why work for twenty directors, each making about three pictures a year, when I could just go out and work on one for myself? So I quit. I went out to play golf, and I ran into the head of Fox and he said, "What are you doing?" and I said, "Playing golf." He said, "No, I mean what are you *doing*?" and I said, "Playing golf." He said, "Well, aren't you working?" and I said, "No," and he said, "Do you want to work for Fox?" I said, "I don't want to do that." . . . I meant "just do what I have been doing." "I want to direct." So he said, "Well, bring in any story you want to do." I tried a very dramatic, downbeat kind of story, *Road to Glory*, and made the film. He said, "You showed you could direct, but for Christ's sake make a picture people want to look at." So I did a comedy story called *Fig Leaves*, and it got its cost back in one theater alone. And I always remembered what he said to me . . . make a picture people want to look at.

EDITH HEAD: Schoolteachers at that time only worked nine months a year. I answered an ad in the paper for a designer to work on a [Cecil B.] DeMille picture during the summer. And I think about twelve of us answered. And all twelve of us got hired. We sat in rows. I think the picture was called *The Golden Bed* with Leatrice Joy. And I know we all sat in little rows with little pads in front of us and were told to design. We were all given the same thing to do. It was like an elimination contest. "All of you draw riding habits today, and the next day all of you draw something else." One by one we dropped by the wayside, and finally there were only two or three of us left.

I had walked in with a portfolio that wasn't any of my own. Years and years and years and years ago, to be a sketch artist you had to have a portfolio showing that you could do men, women, children, and period. And at that moment I was studying seascape. And all I could draw was oceans. I needed a portfolio, so I asked everybody in my class for a few sketches on costume designing. And I had the most fantastic assortment you've ever seen in your life. When you get a class of forty to give you sketches. . . . I took the sketches in and showed them, and they said, "I have never seen such amazing talent in one person."

You know, when you are very young, you have no sense of morality, I guess, or what you should do. I thought it was rather amusing to get this big portfolio. It never occurred to me it was quite dishonest. And all the students thought it was fun, too, just like a dare, to see if they could help me get the job.

KARL STRUSS: I went into the Air Corps service in World War I, in the aerial photography division. When I got out, I came right out to California because I heard of this motion picture company that was over at Elbow Beach. So I went over there. You could get a job, I was told.

The West Coast moviemaking had hardly started then, but in those days, they had two directors of photography. They were called cameramen. One would shoot the American negative and the other the foreign negative. You see, they had two separate negatives, so that the foreign negative was complete in itself and the American negative was complete in itself. And when the picture was cut, the two matched. Those were the two camera jobs. The cameras would be running simultaneously, set out side by side, so they needed two men, but they said to me, "You haven't made any motion pictures, so how can we put you on as a cameraman?" So just to get into the business, I started with Cecil B. DeMille, shooting still pictures. Eight by tens. If the only way to get in was to shoot stills, why, I'd shoot stills. They shot stills instead of taking frame enlargements because the movie frames were so small that the enlargement to eight by ten showed considerable grain. When a scene was over, usually before they made a new set-up, the still man would come in with his camera and set his camera in approximately the same place to encompass the same view that they had in the longer shot. And then move in closer. And with Mr. DeMille, after I had set it up, before I would shoot it, he would always check it himself. He'd see the negative upside down on the ground glass. He was used to that. These stills were used for advertising purposes. And we would take hundreds of them. For each set-up, we'd take about four exposures, and there'd be variations: moving in closer, four people in the scene, then three, then two, and so on. We would photograph the high points of the scene. Since there was no dialogue, we could sort of reconstruct the movie by making it look like the movie itself. Yes, I became a still photographer so I could become a moving picture cinematographer. You could move around in jobs back then.

MERVYN LEROY: I was a lousy entertainer in vaudeville. I was in vaudeville for a long time, but my partner's father passed away and we had to break up the act. I was stuck in New York, and I was broke. My cousin was Jesse Lasky, so I went up and asked him for a job. He didn't want any relatives working in his studio, so he said, "Look, I'll loan you some money." I wanted to get back to California and I had only about five dollars in my pocket, so he loaned me train fare and gave me a letter of reference. I went to the Lasky studio, and I thought I was going to be the head of it right away, you know. I walked in and gave them the letter, and they gave me a job folding wardrobe in the wardrobe department. I couldn't stand the stink of mothballs! I was folding North and South uniforms for a picture called *Secret Service* with Robert Warwick, who was a big star in those days. It was a Civil War picture. A man named Hugh Ford directed it. All those uniforms from the Western Costume Company— stinking of mothballs. I got out of that and went into the laboratory. At least it didn't stink in there. Well, it was all new. It was really something. Lots of jobs.

HENRY HATHAWAY: I had a choice when I was young. I was kind of a good-looking kid, and I had a choice of being in front of the screen or behind the screen. Because of my knowledge of the way actors lived—including my own folks, kind of a nutty, goddamn life—I decided I'd go behind the camera. From the time I started, the ultimate goal for me was to become a director. Anybody who's working in pictures, I don't care whether you say it out loud or not, wants to be a director. The actors all think, "When I'm washed up in this, I can be a director." The writer says, "If I write a good script, I'll direct it myself." It's not like that so much now because the unions make it so goddamn difficult, so it's almost impossible, but in those days you could go from being a propman to being a director. It didn't make a goddamn bit of difference. Doors were open. It was new. Things weren't locked down. You could just decide to be a director.

RAOUL WALSH: I worked for a director—I can't think of his name—and I was playing Paul Revere because I could ride a horse. Well, he set up his camera and told me to come tearing down the street. "Come down the street as fast as you can. Stay in the middle there so we can see you." So I went up there and came tearing down, and after I got off the horse and looked, I had been riding between two trolley tracks. So I told him, "They didn't have any trolley tracks back then." He said, "Who the hell is directing this picture, you or me?" I decided right then I'd become a director . . . and I knew I *could* become a director. If he could do it, I could do it.

GEORGE FOLSEY: It was a new business. Open, if you dared to try things, had confidence. One day, you haven't got a job. Then, boom! You got a job.

MINTA DURFEE: At Mack Sennett's studio, we had a big sign out front: GET IN AND GET WORK. And people just flocked to work. They needed money or wanted something to do. People just walked in. You'd get in and get work. And all of a sudden, you were in the movies!

ALLAN DWAN: This business was strange in the early days. Loose. Everybody was getting into it. It was open to anyone. It was growing fast, and money was to be made. Everyone jumped in or fell into it. All kinds of companies emerged with all kinds of names for them. You look back, you'll see hundreds of them: The American Company. Universal. The Flying A. Essanay. Biograph. World Film Company. Zelig. And many, many others. "Corporations" were formed. Here's how you became a "corporation" back then: you sat down at a table and you got a lawyer and you applied for a corporation and suddenly you were a corporation. So you told a reporter, "We're now incorporated. We're called the Jazwatz Film Company." And you haven't done anything except sit at a table and say, "We're a corporation." The same corporation could have four different names before they settled down to one. The American Film Company was started in 1910 or 1911—how can you prove which?—but they just started up, and before they were incorporated they didn't even have a name. They had nothing, so they went over to a building and took a floor of a building where probably some other fellow had moved out because he didn't have any money. They moved in. It was just some desks and a few offices. No laboratory. No studio. No lights. They didn't own anything—they didn't even own a camera. And then they had to go out and find—rent or find—a camera 'cause that was the hardest thing in the world to find. You couldn't go into business unless you had one. Then they would hire a director from some theater stock company. They'd say, "Well, he's a director. He's directing those things. So he can direct pictures." And they told him, "Make some pictures. We want some western pictures, so go out west and make 'em." I was part of a deal like that. We went to Tucson, not California.

The beginning of the movies is a confusing period. All sorts of things went on. Everybody made movies everywhere. People say it was the year-round sunny weather that brought the business finally to Hollywood. There's all kinds of stories about that.

CHARLTON HESTON: DeMille always told the story that he and his group headed west to find yearlong sunshine, heading for Arizona to make a western. When their train got to Flagstaff, it was pissing down rain. I mean, really a downpour. And DeMille got off the train, looked around, and said, "This isn't the weather they promised us. Let's get back on the train and keep going." So according to DeMille, if it hadn't been raining in Flagstaff, "Hollywood" would now be "Flagstaff."

HENRY BLANKE: Why did the film industry begin in Hollywood? Because there was eternal sun here. The lenses were slow. The film was slow. Everything was slow, and you needed sun. Sun. Plenty of it.

ALLAN DWAN: People always say everyone came out here because of the weather, but I think it was more because of the patent wars that brought everyone as far away from the East as possible. And California was the end of the line. The patents companies made it tough for picture companies for a while during the very early years, as tough as they could. It was all complicated—big companies banding together to prevent smaller companies buying stock, restricting free trade. And they actually held certain patents on the camera. I believe the idea of prongs pulling a perforated film through a camera was a patent. But that's just a patent *within* the camera. The use of the camera was not patented. You could buy the camera and use it. Kodak has a lot of patents, but you can go down to a store and buy a Kodak and use it. So it was the *use* of it that they tried to stop. Not the fact that the camera was a patent—they didn't own the camera. It was ridiculous to think that the use of a camera could be patented—just like patenting an automobile and not letting anybody else drive it because you have the patent of putting your feet on the pedal. It was as stupid as that. But what we were all suffering from was their hired gangsters that were trying to put us out of business. So we had to go to war with them. The patents war. It's almost impossible to remember it. But if you lived through it, you can recall that there was something unpleasant going on and that was it. In the end it drove filmmakers west, to California, where there was also better weather for more days of the year.

JEANINE BASINGER: The patent wars were like a gangster movie. When the business first got going—in the late 1800s and early 1900s—nobody paid any attention to machine patents.

SAM WASSON: They just copied any piece of machinery they came across that they could use to make some money . . .

JEANINE BASINGER: . . . and it wasn't just the machinery, but also the creative product itself. There were no copyright protection laws. People pirated movies, stole equipment, threatened each other. It was a mess. Pioneers of the business like DeMille, Walsh, Griffith, and Dwan were working early enough to have vivid memories of these so-called patent wars.

SAM WASSON: Thomas Edison started serving legal writs as early as 1897, claiming he owned all the rights to the motion picture. He had private detectives going all around the country looking for people shooting films! He'd slap legal papers on them.

JEANINE BASINGER: A movie maker had to be ready to pull up stakes and run! The patent wars are a complicated story—but very colorful. In 1908, after months of negotiations, the two biggest companies, Edison and Biograph, former enemies, got together and became The Motion Picture Patents Company. These big guys licensed successful smaller companies to "legally make films": Vitagraph, Essanay, Lubin, Selig, Kalem, Kleine, and Méliès and Pathé. It was an attempt for MPPC to own it all. By 1912, this controlling and threatening company was weakening, and in 1917, it was dissolved by court order. The motion picture game was afoot! And it was anybody's game.

ALLAN DWAN: I started directing early. I know I directed in 1909. I know that for sure. When I say 1909, it could have been down to almost Christmastime. In California, you don't remember—there's no snow, so we don't remember there's a winter. It all rolled rather fast. Things moved quickly then.

The first picture that I put together I did sort of with my tongue in my cheek. My attitude toward the whole thing was rather light. We kept it fluffy and never took ourselves too seriously. So I thought up a pretty good rough title—*Rattlesnakes and Gunpowder*—what else? I prepared to make it in San Juan Capistrano, but because of the proximity to the railroad and the convenience for those patents company men to get at us, I decided to go someplace a little more remote, where we could protect ourselves.

And someone steered me to Lakeside, which is above La Mesa and where there was a pretty good hotel and lots of nice background. And I moved them all up there. It was just a matter of getting in our buggies and on the horses and going up there. So we went to Lakeside, and I finished *Rattlesnakes and Gunpowder*. And then I settled down to a series. We would work Monday, Tuesday, and Wednesday shooting pictures and make two pictures. Then on Thursday and Friday I'd develop and cut them and take Saturday and Sunday off—go down to San Diego or down to Los Angeles for the weekend. I made pictures so fast and so many of them! I wouldn't ship them until I had maybe six finished.

GEORGE FOLSEY: We all worked our fannies off in those days.

ALLAN DWAN: In the beginning, we had to do it all. We had to cut it. We had to look at it. We had to decide everything and make every move. Later on, they had so many executives around doing it that we just stepped back and did our end of it, which was to go out and direct it and turn it in. If they liked it, fine. If they didn't, they said so, and we did it again or whatever way they wanted it.

PANDRO BERMAN: In that period, there wasn't too much artistic effort in too many pictures. Mostly it was a grind operation.

GEORGE FOLSEY: One time I worked two pictures at the same time, one in the daytime and the retakes on the other at night. I worked for seven solid weeks without a day off, night and day. I don't know how I did it except that I was very young and strong, but I want to tell you I'd never do that again. It was too much.

HAL MOHR: In those days, when you made a picture, there was no designation of responsibilities. I mean, four or five people would get together and take the script, break it down and talk it out, have story conferences, discuss the thing and make decisions. All of us together. And women, too. Universal sent me out with Ruth Stonehouse. They sent me out with Ruth to be her cutter and to keep her straight on the filming techniques. I was sent out that way with men, too, because I had done directing, photographing, and cutting. I could help. You know, there *were* women directors then. Besides Ruthie, there were other women directors: Ida May Park, Lois Weber.

ARTHUR KNIGHT: Film history has shown us that in the silent era, women wrote, directed, produced, acted, starred, did stunts, whatever. But slowly, women disappeared out of the top ranks, both in front of the camera and behind it.

MITCHELL LEISEN: I was friends with Lois Weber, one of the great women directors of that time.

GERTRUDE ASTOR: Lois Weber was at Universal when I was there. She was very nice, very sweet, very talented. Her husband used to kind of help her, but she pushed him aside. She was the one.

HAL MOHR: Lois Weber was a damn good director. She knew what she was talking about and knew what the scene context should be. You were conscious of the fact that she was a woman, of course. You couldn't lose sight of that, and there was a greater differential in those days than there is today. But it didn't inhibit her in any way, and it didn't inhibit the people who worked with her. I found her to be very compatible and very nice to work with and very understanding and very intelligent. She knew what the hell the score was.

MINTA DURFEE: Mabel [Normand] used to direct. Sure, she used to direct. She directed lots of scenes.

LILLIAN GISH: I directed a picture when I was twenty. With my sister, Dorothy. She was the most talented of the two of us, because she had comedy and wit. I thought I could bring it out as a director. I was too busy acting to do much more directing, but there were many women directors . . . and of course, writers, too . . . in the early years. The opportunity was there for a woman if you wanted it. It changed later, after sound came in, I think.

HOOT GIBSON: It took us three to four to five weeks to make a silent picture. We worked hard every day. . . . Sometimes we'd work all night. I've gone from nine o'clock in the morning to almost nine o'clock the next morning—that's what even the stars used to do once in a while.

HARRY WARREN: You did everything. Not only that, but when we were on location, I was low man, so I had to find the cop on the beat and make a deal with him that if any police were around, well, we'd pay them to let us shoot. Then, when I went back to the office, they'd bawl me out and say I gave the cops too much. I used to give them three dollars. . . . That was all before I got into the music business.

KING VIDOR: The first year that I made silent films, we didn't have any budget to buy stories, so we just had to write our own.

MERVYN LEROY: In those days, anything could happen. If you made a drama, sometimes when you previewed it, it became a comedy. And title writers—if something wasn't working, they could take a comedy and write a dramatic title and make a drama out of it, and vice versa if it was a drama. You know, when you wrote titles, all you had to do was, when you saw them open their mouths, write a title and stick it in so the audience would know what happened. A lot of good pictures were made that way! It's true!

RAOUL WALSH: We got into the training of just do it and get out of here. Once in a while you'd get a nice one, a gem, but the rank and file of them sometimes were not too hot. You learned to do what you had to do. You made it work. I remember once, in the early years, I made a picture in New York with Theda Bara. . . . It was a Spanish picture. The studio was in Fort Lee [New Jersey], and we built a big Spanish set there—a big Spanish street. The day we started the thing, a blizzard hit New York, and it really was a blizzard. Well, Bill Fox [William Fox, studio executive] was a nice old fellow, and he said to me, "Raoul, what can we do?" I said, "Well, Mr. Fox, I think that if we put a few domes on that set, we can change it to a Russian picture." He called all the people and he said, "Get the Spanish costumes the hell out of here and bring the Russian costumes in." Now, then, we made the thing in about three and a half weeks, and the salesmen came to New York for a preview of the product. Well, some fellows from Cincinnati were saying "Gee, we advertised a Spanish picture. Where the hell is it?" Well, the Spanish picture was now a Russian picture. Because it snowed.

KING VIDOR: Silent-picture scripts were such that you could ad-lib anywhere, and you were *expected* to ad-lib and be off the cuff. Nobody had to write dialogue, which took time, and nobody had to learn dialogue, which also took time. And it took more time in the beginning because there was no such thing as cue cards and teleprompters. So you would actually have a script that said, "Love Scene." Just two words, and that was it. In fact, you had some sometimes that said, "Battle Scene." And you might spend a week on a battle scene. Once we had a script in our hands that said, "Love Scene," and I said, "I've run out of the love scenes I know." We didn't have all the words to explain everything. And we thought in terms of symbols, graphic arrangements, or possibilities. We were trained in those terms. When you had to explain something, you didn't think, what's the exact word that explains this? You didn't think that way, as you do in writing. Or the exact phrase or the exact sentence, you just didn't think that way. You just thought, What's the picture you're looking for to explain what you're trying to say?

FRITZ LANG: You had one page for each scene, so you could interchange pages—scenes—whenever you wanted. If you suddenly thought, I need something before this, you could just renumber the scene of another page and reorder it.

WILLIAM WYLER: We tried to have as few titles as possible and tried to get everything over with pantomime. If we could find a way to eliminate a title by gesture or by getting it over some other way, well, that was supposed to be very adventuresome and very good.

GERTRUDE ASTOR: You worked hard. You worked Sundays. Lots of times, we did two pictures in a day. We never had holidays. I think the only holiday we would get the whole year was Christmas Day. That was the only day. You worked seven days and nights, too, an awful lot, an awful lot there.

At Universal, they had a big stage and thirty-six companies all shooting at once. It was crazy, it was ridiculous, with everyone screaming and yelling, and one doing a western and one doing a romance. Well, it was just unbelievable, excepting that was all that we knew in those days. We didn't know anything else, you see, anything any better or bigger. It was a living, and I wasn't completely dependent upon it. And I always had a lot of nice clothes and liked to dress—all my life I did. And they liked that, and I had a darn good wardrobe for their pictures.

We had to supply our own wardrobes in those early years, unless it was costume stuff or something. I had so many nice things that I had brought here with me, and I had them all in there, and when they wanted to dress a set they would say, "Go in Astor's closet in there, in her dressing room, she's out working today, outside. Go get her stuff and bring it here." And they would dress the set with it, with dresses and hats and clothes and stuff, you know, and so it got to be a joke: "Go get Astor's wardrobe."

GEORGE FOLSEY: There was so much excitement to it all. I worked on two [Enrico] Caruso films. Silent films, incidentally. Think about that. It was around 1918, I think. There was a flu epidemic, and it was quite severe. I was an assistant cameraman by then for the Famous Players Film Company. Caruso was a fascinating man, of course. To me it was wonderful to be around him. I was very young and idealistic. He used to have coffee in the morning or all day. He'd have a small cup of coffee with cognac in it. And he was always complaining about a headache. In my seventeen-year-old wisdom of the world, I was sure the cognac was the problem.

KING VIDOR: The important thing to realize is that we were all learning, trying out things, figuring out how cameras worked, how to create effects. It was just more informal then, no hierarchy. Easy to get permissions and to go ahead with ideas. I could tell the head guy an idea, and he could say, "Yes, go ahead," and this doesn't happen today. He didn't say, "What stars are you going to have?" I didn't have stars. I had unknowns. He just said,

"It sounds good, why don't you go ahead with it?" That's just the way the picture was made. That's the way the best pictures were made. Just by saying, "Okay, go ahead."

GERTRUDE ASTOR: It was just casual around the studio. People could wander in. They used to have a zoo at Universal, on the lot, with animals, out on that back lot. You paid a quarter to go back there and watch the animals. Oh, dear, that was the place! It was awful back there, an awful place! It was dirty, and it wasn't kept up, you know, so it was awfully smelly back there. Well, of course, really, it was fun, and Universal had a bunch of hardworking people around there, I'll say that for them. Mr. Laemmle was nice, and people that he had there loved him. The reason I stayed there was that it was a living and it was fun and I was young and blond and tall and so what? I mean—you know.

WILLIAM BEAUDINE: We directors would sit there while the film was shooting, and you never left the actors alone. I mean, you'd say, "All right, now look at the girl." We used to talk and talk and talk. You'd just cue every move. I had to get out of the habit when the talkies came in. I found myself talking over the dialogue. And you didn't make a silent without music on the set. You were just a dumb cluck if you did that. I used to play "Boy o' Mine" or "The World Is Waiting for the Sunshine."

KING VIDOR: I remember that with the silent films, the director was always asking the cameraman, "What speed? What speed are you going?" And they had a little speedometer on the camera. You don't see that anymore. Films were shot at sixteen frames per second and projected at about eighteen to twenty frames. Charlie Chaplin said to me once, "Nobody ever saw me run around, turn the corner, as I actually do it, because those cameramen would drop down to half speed." That slow cranking speeded him up double, made him faster. Everyone was constantly utilizing different speeds on the camera to achieve a sense of "hurry up." Even Griffith did it. In *Birth of a Nation*, he has horses traveling at seventy miles an hour pulling chariots. After the interlock came in, everything became twenty-four frames per second and it was locked down.

JOSEPH RUTTENBERG: You had to be sure that you were cranking at the same speed all the time. Otherwise, in the middle of the action, there would be slow motion or there would be fast, or whatever. We cameramen used to have a contest to see how many feet of film we could shoot without changing the speed of the cranking. It was a lot of fun.

GERTRUDE ASTOR: You know, Universal always had a kind of tour, like they do today. They had a spieler who had been with a circus, and he was a real circus spieler and he took people around, announcing to them who everybody working was and what they were doing. There was a big balcony all along upstairs, and he walked along, pointing everyone out. They charged twenty-five cents apiece for people to walk through. And that was the most money they were making then, at that time, I think.

You talk about thirty-six pictures being made all at once there on that long, long stage, all open, it was bedlam. You just have no idea what it was like, everybody screaming, battling. We had a thing built up—one of the stages was built up high, with seats on it, for tourists, and they were charged twenty-five cents apiece to sit up there and watch all these companies at work and everything, you know. All the screaming and yelling, oh, it was a madhouse, just a madhouse.

So one day I was going to walk in from this door into this scene here and—into this "room" in the picture—and I walked in, and there was a lady sitting there rocking in an old-fashioned rocking chair. And I said, "What the hell are you doing here?" I was so startled for a moment, and we were working, we were shooting, and she said, "Well, I got tired sitting on that bench upstairs there and it was hard, and I came down here to rest." She said, "I'm from Omaha."

ALLAN DWAN: Very few of us actually lived in Hollywood. We lived downtown. I lived at the Athletic Club downtown. Many of my friends lived all over the lower part of town in that area. And we'd take the streetcars out to Hollywood to work. Of course, some people had automobiles, not too many. As I recall, it was a pleasant gang of gypsy-like people who were getting away with making a living making galloping tintypes—that's what we called the pictures. Hollywood was, I think, a pleasant place. Rural. It seemed as if even the weather was better out there. And also more accommodating. I remember very, very often it'd be raining on one side of the street and brilliantly sunlit on the other. In fact, we'd go across the street to make a rain scene and then come back across to the other side and make a sun scene. The same day, same time. Of course, there was hardly any traffic to speak of. And orange groves and lemon groves everywhere. Not many houses and no big buildings. And, well, it was just a small town, I'd say. It was a virtual wilderness!

Hollywood in those early years was an intimate place. Not the way it was publicized to be. Everybody knew everybody. And we met everybody. We'd meet together, and we had organizations, little clubs and things where we'd gather together, Photoplay Club and things of that kind. And we'd go to parties, and everybody'd be there. It hadn't divided up into cliques. It hadn't become snobbish and it wasn't aloof. Everybody knew everybody and I guess liked everybody or hated everybody, whichever it was, and got along. We were closer together. They hadn't spread out and away quite so much as they are now—all over the place.

TEETE CARLE: There were clubs and things. All the writers in town, the motion picture writers and authors, belonged to an organization known as the Writers Club. On Sunset Boulevard, not too far from the Crossroads of the World, there was an old frame house, and that was the Writers Club. They rented it, and they had facilities for eating, and they also had a little stage, and they had meeting rooms. A lot of magazine writers or publishers and people like that would come to town, and they would be invited to give speeches. And there was the WAMPAS. It was organized in 1921. WAMPAS stood for the name of the organization, which was Western Association of Motion Picture Advertisers. It was for publicity men, not just those in motion pictures but also in distribution and even in theater. There was an urgency among them to try and get an image. Everybody else seemed to have images. Some dignity, some status, and a purpose. To get away from the old so-called hokum press agentry idea. So they organized WAMPAS. After about five years they had about thirty-eight members. Doesn't seem like much today, but those were the early years of that particular movie job. I was in it. We had associates and honorary persons. The dues weren't very much. We had meetings about twice a month. It would be a dinner meeting, and when I first started it was at the old Roosevelt Hotel. We would have a dinner meeting and then a program, just like in some small-town Elks Club. We took turns putting on the programs. We'd have speakers such as Cecil B. DeMille. One time he talked about the fact that hokum was an integral part of show business. We loved that. And we would have directors and actors, like that. WAMPAS started something called the Frolics Ball. The first one was in, I'd say, in 1922. And they got the idea to introduce something called the Wampas Baby Stars. Names were put up—the names of ambitious actresses around town. Sometimes studios would put them up, sometimes just individual WAMPAS members, whatever. The whole membership voted on them, and the thirteen girls who received the most votes were declared Wampas Baby Stars. This was a big deal. There were three thousand people at the first of the Frolics Balls and six thousand at the second. By that time, there were a lot of people working in the business, and everyone liked to have fun. The money that would be made from the Frolics Balls went into maintaining a health and hospital and life insurance policy for the members. And the Baby Stars got a real career boost. Joan Crawford was a Wampas Baby Star. And another thing, in 1926, at the big annual Frolic—which was held on the huge Shrine Auditorium stage—Doug Fairbanks introduced a new game, badminton. Nobody knew what it was, and he had picked it up in England, and he was introducing it here. See, we were like a community then, for real. We had parties and causes and clubs, and people knew each other.

H. N. SWANSON: Sunset Boulevard wasn't even paved.

JOHN SEITZ: I lived in this house about two blocks away from the studio where we worked. The director Ed Sloman lived a floor above and I lived below and the owner of the studio lived on the other side. Henry King lived across the street. We didn't have to bother with the car. We all walked to the studio together every morning. Two blocks. It was easy living . . . and friendly.

LEWIS MILESTONE: Hollywood was very much gayer than it is now. They didn't take themselves as seriously. And the whole atmosphere was freer and more informal. When we got together, we talked pictures, naturally. You talk shop, just like if you're a stockbroker or whatever. And gossip! Not mean gossip, just gossip. I remember people all telling each other about Pickfair. That's the big home where Douglas Fairbanks and Mary Pickford lived. What a big item it was when everyone discovered that a butler in livery actually would come and open the door up there! This was surprising news, you know. I mean, who had a butler?

MITCHELL LEISEN: Pickfair! Charlie Chaplin and myself went up there almost every night for dinner. Mary would go to bed, and we'd run a picture. Douglas would fall sound asleep during the picture and would wake up and say, "Best picture I've ever seen in my life." And he had a Turkish bath and a pool with a three-hundred-pound cake of ice in it. We had to go in every night and take a sauna and then dive into the ice bath. And then everybody would go up and go to bed, because it was late, and climb into the Rolls-Royce the next morning and go to the studio. I would say, "Douglas, I've got to go home first and get some clean clothes." And he'd say, "I've got plenty of clothes here. What the hell do you need?" I had *more* underwear and shirts of Douglas's!

GERTRUDE ASTOR: We were all pals. We worked nights, too, you know. You stayed out there at Universal. If you got out there, you weren't sure you would get home before midnight anytime hardly. You know, the hours weren't counted. You just stayed until they said you were done. But getting out there wasn't so easy, so that's why sometimes you stayed at night. There was a little winding road over the mountains that went down into a gully, and then it went up over the hill around. When Universal first opened, that first year, you got out there the best you could in somebody else's little old car or something, you know. But they finally had a little bus line, and it was really picturesque. They put a regular bus on Hollywood Boulevard. That whole mountain that's back there was where we made our Hoot Gibson westerns. That was where I learned to ride horses so well. It's where that Sheraton Hotel is now. Up there. Everything was open and unsettled back in those days, but we were all pals at Universal.

HAL MOHR: I liked the Universal studio, I liked it very much. We all felt that it was *us*, that it belonged to us. In the restaurant they had a room called the Indian Room. And that was the Executives' Dining Room. There was one big round table where, I think, old man Laemmle used to come and have lunch, and Junior and those of us who were part of the Laemmle family, like Paul Kohner and Willy Wyler, were invited. They were all part of the Laemmle family at that time, and we would have lunch there at the round table in the Indian Room and sit there and gab. But we all felt that the studio was a part of us and we were a part of the studio. It was nice. We didn't make a lot of money, but we had a hell of a lot of fun.

ALLAN DWAN: We all lived and worked together. Raoul Walsh and I were very close friends. We used to spend a lot of time going down to Tijuana and places like that. Having fun. He'd come over. We lived right next door to each other at Malibu. Whoever you were working with on a picture at the same studio you were friendly with, and then you also had your regular friends. I mean, you saw some people practically all the time and others occasionally. There used to be occasions where we'd meet oftener. At least once a week there'd be some function that we'd all go to and we'd all be there. Parties would be thrown. Of course, after the end of a big picture, there was always a big party, sometimes right on the sets. We went to the openings. Sometimes we'd go to the studios and see them when they'd be newly finished. There was so much congeniality. There was no hierarchy.

RAOUL WALSH: Everybody had fun. Everybody. And in those days, if you needed help on the set, everybody, actors, everybody, would lift the table and set it up for you over there. Great camaraderie. You were never sued. And of course it was all easier on the set, looser, because there was no dialogue or anything that you had to learn. Less pressure. We loved it, we loved it. In those days, early days, they would throw a script on your lawn like they do the *Examiner*. You just picked it up, read it, and went to work.

HOOT GIBSON: I would always give a big party at my ranch house on the estate, and we had as high as four and five hundred people there at the party. It was one grand affair once a year, and really a lot of fun. Innocent fun. With a lot of wonderful people.

GERTRUDE ASTOR: I bought my first little house and all the gang from MGM used to come up to my house. Renée Adorée used to sit on my baby grand piano and sing French songs and Russian songs. She spoke Russian, too, and she was a great, great gal.

I felt like I was a part of Universal then, you know. We worked hard and we played hard and there was a lot of drinking going on in those days. They drank hard cider, did you ever hear of that? We had a man up on the corner, the first corner from the studio, that was there two years with his hard cider. Until the law—they had to get the law to get him out.

Everybody was stewed up on hard cider for two years. I remember they used to keep it in jugs in the dressing rooms. I had a jug of it to give everybody. Hoot Gibson had one. Hoot Gibson used to get tight a little bit, and then he would sit there with his jug up on his shoulder drinking hard cider and go to sleep with it there in his dressing room. It was right across from mine. Everybody went in. Sometimes there would be so many going for a drink of hard cider off the sets, the workmen and everything, that they'd say, "What's going on? What's going on?" Hoot had the big gallon jug all the time filled up for people to come up and have a drink of hard cider. And I also had one, too.

HENRY HATHAWAY: At that time, I won't call the movies scurvy, that's too bad a word, but there was a class of people. I don't mean they were all bad. There were some wonderful people, but they were the kind of people that didn't give a damn if they were broke one day and they drank a lot. They always needed money. They were always broke. No matter what they made, they spent it. That was sort of the demeanor of everybody in the business, spent every goddamn thing they made.

GERTRUDE ASTOR: Oh, it was fun! But you had to be young and you had to be strong, pretty big and strong, to stand it, you know. Those were awful cold nights, awful cold nights, and rain. In the dressing rooms there was a little place where the water could run down the middle, and it would run over and come in your dressing room and you would have to sit with your feet up on your makeup table ahead of you to keep them out of the water, to get ready to get out of there and get on the stage to work.

I learned to ride a horse there. Yes, I really did. Hoot Gibson and the boys helped me to learn to ride a horse there. I didn't know how before. Well, the cowboys were wonderful to me. Oh, they were a great bunch of cowboys. I got hurt, broke some ribs one day, and the cowboys' wives took care of me. They took me up to my home and they brought chicken and made chicken soup and everything, and saw that I got all taped up right, and all that sort of stuff, you know, until I could get back to work. They were a great bunch, a great bunch.

HOOT GIBSON: We were very happy with our jobs. We had a lot of work to do—but say we were up in Mammoth Lakes somewhere, and we wanted to go fishing. We'd get up at six in the morning then, sometimes five, we'd put in an extra three hours and quit two hours earlier so that we could go fishing in the afternoon. All of our schedule, that day's work was done—so we went fishing, we had a good time, we had a good night's sleep, and started over again the next day. That's the way the people worked in those days.

ALLAN DWAN: And now people ask me about the wild life, the scandals, the extravagance. Where was I, really? I was just going to work every day. But I guess, maybe, shortly after I made *Robin Hood* with Doug Fairbanks in '22, maybe things changed a little for some people. But before that? I don't know. The Bel Air set hadn't begun. It came in, I guess, about 1922. It began to appear then. Bel Air was beginning to draw people, and they were beginning to build houses. Some of them who had some money. Very few people had gotten into big money at that time. But it was about to start then. I can't recall when practically everybody had to have a mansion.

GEORGE FOLSEY: I think it was about 1920, sometime in there, and one day I was on the stage in the Long Island studio, and I got a telephone call from Florenz Ziegfeld, Billie Burke's husband. He said that he was calling for Miss Burke, that she appreciated so much the nice photograph that I had done for her, and she wanted to give me a present and he wanted to know if an automobile would be acceptable. I almost fell down. I stammered and said, well, it was not necessary, she was wonderful to photograph and a great person to be with. He said, "Well, I'd like to give you a Rolls-Royce." I said I couldn't think of it, and besides, I was going to California—well, really, where in the world would I need a car more than in California, of course—but it would have been impossible for me to drive it there because I didn't know how to drive very well in those days. I told him I really couldn't accept it. It was too much. In a few days, a package came for me from Cartier's. It was a dress cigarette case with a facsimile of her writing that said, "In deep appreciation, Billie Burke." And then a letter for me and in the letter was a check. I looked at the check and I said, "Jeez, isn't that wonderful! Fifty dollars!" That was a lot of money. But then I looked again, and it was for five hundred dollars! She wasn't kidding when she said she was going to buy me an automobile, because a good Ford would have cost me about $650 in those days.

ALLAN DWAN: Money. Everybody got it, and everybody started spending it.

MITCHELL LEISEN: For sheer extravagance, the popular actor Charles Ray did the most crazy things. Charlie was a very funny person. He was probably the most famous hick character on the screen, but in his personal life he refused to have anything to do with such a character. He loathed having to play a bumbling youth. He lived most extravagantly. Couldn't stand the idea of being a hick. That's why he went completely berserk in extravagance. We would go for lunch at his house one day, and the whole garden had, let's say, tulips. We'd go the next weekend, and they'd be camellias or something. Everything was just in pots put in the ground. They'd take them all out and do them over again. In the drawing room some of the upholstery was $125 a yard. And his wardrobe was all cutaways on Sunday and striped trousers. He had a footman and a chauffeur for his Packard limousine.

One day he complained that there was no good place to eat around the studio. I said, "Why don't we have a luncheon club, get a cook, and use that empty building over there, and we could all put in so much a week." We wound up with a hammered beam gothic room with an antique banquet table as long as this, with a $6,000 set of pewter dishes, a butler and a footman and a cook. Charlie paid for the whole thing. Nobody put a dime in, ever. We had lunch there, and if we had to work late at night, we had dinner there. I said, "It would be kind of fun to do some plays Sunday afternoons. We could do them out here in the garden." I went out the next Sunday, and he had built an open-air theater with clipped hedges for wings and everything else. Charlie had the whole thing brought in and set up, and not only that, but he hired a coach from UCLA and we started with Euripides. Well, that lasted a fast five weeks. Everybody got bored to death very quickly. Instead of doing something fun, we had to go through a whole course of Greek tragedy.

The fabulous thing was his last party. He and his wife had, off the dining room in their house, a big rose garden—a pool in the center with a big fountain in it and big urns forged up. There were blue lacquer tables going all around this thing and strolling musicians. This was the day that Charlie and his wife, Clare, declared bankruptcy. And I'm sitting next to her, and I said, "Clare, for God's sake, what's this all about?" She said, "You may as well go down with all flags flying." That was their philosophy. Seventy-five dollars for a pair of shoes for Clare, never less than that. Three hundred pairs in her closet. One night at one of their dinner parties, Rosa Ponselle stood on the stairway in the hall and sang while everybody sat in the living room. I think Charlie paid her $5,000 to do it.

After his career failed, he tried to become a nightclub singer. He couldn't carry a tune for hell nor high water. I was directing a picture of mine one night, and I looked outside the entrance to the hotel, and the doorman was Charlie Ray, doing extra work. I never knew what happened to him after that. Clare opened up a dress shop on Sunset Boulevard, and I don't know what happened to either one of them.

GEORGE FOLSEY: The parties at San Simeon were unforgettable. Marion Davies was delightful, charming. I remember playing in a tennis tournament up there, and she insisted on giving me a really beautiful prize, a lovely watch. We would go to dinner at the castle in that big, beautiful dining room. And we would have a fascinating time at breakfast. Hearst would come down, perhaps earlier than a lot of the guests, who had maybe stayed up later than he had, and it was very interesting to sit and listen to him discuss the world's events. Then we would swim in the pool, and they would take us all on a picnic. Cars came and took us. Some people rode horses to the place, and the servants had prepared a wonderful picnic lunch. Beer and wines and things . . . and we were out on the grassy slope way off in one of the forests up in the San Simeon area, and it was perfectly lovely and charming. Another time I was up there, they had a costume ball. It was the North and the South theme, so they rented or got from Metro all of the costumes for the ladies and gentlemen. Everyone was especially fitted in whatever they were wearing. What a life that was, up there. The director Charles Brabin—I think he was an Englishman—was married to Theda Bara. She couldn't see ten feet in front of herself. She was always out of focus. He'd bring her through that big dining room, and he'd whisper in her ear, "Coming up on your right is Mary Pickford, and over here will be Joan Crawford . . . and then it'll be the president of So-and-So." He'd guide her through, and she'd say, "Oh, darling, how are you?" and call them by name, so nobody suspected. He was a kind of seeing-eye dog.

MINTA DURFEE: I was there right in Hollywood from the first. With Mack Sennett and the Kops and Chaplin and Mabel Normand and everybody. I'm the girl who knows what she's talking about. But nobody ever asks me anything except about all the money and the scandals [associated with her first husband, Roscoe "Fatty" Arbuckle, who underwent a rape trial and was acquitted]. We just worked for a living, you know? As if my whole life was the trial. Roscoe and I were separated by then. Mother and I were back east, and we had to take a train back. We got on a train, and it was so terrible to get on that train and see every newspaper with those headlines about him. Mother said to be silent. She said, "Just say nothing." We sat with nice people for our dinner, and this lady said, "I just love Mr. Arbuckle, and I can't believe this, I just won't believe this." And Mamma says, "Well, he's a favorite of mine, too." And this was all she said. These publicity men were looking for us, just like the wild ass of the desert, just running up and down, jumping on the train and jumping off the train, to see if it happened to be us. It's a good thing I have a sense of humor. I thought I might as well laugh at this as to get scared to death with it. Roscoe never complained about anything. Through the whole of the trial, he never did. It was pretty much of a shock to me to find him in jail and to see the name of "Roscoe Conkling Arbuckle, Murderer." . . . Roscoe wasn't a horrible monster. But you'd think there was nothing going on in Hollywood but a bunch of bad parties and a lot of big spending. And I'm the girl who knows what she's talking about.

CHAPTER 2

COMEDY

TAY GARNETT: I loved the Arbuckle comedies. Arbuckle and [Buster] Keaton and another comic who was a nephew of Arbuckle's, Al St. John. And Ford Sterling and John Bunny and Sennett himself. I loved all of those. The Keystone Kops. And Marie Prevost and Marceline Day and Phyllis Haver and all those gorgeous bathing beauties. I followed all those comedies. I was living in South Los Angeles when I was growing up, and when I was probably around fourteen years of age, a movie theater was opened about seven or eight blocks from my home, and I didn't miss a one.

KING VIDOR: There were a lot of comedies being made in the early years, and they were right at the top of popularity. Chaplin, Keaton, Harold Lloyd, and things that came out of Mack Sennett's studio. Everybody worked with Sennett at some point or another, probably. I know I did. I think when you look back at the silent era, you have to first start thinking about those comedies, those comedians, and Mack Sennett. When you say "silent film," most people picture a Mack Sennett chase, maybe the Keystone Kops.

TAY GARNETT: When I grew up, I got a call from a director friend of mine over at Sennett's, and he said he needed a gagman. I went over there. The old Sennett studio was on Edendale Boulevard, down in the Echo Park area. You know, there's a bridge on Sunset that goes across the boulevard there. Aimee McPherson's church was about a block south of the boulevard on that side of the street, and about three blocks north was the Mack Sennett studio. (I'm not sure which factory put on better shows!) Before Mack died, he moved from there and built the studio that's now the Columbia Studio Center. The facilities at Sennett were awful, just awful. At Sennett, $35 a week was big money. When I walked away and went over to DeMille, I got $250 to start. There you are. The cameras Sennett had were all right, but they had very few refinements of any kind. They were all hand cranked, of course, and they didn't do much with them except iris in and iris out.

JOHN SEITZ: Mack had two rules: you came in on the left, and you exited on the right. Left to right. Well, they had so many people running around . . . this prevented chaos. Mack Sennett may not have had much education, but he was nobody's fool. And although Griffith had no sense of humor, Mack Sennett did. And he understood that a chase is the ideal vehicle for moving pictures. Ideal.

HAL MOHR: In the Mack Sennett era, it didn't matter how you shot it, as long as you exposed it. It wasn't supposed to be pretty or attractive or artistic. Just as long as you could see it, Mack was happy.

TAY GARNETT: The story writers at Sennett worked in teams. There were usually two who worked together. They could go faster that way. Most of the writing was done vocally. There were about eight teams—sixteen writers—all working vociferously in one room. All sixteen of them! That meant eight different stories bouncing off one another for hours at a time. With sixteen gagmen yelling, trying to sell their gags by vocal volume, laughter, and sound effects, the room seemed to shrink visibly. I'll admit a lot of our time was spent talking about dames and football, or baseball and dames, or whatever and dames . . . until we'd hear the old man coming in. When I was there, Ben Turpin was pushing seventy, but every morning when he approached the studio, there'd be a bunch of kids who turned up to watch the stars work. As soon as he saw them, Turpin would invariably do a 108. A 108 is a front flip, except that you land flat on your ass with your feet up high. And Turpin did it on a cement sidewalk. But if he had an audience . . . when he saw those kids, he'd say, "Good morning, kids!" and *whoops!* He'd do a 108, and then he'd say, "How's that for a greeting?" I don't know how he ever survived. It's quite a stunt. There are damned few stuntmen around who can do it today, and he was doing it at the age of sixty-nine! Every comic on that Sennett lot had to know how to do a 108.

FRANK CAPRA: In silent films, creating the comedy behind the scenes was more talking than writing. There was paper around, but nobody ever used it. Mack Sennett was the great studio, the great school for visual comedy. He'd put you in twos. So two people would work. One could talk to the other, try something out on each other. Find out what's a good idea. Now, if we got together on something he'd call us in. "Now, what you got?" We'd tell him what we had, and if he laughed, great. He knew then that the audience would laugh, but he himself was not funny at all. If he tried to tell a joke, he'd screw it up and give you the last line first, but boy, if he laughed, the audience was going to laugh. It was a real litmus piece, canary, whatever you call it.

The directors in those days were miraculous, just miraculous. You just gave them a hint, and they'd take it from there. You gave them a hint. You'd say, "A cat drinks some beer." God, that's all—they'd have five minutes of different scenes out of that. The cat would put on a hat, chase a dog, and that's the way things were done. The idea would germinate with the gagmen, be officially approved by Sennett, and he'd invariably approve of them. He had that kind of a mind. Never a written word. Sennett would not allow a book to come into the studio. He'd say, "No gags in books. No gags in books." He was afraid of intellectuals. He wanted you to be down to his level where you make him laugh and he makes you laugh, you know, with funny stuff. Funny kind of clown kind of comedy, not witty, wordy, but clownish. *Visual.*

TAY GARNETT: Sennett wouldn't read anything.

FRANK CAPRA: The training ground was there, you see, at Mack Sennett's studio. You know, comedy is difficult. It's the most difficult of all the genres in film or in any other medium—stage, books, or anything else. The silent era trained people in the real comedy school: visual comedy, which is quite a bit different from verbal comedy or oral comedy. In other words, people and things had to *look* funny to *be* funny. The silent era had two main schools of visual comedy: Mack Sennett and Hal Roach. All the people who worked there in the earliest years just graduated upward to making feature comedies later in the sound era. That's how I started making comedies.

I started with Hal Roach, making Our Gang shorts. Then I went to Mack Sennett's and was there a couple of years. I think I wrote twenty-six two-reel comedies for Mack Sennett in the year and a half I was there. . . . It was there, over at Sennett's especially, where you found out whether you had any talent for comedy.

TAY GARNETT: At Sennett's studio, a lot of the time, a gagman on a story would go out with a director and watch for opportunities to fatten up a scene or a situation with a gag while he was shooting. It was always fluid, flexible, ready to get made better. Sennett wasn't funny, but he knew what was funny. He knew how to tell a visual joke.

FRANK CAPRA: My first big silent comedy directing job was with Harry Langdon on *The Strong Man*. We kind of invented a character for Langdon. It was an elflike character, a child-man, and he had to think like a child-man, a man-child. Whereas Chaplin depended on wit to get himself out of things and Lloyd on speed to get himself out of trouble and Keaton on pure stoicism where he endured—that's all he did and wouldn't change any expression on his face—Langdon had a very slow mind, the mind of a child, a very slow child at that. You could just see that the wheels were going very slowly and he could do a beautiful triple take in which he'd see something over here, a lion or a beautiful dame or whatever. He'd just look at it and then come back and look at it again and come back again and then suddenly see it on his triple take. And so the character we had, he must not be smart. He must not outsmart anybody. Only God was his ally, so if there was a brick going to fall on him, why, he'd just pick up something at the right time and the brick would miss him. But he had nothing to do with it. So he had God on his side. That's all. God was his ally and took him through life because he was so innocent. He represented innocence. Speed was Lloyd. Innocence was Langdon. Stoicism was Keaton. Wit was Chaplin. One word each for those four great comedians—that's what they were.

But Harry Langdon did not know his own character. He did not know that what made him wonderful was because he was innocence personified. When Harry came to Sennett's, he was a middle-aged little guy who had made a low-level living for years doing a vaudeville act with his wife. They had a little truck that they took around, and they made enough to live on, and she kept the money. They weren't of very high mentality nor very high imagination.

Now, when we invented his innocent character and he became innocence personified—see no evil, nothing—he shot to the top. Well, now, he read in the papers that he was equivalent to Chaplin. Boy that was the wrong thing for him to see because right away he wanted to do what Chaplin did. Chaplin wrote, directed, and acted. But Chaplin discovered and made his own character, so he knew more about the character he was playing than anybody else in the world. Langdon knew less about his character than anybody in the world. But that poor man, in order to be like Chaplin, decided he would fire me and everybody else—because he wanted to play the witty guy like Chaplin. And that's what he did, and that's what caused his downfall. That is his story. It was the only real, honest-to-goodness human tragedy that I have ever run across in a person—that I have personally seen start and come into fruition and then happen—and he died of a broken heart. He died, and he was playing extras when he died—this star, this big star—because he never understood what made him funny.

HAROLD LLOYD: Chaplin, Keaton, and I, we all invented our own characters. I saw a film about a fighting clergyman who wore glasses. I don't know whether it was—oh, probably in those days a three- or four-reel picture—I don't know how long it was, but it was a serious picture. He just had the wire type of glasses, you know, but he wore glasses. And I was sort of intrigued with the nonchalance he had with wearing those glasses. He looked like sort of a milquetoast type, but his actions belied the whole thing. He was really a go-getter. He finished this fight on a horse—I don't remember whether he wrested the girl from the horse or somebody had grabbed her and taken her off—but he pulled her off, and the two of them had a fight in the dust. When the fracas was all over, he treated the whole thing as though it hadn't hardly happened. He brushed his clothes off, got the girl, and went on as though he'd just stopped to get a drink of water at a fountain or something. And I said, "Gee, I like that type of an idea for a character—not anything to do with his being a parson." I thought that would be good for a comedy series, a young college kid that was so studious and shy and so forth. But when they started to work on him, they found out that he was a tiger in a lamb's coat. I liked the character with the glasses, and I liked the idea of a boy that reacted entirely different from what his appearance gave you to believe he would act. So that was more or less the birth of that. With the glasses, the character became very much the boy you'd see walking down the street, the boy living next door to you. I did him as a believable character.

LEO MCCAREY: Chaplin, Keaton, and I—particularly Chaplin—were all good friends, even though we were rivals, and we all met often. I very quickly allied myself with Chaplin, who particularly loved the Laurel and Hardy pictures I directed. One of the most precious souvenirs I have is a fan letter Chaplin sent me in which he congratulates me on my work with Laurel and Hardy and predicts a beautiful future for me.

Keaton worked in a manner analogous to ours. Two or three gagmen were at his disposal, proposing gags which he could either accept or reject. All of us tried to steal each other's gagmen, but we had no luck with Keaton because he thought up his best gags himself and we couldn't steal *him*! Another man everyone tried to steal was Chaplin's gagman.

PETER BOGDANOVICH: Someone once complained to Chaplin that his camera angles weren't interesting. He said, "They don't have to be. *I'm* interesting."

ALLAN DWAN: The great thing about those silent comedians—Chaplin, Keaton, Laurel and Hardy, all of them—they made it look like they weren't trying to be funny. The minute you're *trying* to be funny—well, take for instance, a character like Chaplin. His scenes were sad little scenes. He was a pathetic little fellow. He never went around trying definitely to be a buffoon. His being one was an accident. And Keaton was always serious. Straight-faced. You see these comedians on TV today, and they are striving so hard and the only way they can ever make you laugh is to talk about their mother-in-law or their wife.

RAOUL WALSH: I used to go down to the Sennett studio and just watch Charlie Chaplin. I knew Chaplin very well, and I used to love to see him work down there. He was always interested in my early life and the West, you know. And I knew Mack Sennett pretty well, and most of the people who worked for him. I liked to watch Charlie.

ALFRED HITCHCOCK: You can learn a lot from watching Chaplin. He once made a short film called *The Pilgrim*. The opening shot was the outside of a prison gate. A guard comes out and pastes up a WANTED notice with a picture of Chaplin in prison stripes. Next, cut to a very tall, thin man, coming out of a river, having had a swim, and he finds that his clothes are missing and all he can pick up is a convict's uniform. Next, cut to a railroad station, and walking toward the camera is Charlie Chaplin dressed as a parson and his pants are too long. Three pieces of film, and look at the amount of story they told.

FRIZ FRELENG: An artist like Chaplin could live for a long time on-screen. In fact, if Chaplin made a picture today, I think he'd draw a big box office, if he made the same little sympathetic character, because he had something the others never had, which was a lovable, believable character. The others didn't do that. They just ran around, put on another funny hat, and ran up and down the street. They had a bunch of people chasing them in an automobile that ran away and ran over the people, and they ran into tunnels and the trains came out and they ran away from that, and they fell into the water. They did pratfalls and threw pies—it was just funny. I think some of it's funny today. I admired Chaplin very much because you could see him think and plan, and you cared for him. In these other things, you never cared. They could get run over by a streetcar and ten automobiles, and it wouldn't make any difference. But with Chaplin, you cared if he was even threatened by one. That was the difference. Chaplin wouldn't act like Fatty Arbuckle or Harry Langdon. He'd be Chaplin all the time. Chaplin was a little sympathetic character who you were always pulling for and felt sorry for.

JERRY LEWIS: My friendship with Charlie . . . that sounds ludicrous! "My friendship with Charlie." Just to say it is awesome. I used to say "Mr. Chaplin" until we met, but when I speak of Chaplin, I always think my shirt is frayed. I hope that sounds like I want it to sound, but it's the most humbling experience to be in his presence. It's awesome.

MINTA DURFEE: The way Charlie came to us at Sennett was that the New York office phoned out and told Mr. Sennett to watch out for this Englishman coming out on the musical hall circuit. So we went down to see him, and we watched him, and he entered by falling out of the upper box, and he had this coat on, you know, and the high split hat and the cane. Very funny. And he fell onto the stage. So we went backstage after, and we met him. He said he had a few more weeks to finish out on his circuit, but he said he would come out to us. So he came out the next day, and he and Sennett talked, and Sennett signed him, as you might say, and said, "Be sure to come back" when he was through with his circuit. Chaplin without a doubt had on the dirtiest suit that I have ever seen on a human being. It was a black-and-white check, and it had soup spots and everything under the sun on it. . . . Poor old Sennett, too, was always, when we first knew him, a sartorial mess . . . but they got him a good tailor.

TAY GARNETT: When I was working at Hal Roach's, before I began in features, I was writing there, and in an emergency I was asked if I would direct a picture, a two-reel comedy. I had never directed anything, but I had written the story. The comic was a guy by the name of James Aubrey. He was a nice guy but not a very funny one. Anyway, at one point in the story there was an automobile chase. There was this Ford going through traffic, and I wanted a long shot of it. I got up on a second-story window on Hollywood Boulevard at a busy time. I had notified the cops and made a deal with them so that they wouldn't pinch this guy for erratic driving. I put a driving double in for Aubrey, and he zipped through the traffic. Remember, I was shooting down on him from the second-story window.

You could never find his car in the shot, so I had to do it over. I looked at the shot over and over again. I spotted the car because I knew where to look, but I knew an audience never would have seen it, so I had the chase car drive right through a sort of farm wagon—a buckboard with a barrel of flour on it. And the black car came out white on the other side of that cloud of flour, and it was the only white car on the street. You just couldn't take your eyes off it. It worked beautifully. It was a comedy chase, so the joke couldn't work without the audience seeing the set-up. Silent visual comedy was a learning process in many different ways. I had to learn that the hard way.

LEO MCCAREY: The greatest pressure in our business was meeting deadlines. You had to think of it, shoot it, cut it, distribute it, all within a certain amount of time, about fourteen days. One day we were stuck for the next Laurel and Hardy. I'm sitting in the living room with a highball—somebody said it would be good for my tonsils (I think it was my own idea)—and the phone rang, and it was the studio. They said, "The gang is sitting around here, and they've come up with nothing and Stan suggested we call you and see if you've got anything." And I started ad-libbing. We had a large facsimile of Gainsborough's *Blue Boy* hanging in our living room, so I said, "Yes, I've got an idea. It opens on a millionaire who owns this painting, Gainsborough's *Blue Boy*. It is stolen, and he offers a handsome reward, and there's a big article in the paper. Then we cut to the racetrack, where Laurel and Hardy are two race touts reading this article. They remark about the sizable reward and say how they can use it. Just then a horse goes by, and on its blanket, it says 'Blue Boy,' and" . . . that's the way we did it. We just winged it.

ALLAN DWAN: I was friendly with Buster Keaton, who did all his own comic stunts. When we were making *Tide of Empire*, one night Norma Talmadge and her sisters came out to visit. And we had a scene in this western town. There was some kind of a fight or something going on in a saloon or something about a saloon. And we heard a commotion, and *wham!*—a fellow came out through the air—somebody threw him out through the door. This wasn't part of the scene. I was surprised to see it happening. But *wham!* the doors flew open, this fellow did two or three somersaults, amazing flops, and then slid in the street and sat up and looked around, and it was Buster Keaton. He'd gone in and just did this stunt to amuse the girls. I kept it in. Just a bit of atmosphere. A bum who was thrown out of a saloon. But I didn't expect it. I was amazed. Keaton was a real acrobat.

GENE KELLY: Keaton had a great influence on me. I certainly intuitively copied a lot of his moves in doing certain numbers. I know that I was thinking of him when I did a dance with a squeaky board and a newspaper, and yet I didn't look like him. I often wish I did. He was a complete genius, and there was a lot of dance inherently in his movements. They were balletic.

LUCILLE BALL: Buster was a personal friend. He was at MGM when I was there. He taught me about props. Fabulous, fabulous man with props, and props have been important in my career. He taught me to be aware of the weights of things and about checking your props, using them, making them yourself, knowing how they operate. Buster Keaton was a very important prop actor.

JERRY LEWIS: The silent comedian that influenced me was Stan [Laurel]. He was a very close friend. Stan was a teacher. I had to pay such careful attention because he established all our discussions with "I'm not going to be here long, so pay attention to me." A man you love and admire tells you, "I'm not going to be around long, pay attention," you pay attention. "Place the camera, lad." That was his way of telling me to watch the placement, that the joke could hurt if I wasn't careful.

GEORGE FOLSEY: I worked with a director who had come from the Sennett company, and they were all kind of a little nutty over there, I guess. He never would say, all right, let's get a close-up. If he wanted to have a great big close-up of somebody, he would stand there and he would say, "Choke her, choke her, choke her . . ." I finally figured out that that meant get a great big close-up, up by her throat. If he wanted a medium shot, like a half shot, he'd say, "Medium fried, medium fried . . ." It took me a while to get this jargon in my head. He would say when he wanted a long shot, "Feetie, feetie, feetie, feetie . . ." "Doorknobs" would mean shoot somebody about waist high, and it took a while to get used to that jargon, but he was a very amusing guy and he came out of that Sennett madhouse of comedy. They had their own language.

TAY GARNETT: It would be impossible for any writer to put on paper the sort of physical sequence we used to call a "rally" at Sennett's. It could be a chase. It could be a fight. A barroom fight. Any action scene. But we had no real plan. We let things happen inside some kind of plot context. We all just went out into the streets, onto the roads, and did it. We shaped it as it was rolling, but we let it happen.

HAROLD LLOYD: As far as the development of all our gags, we would have a number of gagmen get together. We called it a gag room—a place to think up comedy ideas. Why they called them gags I don't know, but that was the accepted parlance of the day. I would keep as many as, oh, anywhere from four to seven or eight—as many as I could get gagmen on the payroll. They were very expensive. I know you paid in those days $800. That's quite a figure, and we'd pay several of them $800 a week. I don't know what that would be today—a little over that. I'd generally have complete control over that thing with the boys. I'd come in, and they'd throw ideas at me. I knew what we wanted, and we worked out sort of a theme which could be changed at any moment. Kind of a story line. That's how we improvised.

When we made *Safety Last*, we shot the climb up the building first, and we were very pleased with it, because we already had the finish to the film all set. That was a gag picture. We tried the same thing with the picture *The Freshman*: we went out to the Rose Bowl, and for two weeks we tried to play a comedy football game, and we got no place at all. When we'd come to look at our dailies, they were just sad. We had to start at the beginning for *The Freshman* because it's a character comedy, and we had to build it from there on. In that one, we knew that the whole picture was really about a boy who wanted to go to school, to college, with the idea of trying to be very popular. He'd like to be the most popular boy, and he goes with a completely erroneous idea of how to go about it. He's in nothing but trouble all the time, so we started shooting at the beginning of the story, because that was a character picture.

We didn't shoot sequentially. We never did that. We did to a certain extent, but we didn't do it like you do today. We shot as much as we could in sequence, then we'd kind of jump around occasionally. Now, in being spontaneous, we'd work out a scene, a series of scenes for the day. We knew we had little islands of what we were going to do in a scene. But in between those set ideas, we'd ad-lib them. Now, the next scene we'd ad-lib a little more. By the time we had shot it four times, little islands would be left out and maybe we'd change the whole idea, we'd have all new business. It's just things that we couldn't think of in the gag room, things that came to us, and that's the reason you got adept at ad-libbing in silent comedy, creating as you went through and thinking of different things.

We did it on the cuff rather than on paper. We knew that it had to build, so I put all the gag writers, for instance, on what would happen to a fellow that goes to a party wearing a suit that's just basted together and can unravel on him. It was up to me to make a routine for those bunch of different gags, how they would fit and how they would go into the thing. That was my end of it. We had freedom as we went along. In the scene, I didn't want to pull my pants off. I said, "Everybody pulls their pants off in a scene. Let's not do that old, corny, lose-your-pants situation." So the first two previews I never lost my pants, but there was always something wrong with that section. One of the fellows said, "Harold, you've got to lose your pants." So I did, and from then on it went fine. The audience loved that section. I had lost everything else, and they wanted me to lose my pants.

We always kept the sets up, because we knew we'd preview it and might want retakes. I tried to tell the boys, "Now, let's not take a century to make this picture, because we know we're going to make a hell of a lot of it over. So let's make it as good as we can for the first time, then, after the audience has seen it, we're coming back really to go to work and find out what's wrong with it." They don't do that today. If Hal Roach said, "Harold, you're a comic, you've got to get laughs. Let's go back," we'd go back and work for months—at least a month—and just put comedy-business gags all over the place—sequences.

I think we were one of the very first, even back in the old one-reel days, to start previews. We used to go out here to Glendale. I can remember the old gentleman who was manager of the theater. His name was Howard. He would always put on tails to come out to explain to the audience what was going on, that this picture had never been shown before, they expected to do a lot more work on it. They, the audience, were the judges, and so forth.

LEO MCCAREY: I was lucky to go to work for Hal Roach. I had no job, no prospects, no nothing. It was like the end of the world. My wife and I went for a ride in the car to the beach. On the way, we passed Hal Roach Studios. I stopped the car and told my wife that I had met Hal Roach at the Los Angeles Athletic Club playing handball. Knowing the situation as I did, I'm sure I let him beat me. I established myself as somewhat of a wit. And I found myself telling jokes for drinks. Roach said, "I make my living making people laugh. If you think you can be funny on the screen, stop in and see me sometime. I'll give you a job." So right there, on that day, I decided to take him up on it, and true to his words, he gave me a job as a gagman with his Our Gang comedies. I had so many ideas for gags that he gave me an actor named Charley Chase and he let me direct him. I was fortunate to have drawn a very clever fellow. Chase was a big help to me, and I hope that I reciprocated to him. And our two-reeler pictures were extremely successful. . . . Some of them were really very funny. Most of them dealt with the misadventures of husband and wife. For example, in *Mighty Like a Moose*, the wife had buckteeth, the husband had a very big nose, and each of them saved their money to have plastic surgery. That's about what the Chase comedies were like. Completely different from what we did later with Laurel and Hardy.

PETER BOGDANOVICH: The Laurel and Hardy comedies are paced very differently from other typical silent comedy, such as Mack Sennett's. They're actually quite slow in comparison. But much funnier.

LEO McCAREY: At that time, comics had a tendency to do too much. With Laurel and Hardy we introduced nearly the opposite. We tried to direct them so that they showed nothing, expressed nothing, and the audience, waiting for the opposite, laughed because we remained serious. For example, one day, Babe—that's a nickname I gave Hardy—was playing the part of a maître d' coming in to serve a cake in *From Soup to Nuts*. He steps through a doorway, falls, and finds himself on the floor, his head buried in the cake. I shouted, "Don't move! Just don't move! Stay like that." Hardy stayed still, stretched out, furious, his head in the cake—you could only see his back. And for a minute and a half, the audience couldn't stop laughing.

It's amazing how much thought went into what on the surface looked like low-down stupidity. I came in one morning, and I said, "We're all working too fast. We've got to get away from these jerky movements and work at a normal speed." I said, "I'll give you an example of what I mean. There's a royal dinner. All the royalty is seated around the table, and somebody lets out a fart. Now everybody exchanges a *glance*, that's all." Everybody died laughing, but I got my point over.

With Laurel and Hardy, you had to believe them in order to get the most good out of it. You took a crazy idea—"Let's have them on top of the skyscraper, and one has a crab in his pants"—and it seemed inherent in their characters that could happen to them. *Anything* could happen to them.

HAROLD LLOYD: I think that on better than, oh, 60 percent of my pictures, I could have taken full credit on the direction. I took writers, idea men, out of the writing room, who had never directed pictures before, and they got credit for directing the pictures. My thinking was this: that I was getting all the credit I needed by being the main comic and the audience was giving me the full credit. Why did I have to have the credit for doing the direction? I wasn't going to be a director anyway. I enjoyed being the comic. So it was good for the boys. It helped them get much better. Charlie didn't choose to do that. Chaplin *did* direct all his pictures. He has a perfect right to take directorial credit. There's no reason he shouldn't, because he damn well did. He does lots of music, and everything he takes credit for he deserves. I just didn't choose to do it, that's all.

LEO McCAREY: I was called the "supervisor" on the Laurel and Hardy pictures. That meant I worked on the stories. Everything was original. We never bought any from anybody else. They all came out of our own brains, and I was in charge of getting the material out. I would supervise the whole story layout and then give it to a director, and he'd go out and shoot it.

"Supervisor" meant being responsible for practically everything on the film: story, gags, screening the rushes, working on the editing, sending out the prints, cutting again when the previews weren't good enough. Also, sometimes it meant shooting sequences over again. But in those days, your name often wasn't mentioned in the credits. The industry knew who'd done what. Irving Thalberg, for instance, never put his name on anything. In my modest way, I tried to follow the same path. Though I made at least a hundred Laurel and Hardy films, I very rarely took credit.

I feel I had a lot to do with shaping the characters Laurel and Hardy came to be, but modesty prevents me from saying that I gave them their breath and blood. Stan and I shaped all those things together. Hardy was no good on stories. Right in front of him, Laurel would say, "I'm doing twice as much as he is, and whatever he gets, I want to get twice as much money." So we always gave Laurel twice as much as Hardy. Hardy didn't mind. Laurel was one of those rare comics intelligent enough to invent his own gags. He was remarkably talented. Hardy wasn't. That was the key to the Laurel-Hardy association, Laurel's stupidity and Hardy's impatience.

When I first knew them, they were not a team, but they were both friends of mine. In those days actors would just come to the studio and see if they could be used—if there was any work. Stan got $100 a week when he worked, and Hardy got $10 a day. Laurel also worked for me as a gagman. "Babe" Hardy was just an extra. One day I got the idea to have them act together in a film. I called Hardy, and I told him I had a project for him that would bring in $10 a day, six days a week, and he shouted, "Oh, sir, that's marvelous news—sixty dollars a week! I can't believe it!" I said, "What's more, if the movies are good, you'll earn that much every week." Laurel was already earning a hundred a week, so for $160 a week, I had the greatest of comedy teams. Of course they got a raise pretty soon.

Their first film together had a real payoff. It was called *The Battle of the Century*. That's what the Dempsey-Tunney fight was known as. We knocked off for lunch, and the pie wagon pulled up. And we got the idea of starting a pie fight. Well, it was so successful that the audience forgot about the Dempsey-Tunney fight and *Battle of the Century* became the battle of the pies.

HAROLD LLOYD: We never had a script until we made a talking picture. When I say we didn't have a script, we had a script in our *mind* up to a point. The first thing I wanted to do was get a character, and, of course, they used to laugh at me. They said, "You have your character: your glasses, your straw hat." Well, that is so. It was the thing that identified me as Lloyd, the man with the glasses. But a little contrary to what most of my contemporaries did—most of them—I don't say they did it all the time—but most of them played just exactly the same character. Chaplin played his little tramp. Keaton was the stone face. Laurel and Hardy were practically always the same. But in the pictures that I did, we had in the beginning a variation. One character could be an introvert, a little weakling, and another could be an extrovert or a sophisticate or a hypochondriac. They all thought differently. They looked alike in appearance, with the glasses, which I guess you'd call a typical American boy. Still, the sophisticate thought entirely different from the character in *The Freshman.*

LEO MCCAREY: Lloyd was a great judge of comedy values. . . . He was a genius of comedy, really. And a great businessman.

MINTA DURFEE: I left Keystone in 1917. I didn't work for twelve years at all after that, and I lived in New York City. Things changed after Mabel left the place. Mr. Sennett never got over Mabel Normand, and of course, Mabel Normand was in love with Mack. I'm the girl that knows what I'm talking about. What happened was pretty silly but sad. Mae Busch was a pretty woman, and somebody brought her over to Keystone, which would be nothing unusual because everybody always came over to Keystone. Mabel, with all her kindness, introduced Mae to everybody and asked her to come down to her place at the beach . . . we all lived at the beach. And so Mae did, and this went along for about four or five months. Mae was a very good-looking and clever woman . . . but I don't think she really had a contract or anything. She was just there. Always there, and . . . well, somebody told Mabel . . . I think it was Ann Luther. Ann should not have told her. She said to Mabel, "If you want to catch Mack and Mae together, now is the time." So Mabel hails a cab, and she had on a kind of jockey cap. She used to wear it quite often, and she had loads of long hair down her back in curls, and she went over to where Mae lived, and of course they were not expecting her. There was Mack, sort of standing in his BVDs, and Mae in her nightgown. And when Mae saw who it was, she picked up a vase or something on the table and hit Mabel over the head with it! Along about four in the morning, Roscoe and I were down at the beach . . . and up the street comes Mabel, with her chauffeur practically carrying her and the blood just running all down those pretty curls. Of course we took her in. We didn't have a doctor down there at the beach. We were too healthy to have doctors in those days. Next day we had to bring her up to town to have a hospital, and she went into a coma which she stayed in for nearly four months. And *that* was what Mae Busch did for Mabel Normand! When she got well, Mabel Normand never again went back to work at the old Keystone lot. Well, Mae Busch was one woman none of us could ever take. We didn't have many things of that kind at Keystone. We were all pals. But Mack Sennett never got over this. He came back to the studio for about two weeks after Mabel getting hurt, but he would kind of hide behind things. He wouldn't walk right past all of us because he was ashamed of himself.

TAY GARNETT: He was a victim of his own arrogance, I guess. He was half-smashed all the time.

MINTA DURFEE: Our love for Mabel was so great. We lived with her and . . . we would have torn him into shreds, really. It was the end of something.

CHAPTER 3

SILENT DIRECTORS

ALLAN DWAN: The way the motion picture business was growing, in two or three months a great deal could happen. History could happen, as a matter of fact.

RICHARD SCHICKEL: Things moved so fast in those early years of development. The whole silent era isn't much more than two decades.

ROUBEN MAMOULIAN: You have to realize what a miracle films really are. You know, it's the only art that was not created by the artist. The scientist invented motion pictures: Thomas Alva Edison and George Eastman. First you had these cheap little nickelodeons that were nothing—amusement—you put a nickel in, and you see a ballerina dancing. Then a giant, D. W. Griffith, walked in, and with one film, *Birth of a Nation*, which could also be called "birth of an art," he created a new fine art of film.

KING VIDOR: I remember when I first saw *Birth of a Nation*. They had a comedy, a two-reel Mack Sennett comedy, and then they had the big *Birth of a Nation* with a hundred-piece orchestra, and I think they had a newsreel, probably, too. I took a streetcar from Hollywood all the way downtown and saw the film and came home, and it was an exciting evening. You got your money's worth. It was a big picture, a big show.

RAOUL WALSH: Griffith was there from the beginning. All the hacking around, all the pies in the face, all the growth and just playing around not knowing what it all was or what it could be or become . . . David Wark Griffith was there in the beginning. He was the best then. At Biograph on 14th Street in New York. His pictures had class.

LILLIAN GISH: It's hard to describe the little house on 14th Street in New York City that was the Biograph Studios. Just a normal little brownstone house. That was the studio. That was the office. We'd seen our friend Gladys Smith in a movie made by Biograph, *Lena and the Geese*. There were no actors' names on the films, and we knew her as Gladys Smith from the theater. Mother says, "Oh, what misfortune has fallen the Smiths? Do they have to go into movies to make a living?" Well, the next time we were in New York, we looked in the telephone book and found Biograph, right there on 14th Street, so we went down there and asked for Gladys Smith. They said, "There's nobody here by that name." We said, "Well, we *saw* her in *Lena and the Geese*," and they said, "Oh! You mean little Mary!" They called for her, and down the stairs came Gladys Smith! She had become Mary Pickford. After warm greetings, a man came down the same steps, singing "She'll never bring them in, she'll never bring them in." We felt this must be Mr. Biograph, because he seemed to own the whole thing. We were introduced, and he wanted to know if we could act. My sister, Dorothy, straightened way up and said grandly, "We are of the legitimate theater." And he said, "I don't mean reading lines. I mean, can you act?" Well, we didn't know what he meant because we'd been in professional theater since Dorothy was four and I was five. We had been in the theater for seven years by then. And he said, "Come upstairs. My company's up there. We'll soon find out." And he took us up there, and there they were, his troupe, including Lionel Barrymore. He called out to them a plot, and they started acting it out. It was a melodrama. There were two roles for girls in it. He didn't know our names, so I had a blue ribbon in my hair, and he took a red ribbon off someone and put it on Dorothy. And he called us "Red" and "Blue." He took out a little gun and started chasing us around the room, shooting at the ceiling! We thought we were in a madhouse! When we went back downstairs to Mother, we told her we'd never go there again, and she said, "Well, if there's a Barrymore up there, it can't be all bad." So that was our introduction to Biograph, to the movies, and, of course, to Mr. Griffith.

WILLIAM BEAUDINE: I graduated from high school in the Bronx in June 1909. Two weeks later, I was working for the Biograph. I was there till 1914, when they built a new studio on 175th Street and moved. They were down in a three-story stone mansion at 11 East 14th Street, and the stage we used was the ballroom—the only room big enough to put a set in. The other rooms were offices on the ground floor, cutting rooms on the second floor, and advertising department rooms on the third floor. Griffith was the only director at the time that I joined them. He used to make one single-reeler a week, and two split-reelers every month. His monthly output was three one-reel pictures and two five-hundred-foot comedies.

I was only seventeen years old.

In the wintertime we used to have to keep an alcohol lamp lit underneath the camera to prevent static. Out on location in the middle of winter, there would be a blanket around the tripod, and I would be under it with a box of matches to make sure the lamp didn't go out. I used to have to carry that monstrous Biograph camera and the tripod, which was iron, it wasn't any of this aluminum stuff. It was damn heavy. The camera was twice as big as any camera in existence at the time. I used to have the camera on one shoulder and the tripod under the other arm. I was assistant cameraman, property man, and assistant director all rolled into one. There was no such thing as a wardrobe person at that time, so if there was any wardrobe, that was part of my job, too. I was kind of an all-round guy—for $8 a week when I started.

While D. W. Griffith was working, I wasn't conscious of the fact that he was doing things differently from the other producers—like Pathé, Edison, Lubin, and those guys. I couldn't compare, I wasn't analytical at all. I mean, it was just a job to me.

Nobody that I ever saw got too familiar with D.W. You never felt like putting your arm on his shoulder. There was a certain invisible screen between you always. He exuded that. I don't know whether he demanded it.

He didn't have to demand it, as a matter of fact. He was always by himself. It was "Yes, Mr. Griffith." Nobody ever called him by his first name. He never called any of the actors by their first name that I know of. You always felt you had to keep your distance.

And yet he was a warm person to an extent. He was quite considerate. It was clear he really loved [cinematographer] Billy Bitzer. Billy was his right arm. No question about that.

He was a good guy to work with. He sort of gave you credit for your ability and your integrity and so forth. But if he said, "That's it," that was it. There's no compromising or argument—although I have seen him take suggestions from a grip . . . in a sort of Griffith way. That would be "Yes, thank you, Charlie." And then Griffith would play around with the idea and change it a little so it would be his anyway. It would start him in a new direction. But very few people stepped up and said much to him. He had more guys trying to carry his chair and that sort of stuff. Wherever Griffith started to bend down, somebody put a chair under him.

KARL STRUSS: Griffith was an interesting man to work with because he had strong ideas. And that's what I like. He was in control at all times.

ALLAN DWAN: When I got started directing, I'd seen a few of Griffith's pictures and was beginning to learn. I had to learn from the screen. I didn't have any other way. I had no model but him. All of us looked to each other, and we picked up and manufactured what technique we could and watched the other fellow. The only man I ever watched was Griffith.

RAOUL WALSH: I learned a lot from my work with Griffith: continuity and cutting and progressions—action. I watched the old man. I was always standing in back of him when I wasn't acting or something . . . always did that when I was working for him. I watched how he shot the battles for *Birth of a Nation*. He was inventing and defining . . . when I started directing, I tried to minimize titles and stuff and tried to copy Griffith with pantomime and action. I did a lot of action that didn't require titles, but they'd put them in anyway. "The posse is gaining." You could see it was gaining.

KARL STRUSS: Griffith was the only one who would actually watch all the action through the camera. He saw a moving picture in there.

JOSEPH RUTTENBERG: D. W. Griffith and his cameraman, Billy Bitzer, used to experiment with everything. They used to cut the bottom out of bottles and make a disc for the lens and shoot through that, and they'd get soft focus that way. They started that whole thing.

HENRY HATHAWAY: Griffith used irises and diffused backgrounds. . . . He'd take a piece of gauze and put it over the lens, and then he'd look through the camera and burn a hole in the gauze with a cigarette where he wanted the most light to come through. Griffith was the first one to use the close-up for storytelling, dramatically.

RAOUL WALSH: He discovered the close-up, you know. He perfected it. Never been seen before. Everything had been just set up. They nailed the camera down to the floor, and they came in like it was a stage play and played everything that way.

HENRY HATHAWAY: They considered acting to be full-figure acting. If you look at the old pictures, you'll find that most of them were full-figure acting. All the actors worked in full figure. And the only actor that still continued that clear through to the end was Charlie Chaplin, who considered himself, his feet and his hands and the cane and the shoes and everything, to be a part of him. He was really the one example of a full-figure actor. There was rarely ever a close-up of Charlie Chaplin. Allan Dwan told me that when Griffith first started using the close-up, the exhibitors complained that there were these heads on the screen with no bodies.

TAY GARNETT: The very earliest directors were thinking in terms of theater, and they photographed what they saw in front of them. It never occurred to them to do a close-up. They just got everybody in, got their whole set in, and played the action, put in the titles, and that was it. Then

D. W. Griffith came along, and he said, "We can do so much more. When the hero gets the news about his mother's tragic death, we must see the impact of that tragic news. We must move in close on this boy. We must see what it does to him. The only way we can get a look at his soul is if we get a look at his eyes. This means we must get another angle—be in close." Someone objected. "What are you going to do with that close-up after you get it, D.W.?" And Griffith said, "I'll stick it in there, and then we'll go back to the other scene." It was some time before they realized that if they had a close-up of the boy hearing the news, they should also have a close-up of the man who was telling the news. That put a frame around the entire little bit of business.

LILLIAN GISH: When he started taking close-ups, up in the office they said, "We pay for the whole actor." When Mr. Griffith entered films, he gave it the form and grammar it has today.

KARL STRUSS: In Griffith's battle scenes, everything had been planned ahead of time for any action by those leading the cavalry or whatever troops. The special-effects men with their explosions and smoke pots and things were placed.

RAOUL WALSH: In those days I was his assistant, too, besides acting in some of his movies. I handled the cowboys and the Indians and the rough stuff for him. And I had a tough job. See, they had no telephones, and all of a sudden around five o'clock he'd say, "Raoul," he'd say, "round up about ten or fifteen cowboys for tomorrow," and then I'd have to get in the car and go down to Main Street to find these bastards in bars. I got everything all ready for him because he knew I knew about horses and cowboys and riders and stuff. And I watched how he went through things. You know, he visualized things, and he could get them into a story and take you away somewhere. He had it all in his head.

GEORGE CUKOR: I was told that D. W. Griffith never had an actual script to work from, any kind of script, before talkies. These enormously complicated things were all in his head. Griffith never had a script! He kept it all in his head in every way.

LILLIAN GISH: Nine years we worked for him, and I never saw anything in his writing or anybody's writing except his name on the checks we were paid. You'd be in a big room, a sort of normal room, and he'd call out the plot. You'd walk through that, and it was up to you to find your character, how it moved, what it did, what it said. Of course, we all talked all the time we were doing it. We were in silent films, so whatever the character would say could be whatever we were saying. We just did what we were told.

KING VIDOR: I used to hear about D. W. Griffith, because when Lillian Gish, who worked for Griffith, came over to work for me on *La Bohème* and later *Duel in the Sun*, she demanded in her contract with MGM that we rehearse the same way Griffith rehearsed. And they told me about it at MGM, and I said, "Well, I'm willing to try it." She didn't want any props or any doors or any set. I had a rough set put up, some tables and chairs, but she didn't want anything. She said that interfered. Griffith used to write the script with actors, not with a typewriter but with actors. Because they were all in the stock company, they were all under salary, they were all there, and he used them, had them around on the stage, wrote the stories that way. And apparently they liked that, they got used to it. Lillian Gish was a great admirer of Griffith.

KARL STRUSS: Griffith was a great one for getting out his old pictures and running them for actors while we were shooting. In the morning, at nine o'clock, as soon as we got on the set, we'd be in looking at some of his earlier work. These films that he would show us . . . he was taking them seriously . . . but maybe he was just stalling a little to decide what he was going to do on set. But he was the boss, and I worked very closely with him as to what he wanted, whether it was big battle scenes . . . or scenes where we used the moving camera . . . or whatever. If the camera was moving, he was right on the dolly, you know, and he would dictate the action to us while we were doing it.

GEORGE CUKOR: He had come from the theater, but he invented the whole silent picture. He ennobled those melodramas like *Orphans of the Storm* and *Broken Blossoms* and *Way Down East*. He made them tragic and wonderful. I think he invented screen acting.

LILLIAN GISH: You couldn't "act." You had to "be." If he caught you acting, he knew the illusion was gone. So you had to be whatever you were supposed to be.

ALLAN DWAN: I liked a lot of the little things he was doing with actors. Of course, I had a different kind of acting group. He was using pretty girls and young people, and I was stuck mostly with character people. But I learned a lot of technique from him—where to put the camera and what kind of lighting to use. Griffith's pictures were my school, I'd say. The only one any of us had. There were other pictures we'd see, but I didn't care too much for them.

TAY GARNETT: I'll never forget one D. W. Griffith picture, I'm not sure what the title was. It showed a villain coming up to the house where the heroine lived. We had had very little prior chance to know this character. So it was imperative that the director establish him quickly as a hard-hearted, ruthless type before he met the girl. He was on his way to her front door. There was a bed of flowers bordering the sidewalk, and this guy stepped in them and smashed about a dozen pansies and kept right on going. That was all. But they inserted his foot crushing these pansies, and everyone in the audience knew he was a no-good so-and-so. It sold the point. Of course, as time went on, these symbolism gimmicks were much more refined, much more subtle and sophisticated, and consequently more effective. But they still required a tremendous amount of imagination and creativity. A director had to learn to say things visually. Ultimately he had to say visually substantially everything that is now said with words, sound effects, and music. Griffith knew how from the very first.

LILLIAN GISH: He was at the studio every day, and he did all the work everybody did.

KARL STRUSS: Although he was definitely the boss, I was never conscious of any friction between him and the people who were working with him or who were financing his pictures.

RAOUL WALSH: A very quiet sort of man, sort of a dreamer, a loner. He had very few friends. All wrapped up in the picture, y' know, and the different angles and stuff, and what he could do that was new. How he could mold these people to tell a story without any dialogue. Oh, he was a master . . . he was a master.

GEORGE CUKOR: He really was an *auteur*. He conceived the whole thing. He was the master. In silent pictures where there was no text, he wrote in his head. You don't have to do a great deal of script writing to be an *auteur*.

LILLIAN GISH: He said, "I'm trying to do with the camera what the eye can do. What I am trying to do is make you *see*."

GEORGE CUKOR: My lawyer was his lawyer, Loyd Wright. And he said, "He was a man of great dignity. In fact, whenever he came into a meeting at United Artists, his associates would rise. He carried himself with so much dignity." I had him to dinner, and Mary Pickford came. She was a remarkable woman, fascinating . . . an amusing woman. They were here at my home, and they were friends. I found that interesting because he was a mysterious man. He would keep people at a distance. He was charming, he was very distinguished, carried himself very well, but I should think he was unhappy. I liked him, but . . . you couldn't really tell very much about who he really was. The Screen Directors Guild decided he was the first one to be given a life membership. There was this great meeting and he was introduced, and everybody, all the great directors, rose to their feet and he looked at them and they were expecting . . . something. In a rather coy, silly way, he said, "Oh, go to hell." And sat down. He meant it to be a joke, but he was supremely tactless. They were expecting the master to say something because he was extremely respected.

SIDNEY FRANKLIN: To work with or under this man or even on the same lot with him was a terrific honor.

GEORGE CUKOR: I don't think he was a very good businessman. He ran his own company, but he wasn't only doing his own but also producing other ones. He spent himself. I really shouldn't talk about Griffith, because there are people who know much more about him than I do. Someone said he started to drink heavily, but I never saw that. I don't know. You don't know what his misery was. I think the last years of his life were terribly sad.

RAOUL WALSH: He was a man who lived by himself in a hotel and came to work alone and went home alone. His only interest was in making "pictures." Griffith was only about "pictures, pictures, pictures."

LILLIAN GISH: He died a poor man, but he never owed a penny to anybody.

JOHN SEITZ: D. W. Griffith was a great influence on other directors in the 1920s, but they had Cecil B. DeMille, too.

ALLAN DWAN: I never admired DeMille at all. I think he's a great showman, but as a director . . . no. He was a garish type, a big, big canvas fellow. He was a Barnum & Bailey guy.

CHARLTON HESTON: DeMille was very difficult. He was not a tyrant, but he had very firm control over the set. And nothing escaped him. He never raised his voice, but he could be very tough on assistant directors and propmen and people like that if they didn't provide what he had expected. I once said to someone, after he had chewed out a propman, "Mr. DeMille's pretty tough." And the guy said, "No, he's not tough. He just expects a good day's work. A *very* good day's work." And that's what he got from everyone.

TAY GARNETT: In the industry, among the writers, directors, and producers, DeMille was never really highly regarded. He was greatly respected for his showmanship, but as a director, he was considered old-fashioned, a little hammy, and quite heavy-handed. These were the general opinions of the professional picture makers. But DeMille knew what the public wanted better than anybody in the business. He consistently made great big money earners. His pictures were loaded with top-star casts. He spent money like it was ready for the incinerator. Never had there been anyone in this business who consistently made as much money with his pictures— until Disney came along. DeMille's silent films are magnificent, superb pieces of craftsmanship. Just magnificent. He's the greatest, really.

MITCHELL LEISEN: You know how many times I was fired by DeMille? Oh, oh, quite often! But I owe DeMille everything I ever learned about making pictures. Everything.

Everybody adored him that ever worked for him. He might raise holy hell on the set, but it would be with a propman or with me or with somebody, but never with the star. But what he would do is put the fear into the actor by criticizing somebody else. But the minute we walked off the stage, he couldn't have been more charming. He'd even apologize for blowing his stack or something: "There was nothing personal in that." I'd say, "I know. Don't worry, I've been with you long enough to know that." He had very positive ideas of what he wanted. As I said, most of it was in capital letters, neon tubes. You had to learn to think as he thought.

RAY RENNAHAN: DeMille was difficult. He was the boss. It was his way, and you had to hand it to the man, he was almost a miracle worker with some actors and everything. He had a sarcastic manner, but I think a lot of it was acting. I don't think he was sincere about it, because I was with him on quite a number of pictures. He'd run the dailies at his house over in Los Feliz. He had a projection room there, and the whole crew would go in, cameramen, art directors, costume people, assistant directors. It was a little show every night. Everyone was welcome, but he liked to be difficult. He'd pick his person.

HAL ROSSON: DeMille was a delight to work with! He always had time enough to tell you what he was trying to do. He had a scheme of what he wanted, and nothing was ever too monstrous in size for him to accomplish. My sister, Gladys Rosson, was a stenographer, and she got the job of being C.B.'s private secretary. She was with him for thirty-nine years. He was very loyal.

HENRY HATHAWAY: Everybody worked with DeMille sooner or later. He hired a lot of people. He had one guy who'd grab the megaphone when he let go of it and another guy to be there with a chair so he could sit down without looking behind him.

MERVYN LEROY: I was part of a camera crew on one of DeMille's pictures in the early days. And Cecil B. DeMille always said that I was the first one who invented soft focus . . . because I got everything out of focus.

RIDGEWAY CALLOW: From the point of view of assistant directors, he was indeed a tyrant. He was the most sarcastic man I have ever worked for, and I did several pictures with him in the capacity of "herder."

In the early days of the picture industry—that is, before the formation of the Directors Guild—whenever they filmed mob scenes, "herders" were employed to help out the few assistant directors assigned to the show. Although termed "herders," they were actually extra assistant directors for crowd control. In productions with complicated action of the extras, one herder was employed for every hundred extras. The biggest use of herders in those lush days, was, of course, DeMille, who specialized in epics with "casts of thousands."

DeMille was a master in mob control. He demanded complete silence when he spoke, so much so that one could hear a pin drop. He was addressing his mob one day when he caught an extra talking to her friend in the background. "When I'm talking, young lady, what do you have to say that's so important?" The girl in question was a well-known extra by the name of Sugar Geise, an ex-showgirl and a great wit. Bravely, she spoke up. "I only said to my friend, 'When is that bald-headed son of a bitch going to call lunch?'" There were a few apprehensive seconds of silence. Then Mr. DeMille yelled, "LUNCH!" So he did have a sense of humor.

MITCHELL LEISEN: He was a very religious man on Sunday . . . whenever he wasn't on his boat with his mistress.

The way I met DeMille and was hired by him is typical of the silent era. Ruth St. Denis and Ted Shawn were very good friends of my family, and Ted asked me if I'd like to go out to dinner one night. I sat next to a very charming woman [Jeanie MacPherson, DeMille's key collaborator for more than twenty-five years]. I didn't know who she was, being fresh out of college and just out here for a vacation, actually. She said she'd like to have me meet Mr. Cecil B. DeMille. Well, I'd been raised on all the DeMille silent spectacles, and I was so thrilled. When he met me, he said, "Miss MacPherson tells me about the wonderful work you do. I'd like to have you come and work for me." So I thought, All right, it would be a good chance to see the inside of a studio, so I went. DeMille was making *The Admirable Crichton* (renamed *Male and Female* because he got several letters from exhibitors saying they didn't want another naval picture and who was this Admiral Crichton?). DeMille wanted some costumes designed, and I'd never designed costumes in my life. As I said, I was out here on a vacation, but what the hell. I went through Ted's library of art books and went to the public library and a few other things, and I made three sketches. DeMille said he'd give me $100 apiece for them and a year's contract for $100 per week. I signed a piece of paper, and then I found out I not only had to design these three things, I had to do fifty more, and I also had to make them! I went back to DeMille and said I was sorry but I needed to go back to Chicago, where I had another job. He said, "You have a contract with me." I said, "Yes, Mr. DeMille, but I have a job in Chicago. This is just movies." He said, "Well, it may be just movies to you, but it's still a legitimate contract and you are under contract to me." And I was. And that's where I started. And I've been out here ever since.

EDITH HEAD: On the big DeMille films, we would work sometimes fifteen, sometimes eighteen months in in preparation. But remember, I was one of six designers on those films. We would have designers who did nothing but the men's uniforms or the clothes for the charioteers, and someone else would do the dancing girls. There were designers for specific periods . . . and DeMille did not want accurate clothes. His costumes were not academically correct to the historic period. He wanted what *he* wanted. A lot of people have been rather cruel about the DeMille attitudes toward fashion, but it was what DeMille wanted, and the public got it and loved it, and that was all he cared about.

MITCHELL LEISEN: You see, DeMille had no nuances. Everything was in neon lights six feet tall: LUST. REVENGE. And so forth and so on. De-Mille loved wild imagination. I don't think anybody ever wore a dress like the white peacock costume I made for Miss Gloria Swanson in *Male and Female*. Remember, I did that crazy sketch, and then he wanted me to make it! I'd never made a dress in my life before, and the head of the ward-robe department at that time was not about to have *me* making anything. So she stuck me in a little room about the size of a table with a bunch of women to help me. The train on that dress is batik. The peacock feathers are all painted in with wax, and it was dyed a pale green so you saw the white feathers on this train. Then it was embroidered with pearls for the eyes. You paint it with wax. Then you dye it and you press the wax out of the material, and it leaves the pattern. Plain, ordinary beeswax. You have to be very careful not to crack it, or you'll get a crackle effect. So that was how the dress was made, for the first time.

Gloria was a very small person, very short. To give her height, I had wooden shoes made, which were Babylonian bulls standing on four legs. The wings came up on the sides of her feet, and that's what she wore.

TAY GARNETT: Originally, there was an intense rivalry between the Griffith faction and the DeMille faction, but Griffith was nearly nonexistent by the time DeMille had achieved his enormous stature. Griffith had slipped badly by the end of the silent era, but DeMille never did slip. He was a highly intelligent man with the most fantastic sense of what the public wanted of any man I ever knew. And he gave it to them constantly. I don't think he ever had a flop.

TEETE CARLE: DeMille had his own publicity staff. He had his own personnel all the way from go. He was savvy. If you want to set up a big big picture for sale, I would say just let him do the whole thing. I was his publicity director and was instrumental in bringing in the whole publicity for DeMille on *The Ten Commandments* [1956 remake]. DeMille had two unit men to write copy, a girl who did nothing but promote the religious material, and all the public relations such as women's clubs and things like that, and he had an art editor and a flock of secretaries—it was all his own special publicity staff. Not that of the studio. They were all on *Ten Commandments*, and I have to tell you that *Gone with the Wind* really didn't have as complete and detailed and in-depth campaign that *Ten Commandments* did because *Ten Commandments* not only had the campaign for the picture as a picture, but it went into the uncovering of hidden audiences or new audiences or lost audiences. In other words, DeMille was trying to attract people who had long since stopped going to the motion pictures because of age or whatever. DeMille knew if he was going to have to bring in the ultimate in money, he couldn't just depend on people who were going to the movies regularly. He had to go out and dig up these other people.

MERIAN C. COOPER: Oh, he was a great showman, DeMille was. A great showman.

RIDGEWAY CALLOW: Well, in the end, DeMille is a very famous name. And there's that classic Hollywood joke.

RUDY BEHLMER: I first heard it about the time DeMille's remake of *Ten Commandments* was released. It concerned an imaginary situation supposedly taking place while DeMille was filming the parting of the Red Sea. There were hundreds of extras, special-effects rigs to shake the earth, dump tanks to unleash thousands of gallons of water on the extras, et cetera. DeMille explained that three cameras were covering the scene, since it would be too costly to shoot it again. Then DeMille yelled, "Action!" All hell broke loose. The ground shook, the water came down in torrents. The effect was superb. After the chaos had subsided, DeMille checked with the number one cameraman: his lens had cracked from some hurtling debris. The number two cameraman was so excited he forgot to take off the lens cap. The number three cameraman—way up high on a tower—upon being asked how the action was for him yelled down . . .

RIDGEWAY CALLOW: "Ready when you are, C.B.!"

RICHARD SCHICKEL: Say what you will, Cecil B. DeMille is a Hollywood legend.

HAL MOHR: An influential and important director I worked with in the silent years was Erich von Stroheim. I've been hailed today for things that von Stroheim did on *Greed*, thirty years ago, before I ever did it. He was a fiend for work. Many nights, I never even got away from the studio, I'd just sleep for two or three hours on the set and go to work as soon as I woke up the next day.

FAY WRAY: In those days there was very little consideration about overtime. There were no unions. There was no Screen Actors Guild.

HAL MOHR: Von Stroheim . . . he was a master. He had his own company, a big group of technicians and actors who appeared in all his films, who moved with him from project to project.

FAY WRAY: I came to meet von Stroheim first through a woman who was an agent, not for actors but for books. She was an author's agent. And I was under contract to Universal and was making two-reelers and four-reelers and westerns and that kind of leading lady sort of thing, and anyway, she came to the studio and she saw me and she said that she thought I would be good for von Stroheim's new picture and she would like to arrange to take me to an interview with him. Of course, I was exceedingly responsive to that idea because I admired him very much. I knew he was a strong and important talent, and so I was delighted and we made arrangements, although I was under contract to Universal. It never occurred to me that it would be unethical for me to go toodling off to get myself something else to do.

We went to see him, but we had to go through a man who was the vice president of the company which was organized to make *The Wedding March*, it being an independent situation, and this man, when he looked at me, he said, "Absolutely no." I was not blond, and I was perhaps too tall, because von Stroheim was short and he would be my leading man as well as my director, but my feeling was extremely strong. I had the mystical feeling that the role belonged to me, and so I was not going to be dissuaded.

We went in to see von Stroheim, and it was really a tremendous experience for me to meet him and sense his electric, dynamic quality. I sat in a chair while he told the film's story. He paced up and down, telling it, and I simply listened, and finally he said to me, "Do you think you could play that role?" And I said, "I *know* I can!" The interview was over, and I stood up to say goodbye, and he took my hand and he said, "Well, goodbye, Mitzi." That was the character's name! And in my thinking, he was saying to me, "The role is yours." My tensions had been building up, so when he said that, it was just so beautiful and so simple a way, I thought, of telling me that the role was mine, that I just simply burst into tears. Now, I think up to that point, he was only moderately interested. He was considering a lot of other people, but that really, really got him absolutely excited, and then his whole attitude accelerated and he thought it was marvelous that I was responsive, and so far as I know, from that moment, he never considered anyone else.

And so I went very soon to work with von Stroheim, and it was marvelous. There was a sense that this was not going to be an ordinary experience.

HAL MOHR: Everybody loved Von, and he loved everyone else. Well, it's a funny thing, but I loved von Stroheim, too. I think he was a marvelous man. I think he was truly a genius. I also think he was an exhibitionist . . . and a wastrel . . . and a sadistic guy. He liked to make people suffer. Well, what can I tell you?

I'll never forget the day when actor Matthew Betz had to play a scene where he cut off a piece of meat when he saw Fay Wray for the first time and then shove this hunk of meat in his mouth. Stroheim—he was a sadist of the first order—would keep the cameras running as long as he could until this guy, you'd see him begin to turn pale and he'd throw up. He just couldn't chew the damned stuff. It was hot as hell in that studio, and the set was supposed to be a butcher's shop where the meat had been hanging so long it was full of maggots. Von Stroheim would laugh at Betz. He thought it was funny as hell. And we'd do take after take with the poor bastard throwing up, eating this maggoty meat . . . and Von just kept on and this guy was getting sicker and sicker, Von enjoying it more and more. I mean, it was a most uncomfortable picture to make.

WALTER PLUNKETT: He was very conceited, very superior, an autocratic person. You went to him praying he would say okay. He had very definite ideas of what he wanted and didn't allow you much leeway to create.

MARGARET BOOTH: Well, of course, von Stroheim was a very difficult man to work with. Temperamental and difficult, and he wanted his own way.

HAL MOHR: Yes, Stroheim *was* a very temperamental guy, but when I took over a picture he'd been having some trouble with up to that time, he and I got along so well, we were almost sleeping together. It was one of those things—we were so fond of each other. And it was a very trying picture to make. He was performing in it as well as directing, and he was a man who had to have his uniforms and costumes be the ultimate in perfection. I mean, if a man was supposed to be wearing an iron boot, he *was* wearing an iron boot. There was no nonsense about the man.

RAY RENNAHAN: Von Stroheim was von Stroheim. He was a fanatic for detail. He would see something—if he had a line of solders and he would see something, he would go down and change a button on a man's lapel or something like that. He was so observing of everything. I remember one time we were at MGM, and I was on a four-foot parallel so we could get a high shot of this scene, and von Stroheim was up there on the camera with me and he saw a man's collar that was turned up and he walked right out on the platform. He wasn't conscious of being on a four-foot platform, and he fell down and broke his leg. Just to change a little collar! He could have called in an assistant or anyone to do it, but not him. He broke his leg instead.

FAY WRAY: The detail of every little thing mattered—the locket I was to wear, the cross I was to wear, the earrings—it was all a lovely experience, and to feel that someone had every phase of the film so well in hand, so well in mind, just made you feel secure. That was a lovely feeling.

HAL MOHR: I remember shooting the apple orchard scene in *The Wedding March*. We had these apple blossoms filtering down through the trees constantly, and to match everything up perfectly, the script girl would have to know if an apple blossom hit the star's forehead or landed on her shoulder or anything. . . . If he saw it and she didn't speak of it before the next take, the matching take, he'd raise holy hell about it. . . . You can imagine, with these things slipping down through the trees. It was murderous. He was a real taskmaster. And those blossoms, they were all put on the tree at one time. They were all made by hand and put on one at a time.

FAY WRAY: Fifty thousand handmade apple blossoms! Paper apple blossoms. And some of them were wax.

HAL MOHR: Oh, it was a beautiful set.

FAY WRAY: The preparation, the details and the care and consideration that went into everything! The costumes and the testing and the photography by Hal Mohr . . . when I saw myself up there on the screen, I just couldn't believe it. It had a kind of luminous glow that made you go into a kind of make-believe experience that I thought was beautiful. I was already transported into the feeling of the whole film, and it just continued that way right to the very end.

HAL MOHR: Of course, he *was* a slave driver. But it was pleasant. It was hard work, but it was pleasant. I had no gripe at all other than the fact that Von had to have a patsy, you know. He had to have a whipping boy, and fortunately I was not his whipping boy until I began to see it coming my way. That was when I broke the thing up and got the hell out of there. I refused to be a whipping boy.

LEWIS MILESTONE: I liked working with him. I directed him in two pictures. He never gave you any trouble. He was a very disciplined man.

When he acted, he acted. He never interfered. If I talked a scene over with him, sure, like any actor, he would have some suggestions, but he was very, very easy to get along with. Yes, I liked working with him, and so did Billy Wilder . . .

BILLY WILDER: . . . I always liked his pictures, and I liked him. As a very young kid in Berlin, I collected his autographs . . . ones that he had sent back to my requests. I decided to do that picture, *Five Graves to Cairo*, and we cast him as Rommel. He's not an actor, really, but a tremendous personality. He arrived from Paris, where he lived, while we were out at Indio shooting tank scenes in the desert. When I came back to the studio, they told me that Stroheim was in Western Costumes, trying on his uniform as Rommel. I had never met him before in my life, so Western Costumes is just around the corner from Paramount, you know, on Melrose, and I rushed across and there he is. I clicked my heels, and I said, "My name is Wilder." He says, "How are you?" In order to be kind to him and make him feel good, I said, "Who would have ever thought that little Wilder is going to direct big Stroheim?" And he just sort of bobbed to me a little bit. I said, "You know your problem, Erich, is that you were always ten years ahead of your time." And he looks directly at me, and he says, "*Twenty!*" That was it. That was Stroheim. And then *Greed*, of course. That was the beginning of when Hollywood started to be afraid of directors who are let loose. Somebody told me that Stroheim was shooting *Greed* in San Francisco and he stopped shooting for three days because there wasn't enough horseshit in the streets. They had to collect it from all over, from San Jose or wherever, all over, because that's what he wanted. Plenty of good horseshit.

FAY WRAY: Today people always talk about his extravagance. I suppose I was aware of that to some degree. There were scenes on *The Wedding March* which were to be made in which I was not appearing, and I was not supposed to come to the set at all because those were the scenes that were set in a bordello. I was not allowed on the set. All that was supposed to take ten days or something like it. They started shooting, and it went on and on and on. It went on, I think, for three weeks. And so I became aware that the costs of the movie were going well beyond what had been scheduled. And he spent money on many things that would never be seen on the screen, such as the cost of musicians. He always had music going on the set at all times, and I have only to hear some of those Viennese waltzes to be absolutely transported back into that time.

HAL MOHR: Von Stroheim *was* an extravagant man. He used up a hell of a lot of film, very extravagant. He was not a cheap director as far as the producer was concerned. If he wanted to get an over-the-shoulder close-up and he couldn't get the camera where he needed it, he'd cut a hole in the wall. Today he would be impossible. He just couldn't exist today because he would bankrupt people. He would never say "Cut." He'd just keep going and going. He'd do a scene—say a close-up of a star—and we'd do maybe . . . oh, hell . . . as many as thirty or forty takes of a scene without any explanation as to why he wanted to do it over again. He'd just say, "Oh, let's do it again," you know. Unhappy about it, obviously, but he wouldn't give any new direction or anything like that, just hoping out of the next take could come an inspired performance that would give him exactly what he was looking for because he didn't know what the hell he was looking for. He just knew it had to be a certain thing. And sometimes he'd just get up and say, "Oh, the hell with it." Sometimes he'd print them all. Oh, yes, he was extravagant. With any small problem or any difficulty, he would stay with it until he got it the way he wanted it.

They went broke making that film, ran out of money due to his extravagances. I don't want to say anything about him that would be unkind, and he was certainly no more extravagant or anywhere near as willfully extravagant as this Italian son of a bitch that they got over here to make *Zabriskie Point* and broke MGM. A man that had made *one* picture by accident, a great picture called *Blow-up*. And on the strength of that, he took it upon himself to destroy the American film industry by making *Zabriskie Point*. Have you seen that thing?

FAY WRAY: Von Stroheim had taste in photography. He was very, very demanding about how he himself should be photographed, and that's where it was difficult sometimes for Hal Mohr to do just as he wanted. They would get tired, and the shooting went on very, very long hours, very long. And there was no air-conditioning or any of the amenities or joys of that kind of thing we have today. It was very hard work, just physically, but it was for me a tremendous pleasure. I really adored doing that film, just adored doing it. I would arrive in the morning about six o'clock and perhaps wouldn't leave until nine. So many times, as I drove home, it seemed to me I would have to hold my head in my left hand and turn the wheel with my right because I was very, very tired. But I always went back to the studio with great anticipation.

HAL MOHR: The only thing that he was very alert about on photography was that he had an air cyst behind his head. It looked like a tumorous sort of a thing, but it was just a cyst of air in there. And I think Von was somewhat of a physical coward, because he never wanted that thing punctured or removed and he didn't want to see it on the screen. And his hair, as you know, was always clipped very close to his scalp, so in photographing him I had to be very cautious that there was never a highlight that would hit that cyst. Otherwise I don't recall him telling me a damn thing about how things were to be shot, either on lighting or diffusion or what lenses to use or a damn thing. We'd look at the rushes every night, and the only thing I ever got from him in the projection room was "That's beautiful, Hal. That's beautiful, Hal." He never, never made any comments as to things he wanted differently. I don't ever remember Von looking through the camera or even saying "We should have a close-up here" or anything. So far as I can remember, and I would remember if it had been anything different, he never interfered in any way at all with the way I set the camera, the way I lined up a shot.

FAY WRAY: He could be very despondent. He was moody at times. As an actor, sometimes he couldn't work. He just couldn't pull himself up into the scene. I remember on one occasion, on one evening, he was weary, he was tired, and the musicians tried to play more happy music and so on and he didn't feel like smiling and he couldn't smile and so we all went home.

HAL MOHR: He sometimes thought he was failing, but you'll never find a greater picture than his *Greed*.

PAUL IVANO: I was hired to shoot some of the Death Valley scenes in von Stroheim's epic *Greed*, but there was nothing, no place to live out there in those days. We lived in tents. A hundred and twenty-five during the day, not counting the sunshine, and our tents never got cooler than a hundred and two at night and the paint fell off the cars, cracked up and fell. I think one of our cooks died from the heat. I told the production manager, "Send me back." I was in bad shape. There was no use of staying there. That expedition out there cost money.

LEWIS MILESTONE: In those days, when you spent a million dollars, it was like spending ten times that amount today. Or twenty times. And Erich von Stroheim felt, you see, that his job was to create a motion picture and the cost was the production office's business. And they tried to bring him into the framework of the emerging studio picture business. Things were changing, becoming more organized, more controlled, than in the earlier days. Now budget people were starting to give a director a schedule of "You're going to shoot it in six weeks or five weeks or seven weeks or eight weeks." And if you go over a day or two, then there was a panic. And von Stroheim couldn't care less. See, he was making *his* picture, and that's what he was trying to do. His biggest excess was, of course, when he did *McTeague*—he called it *Greed* eventually—and he wound up with something like twenty-three, twenty-four reels of film, and that's nothing exceptional because maybe that could happen before you assemble the thing, before you actually do the editing. It might be in twenty, twenty-five, thirty reels. But then you edit and you bring it down. But in those days, they said, "Thirty reels of film!" And they wouldn't let him cut it. They wouldn't let him do the editing. Thalberg grabbed the picture away from him, and he did the editing. It started becoming a constant battle between the director and the producer.

Von Stroheim had ideas about how to show *Greed*. He proposed that it would be a wonderful thing to do an important picture on two consecutive nights. And they howled with laughter, and they laughed him out of the office. But subsequently people actually did that. They did it in a stage play. For [Eugene] O'Neill's play that went on the stage, you came to the theater at five o'clock in the afternoon, they let you out for dinner, you came back to see the rest of it on the second session. So it wasn't that crazy, but anything von Stroheim suggested, they immediately ruled out. Look—after he left Hollywood and he went to Paris, he did some wonderful work as an actor. But *Greed* was destroyed.

JOHN SEITZ: Cut down, it was twenty-six reels. Von said he couldn't take out another inch of the film if it killed him. And it had to be shorter. Someone who saw Von's own lengthy cut said, "Well, we asked for a bungalow, and he gave us an apartment house."

FAY WRAY: He had a marvelous talent to find some thing, some mannerism, some attitude that you might have naturally that he liked, and he would say, "Use that." You know? "Do that." He made you feel that you were in fact creating as you went along. And he was not an imposer of ideas. I think he rather freed you, because there was a strength about him that made you feel that whatever you did was all right and that he would just guide you. When you did something, whatever you did that he liked, he would praise you very, very much. He made me feel quite wonderful. Of course, I was relating to him as an actor, because he played opposite me.

I regret it very much that I couldn't do another film with him. I felt I would've grown very much as an actress if I could've stayed—done one or two more. I didn't see him again until some years later, and he went to Europe, came back. There was an evening when he was at a party that was at William Wyler's house, and we talked a lot and I could see his sadness. It was a very, very large sadness, I think, for not having been able to continue to make films here.

HAL MOHR: I think that in his way, Von contributed so much to motion pictures. There's a debt of gratitude that the industry owed him that I think should be remembered. With all of his weaknesses, and there were a hell of a lot of things wrong with von Stroheim, I do think he contributed greatly to the motion picture industry.

ALLAN DWAN: Pictures became big business. We all watched each other to see what the other guy was doing. We admired the foreign films that came over, too. They interested us because they had some effects we liked. They had some very good technical things. . . . And of course we liked their backgrounds. They were different from ours, and that intrigued us. Sometimes we kind of got a giggle out of them, but outside of that there wasn't too much that we got from them that we weren't inventing for ourselves—except the people who made them. We got them, all of them. The minute somebody made a picture that was any good, somebody here would send for them right away. "He's too good—get him away from Germany or France. Get him over here." Mary Pickford brought Ernst Lubitsch over for herself and got a headache. They didn't get along at all. Lubitsch didn't think like she did at all, but we liked Lubitsch. We liked his so-called touches. And Murnau I remember. We all paid attention to Lubitsch and Murnau.

KING VIDOR: I was greatly influenced by the German films made in Berlin, by people like Fritz Lang, E. A. Dupont, and Murnau. They were beginning to free the camera, move the camera. They were showing UFA films from Germany down in Los Angeles in a small theater. I had to go from Hollywood to Los Angeles to see those films. Murnau was breaking through with the perambulator idea in *The Last Laugh*. I think the camera followed somebody through a lobby and up an elevator and stayed right with him.

LEWIS MILESTONE: When American film was influenced and made the first step forward, that real progress was due to the Germans. The Germans invented the angle. They revolutionized the structure of the sets. They would build a real place, so that every place offered you an interesting angle. I remember before the Germans came, if you had a kitchen and a dining room and a living room, it was one, two, three, the third wall was out like on a stage, that was a plane for the camera. So you always had to shoot the one wall that was missing. In other words, what they were doing, they were following the theater. You see, the proscenium arch still ruled, and what the Germans taught me and everybody else, for that matter, that wanted to learn is that there is no proscenium arch in motion pictures. You have absolute freedom—you can make the audience follow you, where you want to go. You can make them go through a key-hole, through a hole in the floor, you can make them look through a hole in the ceiling, wherever you want to go, you can make the audience see what you want them to see. So there is absolute freedom.

HAL MOHR: I worked with Paul Leni, a German director who could speak very little English, and he had manners of directing that were truly of the silent picture. He directed from his director's chair. He had quite a complex of apparatus set up. He had a siren with a hand crank screwed on one side of it. In the pocket of it he had a couple of pistols loaded with blank cartridges. He had a police whistle around his neck, and oh, a big bronze Chinese gong type of thing alongside of the chair, with the thing that you hit it with. He would rehearse a scene, and, because he spoke very little English, he'd lay the scenes out and tell his actors, "On certain signals, when I blow ze vistle, you do so-and-so. When I do ze siren, you do so-and-so. When I beat ze gong, you do so-and-so," and then the pistol shots were to get them excited, and he had these wild chases through the theater sets and it was like a three-ring circus. When he was doing a scene, you would hear the siren going, the whistle blowing, beating hell out of the gong, pistol shots all over the place. That was Leni's way of directing. A little turpentine on the end of a long stick would have helped a bit, too, to wake some of his bad actors up. A touch on the bongo to wake them up. Roy D'Arcy, one of the actors in those days, was a very bad actor. I don't know what the hell has become of him. He was very bad. They thought he was going to be a second von Stroheim or something. They should have put him back where they found him.

Leni and I had a great empathy. He lived up in Hollywoodland. I used to go over to his house, and we would sit down and have breakfast together and we'd talk about the day's work. He used to eat great platters of uncooked ham for breakfast, just slabs of it. He'd eat more food. I have never seen a man eat as much as he ate. I think that is what killed him. He was a very heavyset man, very fat. But he was a charmer. He was a wonderful little old guy and a lot of fun. He had a grand sense of humor, and we had a very close relationship. He'd tell me what the scenes were. He'd have it all written down on little pieces of paper, and we would discuss the scenes and he would tell me what he would want and how he would like to see it and how he would like to do it. And then I would have some knowledge of what we were going to do, and when we'd get on the set, I would know how to lay the thing out for him.

Leni and I would plan on paper. There was a wonderful crane—completely mobile—and you could do anything with it. We'd plan—we knew the length of the arm, and we'd lay it out on paper. And we had a little model of the boom, we built a miniature of the set, we had a scale model of the boom to show the positions we could get it in in relation to the set where the scenes would be played.

We were trying to do things with a camera that had never been done before. That was the entire motivation of the thing. That was the movies in those days.

KARL STRUSS: It wasn't until I worked with Murnau that I did lots of camera movements and tracking shots. He was really the first one. He knew how to use camera movement. He really was a genius when it came to using dolly shots. You see, in other words, you're living with the action. You start, and then you follow the action, and then you go through to a climax. And when you get there, you must not immediately cut to something else. You want to stay with it a little while before you do your first cut. It has to be a psychological thing. So many copied Murnau's style, but they didn't get the feel of the scene. It got to be mechanical—the camera just moves. Of course, nowadays they use the zoom lens quite a bit, and naturally there is a difference in moving in with a camera to a close-up and staying back and moving in with the telephoto lens, with the zoom lens.

MERVYN LEROY: Murnau used a lot of camera movement, but he also knew that you only move a camera when it's supposed to move. Don't just open on a lit cigar and pan all the way back to show the audience that this is a living room with a cigar lit. That you don't need. And one important thing that I was taught by Murnau, a very good director, was that if you have a phone in a room, never put a phone where you are going to use it when you start to shoot, because you might want to change during the action. If they don't see a phone on the set, you can put it anyplace you want to—for when you need it, I mean. If they see it someplace when you start out, you have to leave it there afterwards. Suppose I want to play an action over in the corner of the room and I plant the phone way over there. Then I have to walk over to it. But if they haven't seen the phone on the set, you can put it anywhere you want it. Once they pick it up, then it's planted. Murnau said, "Never put a phone down unless you need it." That was quite a tagline.

FLOYD CROSBY: Murnau had a good sense of where to put the camera. I worked with him on *Tabu*, and in the final sequence the hero is swimming out to sea, trying to catch the boat his love is in. We put the camera on top of three parallels . . . and shot it from a high angle. That was the most difficult but also the most effective place to put the camera for that sequence, and he knew that. He had a very good feeling for camera. Oh, I thought he was a fine director. *Faust* was a very interesting picture because everything was at a cockeyed angle and there never was a right angle anywhere in the picture. He was original. Murnau was very talented. He was imaginative and an experienced director.

I also had the experience of working with [Robert] Flaherty, and he didn't really even direct. He didn't know how. He knew nothing but was a likable person. If you could have combined Murnau's talent with Flaherty's personality, you'd have had a terrific guy.

TAY GARNETT: Murnau's *The Last Laugh* was the talk of the town. Not entirely because of the moving camera . . . He used close-ups that were *extremely* close. He'd show just the mouth in a laugh, eyes clouding up for a big cry. There were several Murnau pictures that were very successful here, but *Last Laugh* was a solid sender.

KARL STRUSS: In the case of Murnau's *Sunrise*, which he made over here, in the beginning he'd never let his actors see the dailies at all. Because he knew that when an actor or an actress sees himself on the screen, they begin to have an entirely different point of view about their performance. They're thinking of their looks. They're not thinking of the action. They're not thinking of the drama. It introduces an element that shouldn't be there in their performance, and a good director always knows what he wants. And Murnau was a good director.

Working with him was a great experience. People talk about "the German influence" of those years. On *Sunrise*, the greatest new difference that I ran into was the fact that he had the sets built in perspective. For instance, in the beginning of the picture, Margaret Livingston comes into this little cottage where George O'Brien and Janet Gaynor live. She comes and stands in the doorway. Well, the actual doorway was built just high enough to accommodate her height. In the hallway beyond the door, the first time I walked on the set, when I went to the doorway and looked . . . why, here was a miniature door across the hall that was only three feet high! She just came in from one side close to the door and stepped in and looked, see. I had to stoop to get through that doorway! And the floor went up. The floor had been going down in the room that she looked into. This was a great effect. It had a little more illusion to it. He liked to make things not too literal. Once I used graduated gauze on my camera . . . overlapping gauzes. I'd add a single layer, then a double, then a triple, then a quadruple, and so on until the image blacked out. I told Mr. Murnau that it'd take at least thirty feet or more to get this slowly disappearing effect. It's an extraordinary fade-out and fade back in giving no illusion of time dimension. He said, "Go ahead and do it." He was a true original.

Everyone started trying to imitate him, but the imitations were never as good as the original. They missed something. It's just like if a story comes out and it's a great success, then you'll find that in the next year you'll find half a dozen imitations of that story. You know, different people, different locales, and all. It's never as good as the original. I mean, that happens. It's plagiarism of a sort, but they can't prove it.

PAUL IVANO: I worked with Murnau. Before he came to California, I was working at Fox with the best directors, Frank Borzage, John Ford—and Murnau's assistant, Mr. Bing Arnold, came to me and said, "Come. I will introduce you to Murnau. He is a great guy." He took me to Murnau in his office. He walked in military style—German military way—clicked his heels and introduced me, and backed out of the room. And the first thing Murnau says is "Mr. Ivano, I understand you're a good cameraman, but you know, it's a great honor to work for me." I was always very indepen-dent, so I said, "There is no honor for me to work for anybody. I don't have to work for you." So I didn't. When they were going to make *Four Devils*, I shot the tests for it on behalf of Ernie Palmer, who was Murnau's cameraman for the film.

HENRY BLANKE: Back in Germany, I thought the most beautiful pictures, the most artistic pictures, were the Swedish pictures: [Victor] Sjöström, [Erich] Engel, and Mauritz Stiller. They were my "foreign" films. And I took Lubitsch to see those. He said, "I hate them!"

CHAPTER 4

SILENT ACTORS

HAL MOHR: We were all paying attention to each other's work, but those of us making the pictures behind the scenes didn't think too much about the actors. We had our job to do. They had theirs. It was the directors who had to deal with them, not us, but Mary Pickford and Doug Fairbanks got married, and oh, boy. Nobody could talk about anything else, and when they went overseas on a trip, millions turned out to have a look at them. We were all just working away each day and we were only starting to learn that for people who went to the movies, the actors—the so-called movie stars—were the thing.

RAOUL WALSH: Actors' names weren't on the credits in the earliest days, but as things moved forward, all of a sudden, there were *stars*! Some were easy to work with, some were not. Some could act. Some couldn't. People just picked the ones they liked and kinda worshipped them.

LILLIAN GISH: I never realized the power of film—and what it meant to act in pictures—until one time Mother fell ill in London and I got on the train in Pasadena to go to her, still in costume and makeup from the set. Every station we passed was crowded with people, and all the people on and off the train were wishing me well. I thought, This isn't about me, really. This is film. This is power. That's when it first struck me—the power of film, of being in the movies. There's nothing like it.

HOOT GIBSON: Everybody liked cowboys. Right away, people liked cowboys ridin' and ropin' and tearin' around. The original five of the big western stars of the picture business in the early teens was Harry Carey, Tom Mix, Buck Jones, William S. Hart, and myself. And my boyhood friend I was raised with and rode with, Art Acord. I always had real cowboys under contract to me, too. There was ten of them. I always kept all of them on salary because I knew that when we got into scenes, we'd have some real riding—that's what people wanted—plus some great stories. Cowboy stars and exciting stories were what people wanted back then. And you needed some real cowboys for that.

MINTA DURFEE: Some people got to be more popular than others, and they became what they call stars. Lots of comics! Roscoe, my husband, was a star because he was so funny. The Kops. And Mabel, of course. Mabel Normand.

Mabel Normand was the greatest comic of them all. And she was a real person. . . . She always gave me a nickname. Instead of Minta, she'd call me "Mintwa," "Mintwitty," "Mintoola." She never had any sense of propriety. If she was passing your house and she wanted to come in, she would come in. It might be one o'clock in the morning or something. You see, we all lived in such close proximity. We were all pals at Mack Sennett's.

GERTRUDE ASTOR: You know, you just worked. You were in a stock company, so, you know, you worked as an extra one day and the next day you're the queen or something else, but pretty soon, you find out whether the people buying the tickets want to see you again or not. When that happened, the people making the movies were happy to pay you more money. You were bringing in money, so you got more money. I did all right. I got along financially very well and sort of got into good money, don't you know.

RAOUL WALSH: All of a sudden, there were these publicity men. A publicity man in those days would come down to interview you, and you had no time to sit and talk, so he'd write whatever the hell he wanted. And you'd read that stuff and what the hell, was this guy drunk? But nobody cared. It sold the pictures, and it sold the stars. And everybody was living a bit wild anyway. There was all this money out of nowhere. Everybody was talking about their money.

GERTRUDE ASTOR: I remember Lon Chaney. He was just learning to do those faces and all those heads and things, or wanted to or was trying to and everything, and he was so mad because he wasn't getting up in the money, and I was. And he got $75 a week and I got up to $125 a week, which, out there, was great! Oh, that was great in those early days. He'd say, "I don't know how you can get $125 when I'm doing this and I'm doing that and I only get $75." He'd say, "I'm going to get out of this place. I'm going to leave this place!" Every day of my life I heard about that. "A hundred and a quarter a week, and I'm getting seventy-five, and I do this and I do this and all." He was a great guy, really, but very plain.

HENRY HATHAWAY: To show you how loose the studio was when it came to production and job definitions in those days, I can cite one person: Lon Chaney. Lon Chaney used to come work (and I know 'cause I was a propman then) at six thirty or seven o'clock in the morning. If there was a stage where they had a cabaret with a couple of girls or something, he would choreograph the whole thing himself. He would show 'em the steps and put on a whole little number. He was under contract only as an actor, and he wasn't paid as much as some of the others, but he would do everybody's makeup. If somebody needed a beard, he would put it on him. He just loved it, loved to work. He was marvelous with drapes, and if they needed a plush home with fancy drapes, he'd get up on a ladder and go and fix the drapes. He used to come by every morning and say, "What can we do for you?" He had his hand in everything, especially makeup. He loved the choreography, too. It shows how our jobs were so loose that they intermingled, and it was easy to be recognized by somebody if you were willing to work to get a better job. He was getting paid less and wanted to move ahead, but he loved to work, too. He became a real star.

HOOT GIBSON: They talk about the salaries of the stars of the 1920s and the stars of today. Well, sure, today they get $150,000 to $500,000, $750,000 a picture—but what does the government get? Harry Carey, Tom Mix, Bill Hart, and myself—I think—were the highest-paid stars in the twenties. I know that Tom Mix was getting around $17,500. I was getting $14,500 as a producer, director, and a star in those days at Universal (these figures are per week), but our tax was only 4 percent. So I think there's quite a difference in the salaries of these days. There was plenty of money, everybody had a good time, everybody made plenty, everybody had a lot of fun. Today, it's really a rat's nest, they're all going to Europe to make pictures instead of staying in the United States—and I think that has a lot to do with it.

RAOUL WALSH: There were great personalities in those early years. Valentino. John Gilbert. Gloria Swanson and Pola Negri. All the comics and, of course, Doug and Mary. Doug Fairbanks was a great fellow for athletics, and I did a little bit of that myself in the early days. He had a gym down there, and he asked me to come down and work out with him. He finally said, "Irish, I'm going to make a picture, and I want you to direct it." That was all. I'd been making gangster pictures where everybody got murdered in the first and third scenes, and all of a sudden he'd picked me for this fantasy, *The Thief of Bagdad*. Anyway, I took a chance with it. They had no budget in those days, but Fairbanks had his own organization and he never even set a schedule because sometimes he'd work for two or three days and then lay off to work on the script or something and then go again. He was a star, you see. He did what he wanted.

JOHN SEITZ: Valentino became a star pretty quick. When I first met him, he was a fine, earnest young man, and modest. I did tests of him for the Nazimova picture *Camille*. She said she didn't want him because he wasn't a villain type, but she gave him the role anyway, and when the picture came out, it said "*Camille* with Rudolph Valentino," but it didn't mention Nazimova. Valentino was the draw . . . she wasn't. *That's* just how quick he became a star, an idol, really.

I liked Rudy. I saw him in Paris in 1924, and he had a beard. I said to him, "For God's sake, barbers all over the States will revolt against you for that beard." He said, "I'm just wearing it for a while, I'll take it off." If Valentino grew a beard, every man in America would grow a beard. I can tell you that Valentino was the most conscientious actor I ever met in my life, a hardworking and conscientious actor. And he was real. One movie was supposed to be set in the Arctic. We were shooting outside at Lake Mary in Arizona. It was generally about eight or ten degrees below zero in the morning, and then it would heat up to almost freezing. We had loads of wind machines, and one of the most industrious helpers we had was Rudy Valentino, who turned up early to help unload and set up. He just loved the exercise. He was in good shape at that time. He helped the grips, and he loved to do that.

Once on location, they served no meals. So we had to go to a Hungarian house three or four blocks up the street. I had heard Rudy had complained all the time about the Santa Fe train service, but he never once complained a bit about this bad food. I said, "Rudy, I hear you complained, but now you're eating like a lumberjack." He said, "Well, you expect something from the Santa Fe, but what do you expect from a dump like this?" That was Rudy.

Rudy was quite a sophisticate. He knew how to wear clothes. I saw him on a Thursday night in New York City at a play at the Belasco Theatre when I went out to take a smoke. He was with some girl, and he said to her, "Excuse me, I want to talk to my friend Johnny." We talked about general things. So Friday morning or Saturday morning right after that, I saw the *Tribune* and it said "Valentino seriously ill." I was so astonished. He had never looked better, never looked better—a little mature, but he had matured beautifully. That's the last time I ever saw him. What a shock when he died so suddenly and so young. You know, a lot of people said, in a way it was lucky Valentino died. His accent and his voice would have probably been a drawback in sound. He was a new kind of leading man, but he wouldn't have made it into sound.

ALLAN DWAN: Gloria Swanson was a big star whose pictures made a lot of money until she teamed up with Joe Kennedy. They had an unfortunate experience. They made a picture called *Queen Kelly* with von Stroheim. Now, I can't tell exactly what the original idea of *Queen Kelly* was, but what it wound up as—such as it did wind up, nobody ever saw it or ever will, it was never released, never was finished, and never could be released—but what it wound up was either a story about a whore turned nun or a nun turned whore. One way or the other. I've forgotten which. Either way, it's pretty ghastly. And von Stroheim really milked it. He gave it the works. And they shot and shot and shot—into thousands of feet of film—getting nowhere. He was going off onto side tracks as he always did, and this time even he didn't know where he was going. So finally they gave up on it. And they asked me to go over and look at the footage, and I simply said, "I don't even want to talk about it. I not only won't tell you what I think about it—I'm not going to talk about it at all. It's too bad. Just kiss it off. That's all." Well, then they asked all kinds of different people for help, and nobody ever has found a solution for *Queen Kelly*. It's still lying dead. And then Gloria asked me to come over and talk about another picture they were going to try to make, *What a Widow*, so I talked to Kennedy and to Gloria about it, and they decided to make it.

Kennedy didn't know anything about the business. He was a financial man rather than an artist. Gloria should have known, but she was surrounded by some sycophants—one of the troubles with Gloria, she let herself get surrounded by some people that weren't too good for her in advising. So when she left Paramount to go to United Artists, I told her that I thought she'd made a mistake, that she'd be much better off to stay there. But she said she wanted to make her own pictures. She felt she could, and she was sick of working for other people. Paramount asked me if I'd use all my influence to try to get her to stay. I said, "You authorize me to make the offer, and I will." And I offered her, to start with, on a five-year contract, $17,500 a week, and it would end up at $22,500 before she was through, with complete control over her story—choice of story, her cast, and her directors. In other words, she'd be as free as if she had her own company. And she turned it down. She said she could make a million dollars a picture herself making her own. And she never made a successful picture because she didn't have that—nobody has that—*expansion*. They may be good in one thing, but they're not good in all things. And it takes a big team to make a good picture. From the top down. And of course, only the big corporations can afford the risks of making pictures because one picture can wreck you financially, and once you're wrecked financially your credit's gone and then you're out with your hat in your hand again.

It's the old adage: They say you're as good as your last picture. Today, I say, you're as good as your last producer. But Joe Kennedy was a nice guy and shrewd as anybody could be. He's a real brilliant brain financially. But I think he was playing with this business. It was a toy. He enjoyed it. It wasn't a thing he intended to make his living at. I think Mrs. Kennedy insisted that he'd be much better if he'd come back to Boston. So back to Boston he went.

HENRY HATHAWAY: Pola Negri was a real character. She came on the set, and there was a metal statuette of a peacock standing there. She said, "Get that out of here!" I explained that it had been in earlier shots and we couldn't move it. She yelled, "I'm telling you to get that goddamned thing out of here!" and I said, "I'm telling you I won't move the god-damned thing!" She picked it up and threw it at me, and it hit the wall behind me and broke into a thousand pieces and she yelled, "Fire him!" She always talked about herself in the third person. She would be looking at the rushes, eating hard-boiled eggs and swilling stuff, and a close-up of her would come on. She'd go, "Shhhhhhh, oh, isn't she beautiful? Look at those eyes!" Then it would cut to a two-shot, and she'd go on eating eggs. Hard-boiled eggs, dark bread, and a bottle of something.

SIDNEY FRANKLIN: Stars could give you trouble. They weren't supposed to, but they could. Mary Pickford tried to exert a lot of control over her films from the very beginning. She was a shrewd businesswoman. She ran the rushes with me one day, and she said, "I don't like that scene right there." I said, "You're talking about yourself, aren't you? You're not talking about the scene." Every star that goes in to look at the rushes, any star, I've found this out—they don't look at the scenes. They only look at themselves. They don't look at the overall composite action up there that's going on. And if they think they don't look just exactly right every minute of that scene, they say they don't like the scene. I told her she looked fine, very attractive, the way she should look. Period. We straightened it out in no time, and finally I didn't run rushes with her anymore. Stars could slow you down.

MARGARET BOOTH: Mae Murray was very difficult. She used to throw things.

WALTER PLUNKETT: Evelyn Brent was difficult, and I couldn't understand why. During fittings, it went along beautifully. Then suddenly on the set, I get word that Evelyn couldn't work because her shoes didn't fit. They were hurting her, and we had to get new shoes in. That would take a couple of hours, holding up work. Then Evelyn couldn't work for some other reason, and it was held up again. At the end of the picture, she said, "Walter, dear, I didn't mean to give you personally all this trouble, I just wanted to hold up the shooting of the picture because that son-of-a-bitch director was going to get a bonus if he got the picture in under schedule, and I was damned if he was going to get an extra dime for it!" That was the only terrifying experience that I had of somebody giving me a bad time! Then having had it explained, all was forgiven and I loved Evelyn Brent, but stars could undermine you if you didn't look out.

ALLAN DWAN: There was a feud between Pola Negri and Gloria Swanson. I think the press agents started it. You know, you always wanted feuds in those days between actors 'cause it attracted the public attention. We all worked on open stages, you know! There wasn't any privacy like there is now. And Pola was on one end of a big stage, and Swanson and I were on the other with our production. And Pola Negri used to make very important entrances. When she'd enter, there would be a hush and everybody would stand up as she floated in to her onstage dressing room from the one out on the lot. All things must cease. Well, that, of course, amused me, so I got a wheelchair with a fellow pedaling it on back. So Gloria would ride around in this thing, and we'd have a man holding an umbrella over her and escort her to the stage. And when she'd arrive on the stage, we'd have a little orchestra who'd play a little theme song just for her. We all had orchestras. And the orchestra disturbed Pola Negri, who said she couldn't emote with all the noise of our music. So she'd walk huffily off her set, you know, to create trouble at the front office. And they'd come down and say to me, "Can't you play the music softer or something?"

I'd say, "No, Miss Swanson has to be greeted the same as Negri has to be greeted."

So that was the feud at top pitch. Something would have to be done to end it. And I thought, Well, I'll put a quietus on this, so the next time the occasion warranted, I had a band come. It was one of the big school bands. It was a huge, full band—uniforms and all. Must have been seventy people in the damn thing. You know the racket they can make, drums and all. So when we were ready for Gloria, out she came and got in the wheelchair, and this band appeared and "Whom-ti-ti-dum-bam-boom-BOOM!" I think they played the "Trojan March" or something. All on the stage. Well, it pretty near shook the scenery down. And that was the end of the feud. Negri gave up. She couldn't top it. And also I said, "We're going to keep the band because the orchestra isn't loud enough. There's so much noise going on on Negri's set that we can't hear ourselves over here—can't hear the music. And so we can't respond emotionally to the mood. So we're going to use the band." That scared hell out of Negri's group. A seventy-five-piece band.

GEORGE FOLSEY: I can remember that Mary Astor was a fragile, beautiful, beautiful girl, very ethereal looking, and young, very young when she first started. She was one of the most beautiful women I've ever seen. Well, she was hardly a woman when she began. She was a girl, but she was extremely attractive and at that time very, very easy to work with. You could just photograph her from anywhere, and she was patient and cooperative. Later on, I made pictures with Mary, when she had grown up and had gone through her career and she was a hard-bitten, pretty tough kind of a person, but she still had that classic look to her face. It had hardened to some extent, of course. She had learned a great deal as she went along in her career. She became very knowledgeable about what was happening with the camera. She was akin to Marlene Dietrich in that she knew a great deal about the technique of lighting. Stars don't generally concern themselves too much with the actual mechanics of filmmaking, but when they do, you're dealing with something else, you really are. They *know* when they look well, but most of them haven't got the remotest idea of how it's done.

You know, it wasn't all that easy for them. Some actors and stars did have a great problem back in those early days with Klieg lights. We had this Klieg light eye problem. We used so much exposure and light, and some actors apparently became affected by it. Believe me, it can be extremely painful. People at that time thought it came from carbon dust floating in the air. Actually, it was from ultraviolet light, and there is now a law that you must not have these lights on without a glass over them. Just a plain piece of glass would have taken care of the problem, because it cuts out the ultraviolet. Now it's a state law, or a law everywhere, that people must not look into open arcs because they burn. Ultraviolet, which is akin to looking directly into the sunlight, and it can get very painful. Many movie stars in the silent era and early on suffered badly from Klieg lights.

HAL MOHR: All types become stars. Different personalities and unpredictable successes. I remember Mary Nolan, poor child. She was a strange girl. As I remember, she had been associated with some New York gangster or some damned thing. She was supposed to have had one of her breasts bitten off by this guy in the very early days. I don't know whether you ever heard that story or not. I'd heard the story. But Jesus, she was a beautiful thing. She was positively ethereal, she was almost euphoria, she was so beautiful. Mary Nolan had a transparent, ethereal quality about her. Just a gorgeous thing to look at. I remember her . . . and then there's Fifi D'Orsay. She tripped over my camera one day, and I raised hell with her because the thing fell down. Stanley Cortez was my assistant in those days, and Fifi tripped over the camera and knocked it down, and Jesus, it was *my* camera. It belonged to me, and I raised hell with her about it. I've hated her ever since. She was just a big exhibitionist oaf, like she still is today.

SIDNEY FRANKLIN: John Gilbert was a little sulky boy in those days. I remember, it was practically his beginning. He was such a problem. He was always very moody, a moody lad.

GEORGE FOLSEY: Colleen Moore used to call me up on Sunday mornings and ask me if I was going to Mass, and I would say yes, I was, and she'd say, "Could you pick me up?" This was a woman who made $10,000 a week at

that time, and she didn't want to awaken anybody in her house to get her
to church. That was the kind of girl she was. She was a very humble and
very, very sweet person.

KING VIDOR: William Randolph Hearst wanted me to direct Marion Davies in a film. And I wouldn't do it, I wouldn't make one of those costume
dramas they were making. Hearst always had her in costume dramas. We
went up to the San Simeon castle—I say "we," a writer friend of mine, Lau-
rence Stallings, and I. We happened to see her clowning all over the place.
We realized Marion Davies was a marvelous comedienne. A custard pie
was the symbol of the slapstick comedies by Mack Sennett, so we wrote a
movie for Marion where someone would hit her in the face with a custard
pie. This was the idea—make her a comedienne. When it got time to start,
Hearst was adamant. He wouldn't give in. He wouldn't okay the script or
anything. We finally found out he refused to have Marion be hit with a
custard pie. So I stood pat, and I said, "No, that's the whole symbol. That's
the whole idea." There was a standoff. Finally, wanting to go ahead, we
compromised with a seltzer bottle and a blast of water in her face. And to
get him out of the way so we could really hit her with a powerful hose, a
strong stream of water, we had him called away from the set to a conference at the *Examiner*. Then we used a hose with a lot of force and hit her
in the face with it. It was a hit! And Marion herself loved it and would do
any kind of stunt you'd ask her to do.

SIDNEY FRANKLIN: In those days, you didn't have doubles. Any star did
what they were told. They were obedient in those days. It wasn't like today, where the star tells the director what to do. But when I think of what
we did with some of those people! We were all young and foolish, and we
didn't think.

HOOT GIBSON: I became a western star because I could ride and rope and
do stunts. In fact, I was the first stuntman in California. I doubled the stars,
rode for them, and when we played Indians, why we'd put a feather in our
wig on our head, and we'd put the makeup all over us with a breechcloth
on—we'd play Indian in the morning. We got two and a half dollars for fall-

ing off a horse, if we got shot off one playing an Indian. In the afternoon, we'd put our western clothes on, became cowboys, and chase ourselves all afternoon, and if we got shot off of a horse in a saddle, that was five dollars, because it was harder to fall out of a saddle. That's how I became the first stuntman in Hollywood—or at that time Edendale. They hadn't gotten to Hollywood yet.

We used to have real cowboys as western stars. I was a rodeo champion. They stick a big hat on anybody today and an old pair of run-down miner's boots instead of cowboy boots on them, and boy, they're cowboys. Most of them won't get on a horse. That's your difference in the TV cowboy of today and the western star of yesterday. If you want to see some jokes, they've got 'em on TV.

CRANE WILBUR: I was an actor with a New York show, playing a small part. A fellow I had been together with on a play on the road called me up, and he was at Pathé. He said, "They are going to do a picture with Pearl White, and it's going to be called *The Perils of Pauline*." He said, "It's a picture full of stunts, and they need someone who can ride a horse. I know that you can ride anything. I've seen you do it." I signed up to play Harry. That was the name of the hero. It was his job to save the girl in practically every episode. They already had signed up Pearl White. The funny part of it was that she was supposed to be the daughter of a westerner who had lots of horses and cattle and that sort of thing. She was supposed to be able to ride like blazes. She was supposed to go after me and save me. Well, I could ride, and she couldn't. As we were shooting the scene (remember there was no sound at the time), she was crying "Mr. Wilbur, don't go so fast. Wait. Wait. This thing is going to kill me." She couldn't stop her horse. She kept sticking the spurs into him in her excitement. So I threw my horse, which I knew how to do. I made him fall, because I knew her horse would naturally stop anyway. I, who was to be saved, had to stop the blooming thing. Lots of those things happened.

Eventually, Pearl White, of course, could ride anything and could do anything. She feared nothing. She was absolutely calm. I did everything but undress her in pictures. I was saving her life all of the time. We jumped overboard in the ocean off the Florida coast because we were on a yacht and were supposed to be escaping. All I had on was pajamas, and I was disguised with a beard. She had a nightgown on, and we landed right in the middle of a flock of sharks. Luckily, we were both good swimmers. We did high dives. We jumped off cliffs. We were driving cars and racing trains and beating them to crossings and going around in front of them. It was no fun for the other actors riding with you.

There was no dialogue, but we used to put dialogue in for our own fun. We knew that the camera of that day did not pick up the dialogue. I was liable to take a pretty girl in my arms and say, "Come here, you sweet little thing, and I'll punch you in the nose." Then I would kiss her on the mouth. Things of that nature happened all of the time. To the hero we often said, "Who's afraid of you? I'll slap you down with one punch, boy." Then the letters began to come in. The letters would come in from schools where they were teaching them to understand how to read lips. The letters would say, "For heaven's sakes, stop that. You are saying words that you shouldn't say." We were swearing a little bit, you know.

There was never any romance between Pearl and me. We were friends. We understood each other and laughed at each other. While playing love scenes, we would whisper things to try to break up the other one. The camera couldn't hear. The whole thing was a lot of fun. We made appearances in some small neighborhood theaters. At that time there was quite a good return of money for people who were so-called stars in the pictures and particularly in *Pauline*. You would get anywhere from $25 a performance, which would mean maybe two or three appearances. You would go out and just talk to the audience. From that you would go to $50 for an evening. I think I got about $75,000 for the series I made with Pearl over a three-year period. We were very popular. It was all about the stunts.

ALLAN DWAN: When I began making pictures, we had no stuntmen. Every actor had to be his own stuntman. Things could get real and really terrifying because we would have an actor running through the streets being pursued by somebody, and any minute, you know, those people in that area would take a swat at you, thinking you really were a crook. They didn't know we were making a picture, see, because we had our cameras hidden in trucks. They saw a guy running and people chasing him—it's a wonder somebody didn't take a potshot at him. But we were lucky, and they didn't.

LILLIAN GISH: You know, for *Way Down East*, we spent three weeks on an ice floe. We were going down the river on that ice floe, and they got the brilliant idea of having all my hair . . . which is long . . . trailing in the ice water, along with my hand. Well, if you look at my finger on that hand today, you can see how crooked it is. That was on the hand that hung off the iceberg. We were at White River Junction in Vermont, where the White and Connecticut Rivers flow side by side. I did everything myself. I had no doubles. I didn't even put paper between me and the ice. You just did what was in the story, and you did it as well as you knew how. I thought it was effective that my hair froze. They had no platform over the ice. I just started saying my prayers, but we made it, and when I see it now, I think, Well, weren't we silly to do that? But that's what you did.

MINTA DURFEE: Mabel Normand always did her own stunts. We all did.

HOOT GIBSON: Some of our stunts in the picture business were very harrowing. I remember one time at Long Beach, California, doubling Helen Holmes—I had on a wig and a skirt—I had to ride a motorcycle off the drawbridge, which I think was forty feet down to the water, and when I left for the end of the bridge, the skirt wrapped up in the chain on the motorcycle—so I rode it all the way to the water, and when I hit the water, it didn't take me long to come out of that skirt. We never did find the motorcycle, it went in I don't know how many feet of water. That was only one of them.

Another time, I had to jump a horse from a platform at a train depot onto a flat railroad car going by. Well, we didn't know the speeds too well in those days. They were all hand cranked—the cameras—so we ran the train through at about twelve or fifteen miles an hour. I hit the flatcar all right with the saddle horse, but the momentum carried us clear on off the other side of the flatcar, and we piled up on a ditch on the other side. Fortunately, neither the horse or I were hurt, just skinned up a little bit.

We fixed up all our stunts to keep from hurting the horses as much as we could, but the rider was on his own. We used to dig trenches—oh, six feet long, six feet wide, and about two feet deep—and cover them with dirt. When the horse hit it, he had to go, but the rider had to take a chance on where he was going. Then we had one called the "running W," where you'd jerk the horse's feet out from under him. I've never seen a horse hurt with this, but I've seen them take some awful falls, and especially the riders.

We also jumped horses off of cliffs. I was one of the first to jump a horse off a cliff. We measured that, too—one time it was forty-three feet to the water. Well, all we'd do, we'd blindfold the horse, run him off the end of that—well, the horse would automatically turn over because there was nothing to stop him We'd have to leave him in the air. But we finally cooked up an idea to make a slide—I think Jack Ford was one of the first ones to conceive the idea of making this slide, and we covered it with sagebrush—we'd run a horse to it, jump him off there. He would slide off the end of the chute and go straight in, which was better—he didn't turn over in the air. So that made that stunt comparatively easy after that. I remember I used to get $25 every time I jumped a horse off a cliff, and I used to try to jump one off whenever I could. But today, the boys who do that stuff get—these great stuntmen they have today—they get $500 for that stunt—that's quite a bit of difference.

I have raced automobiles, I've ridden bucking horses, I've punched cows, I've run wild horses, I've raced airplanes. I learned to fly in 1927. Had all my ribs broke, my back broke, my hip broke, my left shoulder torn loose from my neck. I was cut to pieces. I was never knocked out, but I was in the hospital once for thirty days, and then I was walking around on two canes. I have made and worked in—as near as we can figure—about 310 pictures. That's through fifty years I was in the business.

HAL MOHR: Doug Fairbanks, Sr., did most of his own stunts, but for the really dangerous ones, he had this troupe of Italian-German acrobats, and one of them was a very handsome boy. There were six brothers, I think. Most of them got killed doing stunts.

HOOT GIBSON: One of the other great men that got into the picture business as a stuntman, and one of the greatest bronc riders I've ever seen, is a boy by the name of Yakima Canutt, one of the greatest stuntmen I've ever seen. He's also a second unit director in Hollywood and is responsible for making the great racing scenes in the 1959 *Ben-Hur*. He's still down there doing a great job and, as I say, one of the great champions of all times. He won the cowboy championship not too long after I did, in 1918.

KING VIDOR: So this was the magic of silent film . . . stars and stories and stunts . . . and I don't know whether someone else has talked about what happened when sound arrived, but I know that most of my friends and other directors were just horrified with the idea of being able to use words, not musical accompaniment, not sound effects, but words. It was just a terrible idea. I'm sure that anyone at that time felt that we were being ruined by words, and it was true for a while. But why? It was just like saying to Marcel Marceau, "We've had enough of your pantomime, you've got to start speaking tomorrow." You could imagine the feeling of Marcel Marceau if they told him that, and that's the way we felt about it.

PETER BOGDANOVICH: Charlie Chaplin said, "Just when we were getting it right, it was over."

HOOT GIBSON: I think about the time that sound changed everything, I was making *King of the Rodeo*, because I remember very well I was producing at that time, and Universal called me and told me to scrap everything I'd made that was silent. We were going into sound. I had to scrap about a hundred thousand dollars' worth of film—go back and make it all in sound. Of course, it was very interesting, because none of us knew what it was all about at that time, but believe me, there was a lot went in that scrap heap when we had to throw that hundred thousand dollars' worth of film away and start over again.

GERTRUDE ASTOR: When sound came, making movies got to be a business, you know. I mean, it had just slowly developed into a business. Before, it was an idea and catch-can sort of thing. I was kind of in all of it. I saw it happen, but I wasn't smart enough to understand how big a change was really coming.

CHAPTER 5

SOUND!

JOHN SEITZ: Suddenly Warners brought out *The Jazz Singer*. Gave all the silent-picture people headaches, I assure you. But it was the best thing that ever happened to Al Jolson!

HENRY BLANKE: Western Electric [developers of sound] went to every-body in the business before the Warner brothers were offered it. All the big studios at this time turned it down. Western Electric finally came down to the small Warner Bros. studio. There were three brothers: Harry, the financier; Sam, who was interested in sound; and Jack Warner, who did the silent pictures. Harry was invited to come to the Western Electric studios, and he went there and there were speakers, and he heard music. Western Electric always had the idea of using sound for talking, which Harry Warner never thought much about. His idea was not to record voices but to use music for accompaniment. He says, "I can give every little town in America a hundred-and-ten-piece orchestra, the same as New York has at the Roxy" with this system. And that's how they began. Harry had the idea of starting out by giving every little theater a big orchestral sound . . . and Sam perfected it.

HAL MOHR: Vitaphone—sound at Warner Bros.—was created by Sam Warner. He didn't invent it, but he was instrumental in the introduction of it as a kind of novelty thing. They started making short films of people singing or a band playing or dancers dancing to music or little comedy skits. It was a novelty for the theaters.

HENRY BLANKE: Warners put sound on discs. And that's how they did *Don Juan* with John Barrymore, which had a complete score . . . and then the shorts, the Vitaphone short subjects with [Giovanni] Martinelli singing or Al Jolson singing or Edgar Bergen and his dummy. That's how it started, with all those shorts, which were the real first "talking pictures." Sound on disc. Sam comes to me, and he says, "Henry, come and join me." And I went to Jack Warner, and I say, "Sam wants me." Jack says, "That sound thing will be dead in two weeks." So you see, even the pioneers of sound weren't all that convinced, but Sam believed, and he ran with it. Sam worked so hard on sound. . . . He worked so hard he died.

JEANINE BASINGER: Sam Warner's sudden death the very day before the premiere of *The Jazz Singer* brought real-life melodrama to the proceedings. And Sam, the Warner brother who had been a real advocate of sound, was married to one of the most famous and glamorous movie stars of the era, Lina Basquette.

SAM WASSON: Everybody knew the Warners were in financial trouble, which was drama enough, and now a sudden death with a beautiful widow in furs and diamonds . . .

JEANINE BASINGER: . . . and Al Jolson, the star, coming to the opening in person and crying about Sam and going out into the audience and personally shaking every customer's hand . . .

SAM WASSON: . . . you couldn't write a better script . . .

JEANINE BASINGER: . . . All this drama off-screen is part of what made *The Jazz Singer* the movie that everyone latched on to, including the business itself, to be defined as "the first all-talking picture" . . .

SAM WASSON: . . . which it wasn't . . .

JEANINE BASINGER: . . . the first all-talking movie was Warner Bros.' *Lights of New York. The Jazz Singer* was one of the early part-talkie experiments that Warners did. It was the most successful one . . . and certainly the one with the off-screen drama.

HAL MOHR: When Warners got the idea they wanted to use sound in a regular theatrical feature, they had a bunch of properties. One was called *The Jazz Singer.* Well, this awful little man—what the hell is his name? Horrible comedian. Thought he was a comedian. George Jessel! George turned *The Jazz Singer* down. Alan Crosland had been assigned to direct the picture, and I was Alan's cameraman. So they were going to make a test of another person, a test of Al Jolson. Jolson agreed to make the test, and if he liked the way he looked and liked the way he came over, he would agree to make the picture. So the fate of the studio hinged on whether or not Jolson liked that test. I made the test myself, and he liked it and agreed to do the picture, and we did it, and it actually saved the studio. I don't think they would deny this because they were really in pretty desperate circumstances at the time. But *The Jazz Singer* actually saved their necks. Just before we made *The Jazz Singer,* they were really in bad shape financially. I think without Vitaphone—Sam Warner was the angel of that Vitaphone thing—well, hell, they had people who were taking stock instead of their salaries. Right after *The Jazz Singer,* that stock just went *zoom!* That movie made a lot of dough.

HENRY BLANKE: People stood in line for blocks and blocks just to hear someone talk. And Jolson sing.

KARL STRUSS: Everyone suddenly seemed to think sound was the most important thing in the world.

KING VIDOR: I was in Europe when *Variety* had a headline that said, "Hollywood Goes 100 Percent Sound." The Jolson picture had been a big hit.

ALLAN DWAN: Well, the talking picture stimulated the box office. It was one of the new gimmicks that brought people back. Sound came at about the time when the silent picture needed some stimulating.

TEETE CARLE: As a matter of fact, sound probably saved the industry. The business had come to a crisis where the entertainment dollar was being attracted by so many competitors. The motion picture business needed a shot in the arm, and the shot in the arm came with sound. It was a whole new field. It was a time when they could hear Garbo talk.

JOHN CROMWELL: It's a little difficult today to realize how extensive the arrival of sound was, affecting everybody in the business. There was a fundamental philosophy about motion pictures: a day lost, a day when theaters wouldn't be open, was a day that was irrevocably gone and never could be recovered again. This governed their entire thinking.

The big producers had to think about a multitude of problems, like how they could get the new equipment that they needed. They had to find out how they could get a movie made in time to make a transition from silent pictures to sound pictures and with no delay. The shift to sound intensified business thinking.

They had to think what they were going to do with these silent pictures that they had already prepared for the forthcoming season while sound was being developed. These pictures represented millions of dollars in investments. The minute that sound came out and the public accepted it, these pictures would be obsolete unless they did something. This was their greatest immediate problem: how to save these pictures representing millions of dollars of investment. They couldn't go back and remake *all* of them from start to finish.

There was an elapse of time from six to eight months from the completion of a picture to its release. This meant that most of the silent programs for the coming year were already on the shelf. This was somewhat of a desperate situation, and solving it produced some weird and amusing results. It was impossible to transform all of these pictures into the new medium. Lack of equipment, time, and the availability of actors prevented it.

Therefore, it was decided to fill the first nine reels with sound effects and have the last reel burst into full dialogue. Characters who had mimed their way through nine reels suddenly found their voices. The audience reaction was first one of surprise and then delight and amusement.

Beginning with the actors, who had the most important problem, down to the cameraman and the electricians, who had to learn a whole new lighting system, everyone was suffering from varying degrees of apprehension for their careers.

The vast and entirely new problem of sound and what to do with it seemed such an enigma. There was not even much assurance for the few actors who had previous stage experience, for there was always a chance that this new and mysterious machine would discover shortcomings in their vocal equipment which would force them into some other profession. It would be about the quality of their voice. It hardly mattered what your voice was really like. No one knew just what this recording business was going to do. It may distort it or require certain tones in your voice that you might not have. No one knew enough about the vocal equipment to know that any shortcoming could be eliminated or corrected.

All of this concern was not alleviated by the attitude of the sound crews sent by Western Electric Company, who controlled the sound patent to install the system and break in new men. No magician ever worked harder to preserve the mystery of the unknown. In fact, this attitude was so persistent that one was led to believe that the electrical company hoped in some way to get eventual control of the industry.

HAL MOHR: I shot *The Jazz Singer*. I did the whole picture. It was a completely new world: new film stock, new techniques, new everything. There were soundmen on the set for the first time. They were just sound recordists, but they were our main obstruction. They became the kings of the set. If they said a microphone had to be right here, it had to be there. And we had to do the best we could to hide the microphone so it wouldn't be in the picture. We used to hide microphones in telephones, behind vases of flowers, in bowls of fruit. . . . We used multiple cameras on the sound scenes, and those dialogue scenes were rehearsed. I mean, they were rehearsed as much as you could ever rehearse Jolson, but the way we had to operate—we shot most of the picture silent, of course. And we had to use a different kind of film stock for dialogue scenes because the old orthochromatic stock needed arc lights and those arc lights are very noisy. Eastman had been experimenting with a new film called panchromatic film, and we had been using a little of it for certain special-effect things. We figured, what the hell, we can use an incandescent light if we photographed on panchro, so that's what we did, but only on the talking sequences. There were just a few of them . . . the movie wasn't 100 percent talkie, you know. *The Jazz Singer* was partially dialogue and partially silent. Could I just stress this point? *The Jazz Singer* was not the first sound picture. There had been Vitaphone pictures made, orchestras playing and all that sort of thing.

Little May McAvoy, who was the leading lady opposite Jolson, had red hair. Red is not sensitive to orthochromatic stock, so a girl with red hair looked like a deep brunette when she was photographed on ortho. So when it got to the scenes that were photographed under incandescent light on the panchro, which was sensitive to red, she'd walk out of a silent scene into one that was going to have dialogue and suddenly she'd become a blonde. She'd be a brunette on this side of the door and a blonde on the other side of the door. Yeah, we were solving problems and creating new ones.

Jolson sang without playback. He sang live, with an orchestra on the set. If he didn't have a good take, we'd have to start over again because we couldn't edit sound in those days. If you had a nine-minute scene of dialogue, you shot for nine minutes continuously. That's why we started using multiple cameras. They hadn't yet learned how to dub sound. They'd cut from one record to another till one of the musicians at Warners figured out how to dub bits of sound from many records into a single record. Up until that time, if a scene ran nine minutes, it ran nine minutes. If it ran over nine minutes, you'd have a second camera standing by where you figure you're going to cut that one in when this one runs out of film. You'd bridge the two cuts with the close shot that was being made by that one over there or this one over here. You had to be a mechanical engineer to make film in those days!

TAY GARNETT: I was under contract to the Cecil B. DeMille studio. A pal of mine—they called them supervisors then—was functioning the way a producer functions today. His name was Ralph Block—a lovely man and a brilliant mind. I got this idea for a story and told it to Ralph, much in the manner the TV writers today would tell an idea to a TV producer. He sparked to it and gave me the green light. So I wrote the story line. It was an original idea played against the background of a carnival, the tale of the regeneration of a confidence man who fell in love with the girl who owned the carnival.

Alan Hale was a contract star at that time at the studio, so I designed it for Alan. We borrowed Renée Adorée from MGM. She had just made a big success in *The Big Parade*. She was very hot—a lovely girl. It was, of course, a silent picture, and we called it *The Spieler*. We had all heard rumors about Pathé's photophone sound process. This photophone equipment—it would be here tomorrow. It would be here day after tomorrow. Next week. This went on for weeks and weeks, these rumors. Suddenly, I was halfway through shooting, and I got an urgent message from the front office to come in and see the boss when I finished work that day. When I went in, they told me our photophone equipment had arrived. They added that there were engineers from the photophone factory coming with it— men with the know-how to operate this equipment and how to record with it. Then they gave me the double whammy: "How long will it take you to convert the last three reels of your movie—or two reels of it—into sound?" *The Spieler* was going along beautifully as a silent picture, and all of a sudden, *whammo!* Right in the middle of shooting, it became a sound movie.

TEETE CARLE: When talkies started coming in, everybody had to get on the bandwagon. Movies in the pipeline near the end of the silent era were brought up to date by the studios putting sound sequences in them at the last minute.

ALLAN DWAN: I was getting ready to make *The Iron Mask* with Douglas Fairbanks, Sr. I said to Doug, "You know, we're just under the wire with this one. And I think we'd better beat them to the punch." So we made a prologue and an epilogue, and in the prologue, Doug, in his character of D'Artagnan, made a speech before the picture unfolded. And at the end, the older D'Artagnan came out and said a farewell kind of thing. So Doug had voice on the front and voice on the end of the picture. It made the picture very up to date.

WILLIAM WYLER: During the time that sound came in, I had just made a picture, and the New York office sent the picture back and said, "Put in 25 percent sound," which was supposed to be a compliment. That meant that they liked the picture. And now they could advertise a picture "25 percent sound." Then came "50 percent sound," and finally came "100 percent sound." So this picture I made, which was sort of a prizefighter picture called *The Shakedown*, they said, "Make it 25 percent sound." So I picked out a couple of scenes, and we made those scenes over with dialogue.

JOHN SEITZ: *Hell's Angels*—Howard Hughes decided he had to redo that whole thing for sound because it had been started as a silent picture. That's the one in which they discovered Jean Harlow, because the original girl in the part before her couldn't speak English well enough.

HAROLD LLOYD: Everybody went sound happy, but some of the comedians, most all of them, weren't quite equipped for sound.

KING VIDOR: Take Chaplin, for example. I think you can take all the comedians, Buster Keaton, Laurel and Hardy, and all of them. They were the product of silent films. They couldn't just sit down and have a conversation.

HAROLD LLOYD: It was difficult to keep the same kind of pace you had in the silents and still have your sound. They thought because you were making a sound picture you had to talk all the time. You had to go to the verbal. Verbal comedy was cheaper to do. You can get verbal gags much easier than you can get sight gags.

KING VIDOR: Chaplin fought it for a long time. Sound was practically the end of Mack Sennett, but Chaplin resisted for five years. It must have been five years before he made his first talkie.

HAROLD LLOYD: I had just completed a picture called *Welcome Danger*. I had finished it silent, and we previewed it, and on the bill was a little one-reel sound comedy, and they howled at this comedy. They had the punkest gags in it, but they were laughing at the pouring of water, the frying of eggs—it didn't matter—the clinking of ice in a glass. We said, "My God, we worked our hearts out to get laughs with our thought-out gags, and look here, just because they've got some sound to it, they're roaring at these things." I said, "We missed the boat. Let's get on the ball. Maybe we ought to try and make this a sound picture. I think we can. Let's see how much we can keep of it and dub it." We didn't know much about dubbing in those days, either. So that was the one that cost me the most: close to a million dollars!

HENRY BLANKE: I was terribly disappointed at first about the coming of sound. We had our own language in the silent days. When you saw a clock that showed twelve o'clock and we dissolved to three o'clock, you knew three hours had passed. That's only a simple sample, you know, but this was how it was.

ALLAN DWAN: I thought it was the end of a fine art. I thought, That's it! and I kissed it off. Because I don't think talking pictures compare with silent. They're a different thing. They're just not the same. I think they're an extension of the theater. They're the theater with more sets, bigger sets, and more expanse but still the same as the theater. Everything's based on what you say or what is the sound. And I liked pictures as pictures. I like the idea of pictures in motion. We always got the best effect from doing something rather than saying something. And we said as little as possible.

KING VIDOR: When sound first came in, that's when popcorn and all the drinks started and necking in the theater started, because you could turn away and do all sort of things and you could still hear. You wouldn't miss anything, you know. The sound would take care of it. In silent pictures, you had to pay attention the whole time. You had to sit there and try to figure it out. The uppermost thought of directors who grew up in silent films was that the photography was it, was number one. That was the reason that when the accent on dialogue came, it was a shock. For quite a while into the sound era, I was aware that directors who had made silent films produced work that was much more interesting than that of those who hadn't. They were still thinking in terms of photography. It's much more articulate and much more dynamic than the soundtrack coming through loudspeakers. I still think that's true. We had developed a sort of language of pantomime and gestures and so forth. When sound hit, everything went static. It meant the end of movement, of pantomime, of ballet. I used to think very much in terms of choreography in films. I think I still do. There were quite a few directors—René Clair, Sergei Eisenstein, Clarence Brown—there's quite a list of fellows who were sad about sound coming in.

HENRY HATHAWAY: I loved it! We had about used up everything there was to do in silent pictures, and it gave a new dimension to movies. Change always happened. Later color would come in and add another dimension. Then there would be the new size of the screens and Cinerama would be added. Sound was just an added dimension. The latest dimension is smut—pornography.

WILLIAM WYLER: The transition from silent pictures to sound pictures affected different people different ways. To me it was a very welcome thing. I was just starting directing, had made just a few pictures, but I always loved the theater, and I always felt the restriction of the silent screen, and while many people hated the idea of sound, I welcomed it. I knew that to be able to hear what people are saying would be an added value to pictures.

RAOUL WALSH: When sound came in, it didn't hit me as a problem. I just kept the thing moving regardless of the sound. I just kept going. Of course, it was pretty tough on a lot of actors and actresses who'd had no stage experience, but I handled directing the same way I always have. Of course, there was a great upheaval amongst the directors when talking pictures came in. They called me a renegade because I was one of the first ones to do an outdoor talking picture. They said that they'd created such a medium with pantomime, you know, and now this talking stuff was going to destroy it all. I said it was going to destroy *us* all if we didn't go along and get in with it. So they finally all came in and faced the problems.

KARL STRUSS: If we had technical problems, it was always up to the camera department to give in to the sound department, which I resented very much. Sound became the important thing. Photography meant nothing. It was a stupid arrangement from the start.

HENRY HATHAWAY: The sound technicians were busy telling everybody what they couldn't do.

HENRY BLANKE: Rule number one: Dialogue! You just took a stage play and translated it . . . well, you didn't even translate it . . . you just took the whole play verbally and put it on the screen. They talked themselves into this. Later Lubitsch and other directors would say, "Let's go back partly to the silent technique, let's not use so much dialogue," but this transition was quite a big step, you know, or quite a big *jump* into sound.

KARL STRUSS: They went into sound too fast. They should have waited until they had thought it all out and figured that recording it on film was the only way to do it. They had these discs, you see. Warner Bros. developed sound on discs, not on film. Fox Movietone was the one that recorded directly onto the film. They did that first with making their news weeklies, then on to movies. But a disc's not flexible. You can't cut it, cut things out, and you can't do anything with it except possibly drop it and break it. And synchronizing those things! They could get out of sync with the picture. It was messy. Sound on film, of course, soon replaced sound on disc. And anyway, after sound suddenly came upon us, the first thing—and the main thing—was that the cameras had to be silenced. The cameras sounded like threshing machines. So it was necessary to make a soundproof booth. Enormous, heavy things in which we put as many as three cameras, one on a sort of table and two others on the tripod. Shooting in the same direction but with different focal length lenses to get different sizes.

TAY GARNETT: We used what you call barneys, you know, blankets over the cameras. We pretty much had to stop making moving shots. We had to forget them because of the heavy box that housed the cameras. It looked almost like the portable dressing rooms on the studio stages—those square canvas things that appeared to be made up of a lot of black flats, wooden frames with black canvas tacked to them, only these were sound insulated. The box was on casters so it could be turned and jockeyed. The mike was in a huge wooden box the size of an apple box. It probably weighed twenty or thirty pounds. So they'd hang it over a set in a spot that approximated the center of activity, and that was it. Then later somebody thought of putting it on a fish pole, and they made a long iron rod and hung the mike on the end of the pole. And the original mikes weren't all that sensitive.

KARL STRUSS: The cameras were in a big, heavy booth. You might almost call it a house. It was about six feet square and had plate glass in the front, and there was no ventilation. And we had three men, camera operators, and three assistants in there. And they used up that air pretty fast, and it got pretty hot. And when the scenes were running one, two, three, four minutes long, everybody would be exhausted by the time the scene was over, and they'd tumble out of the back of the booth . . . I guess you'd call it a "booth." It was heavy. People dubbed it "the icebox."

ALLAN DWAN: It was ridiculous. Cameras locked up in soundproof vaults with cameramen in there looking through a window and suffocating? It was all ridiculous. And everything was padded like telephone booths. Thick walls. *Everything* was padded. And a glass window?

WILLIAM WYLER: The glass booth! Oh, my. I made the first all-talking outdoor picture from Universal. We were in the Mojave Desert, just off Death Valley, in July and August of 1930. It was 120 degrees outside, and in the glass booth it was 140. We opened the booth sometimes after a shot, and the guy had passed out. We had guys pushing this thing, with microphones hidden in a cactus here and in the sand over there. Guys walking, sweating, and pushing this thing.

KING VIDOR: No portable sound equipment. Cameras in big boxes. You couldn't get a low set-up, couldn't get a high set-up, couldn't do a pan-around, because with just a window looking out, you couldn't do anything.

GEORGE FOLSEY: The introduction of sound, as far as I was concerned, started in New York. I went to New York because someone in my wife's family had died. While I was there, I went back over to see my old friends in the Long Island studio, just to say hello. They asked me if I was working, and I said, no, I wasn't, and they said, "You want to work?" I said, "Sure." So I started in New York just as sound arrived, instead of in Hollywood, which meant I was in a place where there was no equipment for sound of any kind. There were no booths, no "iceboxes," nothing. We had to build our own contrivances to keep the sound of the motor on the camera from recording. We joined together pieces of wood, put a plate glass in front of it—a glass we could shoot through, an optical glass. We put lots and lots of coverings and cloths and things over this assembled "booth," and we got a big, long, flexible cable that ran to the camera. We just made our own kind of soundproof booth this way, and it was easily disassembled and put together again as needed very quickly. Our whole operation was a sort of "just figure it out" transition to sound, away from Hollywood on our own.

HENRY KING: You know, necessity is the mother of invention!

TAY GARNETT: It was a fight in those days to try and devise camera movements using those booths.

JOHN SEITZ: I remember that we didn't move the camera much, that's for sure.

KARL STRUSS: It was with the coming of sound that cameramen or the director of photography not only had a challenge on moving the camera inside those booths, but it was also the time in history when he ceased to operate his own camera. It was impossible for him to continue to do all the necessary things such as to attend to the lighting for the multiple cameras and all the necessary details of supervising properly all the important factors essential to successful photography.

HENRY KING: The great problem about sound pictures when they first came in were the technicians who came in with sound. They figured everything had to be built for sound. They discounted the pictorial part of the picture entirely. It was all just to the specifications of the soundman. Everything else was out. They cared for nothing else. The soundman would walk around and clap his hands together and say, "This set is no good. Tear it down." I had one tell me, "You can't make the picture in here." I said, "*We* can make the picture in here. I don't know whether *you* can make the sound in here, but fundamentally we're in the picture business. We're not in the sound business." He said, "Well, you want sound, don't you?" and I said, "We want sound, and we're going to have sound. If you can't do sound in this room, I'm sure I can find someone that can." And I let it go at that. After a little while he came back and said, "I've worked it out now. I believe I can make it."

ALLAN DWAN: We were slaves to sound. Any little extraneous thing that the engineers picked up . . . we'd suddenly hear "Hold it! Hold it! Cut!" You know, from the soundman. "Something dropped. I heard a bing." Or a click. Or a rattle. As if it mattered, you know. Well, they were that way. And they drove us out of our minds.

WALTER PLUNKETT: At the door of the stage, we had to take off our shoes like entering the door of a Japanese temple and put on felt things to walk in. We stood there trembling for fear we'd sneeze and there would be some kind of a sound. We couldn't move a muscle. The jewelry we made for actors to wear—a lot of the jewelry had to have net wrapped around it, backed with velvet, so that it wouldn't be heard moving against the fabrics. Fabric! Taffeta was out almost completely. Oh, the rustling, rustling sound of *that* fabric. The early hoopskirts that we made, which should have had crinoline underneath, had, as I recall, felt petticoats instead because felt was the only thing that would deaden the sound of those starched dresses. Dance costumes all were made of soft fabric.

ALLAN DWAN: I remember one time when somebody was struggling to get the sound of water dripping. Dripping water. They tried everything. They tried pebbles, buckshot, everything in the world, until somebody came along and said, "Why don't you try water?" And it worked perfect.

JOHN SEITZ: Of course, the sound people had a lot to learn, too. About recording, amplification, and so forth. Movies were a new business for them, too, you know. And sound had been around but had been ignored and treated as unnecessary for the most part. I was in New York in 1924. Lee de Forest had the top floor of a studio on 48th Street, and he was making talking pictures and showing them at the Rivoli. When we were there, he had Jimmy Walker, the mayor of New York, and Al Smith, the former governor of New York, all coming by, but sound went nowhere at that time.

ALLAN DWAN: Actors would get into arguments. One would jump over the other fellow's line, beginning his speech before the other guy's sentence ended, because that made it natural, the way people talk. And the sound people would stop the recording machine immediately and say, "You've got to cut there. He was talking over his lines." "Well," I'd say, "but we want it that way." "Well," they would come back, "you can't record it that way. You haven't got the mike right. The mike's aiming at him, and the other guy's talking. You haven't got a balance." And I'd say, "Well, put two mikes on it. Let them each have a mike." "Oh, no, you can't do that. You gotta work with one mike." And the mikes were hidden in bouquets, in backs of chairs, no mike up there on a rod yet. They hadn't come around to the fish pole. That's when the rule went out: "Don't overlap any dialogue." And we were up against that bunch of soundmen who were as green as grass, you know, and their rule was "every syllable must be heard." That meant that if somebody was talking to you, you've got to wait and say one-two-three before you answer. "My mother's coming this afternoon" . . . then you count one-two-three before you say, "What time?" I'm explaining the terrible slow pace you find in a lot of early talking pictures.

HENRY HATHAWAY: At that time they could only work with one track. They had multiple microphones, but they had only one track. When they went from room to room, everybody carried a microphone on them. It used to take them a day to rig up those things. You know, in the early days, when there was no rerecording, we put in all those sound effects as we went along. We would have a siren or a doorbell or a telephone with us.

We had to record it on the original track. It never entered their minds that they could put two tracks together. Even a boat whistle way off to the side had to be carefully done on the original. If you had an explosion and you wanted to cut to another angle, you'd have two or three cameras, and it would be on the soundtrack through the whole thing.

GEORGE CUKOR: There was a streak of absolute panic because everything they'd learned before in silent pictures they abandoned when they became infatuated with sound.

HENRY KING: They always thought only of sound then. They were not thinking that the picture was necessary at all. They soon found out that it was!

MERIAN C. COOPER: I was excited about sound. I had a big outdoor picture I wanted to do, in 1928, but I was at Paramount and Adolph Zukor put his foot down and said no. "It's only a passing fancy," he said. "The only pictures you can shoot are things like stage plays," he said. I wanted to do a whole wide-open picture and use all the extraneous noises, which the sound people didn't believe in at all then. They wanted to shoot what I called bad sound. You look at some of those very early 1928 and '29 pictures. The sound is dead because there's no background to it. They pulled everything out except what goes into the mike . . . using just the dialogue, you know . . . and it's no goddamn good. The sound should be alive.

KING VIDOR: What they were doing at first—because it would work—was that they were just photographing stage plays. Two people on a couch, and everything was like photographing a proscenium arch in a theater. If they dug up all the stage plays, the camera could stay in one place, so that's what they did.

TAY GARNETT: Our first talkies were très talky.

ALLAN DWAN: Technically, sound was wrong when it began. It was wrong for a long, long time. By that I mean in pitch. If your voice was high, it made it higher, no doubt due to the speed . . . very much like the tone if you speed it up. The voice becomes shrill. Actors like John Gilbert just didn't have the kind of a voice that went with his personality, and Doug Fairbanks didn't, either. Doug was manly looking, but he had a high voice. So the sound didn't fit them. Today it could be corrected, or they could have some vocal lessons. But up until that time, they hadn't had to talk, so no one had cared or noticed.

JOHN SEITZ: All these silent-picture players that couldn't talk were gone, too. Poor Jack Gilbert. I think he died more of a broken heart than anything.

GEORGE CUKOR: Some silent stars had no trouble moving into sound. Norma Shearer went straight in. She was wonderfully guided by her husband [Irving Thalberg]. Garbo's transition was very interesting. I remember in the first picture she did, the voice was not flexible. However, she did it wonderfully visually. She was very gay and lifted her hands and smiled. But the voice remained inflexible, although she'd had some theater training. But as she went on, she was so intelligent and gifted, she came along. Some made the transition, like Joan Crawford, and then some new ones appeared. The business tried to keep the great stars going across from silence to sound, but it didn't work for everyone. It was just an era of transition and change, all very sudden, it seemed.

GEORGE FOLSEY: It was a new kind of industry that had sprung up overnight, and everybody had to learn and find out. The most intelligent thing was to be cooperative and helpful and get the thing on the road.

KING VIDOR: Along came dialogue, and the studios thought you didn't know anything about it. And in fact, we didn't know too much about it. We thought in terms of movement and photography, more like cameramen . . .

ALLAN DWAN: . . . so they imported directors from the theater. Well, of course, they were like lost sheep. They didn't know where to put the camera, what to do with it, or how to direct movie actors, and they didn't understand that scenes had to be stopped and cut. They wanted the act to go all uninterrupted as if the film in the camera would never run out. But any of us who'd been in silent pictures were told, "You just sit back there and watch the real director who we're bringing in from the theater who knows how to work with people when they're talking and see if you can learn something from him." Well, of course, these fellows came in, and all they could do was listen to the talk 'cause they didn't know what else to do. So we sat back and let them murder themselves. And pretty soon the people at the top said, "We've got to get back to action, so you better try and see what you can do with it." So we did.

KING VIDOR: Cukor was one of the ones who came directly from the theater. In fact, I think he came out here originally hired as a dialogue director.

GEORGE CUKOR: When talkies came in, the movies imported everybody from the theater who knew anything at all about how to speak. We were all sent out here. I had been running a very good stock company which I sort of originated in Rochester, New York. At that time, in the old days, stock companies were resident companies and the great stars would come and play, people like Billie Burke. It was a great preparation for this new Hollywood! I became a dialogue director at Paramount. That was a very peculiar job. You had to be very tactful, because there was a man in charge—the movie's actual director—and you could make "suggestions" to him. If you were clever and the man was intelligent, you could influence quite a lot. I was loaned from Paramount to be the dialogue director on *All Quiet on the Western Front*. I made all the tests on *Quiet*, and I had a lot to do with directing the intimate scenes, but the strength and vitality of the movie came from Lewis Milestone, who directed it. He was sort of mystified by— but also very sympathetic and appreciative of—what I did. What makes *All Quiet* extraordinary is what *he* did, the vitality of it. In the meantime, while directing dialogue and being as effective as I could be, I was watching and learning his job. I didn't know a goddamn thing about the camera or about pictures, and that was an obstacle. But I was also very lucky because nobody knew at that time. It was like the parting of the Red Sea, and they allowed a lot of people in. I didn't really know a great deal about it, but I learned. It took me a long time, but I learned.

KING VIDOR: Finally, when *everything* started going to sound and movies died in front of us, I said, "You can't say no to sound any longer. We've got to learn . . . and fast."

HENRY HATHAWAY: At first the soundmen were the directors on the set, but picture directors started learning. I was with Vic Fleming, and we heard they were making a sound picture at Paramount, so we went over to take a look. Well, there was a cop on the door to the stage. He wouldn't let us in. Vic told him that he was a director on the lot, but the cop knew that and still wouldn't let us in. So Vic went down to B. P. Schulberg [in the front office] and said, "Jesus Christ, are you only going to have one director for sound? What the hell is this? We are all going to have to learn." So they let us in.

KING VIDOR: If you were a resourceful director—and being resourceful is what movie directing is—you would adapt to the new methods and the new techniques. And pretty much everyone found out that the directors could adapt themselves very quickly to sound . . . and solve their own problems.

ROUBEN MAMOULIAN: I was a director who came from theater, but I created a breakthrough in sound with my first film, *Applause*, in 1929. I used two channels to record sound for the first time. It was revolutionary. Now you can use fifty, but two then was a breakthrough. I was lucky enough to have done a series of very successful shows on Broadway, both commercially and critically. So Paramount came to me. Sound had just come in, and they wanted me to sign with them to make some films. On the stage you deal with sound. When they asked me to direct dialogue, I said, "Why would I want to go into films to direct dialogue? I can do it on the stage and have the whole play. What attracts me to films is not the dialogue, it's the imagery, the magic of the camera, and the dialogue should be subservient to that." They wanted me to sign a seven-year contract and help a silent-screen director by directing the dialogue for him for a couple years, and then, if the studio felt I had learned the business, they would let me direct a film. And they would have me for seven years. But I was in a lucky position. I didn't need films. I was going strong on Broadway. So I laughed at the whole thing. I said, "I'd like to do only one film. No seven years. No options." They said, "Well, right there you're dead." I said, "Well, I don't think I'm dead. I'm quite alive." They said, "You're dead for films because we never sign a contract without options." So I repeated, "No options. And there's only one way we can do it. Let me go into the studio and learn." In those days there was Astoria Studios in New York, where films were being shot. I said, "Allow me to be on the set, watch the shooting, the projection of the rushes, the cutting, and so on and so on. And when I come to you and tell you I am ready to direct, that's when I do a film." I guess they wanted me enough to finally say, "Well, we're dealing with a crazy man, but let's do it." So I went to the Astoria studio to learn about directing movies.

Anyway, watching these things, I learned *ad adversus*. In other words, I really learned what I *didn't* want to do. I'd say when I saw a scene done: that's the last thing I would want to do. I would do it completely differently. Learning the mechanics was one thing, but everything I saw I felt should be done another way. Oh, I remember I saw a movie being shot in which an Englishman was supposed to be a kept man, a gigolo. The director tried to tell the actor, "No, no! You don't walk right. You don't sit right. You don't talk right. That's not the way a gigolo does." And the actor said, "Well, that's the best I can do," and the director said, "Now, look, believe me, I was a gigolo for ten years. I know what I'm talking about."

Anyway, after five weeks—as you know, there's no great mystery to the mechanics of motion picture making. You can familiarize yourself with all of it in five weeks—I felt I knew enough about it. So I went to Mr. Lasky and Mr. Zukor, and I said, "I'm ready." They said, "Ready for what?" I said, "I'm ready to direct a film." They laughed at me. I said, "When I tell you I'm ready, I'm ready." They said, "What would you like to do?" I said, "What have you got? I'd like to start out by making a short. It's all about a dog." They knew for sure they had a crazy man then, so they wouldn't let me do a short. So I said, "All right, I'll do a feature film." I read this

book called *Applause* by Beth Brown. I thought that was interesting. I had
a writer by the name of Garrett Fort. We worked on the script, and we
had the script ready in eight weeks. So I started shooting. They gave me
George Folsey as a cameraman.

GEORGE FOLSEY: He's very artistic and a very capable man. I must say
that he was one of the most impressive directors that I worked with . . . at
any time in any field. I think he was extremely capable . . . a very unusual
man. I don't understand why he wasn't more . . . you know . . . didn't do
more successful pictures, because he was certainly an innovator.

ROUBEN MAMOULIAN: One should be able to do things on the screen
that would be utterly impossible in life or on the spoken stage. There's a
scene in *Applause* when the young daughter is put to bed by her mother,
Helen Morgan, and she can't sleep, and Helen sings a burlesque song in
the manner of a lullaby. I wanted the daughter to take her rosary from
under her pillow and whisper her prayers. Well, in those days, there
was only one microphone, hanging in the middle. You had to rehearse
all the time to find the right balance. I could hear Helen's song but not
the daughter's prayer. I told the sound people, "I want to hear both the
prayer and the song." They said, "We can't do it." I said, "Why not? Let's
get another microphone and put it under the pillow. That's for the girl.
This one is for Helen Morgan. Get two channels. Record it on two channels. Photograph it later on." They said, "We've never done that. It's impossible."

That was it. That got me real burned up. I had a little megaphone—we
used to have megaphones in those days. I threw it on the floor. I ran upstairs. It so happened all the executives were having an important meeting. So I ran in like Mr. Hyde, full of hostility. I told them, "Nobody does
anything I tell them. Am I a director, or what am I? Why don't they do it?
They tell me it shouldn't be done that way. They wouldn't let me make
Helen Morgan look blowsy. Mr. Folsey tells me it's impossible to do the
whole scene in one shot, with one camera, moving. The sound department
says what I want is impossible because they've never done it that way." I
made them bring upstairs the wardrobe man, the cameraman, George Fol-

sey, and the soundman. The wardrobe man said, "Well, we usually have a star look glamorous, and he wants to make her unattractive." Folsey said he respected me but "he's done things on stage and I've been a long time in this business and I know what can be done and what can't be done. I'm only trying to save the studio a whole day's money." And the soundman said, "He's asking for something we've never done, and it will probably be a mess and cost money." Two of them said something pleasing to the big moguls, who are always worrying about the shekels. But they told all three *I* was directing and to do what I said. We went downstairs, and by five thirty we made a take, and then I went home.

GEORGE FOLSEY: Occasionally, like in everything, you find personalities who will only see their own point of view. You get a character like that, and there's nothing you can do . . . except give him all the rope you can.

ROUBEN MAMOULIAN: Well, *Applause* received unprecedented critical raves, but commercially, it was not a success. In fact, the reviews did me a lot of harm in Hollywood. They kept saying "This young newcomer from the stage who's never done a film does something which Hollywood needs to look at and learn." So of course they hated me here. The heads of Paramount called me in, and Mr. Zukor invited me to sit in his chair. They always do that. They think you'll feel you're occupying a throne for two minutes. They all made speeches about what a wonderful film I'd made. Zukor said, "I just hope they don't give you a swollen head, my boy. We want you to know right now that no matter what, we want you to sign a contract with us. You've got to be with Paramount. So we'll call you. But take a two-week rest. You've worked hard." I was almost in tears at their kindness. Well, I never heard from them. Two weeks. Two months. Eight months. A whole year. I never heard from them. Then I made some other hits on Broadway and they called me back, and the whole rigamarole started over. This time I once again signed for only one picture. Then they said, "By the way, we want to tell you, go easy with Mr. Schulberg." He had become the head of the studio. I said, "Oh?" They said, "Yes, because he hates you. He didn't want you. He fought us. He said he wouldn't have you in his studio." By the time I made the movie—which, incidentally, was *City*

Streets in 1931—he and I had become friends and the transition to sound in the movies was pretty much done and I had created one of the break-throughs in sound.

HENRY HATHAWAY: It was by sheer perseverance that directors finally got it together during the transition to sound. Over time they broke down all the rules of everything, from the cameramen to the electricians to the sound guys, to make it all work. In the end, it seemed to me that a picture was made exactly the same way as it had always been during that time, except that the cameras at first were in a booth . . . which we all loved because we couldn't hear the cameramen.

GEORGE FOLSEY: Looking back on the whole thing, I would say the business used those "iceboxes" and those immobile booths for about a year . . . maybe a year and a half . . . then we all moved forward.

FRIZ FRELENG: Sound developed very fast. At that time, it didn't seem that way, but when you look back, you can see that it developed quickly.

ALLAN DWAN: Sound brought on the building of the bigger studio lots. The original studios, which were started up about 1911 or 1912, were smaller, more like offices with some facilities attached.

KARL STRUSS: When I first came out here right after World War I, there was the Famous Players-Lasky, which became Paramount, and Metro, which became Metro-Goldwyn-Mayer, and Universal, of course, and maybe Columbia. But that was about it. There were a lot of independents like Sennett, and small outfits with small studios. These places had employees like cameramen and office people, but they were not like the big studios that emerged and became the Hollywood studio system of the 1930s onward. Not really.

FRANK CAPRA: Sound marked a big change in the business. It drove filmmaking indoors. In talking about the history of film, we're dealing with something that was living and growing. Most people think about Hollywood as a fixed place, one thing, never changing from its beginning to now. Just, you know, "Hollywood."

GEORGE FOLSEY: We all had to learn a new way of making movies with sound, but one thing that didn't change was that we kept on working incredible hours. We still worked every single Saturday, all day and all night until the morning. We would be shooting exteriors . . . night stuff . . . and the sun would be coming up and the daylight would be there. You slept all day Sunday so you could come back and work on Monday. And there was no overtime pay. Eventually, after the unions, they had to pay overtime over sixteen hours, so then they only worked you to sixteen hours.

JOHN CROMWELL: You can see how sound brought in the formation of a dominant business system. It pulled people together into bigger buildings, onto lots, into a working hierarchy, and it created a structure to assess product, budget product, and make product.

FRANK CAPRA: "What's your product for next year?" That's what you started hearing. The original slapdash, out-in-the-field, shoot-it-and-cut-it-and-let-it-go silent moviemaking world became a studio system, growing into it from about the mid-1920s to the arrival of sound, when it really formed up. We began to turn out a manufactured product—expertly manufactured, of course. It had all started out with men like D. W. Griffith making their own pictures. But then, where the hell was he going to show his pictures?

Well, somebody had to find or build theaters, and they built these little nickelodeons, and the finance people came in and built bigger buildings for theaters. Then they had to make bigger pictures to bring in there. It was, in a sense, the growth of the theaters . . . the growth of the demand of this new thing, moving pictures, that practically dictated the advent of the large studio where they could make pictures in some kind of order and on a regular schedule. It was the theaters that needed to be supplied with product once a week or once every two weeks. They needed a steady diet of pictures so they could have audiences every night. This is what probably created the vast empire that in the 1930s and 1940s became the official definition of Hollywood: the studio system. You see, the major companies owned their own theaters, owned their own distribution, owned their own studios. This, of course, led to some kind of an industry, and every industry likes to have it all neatly done, you know. I mean, you start this today, you finish it that day, and these things you're making come off an assembly line costing so much a foot. And I think that the large studios, in a sense, had their origin in the need to supply their own theaters. It wasn't the coming of sound that made this happen. Sound just made the demand bigger. The studio system had begun in the 1920s.

ARTHUR KNIGHT: For the most part, from the 1920s onward, if you wanted to be a filmmaker, there was one place to do it, and that was in the studios.

FRANK CAPRA: Every studio began to make fifty, sixty, a hundred films a year. That meant one or two a week had to be started and finished, and they had to make budgets to do this. They had to create a business hierarchy and have department heads and compartmentalize the work. Centralize everything. They were going to turn movies out like sausages, and that turned out to be a very good idea: the assembly-line concept. And they could make good films that way. The compartmentalization made them become very expert in all departments: in the camera department, in the sound department, in the laboratories, and very expert in distribution and sales, very expert in finding and building beautiful, attractive theaters. This was all big money and how best to use big money in turning out what they began to call "product." They weren't our films then. They were called our "product."

RICHARD SCHICKEL: The excitement and novelty of sound carried the business, with its strongly emerging studio system, across the earliest years of the Depression. At first the business was not directly affected by the stock market collapse. It hit them later.

MARGARET BOOTH: When the stock market failed, we realized that everyone else was out of work, but we weren't out of work. It finally hit Hollywood, but only after the first couple of years.

PANDRO BERMAN: I think the film business suffered from the Depression to a certain extent, but mostly after the first two or three years of it had already passed. Strangely enough, it suffered less than many other industries for two reasons: One, the cost of making films was reduced drastically during that period. And two, the public seemed to want entertainment very much, and they could still buy it at a reasonable price at the movies. So that actually I found the period during the Depression my most successful period, financially speaking, and others may have done so, too. Costs were down, therefore you could make a profit.

WILLIAM TUTTLE: We went through the first years of the Depression on the success of sound movies. This was a couple of years after the market crash in 1929, and just prior to Roosevelt coming into office. The Depression was in full swing then, around 1931. Believe me, I felt lucky to have a job in the studios, any kind of job. Outside, there were people begging for work. In general, the film business kept going fairly well, not untouched but operating. The studios suffered, some more than others. I doubt if MGM was hit very hard.

JEANINE BASINGER: When the transition to sound settled down, you were looking at the major studios more or less the way they were going to be for the next three decades.

SAM WASSON: There were some mergers to come before the midthirties: First National and Warners, and Fox with Twentieth Century, but by the time 1935 rolled around you had the big seven studios of the so-called golden age of Hollywood in the 1930s, '40s, and '50s.

JEANINE BASINGER: Most historians refer to the "big seven" of the "golden era" as the actual producing and releasing studios of MGM, Warners, Paramount, Universal, RKO, Twentieth Century–Fox, and Columbia. They had working lots and all but Columbia (and later Universal) had theater chains . . . Columbia was founded in 1920 by Harry and Jack Cohn plus Joe Brandt as CBC, which became Columbia in 1924 with Harry Cohn as production chief. Fox was founded by William Fox in 1915 and merged with Twentieth Century in 1935 with Darryl Zanuck as vice president in charge of production. Loew's/MGM was a 1924 merger of Metro (founded by Nick and Joe Schenck and Marcus Loew in 1910) with Goldwyn Pictures (without Sam, who had left) and Louis B. Mayer Productions. Paramount was founded by Adolph Zukor in 1912 as Famous Players, and became Famous Players–Lasky in 1916, at which time it acquired Paramount as a distribution arm. RKO was a 1928 merger of FBO with the Keith-Albee-Orpheum circuit. Disney distributed through RKO from 1937 to 1954.

SAM WASSON: Universal was founded by Carl Laemmle in 1912 and opened Universal City Studios in 1915. Warner Bros. Pictures was formed by the brothers in 1923. They absorbed First National as a wing in 1928, and officially combined the two in 1930 as Warner Bros/First National. United Artists was founded by Douglas Fairbanks, Mary Pickford, Charles Chaplin, and D. W. Griffith in 1919. It was essentially a distribution company, not a production company, so its history has its own trajectory.

JEANINE BASINGER: . . . There were B level studios, too, like Republic and Monogram. The business settled down, centralized, and vertically integrated, and, of course, became officially located in what everyone called "Hollywood."

HARRY WARREN: It *was* sort of a factory.

GEORGE CUKOR: I want to tell you something in principle. There are all sorts of books written, very authoritative books, about how it was in those days, all written by people who were not there. And there's sort of a cliché, "Oh, how could you live in that factory thing? How awful it was! You had no freedom of expression. They were crass and commercial, and now we can express ourselves with no restraints," and all that. Well, actually, I do want to say something *for* the studio system. And I was *not* a company boy.

I think the men who built the studio system were very smart show-men. If you worked for them, they provided you with all kinds of things. You had the best stories, the best actors, the best technicians, the best scripts you could get. You were helped enormously. There *were* certain restraints, but they were intelligent restraints, you know. People were not allowed to indulge themselves. A director couldn't say, "Get out of here! I'm going to do this my way! I don't want to see you at all!" And all that. I think those balances . . . and working with people you respected . . . were very salutary and helpful. Of course, the studio system is all gone, it's in the past, and it'll never happen again. But I do want to say that the studio system was not a prison. It was not mainly full of buttonhole makers and people who didn't know anything and they were crass and they crushed artists to the ground. That was not the case. It was tough but certainly no tougher than it is now. And they were very helpful. I worked with those studio tycoons, and if you had anything at all to give, they encouraged you. Why? Because it was to their advantage. They realized that talent was the coin of the realm, and they were very sympathetic to it. And patient, very, very patient. You had enormous help and sympathetic help, and that had a lot to do with the success of the cinema at the time.

WALTER REISCH: It was the New York press that dubbed Hollywood a "factory" system, which it wasn't at all. Everything was about teamwork, a wonderful collaboration, and everyone taking time to get things right.

WILLIAM TUTTLE: Although time mattered, you were given sufficient time to experiment, to play around. Try. Test. See it on the screen. Try again. Remake it. Revamp the thing. Redesign it. Try it again. This was in the *preproduction* stages, where all the craftspeople were involved in planning and doing what was their own particular talent. Everything was thoroughly approved . . . and thought about . . . *before* whoever it was starred in the picture. You know, even if they had to hold up the picture before shooting it, they got everything right first, thought about what they wanted first, and took the time with that. The "factory" came after the first stages of filming, when it was all in place, and because it was in place, you could roll it out. And there was no problem in holding up a picture's start, because everyone working on it was under contract, as opposed to today, when we're subject to availability of sets, actors, writers, and directors. Now there's very little time for the technicians to do what they have to do, and that creates lots of pressures and in the end is very limiting.

FRED ZINNEMANN: There are two sides to the studio system format. A lot of people feel, quite rightly, that the studio system was oppressive in many ways. The bureaucracy was enormous. They could fire you, but you couldn't quit because of the ironclad contract you had to sign. On the other hand, the studio gave you a chance to learn your professional craft in a continuous manner without having to fight from one thing to the next. You were employed. There was a job progression. I made silent shorts, then sound two-reelers for a series called *Crime Does Not Pay*. Well, those shorts were a kind of warm-up. You knew that if you did all right with those, you'd be offered a seven-year contract and a chance to direct features. And you'd get a raise. You were learning, and you were making a good living.

GEORGE CUKOR: In all the literature, you read about how terrible everybody was and that it was just a soulless, heartless factory. It really wasn't.

ANN RUTHERFORD: It was not, believe me.

GEORGE CUKOR: It was not fairyland. It was not perfect, but if you wanted to work, you could work, and you could live. That was a great thing.

ANN RUTHERFORD: As far as I was concerned, it was not a factory at all. It was absolutely incredible. They created a climate for young players, where it was almost like you were in a nursery and they weeded and weeded and hoed and watered you every day. If you had a spark of talent, they found it.

ADELA ROGERS ST. JOHNS: All the studios looked for talent, nurtured it in all categories. They were in business!

CHAPTER 6

STUDIO HEADS

ADELA ROGERS ST. JOHNS: MGM was *the* studio. It defined Hollywood. Everyone wanted to work at MGM.

NORMAN TAUROG: MGM was the biggest of the studios. It was the best place in the world to work. They bought the best properties. They made the best pictures. In the days when Louis B. Mayer was there, it was the most perfect set-up in the whole world as far as making motion pictures was concerned.

KATHARINE HEPBURN: I thought it was like a marvelous school from which you never graduated. That's what it seemed like to me. . . It was like a Chekhov play. It was so comfortable.

WALTER REISCH: I can say that at MGM, it was an age like that of Athens in Greece under Pericles. It just worked like a beautiful Swiss clock, the whole MGM machinery.

HARRY WARREN: I liked it better at 20th Century–Fox. It was a more pleasant atmosphere.

NORMAN TAUROG: You knew you were in a different studio when you came to MGM. You knew because of the people they had. You had plenty of brains to call on. You had the finest back lot of any studio in the business. They could make anything, do anything, depict anything that you needed or anything you wanted. I shot scenes right there on the lot where I would defy you to know whether I was in Germany or France or wherever.

GEORGE FOLSEY: The back lot at MGM was the most expert place I've ever been in my life. They could do anything. Ask them! They'd do it. They were remarkable people. A studio like MGM had such a tremendous variety of crafts. You can't believe how many different things there were. When I first came there in the early 1930s, however, my impressions of Metro-Goldwyn-Mayer were that you practically had to be a duck to work there. It was the wettest place! It was a very rainy winter that year, and they had boards all over the place so that you could walk. You couldn't go anywhere without getting your feet wet, and so I went out and bought a very heavy pair of Florsheim waterproof shoes so I could walk around and get into that darned studio from my parking lot without getting drenched because there was a tremendous amount of water there. There I was, at the great, great studio of MGM with all its expert departments . . . and I had wet feet.

WILLIAM TUTTLE: The MGM back lot had everything. We had such fantastic sets because they had a vast amount of acreage to expand into and to build on. They were constantly building more and more sets. A different type of picture would come along, and they would build another type of set. For instance, we had jungle sets that were enhanced and embellished from the *Tarzan* days and carried on through to represent all parts of the world. Anytime they needed a jungle set or a thickly forested area, you had it. You had a river that you could put boats in. *Show Boat* was made on the back lot except for the long shots, which we did on location in Mississippi. But we had a—I think it was a seven-eighths-scale showboat that actually floated in the river on lot three. It was almost like going to Disneyland today, only on a larger scale. Then we had New England docking facilities. They used some of it for *Mutiny on the Bounty*. They had one tremendous miniature tank. You know, I think most people thinking of miniatures are thinking of something like a tabletop size. I think our miniature tank was something like three hundred feet long by two hundred feet. They had wave-making machines that could make waves of any particular size that needed to be represented. We had a tremendous western street that was changed and embellished and expanded or reduced in size depending on what type of picture you were doing. We had an army barracks that we used for war-type pictures. We had a St. Louis street. And I never forget the first time I happened to go to St. Louis on a tour. I looked out the window of the hotel, and I thought, My god, it's the back lot of MGM. It was that exact.

TAY GARNETT: There was a French village street, a small river with a stone bridge across it, French countryside, and any number of French sets you could use. They built some prison sets, ships and trains, everything.

NORMAN TAUROG: We had the best goddamned electrical department. You had the best of everything. You can say, "Well, Mr. Mayer didn't do all of that." But the man surrounded himself with the best. And he let you retake if you had a reason. You just couldn't go out and retake, of course. If it played well, they would tell you to hold it. They would say the picture wasn't worth it. But if I felt I had blown a scene, I could tell Mr. Mayer, and he'd ask if I thought I could do it better. If I said yes, he'd say, "Find out if you can get the cast back" or "Find out how much it would cost," and then we could talk it over.

VINCENTE MINNELLI: I was at MGM for twenty-three years. I did most of my pictures at MGM. I did two and sometimes three pictures a year. They had an enormous amount of top actors and actresses and the very best designers and musicians and special-effects men and the very best cinematographers. When you got ready to make a picture, if one was busy, you could look down the MGM list and get someone else equally good.

BRONISLAU KAPER: MGM was a big studio, successful, a rich studio. They only hired people of quality. They would not waste time with anybody who was not first-class. If you went to work for MGM, nothing was impossible in your life. Not just your working life, either. Anything you wanted done that would take two or three weeks, they could do it in one day. Unbelievable. They'd get you a visa. They'd get you a passport. They had someone to get you anyplace or anything. All those formalities—just gone. I think they could even give you a vaccination without you being around!

GEORGE CUKOR: You have no idea what it was like to work with that kind of support in all the departments. I'm not only talking about the taste but also the execution. The best cameramen, the best costume department, the best everything. One was dazzled by the resources and the help one was given. I remember when I directed *Camille*, there was a scene in a gambling casino. I thought something should indicate the setting was for gambling. It was decided that there should be the Goddess of Chance, or whatever the hell she is. This was at five o'clock in the afternoon, and we were shooting the next morning. I came in early, and there she was, larger than life.

GAVIN LAMBERT: Mr. Mayer knew the currency in which he was dealing was talent. From some of the stories or myths about him, you'd think the opposite was true.

ADELA ROGERS ST. JOHNS: They talk about Mr. Mayer driving Judy Garland into things or doing things. You would think that Mr. Mayer—or anybody—that none of us were human beings. Just because we were in the picture business. This isn't true.

GEORGE CUKOR: Stupid, stupid! Mayer nurtured people. He was very long suffering, even though he was tough. The proof of that is he and Thalberg built this extraordinary studio, and when he left it sort of went to pot. It needed to be fed and sustained every day . . . and kept organized. It was a wonderful organization, you know, but a very big one. Someone had to keep it all functioning, and that was Mayer. He kept it all going, and it wasn't a heartless assembly line at all.

BRONISLAU KAPER: Yes, organization. MGM had many old-time directors under contract and on the staff. And those directors were reliable. They were employees. They never did a great job, and they never did a bad job. The pictures were smooth, and they were delivered on time. Those movies were kind of like a man who has a haircut, very smooth. Not one hair is sticking out. It's like English grass. Cut very evenly. The sound was smooth. Everything was not too loud and not too soft. People all spoke the same way. Monotony. People could sleep during those MGM movies . . . that was the good thing.

HOWARD STRICKLING: See, MGM made fifty-two pictures a year. That's how that factory idea got going. Like . . . they would make three Clark Gables, three Jean Harlows, three Joan Crawfords, three Norma Shearers, three Bob Taylors.

RICHARD THORPE: That sort of "factory" idea was the beautiful thing about Metro. They had so many people, they could manage to fit a personality to yours or your personality to somebody else's for the working situation. So you all got along. That's why it was such a great empire. I don't care whether people were scared of L.B. or not. There was a feeling at MGM that you belonged to one another and that you would do anything for one another, and you would. You would work Friday night, all day Saturday, and then Saturday night. Joan Crawford would come over to a set and watch somebody else making a scene and say, "Jesus, that was nice." You don't find anything like that nowadays. We all ate lunch together in the Commissary.

HARRY WARREN: The MGM Commissary was quite famous. It was quite a spot. Bronnie [Bronislau Kaper] used to be there. We all worked in different bungalows, crummy-looking bungalows, really crummy, all on a little side street with a line of trees along it. But we all would see each other at lunch in the Commissary. And the foreign contingent were always in there around four thirty, having cake and coffee. Yes, at four thirty, that place was filled. Then there was nothing but German spoken. They should have put a sign on the window that said, "English spoken here." It was the German kaffeeklatsch.

RICHARD THORPE: Chicken soup was Mr. Mayer's thing. They always had good chicken soup, and even after the Commissary changed hands three or four times, they still had good chicken soup. MGM was the top! It was a little city. There was a police force and a fire department. There were two dentists on the lot, but they didn't belong to the company. They charged like hell.

RICHARD SCHICKEL: MGM in the 1930s was dominated by, and defined by, two men: Irving Thalberg and Louis B. Mayer.

IRENE MAYER SELZNICK: My father came from Russia when he was age three. He didn't even know when his birthday was. He picked out July fourth for it, because he was crazy about America. I think that he always worked very hard. My grandfather was in the scrap business. He would send my father to an enormous ship that had sunk in the St. John, New Brunswick, harbor to salvage things. He would also go to large factories after there was a fire, and there would be a great deal of scrap metal. My father would be sent out to bid at auctions, and he would have the money sewed into the lining of his coat. It never occurred to anyone that this pale, undersized boy was a serious bidder. I think he did very well because the other bidders didn't take him seriously, and he learned about negotiating, when to speak up and when to make a move, and he learned to make judgments early. Later, around 1909, he began acquiring theaters in nearby towns, and he got this company together and moved into show business through exhibition and then production. When we came out to Los Angeles, he rented space at 3800 Mission Road and built a studio there in stages. The die was cast for film production. We kept a kosher home until we came to California.

HOWARD STRICKLING: MGM started out as Mr. Mayer's little studio on Mission Road. The movie business was growing, and the theaters needed pictures. Paramount had theaters and Warners had theaters and Fox had theaters, so Mr. Mayer had the idea of having a merger of Loew's Metro Pictures and Goldwyn [the Goldwyn Pictures Corporation] and his own company [Louis B. Mayer Productions] that could make a lot of pictures. He went to Marcus Loew and Nicholas Schenck, and they got together and formed the Metro-Goldwyn-Mayer company, which Goldwyn was never a part of. He had left Goldwyn Pictures by the time the company was incorporated.

JEANINE BASINGER: The merger was accomplished by Marcus Loew in 1924, and the company MGM was the production arm of Loew's, Inc.

IRENE MAYER SELZNICK: I remember that when my father was still out on Mission Road with his own company there, I used to take drives with him on Sunday mornings. We drove by the Metro studio when it was a little white building, at least the offices were white. It was in an area that was kind of a residential part of Hollywood. My father said, "Would you be surprised if someday I became the head of that studio?" Joe Engel was the head of production at Metro then. That idea just overwhelmed me. Little did I know that something much bigger was in store. I became the daughter of a significant movie producer, but no one paid any attention. In the Hollywood School for Girls, nobody ever paid any attention. My father wasn't very well known even though he was producing films. The picture business wasn't something that was big and startling in those years in Hollywood. However, my father was afraid that people would use my sister and me to find out what was going on. Was someone going to get this part? Was someone going to get fired? We were young girls, and people were bound to get something from us. At previews we were not allowed to comment too much or note too much. No opinions. We could be enthusiastic or we could be noncommittal, but we could never indicate that we didn't like it. We were to be tactful and never lie. And we were never to repeat anything.

MARGARET BOOTH: I was hired at the Mission Road building when Mr. Mayer's business was still Louis B. Mayer Productions, before the merger. Nobody was at Mission Road except Irving and Mr. Mayer, but I don't know anything about Thalberg's being hired. I was taken sick with diphtheria, and I was quarantined at home. I was off the lot for months, and when I came back, Thalberg was there, and he introduced himself to me. I loved him. I thought he was a darling. He was wonderful. He was just plain darling, and he was very sweet to everybody. Everybody loved him and adored him, and Mr. Mayer loved him and adored him. He always did. I don't care whether he said it or not. He loved him.

ADELA ROGERS ST. JOHNS: Most people loved Irving.

MARGARET BOOTH: Mr. Mayer did all the money thing, and Irving did all the creative work. It was separated that way, and any kind of creative work, Mr. Mayer never entered directly into. In 1924, when we merged, nobody knew about it beforehand. It just came around to us working there that the studio would now be MGM, and we moved our offices. Nobody was afraid for their jobs or anything. Not ever.

JOHN SEITZ: Thalberg was running the studio. Mayer was running the financial part. He was the general manager in charge.

MERVYN LEROY: If you met Irving Thalberg right this minute, you wouldn't think he knew anything about the picture business. He was simple, sweet, direct, not tough at all. Well, he was tough in a way, but when he told you something, it was worthwhile listening to it. He was in a class by himself, the sweetest, most unassuming man that you ever met in your life.

DONALD OGDEN STEWART: Thalberg couldn't actually create scenes, but he had such a memory of every scene he had read or watched . . . he was like a computer. You put your script into Irving, and the wheels went around and came out "yes" or "no." And he was right in so many cases.

IRENE MAYER SELZNICK: My guess is that it was about 1922 when Thalberg joined my father on Mission Road. Thalberg was having terrible trouble at Universal, an awful lot of trouble with Mr. Laemmle, so they made a deal rather quickly. My father made Thalberg a partner. He was very keen to have him. Thalberg was very talented and very bright. My father just adored Irving, and Irving was adoring of my father. He had been with Universal for quite a few years. He had gone up very quickly. He had become old man Laemmle's secretary at one point. He had traveled with him, which is how he came to Universal City. His opinions on films were so good that he began to produce pictures. His views and his taste were not what Universal was used to or what Mr. Laemmle was used to, and the place had become a hotbed of relatives. Nepotism reigned supreme at Universal, like it never reigned at any other lot. Mr. Laemmle had come to America from Germany, and he imported every damned relative that he had. They all had jobs at Universal City, which made it harder for Irving, who was not a relative. It was an enormous joke. Some of the relatives Mr. Laemmle had actually never seen, but they came on and were hired anyway. I think Irving got his job originally because one of his mother's parents had come from the same place in Germany as Laemmle. They knew people in common, which was how she was in a position to ask to get the first job for Irving. But as I said, he went up very quickly. He had already made a reputation for himself by the time he came to my father.

MARGARET BOOTH: Irving had proved himself as a young boy, about twenty-one years old, over at Universal with Carl Laemmle. Laemmle had left Irving in charge of Universal while he went back to New York. . . . Irving had a mind like a buzz saw. He would come out of a theater with the director and say, "Take this out, and take this and put it over there." He had a great, great mind. When I worked with him as an editor, he used to mumble something to me, "I don't like that." I'd do something with it, and he'd say, "Now I like it." All our writers were really good writers. We had the finest in the country. I forget how many writers we had under contract when we finally merged. Many, many writers. They all had such respect for Irving. They'd kill themselves for Irving. I don't know if Mr. Mayer ever had an innate knowledge about how pictures were made. He knew how they *should* be made, and that's the way he wanted them made.

GEOFFREY SHURLOCK: Believe me, Louis B. Mayer had practically 97 percent to say about the making of a picture, except that 95 percent of it he delegated to Irving Thalberg.

WALTER REISCH: First of all, Louis B. Mayer never read a script. I had to tell him the story in a few lines, and that was all. He never read scripts. There were ten or twenty executives who had that job, like Eddie Mannix or various producers or Bernie Hyman and Kenneth MacKenna, who was his first literary adviser, a whole staff of people who read for him. He'd see the finished picture together with the audience at the sneak preview, and *then* he'd make his recommendations.

MERVYN LEROY: Thalberg never had his name on anything. The only thing he had his name on was the Thalberg Building, and they took that off when the new regime moved in.

MERIAN C. COOPER: Irving Thalberg never put his name on a picture. Best producer that ever lived. He did a lot of great pictures. Hell, he was head of Universal Studio when he was only twenty-two years old, for Chrissake. The production head of it. He died at thirty-five or something, and in the last two or three years he was so sick he couldn't work. The last two or three pictures he made were not very good because he was too sick.

MARGARET BOOTH: When I first met Irving Thalberg, he was a young man but not robust. He had wide shoulders, but he just didn't appear robust. He didn't look sick or anything, but Mayer was a different type of man. Mayer was a big man, kind of plumpish. But Irving looked like a delicate man. He always looked delicate to me. When I think back upon it, I don't think he was ever a very strong man, but he worked very hard. I don't think he was ever a big talker. He was a good listener. I met his mother, the famous Henrietta, and his sister, Sylvia, became a very good friend of mine. Henrietta was like a Jewish mother. His mother and sister were very proud of him. They loved him. His mother was a very nice woman, and his father was a nice man. Irving lived at home. I don't think Henrietta was as much of an influence on him as everybody says she was.

IRENE MAYER SELZNICK: Thalberg was thin, but he had very broad shoulders. He had an underdeveloped body, because he had been an invalid. He had had rheumatic fever and had a heart complaint. He had been in bed during his midteens, and therefore he was quite frail. I think that from the ages of thirteen to seventeen, he couldn't participate in sports or have friends or go to school. During this time, he read, and he had done a great deal of reading, but he was not an intellect. No, never. He thought of himself as being an invalid. His mother was very protective of his health. He was very handsome, very good looking. If he had been well built, he would have been enormously attractive. He had beautiful eyes and a lovely brow, a marvelous hairline. He was a very kindly looking man. He had great humor. His interests were work and his family, and that was all. He wasn't a "father" kind of father, but he was a passionate family man. His wife [Norma Shearer] and his children meant more to him than they did in other families. He sometimes went to a baseball game, but that was the extent of his leisure. He was not gregarious, and he was not interested socially. He wanted to get ahead. He wanted to manage and accomplish things and know about things. He was terribly serious.

KING VIDOR: Irving Thalberg aimed very high. He aimed very big. When he saw a finished picture, if something failed, or something missed, he'd be willing to take it over, if the director would agree and sometimes even if he didn't agree. We changed the leading woman in one picture after it was finished. We just reshot it. In *Big Parade*, we changed the cast of the American family because when he saw the picture he said, "The people are not important enough." But he was so busy running the studio, making fifty pictures a year, that he was inclined to let you just shoot on your own. He didn't interfere at all. He'd see the picture mainly after it was finished. Then you'd get in to see him and talk about redoing something. Maybe you could talk him out of it, maybe you couldn't. Maybe you wanted to. I often wanted to. But he aimed high, very high.

TAY GARNETT: Thalberg was very sure of himself and rightfully so. He was probably as near to being a genius as anyone we've ever had in the picture business.

CHARLES HIGHAM: "Thalberg the genius." I can't understand the genius tag. I've always wondered what that meant. Because as far as one knows, from all the records, all Thalberg did was to add things to films. To have scenes reshot and to add elements to pictures.

TAY GARNETT: Well, that's not quite true. Take *China Seas*, for instance. I can speak about that movie because I directed it. Clark Gable, Jean Harlow, Wallace Beery at MGM. I know about the history of that one, so I know the general pattern under which Thalberg worked at that time. When Thalberg decided to make *China Seas*, he said, "There are some elements in here on which we can build a fine story." I was signed to direct way early, before the script was written, before a word of it was written, because he wanted me to work on the script, too, as an idea man, which I did, although I didn't do any of the actual writing. Jules Furthman wrote it. The way we worked, we would have huddles—Thalberg, his assistant, Albert Lewin, Furthman, and me—and we'd discuss the story: What elements were we going to use from the book it was based on? Why don't we add this? Why don't we do this? And it began to blossom with Thalberg sitting in judgment on every suggestion. He had the most uncanny judgment. Thalberg actually didn't write anything, but everything that went into that script was something he had examined under a microscope. And when he said, "That's right, that's good," it was damned apt to *be* good. His percentage was very high. I think the "genius" tag applies to Thalberg. He was the first man to conceive reshoots or adding new scenes as a practical method for putting a high polish on a picture. Thalberg didn't do little things or retakes just to make a show releasable. His pictures were all right, but he knew these little things would make them much *finer* pictures. He was always shooting for perfection. I hate the word *perfection*. In the picture business it's been kicked around like a dirty beanbag, but I think if anyone rated it, Thalberg did.

MERVYN LEROY: Would you like to hear a story about Irving Thalberg? That sums him up? I made a picture called *Tugboat Annie* with Marie Dressler and Wally Beery. And we had a wonderful preview in San Bernardino. And Irving, after every movie, would bring you back to the studio. He'd take three directors to the preview, three writers, three producers, three cameramen, everybody, because he wanted people there that knew the business, that knew about making great pictures. We sat around together after *Tugboat Annie* up in the Metro-Goldwyn-Mayer dining room, way upstairs, where he brought everybody back after the previews, and everybody was saying "Well, you made a fine picture," "You had a wonderful preview," and Irving sat there. He never opened his mouth unless he could improve, and he finally said, "Mervyn, I'd like to ask you a question." He says, "You know the scene where Marie Dressler is in the school auditorium speaking to the class of kids and grown-ups and so forth?" I said, "Yes." "And when Wally Beery comes down the aisle from the tugboat, drunk?" I said, "Yes." And he said, "He tried to sneak in so that his wife wouldn't see him as she's speaking on the platform." And I said, "Yes." "Wouldn't it be funny if he just left the tugboat and he came in and his shoes were soaking wet and as he walked down the aisle the shoes squeaked and squeaked and everybody turned around, and she was so mad because he was drunk that everybody laughed?" I said, "Yes, Irving, but the set was already torn down, and we'd have to have the same actors to match. It would cost about forty thousand dollars to do it over." Irving looked at me for a second and said, "Mervyn, I didn't ask how much it would cost, I asked if it would improve the picture." And I said, "Yes, it would." And he said, "Shoot it." And that sums up Irving Thalberg.

ADELA ROGERS ST. JOHNS: Well, Thalberg had people advising him, too. [Screenwriter] Frances Marion was Thalberg's other self. Every picture that Thalberg did, Frances was involved in or wrote. She was the great scenario writer, and she sat with him on every picture. And she was the greatest scriptwriter the business has ever seen.

PANDRO BERMAN: Thalberg ran a very tight ship with everything under his control. He made all the decisions. He had a very small group of men assisting him. Louis B. Mayer was the exact opposite.

ADELA ROGERS ST. JOHNS: I first met Mr. Mayer when I was western editor of a magazine called *Photoplay*. And Mr. Mayer was just a guy running a kind of junk studio. I had sort of picked up some *Photoplay* material out there, just stopping by the Mission Road studio. He looked exactly the way he looked at all times, only a little younger. I don't think he changed at all in appearance. He got older, but there was no vital change. Even toward the end. He kept himself in pretty good shape. He didn't talk the way Sam Goldwyn did or Carl Laemmle. He was a Canadian and very conscious of it, very proud of it.

MARGARET BOOTH: I remember the first time I ever saw Mr. Mayer. My first reaction was—I liked him. He was only about thirty-two years old then. He was a young man, of course, but I thought he was older because I was so young. I thought everybody was older. I was working in the cutting room, and all of a sudden I turned and looked, and Mr. Mayer was standing in the doorway and he said, "Billy over here tells me you're a very loyal girl and work very hard." And then he said, "We'll get along fine." He was quite plump then, quite a plump man. Very nice. I always liked him very much. And he paid me as much as he did the men—more, actually. When I first went there, I got $35 a week, and then I got $50 a week. I used to get on the Red Car, and I'd say to myself, "I'm getting more than anybody on this car, I know it." I was very happy. It was a very big salary for a young girl.

BRONISLAU KAPER: I knew Mayer very well. I was very close to him because he brought me to Hollywood. I was his protégé. For years we had a wonderful relationship. And whatever bad people have to say about Mayer, I always defend him because I have to. He saved my life and the life of my family. So to me he did only good things. I know the bad things he did, but they were not crucial. He never killed anybody. He never ruined anybody.

KATHARINE HEPBURN: He was a tough man if he disliked you.

BRONISLAU KAPER: Yes, he was tough. That's why he was Louis B. Mayer. And I'm not tough, so that's why I am Bronnie Kaper.

KATHARINE HEPBURN: He happened to like me and I liked him. We were friends. When you went to Mr. Mayer you got an answer . . . and you didn't have to go to five thousand people to do it either. They are all a bunch of nincompoops today compared to him.

JOHN CROMWELL: I met Mr. Mayer, of course, and I found him to be the type of man that I could not admire. To me he was domineering, ruthless, and humorless. He had worked hard and driven himself all his life for a success which seemed to reveal all of the unattractive traits of his character.

PANDRO BERMAN: Right. Oh, Louis Mayer *was* a great man. There's no question about it. He was not necessarily a nice man, and a lot of people had a lot against him. But he was a great man in his job.

WALTER REISCH: I disqualify myself to pass judgment on him as a person. I'm immeasurably grateful to him for the rest of my life. He was good to me, and he was good to my family. We were invited to his house two or three times each year, and he loved my wife and adored beautiful people. If it hadn't been for him, I would have been stuck in Europe. I would have been bombed out or killed. I have absolutely no wish, nor am I in a position, to judge his personal status. It was his business, not mine.

BRONISLAU KAPER: Mayer was very conservative, old-fashioned. His favorite song was "Ah, Sweet Mystery of Life." Every year, at his birthday party, in his private room, Jeanette MacDonald would sing this song, and I would accompany her on the piano. Don't forget, when you ask about Mayer, I was raised for twenty-eight years on the MGM lot. That same studio every week. MGM. I was there *every day*. It's a different thing when somebody is freelancing or borrowed from another studio or goes on long vacations or takes sick leave. With me it wasn't like that. I really worked there. For twenty-eight years. Every day. I knew what was going on, and I heard all the rumors. I saw Mr. Mayer in every possible situation. He was there every day, too, and you could meet him in the Commissary or at the barbershop. When we were at the barber's, you know. Jokes. We told jokes. But Thalberg? Of course, he was a very hardworking man. You didn't see too much of him around.

NORMAN TAUROG: Whenever I started a picture, I either got a phone call from Mr. Mayer or a note saying "Congratulations, I hope this is the way you want it." Or he would stroll by the set with Howard Strickling. He was always with someone. He would say, "Norman, good luck." Then he would shake hands with the stars or whomever I was with. If I was working with Spencer Tracy, he would shake hands with him. He always made it like a family, and he always knew when you were starting to shoot a new picture. Always! If a day went by and he missed your first morning, he would pick up a phone to say, "I'm sorry I missed your first day, but I was tied up with a conference." If someone came out from New York, Mr. Mayer brought him down to your set, and if the guest wasn't familiar with you, Mr. Mayer would say, "This is Norman Taurog. He made *Boys Town* and *Girl Crazy* and this and that and so on."

Under Mr. Mayer, we were always allowed to work as a team. Making a picture is like playing football. If the line doesn't hold, then the quarterback doesn't have a chance. You must have teamwork. If the art director, the casting director, the music department, the cameramen, and all the different departments aren't of top-notch quality, no matter what I put into it, I will not get a top-notch picture. This is where Mr. Mayer was great. He was great at picking people. He hired the best in all areas.

KATHARINE HEPBURN: He was an amazing man. He was a real entrepreneur in the old-fashioned sense. He had the courage of his convictions. I liked that. He'd go along whether you agreed or disagreed with it. He wasn't afraid to make up his own mind. If you thought you needed another two million dollars to do something, then he'd pay for it. . . . He was conscious of the impression he made, but also rather unguarded. He knew more without any formal education than all these fancy fellows with a lot of education. He had a sense of smell for the business. . . . He was not stupid, not crude . . . and extremely honest. With all my dealings with Mayer, I could say that he was the most honest person that I ever dealt with in my life.

ADELA ROGERS ST. JOHNS: Mr. Mayer knew how to be part of a team. I think Mayer and Thalberg were a great team. I think they fitted together. And Mayer knew about people. I think he proved with Gable and Mickey and Judy, with all the great stars at MGM, that he knew how to handle people. That was his gift. He knew and believed that Thalberg was the greatest maker of motion pictures in the business. Mayer said Thalberg was a genius. And I think Mayer desired to give Thalberg's genius a place to work. That's why Mayer got all that money. Because *he* could make Thalberg work and make all those people work. And I think that Mayer's one idea was to make Thalberg happy and keep him happy and keep him alive. That was his whole intention: to keep Thalberg working.

SAM MARX: Mayer and Thalberg had a marvelous concept, which was "Get the best and pay for it." Mayer said to me, "Look, I hired you because I think you have brains. Why should I say no to you?" He was always willing to listen to me, even though he may have felt another way about what I was saying. That was their policy with all the department heads. If the department head wanted to do something, they backed him up. The department head at MGM had the authority to do what he thought best . . . until he made some colossal mistake or proved to be utterly incompetent . . . they would back him up. After I left Metro and went with various others, I realized how valuable that policy was. It doesn't happen very often, but you could count on it with Mayer.

ARTHUR FREED: When I first signed Gene Kelly, nobody in the studio liked him. They said, "You're not going to put him opposite Judy Garland in *For Me and My Gal*?" I said, "He's perfect for it, he's an Irishman." Eddie Mannix said, "But he's the wrong kind of Irishman." I had lunch with Mayer, and I said, "I want to tell you something: I'm starting the picture next week, and everybody thinks that I'm doing the wrong thing putting Gene Kelly opposite Judy." He said, "How do *you* feel?" I said, "I love him." He said, "Well, then, don't listen to all those schmucks."

NORMAN TAUROG: Look at the number of men that Mr. Mayer assembled around him. And look at the class of the people. There is one thing that I do know about Mr. Mayer: he would give you an option. Many a time I went in to Mr. Mayer with complete sincerity. I asked to see him, and he told me to come in. He asked me what he could do for me. I said, "Mr. Mayer, I was given a script to do, but I cannot make the picture. I do not believe in it, and I cannot do a good job." I never heard the man rant and rave, so help me. I never heard him say, "Take this man off salary" or "Give him a suspension." He said, "Is there anything else on the lot that you would rather make? Why don't you talk to the other producers? If you can find something, I will let you off the hook. If there is nothing, then I think you should give this script a second thought and see if you can't possibly get yourself to make it. If you can't and you honestly feel that way, then we will put someone else on it."

KING VIDOR: Mayer held the thing together at MGM, and he persuaded stars and star material to stay there. He had a "family." He believed MGM was like a family. He was holding that together, and that's a great ability in itself. That's a great talent, to be able to keep all those stars and actors satisfied, keep the directors there. If you started to leave, he'd practically break down and cry. You're walking out on your home and all sorts of things like that went on from him to keep people there. One actor went in to talk about a raise with Mayer, and he went in without his agent. When he came out, the agent says, "Did you get the raise?" And the actor says, "I not only didn't get the raise, I got Louis B. Mayer for a father." But Mayer would do that. He'd say, "You're my son" and so forth. He was very adept at it. He wanted to hold that big organization together. I don't think you have studio heads like that today. They don't want to build up a studio. They're as interested in Las Vegas and running a hotel as they are in running a studio. It's all divided up today, cut into pieces.

ADELA ROGERS ST. JOHNS: Louis B. was very kind to me. And that doesn't necessarily mean soft. It means kind. And he was quite thoughtful. He said to me one day, "I like having you on the lot. I like having you come up to have breakfast with me occasionally. I would like to have you for a sister. You would be my ideal of a sister." Maybe that's the right line to take with me. If so, it's pretty perceptive of him to get it. And if he could get that right line with everybody, well, then, that's the way he could handle them because I still regard myself as a sister to Mr. Mayer.

KATHARINE HEPBURN: He said things that would really charm me. I finally said, "You know, Mr. Mayer, you are charming me. I know that you are charming me and still I am charmed." That's a real artist.

MARGARET BOOTH: Well, one thing to remember, Mayer had a very bad temper. He had a really bad temper, and he used to go into fits real bad, so much that people were afraid of him. He'd yell and scream. I never heard Irving do that. Mr. Mayer would be angry, and he'd look at you with those big eyes. When he wanted something, he wanted it. Mr. Mayer could be vitriolic, and if he got mad at you, you knew about it, but I always found him to be very honest as far as his dealings with people went.

ADELA ROGERS ST. JOHNS: People talk about Thalberg and Mayer. But they don't know. I knew them. I observed them, and I was a reporter, remember. Observing people was my job. I can remember once when I was sitting in Thalberg's office. Both of their offices were in the same building, Mayer's office and Thalberg's office. There was a balcony, a long strip of concrete balcony, that ran outside them both and then made a little switch and went down the staircase. I can remember sitting there in Irving's office and there would be a pitter-patter of feet and Mr. Mayer's head would come around the side, and he'd say, "Irvie, do you have time for me?" He called him "Irvie." And Irving would say, "No, Mr. Mayer, not now." And Mr. Mayer would say, "All right," and go back to his own office. I can always remember his head peeking around the side of that door.

IRENE MAYER SELZNICK: My father was very intimate with Thalberg. If he had been his own son, he couldn't have been more passionate about him. And Irving was very adoring to my father. Irving used to come around to the house a good deal. He often used to come to dinner. My father had him around, but he made one point very clear: he indoctrinated my sister and me about how sick Irving was and that he would never live to be the age of thirty. My father believed this. He really believed that it would be a miracle if Irving lived beyond thirty. He didn't want his daughters young widows. He made it very, very clear that his girls were not to be taken out. They weren't going to go out for years anyhow, and he wasn't even going to let us go with boys, let alone men. Irving was not to pay any attention to either my sister or myself. Irving was watched like a hawk as far as we were concerned. My father was very firm about it and very frank about it, too. If either of us had gotten any romantic inclinations, it wouldn't have helped. We couldn't talk five minutes to Irving. We were never alone with him. We did see a lot of him . . . we had a lot of parties at our house . . . but one dance each, and that was it. In general, my father thought that no good would come if we were around people who were too modern. He didn't approve of cigarettes, and obviously he didn't approve of drinking. He didn't approve of low-cut dresses or flirtations, and so on.

HOWARD STRICKLING: People that Louis B. Mayer had faith in and trusted, he built up. Like he trusted Thalberg. See, he never had a son, but as near a son as he could have was Irving Thalberg. He gave him everything.

MERVYN LEROY: When Irving Thalberg was head of production at Metro, he was possibly the head of the whole business, because everybody looked up to him. And he was also the head of the motion picture producers association. He was the head of everything. And there was no jealousy of any kind.

GEORGE SEATON: Getting to Thalberg was a problem. You've read all the stories about how difficult it was, and it was. No doubt about it. Even the high man on the totem pole used to sit for hours and hours outside. I don't know whether it was an affectation or if it was by design, but it really *was* that difficult. Everybody waited for Thalberg.

ADELA ROGERS ST. JOHNS: Yes, but Metro-Goldwyn-Mayer *was* Mr. Mayer. I used to watch him with Thalberg, and he deferred to him, but because he wanted to. The Mayer studio in those days . . . well, there has never been another studio like it, and there never will be such an array of stars, pictures, ever again. That was Mr. Mayer. You can't do that if you are not the person who can do it. And he could.

FRANK CAPRA: How big was Mayer? He had all the stars. He had a tremendous position. Men like Harry Cohn took aspirin every time Mayer sneezed.

TAY GARNETT: Thalberg's theory was that pictures are not made, they're remade. That's why MGM was called "Retake Valley." But he was thought of as sickly. His health was always an issue. Thalberg ceased being the head man in all of MGM's productions on his own decision. He refused to do that anymore on doctor's orders. Thalberg was working very much on an island, and you felt as if he wasn't working for MGM anymore. If you worked for him, you were working for Irving Thalberg. So L. B. Mayer had to take over running the studio, and I believe that's when some kind of feud got started.

ADELA ROGERS ST. JOHNS: Remember, Irving was very young, very extravagant, but he was the producer. Irving actually produced the things that other producers, like Hunt Stromberg, have their names on. Irving was the man. I think Irving never once in his life thought about what a picture cost, how much it cost. I think that if Mayer got mad at Irving, it was because he was trying a little bit to keep the cost down, because he treated Irving as though Irving had been sent down to him from God. Always like that. He thought of Irving as the artist, the producer of these great movies. Without Mr. Mayer there wouldn't have been any Irving Thalberg. Mr. Mayer gave him the money. He gave him the protection. He gave him the stars. He gave him the directors. He gave him this great big studio, which he kept running and solvent with Andy Hardy movies and God knows what. Thalberg had what many a great artist has not had. I think Mayer gave him the opportunities to do the things he did.

NORMAN TAUROG: MGM was the biggest of the studios, but Mayer always ran it with an atmosphere that everybody was pulling for good pictures. I never heard anyone saying that someone had a flop on their hands. I would always hear people say, "How did it go?" If you said there were rough places, they would say, "Can you edit it?" That didn't happen at RKO when I was there. That is why Metro is Metro. That is why Louis B. Mayer was a great, great production and business head. He knew people. I have never seen the side of Mr. Mayer when he resorted to screaming.

I never saw that. Never! On the other hand, I have seen him cry and give an Academy Award performance. He did it when it meant something. Like if someone asked for a pay increase during World War II, when everyone was making so bloody much money that you couldn't see straight. You went up for more money, and he'd say, "Wouldn't I give it to you if we were making it? I would give it to you in two minutes. I would give it to everybody. I would give it to anybody. But we're not making it." You would go out of his office and down to the barbershop, and there would be a report, "Metro made $33 million this year." But when you walked out of his office, you had been thinking "Why in hell did I ask that poor man for more money?" He was a great performer. Great! I also saw him tell actors off when their heads were too big, but I never did see him scream.

RICHARD THORPE: I once went up to Mr. Mayer's office with Myrna Loy. She didn't want to do some picture she was scheduled to do. And L.B. was a great actor. He'd learned to get up and stand on his chair or get right down on his knees and plead with women stars with tears in his eyes. But in this instance, he passed out. And I have never known whether he actually fainted or had a slight heart attack or just pretend passed out for dramatic effect. They called his doctor, and she showed us all out of there. I've never really known whether he just did it or not, but I do know one thing: Myrna did the movie.

ADELA ROGERS ST. JOHNS: I remember when he talked Greer Garson into playing Mrs. Miniver. At first she didn't want the role because she'd be playing the mother of a grown son. She came into Mr. Mayer's office, and I was there, and he started telling her how great the part was. He got down on his knees and acted out the role, and he played it a gosh-darned sight better than she ever did. And when he finished, I was crying, she was crying, and she says, "I'll play it," and went out the door. See, if Mr. Mayer had been the man some people say he was—so mean—he couldn't have pulled things like that off. I used to watch him with Thalberg. He loved him. And with Clark Gable. Gable was Mr. Mayer's youth. Gable was the guy he still wanted to be.

PANDRO BERMAN: The talent department at MGM was very good. They had diversification. You see, that was the secret of Mayer. He diversified in the talent department by having Rufus Le Maire, by having Billy Grady, by having talent coaches who would instruct the young stars, starlets, and the young hopeful actors and educate them and bring them along. It wasn't left to chance. He did the same thing in the story department. I recall that where the average studio would have one story personality, maybe one in New York and one out here, Louis had not only the New York office very well organized under J. Robert Rubin and his staff in New York, who were the most efficient eastern organization of that kind, but he also had people like Lillie Messinger, Kenneth MacKenna, Voldemar Vetluguin, and others right here in the studio operation, contrary sometimes to each other, you know. Mayer did not have one funnel through which everything went in the way of himself as the studio head. He tried to avoid that funnel in the story department, too, figuring that if one person turned down a story and didn't bring it to his attention that it wouldn't be lost if it was good because one of his other story department men or women would come up with it. He had a very competent woman named Harriet Frank, in addition to these others, who would tell him the stories of books that he never had the time to read. He didn't like reading synopses. He preferred to have these stories told to him.

The talent department was given a great deal of leeway under Mayer. They were more apt to accept the recommendations of anybody qualified than you would find the case in most studios, you know. In some studios they'd rule out Clark Gable because his ears were too big or this, that, or the other. But Mayer had a very open mind about those things.

TAY GARNETT: Mayer had a big thing about mothers. His own mother must have been pretty wonderful to him, because anytime we had a story with a mother in it, a good character, we were halfway home. If you had a story with a mother in it that was bad, forget it. Just get lost. Either that, or don't ever mention the fact that she was a mother. Oh, he was a strange character, but especially with the outset of the war [World War II] and a lot of boys going away from their families and their mothers were standing by . . . no bad mothers.

ADELA ROGERS ST. JOHNS: He would talk about his own mother from when he was back in Canada. His mother taught him about echoes, and this was one of his great things. He told it when he wanted you to understand about certain things. He said that when he was a little boy, they lived on the side of a hill, and his mother used to take him out on this little porch and make him holler. And it would come back—an echo—but he would hear his voice. And she taught him that that's what life was like: you got back what you sent out—echo of what you created or what you said or did is what came back. And nothing else could.

BRONISLAU KAPER: Mayer had a house in Bel Air and a house at the beach. He had people over to play bridge, and he gave luncheons. He used to play cards with me and Walter Jurmann when we first came over from Europe. Because he knew how much we made, because he owned our contracts, he never wanted to play for high money. And we wanted to impress him, so we'd say, "Let's play half a cent a point." How can you impress a man who knows how much you make? And he said, "No, no. It's too much. Let's play one-tenth . . . or one-twentieth." We finally got the message.

ADELA ROGERS ST. JOHNS: Mayer was very prone to tell stories about his early days in Canada and about his mother and the things that happened to him then. I knew him all through those years. And Mrs. Mayer, his wife. I was devoted to Margaret Mayer, and so was everybody else. She was a great woman, you know, and she understood him. I once told her, "Margaret, you're a very lucky woman." I think any woman who married the right man and stays married to him all those years is very fortunate, because every change you make is for the worse, and all women know that, actually. Maybe you stick to one of the later ones, but they're all the same. Once a man is a husband, he's a husband, and there you've got it. Anyway, I told Margaret Mayer, "I think you've been very fortunate, because you've only been married to one man." And she said, "What do you mean, I've only been married to one man?" Well, I said, "Margaret, you yourself told me that when you married Mr. Mayer, he was so young and inexperienced and his clothes didn't fit him, and I always remember your describing him as his coat was so tight for him that the sleeves came up halfway up his arm. So

I don't see how you were married to anybody before that. You were kids, you said, and here you are still married to him."

"Oh, yes," she said, "that's perfectly true." But she said, "My dear girl, you do not understand that I have been married to more men than you ever dreamed of. You don't think there's anything exactly in common between that shy, idealistic, frightened boy with his wrists sticking out of his coat cuffs and the ruthless, dominant man that's run the picture business all these years, do you? That's not the same man. I think he's the most complex man that it would be possible for any human being to know anything about. And he is so complex because each piece of him is completely sincere and completely uncontrolled and as dynamic and violent and complete as you can get. And they are utterly at variance with each other. The man who gets the biggest salary of any man in America and keeps it and who controls the kind of people that he's got on the Metro-Goldwyn-Mayer lot—and he controls 'em, every one of 'em, Thalberg, Gable, Mickey, Judy—every one of 'em. He's got that other end of the string in his hand. And that's why we have the greatest studio and the greatest stars and the greatest everything that has ever been in the world." And besides, she said, "I just loved to dance with him. He's the best ballroom dancer in Hollywood. I'd rather have him come and ask me to dance than anything."

PANDRO BERMAN: Louis Mayer took great pride in the fact that he spent time in the White House as a guest when Herbert Hoover was president. He was a strong Republican, and he took a great interest in politics. In fact, Ida Koverman, his principal secretary, not the one who took dictation but the one who made engagements for him, was hired because of her political know-how. She became a kind of a casting talent in the course of events but actually was originally put on because she knew politics.

L.B. was rabidly anti-Communist and strongly supported the Motion Picture Alliance [for the Preservation of American Ideals]. And at one time he turned his editorial staff into what you might call a kind of secret service to examine every script for any Communist propaganda, et cetera. He was the "Mister Republican" of MGM, and Nick Schenck in New York was "Mister Democrat." And they both made their contributions to their respective parties, so that MGM always had a friend at court. And, whoever became president or governor or whatever you call it, there was always somebody in the organization who had an entrée to him. *They* knew how to do business!

DORE SCHARY: Mayer had marvelous, cocky guts, real chutzpah. Most of those men had that. Your Warners, your Cohns, your Mayers . . . they all had this one thing in common. It's a crazy idea, really, the studio system. A hundred stars, 110 writers, and 100 directors or maybe 50 directors. Put 'em all under contract. You're crazy to do that, but Mayer did it: more stars than there are in the heavens.

ADELA ROGERS ST. JOHNS: All Louis Mayer wanted out of life was the power to make great motion pictures.

KATHARINE HEPBURN: He loved the business. He just loved the business. His life was his work. When the work ceased, he really sort of died. What was Mr. Mayer? Mr. Mayer was his work.

RICHARD SCHICKEL: Thalberg and Mayer were a team, really, and everybody debates which one of them was the genius. But they were a team, and one of the team members died, and the other one carried on and ultimately has to be seen as the true definition of MGM, and that's Louis B. Mayer. He hired Thalberg and gave him what he needed to thrive, and he was there after Thalberg was gone. They had started working together when Thalberg was twenty-three. Thalberg died at the age of thirty-seven in 1936. Louis B. Mayer kept on running MGM until 1951.

ADELA ROGERS ST. JOHNS: I remember exactly where I was when I heard about Irving's death. I was at Warner Bros. in New York City. Someone back there was trying to get me to do a movie, and I was trying not to do it. And we got the news. And he looked at me, and he said, "You don't look surprised," and I said, "No, I've expected this from the first day I ever saw him." He was frail. You could see through him.

RICHARD SCHICKEL: Mayer and Thalberg are two big names, but there were other men who ran these businesses, oversaw the making of those memorable films, and shaped careers for iconic stars—a bunch of amazing men: Harry Cohn, David O. Selznick, Darryl Zanuck, Sam Goldwyn, Jack Warner. These were real blood-and-thunder guys.

ADELA ROGERS ST. JOHNS: These are men who are ruthless. With themselves first. They did not let themselves be used, and they did not let other people dink away their time. They had some kindness with it, but they worked so hard and so tirelessly. Maybe ruthless is a bad word. No, I know exactly what I mean by it. They knew how to get things done.

GEORGE CUKOR: All those men were rough, tough men, but they were showmen and they were confident and bold. They didn't have popularity polls and they didn't have Nielsen ratings, but they were capable of making big decisions without flinching and sticking by them.

VINCENT SHERMAN: They had a nose for what the public seemed to want, but sometimes they made mistakes. I don't think we have to look at them with reverence or with any great halo of mystery about them, but they kept a finger on the pulse of the public.

MERVYN LEROY: These men wanted you to succeed.

HARRY WARREN: Zanuck—a lot of people didn't like him. I liked him. A lot of people didn't like L. B. Mayer, but I liked him. I liked those two men. They were very polite. I don't know if they did dirty work on the side, but as far as I know, they were very polite. But not Jack Warner or Hal Wallis. They weren't polite at all. I thought they exceeded the bounds of being a gentleman.

NUNNALLY JOHNSON: Zanuck was the master of the story conference, and I never realized how good he was until I worked with some other people. I knew that he was a definite collaborator, contributor to every picture that he ever had anything to do with. I always thought he had a Geiger counter in his head. Darryl was a great editor. He'd read a script, and the minute it got dull or didn't move or went off the track—*tick, tick, tick*—he said, "It stopped. Now, where did *that* start?" And he'd go back two pages, three pages, and then he'd figure where the movement stopped or the movement went wrong. So when you came in to talk to him about your script, he knew exactly where it wasn't moving right.

Darryl's idea was to read a script and then call in the director. Then the director was not only permitted but expected to make suggestions, make his contribution, but it all had to be written on paper before he went out onto his set. And Darryl had to okay it. There was none of this "the director takes charge" while Zanuck was making a picture. The director never took charge. Zanuck was in charge.

HENRY KING: Darryl Zanuck, in my estimation, was one of the fairest men in the world. I always found him to be extremely fair. He was very definite, a man who can make decisions. He had a kind of radar approach, always listening. He was a great man to work with. He could see more defects in a script than any man I ever saw in my life. He's got the keenest eye for reading. He's got the keenest ear for listening of any man I've ever been associated with. He helps you in every way on Earth. He never interferes with anything in the world. He wants to stimulate your imagination for you to go right on, yet he doesn't want you to throw all the money away. He inspires you to the point that you want to be economical with what you are doing. Zanuck is one of those people who can't wait. He's read the script you sent him by the time it's there, almost. This man can read a script and remember every word in it faster than any human being I've ever seen in my life. Remember every word in it. He can remember every movie, everything that was in it. Everything. I think he's the best executive I ever saw at the head of a studio.

GEORGE SEATON: I learned a lot from Mr. Zanuck, and I have the greatest respect for him. He ran a studio as well as anybody ever ran a studio. You could always get to see him, and you could get an answer "yes" or "no" within five minutes. He would get an idea, and he would come over to the writer—he had a great respect for writers—and he would come over and say, "What if so-and-so and so-and-so?" And the natural tendency of anybody listening was to sort of nod your head. That means "I understand what you're talking about." Then the next day you would get a transcript of the meeting from his secretary, who was there taking it down in short-hand, saying "Mr. Zanuck suggested so-and-so, and Mr. Seaton agreed to this." And I realized quickly not to nod my head. So the next time he did this to me, I just sat there with fish eyes and didn't move a muscle, and finally after about two minutes, he would say, "That stinks, doesn't it?" And I would say, "Well, I don't think it's very good." That was a trick I had to learn, because he would put more writers on the spot by having them just nod.

RANALD MACDOUGALL: Zanuck was a craftsman. It wouldn't matter whether he was the president of 20th Century–Fox, chairman of the board or whatever it is, or just a human being in a room, he had enormous craft and talent, quite aside from everything else. And he is one of the one or two major creative talents that I have encountered in my entire profes-sional life. He was personally involved in every motion picture that was made—no matter who produced it, he was deeply involved—and he had a tremendous skill at assessing a story, knowing a story. I'll tell you a story about him that illustrates the point: when one writes a script, there are—particularly in the first draft—there are things in there you do for conve-nience. You do a little bridge scene that you know isn't quite right, but you do it so you can get on to other things. And you know as you read the script progressively, and the next week or the week after, you always notice that little two-line bridge scene, whatever it is, and it's a little blister on your creative skin, and you say, "Well, I'll fix it next week" or "I've got to fix that." You understand? You never really lose track of the fact that that is not the right line, but you are doing the whole script so you'll get to the finer points later. I did one such script at 20th and took it—at Zanuck's request—down to his house in Palm Springs, and I sat on his patio while he read it. Now, there were only two people who had really read it, myself and my secretary. With an unerring precision, as he read it through, he made little marks, and I watched him, not conscious of what he was doing at the moment. He's reading but making little marks. He got all through reading the script in a remarkably short time—he was a very fast reader, another aspect of creative ability, by the way—he got through reading it in about an hour and a half, and then he went on back to the beginning and he said, "Now, on page twelve you said so-and-so, and on page thirty-eight you said so-and-so. Why?" With unerring accuracy he picked out every one of the things that I would have fixed, as a writer, and that I knew were not right. It was an astonishing display of his *grasp* and his *recall* and his *ability* to *focus*. He *knew*! He *knew* what all of the little things were and some of the not-so-little things, and not only had he done it all in one reading and made little notes and focused on it, it was an astonishing display to me. I have never been quite so impressed in my life as I was by that.

He worked differently than I was accustomed to do, and the studio worked *his* way. Zanuck's approach to making a motion picture was to start with the novel, have it put into a synopsis form, which reduces itself to its main essentials, then take that synopsis and put it into a treatment. First, a story line, which is perhaps a forty-page motion picture sort of breakdown, then the story line expanded into a treatment, which, in essence, is a prose visualization of a screenplay without the dialogue. Sometimes there are sketchy indications of dialogue, but not many. But the treatment then, which can run eighty pages or—I've seen treatments which ran three hundred pages—but they become very meticulous treatments. When they are done, they are very meticulous descriptions of a screenplay, if you will, or a motion picture. And that was Zanuck's way of working and of assessing. He wanted one paragraph to start with, and then it began to expand and finally would culminate into a screenplay, which would become a shooting script, which would be done. And that was his work process, and that was the way 20th Century–Fox, his studio, operated.

HARRY WARREN: Zanuck was actually the producer of everything on that lot. He had the last word, and he cut the pictures. He was a nice fellow to work for. We never had any trouble with him. In fact, I think the only fellow we had trouble with was Jack Warner. I never heard Zanuck talk about "How much is it going to cost?" Zanuck was much more interested in what we were going to do. Remember, he had been a writer. And with us he was very polite. If he didn't like a song we'd written, he didn't say,

"I don't like it." He'd say, "Save it. Maybe we can use it some other time." But others, like Hal Wallis at Warners—he was one of the bosses—he used to say, "That's lousy. Write something else." But Zanuck wasn't like that.

GEORGE SEATON: With Zanuck, things could be a little tense. It was difficult at Fox sometimes because he liked to run rushes at midnight, and if you were directing—he wouldn't ask the directors to come in *every* night— but often when you had to run your rough cut for him, you ran it at two o'clock in the morning. Zanuck didn't get to the studio until twelve noon or so. Everybody else got there at nine. So if you were there until four in the morning, it was a long day.

JOHN BRAHM: He had the sort of mind that was perfect for movies. He *thought* pictures.

BARRÉ LYNDON: He was very open minded. He would make suggestions and then you could try them, and if they didn't work, he would say so.

JOHN CROMWELL: I was grateful to have the chance to know something of Darryl Zanuck and how he worked. A man of impelling ambition and energy, he had forced his way up from being a somewhat less than indifferent writer. He qualified eminently as a high-powered Hollywood executive. He was running one of the largest studios in town, personally supervising one or two of the most important films on their schedule, and editing all of the studio's output. There was also the supervision of story material, keeping up with the world's supply, planning the next year's program. He had to get stories for the contract star and constantly be sensitive to the pulse of the company's policy.

Within the range of his limited taste in what constituted entertainment, he had an aggressive story mind. By that I mean that he thought of a story mostly in blacks and whites. Shades of color and shades of meaning interested him, but he felt safer where the going was on tried-and-true grounds. He was utterly devoid of humor. He allowed absolutely no interference with his ideas unless divergent opinion would be presented through the medium of an obviously valid story point. In conference he

gave lip service to open-mindedness. Consciously or not, there was definitely a Napoleonic complex.

In talking about a story point in conference one day, he talked about
a millstone when he meant milestone. The writer, new to the studio, used
the correct word later rather emphatically. After the writer left, Darryl
turned to the producer and said, "Where did that guy come from?" Upon
receiving the answer, he said, "Fire him."

In one corner of the large Fox Commissary, there was a small private
dining room reserved for Mr. Zanuck, members of his staff, and any producer who cared to use it. An occasional writer or director might be invited. Then there were four to six of Darryl's henchmen, usually referred
to as "yes-men." This coterie consisted of the studio's head cutter, a producer or two, and at times the court jester, Gregory Ratoff, an amusing
and ingratiating Russian actor.

It was inevitable that Darryl would have such a retinue. The pace of
his existence demanded such relaxation. Having been there on one or
two occasions, I knew what the usual conversation was like. There were
the prevailing studio jokes and gossip for the right amount of diversion.
But I also knew that studio problems, if they weren't too secret, came up
for discussion, as did recent previews, first cuts of new pictures, and the
box-office potential of confirmed new material. Zanuck cared about everything, and he asked for opinions. This gave rise to the idea he always
wanted to hear a "yes" from his tablemates, but "yes" or "no," he would do
things his own way.

WALTER REISCH: Zanuck left you alone until the day came that he needed
you. You got an appointment via Esther [Roberts], his secretary. She'd
say, "Tuesday, four p.m., half an hour," and on Tuesday at four in the
afternoon you got your half hour. You walked in, and he told you exactly
what you needed to know. There he sat with his cigar—he didn't even
know your second name, addressed you only by your first name. He'd
say, "I have to start a Clifton Webb picture on December first, and today
is June fifteenth. I need the script within eight weeks because Webb has
to read it, and as a perfectionist he takes a long time to learn his lines."
He told you what he wanted, whether he wanted a comedy or a mystery

story, whether in black and white or color—he gave you the whole production set-up.

He'd say, "I don't want to make a picture that will cost more than
$1,200,000 or $1,500,000, or even less. I have three directors lined up; let's
see which one of them likes it well enough to do it." He wouldn't argue
with a director. He'd give the script to Henry King, to Jean Negulesco, to
Henry Hathaway or to George Cukor, whoever came in first, and say, "I
want you to do it," and they got the picture. Then you didn't see him for
ten weeks, and he didn't ask you to see him. You'd get another call from
Esther saying "You're supposed to see Mr. Zanuck and tell him the story
on Wednesday at three o'clock in the afternoon. You have forty minutes—
use your time well." You walked in—he didn't want to read what you had
written. No director was present, only a secretary, no witnesses. She always took minutes of the conversation during which you told him the
story. Either he hated it and you walked out—and there was no argument,
you couldn't convince him that you could do better—or he loved it and
you had the assignment before you returned to your office. After that he
read the finished script, took it home on Friday at twelve o'clock, came
back on Monday at eleven in the morning with his marginal notes, and
those notes had to be observed. He knew you would observe those notes.
I don't think he ever read it the second time around. He knew that his
amendments would be followed.

As far as I was concerned, he was an ideal executive. To begin with, he
delegated power: if the picture was good, it was *your* success. If the picture
was bad, he took all the blame and said, "I never should have let it go into
production." He never interfered on the set with a director or with an actor. He saw the rushes, he wrote notes to them, and these notes had to be
observed, too: "Let the actors speak more slowly" or "more dramatically"
or "more tempestuously" or whatever. Then came the great moment when
he took over everything, and for many, many productions, that was very
dangerous. Once a picture had been shot and the director had, according
to his contract, submitted the first cut to Zanuck's office containing everything that had been shot, regardless of whether it was long enough or too
long, Zanuck took over and edited the picture every day from after dinner
till long after midnight.

HENRY KING: Zanuck would come on the set, but only to bid me good morning. He never made a suggestion on set. Zanuck is the greatest office man in the world. He can tell you more about your story just sitting in his office discussing it than any other five men that ever made motion pictures.

BARRÉ LYNDON: Zanuck had a big office, and near the end of it was an archway, and his desk was at the far end behind the archway. You didn't go through the archway. You sat outside. I remember taking a script there and hearing him say, "This is about eighty-five percent to ninety percent right. Now let's get it to one hundred percent." The film was *The Lodger*.

He wanted a different ending. I remember him coming out and acting out a scene. The big trick with Zanuck was to take the "shape" of what he would suggest, to make it work, but not to do exactly what he said, because he would use whatever he could use to get his idea across to you. He was always right, because he had a very good dramatic mind, a marvelous mind.

He thought in terms of dramatic scenes and structure. I remember that he called everybody in to see the rough cut on *Hangover Square*. He ran that in his private projection room near his office, and he had everybody in there, the writer, the producer, the wardrobe people—everybody who'd had anything to do with making the picture was there. He ran it reel by reel, and at the end of each reel he'd stop it and make his remarks and ask his questions—and you'd better have some answers, too!

He wanted straight answers. We weren't yes-men. Then he'd criticize the scenes and say, "Well, I think instead of this, we could do that." He'd consider shooting new scenes or cutting others out. He went right through it, and we were there till past three thirty in the morning and back again at nine the next day.

GEORGE SEATON: Frank Nugent was the film critic for the *New York Times*, and Zanuck had an idea: "Well, if this guy's so smart, he can tell us what's wrong with a picture after it's made. Why don't we hire him and let him come out here and read the scripts and tell us what's wrong with them going in?" So Frank Nugent came to the studio. The first script that he ever read was *That Night in Rio*. He was there at that conference at two o'clock in the morning, and finally Zanuck turned to him and said, "Well, we have Mr. Nugent here. Perhaps, Frank, you can tell us your opinion of the script." I sat back, waiting for the critic of the *New York Times* to be very profound. There was a scene in the stock market where Don Ameche held up his hand, trying to get someone's attention across the room. He doesn't realize it, but he's buying stock by this gesture. The upshot of it is that he comes out with a $50,000 profit. So Nugent said, "I've read the script, and I think that scene where Don Ameche makes $50,000 is excessive. I think if he made $25,000, it would make the point and it wouldn't be quite so ridiculous." So Zanuck says, "Fine, what else, Frank?" Frank says, "That's all." Zanuck looked at him, and later when Frank left the room, he said, "My God, there's our critic, and all he can think of is saving $25,000. It's not even in the cost of the picture. It's just a line of dialogue." That was our last conference with a critic.

CHARLES LEMAIRE: After Zanuck left the studio, there wasn't a head anymore. There wasn't *that man* in the office, third door to the right, you know? The man wasn't there, and there wasn't a fellow you could go to who you felt was the boss and who you felt knew what he was talking about. The thing that I admired so much about him was his perfection. He spent the money and took the time to do it right. *His attention about detail!* He loved detail, and it was exciting. That's why I say that there are the two great men, Zanuck and Ziegfeld. Ziegfeld used to say, when first I met him, he said, "Those girls' costumes have to be lined in silk. Don't forget, lined in silk." And the woman who was making the clothes for him said, "But Mr. Ziegfeld, lined in silk?" You know, she had never worked for him before. "Lined in silk, that's going to cost a lot of money." He says, "Don't you worry about it," he says. "People can tell class even if they don't see it." And the girls felt better, too. And Zanuck understood that, too.

IRVING RAPPER: Jack Warner never went to the extent that someone like Zanuck at Fox would go in critiquing product. Oh, no, no. He was much too busy. Zanuck or Selznick or Goldwyn could do one picture at a time, at their will, but Warner had half a dozen going at one time, seventeen or so. It would be a hell of a thing to be able to do. Warners popped 'em out. Warner had a different approach. He wouldn't have a hand in the beginning or the formative part of the picture because he would rely on the cutters . . . at Warner Bros. the cutters were masters of their art . . . and the average producer there was also a very knowledgeable man, like Robert Lord or Henry Blanke, for instance. And so when the director, together with the cutter and the producer, would make suggestions in the dailies, this would all be in the formative stage until a rough cut emerged. That's when Jack Warner would look at it at home, and that's when you got to see the fabulous mansion of Jack Warner, which was most impressive and where he revealed the other side of his nature. There he couldn't be anything but the most hospitable. He was a great host and a great guy at his house. I wish he was like that at the studio. Everybody would be working for him forever. At the studio, everyone who knocked at the door to see him heard "What does *he* want?" It was one complaint after another. Jack Warner was a bit of an ogre.

GORDON DOUGLAS: I was under contract to Warners for at least twelve years. In those days, Jack Warner ran the studio. He had an assistant named Steve Trilling who was his right arm. They would make the decisions along with the head of the story department, almost as a team in the front office. They would call in a director and talk to him about a project. And before you knew it, the wheels were rolling. Or not. If I didn't do the project they talked to me about, I could get suspended. So I would do it.

RANALD MACDOUGALL: Jack Warner never got my name right all the time I was at Warner Bros., but you know, I'd meet him and perhaps go to a preview in Glendale and then be in the manager's office in Glendale while Jack would invent things that could be done to improve the picture. But at any rate, I knew him quite well, and even up to the last two years I was under contract, he was always after me. "You're the one who doesn't come in on time," he'd say. "You're the one who doesn't come in." And he used to go over the time sheets in the morning, and anybody who came in after nine was marked in red: 9:07. Me? I was always 10:45, 11:10. When they got after me, I'd come in at two o'clock just to show them. And all of that stopped and I found out that Steve Trilling had cured the whole situation: he decided that I was never going to change, so he gave orders at the gate and the policeman always wrote me down as nine o'clock, no matter what time I came in.

HARRY WARREN: The Warner studio was a one-man lot. If it wasn't Jack Warner, it was Hal Wallis. They were very autocratic and acted like the heads of countries. Also, the difference between them and Zanuck was, Zanuck was a one-man lot, but he never acted the way they did. Warner and Wallis were very ruthless with people. I know of instances where a fellow—a cutter—who left the light on while he was out of his office was fired. This was before the unions. And they kept actors up all night. If an actor worked until three in the morning, he had to be back on the set at eight o'clock the next morning. That's the way they acted.

IRVING RAPPER: Jack Warner was not to be coped with. He was tyranni-cal, unreasonable, and didactic. At home, he was a prince and an angel, the greatest, kindest host in the world. And he had a most charming, won-derful wife, whom I adore and who helped cope, but really, he was not to be coped with. I suffered. Once Bogart saw me, and said, "What's the matter, you look down," and I said, "Another suspension." And Bogie said, "One more, and you'll be the San Francisco Bay Bridge." He admitted he was doing a "lousy thing" that he hated, so I told him, "Well, you've got a little more money than I have, why don't you take a suspension and see the world or something?" And he replied, "No. I want Jack Warner to have to look at my puss every day of his life."

VINCENT SHERMAN: Errol Flynn had a great sense of humor, a great sense of fun. I asked him once if he did much reading, and he said, "I read every night." I said, "What do you read?" and he said, "Law books." Well, then he said he did it so he could see how to protect himself against Warner Bros. He was always having fights with the front office, with Jack Warner. I had to work with Flynn, and I tried to keep out of the fights as much as possible. Warner used to call me ten or fifteen times during the making of a picture with Flynn, and he'd say, "You tell that bastard this. You tell him that." I said, "Yes, Mr. Warner. Yes, Mr. Warner." Finally one day, I couldn't take it myself anymore, so I said, "Mr. Warner, you pay him . . . *you* tell him." Maybe he did. I doubt it. Jack Warner had trouble with all of them: Flynn, Cagney, Bogie, de Havilland, Davis. He drove actors crazy.

BETTE DAVIS: Well, there was an enormous difference between the artistic side of the industry and the money side, the men who ran the studios and those of us on the stages. Neither of us understood each other at all, except if you had intelligence, you knew they had to be there. But artistically it was extraordinarily difficult always. The absolute worst was Jack Warner. We all felt the same way about him.

ADELA ROGERS ST. JOHNS: Look at what they went through out there at Warner Bros. with all those unhappy stars. They gave out so many suspensions that their people weren't working half the time. Bette Davis wouldn't work for that son of a bitch Jack Warner, and she ran off the lot to England. Of course, they forced her back, and when she comes back, Cagney runs off the lot. I mean, you know, those things didn't happen at Metro. Maybe at Fox or Paramount, I don't know. But not Metro.

VINCENT SHERMAN: Everybody today lumps Jack Warner in with people like Louis B. Mayer, Harry Cohn, and Darryl Zanuck. Mr. Warner was the head of the studio, that's true, but when I worked there, Hal Wallis was running the studio. Mr. Warner's activity was not as full as it became after Wallis left. The responsibilities for getting scripts ready was Wallis's. Warner wasn't as close to the studio in those days as he became later when Wallis left. But it was Jack Warner's interaction with the stars who fought him, like Bette Davis, Jimmy Cagney, and Olivia de Havilland, that got attention.

HENRY BLANKE: I have a great admiration for Jack Warner. He had his difficult side, but he also had some great, great, really very great judgments. Sometimes he was wrong, but he was 90 percent right, purely by instinct, on movies. People like to tell jokes both about him and by him. For instance, when he said that if John Huston took any longer shooting *The Treasure of the Sierra Madre* in Mexico—if he didn't find that gold pretty soon—he'd have to hock the whole studio. Or when I gave him the script for *The African Queen* to read and he misread it completely and said,

"I wouldn't make a picture in which the leading man gets bitten by a mosquito." Or I remember when Wallis was in Canada and I had to send him the script for *The Story of Louis Pasteur,* and he hated it and said, "Fire those two writers immediately! Who wants to see Paul Muni with a beard looking through a microscope?" But he said I could show it to Warner, so I did, without telling him about what Wallis said. So Jack Warner says, "This is great! This is a prizefight story, isn't it?" So naturally, having been in this business so many years, I said, "Yes."

But 90 percent of the time, he was very knowing, very cutting. He can tell you right away when he sees dailies whether the director knows his directions, purely in regard to the film on the screen. He'd say, "This son of a bitch, doesn't even know how to shoot it." By seeing dailies, he knew whether a film would work or not. Jack Warner was a gambler. And if you were able to sell him some idea, most of the time he'd go with you. In the olden days, if you could more or less convince him that something would make a great picture or tell it dramatically to him, he was enough of a gambler to know to do it. "That I gamble on!" he'd say.

GEOFFREY SHURLOCK: They were all gamblers, but Harry Cohn is the favorite studio head to pick on. He *was* coarse. But it was an act in his case, because I got to know Harry rather well. And he put on that act because he wanted to scare you or impress you or terrify you.

Cohn had a trick of terrifying you when you came in by jumping on you as soon as you got in there with a script you wanted to discuss with him. And he jumped on you to ask you a quite irrelevant question in a very belligerent tone of voice. That got you off base. I'll give you an example. I went in there once with some script, and right away, he jumped on me for no reason at all. He said, "I want to ask you something. How come you haven't got a Jew on that staff of yours?" Right away, I figured, he's got me, but I thought very fast. And I said, "That's right, Mr. Cohn, I haven't got a Jew. And you asked me why?" He says, "Yes, I asked you why." I say, "I'll tell you why. Mr. Cohn, no Jew in his right mind would work for the salaries you pay us over there!" Well, Cohn threw back in his chair and started to laugh. And he said, "That is the best answer I've had this week." From then on we had an increasingly friendly basis.

FRANK CAPRA: This is what Harry Cohn gave you. . . . To deal with him, you had to have a lot of brass and a lot of chutzpah. Harry was one of those very crude guys that only believed in you if you believed in yourself to the point where you could tell him to go to hell. Otherwise you couldn't get through the door. If you had your hat on, ready to walk out . . . if you were not servile to him . . . if you didn't let him bully you . . . you were the kind of person he wanted. He trusted people who could stand up to him. Then he would sleep better at night, knowing you were spending his money. He ran his studio on the very crude idea that a creative person without mettle, without guts and a complete belief in himself, was not a good man. He would constantly challenge you by saying you stunk, your work stunk, and, well, if you agreed with him, out you went, but if you didn't agree with him, you stayed. That's what Harry Cohn gave you. I never lost a battle with him. I never let Mr. Cohn argue with me, even when he was completely right! Because he'd lose confidence in you. This is an extreme example of the ingenuity you have to use in the making of films. There are not many Mr. Cohns in the business, but when you find one, you have to be ready for him. And by his crude methods, by the crude perimeter of his guts, he raised that rinky-dink joint he had down on Poverty Row into a major studio. Think about that.

RANALD MACDOUGALL: Harry Cohn was a pirate. You can't call what he did chicanery. Chicanery is when somebody sneaks up on you and takes a wallet out of your pocket, but Harry Cohn was a *pirate*! There was no other word for him, and he could be depended upon to act like a pirate under any circumstances, and there is nothing deceptive about that.

FLOYD CROSBY: Nothing escaped Harry Cohn. The guy who was my gaffer on *High Noon* was working as an electrician at Columbia. He'd just started. He'd only been there a short time. They needed a black car to use in a sequence and he happened to have what they wanted, so they said they'd rent it from him. They said, "How much do you want for the rental?" He said, "Twenty dollars." So the production man okayed it. Pretty soon the car owner got a call to go up to Harry Cohn's office. He went up there, and Harry Cohn said, "You know you're a young man just starting in this business, you got a big future in this business, we feel you're going to do well here. . . . Can we have the car for ten dollars?"

JOHN BRAHM: I had one of the oddest relationships with Harry Cohn. He loved me. Oddly enough, he was utterly charming to me personally. I did very well with him, but he'd do nasty things, stupid things. For instance: Christmas at Harry Cohn's office was really an experience. Everything was taken out of the office. The carpet was laid over with linen so it wouldn't get dirty, so were the chairs, and cardboard was put on the piano. It was as un-Christmasy a spirit as possible. There was a policeman at the entrance, and so on.

So I come in, go up to him and say, "Merry Christmas, Harry." And he shakes my hand and says, "Two and a half days behind!" That's the kind of guy he was. And that was the guy who loved me! But he couldn't help that, he had to say it. While the other guy, Sam Briskin, who was usually up there with him, was a bastard, a real son-of-a-bitch bastard. Cohn wasn't that—Cohn was a *charming* bastard, let's put it that way. But Sam Briskin was a horrible guy, a bastard of a guy.

VINCENT SHERMAN: Cohn usually had an executive producer working with him. At one time, Sidney Buchman was his executive producer. At others, he had Sylvan Simon, Virginia Van Upp, or Sam Briskin. He liked to have somebody helping out . . . so sometimes he had a second in command. Jack Warner always had that system. Studios like Fox were more places run by hands-on heads like Zanuck, but Cohn sometimes would have an executive producer.

FRANK CAPRA: Sam Briskin was primarily a businessman, and he looked at things as a businessman would look at them. He was just the opposite of Harry Cohn. Harry was a hunch player. He'd play a hundred-to-one long shot if he got the hunch. Sam Briskin would never play. He'd bet on favorites only and bet them to show. So you had this kind of combination there—one who took care of the money and did very well at it, and the top guy, who was a nut, who got strange ideas and followed them up. He was a gambling fool. There would be no Columbia without Cohn.

FRED ZINNEMANN: In the old days, the studio heads were people who delivered enormous practical experiences from their lives as showmen. If you'd like an example: Harry Cohn, who was, some people say, a very crude individual and very rough, et cetera, but who had an enormous instinct for the audience. He bought the book *From Here to Eternity* at a time when everybody thought he was crazy. This was still toward the end of the McCarthy era. And the idea of doing a film which was critical of the army, at that time, seemed more than courageous, it seemed preposterous. People called it Harry Cohn's Folly. He said, "We are going to open in August in the Capitol Theatre in New York on Broadway." Now, this was in 1953, and there was no such thing as air-conditioning. And New York in August was a red-hot box, and nobody in their right mind would have opened a picture that month. In August. And then he said, "There's to be no publicity, no advertising, except one full-page ad in the *Times*, which I will sign as president of Columbia, recommending everybody see the film." And people really thought he was out of his mind. Well, to make a long story short, I was out here when the picture opened. And at about eight o'clock in the evening, a call came from New York, which was from Marlene Dietrich, whom I didn't know, but she called and said, "You might like to know that people are standing in line all around the block, in spite of all the heat and everything else," and I said, "How is that possible? There's been no publicity." And she said, "They smell it." Harry *knew*.

FRANK CAPRA: He knew that he didn't know anything about photography or directing. He said, "I know things by the seat of my pants. If my ass squirms, the picture stinks. If it doesn't, it's great." Which produced that wonderful crack from Herman Mankiewicz: "Harry, what makes you think the whole world is wired to your ass?" But that's the way it was with self-confidence, personal confidence. It will get you a long way in a field as fragile and intangible as show business.

DENNIS HOPPER: Harry Cohn was very famous for psychologically dealing with everybody, so he had a long, narrow room for his office, you know, where you had to walk forever, and at the end of it was a big desk where he'd be sitting. And behind him were rows of Academy Awards, sparkling like rainbows. I'd never even been in a movie studio before when I first went there. And I'd never seen an Academy Award, much less fifty or a hundred of them. How many I don't know, but you get what I mean. So Cohn was sitting at the end of this room at this desk with a man by the name of Abe Schneider, who was second in charge there at that time. Later, his son, Bert, gave me the money to make *Easy Rider*, but that was fifteen years later. So anyway, I came up to the man. And Harry Cohn said, "You are the most natural actor since Montgomery Clift. I've never seen anybody as natural as you." Blah blah blah blah. On and on and on and on. Praising and praising and praising. I was sweating. I was so nervous, you know, and I was shaking all over. I was looking up at a crack in the ceiling, and he said, "What have you been doing recently?" And I said, "Well, recently, Mr. Cohn," very proudly, I said, "I've been playing Shakespeare." And he goes, "Oh, God, no! Oh no, oh no, not Shakespeare, anything but . . . oh, no." And I stopped sweating and I looked at him, and I said, "Go fuck yourself." Well. At that moment, at the age of eighteen, I'd just finished my career immediately in a few words, and I hadn't even started yet. So I was banned from the studio, my agent was banned from the studio. . . .

KING VIDOR: Samuel Goldwyn was one of the big studio men. He really aimed high, but he was inarticulate. He couldn't tell you what he had in mind. Sometimes to prove a point, you had to go ahead and shoot it the way you wanted it and show it to him on the screen before you could convince him.

HENRY HATHAWAY: Samuel Goldwyn, who began as a glove salesman and was really sort of an uncouth fellow, a rough businessman, had the idea in his earliest days in the business that the important thing was the *story*. He started a program called "the play's the thing" and he hired what they called "famous authors" and brought them into his studio. That's where they started to make films like *Madame X* and *Noblesse Oblige* in the silent era. And he never lost that belief in the story as *the* thing.

JOHN CROMWELL: Sam, pretty much throughout his life, had a reputation for having a difficult time getting along with directors. I didn't think much about it, as I had been an admirer of Sam's since I had come into pictures. I thought that he was one of the three best producers in Hollywood. He had very good taste. He never spared any expense to get things the way that he thought they should be. Fundamentally, he was a very endearing man in spite of his habit of exasperating people. No man in this country in this century has had more stories told about him and the things that he would do with the King's English. People don't repeat such things to anyone who has not captured their affection.

DONALD OGDEN STEWART: I was in Sam's office, and he was firing an actor. He was letting the actor have the words . . . I mean, "You son of a bitch, you goddamned . . . get the hell out of this office! I never want to see you again." As the poor guy walked over to the door, Sam added, ". . . unless I need you."

RICHARD SCHICKEL: Goldwyn was the famous "include me out" guy.

MERVYN LEROY: He told me he could sum up a film in two words: "Terrible!"

BRONISLAU KAPER: Sam Goldwyn would say, "I do not always win, but I never lose."

EDWARD DMYTRYK: Sam Goldwyn once said, "Nobody walks out of a picture in the first fifteen minutes." Well, I do, but he said nobody does. What he meant by that was that you can't take more than fifteen minutes to establish your mood, your characters, and do something to grab your audience and keep them in the seats.

LEWIS MILESTONE: Men like Samuel Goldwyn—and Warner and Cohn and Zanuck and Mayer and all those guys—they would sit and control the money, and so if you wanted to work, even if you were a successful director, writer, or whatever, you had to play the game. Take Goldwyn for an example. He happens to be a very vain man, and he's convinced that he is the one making the pictures. I've worked with him, so I know. As a matter of fact, there's a great anecdote involving Goldwyn and William Wyler. Goldwyn ran a picture he produced and Wyler directed, and they had lengthy arguments about it after. Goldwyn claimed that the point doesn't get over. He doesn't know what the movie is trying to say. And Willy said, "It's as clear as the nose on your face." So Goldwyn's son, Sammy, was just a young boy then and in the projection room. So Sam says to Willy, "Why don't we ask him what the point is. Will you abide by the decision?" Willy says yes and asks Sammy if he understood. Sammy said, "Of course," and offered up a perfect explanation. Willy said to Sam, "Well, you see?" And Sam said, "What the hell are we doing now . . . making pictures for kids?"

RANALD MACDOUGALL: When I first came out here, I was personally interviewed by David O. Selznick. And the interview had an aura about it. You know, my idea of Hollywood was fellows with puttees, slapping them occasionally with whips and carrying on like that, and I was a little astonished every time I found out some of those things were true. Zanuck used a polo stick and banged on the desk occasionally when you had an interview with him. Michael Curtiz wore puttees. All of the things that confirmed all of the clichés. And I knew Selznick's reputation, I admired his work and his pictures. But I was not prepared for the aura that surrounded this: a personal meeting with David O. Selznick.

When I got to his office with my agent, we happened to be there at the changing of the guard. All of the secretaries—there were about eight or nine of them—it was about four o'clock in the afternoon, and they all finished their work and went out, and a whole new set came in. Selznick, as I afterwards learned, worked at night. He started at about five o'clock every afternoon, and he worked at night. Which was okay with me, because I have always done most of my work at night. When I finally got in to see Selznick, he said, "We've heard of you, we know how good you are," and he said, "I have a special project that I want you to work on and it's very secret and I can't tell you too much about it, but it's sort of a combination of the best aspects of radio and motion pictures." And I said, "Well, you must mean television." At which point Selznick turned to ice and terminated the conversation, which was rather astonishing. I had already worked in television. I'd been working in television off and on for two or three years by then, at both NBC and CBS. But to him, it was *his* secret.

MERIAN C. COOPER: David has to interfere with every goddamn detail for a picture, and he has to think he owns it all. I'm a pretty good interferer myself, but not that much. I can tell you this. I worked with Selznick at RKO, and David Selznick wanted credit for things. I invited David to the preview of *King Kong*, the first preview at San Bernardino. He telephoned me at least two or three weeks afterwards and said, "Don't you think it would be fair if you put me on as executive producer?" And I said, "David, you sure as hell backed me on this picture, but you didn't have anything to do with producing it." He said, "Well, I had just as much to do with producing it. I backed you, and I think I'm entitled to credit," and I said, "Okay, I'll put your name on."

GEORGE CUKOR: I had worked with David Selznick before he became the head of RKO, and I think that was a very happy collaboration with David, who had what all great showmen had: he had an enthusiasm for people. He encouraged people, he wanted the best out of you. He happened to be a great friend of mine. A lot of these gentlemen were tough tycoons, but if you had anything to give, they encouraged it and they *wanted* it. They weren't awfully busy making geniuses of themselves. They made a lot of money, but they were *showmen*. With David it was a very happy collaboration, because he was full of beans, and twenty times a day he'd say, "What about this . . . let's do this, and let's do that." And it was very exciting and very pleasant.

PANDRO BERMAN: Selznick and I were friendly. He was good to me and gave me an opportunity to produce, and at the same time I was working as his assistant. He didn't stay at RKO too long. He left to go to Metro within a couple of years. But during the period that he was there I enjoyed working with him very much, and I had a lot of respect for him. But he was a strange fellow in some ways. For instance, in his communications with people, I've never known anybody to write so much. Telegrams, letters, reams of stuff. In fact, he used to come in the morning sometimes with a roll of toilet paper that he had written on. During the night he would awaken and think of things he wanted to say to people and had no other paper to write it on.

JOHN CROMWELL: David Selznick was a shrewd judge of material, and he was a perfectionist of the first order. Nothing was too small to receive his searching consideration. He was one of the few producers to understand the value of such care. I directed his production of a remake of *Little Lord Fauntleroy* in 1936, and I would have thought that material was too far back in people's memory to be of any great value. Also, the young were a growing picture audience, and to them it could only be hopelessly old-fashioned. But David's cleverness was to take advantage of material that offered the maximum opportunity for exploitation. He subjected the reputation of the story to a vigorous publicity campaign. His plan? Inject the excitement of a search nationally for a boy to play the leading part and fill out the cast around him with players of high reputation. Select a script by a new and fresh storyteller, and top it off with an impeccable production. Go as far as it is possible toward success in the preshooting process. The writer he chose was Hugh Walpole, a famous English novelist, and it was a privilege to work with him. And his cast members, surrounding the talented Freddie Bartholomew, were such stalwarts as C. Aubrey Smith, Henry Stephenson, and Constance Collier. These were very well known names wherever English was spoken. He aligned them with pure Hollywood in the presence of Dolores Costello, Mickey Rooney, and Guy Kibbee, and you have a cast that stands out for its brilliance . . . and draws customers into theaters. Selznick was deeply involved in every aspect of producing his films.

GEORGE SEATON: When I was an innocent beginning screenwriter, I was working with a bunch of writers, sitting around in a motel, although they didn't call them motels in those days. It was a little bungalow court. My room cost $5 a week. But a big screenwriting problem came up, and in my innocence I said it wasn't that big a problem and I'd think about it. So I did and came up with two solutions and brought them to the team. When I told the first one, Herman Mankiewicz, God bless him, said, "That's it!"

Everybody agreed, so they took it to Selznick. (By the way, it was a forgotten film called *Meet the Baron*. The picture was miserable.) Selznick called me in to talk to me, and he said, "Young man, do you know the reason you got the solution?" I said, "No, sir." He said, "Because you didn't know how difficult it was." I thought that was a pretty silly statement at the time, but over the years I've learned he was absolutely right. You can get yourself so involved with the don'ts of writing a screenplay . . . until somebody comes along with a very simple solution. Of course, the picture was horrible, but Mr. Selznick was right.

PANDRO BERMAN: There's no question about the fact that he was a very strong collaborator in the construction of screenplays. Whether he did a great deal of dialogue writing, I don't know. Maybe he did later in life, as he went on making independent films. But when I worked with him at RKO in the 1930s, he didn't do much actual writing of words. He did an awful lot of collaboration of editing, of revising of story and script, in terms of scenes and construction, working with writers. But he hired the best writers. He always knew enough to go and get somebody who could write. Whereas I think the man who really wants to write himself won't do that. He'll either write it or he'll hire some writer he'll bend to his will. David always hired the best.

RIDGEWAY CALLOW: Selznick made a lot of people mad. He took care of himself first. We had to work late with him always, and one night, his butler brought in his dinner at nine or nine fifteen. None of us had eaten, and he ate in front of us. So the next night, [production designer] William Cameron Menzies said, "I'm going across to the Coral Isle," which is a Chinese restaurant opposite the studio, and we all went over there. At eight thirty the phone rang and a secretary said that Mr. Selznick was waiting for us, so we made him wait another half hour while we finished our dinner, and then we went over. He got the message.

Selznick went by trial and error or process of elimination. That was his method of working. I remember on *Rebecca*, we shot an insert of a letter nineteen times. He didn't like the paper, he didn't like the handwriting, he wanted a different type of handwriting, he got another type of handwriting, he didn't like that, he didn't like this. His percentage of retakes was probably more than any other independent producer. I think any director will tell you that if he reshot a scene he could make it better the second time. Selznick had a terrific record with retakes. His forte was editing. He was a damn good film editor—excellent.

PANDRO BERMAN: Selznick was the greatest stickler for secrecy and for detail of any man I've ever met in my life in any business. To him detail was vitally important. He was one of the producers, of which there were some number at that time, who really made films that represented *their* point of view no matter who directed, no matter who wrote. The picture was David Selznick's point of view always.

I don't think David ever really wanted to direct a film himself. I don't think he was ever inclined to sit on a set and direct actors, but he was so enormously impressed with the necessity for detail to be perfect that he would do the same thing to a director that he would do to anybody else in writing, in sets, in costumes, in decorations or settings. He would look for a certain perfection. So naturally, he would always be able to say to the director, "I wish you had done it *this* way, or a little more *that* way." But I don't think David himself ever wanted to direct films. It's just that he influenced the director more than producers usually would. And I think, in that regard, he was like Thalberg, Zanuck, and others who were actually making pictures their way.

JOHN CROMWELL: The first thing that ever impressed me about David was his excellent story mind. He understood the elements of dramatic fiction, a somewhat rare quality among studio producers. The great majority of them were manipulators, including him. He could be a very persuasive arguer, and his persistence could drive you to destruction. I could only conclude that he was conscious of every detail and how he wanted it to be. He lacked only two things to have become a fine director himself: experience and self-discipline. And perhaps organization.

KING VIDOR: When we started out making his production of *Duel in the Sun*, the first time I talked to him, he said, "This is going to be a nice little picture. You'll be completely in charge. No interference from me. I'm going to be doing something else. No interference from me." And the first thing he did when I started was he had me looking at *Gone with the Wind*, so I could make him another *Gone with the Wind*. He'd keep expanding, expanding the story, and he had no idea about cost or money, and he'd just keep making it bigger and bigger. He took over the script himself. He would arrive at 3:00 p.m. with a rewrite of his own, and I'd say, "We started shooting this material at nine and we're almost through." He wanted it done over, but I told him he should get new material to us in the morning. What he did was, he'd walk up and down all night and dictate, and when he finished, the secretary would need a few hours' sleep, and then she'd go in and start typing. He would sleep all morning, and then he'd arrive with the script and try to get me to do it. And he was the producer, so I won about once and he won about three or four of these battles. His idea was to make a western *Gone with the Wind*. Walter Huston worked only about three days, and they asked for $40,000 for that . . . $4,000 per week for ten weeks minimum . . . but it was only about three days' work. In the end, with all the rewrites and changes, we needed him more than ten weeks, and so they had to pay him more than the original $40,000. So that's the way Selznick worked.

MERIAN C. COOPER: Selznick was a very brilliant man, very brilliant, a great producer. Jack Ford never thought so. He thought he was a very bad producer. He thought Selznick overrefined his stuff, and so did I, for that matter. He killed *Duel in the Sun* by overrefining it, you know. Selznick wasn't a chance taker like I was. He would get the best directors, the best cast, the best cameraman, the best everything. *Gone with the Wind* was a hit because he got the best of everything. He couldn't get any better than he got. He got the best that money could buy.

KING VIDOR: In the end, on *Duel in the Sun*, I disagreed with Selznick on something and we had a kind of a big disagreement right on the set, and he started blowing off, losing his temper, and I warned him. I had already told him three times that I'd quit. It was about two days from the finish of the picture. And I quit. We had a lot of people out there, a lot of cows, a lot of cavalry, and a lot of everything, and I just gave him the megaphone and left. I said I'd had it. He started yelling and screaming and blaming me, and I quit. After I left, he called me up and tried to get me to go back, and I didn't.

RAY RENNAHAN: You know, David was notorious for sending down his yellow sheets. They were memos. After he'd run the dailies, he'd send out a bunch of these yellow sheets to the director, the cameramen, the stars, or anyone that he disliked something about here or there. The only reason he ever put memorandas down was to criticize. He'd sit in his office and he'd have his secretary type them out, and down they'd come. Oh, boy. I've worked with him a lot, but I've never known him to send down a yellow sheet of thanks to anybody on anything. But still, I rate David Selznick as one of the best producers we've ever had in the business. He very often would come down on the set and talk with the director about something or other. And he'd retake the whole thing. He did that on *Gone with the Wind*. We had a scene in the blacksmith's shop inside a barn, and the barn was a little bit small, and the whole cast was in it. It was a big scene, a beautiful scene, but he sent word, "Build that set bigger! Retake the whole thing and make it bigger!" We did. We rebuilt the whole set. Made it a real big set, and then we shot it the same way we did the other one, and the action and everything was about the same except that we had a big barn instead of a small barn. When he made up his mind, nothing would change him, and he wasn't afraid to spend money. But he knew what he wanted. He was a marvelous, marvelous producer.

ADELA ROGERS ST. JOHNS: David Selznick was very independent. He moved from place to place and then became an independent producer. He was at MGM for a while, of course, but he and Mayer never saw eye to eye. They had this awful feud because of Irene [Irene Mayer Selznick, Louis B.'s daughter]. For a while, David replaced Thalberg as head of production at Metro when Irving removed himself to go to Europe to take a long rest for his health. Selznick and Mayer didn't speak during most of that time. After Irene married Selznick and Mr. Mayer had done everything in God's green Earth to prevent it, he wouldn't allow David in the house. Told Irene that if she married him, he'd never speak to her again. Mr. Mayer told me all about it. He said, "I told her, don't you marry that man, he's a Selznick, they're no good. No Selznick was ever any good." And he said she went right ahead and married him.

RICHARD SCHICKEL: People usually don't discuss Walt Disney alongside the famous studio heads like Mayer, Zanuck, Selznick, et cetera. But he *was* a studio head, and in fact, Disney was a studio, too, but it doesn't get mentioned because it was making animated films for the long period until it went into feature films, live-action stuff, and television. But Walt Disney is a classic example of the man who came to Hollywood and built his world and made a fortune from it.

MERVYN LEROY: I first met Walt Disney at a party. He was a simple man. He was an absolute perfectionist and a genius, because he created all those things. Not that his men didn't have a hand in what he created with them, but Disney was Disney. When I first met him, he was making shorts. You know, he was a cartoonist. And we got to be very good friends. He used to invite me out to his studio very often, and he'd run his rushes for anybody. There were no secrets with Walt Disney . . . but he was a creator. He had a bed in back of his office, and he slept there many nights just drawing and working.

RAY RENNAHAN: Disney was on the set most of the time anything was going on, but of course he did leave things pretty much up to his technicians, too. His personal control was into everything, but not objection minded. He was a perfectionist, and everything had to be just the way he wanted it, but he had such marvelous technicians there and they knew him so well that he didn't have to do much actually physically on the set or anywhere. But he was creatively responsible and knew just what he wanted and always got it. He was a genius. And that marvelous bunch of technicians . . . they could build anything . . . they could *do* anything . . . and those musicians he had! The music was out of this world. But Walt Disney was the master. There was no doubt about it.

FRIZ FRELENG: I lucked out because I went into the animation field when it was a new field. If it had been some time later, I might never have made the grade. I went to the theater and saw one of the cartoons that Walt did out on the coast, and I got quite a thrill out of it, and naturally I wanted to be a part of it. I met Hugh Harman, and I started corresponding with him. He was with Walt Disney. Hugh wrote that Walt was interested in me and wanted to know if I'd be interested in coming out to the coast, so I wrote to Walt and told him that I was very interested in becoming an animator but I had very little experience and that I'd have to go through some kind of training experience and he'd need to be patient with me. Walt was just finishing *Alice* [*in Wonderland*] and was starting *Oswald the Rabbit*. He had a little studio on Hyperion, just a little spot. He told me to come ahead, and I sat right next to him. I animated scenes and turned them over to him, and he timed them and made small changes. Ub Iwerks, Hugh Harman, myself, and Walt Disney sat in one room and worked on those pictures.

LEWIS MILESTONE: No producer could be more hands on than Walt Disney. He used the storyboard from the year one because he had to do with animated cartoons. He would do them on thin paper, and I understand that if he didn't like it, he would just tear it off and redraw it. Then when he was satisfied with it, it would get sent to the animators, and then the number one artist would draw the first picture, and then it became like a production belt. The most important drawing was the first, and after that they were all copies made by the rest of the girls.

FRIZ FRELENG: I started putting personality into the little characters, and Walt recognized that right away, and he used to compliment me on it. Ub Iwerks was more advanced in the technique of animation than anybody else, more than Walt or myself or Harman and [animator Rudolf] Ising, but he was limited because he approached it mechanically. He learned to make a walk or a run, but he never thought about personality in the characters, and that's what makes the difference. After the mechanics of motion became easy and simple to us, that's when personality started creeping in. Sound is what helped us. It helped things become more human and realistic, and when that happened, the funnier it became. The big change was when Walt did *Snow White and the Seven Dwarfs*. There was a distinctive personality for each dwarf, and you recognized one from the other. Disney was a genius. Nobody had ever really done anything like that before in animation. But he wanted things done his way. Most of those people that worked for Walt Disney always worked a little reluctantly, a little worried about what they were doing, what Walt wanted. I think that stopped progress in the Disney short subjects. When Walt got going in features, he just couldn't be on every detail all the time. The artists who were working on the shorts were afraid to put down what *they* liked because Walt might not like it. They weren't going to take any chances. They just didn't go beyond what Walt might like. The Disney people looked with envy at Warners, because they did some wild things. Walt would say, "That's all right for Warners, but don't give me a Warner gag here. We don't go for all that Warner stuff." He used to tell them that Mickey wouldn't do this or Donald wouldn't do that. He set rules and regulations for all his characters. So his animators could only do what they had done in the past. This restricted them immensely. Disney stayed with the same old characters year after year. After I went over to Warners, I had no rules or restriction. All we had to do was stay within the bounds of good taste. If we had a bright idea and it was a wild one, we tried it out. If it failed, we just didn't do it again.

But Disney was a genius. You never could look down on Walt, really, because he was always one big, long step ahead of you. I left Disney because Walt and I never got along too well. We just rubbed each other the wrong way, apparently, or he rubbed me the wrong way. I guess I rubbed *him* the wrong way. We just didn't get along, and finally I told him I was leaving. I left Walt regretfully, though, because he taught me, and, really, Walt Disney was a genius.

CHAPTER 7

STUDIO STYLE

RICHARD SCHICKEL: Each of the old studios more or less had its own style . . . and really, each had its own personality, its own atmosphere.

JOHN CROMWELL: I had gone back to New York for a while after sound came in, so when I came back, I looked over all the studios to sort of see what each one was like and where I might want to work. Paramount had impressed me always as having a staid, conservative atmosphere. RKO, which had been a financial football for its promoters, had an air of reckless excitement. Everyone who worked there had the feeling that it might close down right after the picture was finished. MGM posed as the aristocrat of the industry, undoubtedly stemming from its reputation for extravagance. . . . Warner Bros. was a rough-and-ready place, willing to try any idea for a picture as long as Warner felt that it would make money. They paid no more than they had to. 20th Century–Fox was a big, sprawling lot on Pico Boulevard, and it suggested the opportunistic. Headed by Darryl F. Zanuck, a disappointed screenwriter—he never outlived it—it emphasized the obvious. While shunning sensitive material, the studio kept one standard of taste and discrimination to which they might point with pride when challenged. Otherwise it was very much the factory. Universal was a happy-go-lucky place, seldom getting top-budget pictures. But they were pretty unconcerned about it. Everyone was completely relaxed and enjoying themselves. At United Artists, not a studio in the same way, one felt relaxed and free. Most of the productions were independent, which usually removed distribution pressures. The schedules were apt to be more generous. Every department was smaller and seemed to be more efficient. I always regretted that I made only one picture there.

JOHN BRAHM: You'd find different atmospheres at each studio. They each had a certain forte for certain kinds of pictures, and that meant they hired specific types of people who could give them that style, that genre, that look that they wanted. Where they were alike was in business efficiency, bottom-line toughness, and a dedication to getting a quality job done efficiently.

BILLY WILDER: You belonged to the studio that put you under contract. Every studio had its own handwriting, its own stable of big stars and supporting actors. You walked into a movie house, and you knew "This is an RKO picture." Because they had a style, you know. Studio style.

VINCENT SHERMAN: There is no question that the different studios had different styles and the content they made was different. There were things that Warner would do that L. B. Mayer wouldn't do and vice versa. But all the studios were aware of what the others were doing, and if something became a hit, it would get copied by everyone.

RAY RENNAHAN: At Paramount, they didn't bother you at all. When Buddy DeSylva was in charge, he actually never—well, very seldom—actually came on the set. He'd see the dailies and see the cutting, but I think in those days Paramount was the most homey and pleasant place to work of all of them. MGM was a little too commercial, and Fox was too clannish, and Warner Bros. was . . . Warner Bros. And, of course, only a certain group would like to work at Columbia. It was very difficult at that time to work for. But Paramount was amiable. They had a marvelous group of executives and production managers. It was very friendly.

GEORGE SEATON: Ah, Paramount. Frank Freeman was head of Paramount when I worked there. What a gentleman he was! He quite honestly confessed that he knew nothing about films, so he just let the filmmakers make the films. His talent was the business end of it and keeping everybody in the studio content, which was quite an accomplishment. Paramount was the pleasantest studio to work for in those days, a big family, no doubt about it. He was a gentleman, courteous, appreciative. Never passed the buck. Like Harry Truman, he said, "The buck stops here." He took the blame for anything he should have taken the blame for. Paramount was a different sort of thing from working at Fox. Mr. Zanuck, in my opinion, was probably one of the best heads of the studio that one could possibly imagine. You could get an answer from him, yes or no, very quickly, but he was the boss, no doubt about it. Sometimes, in my opinion, he made mistakes, but he didn't make too many. But Fox was a bigger place, and people didn't know each other quite as well. People came and went. Paramount was a small lot, so everybody saw each other. The Commissary was a sort of club. C. B. DeMille had the head table there. Everybody knew everybody else, and it was very *gemütlich*.

WALTER REISCH: I loved MGM, and I adored every day I spent there, but I changed completely when I moved studios. I changed to suit the climate of Fox. That is my only talent, that I can adjust myself at will. Fox was totally different from MGM. At Fox it was like being in a big newspaper office. Everything was according to Zanuck's taste, to Zanuck's speed, to Zanuck's way of making pictures. And that was like a newspaper: fast, topical, very little conversation, very few arguments, and I personally just loved it.

HENRY HATHAWAY: It was a factory then. I worked for Fox for twenty years, and in that time I never turned down one script they gave me. I'd figure out some way to make it, and I was never restricted from changing it. It was an open world.

WALTER REISCH: It was not just one picture that was important to 20th Century–Fox. It was the annual product. When they came out with their financial statements at the end of the year, no one said, "This picture brought in $200,000 more or half a million more than that other one." No one said, "This picture lost money" . . . which, actually, I think no picture did at all. I don't believe any Fox picture lost money. They had their own motion picture theaters to release them in for as long as they wanted. 20th Century–Fox put all its money into a production program, and then a statement would come out at the year's end disclosing how much profit they made on all that. They didn't single out pictures. That made for a happy situation. It made people feel part of the whole. I mean, have you heard of Random House concentrating on only one book or Ford differentiating between cars? They say it's Ford Motors that grosses so much in a given year. But Fox was the studio that had that idea . . . it was a team, all working for the bottom year-end profit.

BARRÉ LYNDON: I always thought Fox was the busiest and best studio. Their craftsmanship in those years was fantastic. I worked at Universal, too. You find a different atmosphere at each one of these studios. Universal was tremendous. Everybody was busy. Nobody was playing shove ha'penny or cards. Everybody worked on the Universal lot. You could feel it in the atmosphere when you went in to do a job. Paramount was more relaxed, and in a way so was Fox. I've only worked a couple of times at MGM and didn't care much for that.

KARL STRUSS: When I was under contract at Paramount . . . they kept you working steadily, no downtime at Paramount. At Paramount, it was more a director's studio. MGM was a producer's studio. What they would normally do at Paramount, where I was for sixteen years, was have a big conference *before* they'd start to shoot, which is the right way to go. I mean, everybody, all the departments, would be in there. Course, sometimes on the smaller pictures with lower budgets and all, they wouldn't have the time for that. You'd just get the day's work from the director when he came on the set. We'd always say, "Well, we're flexible." That's the word. We're *flexible*. We'll do anything you want.

RIDGEWAY CALLOW: I worked at Selznick's and then RKO, and then I landed at "Poverty Row," Columbia. The main difference when you go from what you might call quality pictures to "quickie" is in speed and economy. In other words, if an actor mumbled his lines correctly, they'd say

"Okay" and go on to the next take. They'd never strive for quality because they didn't have the time to do it. At Columbia it was economy, economy, economy, because Harry Cohn was there at the time.

Cohn ruled absolutely.... It was the difference between night and day when you compare Columbia with MGM in those days. They used to call MGM the Tiffany of the picture business, and MGM believed they were the Tiffany and acted that way.

None of the directors I worked with paid any attention to a schedule at MGM, but they had a very peculiar system at Columbia when I was there: you had to phone in the time of your first shot in the morning. So most directors would start off with an insert which they could knock off by 9:05 on a 9:00 shooting call. And then the front office would say, "Well, that company is in good shape," and they'd leave you alone. Then after you finished an insert at 9:05, you'd set up for an hour on a big boom shot. You should have started with the boom shot, but you wouldn't do it, you'd start out with some simple shot to get them off your back for the rest of the day.

At Columbia, if the director went beyond four takes on any given shot for any reason whatsoever, the assistant director was supposed to call the production office. The production manager would come running down to find out the reason. And actually the reason was quite simple: on the first take, for instance, the camera operator might miss the shot. On the second, an actor might forget his lines. You know, there's a million reasons why you could go beyond four takes. But at Columbia, you only printed one take.

IRVING RAPPER: At Columbia, everybody had to do his duty, no matter what. I couldn't speak to the writer too much. I couldn't even speak to my supervisor too much. Everything was on schedule. And it was kind of cruel and the most wicked kind of discipline I ever knew in my life. Efficiency was being carried too far. It was being carried to a point where it hurt.

RIDGEWAY CALLOW: Warners was a cross between Columbia and Metro. It wasn't quite as deluxe as MGM, but it wasn't as cheap as Columbia, although Warners was a cost-conscious studio. It wasn't as bad as Columbia, but yet it wasn't in the class of MGM.

RANALD MACDOUGALL: It was different at Warner Bros. from working at either Columbia or 20th Century–Fox. It was true that each studio had their own methodology, their own way of approaching the same thing. Columbia was no exception to that. Columbia was, to me, like Warner Bros. What was wanted, was wanted as quickly as possible. There was little or no standing around waiting for decisions. The definitive "maybe" was not in their way of doing things, and it, I must say, suited my working temperament much better than had been the case at either Paramount or 20th or ultimately at Metro. The two lots that I have worked on over a period of years that I felt were closest to my tempo and mood were Columbia and Warner Bros. That may possibly be because of certain business resemblances between Harry Cohn and Jack Warner. Both of them thought, "Art if possible, but business first." That suited me. I tend to be rather practical, down to earth, pragmatic. I accept the limitations of the medium and the budgets and the tempo.

HARRY WARREN: Everybody talks about the cheap studios, the "Poverty Row" Columbia or the B studios, Republic or someplace like that. We used to call it "the hinterlands." You had to get a passport at Coldwater Canyon to get to one of *those* studios, but let's not forget that on the Warner lot, a fellow was fired because he was using the studio vacuum cleaner to vacuum off his clothes. He'd gotten dusty. Another fellow was fired because he left a light burning. And then, another time, there was a property man on the Warner lot who was waiting for a cue to ring a phone bell. And he was caught reading the newspaper. And *he* was fired. Warners paid its stars less, too. They watched the pennies.

HENRY BLANKE: And at Warners, nobody ever got credit. Warner wouldn't give credit. That was true for Jack, and the same policy held under Wallis when he came in. And then finally, those of us producing did get Associate Producer credit. Warners watched the credits . . . and the pennies.

HARRY WARREN: Going out to Warners in those days, when you went over Cahuenga Pass, it was a narrow road. And on rainy days you had to be very careful, because rocks used to fall on the road. And you could get hurt. I remember a terrible rainstorm where the bridge was washed out before they got to Warner Bros. They issued blankets to us. We were going to stay all night. It was like a war experience.

BRONISLAU KAPER: Being at Warner Bros. is like being at Warner Bros., not in the United States. That's like extraterritorial. It's a different country.

RANALD MACDOUGALL: I thought the whole Warner Bros. outfit were absolutely insane, the lot of them.

PANDRO BERMAN: Warners had its own ranch . . . and at RKO we had a ranch, too. RKO's was located in quite close juxtaposition to Hollywood, as compared to some of the far-off ranches. There was no back lot big enough at RKO to do anything, so the filming always needed to be at the ranch when we had exteriors to do. It needed to be close. I remember we did *The Hunchback of Notre Dame* [1939 version] out there at the ranch. And whenever we had outside stuff that required set building, we usually went there. On occasion we'd go to a natural location and build sets, like we did for *Gunga Din* up at Lone Pine in the mountains, but mostly we used the ranch. Some richer studios went to farther places, even England, to make movies, but those were richer studios! MGM or Warners. People who had money in those days. But RKO was pretty hard pressed for money always. But we had the ranch.

JOHN BRAHM: We built all kinds of things at Fox. In *The Lodger* we built London streets especially for the production. You see, in those days they built things without worrying so much about money because the sets could stand for years out on the lot, if you had a lot. They would be useful for years. Those were the good days when such things could be done. I remember, for instance, that for *Singapore*, which I did at Universal, they built a lake for the evacuation of Singapore that's still standing there today. They call it Singapore Lake, and it's been there thirty years. The things were so well built and so useful. I don't know how many subsequent pictures needing water . . . maybe hundreds . . . were shot on that lake.

RIDGEWAY CALLOW: And sometimes studios would borrow from each other or use each other's property. There was Eagle-Lion, a small studio that emerged in the 1940s. The little pictures they made with directors like Tony Mann made a lot of money. They had a compact studio. I thought they functioned beautifully. But a studio of that type couldn't compete with Warner Bros. and particularly MGM with big-budget productions. To economize, we shot most of the exteriors at Universal on *their* back lot. We made interiors at our own studio.

NORMAN TAUROG: I worked for three companies in my career: Fox, Paramount, and MGM. Everybody that came to Metro generally took a little less money, because they wanted to be at Metro. Louis B. Mayer had assembled such great brains around him. Even the second team could make first-class pictures. For their lower-budget movies they'd give you Jimmy Craig and people like Rosalind Russell. And if you were working on the high end, in their top films, you could get Gable and Loy to star and someone like Frank Morgan as a character actor.

HARRY WARREN: You can shoot deer on some of those places now. But sometimes, back then, you couldn't even get into the café to have lunch, it was so crowded. Not only with the people who worked there every day but with extras brought on for specific movies, with actors and everybody. Sometimes you had to wait for a table.

RANALD MACDOUGALL: When I decided to come out here from New York, I had lots of interviews at all the studios. So I sat down to make a list of the pictures that I really thought I would have liked to have written or been associated with. Most of them turned out to have been made at Warner Bros. *I Am a Fugitive from a Chain Gang*, the biographical pictures, [*The Story of Louis*] *Pasteur*, *Juarez*, [*The Life of Emile*] *Zola* . . . these were all Paul Muni starring roles.

HENRY BLANKE: Warners knew how to tell a story. And retell a story. They did *The Maltese Falcon* three times, first as *The Maltese Falcon* in 1931, then as *Satan Met a Lady* in 1936, and then again as *The Maltese Falcon* in

1941, with Bogart. But people remember that last one. Warners made a lot of movies that people remember.

HARRY WARREN: And now Warner Bros. has bit the dust, and who owns it? Some parking lot people or something? Is it Kinney Shoes or Kinney Parking Lots? Do you know?

JOHN BRAHM: I left Columbia and went over to Fox to work under Zanuck. There's actually no comparison between the two studios, because at the time when I was at Columbia, the only really worthwhile productions going on were those Capra did with Briskin. Harry Cohn accepted this fact and just supervised the other pictures without influence of any kind. I assume that at Columbia the decisions as to what pictures should be made—for instance, the remake I did of *Penitentiary*—were taken by Harry Cohn. I don't know who else it could have been. There was no one doing what Sam Briskin later did. I don't think Cohn had a second in command then. He just decreed that this and that would be done. Things were done fast. And it was a lot of fun. I do not recall any particular supervision at Columbia, while at Fox everything of importance was seen by Darryl Zanuck. You were aware of his dominant will, of his dominance.

BUDD BOETTICHER: When you went to Universal, and I imagine it is still the same, they just assigned you a picture. If you didn't like it, you went on suspension. They gave me a western. Well, I had grown up on horses. I could ride before I could walk. So I did a western. I had never made a western until *The Cimmaron Kid*. I had given up bullfighting for what I now consider to be a more dangerous profession.

HAL MOHR: Universal was looser than some other studios.

WILLIAM TUTTLE: In the 1930s, with *Frankenstein* and *Dracula* and that type of story, Universal gave birth to its forte in motion pictures, the horror film. Although there had been science fiction and impressionistic horrors made in Germany and in the silent era, it's easy to think of the American horror picture being born at Universal with Boris Karloff. He was a relatively unknown actor at that time. A bit player. Universal gave him a career that spanned quite a number of years through this one makeup that I think was quite a contribution, and that was at Universal, where there was the great makeup artist who did it, Jack Pierce. He was in charge of makeup at Universal Studios. The studio gave him the freedom to "spit and pray," as we refer to how you put things on in makeup. He used cotton, collodion, spirit gum, tissue paper. So many different things—putty. He managed to build up this head and the bolts on the neck and all those things. And he produced a character and laid it on a man who is probably one of the most gentle men that ever lived—Boris Karloff—and turned him into a monster that became immortal. Even today you say the word *Frankenstein*—and the monster's name isn't even Frankenstein, as you know—that was the doctor—Karloff is known as *the* Frankenstein. And it took him about four hours every day to get into that makeup. That was Universal. They let it be created by an individual. They gave Jack Pierce free rein. But of course, he wasn't allowed to copy it. Or copyright it. Universal has the copyright on that makeup.

ALLAN DWAN: Republic is the studio everyone forgets. Herbert Yates bought the studio from Mack Sennett, I believe. The one he built over in Studio City. It's a fine studio. A nice place to work, good facilities, and Yates had nice people around the place. It was quite a nice place to be, but it was a B level picture studio for a long time, and that was the trouble. Yates kept Republic in the B class for no reason. I had all the freedom in the world at Republic except that the final decision as to whether a story would be made or not and what the case would be was up to Herbert Yates, the head of the company. A fine man, a good businessman, and a *lousy* producer. And that was the trouble with Republic. It was a matter of the top man's taste, and it wasn't the best.

After we got the go, it was all ours, however. Nobody bothered us. Of course, they looked at rushes, but we played tricks on them in rushes. We'd have scenes made with dialogue that nobody ever wanted to hear— talk about today's dialogue! This really makes today's a blushing bride compared to some of the stuff we put in. A fake scene, just to drive them nuts. They'd see it in the projection room and send word down or come rushing down. "You can't use that!" And we'd say, "Well, why, what's the matter with it?" And so horrible that nobody in the world could get away with it.

GEORGE SEATON: I worked on the Republic lot. A cesspool! We had a little room which also served as a dressing room, and you had horse smell all over the place. They were making so many westerns, you know. Herbert Yates was in charge, but we never even met him. Phil Goldstone was the producer there, and he knew his business. I remember his first words to us were "Fellows, we've got to make this picture 'echo-man-nick-aly.'" Describing our leading character, he said he wanted a "soo-ave man." He was sort of the king of those cheap pictures over there.

ALLAN DWAN: Herbert Yates was a fine person. A very congenial host. Jolly. A very pleasant man, but he was a real dollar man, too, but like so many of those guys that take over as head of a studio, he just wasn't equipped to make pictures. He wasn't gifted that way. He didn't have very good taste, and then, of course, he fell in love with Vera Hruba Ralston. She was a skater, Czechoslovakian champion. And he saw her skating in a café. She used to skate in restaurants. Very graceful skater. The first thing he did when we got her over there at Republic was build her a skating rink in one of the little stages and he had her give him skating lessons. It's a wonder he didn't break his ass. But he learned to be a skater in this little rink. Well, what am I going to say? A man goes nuts about a woman, what *can* you say? It's a hopeless situation. He was genuinely fond of her and eventually married her, but the story is, he was just stuck on the girl and he wanted her to have a big career and *she* wanted to have one. He didn't exactly wreck his studio with her, but I would say that he wrecked a lot of my pictures. She tried very hard and was very pleasant. Very nice girl. But she hadn't been trained to be an actress long enough to star in pictures. She was a skater, and you can't just come off the ice and be a dramatic actress. Unless you slide off with the right finish. Well, eventually he just stopped making pictures. He sold the company. But he fixed Vera up real fine in real estate. They own a lot of apartment buildings over in the valley and in various places. Pretty rich.

GEORGE SEATON: I just didn't know Republic's kind of picture making, coming from Metro, where everything was so lush, Cedric Gibbons sets, et cetera. I had one scene at Republic where a man gets off a train and he's greeted by his wife. I said, "How are we going to do this?" Phil Goldstone, Yates's producer, said, "Don't worry about it. The Lark from San Francisco gets in at Glendale at 9:03." We went out to see how in the world they were going to shoot this. The train pulled in, the leading man jumped on and knocked passengers back. The leading lady rushed in, he came off the train and said, "Darling," and the porter stood there with his mouth open, and then the train pulled right out. It just stopped there long enough for people to get their luggage out. They stole the shot!

PANDRO BERMAN: I worked for RKO for so many years—the dates are so vague. I went through so many different ownerships and administrations, but I do recall spots of each. I recall many times when I was in contact with old man Joseph P. Kennedy during his operation of the company when he would come out here for a few months at a time or a few weeks. In fact, I once talked him into giving me a $5 raise when I couldn't get it from anybody else in the organization. And I did it by waiting, laying in wait for him, at the gate at midnight one night, when I knew he was going to have to leave the studio and when his resistance was low. He was a nice man, Joseph P. Kennedy. I liked him. He had the studio filled with Bostonians who were his men: Charlie Sullivan, E. B. Derr, Ed King, all men who knew nothing about the film business but who were his watchdogs and who operated for him. And as I say, during the seventeen years I was with that company, before I left in 1939, I honestly believe there were nineteen administrations! People came and went to run that place!

RKO had a history of changing studio heads, starting with William LeBaron, going onward through Selznick, and then finally with Merian C. Cooper and myself. That ran from about 1929 to '39. That was their good period, and after that they went down. They just didn't get the proper people. After me, there was Charles Koerner, Jerry Wald, Norman Krasna, Dore Schary . . . they kept changing heads, and eventually RKO was sold to Howard Hughes.

JOHN SEITZ: The first time I met Howard Hughes was on a picture I did retakes for, a Billie Dove picture for Frank Lloyd in the early thirties. That was the first time I ever met this strange individual.

BRONISLAU KAPER: What are you talking about? You don't meet Howard Hughes. You meet his money.

JOHN SEITZ: Well, every Sunday night Preston Sturges had a party at his house, and a constant visitor was Howard's uncle Rupert Hughes, a great writer and a great wit. He always referred to himself as the poor uncle of a rich nephew.

BRONISLAU KAPER: The best head of RKO was Pandro Berman. Pandro was a powerful person. Small. When he tried to smile, he hit you with his eyes. It was the smile of a cannon. He looked at you like Napoleon. He used to run one of the studios, RKO. But you see, sooner or later, everybody used to run RKO. There are very few people who did *not* run RKO. There is a private club of people who *didn't* run RKO.

PANDRO BERMAN: There were a small number of writers under contract at RKO because everything was on a much smaller scale there than at Metro or some of the bigger studios. You know, Metro had maybe fifty, sixty, seventy writers under contract. At RKO we probably had about five or six. Not too many. Ten maybe. We had Jane Murfin, Allan Scott. I remember those two particularly. And Dudley Nichols. Not too many writers—or anybody—under contract. RKO was smaller.

MERIAN C. COOPER: Pan Berman is a wonderful producer. I made him head of RKO when he was twenty-six years old, because he was the best man. He followed David O. Selznick's approach, which made him one of the top producers of all time. He got the best directors, the best stars, the best properties, and the best everything, regardless of cost. You could do that at MGM when it was on the top, and you could do it easily. But you couldn't do it with RKO when it was broke, you know. They didn't have the money, and it didn't have the distribution. Look, MGM could sell the same picture that RKO would, but RKO would get 20 percent and MGM would get 40 percent of the theater gross. Metro was king of the business, and the theaters wanted to do business with them. Metro was the king. Paramount had been, but Metro in those early years . . . there was nothing like it. It had everything.

WALTER REISCH: In all my years with MGM, I only heard of one picture habitually referred to as having lost money—I'm talking about the period covered by the Louis B. Mayer regime. After that, under Dore Schary, every picture was very much in the news both critically and financially, *especially* the losses. But for twenty-five years at MGM, they only talked about *Parnell*, with Clark Gable as an Irish diplomat or politician. That was a proverbial reference, just as you'd cite Camille's dying cough or Edward Kean's going crazy on stage. You'd always hear people say, "Don't make another *Parnell.*" But in my whole memory—and I'm as familiar with MGM pictures as I am with my own private financial statement, which is much thinner than MGM's—nobody ever said, "That picture made more than another." We knew that *The Great Ziegfeld* was a majestic success. We knew that everything with Jeanette MacDonald and Nelson Eddy was a tremendous success, and *San Francisco* with its earthquake. But out of five or six hundred MGM pictures of that period, you only mentioned *Parnell* as a loser. It was just like a word in the dictionary, identical with "failure," and it opened the way wide for English actors because they said Gable was not an Irishman and therefore people couldn't believe in him and the whole thing collapsed. Gable never made another picture in which he didn't play an out-and-out American.

PANDRO BERMAN: Well, Metro was always accused of mounting their productions too well! As a matter of fact, the average critic used to claim MGM films were overglossy, overdressed, over–made up. And I guess to a certain extent that was true, because Louis B. Mayer had a philosophy . . . and this was his, not ours . . . which was that we were selling pictures of beautiful women, for the most part, with Garbos and Shearers and Crawfords and Lana Turners and Ava Gardners. And he said, "If you're selling beautiful women, *make* them beautiful. Dress them beautifully. Make them up beautifully. And photograph them beautifully." And that was what some of the critics used to resent, that glossy finish, you know.

KATHARINE HEPBURN: Oh, hell. We read fairy tales for years, didn't we? Are they throwing all that out? Do you think that *A Clockwork Orange* has a lot more to do with reality? I don't. . . . You've got to dream up your own life. You've got to dream up everything.

CHARLES LEMAIRE: MGM loved its glamour, and their costume designers were famous. Yes, they had big glamour things and were famous for their style. They had lots of things that cost a lot of money, but sometimes I wasn't particularly interested in them. All of us in design started trying to stockpile our costumes. I had a great stock, and the other studios knew this. So by being at Fox, where they let me handle the business of the costumes, I always had something to dangle in front of other studios. You know, "I'll lend you my farm clothes if you let me have six ball gowns," you see? RKO, the smaller studio, didn't have much of a stock. Columbia held on to whatever it had. Warners had a lot of stock, really a lot of stock, because they hung on to things to reuse them, and, of course, MGM had stock, but I built up the wardrobe at Fox in my years there, and I sometimes rented out costumes to other studios or even sold them our old stuff! I made money!

FRANK CAPRA: Nobody gives Hollywood any credit for business sense. Every studio looked for ways to save, to make profit off something lying around. And, of course, studios would make deals with one another to loan or exchange stars. The poor stars were just traded back and forth, and there wasn't anything they could do about it. That's how I got Clark Gable for *It Happened One Night*. Louis B. Mayer wanted to punish Gable, teach him a lesson, so he made him come down to our Poverty Row studio in Gower Gulch, the awful low-budget Columbia. And that's also how Clark Gable won an Oscar for his performance in our film. Some punishment! And studios had B units, strictly created to make money the cheap way and recycle old stuff and develop talent.

PANDRO BERMAN: The B movie unit was the studio's testing ground. That was the field where we developed all of our people. B pictures developed directors, writers, actors, stars, and producers. It was such a smart system, a little film school where you got paid when you were learning. You could grow up from B pictures to A pictures in all categories, and sometimes, as juveniles and leading men got too old, they became character actors and were very happy often to move down and get jobs in B pictures. It was good, steady work in movies that were well made, just cheaper and shorter. Good business policy.

WALTER REISCH: Studios would have specialties. The so-called special effects department at 20th Century–Fox became, in the 1950s, the best in the universe. They could combine shots of wild animals with scenes played by actors or explosions or catastrophes. It was very expensive. They had a complete stage of their own, the biggest stage ever built in the world, with backgrounds and a million gadgets and machines, a staff of twenty or thirty experts, and all the time and money they wanted on a special lot of their own. And nobody interfered with them. They got their assignments, and they came up with their own stuff.

PANDRO BERMAN: And there were "shorts"—sports films, little musicals, big-band shows, crime dramas, comedies, travelogues—made by some of the studios, and cartoons, of course, and previews, and then newsreels. But the RKO Pathé News wasn't handled in Hollywood. We knew nothing about it at the studio at all. Nothing. It was all out of New York, strictly a release set-up. All the newsreels were done that way, I think. Hearst for MGM. Previously the Hearst newsreel was handled by Universal. It was run then by a friend and associate of my father's, Ed Hatrick. My father released the Hearst newsreel at Universal. Incidentally, Ed Hatrick's daughter lives the second house down from mine. She's Mrs. Jimmy Stewart. But studios created shorts of their own, all original.

HENRY HATHAWAY: There were some shenanigans in those days. I was a junior writer at MGM about 1930. They had just stolen Jackie Cooper away from Paramount after he had made *Skippy*, a big hit. Thalberg said, "I want a picture with him and Wally Beery. I have to get it ready in a hurry, because we're getting the kid from Paramount and we've got Beery under contract." So they went down to the juvenile department, and they offered anyone who could come up with a story idea for Beery and the kid $10,000 if they used it. They used to give that all the time. As a matter of fact, at Paramount, if you could bring in a story, just a page with an idea, and they accepted it, you made ten thousand bucks. We made forty pictures a year! Charlie Furthman was the one that turned in the most stories. He used to get six or seven of them every year. He was makin' fifty, sixty thousand bucks just on one-page ideas. So Charlie was coming up with ideas hand over fist, and somebody got suspicious and investigated. They found out he was takin' 'em from the *Saturday Evening Post* from 1902, 1903, 1904!

Paramount was the studio that had the infamous "talking writers." They had five guys. They had Grover Jones, Keene Thompson, Lloyd Corrigan, Bill McNutt, and a skinny guy. His name was Clarence something. Anyway, these guys would sit around on the top floor in the writers' building and play word games all the time. No working. When the top people came to some kind of impasse, when they got narrowed down to one idea and couldn't see beyond it, the "talking writers" would be called in and told, "Now, this is the situation." And those guys would come up with forty ideas! A million things about how a boy and a girl could meet: "You start in the sand. The boy and girl are in the sand. You pull back, and we find it's the sandpile outside of a building. They're gonna make cement with it." Grover was especially good at this. He had a wonderful mind. It was a fountain that just flowed all the time.

Grover Jones told me that one day Schulberg called the "talking writers" in and said, "Last night I had a good idea about so-and-so. Go to work on it right away. I think it might be a good story." So he told them the idea. They went back upstairs and just started playing word games again. Pretty soon they got a call from Schulberg saying he wanted them to come down and tell him what they had. They said, "Jeez, we have to go down and tell him something" and "What the hell *was* that story he told us?" They talked awhile, and Grover said, "I'll tell you what we'll do. I'll get up and start to ad-lib, and when I put my cigar in my mouth, you take it from there. When you get stuck, put your hand in your pocket, and somebody else will take it. When he gets stuck, he'll start rubbing his head." So they went down and ad-libbed the whole story, and the damned thing got made.

ALLAN DWAN: We pulled things . . . some real deals. We stole a B-29. We needed a B-29 in a movie, and the military wouldn't give it to us. So one night we put it on two of these gigantic trucks, drove it off the base at Tucson, Arizona, right through the gates and past the guards and up the road to our studio all through Arizona and California. These things were so enormous that they were violating all the laws because you're not allowed to drive anything that wide up the streets—they're allowed to move at night only, and they had to have motorcycles out in front of them to warn anybody off the road when we were approaching. They came that entire distance and drove right into the Republic lot and back to the special-effects department. They took it off the truck, sent the truck back to Tucson, Arizona, without a single permit, without anybody knowing we were doing it. Yes, we stole a B-29.

Well, first thing we did was cut it right down the middle so we could get in and photograph it from the side and in doing so discovered that it had hundreds of motors in it, all over the place—underneath to operate the bomb doors and all the rest. Everybody in the studio had a motor he took home. Either he put it on his garage doors or did something with it. Those motors scattered like chaff on the wind, just *whang!* And everything was removed that we didn't need, and I had a perfect B-29 to use, and we put it up on rockers so we could move it and do anything we wanted with it in sections. Then, after it was all done, there it was stacked up in the backyard, and our picture was out and shown in release and nobody asked about the B-29. All of a sudden, we saw MGM put in a bid for a B-29 to use in a movie, and somebody remembered that *we* had a B-29 or parts of it. So we wound up selling it to MGM. They would buy anything. We hauled it over to MGM to make a picture that Robert Taylor was in. I don't know what happened to it after that. That was the case of the B-29 that never was returned . . . and it made a profit for Republic. MGM bought a used B-29.

HAL ROSSON: Sometimes when I look back on it and I think of all of us who worked on those pictures, I think we should have paid the studios just to be able to work on them. We had such darned good times. Nobody had an ax to grind. We were all paid to do what we were there to do, and we all did it in a happy frame of mind. And we did have fun with our jokes, our little games with each other, all while we were working together.

CHAPTER 8

THE STUDIO WORKFORCE

MERIAN C. COOPER: A studio, in those days, actually was a kind of factory. The people at Metro were the only people who really understood that. MGM got that it didn't really cost more to do forty pictures a year than it did to do ten pictures a year. To make pictures, you had to hire stars, directors, personnel, and undertake physical costs with lights and props and buildings and all that stuff, so they got the stuff, kept it, and put the personnel under contract. It didn't cost any more to publicize forty pictures rather than ten because you had the same guys selling all of them, and the actual distribution didn't cost much more. The more pictures you could push through, the more money you made. The Schenks out on the East Coast understood this perfectly. They were moneymen. This is why MGM was a success and also Warners was a success and Fox was a success . . . they pushed stuff through the system. The studio system. It *was* a kind of factory.

RAOUL WALSH: The factory? Oh, yes, the factory. No doubt about it. We got 'em done and out the door, but what kind of a factory has a bunch of conniving, creative, independent, determined manipulators running around inside trying to get everything their own way all day?

JEANINE BASINGER: The studios were an economic force, tightly organized to be efficiently run and controlled by top executives, with a defined and detailed system in place, a table of organization, really. But the employees were *creative* people, with highly specialized jobs and autonomy in their own areas because of that specialization. When you think about it, since it was the business that was an art, or the art that was a business, as has been said, it's a miracle the complicated studio system worked at all. The studios developed separate departments, each with its own head and each assigned a specific job: makeup, costumes, cinematography, publicity, music, direction, production, editing, writing, building, designing. A complex system, department by department.

To understand how the studio system worked, it's necessary to consider all these various departments, the jobs on the payroll. What was the definition of each job? The level of responsibility? Each department had a definition, whether they abided by it or not. The cameramen, writers, editors, costume designers, art directors, script girls, all had their own hierarchy and tasks. The department heads got credit for the work done by their staff so only their names were in the credits. The way each department grew—and operated—is the true story of Hollywood.

ROBERT WISE: I grew up inside the studio system. I came in early 1933 and left in 1949. I was at RKO in the editing department, and then I became a director for the five years before I left. I had never worked anyplace else. After I escaped from RKO, Fox signed me for three years . . . I was a little afraid of what it might be like because RKO was a major studio but still small and sort of a family studio. I found Fox wasn't all that different. In fact, through the years, as my career grew, I worked at Fox and then Warners and then MGM and really became a part of the "golden age" studio system. And what I learned was that the one common denominator in working at all the studios was the creative departments and support systems. Oh, yes, there were great cinematographers and so-so ones, good designers and weak ones, et cetera, but really, the business structure, and the departments . . . the same.

VINCENT SHERMAN: One thing all the administrations had in common were the contracts that bound you to them. And so no matter how ambitious you were, you had to do what the studio assigned you.

LEWIS MILESTONE: As the studio system took over, you learned how to work within their business system. They were all more or less using a supervisory system of producers, which meant someone was watching what you did.

IRVING RAPPER: There were echelons of power. The top was the top, but as you went down the ladder, each department had its own echelon of power.

FRANK CAPRA: There was a definite lineup about who had decision-making power, but you had to negotiate with all your other creative people in the departments. You had to talk your way through. You had to smile. You were a fool if you didn't listen to your cinematographer or work with your writer or take the suggestions of your costumers and set decorators, of course. It's a collaborative art, and collaboration within the studio system was imperative, but the most confident person—the one with a vision for the project—could carry the day about decisions and choices.

LEWIS MILESTONE: In the new system, there was a constant fight about things, but if you knew how to live with the system, you could get by . . . you could get your own way. But not in a frontal attack. You had to sneak up on them from the right or left flank. If you started saying "I want my way, and that's the only way," well, no. You had to be smart about things.

PANDRO BERMAN: There was the system on paper and the system that happened on any given working day. Who knows who might have had the last word or have come up with the idea? Or persuaded the others? Think of all the departments, from the top down, and imagine how complicated it all really could be. And yet people really worked together. Everyone wanted the finished product to be good. The department system worked.

FRED ZINNEMANN: At the top, just under the studio head, were the producers. In the first decades of sound, there were all kinds of producers: executive producers, assistant producers, associate producers, production supervisors, what have you. They were all geniuses who were hired to tell directors and writers how to make films. And they had their rules and ideas . . . and if you go back and examine the kind of rules that were put forth, you find they were totally arbitrary. "No matter what happens, you've got to see the star's face in good light" . . . even if it's in the middle of the night in a railroad town. There were a whole slew of rules and regulations of that kind, and no matter how hard one fought against it, some of it insidiously stuck. And yet people found their ways to deal with it. But even more surprising, the most surprising thing of all, in the thirties the Hollywood films probably reached their all-time high as far as quality is concerned. That's the extraordinary thing. And it's because of all those departments, each one dedicated to its own craft, its own task. Top to bottom, people who knew what they were doing were doing it, finding a way to work with each other, avoiding stupidities wherever they could, and asserting themselves when it really mattered.

PANDRO BERMAN: Well, in the early days the word *supervisor* was used to designate a man who was assigned to work on individual pictures by the head of the studio but who didn't have any great authority in connection with the important matters, such as the purchase of [story] material or the assigning of stars. Later these men became known as associate producers. They were more or less expected to carry out the job after some policy was laid down by the head of the studio. And the labeling's progress went from "supervisor" to "associate producer" to finally "producer." And then eventually the independent producer came into being. That was the gradual stair upward, but in those early days, "supervisor" was about the only thing they called them at any studio. It was the first job that really started to strip away some of the authority of the director . . . the one who had controlled most everything in the silent era.

After sound came in, productions became more elaborate, needed larger crews, more shooting time. And this is one reason the producer became more necessary. There was a general feeling at that time—growing even before sound—that directors were becoming too extravagant, and Louis B. Mayer was in the forefront of those men who decided that he had to put some kind of control over his directors. And he instituted the producer system. And little by little it grew until men like Thalberg had staffs of producers around them who were held responsible for the cost of the picture and, as a result, eventually became responsible for its artistic value as well. So slowly the producer grew in stature and the director, who had formerly done the whole job, became the director of the actors on the set. And for a long period of time *that* remained in effect. I recall that when I was producing at Metro, in the years from 1940 to 1960, some directors used to be assigned to the picture only a couple of weeks in advance of the actual production. A director had nothing to do with the purchase of material or the development of screenplays. And he used to be yanked off the picture about four days after he finished shooting. He usually had nothing to do with the editing. The producer had the major responsibilities during that period. Of course, now that has reverted back to the days before the producer.

MITCHELL LEISEN: There was a producer on each picture, and he picked his director. The producer had absolute say-so, and if a producer chose a director who didn't want to do it, he went to the front office and said, "Look, I'm going to make a mess of this thing because I don't believe in it. I'm sure that some other director can make a very fine picture out of it." If you told the producer—or the studio head—that you were going to make a mess of it, believe me, they weren't going to insist you do it. You could talk the studios into things.

PANDRO BERMAN: You know, I've always believed that although this is a business of collaboration and nobody could ever make a picture without all the elements working together . . . that is, never make a *good* picture without all the elements working together . . . nevertheless, I believe there's one mind that usually dominates every successful picture. It could be a producer or it could be a director or it could be a writer. It could be anyone with any important function that could *lead* the others. In fact, without a doubt, there have been pictures that have been made really from the point of view of the star if their personality is strong enough to influence other people. However, I think that era we're talking about was the era of the producer. The producer was dominating the film and the film bore his trademark, just as today is the era of the director.

In 1940, when I went to Metro, they had a very interesting and quite complicated organization unlike anything any other company has ever had in the business. After Thalberg got sick and left the company, Mayer diversified by getting in producers who were given authority beyond that which they had ever had under Thalberg. And in order to keep a close check on what everyone was doing, he set up the following kind of organization: every producer worked under an executive. There were at least three such executives: Sam Katz, Al Lichtman, and Joe Cohn. These executives are differentiated from the staff of executives that one finds in a studio normally, which Metro also had from the top down: Louis B. Mayer, Eddie Mannix, Benny Thau, L. K. Sidney, and others fulfilling the usual functions of studio executives. This was a group of *special* executives who did nothing but "service" the producer. In addition to this set-up, they also had a group of so-called editors differentiated from film editing: editors of script. This group was headed by a wonderful man named Bernie Hyman, and he had a couple of assistants, who were also called editors. I believe at one time Larry Weingarten was one of them. The so-called foolproof formula, therefore, was that the producer could develop the property. A certain amount of executive supervision related mostly to finances would come from the executive, whoever he might be. In my case I was with Sam Katz. Louis Mayer asked me to go with Sam Katz, which I was reluctant to do because I knew a lot about Sam's reputation in the business and I wasn't enamored of him. But Mayer put it on a basis I could not reject. He said Sam was closer to him than any of his other executives. So I'd be closer to Mayer by working with Sam. This supervision by the executive was, as I say, purely a financial one. It had nothing to do with anything except how much you paid for your property or your writer or your actors and so on. However, the other set-up was the one that was calculated to bug me and probably some other producers: the script editors. They would swoop down on every script that was finished, ready it, and come bursting in to tell you what was wrong with it! And it took me very little time to get my dander up and to get angry enough to go in and threaten to resign when on my very first picture— after going through the usual discussions with the editors and more or less winning my way in spite of everything through the early stages and through the shooting—I suddenly found Bernie Hyman, whom I didn't know at the time, and Margaret Booth, who was his editorial assistant, were down in the editing room undermining all my decisions. I took care of that.

MITCHELL LEISEN: The producer became the kingpin. He was the independent set-up *inside* the studio. The front office had nothing to say about it. He did what he wanted to do, functioning as an independent unit. Nobody seems to understand this now. If the movie was a flop and he had a red figure after his name, he was a lousy producer. If he had a black figure after his name, he was a good producer. I am talking about the working day on a studio set. Things had to get done. Producers had to have say-so, and they had it.

HAL WALLIS: Well, there were so many variants of "producer" or "head of production" in the old Hollywood. Head of production could be general production executive, and all production at the studio would come under his wing, but then there were executive producers, associate producers, and line producers. Of course, in the Warner days, there was Jack Warner, and I worked closely with him, but in the day-to-day operation I made the decisions—and, of course, took the blame if there was any to be taken. And I selected the director. A director was very much a component, supported by technical departments working at peak efficiency. In that period—my Warner period—the director was important, as they always have been, but he probably had not reached the degree of prominence that he enjoys today. And often today, "executive producer" might mean an actor's agent or business manager.

There were some subtle differences from studio to studio. At Warners, the directors there, for the most part, were under contract, and we assigned directors the way we assigned actors. They made Warner Bros. films which were "directed by" . . . and these people were under a Warners contract, so that while they were shooting a picture, we were acquiring other properties for them which we would pencil in for their futures. The director directed on the floor. That was the system at that time at Warners.

BRONISLAU KAPER: There was one trouble with this producer system. I'd like to explain it. Take William Wright, a very sweet man. I liked him very much. But somehow he was one of those producers who was eager to make a picture, regardless of whether it was good or bad. You see, the trouble was that a producer was under contract to the studio. His main object was that before the option on his contract came up, he had to have something good on his record. And—if not good, to have *something* on the record. This was at MGM. If a producer was sitting at MGM for two years and did not make a picture, obviously he was out, because they said, "Well, he couldn't find the story."

CHARLTON HESTON: I think producers can do their job in three general ways. There is the producer who is a logistician, who deals with the logistics of film, and whose expertise has to do with schedules and the mechanics of making a picture. And this, never doubt it, is vital. Then there are producers who are promoters. Arthur Jacobs was one of those. So was Sam Bronston. There are many such. Sam Spiegel is such a producer, really. Then there are producers whose primary instincts are for some of the creative aspects of filmmaking. Perhaps script, perhaps cutting. I would say Hal Wallis was an example of that, a man who knows a great deal about editing and who feels that his prime creative contribution is in the editing stage. There are producers who, like David O. Selznick, said the producer is the conductor of the orchestra and the director is merely the first violinist.

GEOFFREY SHURLOCK: They used to say a producer was a man who knew what he wanted but couldn't spell it.

BRONISLAU KAPER: I saw cases where a producer would ask me to do the music for a movie or would ask the music department to have a movie assigned to me. And he had to start it in three weeks. He gives me the script, and I read it, and, being honest, I tell him, "I think this should be changed." And he says [whispering], "Yeah, I know. But look, let's not talk about it. I want to do this picture, *but—*" what they said in the studio jargon: "I don't want to open a new can of beans. Let's not open a new can of beans." You heard it all the time. They were all afraid of their jobs. You'd say to the cutter . . . "fix this and this." "No! *They* liked it already." The mysterious *they*. *They* already okayed it. Never mind the quality of the picture. "Let's not open a new can of beans." There were many producers who were not too secure, so they would rather do a bad picture than not do a picture at all. It was very sad. But that was the studio system at MGM.

HAL WALLIS: I can tell you that what I do as an independent producer today is pretty much the same as what I did as the executive producer inside the old Warner Bros. studio system.

JOHN CROMWELL: Producers maintained their status by using the creativity of the men they worked with. The studios developed an efficiency with this. They maintained their own budgetary and creative control through the top level—the producer—but freed up everything below that to function. If the producer wasn't a man like Hal Wallis, a head of production at a studio, then a description of the basic producing process became a standard format. A producer would select or be assigned a story by his superior. As he grew more influential, of course, he would have more to say about who the writer or director would be who would be working with him. A meeting would be called to discuss the material, be it a novel, a play, or an original. These meetings would go on for a week or perhaps even longer, until a line was decided on. The writer and director would be allowed to express their ideas. The writer was the one who was going to put it in its first form, and the director was the one who was going to bring it to life on film. The producer, talking with them, had the opportunity to guide, to reject, to weigh their ideas and form an opinion. He might contribute little or nothing to the final result . . . or he might define it totally. You see, these things were always flexible according to types of personality and levels of persuasion. A director, on set, could assert himself and find his way to his own vision. It depended on him, but he'd always need a good producer.

MITCHELL LEISEN: A good producer does the same thing today he did in the old days. The difference is always the level of authority: Who's the boss on the project? Who picks the collaborators in all the categories? Who gets final say-so or final cut? These issues are why so many big-name directors ultimately became their own producers: Frank Capra, John Ford, Cecil B. DeMille, Alfred Hitchcock, and so on. They became producer-directors.

CAMERAMEN

JEANINE BASINGER: There was excellent collaboration and balance to the creation of a motion picture in Hollywood, but there was frustration, too. The writers often felt unappreciated, even abused, and the cinematographers, whose work was vital and not as subject to constant change as the writer's was, were still often men who felt they did not receive the credit they were due. Cinematographers differed in their opinions, but many felt *their* job was to define the film totally and others felt it was to support the vision already defined. I think the cinematography department was the one that kept itself most separate from the others, with a sense of some superiority due to the specialized technical knowledge that cameramen possessed and no one else had. Cinematographers tended to work as a unit with their own crews around them, but it was essential that they work in collaboration with everyone on the set, especially the director.

JAMES WONG HOWE: The man behind the camera has to keep the people in front of the camera comfortable, so they have confidence in him. A picture is kind of a family group. The cameraman has his own family: operator and assistants, the gaffer, the head electrician, his grip, and his standby painter. These people are all in his one family, and usually, when you're under contract, you keep that unit together.

JOSEPH RUTTENBERG: I was fortunate to have started as a cameraman very early, so I had the opportunity to do many things that are not controlled by specific members of a camera team. I learned all aspects of photography. So I impress on you gentlemen who want to be cinematographers . . . I mean, you *ladies* and gentlemen who want to become cameramen . . . or camerapeople . . . learn photography. Know *everything* that you can do with it. Learn the things that aren't conventional, you know, that they don't teach you. The cameraman and his crew are the people who understand photographing an image. None of the other departments can do that.

JAMES WONG HOWE: You're the head man on the set. Under the director, of course.

HOWARD SCHWARTZ: The guys who set style are the directors. They set the style of photography they want. And they're the guys who are telling the story, and it's right that you should accommodate yourself to their ideas.

FLOYD CROSBY: When I was working in old Hollywood, 90 percent of the time I went along with whatever the director wanted. You more or less have to, you see. They are the person responsible for the picture. And I don't think it's up to the cameraman, unless the director is a new director doing his first picture and he needs help . . . I don't think it's the position of the cameraman to try to tell him how to direct the picture. I think any cameraman has ideas of what his conception of good photography is, and your technique you learn from watching and doing so you know how to accomplish the results you want. Most cameramen have their own ideas of what they want to do, but your job is to work with the director and to give him *his* vision the way *he* wants it.

HOWARD SCHWARTZ: The director should be able to communicate with the cameraman and not waste time looking through the camera, except after the cameraman has set the shot up. He should be utilizing his time to work with the actors to rehearse and get the scene to play properly. It's amazing to me how many directors today—and they are the ones who are telling the story—cannot communicate.

STANLEY CORTEZ: Directors should learn how to talk to a cameraman in a few words and tell him what they want and then get out of the way, let him do his stuff, and come on back and check and see that he's giving you what you wanted, and you save a lot of time. But if a director likes to line up his shots through a camera, that is his prerogative, of course.

HOWARD SCHWARTZ: Directors? They're the boss. Unfortunately from our standpoint, photography isn't the most important thing to the ticket buyers or the studio executives.

MILTON KRASNER: We only contribute.

HOWARD SCHWARTZ: We're just doing part of it, even though sometimes we feel it's the most important part. We have to be subservient to the story and the director's point of view in telling the story. You just have to learn to accommodate it, and the earlier you can get that feeling, the better off it is for you. Don't start fighting it like I used to. You'll be making yourself a lot of trouble.

STANLEY CORTEZ: There are certain directors who never even look through the camera. Orson Welles is *not* one of them.

HOWARD SCHWARTZ: You cannot have two men creating the mood, both a director and a cameraman. The cameraman is the one who, three-quarters of the time—more than that, 90 percent of the time—creates the entire mood of the picture, because most of the directors don't even consult with him about what they want, but even when they do, it's still in his hands—the way *he* envisions what the director wants. He is the only man on the set who knows what he's striving for. He must tell his gaffer, who's his head electrician, what to do. You wouldn't need a gaffer if you didn't have time restrictions, and it would be a pleasure to set all your own lights, but you don't have time for that. You've got to set up the dolly shots, the zoom shots. You've got to check backings. You've got to set your scrims for your breaks on the walls. You've got to work with your fire effects. You've got a thousand things to do, but the first thing you do is you tell your gaffer what you're after, the mood you want to work in, the key you want to work in, where you want the light source to come from, whether you want the faces to be down in the front. You tell him what key you want to work in, because you may want to stop down more on a sequence to carry focus. The thing is that you're the guy that's in control and you should never relinquish any of this, because when you do, you're losing part of your creative definition of the picture.

ROBERT WISE: I usually look at each project in terms of what it ideally wants to look like on the screen. Then I try to cast a cameraman like I would cast an actor, the man I think would be closest to ideal.

LEE GARMES: Josef von Sternberg is a director many people think controlled the photography totally on his films. He didn't with me. He's a very, very fine picture maker. *And* a card-carrying cinematographer. Also a very exacting, very self-centered man. However, I'll tell you that from a cinematographer's point of view, he was probably the easiest director to work with, because he never made any scenes that ran any length of time. If there were three people in the room and three people talked, he would be on that one person for that one line and he'd stop the camera and go to the next person. Then he'd come back to talk with you. He wouldn't stay there and do the whole scene, you know, so you could get good lighting and you got it most every time you came back because you could light again, but it took forever and a day to make a picture that way.

STANLEY CORTEZ: I think any creative cameraman or director of photography really is an interpreter, the interpreter of the drama, so to speak. And they, all of us who are in our field, basically are dramatists to a very high degree, as a writer is. But we do it with light, with optics, with the camera, with all kinds of gimmicks and things. Who cares who creates it? If the result is there, this is what's important.

KING VIDOR: The feeling I always had—and I was always having difficulty fighting the studio—was to get the cameraman on long enough ahead of time. If I went on location, I always wanted the cameraman there, because he would then have a feeling of what time of day was the best time to do certain shots. He could think in terms of light. And I was always having to go to the head of the studio, Warner Bros. and so forth, and they said, "Why do you need the cameraman? You just pick the location, take the production manager, assistant director along, and art director. What the hell do you need the cameraman for?" It was always so that he could contribute to it. And to get him in on what we were trying to do, let him have time to get in on it. There was always a fight.

STANLEY CORTEZ: You walk on a soundstage. There's a set. It's black. The sequence calls for so-and-so and so-and-so. How do you start? You have a preconceived idea. All of what you've experienced in your life comes to a focal point, and from that focal point, ideas build upon ideas. All of us in the movies are creators. There are no set rules. You are receiving input from others. It's the art director at the very beginning, and it's the costume designer at the very beginning. When a costume is designed, the director will invariably check the costumes, because of the designs, styles, so forth and so on. Then the cameraman is called in by the director or the producer and they say, "What do you think of So-and-So?" "Oh, great." Or "I think this, I think that." And the reason why I would think this or think that would not be based primarily on the set, although that is a factor, but based on the structure of the person's face, the color of the person's eyes, et cetera, et cetera, et cetera. The audience is ready to drink in and watch the performers. They become part of it. You relate to them. This is the whole point.

HAL MOHR: A director says to you as a cameraman, "Now, in this room, I don't want to see anything at all. I want the room to be absolutely dark. Nothing!" And this is happening, that is happening, the other thing is happening, but he insists he wants no light at all. But there must be something on the scene besides just blank film. There must be some identification of some kind—a corner of a highlight on an arch or something. So I've had directors say when I've had the set lit for one of these effect things, "This isn't what I want." And I tell them, "Look, will you just wait until you see it on the screen? If it isn't what you want when you see it on the screen, I'll be very happy to apologize and come in on my own time and do it over again for you. But see it on the screen, because if you don't, what you might as well do is not photograph it at all and just run blank film on the screen with sound over it. If that's what you want, do it that way. If you don't want to see anything but just hear sound, then I strongly advise you not to waste your time directing these people on the set, just make a soundtrack and run blank film over the soundtrack." Well, most see the logic of that to some degree, and in one or two cases, I had to actually do it all over. I had to kill all the lights on the set and go through the motions of photographing a scene that was never photographed. So that they would soon damn learn that there's a certain technical variance there. I mean, there are laws of physics that have to be observed, for Chrissake, and laws of rationality. You say, "Let *me* say it for you. Let *me* say it *visually* for you." That's the cameraman's job.

HOWARD SCHWARTZ: Some of your best stuff comes out of adversity.

JAMES WONG HOWE: Sometimes a cameraman goes out on a bad day and the lighting is bad and the director says, "I want this last shot." The cameraman says, "It's no good. I don't want to shoot it, but I'll shoot it under protest," and he'll write on slate, "Shot Under Protest" and hold it up and then in the dailies it comes on the screen and it's beautiful. Very embarrassing.

ALLAN DWAN: Jimmy Howe—I've walked into Jimmy Howe's sets and said, "Well, aren't you going to turn the lights on?" and he said, "They're on." And I didn't even know that the thing was lit, it was so well lit. He always got gorgeous effects 'cause he knew how to handle it. Most of them want a lot of light. They blaze it in. People are squinting. Get a good cameraman, and trust him.

JAMES WONG HOWE: There's always problems. The writers put in certain things they have imagined, and then the cameraman has to figure out how to photograph them. Being a cameraman is very interesting that way but also very frustrating at times. When I was making *The Old Man and the Sea*, Mr. Hemingway had his character right out in the middle of the ocean at night, and a bird flies in and lights on the man's fishing line. Just then, the fish grabs on the line and jerks it and scares the bird and the bird flies away. Beautiful. But how do you get a bird to light on a fishing line so you can photograph it? The production office never thinks about that. They leave it up to the people out on stage. So we have to get a bird man in, and he brings his bird and puts a rubber suit on him and takes him out into the middle of the tank, and he holds the bird up, ducks under, and lets the bird loose. What does the bird do? He flies up into the rafters. Try another bird. Same thing. You can't get those birds to come to into the boat. This was taking forever. Finally we took the bird, put BB shot on his wings, and weighed it down so he could only fly so high. The first time I overdid it, and he flew five feet and went right into the water. But we dried him off and got him up, lightened the load a bit, and got the job done.

HOWARD SCHWARTZ: One little tip in that regard. You don't want to say no to a director, because right away, he takes a dislike to you as a cameraman. If you say no to him, that you can't do this shot, he just doesn't appreciate your attitude. He doesn't understand your reasons. So what you say is "Sure, we can do this shot. It'll take about two and a half hours to do it this way, but if you want to confine it a bit and do it over here, why we can do it in fifteen minutes." And usually they'll say, "Sure, let's go this way." You don't ever say no. You say, "Sure, we can do it. Great! But it's going to take a little time." "How much time?" Time is money. You have to be a diplomat.

JOHN BRAHM: Every director like me is looking for a cameraman he can work with. My association with Lucien Ballard began at Columbia, and I used him on every picture I could. We just understood each other. He did what I wanted him to do, and he liked what I was doing. His work was sharp, precise, intense. He had fun with me, and I had fun with him. It's very hard to define our working relationship, except to say that it worked perfectly for both of us. And I should think that's what every director and cameraman want and are looking for.

MILTON KRASNER: I don't know where to start to tell you about working with directors because they are all so different. Some of them are writer-directors and also director-producers. Some of them will leave it to the cameraman to do the lighting and plan the shots. Some of them really want to do it themselves. And still others are like George Cukor, who won't look through a camera.

ALFRED LEBOVITZ: He's afraid of the camera.

MILTON KRASNER: Howard Hawks is a dream. We play golf on the set most of the time. You know what he did? He got a big net, and we used to stand around and hit golf balls into the net. The producer comes on set and says, "Is anybody doing anything here?" I said, "I don't know."

HOWARD SCHWARTZ: You did ten weeks of production and four weeks of golf.

JAMES WONG HOWE: I'll give you a little example of working with Howard Hawks. When I was working at Warner Bros., I was on his film *Air Force*. Howard Hawks was the director and a fine director and a wonderful man. Went down to Tampa, Florida. We had nine B-17s. This is during the war. We had nine B-17s down there for a movie. So he had a shot where they're supposed to be coming in to land. They're supposed to be in the Philippines or someplace. But we made it in Florida just after sunset. It was dusk. So I had to line up all my lights and get the generator. About two, three hours before the shot, I asked the electrician to hit the generator and light all the lights up to try it out, and he came back, he said, "Jimmy, the generator doesn't work." In an hour or so, those planes are going to come in, I said, "Howard, we're having problems." He said, "What's the problem, Jimmy?" I said, "Generator broke." He said, "Don't tell me that. That's not my problem. That's your problem."

I went to the special-effects man. I said, "Look, do we have any flares?" He said, "Yes." I said, "How many you got?" He said, "I got a flock of them." I said, "Great!" So what I did was to take the mirror off of the back of the lights and I hung them onto the reflector stands. I stuck the stick down with a flare in it. Had the electrician wire them up. We tried out a couple, and it worked. So here they're all lined up and here comes these planes and I said—if I ever prayed to Buddha—I told him to hit the switch and all these flares came on and they flickered and it was wonderful because the landing field was supposed to be on fire—in flame—during the war, you see? And the smoke from the flares drifted across. And these planes coming down with the landing lamps going through this smoke and the propeller swirling this smoke—it created a lot of drama. And Hawks saw the rushes. He saw the scene, and he said, "Gee, that's great,

Jimmy." He said, "Wonderful effect. Send the generator home—shooting this with all the flares—" So now, if the generator didn't break, I wouldn't have got this effect. And if Howard Hawks hadn't said, "It's *your* problem," I couldn't have added a big moment to the movie.

STANLEY CORTEZ: So much depends on your director and your relationship with him. We are the ones who solve the problems and create the effects, so the director must accept that and trust you and also have an ego that allows your own control. Charles Laughton was the director of a film I shot, *The Night of the Hunter*. He and I became the dearest of friends. We met in Paris and did many films together, and we enjoyed a very warm relationship. He would observe me doing a couple of things on my own, and he would say, "What in hell are you doing, Cortez?" I would say, "None of your goddamned business, Laughton!" All this in a nice, lovable way, don't get me wrong. The respect was there. Of course, he would insist I tell him what I was doing, but on *Night of the Hunter* I told him at one point that I was thinking of a piece of music for the scene when Robert Mitchum murders Shelley Winters. I told him it was "Valse Triste." And by God, his face turned purple and he said, "Stan, how right you are!" He immediately sent for the film's composer, Walter Schumann, and he came on the set for the purpose that Charles asked him to—to see and absorb what I was doing visually, so he could interpret it into a waltz tempo for the scene. This is a true story. With a director like Charles Laughton, you could stretch out your influence from your own area into another's, like from photography to music.

I think every creative cinematographer has a style. And from this style, he varies. He goes from this point to that point. There is a variance, but the style is basic.

FLOYD CROSBY: You know, I never thought in terms much of the style of photography in a picture. I created almost every individual scene with what the basic photographic requirements were for that scene, and I suppose that unconsciously I had a certain style of lighting that I followed more or less, but to me the requirements of the individual scene were much more important than trying to prefer any style of photography through a whole picture.

JAMES WONG HOWE: A lot of the regular directors in the studio system left the style of the movie's photography in the hands of the camera department. Not all of them, of course. Not your Hitchcocks, Capras, whoever. But stars were often vocal about cameramen.

HOWARD SCHWARTZ: The star system is not as prevalent today, but back then a star could push—or even insist on—a certain cameraman. Today it's more a situation where the director hires and chooses the cameraman and the star pulls less weight. Most of the stars today don't do that many pictures, and they don't do them for a specific studio under a contract. And the audience is perhaps not as star crazy, either. It's a different filmmaking world now. When Jimmy Howe was doing most of his work, one of the most important elements of a photographer's job was the look of the star. That mattered to the audience, so it mattered to the bosses. And, of course, it mattered to the stars themselves, and that could be a juggling issue.

JAMES WONG HOWE: When I came on the set for *The Prisoner of Zenda* [1937 version], I was faced with the star, Ronald Colman. He sits in front of the camera, and he feels strange because they've changed cameramen on him and I had never photographed him. The female star, Madeleine Carroll, I had shot her hair tests and she was very happy with how she looked in them, so she was fine. Colman took me to one side. He says, "Jimmy, my left side is the best, you see?" And Madeleine Carroll says her left side is the better. Now, I didn't know what to do, so I said, "Yes, Mr. Colman, I'll take care of that."

You see, besides being a cameraman and knowing the technique, and how to use a meter, and how to use different lenses, there are other things besides. You have to deal with personalities, especially stars, and it's the stars that can be the ones that can make you as a cameraman or can break you as a cameraman. If a star liked your work, the bosses put it in their contract. Like William Daniels. For many years, he was Greta Garbo's cameraman. She didn't want to do a film without him. So that gave him a great security. So when you were working in the old studios, you needed to know technique very well, but often you were not dealing as much in technique as you were in people in front of the camera: how to deal with them and how to deal with the director. The producer you don't see very much, so you can forget him. He's mostly the moneyman.

JOHN SEITZ: The duty of the cinematographer is to tell the story in the best way possible.

GEORGE FOLSEY: I don't think that a picture that is photographed in a manner that constantly keeps calling attention to the photography has served its purpose as photography. It should not do that. It should always tend to help the story, further the story, carry on the idea, and not in any way intrude upon it. You shouldn't be aware of the photography as such. You should be aware of the story and the plot and what's going on and how the people are doing it and the characterizations. The photography should be an adjunct to all that. It should not intrude itself. . . . People might say, "Oh, what a beautiful shot!" It should not be a beautiful shot if it isn't supposed to be a beautiful shot. I think the fundamental thing is still what it is about, what is the story. "The play's the thing." That was the idea in old Hollywood, anyway.

WRITERS

GEORGE SEATON: Nobody wants to talk about the writer's life in old Hollywood. When I first came to 20th Century–Fox, at that time there were seventy-six writers under contract at the studio and about forty-two directors. More writers than directors. Some of us were just brought out to Hollywood and allowed to vegetate. For instance, there's the famous story about William Faulkner. He was brought out and sat around, and he said one day, "Do you mind if I work at home?" They said, "No." So he went back to Oxford, Mississippi, and he was there for six months before anyone figured it out. His agent kept sending him checks the whole time.

Those were pretty lush days in the studios, right after the Depression. This was just after Roosevelt came in, and a lot of money was pumped into the economy. I suppose people who were out of work had nothing to do except go to the movies to kill a couple of hours, but in those days, you just couldn't lose money on a film. The studios couldn't make them fast enough, and because of that, lots of writers were hired and brought to Hollywood without any plan for what to do with them.

HENRY HATHAWAY: A producer's job in those days was to hire writers, lots of them, and get scripts done so that as soon as a director who was under contract finished a picture and was free, they could call him in and say, "This is what you're going to do tomorrow." Yes, it was a factory. I worked for Fox for twenty years as a contract director and never turned down one script that they gave me. I'd figure out some way to make it, and I was never restricted from changing it. How do you think the writer or writers liked that? Not much, I would say.

GEORGE SEATON: They hired us as "junior writers," paying us at the same scale, and just threw us together in random pairs and told us what to do. One junior writer that I was thrown together with to make us a team was Robert Pirosh. They said to us—and we barely knew each other—"You fellows better think of something because your options are coming up." That meant if we didn't come up with something, we'd be let go. So we just took a thing they had called *The Winning Ticket*, and we wrote it. In those days, you did what you were told to do. You wrote it.

DONALD OGDEN STEWART: Toots, they owned you. You were a commodity. They would give me a script to write, and I would function along with the director and the producer and the star and everything else in the creation of something. I didn't ever think it was mine.

GEORGE SEATON: There was a guy around who just came up with ideas. That's all he did. A man called Hopkins. Hoppy. He never had an office, but he was an "idea man." He'd go on the lot and call up a producer and say, "I've got an idea. How about a picture called *San Francisco*?" Many times he'd stop us on our way to lunch, and he'd say, "I've got an idea for a thing called *Snug Harbor*." I think that one was about a commune of old vaudevillians. We worked on that. We worked on so many scripts that never materialized or went anywhere, but we were getting paid. And we were learning how things were done and learning the lingo that the business used. Hal Roach said, "We have a script here for Laurel and Hardy, and we're going to make a feature out of it. But it was written by gag writers, and they don't know English . . . so you two fellows put it into English." That was our job: "Put it into English." It was quite an experience, because we read the script and it was sort of film business shorthand. It said, "Ollie gives Stan the office." You'd have to have a glossary to figure this out. Or "Stan gives Ollie half an Oakie." So we had to go to one of the writers and ask him to tell us what it meant. Giving somebody the office meant tipping them off. "Half an Oakie" was based on Jack Oakie's triple take. Stan Laurel used to do a take and a half. There were so many things like that to learn.

WALTER REISCH: Talkies inspired all the studios to hire lots of writers, especially big-name writers. At MGM, on the second floor, which was the writers' floor, there were doors carrying names like Anita Loos, Michael Arlen, Donald Ogden Stewart, Charlie MacArthur, Ludwig Bemelmans, and I was proud to be one of them. There were the Spewacks, the Hacketts, and anybody who had a name. Paul Osborn, Claudine West, Alice Duer Miller, who wrote *The White Cliffs of Dover*. It was an endless procession of great names, and really and truly, with the exception of James Hilton, who at that time also had an office there, they did not know how to write an original story for a motion picture. Either it was beneath their dignity or they didn't have the knack to do it.

WALDO SALT: When sound came in, Goldwyn went right after George Bernard Shaw. I worked with Ogden Nash for a year. F. Scott Fitzgerald was working for Joe Mankiewicz, and I was, too. Fitzgerald was a very sweet man and very modest, extraordinarily modest. It was toward the end of his career, and he was trying not to drink. And he wore an overcoat and rubbers to the studio in the summer. He was a friend of Ogden Nash's. That's how he got the job.

DONALD OGDEN STEWART: Fitzgerald really didn't understand movies.

H. N. SWANSON: Neither did Faulkner. He had a drinking problem, too, but he was a god to all the writers. He had no interest in motion pictures, really. But those two were narrative writers, not dramatic writers. They both tried, but they didn't understand the medium.

WALTER REISCH: The men who at that time dominated and ruled Hollywood did the right thing in not leaving it all up to one man, as they do today. The results today are very sad—the so-called *auteur* directors who write everything, direct everything, cut and edit everything themselves—the end results turn out to be lopsided, cockeyed. The results are not always 100 percent happy when one of these "great" directors does everything himself. There is no control, no supervision. The pictures we made at MGM in the studio system conquered the earth for one reason: whether right or wrong, the attitude of those dialogue writers towards the original stories was unmolested by their own vanity, had an open mind towards them, a critical distance. It wasn't their own stories the writers had to defend, to improve upon, or to polish. So they had detachment. Thus all the departments together under the producer and director, with the objective control by the studio . . . it just worked like a beautiful Swiss clock, the whole MGM machinery. I laughed—and so did everyone—at New York reviews that referred to us as a "factory" because two or three writers' names always appeared on a script. *That's* why it worked. It took collaboration. I made myself an integral part of the whole machinery.

PANDRO BERMAN: While I can well understand the anguish that writers suffered during the days when there were four and five and six writers on a film, I must say I also understand the predicament of the producer who time after time would find he couldn't get a good screenplay from *a* writer and had to get certain values from other writers. I recall many instances where a collaboration was the only way you could get a successful result.

HENRY HATHAWAY: Harold [Hurley] had an idea about scripts. To make them fast and get the best out of them, he was going to have four writers work on one script. There was gonna be a guy to do the plot, a guy to write the love story, a guy to write the heavy, and a guy to write the comedy. I got a script for a western out of the deal that had the love story written by Joe

Mankiewicz, the plot by Bill McNutt, and the comedy by Nunnally Johnson. These were the guys that had just come to the studio to go to work. When I read the love story, I went to Harold and said, "Jesus Christ, this is great. He's probably getting Herman [Mankiewicz] to write his stuff for him." We always thought that Joe was getting his stuff written by Herman, and we found out later that Herman was getting his stuff written by Joe.

PANDRO BERMAN: Certain collaborations came about where they'd bring a talented man like Sam Behrman out here from the stage, a man who knew nothing about motion pictures, and team him with some very, very competent craftsman like Sonya Levien. They made a very successful combination, she supplying the screen construction technique and he supplying the creative ideas.

WALTER REISCH: The story of my Hollywood career as a writer is simple. Whenever they needed construction—a beginning, a new middle, and, more than anything else, a new ending or a finale (which they never had, you know)—I was called in. Fortunately, I was always teamed with a very important dialogue writer. This was their great forte in Hollywood: these people could write magnificent words, beautiful lines, but somehow they always lacked a sense of story construction. I was always called in to write a story, to invent characters, to give the outline scene by scene as in a shooting script. And I could write exactly within the budget they were going to shell out for a picture. If they'd allocated, say, $1.2 million, which at that time was a lot of money, I could write exactly 150 pages that would cost exactly that.

RANALD MACDOUGALL: They wanted me to collaborate. That was the way things were done. Committee writing. It was incomprehensible to me that two or three people could work on something, that a screenplay was a group effort. I did collaborate for about a week with a fellow. We sat down, and it took longer for me to explain to him what I had in mind than it did to sit there and write it and show it to him. I found myself writing for a fellow writer. So I couldn't collaborate, and I never have since and never did after that. At that time, however, when I first started in the studio system, it was quite commonplace and ordinary and the usual thing for every film to have four, five, six, seven writers.

WALTER REISCH: I can work with any collaborator, man or woman, famous or not famous. I don't care. I can adapt myself to any possibility. I can say this without any false modesty. The reason why I have a record of at least eighty or ninety pictures, silent and talkie, and am still around (although I am not that old for an old-timer) is that I can adapt myself to any personality. If I'm assigned by Lubitsch to write for him, I'm writing a Lubitsch picture, and if I'm working for King Vidor, I'm not writing a Lubitsch picture for him, I'm writing a King Vidor picture. When I worked for Charles Brackett, I never wrote a story which Cecil B. DeMille could have made. I wrote for a Charles Brackett production, adapting myself cleverly, I must say, to the tastes of that man, not only because I liked him but because it was easier to convince him if I worked towards his style. If you had come to Lubitsch with a Hitchcock set-up, he wouldn't have made it. You had to come to him with a Lubitsch idea, and the scenes had to be Lubitsch-wise, and so forth. That is why, for instance, I've never worked for my oldest friend—and I am *his* oldest friend—Billy Wilder, who in the meantime has become a very famous director in his own right. For twenty-five years he never asked me and he never let me write a screenplay for him. Why? Because the things I know he knows, too. He wouldn't get anything new out of it. He knows how to write a well-made screenplay, he does not believe in dirt, he does not send out messages. In short, he makes total entertainment, and for that, unfortunately, he doesn't need me. But I worked on all his pictures as a constructionist sub rosa as a friend, and he helped me with my stories sometimes. However, I've never had my name on a Billy Wilder–*directed* picture. Many people ask me how come and why, and that is the answer: whatever I can give him, he knows himself.

BILLY WILDER: I write with a partner, and the question I always get is: When there are two names, three names on a screenplay, does one write one scene and the other another scene, and then you meet every Tuesday and compare? Or does one write the action and the other write the dialogue? I'm already very gratified if anybody asks that question, because most of them think the actors make up the words. So the mere fact that they ask, "Which one of you two writes the dialogue and which one writes the action?"—that already is a high compliment.

CHARLTON HESTON: A screenwriter has to recognize that film is a collaborative undertaking. You can't write a film script totally in the typewriter. This is a highly controversial point, and the next time you have a writer in front of you, quote me and hear how mad it makes him. But there are things that are true about a film script that you aren't going to find out by typing it again and again and again and again and talking about it. You've got to be there on the ground. The economics of film deny the writer the opportunity to collaborate at that stage. He's long gone and been paid off, and his phone number's been taken out of the Rolodex. It becomes more the director's responsibility, and also I feel, of course, that an actor should be able to make a contribution. Part of my equipment is an ear for language, for the way people talk, the way people from different regions phrase things. I can contribute. I've also done a great many period films, and in period films, speech is extremely difficult to bring off. Many very good writers have no ear for it at all. When I first began in films, they still used to write some of those pictures in what they called "MGM Medieval." There'd be Tony Curtis saying "Yonder lies the castle of my father. Gladly will he give us shelter." The actor who finally has to say something like that and make it work is faced with a very special problem in projecting a character or situation from a remote time period, and some improvisation or discussion on the set with the director can be a good thing.

KARL STRUSS: The writers are usually not around. They write it, and that's it. They're sent away.

BUDD SCHULBERG: I believe very strongly that one of the evils of the Hollywood system is that the writer turns in a script, and they can't wait to take him off of the payroll. I do think that the writer should be right with the director all of the time, as is true in the theaters, to make changes and alterations as it unfolds. But in movies, you can't stop to alter the script to best accentuate the actor's attributes. You end up with something sort of plastic in the course of making the film.

DONALD OGDEN STEWART: I was a commodity, as I said. I was paid by the week. A writer really had very little say after he turned in his script. He just had to wait and see if they liked it or if Norma Shearer liked it or Lana Turner liked it or if the director liked it. The writer couldn't defend his script. He was the lowest cog, really, next to the electrician or the cameraman. The first thing you had to learn was not to let them break your heart. Don't care so much about what you're giving them. Because if you had creative feelings—like we all did—you could get your heart broken.

BILLY WILDER: I work with someone who can give me something . . . anything. People want to know our writing plan. Our plan? How we plan out what we do every day and how we work. In our case [working with I. A. L. Diamond], it's very prosaic. It sounds very dull. We meet at, say, nine thirty in the morning and open shop, you know, like bank tellers, and we sit there in one room. We read *Hollywood Reporter* and *Variety*, exchange the trades, and then we just stare at each other. Sometimes nothing happens. Sometimes it just goes on until twelve thirty, and then I'll ask him, "How about a drink?" and he nods, and then we have a drink and go to lunch. Or sometimes we come in full of ideas. Let's say we have finished in the middle of a scene the evening before—we open shop and we close shop, you know. This is not the muses coming through the windows and kissing our brows. It's very hard work, and having done both, I tell you that directing is a pleasure and writing is a drag. I mean, directing can become difficult, but it is a pleasure because you have something to work with: you can put the camera here or there. You can interpret the scene this way or that way. The readings can be such or such. But writing is just an empty page. You start with nothing, absolutely nothing, and I think, as a rule, writers are vastly underrated and underpaid. It is totally impossible to make a great picture out of a lousy script. It is impossible, on the other hand, for a mediocre director to screw up a great script altogether.

I. A. L. DIAMOND: A writer named Hal Kanter once wrote a monologue for Groucho Marx which had the following line: "Who needs writers? Give me a competent director and two intelligent actors, and at the end of eight weeks I will show you three of the most nervous people you ever saw."

HENRY BLANKE: I knew other writing teams. Ivan Goff and Ben Roberts worked for me for years. They had a system of their own, which is a very tough one to make work. They split the script. The first one does his scene, and the following scene was done by the other one. That way, they are both writing for the same characters all the way through. Goff writes dialogue for the same characters that Roberts writes for. Each character has a style in the way of talking, and both writers can do it. They maintain the style in the way of talking . . . you know what I mean, you and I talk differently. The way they did it was they went over everything together, and they read aloud to each other what was written. And then they made corrections, each of them, on the scenes they were responsible for if the dialogue didn't match. They made that work. It was hard to do, but it worked for them.

FRANK CAPRA: As a director, I work together with a writer, and you spark each other, you know. And when you get somebody that you're really in cahoots with, why, that works just wonderfully, because you're your own audience and your own entertainer. But also, I work a long time on the script in preparation, a long, long time—maybe five months, six months, writing the script. I may throw it away, throw all the scenes away, but the body of it is there and the idea is there, the structure is there, because I don't fool with that structure, I only fool with details. So a great deal of preparation goes into it. What I look for is entertainment, interesting characters, interesting people, and a writer who can spark me.

WALTER REISCH: The spark of inspiration is if a producer calls you in and says he has a certain actor and wants you to write for this actor. I am a tailor: I can make tailor-made "clothes," and this is my great preference. If a producer calls me in and says, "I have Lilian Harvey or Clifton Webb or

Joan Collins or Greta Garbo," my mind immediately functions in that direction. Half the battle is won. It's all geared towards a personality. One of my biggest successes was when Gable was at MGM and L. B. Mayer called me in and said, "We need a story for Gable," and I wrote the original script of *Comrade X*. You write *exactly* for that guy, you know, and they read it with Gable in mind, and, as I say, half the battle is won. That is my favorite starting point.

ABRAHAM POLONSKY: If you wrote a screenplay that actually described the movie, it would be maybe twenty or thirty volumes long. If every single thing that had to be done by the director and the cameraman and the editor and the art designer and the costumer and everybody else were described in the screenplay, it would be the *Encyclopaedia Britannica*.

WALTER REISCH: I've no real method. I'm a man without any message. I don't care. I can write in an airplane, in a train, in a hotel deluxe, in a motel, anywhere that a down payment may be expected. I can dictate it, or I can write it by hand. I can adapt books, and deep down I'm an original story writer. I believe in the well-made film, but not necessarily. I can write anything as long as somebody wants it. Just give me a topic or a title, say it's the frame around this picture on the wall, and I can tell you right now a mystery story with a beginning, a climax, and an ending. From my earliest beginnings, I've been a motion picture man. The next step is if somebody says, "I have money to make a film . . . have you got an idea?" Nothing is more inspiring to a motion picture man than to hear a man say, "Here's a down payment!"

ABRAHAM POLONSKY: In the studio system, this business of Hollywood, there's a conventional attitude toward the form of the screenplay. You mustn't have too much text on one page. There mustn't be too much description, because they get bored when they read words. Out here they hate words.

WALTER REISCH: Your plan has to fit the system.

RANALD MACDOUGALL: You know, screenwriting is basically a problem-solving exercise. You have a little problem, and you solve it. And you have another one, and you solve it. And you have another one and another one, but by the time you get through, hopefully, you've solved the problem. When you take a novel and you are going to dramatize it, the description by the novelist is what's happening in people's minds. Your problem in straightening out the example is how to express that outwardly so that it will photograph.

HENRY BLANKE: During the thirties and into the forties, screenwriters were often switched away from a picture they were assigned to, and someone else came in on it, so you ended up with several uncredited writers. I never, never switched. I never switched. Once a writer started, I kept him on. I never took a writer off a script once I had assigned him. A writer that started had to do the finished job. I never believe in switching writers, which other people do, especially nowadays. That's impossible. Either the script is good or it's bad, but not several writers, please. Every writer, unfortunately, through the Writers Guild rules, must write a certain percent—I think it's at least 25 percent of the script—in order to get screen credit for it. So every writer you bring in on a script throws everything you have out and does it all over again in order to get 100 percent of the credit. It's a terrible sin in this business. It's like the John Ford story that everyone tells. You know, someone comes to his set and tells him, "You are sixty days behind schedule," and he takes the written script and tears it in half and throws half away and says, "Now I'm on schedule." And he was. He was.

HENRY KING: You must understand about screenwriting . . . when everything is decided upon and ready and the finished script comes out and mimeographed, that script is put on the schedule for production. It goes into the system, and it's not about the writer anymore.

GEORGE SEATON: Every writer working in a script department in the old studio system learned what it was all about. There was maximum support for you to get it done as fast as possible. When you were finished, you could take it to the end of the hall in the writers' building, and there was somebody waiting to type it for you. You didn't have a secretary as you worked, but when you were ready, they were ready. When your script . . . or the one you and your collaborators and maybe the other writers who were brought in, all of you together . . . the one that you had turned out had been finally approved and finally typed and copied, you had gotten it ready to go on a journey away from you and out of your life.

HENRY KING: You see, the head of the Art Department gets maybe two copies of a final, approved script. Men's Wardrobe and Ladies' Wardrobe get a copy of it. The Transportation Department gets a copy of it. The Construction Department gets a copy of it. Every department head gets a copy of this, and they read it. Now, you have a long room that's a rectangle with a long table across the end of it. The director sits in the middle of the long table, and he has his assistants sit over here, and you have the studio executive sit over here on either side of the director. All through the middle of the room are the department heads. Transportation wants to ask you so many questions. You have to sit there, and Transportation says, "I note on such-and-such a location, how many people you're going to have. Are these people going to be housed there, or where are you going to house them?" He's got to figure what kind of transportation you'll have for that. The Animal man over here says, "How many horses are you going to use for so-and-so and so-and-so?" "How many automobiles are you going to have there?" Wardrobe has a budget made out. "You're going to change the clothes at such-and-such and such-and-such a time. All right. Now, we figure in these fourteen sequences, there'll be fourteen changes of costume." You'll say, "Don't you think we can double back on a costume from here to here? We can be very consistent. And the men's costumes, the same thing." Now you sit and answer all the questions they have in there. The Assistant Director has what you call a breakdown sheet, and on page so-and-so, such-and-such, it tells you what's going to be in it. Everyone has all that. Then they ask you questions about it. From this, each one from every department makes up a budget. Then you add all that budget together. Then the headaches start! You may think I'm not talking about the script, but I am. You need a good working agreement between all the departments, and the Writing Department is only one of them. If you handle yourself right, all the departments are for you.

The department that often feels the least happy is the Writing Department, especially if that writer was only one guy. When you're bringing a story to life with props and clothes and lights and actors and music and so many elements, it often changes or doesn't look the way the writer envisioned. He's only one part of the whole, the whole collaboration. But all of us—and usually the writer, too—all of us were always trying to make the best picture that we could possibly make, turn the script into the best it could possibly be. You can't be lazy and make good pictures, and you don't make them alone, either. Everybody adds something to the story . . . and the script is one piece of that collaboration.

Picture making is not a haphazard, catch-as-catch-can thing. It's all thought out and carefully debated. And ideas can come from anywhere, ideas that end up in the picture. I've had people in the Property Department come up with some tremendous ideas. There's a famous scene in one of my movies, *Margie*, in which the young heroine, Jeanne Crain, sits in a bathtub, taking a bath and singing. Props turned it into a gigantic bubble bath, all their idea, and they had to solve the problem of the bubbles, when they would hit her, how they would float in the air, and could they make them bounce? *They* thought it up and *they* made it work, and when people talk about *Margie* or choose stills from it, it's always the bubble bath scene, which ended up in *Life* magazine. The props guy wrote the bubbles, not the writer.

EDITORS

RICHARD SCHICKEL: One of the most important aspects of any movie is the editing. And yet you hear so little about any individual editors from the studio system era. Margaret Booth, of course, the grand dame of it all . . . but mostly you hear about specific directors and their ideas about cutting and how they worked with an editor or whatever.

MARGARET BOOTH: I worked all my life as an editor, but I never became head of the editorial department. I was the supervising editor of all the pictures made at MGM. I had offices, and I had influence, but I didn't have anything to do with the hiring of cutters or daily problems or budgets or departmental business. I used to tell them I wanted such-and-such editors on such-and-such pictures . . . I could choose . . . but being the head of Editorial . . . to keep books and make release prints up . . . that didn't interest me. Mine was an artistic job. I was a creative editor, not a businessperson or an office manager. A department head was more a businessman than a cutter. Garbo's *Camille* was the last picture I ever sat at the bench and actually cut. I had a projection room of my own at MGM . . . Room F . . . and I used to supervise all the editing of all the pictures.

JOHNNY GREEN: Margaret and I were very close friends. I learned 90 percent of what I know about film from her. She was the supervising editor at Metro from the time it first came over from Mission Road, going back to 1924. She's a very, very old lady now, but she's still working and is the supervising editor for Ray Stark. She had a mind for editing. She knew how few frames it could take to make a difference.

MITCHELL LEISEN: Cutting is of vital importance. Six frames in a cut can make a great deal of difference, whether the film is smooth or jerky. You must always cut on a movement, not a static scene. I mean, cut on a movement of the person you're cutting away from to the other person you're cutting to. It need only be the lift of an eyebrow or a suspended motion, but as long as there is movement going on, you are less conscious of the cut. Directors need to know this, and you'd be surprised how many don't. But editors know it. They're there to help. The old system gave the producer or director editors to help you, to carry out what you'd planned.

DEDE ALLEN: There were very, very prestigious women in the 1930s who were editing in Hollywood. But of my generation, very few women became prominent editors. When I started in 1943, it was right after the Depression, during World War II. I got a lot of good breaks, and I worked very hard to make them work. That's what it takes. You know, in the olden days, especially in Europe, montage was always done by women. It was considered women's work. Very few men were editors, but there were a lot of husband-wife editing teams. The woman was the negative cutter and the husband was the positive cutter, and later the woman would become a positive editor.

GEOFFREY SHURLOCK: I became a Scenario Editor at Paramount. They were very well organized at that studio, and they told you how to get the job you wanted. B. P. Schulberg told me how to get the title of Scenario Editor: "You've got a pretty good analytical mind. Go read every script, and make me a sequence analysis. I want you to tell me in fifteen lines how much the section in each sequence develops the plot of the story . . . or tell me instead if it's deadwood as far as the plot is concerned." That was *his* definition of editing. You could read it on the page.

ROBERT WISE: I was a film editor before I became a director. Yes, I am the man who edited *Citizen Kane* and took over to finish *Magnificent Ambersons*. An editing department was, to my mind, of primary importance in the creation of any motion picture. In editing you deal in much of the visual sense of the film—in composition, camerawork, coverage, all of that. In the old days, the strong editing departments of the studios helped a director not have to be concerned about how to physically treat scenes on the set or how he was going to handle the camera. For instance, as an editor I was sent to the stage to stand by Garson Kanin when he directed *My Favorite Wife*. Gar had come fairly recently from the stage and had done only a couple of small films. He was very uneasy and unsure about how he handled the camera and how he put his scenes on film, so he always had an editor on the set. This function of an editing department on set support for a director has largely been overlooked in film history.

PETER BOGDANOVICH: Probably the central thing I heard from almost all the old directors I spoke to—Ford, Hawks, Hitchcock, Lang, Dwan, McCarey—was that they basically cut in the camera. Generally, the old masters didn't shoot a lot of coverage. I saw Ford put his hand over the camera lens one time as if to say, "That's enough." These guys knew where they were going to cut when they were shooting the scene. Being young in the business, I assumed that was the way everybody did it, but I found out later that some directors, like Capra and [George] Stevens, would shoot a lot of coverage.

ALFRED HITCHCOCK: How much work do I leave for an editor? None. This is the point. It seems to me an extraordinary thing—I hope there are no cutters present—that you have, say, $6 million of film, and it might get into the hands of a very indifferent editor. That's a problem.

ALLAN DWAN: When you're directing, you're working with a pair of scissors in your mind all the time. You're always thinking ahead. You take care of problems on the set.

FRANK CAPRA: Film is a funny thing. You can take a series of five scenes, and there are perhaps twenty-five ways you can put them together. But there's probably only one way that makes any sense, and you've got to find that one way. It's almost like music. If you put the notes of a piece of music together, you get something wonderful, but if you take those same notes and alter them a little bit, you get dreck. It's the same way with scenes. You get a chance to compose in the cutting room. A film is made both on the set and in the cutting room. But if I didn't want a shot I made on the set in the film, I wouldn't have let that shot get into the cutting room. You can improve a film in the cutting room, but you can't find a great, great film on the table, because you're only working with what you brought in. Never bring in anything someone else could use to ruin your picture.

HENRY BLANKE: As a producer, I closely supervised the editing of all my films. I watched every foot of film cut. Most of the directors, with the exception of Lubitsch, came in and you showed them the finished product. John Ford oversaw the editing, and maybe somebody like Flaherty. But those directors are very few. I learned about editing. Characters could bore an audience stiff no matter how fast the picture moved. Don't mistake fast cutting for tempo. Each character has to have his inner tempo. If you are fascinated by a story, by the characters, it can be as slow as you want, but if the audience doesn't care, they start yawning or walk out on you no matter how fast you cut. Tempo is only what is in the story and the characters. If they fascinate you, it seems fast. But if they bore you, fast cutting can't fix it. Fast cutting can be of great advantage if you want to show a montage of something, but that's a different thing. Tempo, of course, is also part of the writing of the script.

ROBERT WISE: One of the things you have to remember—and it's difficult for actors, and particularly stage actors, and even I have to remind myself of all this all the time—it's that there is a tempo for the overall picture and a tempo for a particular scene. It's very easy to play a given scene for its own value, play it for the fullest in terms of the actors and performance, only to find that in its place in reel five, that it may be a little slow. Rarely do you find yourself saying "Gee, I wish I played it slower." It's always the other way. Dick Wallace, an old-time director, once told me, "Bobby, I've only got one piece of advice to give you. If it seems a little slow on the set, it will be twice as slow in the projection room."

GEORGE CUKOR: We directors now have the right to make the first cut of our pictures. And even when in the past, we didn't, I always stuck my nose in. I was right in there. At times I was overridden, and I yelled and yelled. But the final cut—the actual cut—was always the property of the studio. They owned it and had certain rights over it. I never found them to be blatantly against your cut. I'll tell you something about the old tycoons who are supposed to be such villains. They were showmen and perfectly practical men. If you had anything good, they wanted it, and they also handled you in a certain way, and I don't think there was all that bullying that people talk about. "How did you work in that terrible system?" Well, the pictures you see from the 1930s and 1940s were done under that system. They were smart, clever people. You give a little, and you take a little. And you paid attention to your precious first cut.

BILLY WILDER: Any first cut of the picture makes you feel suicidal. It's just the worst moment of your life . . . but then you start cutting and a little music comes in, and then you kind of polish it and it's all worth it.

SAM FULLER: I stand over the editor. Very few guys do that. I just like to do that. I myself am a very bad cutter. I can fall in love with the scene and then hang on to it, but I want to be there for every choice.

CHARLTON HESTON: George Stevens said, "Every time you make a cut, you let blood out."

MERIAN C. COOPER: Whoever cuts a picture has to be real tough, you know, because to somebody . . . it may be the director, the producer, the actor, or the writer . . . some scene is so close to their hearts and so good . . . they just can't bear to see it go. And they'll fight you for it.

SAM FULLER: Film *editing* is really what it is: it's editing. Cutting things out and deciding.

COSTUME

MITCHELL LEISEN: Two of the most important departments, because they involved the overall look of the film, its appeal to the female audience, and, of course, the working relationship with the stars, were the costume and makeup departments. The producer couldn't neglect them, no matter how little interest he might have in clothes and lipstick.

CHARLES LEMAIRE: I had complete charge of the costume department at 20th Century–Fox. I wanted to run a department and not design clothes anymore. I'd had *that* career. I wanted to run a big department and be able to see that the pictures from my shop were better costumed than all the other pictures I had seen. I believed that the greatest costume shop would be run by a man who would get the best possible people and let them do the best possible thing they could do. My contract read that I was responsible for everything that was put on the screen, everything that appeared there regarding clothing and costumes. Zanuck put it in my contract that I had absolute charge, and so I came to Fox and installed myself as department head for costuming.

The department, when I arrived, had a bit of a bad reputation, and

I wanted to learn what that was all about. For the first two weeks, I did nothing but look at the last motion pictures that had been made there. Day and night, until in the morning, I looked at *all* of the last pictures, and I saw they needed someone in costumes very badly. There was no coordination. Nothing looked right. Everything was wrong. It was just wrong. So what did I do? I fired no one in the department. I allowed everyone to stay. I'd heard many things about the intoxicated wardrobe girls and that this wasn't going well and that wasn't going well, but finally, after I'd been there two or three weeks, I called a meeting in the workroom and I said, "I am the new boss, and I'll tell you how I work. I like everything to go like it's supposed to go. You cannot drink on the lot, ever, and you cannot come to the lot intoxicated. You cannot come in at ten minutes after nine. You have to be here at nine, and if you're supposed to be on the set at seven, you have to be there at seven," et cetera. "And as far as the sewing rooms are concerned, I insist on very sanitary conditions. I have been in all the workrooms of the best designers in New York, and I know how they work. *That* is how *we* will work. Now that I've explained this to you, if you feel unhappy, you may leave. Come to me and tell me you want to go. I won't fire you unless I have to. I would rather you decided to leave on your own." One by one, they decided. Many left, and soon everything was going very well and they all knew what I wanted and what I expected. I then had a wonderful group, and I had set up a proper costume shop. And I was the boss. My job was to see that any costume you had on the screen was appropriate . . . that it looked good on the star . . . that it was there on time for filming and was fit correctly . . . and, above all, that it was affordable within our budget. That was the studio way.

It was always about the department in the studio system. There was a department for everything, and we worked on the films we were assigned. First, we collaborated in our own department, working under the department head, and then we sent what he approved to the producer of any one film. And everyone was there every day. My costume designers were under term contract. They were paid regularly, not hired on a job-by-job effort. There were no layoffs for down times. It gave them security. They knew a check was coming in. They knew they had a job, they knew they had something to plan for, and they were never afraid they were going to lose their jobs. We were too busy in the department! And since we were all there together every day, every week, we learned from each other and had time to develop ideas and specific strengths in design.

I had arrived at just the right time. I came to Fox when the studio—and Hollywood in general—was moving into the plush, lush years of the motion picture. Oh, God. There were times when our department was doing hundreds of clothes for ten and twelve films at a time. I built up a great stock of costumes for future use. Central Casting sent you extras who got an extra seven dollars if they wore their own clothes, so often they didn't want to wear your stock, because they lost the seven dollars, you know, but you could instruct Central Casting that these people would not be wearing their own clothes. We kept enough modern clothes in stock to be able to dress a crowd the way we wanted. Of course, if you had two hundred people . . . I could dress a hundred of them, but I couldn't dress the other hundred. You'd put those hundred you didn't dress the farthest away if they were wearing the wrong thing or something you didn't like. Sometimes if they were wearing the wrong thing, you sent them home. If they were told not to wear black or told not to wear purple, you sent them home even if they were the sister of the casting director . . . you sent them home. "Go home."

You had to think when you were using stock. Would the clothes be recognizable from other films, or would they not fit in well in the background? But you know, over all my years, I never have had anyone say, "You used that stuff in" a particular film. I never had a producer say, "I remember that from another picture." I never remember a viewer, a theatergoer, writing in to say, "Oh, I see you used that pink dress again." Never. I always knew where the costume came from. I don't think producers or directors ever knew. They arrived on the set, and the director would look things over and say, "Fine. Let's go to work." You could even use a star's former costume in the background. A dress that had originally created a lot of attention could be made over with the bodice changed or the hemline raised or a veil added or something. Well, one time a star was not fooled. A costume house called us and said they had the entire Loretta Young wardrobe made for *The Men in Her Life*. They had never been able to use any of them because they were so distinct, so they wanted to sell them to us if we wanted them. I made a price and bought them all and used them all. But there was a very special dress with tiger lilies embroidered all over it. I veiled the whole thing with two layers of net, and no one recognized it . . . except, of course, Loretta Young. She remembered it. It wasn't even the tiger lilies . . . it was the cut of the bodice. She said, "You didn't fool me with that one."

EDITH HEAD: A good designer is responsible for every costume worn by everybody on the set of the film she's assigned to—unless, of course, it's a mob scene or something you shoot out in the streets in real life. And a good designer is responsible for the director's feelings. He should feel when he comes on the set that he can go ahead and shoot and not have to say, "Move that lady in the bright orange dress with a purple flower out of the way." You know, movie costumes weren't just about making good-looking clothes.

We designed sometimes what we called backgrounders, a dress that you didn't want anybody to notice. All of my clothes are specifically designed mostly for the star, but I also am in charge of actresses' clothes for actors who are not as important as the star. Either way, I always try to emphasize the girl rather than the costume she's wearing. But a "background dress" meant that the dress is there, unnoticeable for story reasons. A good designer tries to still have that dress work for the story.

In contrast to the backgrounder dress, you would design the deliberate eye-catcher dress. The eye-catcher is for where the woman comes in the room and the dress is supposed to be noticed for itself, for reasons of story and character. Like Grace Kelly's first appearance in *Rear Window*. And then we made dresses that were mood dresses. If you have a mood dress, it's because the tempo in the scene is to be played, and so the garment would be a quiet dress. In other words, if it's a mood dress, it shouldn't have a lot of crisp ruffles and frippery. It should be a simple dress, a soft dress. It's a very fine distinction, but any designer who works with an intelligent director can get his directive easily. He might say, "I want a quiescent look." Or, "In this scene, it's necessary that I have an aggressive dress" or that "the dress dominates the scene." These are just words, of course, but a director can give you a word picture of what he wants and you need to be able to understand him. I liked to do the deliberate eye-catcher dresses.

MITCHELL LEISEN: My biggest problem after I became a director, having been both an art director *and* a costume designer, was that I couldn't get them to do anything for me. They said, "You do it. Tell us what you want, and we'll make it for you." So the result was that half the stuff Edith Head got credit for were my own designs. I had to go up to the art department or the costume department and sketch out what I wanted. It took me a long time to get them to go on their own. I never took credit, but I almost always designed the dresses in every one of my pictures. Edith used to take all the bows.

They had a fashion show at a big dinner party the costume designers gave, and Edith Head showed a dress that Travis Banton had done for Mae West and claimed it was hers. And she also then announced that the most beautiful dress that was ever made for the movies, which was the mink dress from *Lady in the Dark*, which *I* did and she had nothing to do with, was her own design. My table practically got up and threw things at her. And I sent her a wire the next day and said, "With fifteen Oscars, do you have to claim other people's clothes as your own?"

CHARLES LEMAIRE: Department heads got credit on a film for the costumes whether they designed them or not. This led to some hard feelings and rivalries. I took the title "director of wardrobe." On the screen you saw "Director of Wardrobe Charles LeMaire." Not costume designer or whatever. Then you saw "Costumes Designed By Bonnie Cashin," which meant that Bonnie did the clothes for the principal people, sometimes also for some of the people in secondary roles. Oftentimes, due to money or time constraints, she might have to take something out of stock and redo it, but she designed the movie's clothes. The look of the men and the women that were on the screen was put there by the director of wardrobe, who at times *might* also have designed the picture. Bonnie was working under me in my department, and I chose her to do certain films, so I was responsible for the overall look, but if she designed, I gave her credit for designing. Edith never did that.

EDITH HEAD: A great many films are made nowadays where you do not have designers. The actresses and actors wear their own clothes, or they have people who go out and shop for the clothes. I think that's impossible.

JEAN LOUIS: The costume designer was so important! I would read the script, and after I read it, I had to know who was the star. You can't make clothes for somebody you don't know! You can't just "make a design." If it's Rita Hayworth or if it's Lucille Ball or if it's Joan Crawford, it's a different woman. Of course, her character may be rich or poor or old or young, but clothes are personal and must fit a body correctly. You can't buy that off the rack.

EDITH HEAD: Years ago, we transmitted the mood of the actress to the audience by the way we dressed them. We were so much a part of the storytelling image. If we had a girl in a low-cut, tight-fitting black gown, you know, she was a sexy girl in the right mood. If we had the Mary Pickford image, the girl in white organdy with ruffles, she was innocent. Today directors want you to play against the mood in costuming. They don't want to telegraph to the audience that we are about to have a sad scene. We don't want people to know it's going to be a love scene. You know, we used to do what we called "moonlight and roses." Carole Lombard was about to be proposed to by Clark Gable, so we would put her in a lovely, soft, fluffy chiffon dress, even if the movie were black-and-white. It seemed that the dress was pink and there was moonlight and then the music—the sound of violins and everything—and people said, "Aha! It's going to be a love scene." So what is important here is that then or now, the costumer has to get that decision from the director or whether you are supposed to help the mood, show the mood, or work against the mood and surprise the audience with your clothes. People don't wear a black dress because they're gonna get killed later that day. In the old days, we telegraphed: the white horse, the white hat, you know.

JEAN LOUIS: When Rita Hayworth was pregnant in *Down to Earth*, we had some challenges. Sometimes she just covered her middle with her hands. But we had to be clever with the costumes when stars were expecting. There were a lot of big purses and muffs designed to be held in front of movie stars. And lines created on tops to disguise the fact that the waistline was thicker than usual.

WALTER PLUNKETT: Kathryn Grayson had a big bust. Designing for her could be a challenge. The cutter and fitter just said, "What the hell do I do?" When she made a 3D film, *Kiss Me Kate*, it was a real challenge.

We had to be careful because of the law of cleavage. You couldn't show cleavage at all. The slightest suggestion of a line in the middle of the chest was out. The theory was if it was an essential feature, you could suggest it. In *The Three Musketeers* with Lana Turner, I had shaped jeweled pieces that fitted into her cleavage and made a great ornament there and then cut the dress so low that it showed the full round outside of her breast. The law was abided by with what we called "cleavage pins." It was a stupid ruling, because I remember that in *Gone with the Wind* Selznick was wanting cleavage because it was a period that showed it. The trouble was that Vivien Leigh had a very high rib cage. I think they call it "pigeon breasts." The ribs stick out prominently, which meant that the breasts hung to each side a tiny bit. Not to a point of being grotesque, but a woman of that figure does not have a cleavage. It's the pressing of the breasts together that makes cleavage. So we had a hell of a time. I had to get in a fitting room with Vivien and a woman, and we pushed her breasts and put adhesive tape to hold them closer and put pads on the outside to make a cleavage, which must be terribly painful and quite absurd. It was not that she was small, it was that they weren't built for cleavage. And of course Ona Munson, who played Belle Watling, the madam, had the chest of a boy, and she *had* to have cleavage because, oh God, Madam Belle Watling must have it. I actually think it must have been her stomach that we taped up there after all the fuss.

CHARLES LEMAIRE: One of the trickiest issues was dealing with sensitive issues with stars and their bodies, their feelings about clothes. I worried about everything. I worried about everybody. I worried about the producer, I worried about the director. You have to be diplomatic about anything and everything. You're dealing with people who have temperaments.

You must never tell them they're wrong. You must, above all, never tell them they don't look good. It can be a challenge. Think about fitting a costume on a star. It all depends on how you go about it. It causes friction if you say, "That's a lousy fit." But it doesn't cause friction if you say, "I'll bet you any money that if that waist was lifted a little bit, if the waistline was adjusted, everybody would be happier about it, so why don't we try it?"

JEAN LOUIS: I had only one problem with a star, and that was Betty Grable. I only did one picture with her, and she was a very, very big star and she was really nice, but she did not like long, long dresses with no breakdown. She showed me one day. She said, "Here's why I don't like those things: look at me." Of course, she had her bra up to her chin. She'd bring her bust up as high as she could, and it didn't give her any neck. So I said, "Well, look at your neck." She said, "Yes, but look at my legs." You see, she wanted her legs to seem longer. They would seem to come up higher. So I fixed this one dress for her and loosened it up. I was not happy, but she was the star. And she knew how she looked. And she knew what made her famous. Her legs.

WALTER PLUNKETT: With Ginger Rogers you'd always have to go into her dressing room before shooting because she would have found some artificial flower to pin in her hair and a bracelet or two to put on, because she just loved to overload herself.

JEAN LOUIS: I always liked Ginger. She had a marvelous figure. I had no trouble with her except she was always adding a little bit to her outfits, bows on her shoes and something on her hair and something you'd never expect until the last minute. One of the other designers said about Ginger, "If she couldn't wear it on her Christmas tree, she wore it on her dress."

WALTER PLUNKETT: I was terribly amused recently when I noticed some interview in a magazine or newspaper saying that she is doing the thing for Penney's store and that Ginger was always a great authority on clothes and designed so many of her own things for her films. She had the most incredibly bad taste of almost anybody in films! I remember once, I think it was a party that Betty Hutton gave at the Beverly Hills Hotel, Ginger was there in some black-and-gold lace thing with ruffles on and orchids and a clamp in her hair and everything you can think of. I just stood there and looked. I heard other people come up and say, "Oh, Ginger, darling, you look divine, you look wonderful tonight." I just stood and stared. Then Ginger said, "Walter, you don't seem to join in saying how good I look." I said, "I couldn't possibly, Ginger. To me you just look awful. Because you're a very beautiful girl, you have beautiful hair, you have a lovely body, and why not show it off in something simple instead of hanging yourself in this? Come on over for dinner next week, and let's talk it over. Do you know what night you'll be free?" So we set up the evening. Ginger came to my house with no makeup, her hair in a couple of little pigtails, and a very simple gingham dress and was the sweetest, most beautiful looking thing you've ever seen. It's like meeting the Queen Mother here, who is a handsome woman for her age, with gorgeous jewelry, and if she would only know enough to wear a simple dress in a deep tone of velvet showing off rubies and emeralds, she'd be glorious. Instead of that, her royal duty things are covered with sequins, lace, and beads. The fabulous Tower jewels on her are lost completely. Ginger tried out every hair color there ever was. She utterly destroyed her hair with all this dyeing. But with Ginger I only recall an absolutely sweet, lovely girl, very easy to get along with. She proved that she had much more talent than people had given her credit for. It is too bad that it went to her head a bit.

JEAN LOUIS: I liked designing for Rita Hayworth. She was a beautiful girl. I designed her famous dress for "Put the Blame on Mame." She did a very strenuous dance wearing it, so it was a real construction, because we had a piece of plastic on the top. We heated a warm iron and bent the plastic to fit the exact shape of her body. We put no bones in, no boning in the bodice. We didn't have a chance to try this dress out before the shoot. Many times we tested a dress, but this one we didn't try on her because the number came up at the last minute. The hairdresser at Columbia was a woman named Helen Hunt. We were always fighting. Helen was always adding a flower or something. Sometimes you had Costumes versus Hair. That could happen.

EDITH HEAD: Some directors are suspicious of designers, did you know that? Why? Because they always feel a designer is trying to sell a dress. An actress would love to have people look at her in your dress and say, "Isn't that actress beautiful in the scene?" And the designer would love to have them say, "Isn't that dress beautiful on that actress?" And the director just cares about the scene. In other words, some directors just don't trust us. Billy Wilder was not like that. I spoke with Wilder about *Sunset Boulevard*, and he said, before we started designing, "I want this to be completely honest, an authentic costume job, because I think the clothes are terribly important." This is ideal. A good job is when the set decorator and the art director and the cameraman and the designer all work together and show each other sketches and have discussions. We used to do that in the past, in the old system. We used to make actual photographic film tests of the stars in their costumes on the sets they would be using. These were the good old days. We could see how it all fit together, all of us, each with our own craft.

WALTER PLUNKETT: It was so much fun doing the costumes for *Singin' in the Rain* at MGM, because we all worked together and the musicals made there by the people in the Arthur Freed unit were usually successful. It made for happy workdays. The reason *Singin'* was one of my favorites was that they let me make these accurate, funny 1920s clothes. It was exactly where I started in pictures, doing clothes for silent pictures when sound came in. I was doing overly lavish things as soon as I had the opportunity to design, adding more fur and feathers on them than was humanly sane. So I was in a good position to redo it and know how funny it was when the occasion of *Singin' in the Rain* came along. Also I had occasion to realize how funny my own clothes had been and had a chance to make fun of them by reproducing some of them for Donald O'Connor and Gene Kelly . . . plus fours and knickers and that sort of thing.

EDITH HEAD: If you were under contract to a studio as a costume designer, they gave you a script to do. At first we had the design rule that everything was glamorous, whether it should be or not. You know, the lady who escaped the tenement and moved into a penthouse and rode in a limousine, wearing a leopard skin, getting out of the car with a live leopard on a leash. That was supposed to be realistic.

I know I did a picture about a woman who went across the prairie with a wagon train. I think it was Joan Bennett. Every time you saw her, she had fresh white ruffles. She had gone through rainstorms, floods, prairie fires, and Indian attacks, but every day she appeared with a new dress with frills around her neck. I went to the director and said, "Don't you think it's a little odd? She's crossing the prairie driving a herd of whatever . . . it was mules or horses or whatever . . . she was driving a covered wagon." But no. Glamour. And the audiences liked that. It was unrealistic, at first, for the most part. During World War II, we were still going mad dressing people in sable and diamonds, but Washington told Hollywood that due to the importance of films regarding shaping public taste and feelings on the home front, studios should not use pleats, wide lapels, or any waste of material that needed to be used in the war effort. That helped to make us realize we had to quit fashion Neverland, the design fantasy we were living. We started to do more realism in clothes.

WALTER PLUNKETT: Costume designers all did copious research regarding realism. Studios had big research libraries. I remember a very important thing about the shoes in *Gone with the Wind*. There were shoes worn by Olivia and several people that were made of blocks of wood with bits of carpet tacked over them, which actually did happen in the South when they couldn't get leather and they couldn't get shoes. They made their own, and I saw them in the Confederate museum, and I made sketches there and I had them copied exactly for a lot of the people during the war scenes. And at the end of the war, when the low-class Isabel Jewell gets out of a carriage and Scarlett is shocked by her appearance because she's dressed by all that money from the North, Jewell pulled up her skirts and there were two-colored shoes with tassels hanging off them and Scarlett looks at them, and God, she's wearing her homemade wooden block and carpet shoes underneath.

CHARLES LEMAIRE: You could get some crazy costuming. I remember a pseudo-Egyptian movie called *Land of the Pharaohs*, a gaudy kind of a film, with gold lamé things wrapped around men's bottoms. But when Fox did *The Egyptian*, I promised Mr. Zanuck we would do real research and do the most honest job we could and that I would design the film. And I said, "You understand the costumes have to .be designed from scratch. We have to start right at the very beginning, right down to the feet with the sandals." And he said, "Fine, okay." The Brooklyn Museum had one of the great, great departments, and I had a wonderful woman brought to the studio after I had spent two weeks in Brooklyn every day. I had this woman brought to the studio as an expert on Egyptology, and she became our reference woman. We also bought, from the Brooklyn Museum, a chair that came from the tomb of Tut. There were three and they only needed two, and they were willing to sell me one. We bought one, copied it, and we used it in the film, all through the film. I went to the pleaters—people who did pleating in New York—down on 7th and 8th Streets and had them make me new paper patterns for long pleating. I had to use crepe materials for gauzes and things like that. Everything in the film was made, and everything was authentically made. They really looked like Egyptian clothes. There was no fantasy to it. I found little thin, thin fabrics that looked like they were thin woven cotton, with little stripes in them, like irregularities. It was perfect. And Gene Tierney, the star, loved being who she was. They all loved being Egyptians.

So men, women, soldiers, shields, banners, everything was designed specifically for the film. When the museum in Brooklyn closed, four o'clock, four thirty in the afternoon, I was allowed to stay for another half hour, and they'd open the cases and I could feel the jewelry and look at the backs, the original jewelry. The jewelry we made was so authentic looking that Aly Khan, who was courting Gene Tierney at the time, was around the studio. And he came to me and said, "You know, Charles, I have never seen such beautiful jewelry. Where was it made?" And I said, "Here in the studio, on the lot. We have a man with four other men who does nothing but make the molds to pour the stuff in to make the pliable metal." And he said, "I have two of the originals from the museum in Egypt, and I could take these you've made and put them back in there and no one would know the difference. They are so good, they are so right."

Over on the set for *The Ten Commandments*, DeMille looked at the

Egyptian scene they set up for him with all the people on it one morning, and he said, "What is this?" And they said, "Egypt," and he said, "Doesn't look like Egypt." DeMille said, "Can't you get Mr. LeMaire's Egypt over here? Is there any way you can get Mr. LeMaire's Egypt from that picture he did? Because that's what I'd like." And they called me. I sold those costumes—I sold some and rented out some—when I sold those costumes and rented them, it paid for half of the budget of the costumes for *The Egyptian*.

Everything about costumes really mattered at Fox. And at all the other studios, too, actually. The costumes were so important to the audience. They were so much a part of Hollywood's mystique. And at Fox, I was overseeing all of it. You know, every film was taken as seriously as any other. There were no B pictures in our costume department. There were pictures that the studio called or labeled B pictures, but they needed A attention from us, you know, whether they were B pictures or not. And remember, sometimes there were situations such as when some of the people who had been stars in Technicolor movies but who began to fade a bit, but were still under contract and were now being shown in some black-and-white movies . . . like Carmen Miranda and little Vivian Blaine . . . they would be finishing out their contracts in films that cost less to make, but they still had to look just as pretty and glamorous as they had in their more expensive movies. We took it all seriously and did our best at any level. And so did the makeup and hairdressing people. Their creations for the looks of the stars define Hollywood glamour.

MAKEUP

WILLIAM TUTTLE: I will tell you how I came to work in makeup, what the job was, how the department looked, and how we worked. I'll give you the whole history. Nobody ever asks about us makeup and hair people. I was twenty-five years under contract in the makeup and hairdressing department at MGM, the biggest, most glamorous studio in town. The studio with "more stars than there are in the heavens," and they *all* needed makeup.

I arrived in Hollywood in 1930. February 11, 1930. At that time the

Depression had just started seeping in out here. I found a nice, clean, cheap apartment hotel to live in, and the landlord and landlady seemed to know people in the industry. I expected to be a professional musician at that time . . . and they said they'd try to help me find something. They knew a man who was a contractor for musicians at the Fox Studio. They called and made an appointment for me to go out and audition. I could play well enough, but they suggested I come back and see them in a year or so. My mother was with me . . . I was very young then . . . and she said, "We have no money." I said I'd do anything because we had to eat. So I did odd jobs around the studio and also worked in the mail room. I ended up with getting in through a series of accidents and unexpected events and finally went to work for a man by the name of Jack Dawn, who had been in the makeup department at Fox Studio. He was kind of an old bear in a way. He was surly. He said, "I've been thinking about starting someone in the makeup department to become a makeup artist. We have no way of training anybody," he said, "but I just have an idea that a sort of apprenticeship would be a good way of doing it, and I'd like to start you in." I needed money, and the pay was going to be good. I thought, What have I got to lose? So I accepted the job and went to work for Jack Dawn. This was at the end of October in 1933.

Well, here is how it was in those days. I started working as an "apprentice" with him, which meant I did everything. When I say I had an "apprenticeship," I can tell you no one ever had an apprenticeship like it. It included sweeping the floors, cleaning up after the janitors, who didn't do a very good job, and typing everything for the office. I typed everything out with two fingers, all the letters and forms and requisitions and so on. And he was an absolute stickler not only for cleanliness, but also if I made one strikeover or one erasure, I had to do it over. He would tolerate no mistakes.

He wasn't a very well educated man as far as formal education was concerned. He had knocked about since he was a kid. He had been in the merchant marine and had worked as an assistant director in pictures. Had been an actor but had finally settled in makeup. And he was quite artistic. He was quite good at character makeup. So he taught me how to break down scripts. The third day I was on the job, I had to attend a budget meeting on *The House of Rothschild*. I was scared to death. I didn't know what it was all about. Because I never had any exposure to that side of it at all. Something happened and he was busy, and he sent me over to attend this meeting. I sat there just afraid they would ask me something I couldn't answer. In the meantime he had contacted MGM and they were quite busy, and he was appointed head of the makeup department at MGM. So he took me with him. At the time we came there, many films were in production. There was a picture with Marion Davies called *Operator 13* about the Civil War; *Treasure Island* with Wally Beery, Jackie Cooper, and an all-star cast; a Tarzan picture going on with [Johnny] Weissmuller; *The Merry Widow* with Jeanette MacDonald and Maurice Chevalier. They must have had eight or ten pictures shooting, big ones that were in progress when we came into them. Now the time came for me to go out on sets and everything. I would go here and there and stand by with tests and powder puffs and things like that.

One day we were starting a picture called *Mark of the Vampire* with Bela Lugosi, Lionel Atwill, directed by Tod Browning, who was considered one of the top horror picture directors. The morning that they were supposed to start shooting, the man who had been assigned to the picture had a heart attack. He didn't show up for work. So in an emergency I was told to go down to the set and take care of it until they could get a replacement. I guess they never found one . . . I stayed.

And so here is my story. Jack Dawn told me that one day I would be head of the makeup department at MGM, the biggest studio in town. He said I would take over, which I did. I was his assistant for seventeen years, and then, for twenty years after he retired, I was department head at MGM. And the department head was king at MGM. They put you under an iron contract. If you were good enough to be a department head, they wanted to sew you up for good. I was king. And it was the same in every department. Cedric Gibbons was the kingpin in the art department and Doug Shearer on sound, and it went right on down the line. Everybody was contracted, and they really sewed you up. You couldn't do any outside work of any kind. And you were responsible for every penny that went through your department and answerable for it. My budgets, overhead plus production, would run from $1.5 million to $2 million a year. That's a lot to be responsible for in those days. You had to do the business end of makeup, and you also had to do preparation and production.

It was a tough job but a very rewarding job, and you made good money. So what were the responsibilities of the head of a makeup department at the most glamorous studio in town? You did all the creative work plus the business managing. You were responsible for all the money that was spent in the department. You did all the hiring. All the setting up. All the preparations. You approved all looks for each individual star. I would design practically all the makeups for whatever picture. And then I would turn it over to somebody to follow through for production. Believe me, when you had as many as eighteen features at once, you were busy. You were plenty busy. I went to check the sets. And I'd have to see all the dailies of everything that was shooting. Every department head had to attend these runnings. You were always looking for continuity in makeup or any defects. That's the reason you were there. If anything was wrong, you had to answer for it, no matter who did it. They weren't interested in *who* did it. *You* were responsible. So if I saw something wrong, I contacted whoever did it and said, "Look, watch this" or "Watch that" or "That isn't right" or such-and-such. Then in the mornings I usually walked around and supervised, saw that everything was going right. And I had an assistant. I had two assistants at one time who would do a lot of the legwork for me. How the stars would look was more or less in our hands . . . of course, along with the cinematographers and designers and clothing people . . . well, everyone, of course, because it was a collaboration. But our work was key, and everyone took us seriously.

I had wonderful contemporaries. Perc Westmore made some tremendous contributions. He's credited with inventing the panchromatic makeup, and Max Factor perfected it for film. We went from a more yellowish tone to a more orange tone of makeup. The older makeup was almost white. It was kind of pale—for one thing, to see the face they wanted as much light as possible. And they couldn't use any orange colors. It made them go dark. The old ortho shades were kind of a pinkish cast to them and very light in relation to what a realistic effect would be. Then they came in more to yellow and gradually into the red or warmer tones. Perc Westmore was first to use latex to make a different type of mask. It was more or less a fixed mask, no mobility. Jack Dawn played around with that, too. And they were pretty good friends, so they sort of exchanged ideas. Perc could really do grotesque faces. He did all the masks for *Alice in Wonderland* [1933 version] in latex. They didn't resemble human beings, really. When people think of makeup today, they think of horror films. Like what Jack Pierce was doing at the time, all those horror makeups at Universal. He wouldn't let anyone near him. It was all secretive. I never worked with Jack Pierce at any time. He spent most of his life at Universal. I would sort of call him the father of monster-type makeup. And he produced it with nothing to work with.

The whole Westmore family were amazing. There were so many of them! I knew them, of course. There are second-generation Westmores. One of the first generation left—Frank Westmore—he and I never worked together until a TV series this last year. All these years he has been in the business and I have been in the business, we never had an occasion to work together. But all the others are deceased now. The oldest, George Westmore, who came over from England, was a wigmaker. And then he had six sons: Montague—Monte Sr.—was the oldest. Perc and Ern were twins. And then Wally and George Jr., who was known as Bud Westmore, who was at Universal, just died about a year and a half ago [1973]. And Frank was the youngest, and he's the only one left. And at some time or other they each one had been in charge of a particular department. But George Westmore was the original department head at MGM, as I understand it. He was dead long before I ever got into the business. He was succeeded by a man by the name of Cecil Holland, who was quite a fine makeup artist, who in turn was succeeded by Jack Dawn. Perc and Ern Westmore were at one time employed by Max Factor as head of their wig department.

Max Factor is the one that supplied all the makeup for the studios at that time, because no one made their own makeup. No studio made its own makeup. Max Factor was one of the earliest people to get in motion picture makeup. He started a little store downtown on Spring Street, manufacturing theatrical-type makeup. And one of the early cameramen, Charles Rosher, was shooting all of the Doug Fairbanks and Mary Pickford pictures at the time. And he felt that there should be some improvements made with the makeup. This was way before my time. Maybe they were using some kind of a stage makeup. But he felt there were certain things required, and he went down to see Max Factor and described what he needed. And that's the way Max Factor sort of got into the film business. And he would make special colors for this one and special colors for somebody else.

We never made wigs to any extent at MGM. We had wig repair people there and so on. But the better wigs came from Max Factor. They don't make wigs anymore. And there are many others who make very fine wigs today. But they are very, very expensive. I mean, as a comparison in price, of course. Some of it's due to inflation, but some is just a gradual increase in the price of material due to difficulty in obtaining it. Because some of the best hair comes from behind the Iron Curtain. Up until recently we had no way of getting it imported. Before World War II, we could get the finest possible wig for $100 to $125. Same wig today costs you about $650, $700.

Wigs were very important and used constantly for several reasons: sometimes to expedite matters in the time used for hairdressing. Sometimes because a person's own hair was the soft, silky kind that didn't hold any kind of dressing for very long, which meant that you had to keep puttering with it all day long to keep it looking right, and many times to effect a hairstyle of long hair or short hair when it did not exist on the person. And of course, period hairstyling might call for not only a wig but several switches and pieces to go with it to build it up to whatever particular fashion was necessary for the period of the picture.

My responsibilities as far as hairstyling was more of a business management aspect, because I am not a hairstylist per se. By that I mean I've been involved in some of the styling of the hair from an artistic standpoint but not actually *doing* it. Men's hairstyles I have been more involved in, but when we think of hairstyling, we generally refer to women's hairstyles. And I'm not qualified for that from a standpoint of licensing or anything else. You have to have a state cosmetology license to do hair, which I don't have. But the fact that the two have to be coordinated—makeup and hairstyling—it's usually the makeup artist who is the business head of it and sees that they work together, coordinates it.

Oh, I have so many memories. The makeup arts reached a high degree of perfection in the studios in the old days. I don't think people today can picture what it was like back then, on the MGM lot, in the makeup and hairdressing departments. You know, every day everybody had to be made up, shampooed, turned into the character they were going to be, and the women, those beautiful women, had to look their best. Let me tell you, because no one knows and I just want to tell you, how the makeup department was organized at MGM in the 1930s and 1940s. We couldn't duplicate it today.

We had three small rooms, one of which had been cut through and made into two. They cut out the partition between the two of them and made a large room, and then we had a small room downstairs in a frame building, which we used to refer to as the rabbit hutch. And it was all in a building that was put up when the studio was first set up. It was the front wall of MGM on Washington Boulevard. And they were the original stars' dressing rooms, a long line of them. Uppers and lowers. The women were upstairs. The men were downstairs. All the big stars were in that building at one time. As I said, they cut through the wall in one of these and made a large room and a small room. They had a men's makeup department and a women's makeup department. And hairdressing. The hairdressing and women's makeup was upstairs. The men's was downstairs. And most of the people came to the department to get made up or did their own makeup in the dressing room.

When I came here in April of 1935, many of the people, the stars, made up themselves at that time. Jack Dawn set up, I think, an ideal type of arrangement for makeup work: everyone would come to the makeup department. It was centralized. And he, as department head, had the final say on all makeups. Where they had formerly had one man who sort of circulated all the sets and in between times somebody passed out a powder puff, you know, if they needed it. He put one person on each set to stand by. And then that later grew—we had such a volume of pictures in production at that time. He felt he could get better work on the stars by specially trained people. He took the better people and had them do nothing but makeups all day. They didn't have to stand by on the set. They were there where he could supervise everything. He would do many of the tests himself, and then he would direct someone to take that over to the production. So in this way he was able to supervise all the pictures and all the makeups. He would do the creative side of it and then turn it over to one of the staff members, who would do that same makeup every day. Then there was a man who was maybe not quite as competent or newer in the business, who would be assigned to stand by on the set and do the patch-work. And this built into quite a department. Then he brought in some more talented hairstylists and tried to improve the personnel in every way he could. And he was constantly fighting for better quarters and then would get moved around. We had two places: one for the extras and bits and one for the stars.

And then back in about 1940–'39, I guess it was—our own building was put up. I sort of drew up the plans for it. At the last minute someone said, "Oh, we have to move a lot of writers in there." So they revamped the floor plan to put writers in after it had been built for us. Finally they moved the writers out and moved us in. But the floor plan was changed considerably from what it was supposed to be. But we made it work, and this became the main makeup department. Then they still had a place for the extras which is a very large part of the basement of the rehearsal halls, where we had as many as two thousand extras go through in the morning while we were doing several period pictures. There were as many as six, eight men on staff all the time. We had a lab crew who did nothing but the lab work. Others who did mostly beauty makeups. Others more involved in character makeups. In other words, the top talent in each one.

I had my private makeup room, where all the big stars would sit in a big chair. In my office we had the consultations and conferences with direc-tors and producers and stars. And across the hall was my assistant's office and his makeup room. And then next door was where the head hairstylist had an office, and there was a main office where you just came, with a big counter and two desks. We had a day and night shift here. We were usually the first ones into the studio in the morning. We would be here as early as five o'clock in the morning. Five or six o'clock. And one secretary—they only being allowed to work so many hours—one secretary would come in early and stay until about two o'clock. And another one would come in at two and stay until nine. Then they would alternate so they wouldn't all get stuck with the night work or the early mornings. We had an office for the timekeeper or bookkeeper for the department. And that led into the stockroom, where we kept a stock of wigs that I would estimate to-day to replace would cost a million dollars. And on my recommendation, when I departed here five years ago, I suggested that they hang on to them rather than sell them too cheaply. And so they now can be rented for spe-cific things and used on productions which MGM is beginning to make now. We had a stock clerk, morning clerk, and night clerk to issue stuff. It was the only way we could preserve our hair goods. And across was the shampoo room with shampoo bowls and hairstyling. Then came the sepa-rate makeup rooms for the staff members, three separate large rooms, and across the hall was the makeup lab.

In the lab, we would experiment with things. We usually had three or four technicians. But we had altogether a staff of about seven, maybe eight makeup artists who did nothing but makeups all day long. They seldom went to the set. Separate people who took care of the sets did the repair work standing by. The counters used to be full of all kinds of makeup. We had a little stove where we hooked up the materials for making impres-sions. There was a very large oven for baking the appliances, and there was a sort of large open room which we used for sketching and for various special effects and storage space in the cabinets that were there. We had hooks hanging up above, and on those we hung masks of all the stars. Each one had his or her name on it. Those masks still exist somewhere . . . there was Judy Garland and Fred Astaire and Tony Curtis and Anne Francis and everybody who ever went through MGM. We took an impression of all their faces, each and every one. We could practice makeups and hairstyles on them. The stars hated having the masks made. We put marble on top of all the desks, so we could use them for plaster work. It's easier to clean up a marble tabletop. And we kept one single very separate room as a private makeup room.

Does anyone realize the efficiency of all this? The way we assembled what we needed, got the right number of people, trained them, and kept it moving, moving forward?

We found that by putting two hairdressers—staff hairdressers—on each person, that we could turn them out in about half the time. They were so well schooled that they worked very similar to each other. And we had a man, Sydney Guilaroff, whose name is quite famous in hairstyling, supervising their work. He did the creative side. He was not the business head of hairdressing. I represented *all* the department in that respect. But he did the designing of hairstyling, and he'd have two girls working on one head. One would do one side, one would do the other. Then he might do the comb out. But we eliminated a lot of time for the actors and the actresses. Because everybody hates to get in any earlier than they have to when they have to stay on the set so late.

And then we had a little kitchen. We served coffee and something nice in the morning, and it was always kind of a kaffeeklatsch. Oh, that place was jumping! Can you imagine if you could go in there now and listen? You'd hear some fabulous gossip and see some of the most beautiful people in the world, but all of them up early, preparing to go to work. It seems a long time ago, and yet I am still working today. On *Logan's Run*.

MUSIC

HARRY WARREN: The music department was like a stock company. Well, the *whole* studio was more or less like a stock company, but we knew each other's musical skills, so it really was like a stock company. We knew who could best play each part as needed.

BRONISLAU KAPER: There was an old saying: "In Hollywood everybody knows everything *and* music." We had to pull together as musicians to survive!

ALEX NORTH: I think it takes a special flair to write music for film. It takes a dramatic flair. You don't write necessarily for yourself but for a purpose.

BRONISLAU KAPER: Music is only important and necessary in a movie if it makes some kind of a statement, takes some kind of position, means something. *Statement* is a good word, positive or negative. But just to play music is absolutely unnecessary. At Warners people used to write lots of music because Mr. Warner liked music through the whole picture. So there was music, music, music, and finally your ear got so used to this music that it completely lost any value.

LEONARD ROSENMAN: When I first started in films, I worked at Warner Bros., and at that time their films had wall-to-wall music. If the film was an hour and a half long, the score was an hour and a half long. If you see an old Warner Bros. movie like *Anthony Adverse* with wall-to-wall music, after a while you're saying "Stop the music!" Historically this came from silent films, where the function of music was to add sound effects and also cover up all kinds of realistic sounds in the theater, like popcorn, the toilet flushing, the projection machine, and so on. The music helped remove the idea of reality so the audience would be able to suspend disbelief. Jack Warner evidently felt that music had this magical mystery power to make people feel things or make something palatable which didn't seem palatable. Basically they knew nothing about whether the music was good or bad, so they began to use it indiscriminately.

Through the thirties and forties there was a transition whereby you had a film with sound, dialogue, special effects, and everything else, but the filmmakers weren't quite sure about the role of music. It seemed to work in silent films in a certain fashion, with wall-to-wall music, so they just continued to do it. They didn't realize that diminishing returns set in, and if you had music from frame alpha to frame omega, people wouldn't listen to it after a while. It was like an enema in the Jewish family tradition. The idea was that it couldn't hurt you.

ELMER BERNSTEIN: There's a big history for film music that is different from some of the other departments. Well, obviously, it took some time for music to get into films and thus become a part of the film business, because when film first started, there were no soundtracks, no way to use music on the film itself. Yet I was astounded when I found out that the films of Georges Méliès, made just before the turn of the century . . . and right after . . . actually had scores written for them. I was really astounded, but these scores exist. They were written especially for a specific film, and they were to be played on the piano. These scores were very much like our sketches for music today in the sense that there were timings on it, descriptions of what would be happening on the screen at this particular phase of the music, so you could time yourself out. They were very neat little scores. Now, it's interesting to note that when films back then were longer and accompanied by a full symphony orchestra in a big first-run house, these were *not* any original scores as there were with the Méliès films. There was a fellow, Dr. Hugo Riesenfeld, a very early pioneer in the use of music with film, and he took the works of standard fare . . . like Dvořák's *New World Symphony* and some pieces of Wagner's . . . you know, the real concert hall warhorses . . . and he cut them up and kind of put them together in such a way that they accompanied the action of the film. He created a score from already existing music. They would have a conductor in the pit with a full symphony orchestra playing the "score" live at each performance of the motion picture.

One of the first men that had a real indication of the importance of film music was David Griffith, who, of course, is noted for many more important things in the history of film, but it is interesting to note that he used to have musicians come to the set to play for the actors. He saw it as an emotional aid to the actors to get them into the mood for what they were going to do. Of course, this is something you could do in those days, there being no sound on film. You could do anything. Griffith had a tremendous appreciation of the fact that music was indeed an emotional art.

I think within a question of two years after sound came in, you will find that the films in the early thirties are scored. One gets the impression that we aren't quite sure why we have music in the film except we know it is kind of better to have some sort of noise than silence. So there are many movies and many scores which sound like a bunch of popular songs strung together, and they kind of drone on and on in 4/4 time. By '36 you'll find some of the very great names in music involved in much of the scoring— just to mention a few, Arthur Honegger, Dmitri Shostakovich, Prokofiev, Aaron Copland in this country, certainly Georges Auric in France. There was quite a bit of excitement about this on the part of many composers who felt that this was a new world, new vistas. It's interesting, they weren't really quite sure of what to do at the beginning, because in film, when you use music in film, you have to make a certain kind of decision about what you're going to do with the music. But the first thing you really have to ask yourself, is: Why music? What is the music supposed to do? What is its function? Because you can do many, many different kinds of things.

It's always been my feeling that most motion picture makers do not understand what music does in a film. They've learned about its importance but for all the wrong reasons. They've learned about its importance, because they've learned that there's money to be made out of the music of films, and therefore they attach a great deal of importance to it, but they still don't understand what music does in a film or what music *can* do in a film. I think what music can do in a film is to create any emotional ambience. This is its greatest use and its most valid use. And it is this use which led to that terribly abusive statement, you know, "The best kind of music in a film is the music you can't hear." Well, that's ridiculous. But there's something behind that that has a great deal of validity. In other words, the music should be melded to the film in such a way that your first reaction is not to come out whistling the tune. Because in a sense the minute you're aware of a tune the music is in trouble, certainly emotionally it's in trouble and your picture is in trouble, to a very great extent.

DAVID RAKSIN: The important thing to a composer is that as long as there are things done in films which may not be seen or spoken—and heaven knows, there're getting to be fewer and fewer of those all the time—there will always be a need for music. I'm not talking about things which might concern the censors. I'm talking about things which are better left unverbalized.

JOHNNY GREEN: The function of music in a movie, as I see it, is to supply some element that isn't there without it.

ALEX NORTH: You try to help and improve what is lacking dramatically or what is lacking in terms of performance. I try to chart a score out as to the key of the music, which is usually affected by the conflict, whether there is a conflict of two people or interpersonal relationships with two or three people or whether it is a spectacle where the music is not necessarily making a personal comment but a physical one. The tough thing to do is to tailor a piece of music to a scene so that it doesn't sound "Mickey Mouse." A lot of the stuff that was done before some of the guys came in from New York was that kind of composing. For example, when you would switch from the Indians to the American army, you would have a fanfare, and then when you went back to the Indians, you would have Indian music. That kind of scoring was very prevalent during the 1930s and the 1940s.

BRONISLAU KAPER: The music department, like all departments, was part of the mechanics of a studio. You are under contract. Your work is assigned to you. After discussions with the executives at the top . . . the men who assign the work . . . a producer would come to you to confirm that he wants you to write the score or compose a song for his film. After you hear about it, he would, of course, have to talk to the man who is running the music department, the man who is scheduling all the composers, lyricists, et cetera. Usually what the producer wants, the producer gets, but the department head might have a problem regarding some other promised assignment or whatever. Anyway, I would be assigned, and I would then start working.

JOHNNY GREEN: Nobody except the director and the editor saw a picture as often as a composer saw it.

BRONISLAU KAPER: When you're a composer, you're paid to see the movie many times. But the producer sees it even more, because he runs dailies every day. And he goes with the picture through cutting. And so does the director. And most times, they watch the picture with some canned music, some temporary music, all the way through all those viewings. This is a great danger, because it connects *that* music to the scenes, to what they are seeing. And finally, after the last cut, after they have manipulated the picture, and to them the picture is good, and everything is peaceful, everybody loves the picture, and nobody has said, "This temporary score is lousy," in comes the composer. Suddenly arrives a guy who writes a different kind of music, and the producer says, "Wait. It's a different scene now." It's terribly dangerous. This canned music is terribly dangerous. The composer is in the danger zone.

How does a movie music composer work? I *always* had to start by seeing the movie three or four times, because if I don't, I'm at a tremendous disadvantage versus people who lived with the movie, who saw every foot fifty times. And they talk about it like clairvoyants. And I talk about it like a man. So I have to know the movie quite well. Then, when I've seen the movie a few times, I have to decide how much music it needs, generally: What are the climaxes, important spots for music? Can you have a theme or not? You can always have a theme, but is it going to be wasted? Sometimes your dramatic ideas and construction ideas sound beautiful on paper or when you discuss them, but then you put them against the picture, and they die, because the picture will not take music. There are some pictures which don't take music, for reasons of construction in drama, because certain situations are too close to each other in sequence. By scoring them, you only reveal the weakness of their being too close together in the structure.

Also, an important thing: Can a picture technically take music? This means: Is the dialogue, the amount of sound effects, permitting you to have the kind of music that you think you should have? You can say, "Here we should have exciting music." But when you see the picture, you see that technically it's impossible, because the music is going to be killed by dialogue, killed by trains passing, killed by planes flying, or whatever our enemies are. And writing music *under* dialogue, under voices, is hard. There's no connection between that and writing *for* voices. That's a completely different profession. To write under dialogue is to write *against* something which is trying to disturb you. Writing for voices is creating sounds *for* the voice. You have to know which vowels are correct and which register. You have to know where to breathe. You can be writing a song, and suddenly there is no place to breathe. It's like swimming.

ELMER BERNSTEIN: When I first came here, the composer wasn't even considered until after the film was done. I mean, the composer was faced with a fait accompli. The film was completely done. Everyone was gone. Things were a bit more mechanized in filmmaking in those days. The studios were turning out, oh, maybe anywhere upward of forty films a year, each of them, and they had vast music departments. It was all handled reasonably mechanically, and the producers and directors . . . well, the director never got into the discussion of who the composer was going to be in those days, and the producer rarely did. The head of the music department made the assignment, and it was done in a reasonably mechanical and very organized way, in fact. Later it became more fashionable to bring the composer in early.

ALEX NORTH: In nine out of ten cases, the music was the last thing done on any film. Unfortunately, that's the way it worked. It was more or less a question of economy, bringing a composer in when the picture is completely shot and cut. Because trying to redo music after retakes, reshoots, and editing would have been a real time and money waste. A composer was usually given four to six weeks, ten at the most, to do the score. The first film I ever did was *A Streetcar Named Desire* with Kazan. The music of any film is in a sense the most abstract contribution to it. The composer often gets away with murder in the sense that often the director will come to the recording, and that's it. He's not able to listen to the score in advance, and what is there is what will have to be used. On *Streetcar*, fortunately, Kazan was at both the recording, the rerecording, and the dubbing, because that is a very difficult moment for a composer. You are coordinating a musical score with sound effects. If the director is not there to support your music, it can be overshadowed by horses' whinnies or anything the sound-effects men put into the track prior to the musical scoring. This is a question of what should take precedence . . . the music or the sound. Very often, if the sound effects are that powerful and important, they take the music out. Many of the fine composers of the thirties and forties used music to cushion a scene, to just have neutral music which didn't comment on the scene but which was *there*. There *are* directors who feel that one shouldn't hear the music. One should bend over in order to hear the music. My feeling about it is that if there is to be any music, then it should be heard.

DAVID RAKSIN: When a picture is in, let's say, its first final cut . . . which means there are still things to do on it . . . the composer then gets together with the producer, the director, the editor of the film, and his own musical editor, who is a guy with a special kind of expertise. Editing for music or sound was a specialized job within the music department. All these people run the film together and share feelings and observations and ideas. They make up their minds where music should start, stop, appear, reappear.

During this, they're all talking about what the music is expected to do, what part it will play in the overall carrying of the burden of that picture. Out of this emerges "music conference notes," which become a "music timing sheet breakdown" that shows the composer how a sequence he is composing the music for will move forward with the picture. This is what a composer works with. He sits there and composes the music and has a stopwatch to make sure that everything is in synchronization.

Why does a composer want to work this way? It's challenging!

I used to have a saying: "Old composers never die. They just fade away in the dubbing room."

BRONISLAU KAPER: Let's take any composer. Even if he can orchestrate very well, he will never have time to orchestrate completely unless he wants to kill himself, because the time element in moviemaking is so tight. You get a cue sheet to work from, but you are lucky to get the cue sheets in time. You usually ask, "What have you got for me?" and the music cutter says, "I cannot get reel three, but I'll get reel five." So you cannot even write in continuity. "Why can't you get reel three?" "Reel three, they're working on the sound effects. We don't have another print. We can give you this dupe, but it's not a good one."

So sometimes while you are already writing and on a schedule, he is still timing the other reel. So you get the cue sheets. They send them to you by messenger to your house. But I couldn't just get the cue sheet and start writing to it. When I get the cue sheet, I have to go to a projection room again and see the movie with the cue sheet. And then I make my own secret notes on the cue sheet. You develop your own technical language when you do movies, or little signs: where the dialogue is going, crescendo or diminuendo, or this is important, or this is sustained, quick descriptions of moods, which you can only mark on the cue sheet when you run the movie again.

All this takes so much time! We were working, of course, with a schedule not only tied to a movie production schedule but also to scheduling a full orchestra session. There are no more studio orchestras. It's a matter of economics. In the days of the old studio system, there was an orchestra . . . with a guarantee. There was no question of the music department sometimes not using them because you wanted to take advantage of their guaranteed hours. They were easily available.

The studio musicians of the old days were fantastic musicians, and they had been carefully selected and hired . . . because a studio orchestra was out of proportion compared to a symphony orchestra in relation to the amount of strings you have. Because of technical possibilities and tricks, and microphones and all that, you don't have the normal amount of strings you have in a symphony orchestra. You have less. You have lots of woodwinds, lots of brass, but it's limping. The strings are not there, but we fix it with recording. That's why, because you don't have so many strings, everyone has to be especially good. You cannot just smuggle a bad player into the movie orchestra. It's too expensive. Time is too expensive. If you have a mediocre musician in the string section, he can ruin a take or a session.

Every music department . . . and every head of a music department in the studios . . . had to be aware of some unique needs regarding studio musicians. They had to be specialists in adapting themselves with quick thinking and quick interpretation. You see, when you have a symphony orchestra, the musicians play a repertoire that they have been playing for years. They know every Brahms symphony, every Mahler, every Bruckner, every Beethoven, Mozart. They played practically everything, but since there are so many recordings of this music, the interpretation has a standard and a tradition. But the studio musician . . . and the studio conductor . . . they have to play music that has never been played before. And they also play music which is usually formless, compared to classical music, because it's the music written for a movie, for a scene. So the interpretation has no tradition. You have to read it from nowhere. And you have to play it according to the conducting to fit the action of the picture. So there must be really extremely smart and adaptable people in the studio orchestra.

HARRY WARREN: In the old days, Metro had a load of musicians on a weekly salary. And Fox, Paramount, RKO. They all had their house orchestras. Under contract. And they had songwriters like me, special lyricists, orchestrators. Music was one of the most important departments in any studio. They aren't making enough pictures today to use enough musicians.

JOHNNY GREEN: A composer was primarily working with his own team and with the director. In other departments, the head of the department and the producer are the key connections, but in music you're usually working with the person who directed the picture. The producer and the head of the department were involved up front. The producer's interest in music used to be primarily "What does this music on the soundtrack of this film mean to the dramatic, emotional impact of the interest entertainment value of this film in the theater where it is being viewed?" That was the former barometer. The barometer today—and if I sound a little bitter, it is only because I am, I disapprove of it—the barometer today is "What will make a good single?"

MERIAN C. COOPER: A musician cannot write a good score of a picture unless he likes the picture. None of them can. All of them have tried. They've got to like what they're writing and what they're writing for. And they need to understand what the producer and director want. Max Steiner understood that. He did *King Kong* for me, and he fell in love with the picture. I had lengthy discussions with him on what I wanted. Before we started, I told him I would not put great restrictions on him. His eyes bulged out when I said he could have "as big an orchestra as you want, you can play as long hours as you want, and you can put as much music in this picture as you want" . . . and then I added, "But, Maxie, I must tell you"—and I'll just clean up the wording here . . . "you can't make love to the female star of the picture, Fay Wray." Maxie laughed until he cried. He damn near rolled over falling down, you know. He'd soared up to the heights, down to the depths, and it was all a joke.

ELMER BERNSTEIN: All directors should know . . . or be taught . . . how to communicate with a composer. I did three pictures with Anthony Mann, a marvelous guy, but he was a guy who never said anything to me about music. I loved him a lot, but not one discussion ever. Ever. That was it. He must have liked my music, I guess, but he never said a word. Another like that in a different sort of way is Otto Preminger.

DAVID RAKSIN: Preminger—although, you know, he's considered a very difficult fellow in the profession—he's a very gallant fellow.

ELMER BERNSTEIN: When I was with Preminger on *The Man with the Golden Arm*, he had me involved in the first cast reading, when the cast first assembled around the table to read the script. And I saw the rushes every day thereafter, the entire run of the picture. Now, he made no demands other than that. Once in a very long while we had a discussion about something, and in those days, although I understand he's changed now, in those days Otto disclaimed any working knowledge of music at all and said, "Look, you do what you think is right, I don't want to even hear what you're doing, it's not necessary, you know, along the way." In those days he was marvelous. I did two pictures with Cecil B. DeMille, one in which he was both the producer and the director, a film called *The Ten Commandments*. He believed in music as a storytelling part. *That* is what he believed its greatest value was. He was a kind of a storyteller. He would sit you down and say, "I'm going to tell you a story," which he did. He believed that every individual and emotion in the film should have a theme. Now, in the case of *Ten Commandments*, there was a specified theme: there was a theme for Moses, there was a theme for evil, there was a theme for God, there was a theme for the exodus. And all of these things worked in a rather literal way.

Cecil DeMille was also a perfectionist on sound. We used to dub a reel a week because of the sound effects. But there are very few producers like that around anymore. Most sophisticated people tend to write off DeMille's work as kind of crassly commercial, and yet I wish that some of the people who write his work off that way were as devoted to what they're doing as he was to what he did. DeMille used to say, "You young film people, you don't even go to look at films." He used to run about a hundred films a year at his home. Every third day, every second or third day, he ran a film.

Even though his principles were often not my cup of tea, it was fascinating to see somebody so meticulous and so devoted to what he be-lieved in. The only thing with him, you'd have to be very careful to give an honest answer, because if you tried to do anything that was designed to please him in any way that he thought was dishonest, you could be in terrible trouble.

ALEX NORTH: I went to John Ford's house in Bel Air. He was lying in bed, chewing his white handkerchief and reading. Apparently, he is a fanatical reader. We discussed briefly the approach to *Cheyenne Autumn*. I got a feeling right then and there that Ford was not really a connoisseur of music or a musically inclined person. He said, "Go ahead, Alex. I respect you, so you go ahead and do it the way you feel." He came to the recording, and I just finished conducting one thing and he ran up to the stage with his ten-nis shoes untied, his belt and coat dragging on the floor, and he embraced me, kissed me on the forehead, and said, "Now, musicians, don't get me wrong. I am only showing my appreciation for Alex's contribution." That is John Ford.

ELMER BERNSTEIN: Sometimes I will get up and boo at the end of the performance. I do things like that. There's one score I really hate. I hated it so much. In the case of *2001* I had to walk out of the theater for a few minutes at one point because I got so infuriated by the ridiculousness of it. Now, maybe that's what Kubrick wanted. I once discussed it with Kubrick, and I still don't know what he had in mind. But the use of the "Blue Dan-ube Waltz" made me very sorry that I wasn't stoned when I was in the picture. Maybe it would have been fine. But just sitting there, normal-like, it was positively infuriating, it was so ludicrous, asinine, totally unrelated, and unless it was designed to be, to me it was like writing "Fuck" on the bathroom wall or something in the girls' dormitory, or something like that. It was just stupid. It was unrelated and smart-assed and dumb.

Kubrick is a literate man. There's no problem about that with Kubrick. He's a literate man and he knows composers, and I think he should have gotten a composer and he should have let him score the picture. It's my feeling about it. In the case of Kubrick, there are certain men whose atti-tudes are bigger than life. These fantastic men who sometimes border on being mountebanks. The mountebanks are Renaissance men, and Kubrick is somewhere in that area.

HENRY BLANKE: I had a famous composer, Erich Wolfgang Korngold, who worked with me very closely. When I brought Korngold over from Vienna, he wrote beautiful music. He wrote *Anthony Adverse* and the Errol Flynn films *Captain Blood* and *The Adventures of Robin Hood*. Ten years later I said to him, "Erich, you don't write as beautiful a music as you did in the beginning," and he said, "I'll tell you why. Now I understand the English dialogue on the screen."

Korngold's themes were somewhat powerful, and not for an intimate tiny little story. Always very Richard Strauss–ish. He was so brilliant that he knew already when a sequence was cut, he clocked it and said, "This is exactly so-and-so many minutes," on the dot, or feet. And then he says, "Take two feet off here, add the two feet on the next scene." A fantastic man. He had new ideas about motion pictures. In *A Midsummer Night's Dream*, characters talk rhythmically to music, so that would have meant we would have 110 musicians on the set, which acoustically isn't ideal, but he had a brilliant idea. He says, "Give me a celeste instrument, and I'll use my earphones and conduct the orchestra on the soundstage." He played right on the set. They could see him. He could conduct them while they talked and everything. He rehearsed on the set. The actors had to be in rhythm to the music. So if something was wrong, he stopped and he'd say, "Do it again." And we rehearsed that for weeks while they learned to talk to rhythm. It was the first time this was done! An idea from a man who doesn't know anything about motion pictures. Brilliant!

HARRY WARREN: I was a songwriter. I worked at all the studios, but I started at Warners. I was in all the studios at one time, moving from music department to music department.

BRONISLAU KAPER: When I came to Hollywood, one of the first people I met was this great, great, great, great genius of songs, Harry Warren. Harry invited me to his house and played for me some of the production numbers for which he wrote the songs. I was absolutely thrilled with the symphonic sound and scope of the numbers. It was like a composition which lasted fifteen minutes, maybe, based on a beautiful theme by Harry and composed by Ray Heindorf. I remember that one of the numbers I was so impressed by was called "Shanghai Lil." It was just like a symphony. Nobody could do it better, with more excitement and more color. This was really a composition, not just arranging, not just adapting.

HARRY WARREN: There were some great songwriters out here. Max Steiner, a very talented composer of scores, would have liked to be a songwriter, too. He was a very funny little guy. He had a great sense of humor. He'd make funny remarks to the musicians in the orchestra. Of course, he was very serious about his music, but he was a very funny little guy. I think he was the forerunner of all the screen composers who wanted to write songs for their own pictures. He had a sort of carte blanche at Warners.

Sammy Cahn was the fastest lyric writer I ever met. You could be laying the first eight bars of a tune, and he had the title already in the first eight lines. He was a busy beaver. He was busy socially *and* as a worker. He never let anything get in his way, and you can get a job out here by just hanging around a certain social set. He played the fiddle. But he was an enthusiastic writer. He was always bubbling over. He was always anxious to go someplace, or he knew a place where you could get something cheap. In between songs, you'd drive over there and take a look at them. Discount houses and everything. He always had something going. Busy beaver, busy beaver. And the other songwriters were all kind of quiet, except Mack Gordon, who wanted to find a new delicatessen all the time.

BRONISLAU KAPER: Oh! Sammy writes fantastically, and he's so fast. He also *rewrites* fast, which is more difficult. You could write a song with Sammy, and then you play it for the producer or the director, and one of them says, "You know . . . this line . . . I'm not so sure." Sammy would have three more lines for it like that! He was like a computer. I saw him yesterday at the Beverly Hills Hotel. He was sitting with three guys. The guys laughed, and nobody opened his mouth, because Sammy was talking all the time. You could hear his voice. He represents, really, show business,

Hollywood, whatever. If he would go to Turkey, he would still be a Holly-wood man. He used to say, if we were at an event, "Let's go. Smart money is leaving now." "Smart money is leaving now" . . . the first time I ever heard that was from Sammy Cahn.

Fox Studio brought a lot of songwriters like Sammy out here in the early days, right before sound. And at first they all wrote subtitles. Grant Clarke was here, Buddy DeSylva, Billy Rose, quite a few of them came out. All lyric writers. George Marion and others. They were in the right po-sition when sound arrived and musicals became popular, because they'd been writing lines set to images. And of course all those Broadway famous names were here for a time: Johnny Burke, Jimmy Van Heusen, Irving Ber-lin, Cole Porter, Jerome Kern, Rodgers and Hart, George and Ira Gersh-win, and many more.

HARRY WARREN: Let me tell you about the life of a songwriter in the 1930s. Not a man who composes a score but a songwriter, another part of the music department. I was at Warner Bros. I came out in '29, and an-other guy, Al Dubin, was there, and he had done a picture with Joe Burke, and he had written "Tiptoe Through the Tulips" with Burke. In 1932, they gave Dubin and me an office, and they assigned us a movie called *42nd Street*. We were the only songwriters on the lot. We had an office all to our-selves. We could look out the window, and there wasn't a house in sight. It was like being out in the wilds in Burbank in those days. I gave Al a cou-ple of lead sheets, and he went away and came back with "Shuffle Off to Buffalo," which was the first movie song we wrote together. Buzz [Busby Berkeley] was brought on the picture, and he stayed on the stage for about a week, thinking about how he could do that song.

It's awfully hard to say how you write or what you're going to write. They assign you to a picture. You sit there and say, "Where will we start? What will we do?" And your writing partner . . . he'll throw some lines at you, or titles. You fool around, you try to get a melody or start digging. So whatever sounds like something, you know, and you go on and on until finally you hit something you think is good and you write it up. You never know where you'll find a title. We got one when a girl in the office was teased because she kept seeing one guy, and she said, "Yeah, he's getting to be a habit with me." She was [music director] Leo Forbstein's secretary. And that's how we got a song for Bebe Daniels, "You're Getting to Be a Habit with Me."

In the early days, like on *42nd Street*, we had to go to budget meetings. We hated it. The budget meeting consisted of everybody who was concerned with the picture: the cameraman, the producer, the director, the assistant director, the head of the music department, the scriptwriters, and, if it was a musical, the songwriters like us. Oh, and the property man and the unit manager. And they all went on and on and on, and it was a big gathering of people in one big room around a big table. They discussed a lot of things that didn't concern us at all. I often wondered why they asked us to these meetings. It was just a big waste of time for us. And also the choreographer. Waste of his time, too.

Buzz was making a movie. And his idea was that when you use a camera, you can do anything you want. Remember, the director of a movie like *42nd Street* had nothing to do with the musical numbers. Buzz Berkeley shot those himself. As a rule, the director of a picture doesn't run in on anything that the choreographer is going to do, because the choreographer gets credit for his own stuff. Anyway, in those days, we were trying to write numbers to fit the script. That was our job. That was what we were hired to do. If we could write a song that would become a hit, too, well that was fine, but the number had to fit the story.

Songwriters really mattered back then. We sat around and sat around and doodled around, but we were working hard, turning out song after song, many of which became big hits. But once they took your music in the studio, once you turned it over for the film you wrote it for, you had no more control of it. It wasn't like in the theater, where the composer had control of his music. Not in the studio. The arranger and the musical director all of a sudden became the owner of your music, and they could do with it whatever they wanted to do.

ALEX NORTH: Hollywood is a lonely place for composers. I had a rough time coming out here, and I was sponsored by Kazan. Benny Herrmann, who has written some brilliant scores, was sponsored by Orson Welles. I don't know if "sponsor" is the right word, but Benny came out here to do

Citizen Kane. It was a closed-shop kind of a place when I came out. It still is very rough to break in. You have to be really good.

BRONISLAU KAPER: We used to be wizards, you know? We learned. I mean, Johnny Green, for instance, who did all those musicals: he was a wizard in sound, in music cutting. He would manipulate things with a great mastery. Another perfectionist, you know. We were all perfectionists. The old music departments were full of perfect wizards.

ART DIRECTION

MITCHELL LEISEN: A department head could help you or kill you. You ended up all right usually, but it was the hours you had to put in with them, working toward what you wanted. In the old days, the departmental days of the studios, the men who did the designs of the world inside the picture were called art directors. Art direction was one of the most important aspects of any film, no matter how small a production, and it's often the one most ignored by critics or people outside the business. It's taken for granted or thought to be part of what the director did or something. But the art department of an old studio was key to what the public saw and remembered and dreamed about.

I worked most of my career at Paramount, but I made a picture at MGM, *Young Man with Ideas*, in 1952, and I had much less say on design over there because I had to fight with Cedric Gibbons every day. MGM was the studio that held on to the departmental system, and Gibbons was the head of the art direction there. He was extremely elegant and a very fastidious man. He was God out there at Metro. He wanted everything a certain way, and that was the MGM style, and that's what you got. My movie had a bookie joint that looked as if it had been done by *House and Garden*. Copper lights with plants growing out of them! It was supposed to be over on Washington Boulevard, so we shot an exterior over on Washington Boulevard, and that was the end of reality.

HARRY HORNER: I am a production designer. That's the fancy name. People want to know: What is the difference between an art director and a production designer? I won an Academy Award as an art director, and yet I am a production designer. To understand about art direction and production design and the departments for these things that Hollywood established and developed is to understand what Hollywood really was as a business. Hollywood is an establishment, and within this establishment there are conventions, and within these conventions you fall, like a pinball machine, into specific categories. The difference between an art director and a production designer is a minimal one. A good production designer per se is the left hand of a director or the mind or left brain cell of the director. The job of the production designer is to stimulate the director into seeing more than he has seen. By "seeing," I don't necessarily mean something visual. It means to have him understand more, to widen or be more curious about a character, about a landscape, about the relationship between the interior and a character. Production designer and art director, really, are thus one concept. It is just when you call yourself a production designer, you get more money. That's the only difference.

There are a great many people needed in production design. Draftsmen. Costume designers. Sketch artists. Perhaps an architect. Carpenters. Matte artists. Who knows what you might need? It's like building a city, actually, and you have to have all the people you need to make or create everything, but you are responsible for all the mistakes. All the people are under you, of course. You start by doing the research on what you are asked to design and make. I look at thousands of things out of which I make little notes and then little studies for the costume designer over in that department. Naturally, the costume designer is one of the people you must work with, because the costumes will probably dominate the backgrounds you are making. He is only one of the people you work with, but when you've accumulated your ideas, you want to talk with the costumer and get his choices or ideas because you're hoping, obviously, to control to some degree what *he's* going to do. You're trying to control, always, the total look of the picture. You make sketches of details, and when you have your layout solidly in mind, then you can deal with the draftsman. You make your own layout first so that the draftsman can do the details, with scales and elevations. The draftsman has to do the drawings that go to the carpenters and to all the specialists you'll need.

HAL WALLIS: The art director would work two or three months ahead, because he would have to go out and see the locations or start planning the sets and so on—and drawing the plans so we could start building in time to be ready to shoot. So the art director—and the production manager—are key people who would be on the job two, three, even four months ahead.

ALLAN DWAN: The art director and his department had to be both practical and creative . . . and reliable. Van Nest Polglase was at RKO, as I recall, and he'd had a misfortune. He'd started to hit the bottle pretty hard, and people lost confidence in him. I had known him to be a very fine art director and a practical one, which is the kind I like. A lot of them are very arty, but they cost you too much money. Van was a practical fellow and a great guy to take an old set and transform it into a new set for you with very little money, and he knew the moves. He created the RKO look, those art deco rooms with shiny black floors, the world of the Astaire-Rogers musicals. He's so important to the history of Hollywood and what people think of as Hollywood.

ROBERT BOYLE: The art director or production designer starts with the script. You have to identify your characters. The art director is a contributing factor right from the beginning, and hopefully he contributes to the overall film and aids the director in getting what he really wants out of the whole film. Let's take *The Birds*. I got a call from Hitchcock. I had just done *North by Northwest* with him, and I got a call from him saying that he had this project, Daphne du Maurier's short story called "The Birds," which, incidentally, had not much to do with the final product. But he wanted to know whether it would be technically possible to make this film. Well, I read the Daphne du Maurier short story, and it didn't give me too many clues except that we were going to have to have birds all over the place—pecking at the walls, coming down the chimneys, doing whatever they had to do to destroy the human race—and that already seemed to be very difficult, but I knew we would have to get into some technical procedures which were not new but there would have to be a marriage of almost every technique that we knew.

I gritted my teeth and recommended to Mr. Hitchcock that we could make the film. At that time it was rather chancy, I thought, because there were many, many problems. But at any rate, we started. The film took on more and more complications. For one thing, we decided that we wanted to do it on the coast, so we went up to Bodega Bay and we had them make our one little town out of about half a dozen little communities around there. So the schoolhouse was in one location, and one place was out on a point which is now the site of a defunct atomic site. There was a woman, Rose Gaffney, who owned the one site we wanted, and it's not very nice to say, but we really had to go out and woo old Rose Gaffney to get her place. In the meantime, we were trying to get all the technical things going, and she was having a big fight because she was a big ecologist and that whole point out there was full of Indian artifacts and she didn't want anybody there. But we finally convinced her that we wouldn't harm the ecology of that peninsula and that if there were any way we could help her in her fight against the gas and electric company, we would. So we made up our town.

Our town, while I hope it had a certain cohesive quality, was actually made up of about six towns all put together. Then the other problem was superimposing the birds over whatever set or settings we had. We tried to do this as nearly as possible without getting into second- or third-generation duping, and for the most part we were very successful.

Hitchcock will push the technical aspect of any shot to any length if it will satisfy what he feels is that gut feeling of whatever he's trying to do: suspense, terror, and so on. And sometimes he'll push it so far that it doesn't quite make it—the shot becomes a little too strange, a little too far beyond the capabilities of the medium. But he never really was worried about that.

There is no one who taught me more than Hitchcock about film language, about how you can shoot a sequence and make the shots count. He will rarely, rarely make a shot for its own sake. Every shot has to make some kind of statement. Many directors that I've worked with will say, "Wouldn't it be great to have a shot here?" or do something with a shot, always talking about the shot. Hitchcock never did that. He might get carried away with an obscure idea or an idea that doesn't work, as everyone does, but he would always start with the statement he wanted to make. He himself had done some art direction, and he knew what he wanted. He knew how important it all was for the film.

HARRY HORNER: In the studio days, the designing profession consisted of art directors—the title of it was art director, and, you know, in the picture business, the credit is terribly important. It's very important. I was an art director, and the great production designer of that period was a man by the name of William Cameron Menzies. Menzies was the innovator. His big and important theory was that designing is not a matter of simply doing backgrounds but must definitely take on active participation in the creating of the scene. William Cameron Menzies was *the* great production designer.

MARTIN SCORSESE: For me, William Cameron Menzies was always the magic of the movies. As a kid, I saw *Duel in the Sun* on its first release . . . I think I was six years old . . . and I've never forgotten it. It's a very important picture for me, and it was designed by William Cameron Menzies.

RICHARD SYLBERT: William Cameron Menzies was the greatest designer that ever lived, the father of the words *production design*. He didn't invent that title. David O. Selznick gave it to him. He wanted to bring him in to do the designs for *Gone with the Wind*. And there was already an art director on the film, so they asked Selznick, "What are you going to call him? Art Director Two?" He said, "No, no, we'll call him the production designer." That's where the term came from.

KEN ADAM: I think the first true production designer was William Cameron Menzies. His function was to design almost every frame of the film, and he did it brilliantly for *Gone with the Wind*. After first discussing concepts with the director, the function of a production designer is to set a style and a visual progression for the film and to physically realize it. Ideally speaking, that means supervising everything that is visual: sets, locations, props, coordination of costumes with settings, et cetera.

HARRY HORNER: Research was so important for production design. I did a film called *The Little Foxes*, where, only through research, did I learn how the concept of "southern hospitality" would look in the home of a wealthy industrialist. People would have their servants swinging a big fan over the dining table while people ate. These are things I didn't know but made my business to find out. The production designer had his hand in all things, not as a matter of ego but rather of total style. So the look of the film was unified, so that it was authentic and believable. On *The Heiress*, I compiled three volumes of my research. One of the three is only about the costumes of the era, the clothing. To start your research, you make a list. You go through the script and put down all the things you don't know. You ask all the questions: Behavior in the South? How does a doctor live? How does the doctor practice in the 1860s? Where does he practice? Does he go to an office, or does he have the office at home? What does the office look like? What kind of instruments? Other things, too: How would a very wealthy man in this social milieu think? How would he talk? Sometimes it's heartbreaking, because when you do not work with a very sensitive director, you find—and this is where you despair—that what you are doing is not only not appreciated, but it isn't used. You suddenly know much more about the characters than an unprepared director does.

One doesn't have to define too carefully where one contributes and where one steps back and says the other one had a better idea. The main thing is the end result. Let us talk for a moment about *The Heiress*. *The Heiress* plays primarily in a house. We did *The Heiress* at Paramount with all the facilities, with a marvelous research department. You can get and put together a period, which in this case was the 1860s. You take a window, and you take the doors, and you know that they had sliding doors in those mansions in Washington Square, et cetera. I am not a background painter or decorator who just says, "This room will look nice in beige with pink curtains." It might look nice in beige with pink curtains, but it has to be right for the character—it's *his* room—and the period.

It is rare that modern filmmakers have the opportunity, because of the budget, to make a historic film, an elaborate, extravagant historic film. We used wallpaper, which at that time cost $15 a yard, which is a lot of money. It wasn't paper, it was damask. At one time we had to fireproof the wallpaper. It was white, and the fireproofing destroyed the texture of it. When we saw it, it was all brown, so we had to reorder the whole thing. So you can imagine, even then, that was a lot of money. Now when someone does a historical film, he will probably try to go on a location, where possibly he will make do with something. This is probably just as well, in a way. My contribution, I think was in another direction.

When you work with others, you interfere. The fancy name of production designer means I am responsible for the production. It doesn't mean that there aren't other people who are equally as creative or better. But there I am. Because this is entrusted to me, I have the right. This works out very well if one is diplomatic. Where one doesn't hurt others' feelings.

HOWARD SCHWARTZ: There's a tremendous difference in art directors. Some can work with us cameramen, and some can't. Some of them are very helpful and knowledgeable. Others you fight. It's just that simple. Some of them are considerate of the fact that the cameraman has to photograph it. They'll come to you—even though they have to have the sets in well ahead of time—and particularly if they see a problem, they'll come to you and say, "What do you think about this?" You'll have a chance to have some input. Others just go ahead and put it in there and you have your grips tear it out and put it back so that you can handle it. Sometimes it's easier to do it that way than it is to fight with these guys if they're very stubborn and opinionated. You learn that as you go along. On the other hand, they can be tremendously helpful to you. You're really in seventh heaven when you get an art director who's interested in your problems.

HARRY HORNER: I worked with Edith Head, who designed the costumes on *The Heiress*. I made rough costume sketches. I wanted to have that black-and-white feeling. I discussed the costumes with Edith Head and William Wyler, the director. Wyler said yes to everything because he trusted me. If you discuss things, the rest of it is left in Edith's hands to get together, but in the same direction as your production design. You execute and contribute more to the total film. You meet several times, and she says, "What is your reaction to this?" I might say, "This is too severe." I won't say I don't like it. Let her say it after she thinks about it. Everybody wants to get it right. Sometimes you disagree. That's inevitable in a business where there are so many people involved.

How much input I have once the sets are built depends on who the director is. I make the sets, and I discuss things with him. It is a question of great diplomacy. You have with and against you the following two friend-enemies: the cameraman and the director love you when you make the schedule. However, when the cameraman comes on the stage and you look through the camera, he says, "Who is shooting this?" Then he gets mad at you. He says, "I can't shoot white things. You have to paint it all gray." There are little private feuds. The director you have to be very tactful with. It is just as well to give him the sketch and remind him what you have discussed with him the night before. Don't cry if he doesn't use it. Nobody is there to fight with anybody, unless it is on something terribly important. The role of the art director is to fight when necessary, which is what all departments do.

STUDIO PERSONNEL

ARTHUR KNIGHT: The large studios of the golden age of Hollywood—the thirties, forties, and into the fifties—employed so many people. It wasn't only the specialized filmmakers that the public knew about but also so many people holding down jobs not associated only with moviemaking—carpenters, painters, seamstresses, builders, gardeners—but also people in jobs associated with the business that were not, on the average, discussed or thought about, maybe even not known, such as script girls, readers, timers, agents, and stuntpeople. It took so many people to run the studio system—so many people in so many jobs.

FRANK CAPRA: Today the business is all about agents, all kinds of agents, and business managers. In the past, the agent did not play the same important role in a star's life or a director's life because everyone had job security. They were under contract.

KARL STRUSS: An agent? Did I have an agent? Did anyone have an agent? Over the years I had three different agents, but they never, not a one, ever got me a job. I did it on my own. I went around myself to see different people, keeping an eye on all the various productions in town. We read about pictures scheduled in the trades, but the studios had their own staffs and that was kind of hard to break into unless they were terribly busy and needed somebody from the outside. The only way you could break into a studio was if they suddenly had some kind of vacancy they couldn't fill, and then you had to fit the type of picture and be liked by the director, etc. And you got that on your own, not through an agent, because basically it was just an accident.

RIDGEWAY CALLOW: At one time, we hired a lot of dialogue directors. Dialogue directors were created because studio executives felt that silent film directors were not capable of directing dialogue. So they brought "specialists" in, and the job lingered on for a decade or so. The dialogue director was completely ignored by most directors. His primary responsibility was rehearsing or coaching players in how to speak dialogue, and that was done off on the side. Dialogue directors were gradually phased out, and I don't know anybody today who has a dialogue director. Now they leave anything needed in that area up to the script girl. You get a very competent script girl, who, between set-ups, will go over lines with the actors.

HANNAH SHEELD: The script girl is an important person on the set. Contrary to what many people feel, she is not a bitch and she is not out to get the director. She is there to service two people: the director and the editor. She is there to mother the actors, to act as a buffer between everybody and the director. The dreadful thing is that she is supposed to know everything that goes on without being bossy or show-offish. She must have patience and be interested in detail. She is terribly important, but she must not let anybody know that she is.

As a script girl, I usually come in the week before the production starts shooting, but it all depends upon how involved they want you to be in the production. I have worked with directors where I was called in for four weeks and I sat in on all of the casting. But that depends upon your individual relationship with the director and who hires you. Did the director hire you and say, "I want you," or were you just hired as a script girl to be there and do the bookkeeping and keep track of closing the stage entrances and exits when they can pause for a cigarette and so on? But ideally, you come in a week before the shoot and you do your breakdown on the scripts, and then you usually have a week after shooting ends to wrap

up the script and do the reports and things. And then you have at least an
hour to two hours after every day's shooting. There is a lot of paperwork,
but it is also terribly exciting if the director allows you to work correctly.

The director, first of all, should not consider the script girl a menace.
She is really able to help if she takes her job seriously. Originally, and this
is a hangover from the old days, the script girl was put on the set by the
producer in order to keep tabs on the director. She was a watchdog.

A script girl has the advantage over the director in that she has the
script with her at all times. It is her responsibility to know what has trans-
pired during any period of shooting. Her job is to sit and observe. She
is the only one whose eyes are riveted at all times. She knows almost as
closely as the director does what is going on. She is his little shadow. She
is there with him in preproduction. She knows his overall intent. Most
script girls—and notice that I am saying "script girls" rather than "script
clerks"—have no ambitions to become directors. It is a very well paying
job, and also it fulfills. Good script girls are very fulfilled. They are very
important. They know when they are done that they did a good job, that
they were needed, and that they were not a waste on the set. They didn't
just sit around and pick their noses.

It is very important for the script girl to have a good relationship with
the cameraman. There are many reasons. It makes her work more pleasant. There are cameramen who do not like you to look through the lens,
but it is necessary to know the size of the image and the frame lines. You
can sit there and knock yourself out, and if he hasn't told you, you have to
ask. I always say, "What lens are you on?" It is much easier for me if he tells
me, "I am on fifty and my frame line is on so-and-so." Otherwise I may be
sitting and watching for things that may not even be on the camera. When
she asks the cameraman what lens he is on, it's not just because she is nosy,
it is because she should put it in her script. It does make it easier for the
director when he goes through her notes. He knows either by his lens or
what the image is more or less what the shot is designed to do. It is also for
the retakes, so that you know precisely what went before. And of course,
it is invaluable for the editor.

Today, nobody but the director and the operator and the cameraman
and the gaffer are supposed to look through the lens. They have these

silly little wars. You may have a cameraman who does feel strongly about this. If he wants to, he can say that you are not allowed to look through the lens.

As I said before, the script girl is responsible to two people, the director and the editor. A script girl can make an editor's life almost a dream if she takes her job seriously. She should be his right arm. She should help him so that he doesn't waste his time and his creative energy. And that will happen if he has to sit and go through take after take after take. He should just look at the script girl's notes and see "Take one was NG [no good] because of fluffed lines throughout." It isn't enough just to put "NG." That really tells him nothing, because a take can be good for the first forty-seven seconds, and then there may be a noise. So all of these extraneous, boring little details should be in the script, because that way the editor at one glance can see what to pull and what not to pull. Anything pertaining to the take should be in the notes. Also, you should mark whether the cameraman commented that he didn't like a particular take. And the same is true for the soundman. Also, mark which one was the director's preference. It helps the editor and gives him time to just sit and be creative and work with what he should do, and that is to edit the film. Detail, detail, detail! I mean, I have bored them all to death.

JAMES WONG HOWE: Before we had script girls, in the early days, the assistant director did everything. He was a production manager and everything. We'd go out on location, we'd have a camera assistant, a second cameraman, the grip with the three, four reflectors piled on top of the car and the tripod tied on the running board of the car, and the cameraman, we'd go out and shoot pictures. Today you go with even more, a lot of people. Now, I remember, there was a shot made in those days of a living room, and they had a little statue of Cupid on a table, and he had a bow and arrow pointing. We went to lunch, and we came back to continue with the same shot. The next day, they put the thing together, and the cupid, right in the middle of the shot, jumped and faced the other way. Somebody had moved it, you see, and we didn't know about it. So then they finally put in script girls, or continuity clerks, as they call them, to watch for things like that, to prevent them and save time and money.

HANNAH SHEELD: Your production manager very rarely shows himself on the set. He takes care of all of the preproduction. He is the one who makes up the storyboards and the schedules and what have you, and he is also the one who rides on the money, more or less. Then you have two ADs, the first AD and the second AD, and the first assistant is the director's alter ego to the point that he goes and informs the stars that they are wanted on the set and all the protocol-type things. The assistant director very rarely gets to direct. The second assistant is just there to keep track of the extras, when they were called, when they were released, when the shot was made, when you broke for lunch, when you came back, and when you got your first shot after lunch. He also does all of the bookkeeping on set.

SAM MARX: There was a big and important reading department. Yes, reading. All they did was sit and read all day. There was always a commander at the head of the reading department. The reading department was under the story department. Over at MGM, Dorothy Pratt was the commander of the readers. There were ten readers in a room, and they were all trying to keep up with the material she would distribute to them to read. She would keep them reading and would bring their synopses of what they read up to the head office. The reader's synopsis depended on the material. If it were a big, long book—if it were *Anthony Adverse* or *Gone with the Wind*—the synopsis might run as many as fifty pages. It depended on what the reader felt the book was worth. There was no set amount of pages for the report.

The readers were also reading for particular material for specific stars. Irving [Thalberg], who was head of production, would send a memorandum reminding everyone about the star issue—"This year I want you to do four Crawfords, three Marie Dresslers, and two Norma Shearers"—like that. What that meant was that out of the readers' suggestions, I was going to have to find four Joan Crawford ideas. The readers made a synopsis of all the material that came through—original scripts, books and plays, everything. At the end of each week, I'd sit down with Kate Corbaley, who worked with me, and we'd decide which ones we'd consider. If we maybe hadn't found anything yet for a particular star, the pressure was on. We had to think about a star's individual characteristics. For instance, a Crawford story would differ from a Shearer story. There was a certain amount of majesty about Norma, because she was married to the boss. Also, she had a certain amount of regal bearing, which showed itself in her general character. Joan, on the other hand, was still young. She was doing dancing films and rags-to-riches films, and she was sexy and alive and very down to earth. They were types. Norma played the married woman or the girl who was close to being married. Joan played the sophisticated adolescent. You had to look for stories that those characters could fit into.

The readers were so important. It all started with them in a way. If they read *Gone with the Wind* and gave it a no—and in fact, I read the synopsis when it came to me, and the story department said that none of the producers seemed to like it, but the readers had. They should have listened to the readers. Nobody worked harder than the readers in those days. We were desperate for material and kept them going around the clock.

MERIAN C. COOPER: Hollywood hired stuntmen. And, of course, standins. Every major star had to have a stand-in to replace them standing under hot lights while sets and photography were being prepared for a shoot. A stand-in was not so much a look-alike as a duplicate in size, body shape, and hair color, face shape, et cetera. That person was a physical replacement while a star rested, studied lines, changed costumes, did interviews, or whatever. The stunt double—or the stuntmen and women—did the hard physical stuff for the star. Some stars, like Errol Flynn or Douglas Fairbanks or later Barbara Stanwyck, could and would do their own stunts, but it wasn't a good idea and the studios didn't like it. If anything happened, it could shut down the movie or even ruin it. Few stars were allowed by a studio to do anything like a stunt, although their publicity might claim they had done it.

GENE KELLY: I wasn't that brave about doing it. A lot of stunts I wouldn't touch. I would never ride a horse. "No," I said, "I can't do it." And then there'd be scenes in *The Three Musketeers* where I had to ride a horse and say dialogue. I would go to the wrangler and say, "Look, I can't ride a horse very well. I'm a city boy." They'd get me a horse that bounced well and made me look good. I can tell you a dozen stars who broke their legs riding horses. See, the horse is the dumbest animal in the world, and you don't know what he's going to do. He can be stupid. We got stunt guys for *Three Musketeers*, and, you know, they were just fellows off the street, but they were real riders. You know, cowboys dressed up with plumes. Stuntmen are very athletic and marvelously good at doing things. They can have a long line or a pointed toe or an arched back like a dancer.

MERIAN C. COOPER: A stuntman is great when he hasn't got a wife and children. Most of them . . . I won't say this is all true . . . but many of them, when they have these dependents, won't take the all-out risks that a good stuntman should take.

TAY GARNETT: Most stuntmen were not what you would call intellectuals, but then, if they were, they wouldn't be stuntmen.

RIDGEWAY CALLOW: Or stunt pilots. Howard Hughes never asked for the cooperation of the army to use their pilots in *Hell's Angels*. He hired barnstorming stunt pilots. In those days, stunt pilots went around to county fairs and did crazy things such as wing walking, which was quite common. Howard felt that the kind of stuff he wanted—planes spinning out of control, spectacular dives, loops, crashes—would be done better by these wild, crazy stunt pilots. Those flyers were the craziest bunch of men in the world. I think they were all wonderful guys, but God, were they crazy.

TAY GARNETT: These stunt guys were constantly getting hurt. Usually they'd get hurt because they wouldn't listen or wouldn't do what you asked them to do. It's a strange thing about picture fights and picture action. The incidents in which men are actually injured are usually not as photogenic as a faked piece of action. They are not as effective.

It's like in a real prizefight—you know, the punch that really wrecks Muhammad Ali—you never see it because it only travels about six inches. In a picture fight, your experienced stuntman reaches way back to Chicago, makes a roundhouse swing, and that misses the other guy by about six inches. The victim snaps his head back hard at the right moment, and you put in a crunching sound effect. It's very effective.

We always had things to protect stuntmen, such as breakaways. Breakaway chairs. Sometimes a lot of them are made of balsa, but a lot of times they will use a real chair, if the guy doesn't have to take it on his head. If your target can take it on his shoulder or something like that, you pad him up pretty well. Of course, the chair, although made of real wood, has been scored so it's just about ready to fall apart. Of course, for a barroom brawl, we had hundreds of bottles made of wax, some made of candy. If you're not going to break the bottle, you use a papier-mâché bottle. But usually you put liquid in them and use a wax bottle. Not an awful lot of liquid. Just enough so you see drops flying through the air when it breaks. And you know, there is no sting at all.

RAY RENNAHAN: Stunts were important. There were stunt directors, too, like Breezy Eason. Breezy was considered and recognized as a stunt director. Of course, his work was called "second unit." Another group of employees that no one talks much about were the famous second-unit directors who took over from the big names, went off somewhere, and shot the action sequences that Hollywood is famous for. So many action sequences or musical sequences were directed by someone other than the name on the director's card. They sometimes didn't get any credit at all, or they got second-unit credit. But Breezy, he was the guy you wanted if it was a big stunt sequence.

WILLIAM WYLER: Well, I must point out that on my version of *Ben-Hur*, the directing of the chariot race was really the work of two other directors, Yakima Canutt and Andrew Marton, two second-unit directors. They were the directors of this chariot race, because this was a separate unit. They worked about four months doing just nine or ten minutes of film, and they had the special assignment to do that. I couldn't spend that much time on it, because I was doing all the other work, and that whole thing took about four months.

RICK INGERSOLL: There were armies of people working and running all over the lot. I was an office boy at MGM, assigned to the publicity department. There were a lot of office boys. I took messages, picked up the trade papers, and gave guided tours around the lot and onto specific sets.

HONORE JANNEY: First I was a stenographer in the script department. Then I got into timing scripts. That's a job which projects from a shooting script the eventual length or running time of the completed picture. I was the first woman to do it. I'd say it took about three or four days to get a script timed. You can work just so long, and then you find yourself going mechanical, and then you've got to put it down and go take a walk or something. You have to make your mind a screen and see the characters and read their dialogue and react as you think they would react according to the story. You use a stopwatch, and you click it on when you start reading a scene and you click it off when you finish. It's a very simple mechanical process, providing you know a little bit about people. The writer always describes locale, sets, props, notes to the property department, the art director, et cetera. From this information you know the type of story and you absorb this information and picture the sets. You read the dialogue aloud to the stopwatch, remembering that these are real people in real situations and not just characters in a movie. The people will be artists acting, and they are going to make as much out of their parts as possible. You have to allow for it. After you've read it all, you translate your minutes and seconds into footage. We worked in units of five feet for the sake of facility in adding the total. You divided your total footage by the number of pages in the script, which gives you a figure of so many feet a page, and this establishes the tempo. Drawing room comedies run pretty fast, and westerns are pretty fast. Musicals are very heavy, and we timers had no responsibility for music. We just asked the music department to tell us how much had been recorded and how long it might take. After I timed a script, it was sent to the right people: the cutter, the unit manager, the head of production, the budget people, et cetera. Once they started shooting, I had no further responsibility.

HENRY BLANKE: Every studio had its casting department. Before you finish any script, you must have a conception of who would be right for it, provided you can get them. In the old days, a picture would have been developed in-house with specific parts tailored to the character actors and stars that were under contract. If you see an old Warners film like *The Life of Emile Zola*, you can see that every character was cast perfectly. Not by name, but by talent and characterwise. As a producer I'd sit down with the director and say, "Who do we take for this?" We'd be looking at the list of Warners contract players, of course, although borrowing from other studios was negotiable.

RAOUL WALSH: Sometimes this "we've got him under contract and he's available" stuff could kill you. I had a helluva fight with the studio once. They wanted me to cast Victor McLaglen as a matador. I said, "In my wildest dreams I can't imagine Victor McLaglen as a matador," and they said, "It'll be all right. He's got a big name," and I said, "He's got a big ass, too . . . let's get somebody else." Christ! He was six foot two, and he had an ass on him as big as a table. What a matador! Bigger than the bull.

RICHARD SCHICKEL: One of the biggest departments in any studio was the publicity office, with all the PR people, the fashion photographers, the still photographers, the admen, the liaisons to the fan magazines, the newspapers, et cetera. This was an area that, as a critic, I dealt with part of the time.

TEETE CARLE: I worked in every aspect of movie publicity. When I was at Paramount in the early years, the publicity staff probably had twenty publicists working full-time, supported by about the same number of secretaries. During the time I was a unit man, unit men had to do all the writing on a film's campaign. You had to do all the publicity. This was an overall thing. We not only worked on our picture, but we worked on *everything*. In other words, you not only just centered on your own little picture. Pictures were made so rapidly and released so rapidly that a unit man probably handled six or eight pictures in a given year. I know press agents today who will be working on the same picture for two years. In those days, nobody worked on a picture for two years.

After a while, the age of specialization started coming along for publicists. A young man would come along who would be particularly adept at posing photographs—creating art ideas. Usually the photographer, unless he was a top photographer such as George Hurrell in those days at MGM, merely made exposures. Hurrell was the man who first created glamour in

Hollywood. Unless you were a brilliant man like Hurrell, your photographer usually just squeezed the bulb, I'm sorry to say, in a gallery. One of the most brilliant young men that I ever knew, John Engstead, is *the* top photographer in all of Los Angeles. He's the *Vogue* and *Vanity Fair* photographer, but in those days, he started as an office boy at Paramount. I mean, he was not a writing publicist. In other words, his interest wasn't in writing. He didn't want to be a writer, so he developed his own job of posing, and he became a famous photographer of stars.

The first move toward specialization came in having somebody concentrate on taking care of all of the writers for fan magazines. It was always a young woman. You are surprised that it should always be a woman? Honey, the truth of the matter is that for years and years, a woman's chance of getting into publicity in a studio was practically nothing. First there were only two ways you could get in, then three. The first chance was to handle fan magazines. Well, there were only eight studios in town, so that's only eight jobs. Studios later decided that somebody should concentrate on fashions, which was getting important. So a woman was brought in to do fashions—a man couldn't do fashions. Then there were so many columnists who came along that publicity directors decided that they should have somebody do nothing but gather gossip. The item gatherers went all over the lots just to get chatter, chatter, chatter.

LESLIE CARON: You know, everything was sort of arranged for you to have a so-called glamorous life to be fed into the publicity mill. Now, if you didn't fit the mold or play the game, they were nice enough up to a point, but there were things you had to do. One of the routines was that you had to be photographed throughout the four seasons, following your appropriate image. I was the gamine, the Parisienne. Always on the bottom of my pictures was the caption "Ooh la!" I have a scrapbook of those nauseating pictures with "Ooh la!" written down there on every one of them. These photos were distributed free to newspapers, and they coincided with the seasons or holidays. For instance, every Easter I would be called in by the publicity department and told to report to the Portrait Gallery, where they had some "darling Easter fashions" for me and we were going to take some sweet and cute little pictures. I would arrive and be handed either a basket of strawberries or a basket of Easter eggs or a bunny costume or a hoop to jump through. At Christmas, I had to have a red dress, with red candles around me and red flowers. Everything would be red and gold, and they would put Christmas tree decorations on your earlobes, and the more you looked like a Christmas tree, the happier they were. In spring you'd be wading in water, holding up your skirt, or sitting in a field of flowers . . . and posing with cute little animals. They thought cats were good for me.

EMILY TORCHIA: We called it "holiday art." Very few of the stars liked it. We eventually stopped doing it, but for a long time every Sunday newspaper and magazine in the country would use it, in color and in good papers. At first it was free, but then we were able to sell it. I sold a picture of Esther Williams, when she was first starting out, peering from behind a barn with a gun and looking at this big turkey. Thanksgiving! She had started her big roles then, and this was a good way of familiarizing the public with her face. "Holiday art" was very popular. No one ever forced anyone to do that stuff. No one said regarding this stuff that "You're on suspension" or "You're fired." We were kind of insistent, I guess, but that's the job of the publicity department. They might not have liked it, but they liked the career, you know?

TEETE CARLE: The fan magazines were the greatest star builders that ever existed for the motion pictures. And then the newspapers in the old days.

RICK INGERSOLL: We publicized stars through the stories in columns. Contrary to rumor, MGM never planted romantic items. At least I never did when I became an apprentice in publicity and worked there. Columnists would pick this up for themselves, you know, as they got around town. Many people believe that planting gossip items about romances was the function of publicity. Well, that might have been the function of the press agent for a restaurant or whatever, but it wasn't our function in the publicity department of MGM.

TEETE CARLE: All publicity directors have to know everything that's going on, because if something goes wrong or if something is wanted, he's the man who was called, whether it's the studio head or the director on the set or the producer or the star. I mean, now and then a star may wind up in jail, and you have to be ready for that. You have that with your clients, with the people you're working with. That's part of your job, protecting them . . . not protecting them but helping maintain an image. There really aren't so many wild persons in the business. But you try to minimize the release of stories which would damage the image of your players, you know. There are certain things which you can't hide. You must always be honest with the press. When they come on a set, there wouldn't be too many things happening, because really the wild, wild Hollywood, if it exists, is in private life. Now and then a handsome, husky leading man, through a bit of clumsiness, gets hurt or something like that, and you say, "Gosh, that's bad for his image—he fell on his face and broke his teeth." Something like that. You hate to have that happen. But if you have somebody on the press that day, he'll print the story, so you can't hide it.

KATHARINE HEPBURN: You were very well protected. If you got into trouble, you called Howard Strickling. Your problems were taken care of. It was a wonderful sensation.

HOWARD STRICKLING: I required a certain number of stories every week from my unit publicists. It was all to keep the public's interest in a star going or to create it for a new person. I read everything they gave me and decided where to place it. Sometimes I had it rewritten or given to another writer better suited for it. We churned it out.

TEETE CARLE: I was a pioneer of all this. We had to write for pressbooks. A pressbook is a newspaper about twenty inches long by about fifteen inches wide. The cover of it is usually a big photograph or something in the way of advertising, with the name of the picture. Inside are ads already laid out, and all the theater has to do is buy the mattes of those ads and insert their own theater and their own dates. In other words, there are ads all the way from one-column, one-inch ads through one-column, six-inch ads, et cetera, all the way to full-page ads. They included a synopsis of the picture and photographs so that you could choose to reprint.

When you are a publicist, whether you're a publicist for a motion picture studio or no matter what it is you're a publicist for, in a public relations field in any regard, the only thing you have to really sell, that you can offer, is service. In other words, you are not any better writer or any more brilliant thinker, you can't come up with any more ideas, than the people that are already on the staff of the newspaper. All you really have is a service to sell to them. You give them very quickly and very readily an idea or the material for a story or a well-captioned picture which they can print without a great deal of rewriting.

I was at Paramount when we first started to send out stories around the country. We realized that the newspapers in St. Louis and Louisville and Dallas and other cities were just as important as they were in Los Angeles. That would be about '33 or '34 or '35, just before I went to MGM. The publicity director and myself at that time made a deal with one of these out-of-town newspaper dealers so that after he had kept papers so long he couldn't sell them and was going to throw them away, he would sell them to us for, I think, a penny an issue or something like that. We'd go through these and find out what the Chicago papers were running and the names on them. Then we wrote letters saying we were about to have a service: "We want to send directly from Paramount Studio to you. What kind of stories would you like to have? Et cetera, et cetera."

We'd go through all players' biographies to note where they were born or they had gone to school. Then we would offer a hometown service where the service was to a certain town about a certain character from that place. If the leading lady or the male star or the director or writer was from a certain city, that would embrace hometown publicity. But basically you will find that the readers in Louisville or the readers in Seattle, Washington, are all interested in practically the same thing. Whatever feature or whatever star or whatever personality or whatever book that will appeal to somebody in Keokuk, Iowa, will also appeal to them in Miami, Florida.

HOWARD STRICKLING: Every picture had a campaign. We would find an idea for every national magazine, fan magazine, syndicate, press service— we had an idea for everyone. We wouldn't get the story *into* every one, but if we got three out of five, we felt okay. For every campaign, we also had a list of stills to be distributed. We didn't just shoot stills hit or miss. We sat down and decided what was key to publicizing the movie. For instance, for *An American in Paris*, it was glamorous, big, a musical extravaganza with a romantic background in Paris. We made sure all our stills and copy emphasized those things. Everything in the old studios was done to perfection and never done casually. That's why the films still play.

TEETE CARLE: The one thing you can't buy is word of mouth. You can buy everything else in the world. You may even find a newspaper who's on the take and you can buy that man to print anything. I've never had to do that and I don't like people to do it, but you can buy anything. . . . You can buy all the ads you want, you can buy television space, you can buy radio, you can buy *anything*. You can even make a book a bestseller by going out and buying every copy in a big bookstore. You can buy anything but word of mouth. That's one thing you cannot buy. And this is the one thing that sells. But how do you create word of mouth?

DIRECTORS

FRITZ LANG: It's a peculiar thing, making motion pictures. The balance of power. If you weren't in Hollywood making them yourself, you wouldn't understand how it really worked in the system.

VINCENT SHERMAN: Men like Warner and Mayer and Cohn and Zanuck built the industry. Naturally, there were many other people inside who participated in it and who contributed, but these were the men who built the business. They were the heads of the thing. You have to say that. They created the studio producer system that made the business grow, but today when we talk about those years, we talk about the directors, and that's because it was the director who was responsible for what came up on the screen in front of the audience.

PANDRO BERMAN: The business of Hollywood in the thirties and forties was a producer's business. We usually put the director on a movie after we had developed the screenplay, because the directors in those days were mostly . . . and I say, *mostly*, certainly at Metro . . . were mostly employees who were on forty-week contracts and who were expected to deliver four or five pictures a year. Of course, any good director would come on the project with ideas of his own, and any intelligent producer would welcome them. But for the most part, months of labor on a movie were generally behind us before one of our contract directors took charge. Businesspeople thought the most efficient way to run a studio was to have each part of the factory set up separately, with specialized talent in each department, so that making a movie was a process that flowed forward from one stage to another. Each stage of creativity, in each department as it moved forward, would develop and polish and make its own contribution—not without discussions back and forth, of course, but with the highest level coming out of experts in each area of filmmaking: costumes, editing, whatever. Other people—and not just directors but usually directors—thought that although departments should make their contributions, the person responsible for putting the story directly onto the screen, the director, should be in charge from the beginning. Today there are thousands—or hundreds of thousands or maybe millions—of people who believe that everything done on any one Hollywood film was done by only one person, the director.

HAL WALLIS: I would say—and I shouldn't say it—Jack Warner looked upon a director as an element in the making of a picture. No more, no less. To him, the director performed a service somewhat better than others, and Warner had a respect for them and their work, what they accomplished, but beyond that—nothing.

Of course, any producer in the past . . . or today, too . . . knows that his relationship with the director *must* be (and almost always is) a pleasant experience because the director is, after all, the key man. The director is on the set and puts everything up on the screen. Come on . . . do you think there are . . . or were back then . . . any directors who wanted to produce and give up directing? No. I don't know any directors who didn't want to be directors. I think a lot of directors would like to produce *if* they could also direct.

WILLIAM WYLER: It depends. I did both jobs on some of my movies, and sometimes it's a burden being your own producer. I never felt that I did a good job as a producer because there was too much to do as a director. They are two different jobs, and the only reason I wanted to be a producer was in order to control the situation and to be able to do exactly as I wanted. Now, I didn't have much trouble with Sam Goldwyn doing what I wanted except in a few small instances where he overruled me. He, of course, had the control, had the final word. But in most cases—not all—he somehow seemed to have more confidence in what I thought than what he thought himself, and he let me have my way.

ALLAN DWAN: We're specialists if we're directors. It's the fellow who's a producer *and* a director that's got the problem of business and art in conflict because he's got to think of the dollar. A director has to think only of the artistic effect. He has to think of the schedule, too, in order to last, and a lot of them didn't, and didn't last, because a lot of them went on and spent millions just wasting their time, like von Stroheim used to do. Well, actually, he was a very artistic fellow, and he created very fine things but things that had to go into the discard. There were two issues: money and creating.

MERVYN LEROY: I prefer producing *and* directing because then you're the boss on both sides. Of course, if you have a big movie, like one I made, *Quo Vadis*, you can't do it all alone. You have to have a producer no matter how clever you are or how clever you're not. There's no rule to making a picture. No rules to show business. And there's no mystery to it. Everybody thinks that the picture business is a big mystery. But there's no mystery to it. Do it as you feel it. Don't listen to anybody else after you're on the set. I mean it. When you're on the set, you *have* to be the boss. You're the one that says, "Print it." And that means you're responsible for it.

VINCENT SHERMAN: These producer/director issues can get complicated. I was under contract to a studio [Warners] for so many years, and I think there was no question but that I was influenced by what I knew the studio heads wanted. Having seen many of Mr. Ford's movies, I can imagine that he felt free to do a lot of things with the camera. We couldn't do that at Warner Bros. If we started doing that, we would have been in trouble right away. We knew we had to cover a scene from many angles so that there would be a choice, so Wallis and Warner could have a choice of what *they* wanted. Sometimes we wanted to have a choice ourselves on things, but the shooting we did was conditioned by the fact that we knew that Warner and Wallis wanted certain things.

ALLAN DWAN: I got involved in contracts which made me do things I wouldn't do under any condition—wouldn't want to do, that is, but I had to. You were drawing a salary. You were assigned a thing, and you did it.

VINCENT SHERMAN: You had assignments. I did some retakes occasionally on other people's pictures. I did retakes on a thing called *Juke Girl* by Curtis Bernhardt, and I did some added scenes on *Sergeant York* by Howard Hawks. You sometimes just got called in to do some added scenes on various things. No credit involved.

JOHN BRAHM: Many directors in the old system were their own producers, and many achieved a status that afforded them decision-making power. I myself had absolutely no say, no "I want to do this" or "I want to do that." Many directors were just ignored.

HENRY HATHAWAY: I once asked Preston Sturges why he wore a red fez on the set, and he said, "So people will know who the director is."

CHARLTON HESTON: The producer/director relationship balance was in play during my first years in Hollywood in the studio system. It was really, by and large, a very harmonious and fruitful relationship. I worked with some producer-directors. Cecil B. DeMille is a good example. DeMille was a superb producer, and his preparation was meticulous. George Stevens essentially was his own producer on many of his films, certainly on *The Greatest Story Ever Told*, which I did with him later in 1965. I think it varies a little depending on the chemistry of the people involved. If you have a first-time director, the producer might feel inclined to hover a bit more. If, on the other hand, he's hired David Lean, he'll probably sort of stay out of the way. Every picture is a different emotional mix. The performers relate in different ways to one another and to the director, the editor, the cameraman. And you can't predict these things. I think part of the producer's function is to kind of make all this work and to solve any problems other than to do with the execution of the scene that's happening right there now. The best job you can do as a producer is keeping the shooting set trouble free. Without the studio system hierarchy, these relationships have grown more fluid, defined more by personality, but of course that was true in its way in the studio days, too. *Some* directors dominated.

RICHARD SCHICKEL: The studio hierarchy put a producer at the top because he had financial control and access to the studio head, but the directors we admire today were men who found their way to their own control of those elements . . . either by their personalities or their talent or by simply being successful and taking responsibility for producing their own movies. What is impossible to document is the on-the-set, day-to-day dominance that can emerge from a creative person in any department who could end up shaping a movie. Over time, directors took hold. They were the men who put the images up on the screen. They were responsible for the creative accumulation from all the departments and for creating the movie that would be seen. Not all of the directors in Hollywood were artists, but the ones who were . . . these are the men we remember and study. Theirs are the films we see again and again. These are Frank Capra, Ernst Lubitsch, Orson Welles . . .

ARTHUR KNIGHT: . . . John Ford, William Wyler, Billy Wilder . . .

DON KNOX: . . . Vincente Minnelli, Preston Sturges, Alfred Hitchcock . . .

RICHARD SCHICKEL: . . . and many others.

STANLEY KRAMER: One man's thumbprint always has to be on a film, because somebody has to make the basic decisions: "We will do *this* story. This script *now* is ready to be shot. We will use *this* actor. We *will* do it in forty-four days." Somebody has to okay all that. Today it's the director. It used to be the producer. That's why I started as a producer when I came out of the army after World War II, because then the producer was the boss and I wanted to make films the way I thought I wanted to make them, and the only way you could do it was to be the boss, so I became a producer. I promoted money and I became a producer, but I always wanted to be a director, not a producer. So I made myself my own director as quickly as I could, which is a reverse on the process.

SAM FULLER: Some producers are men who know everything, but they can't think of it. Some others are excellent.

KING VIDOR: Well, practically speaking, when a movie is being made, the director has to say yes or no, so he's got to be able to say yes or no. You're always depending on a lot of other people, but as far as I'm concerned, if you want to make a good movie—even if the cameraman or someone makes a big contribution—it's the director who has to say yes or no. This is the way I see it.

VINCENT SHERMAN: The director is making the movie. There are things that are not written in the script. Think about this: "A fight takes place." That's the script. I had one that said, "The café breaks into chaos." That took me four days to invent and shoot. They say that Mike Curtiz, who directed *The Charge of the Light Brigade*, had a script that said, "The Brigade charges." On *The Adventures of Don Juan*, which I directed, there was a dungeon scene with a big fight, lots of stunts, and complicated action. My script said, "Don Juan makes his way to the dungeon and rescues his old friend and they get away." I had to write that action, which included scene changes, and produce and direct all that and stay on budget and keep to the time schedule. I was writing the film, directing the film, and producing the film for that sequence.

BILLY WILDER: After I established myself, I became my own producer. I had the final say about the cutting of the picture and the casting and whatever. And also, my primary role of being a producer was that there was one less nose sticking in my pie, you know. I just kept them away. But I would be perfectly willing to welcome a producer who added to the picture, but there are very few.

The word *producer* is such a vast thing. It encompasses such a vast area. The producer today is not the kind of producer that Mr. Selznick was or Mr. Thalberg was or Mr. Goldwyn was. Today he's a guy who has a brother-in-law who has a cousin who has the galleys of a new novel, and he takes an option for $500 and he comes to the studio and he says, "Hey, it's on the bestseller list, and I have an option." They say, "All right, we'll buy it." He says, "And I'll be the producer." It's the first time he's ever been in a studio, but he suddenly becomes a producer.

In other words, what I'm trying to say to you is, no such profession as producer really exists today. Most producers make you feel that if only they weren't quite so busy and not quite so involved in six enormous projects which are going to revolutionize the cinema, they could write your picture better. They could direct it better. They could possibly act in it. They could compose. They could photograph. The truth is that if they can't write it, they can't direct it, they don't know how to write a note of music. But today, if they can't do anything, then they become the overseer of it all.

I. A. L. DIAMOND: The old studio producer system was designed for a different filmmaking process. It's much easier to make six pictures all at once than just to make one picture, because you have no real responsibility. You talk to somebody for an hour. You say, "Go and develop it," and they're left with your mess to clean up and you're busy with something else, whereas with only one picture in production, you're obviously responsible for all of it because you have to spend all your time on it.

BILLY WILDER: It was even easier if you were the head of the studio and you were making twenty pictures, because it's just like you were standing around the roulette table and you've got twenty chips, and you put them on various numbers—black, red, twenty-three—one or two of those chips are going to be winners. Today we have only one miserable chip, and you play it, and if that doesn't come off, we are just out for a year and a half—that's it. There we are with egg on our face. I once talked to a top executive at Columbia, and he was a friend of mine, and he said, "You always look at me with a kind of peculiar glance—you always wonder how the hell I deserve five thousand dollars a week." And I said, "That's right, it has crossed my mind." He said, "Look, the trick is the following: the studio will send down to my office ten projects that they are planning to do. They're not quite sure whether or not to do those ten projects, and I would say no to every one of them, always no, because nine out of ten are going to be stinkers. One will be a big hit, but they will be so ecstatic about that one that they will forget that I said no to it, too. So I just go on and say no, because how wrong can I be by saying no when ninety percent of the pictures lose money?" Producers and directors are in a different business.

HAL WALLIS: The whole notion of the old Hollywood as a place of temperamental artists clashing is romantic fiction. That stuff works in plays and novels but not in getting a movie done. If there were a difference of opinion between me and a director or we were not in agreement, we would talk it out or work it out either beforehand or during the process of the picture, but always with both of us having the same end goal: the best movie we could get. The idea of directors fighting to make a good picture with no help is simply wrong.

MERVYN LEROY: Not with the top boys. Capra didn't have to fight. George Stevens didn't have to fight. Willy Wyler didn't have to fight. I don't think any of the top boys had to fight. Negotiate, yes. Argue, probably. But not fight. You didn't have to fight to make a good picture, you know. Everyone wanted the same thing.

NORMAN LLOYD: Alfred Hitchcock often was *very* unhappy with what happened in his relationship with producers. He was brought here by David O. Selznick. His first picture was *Rebecca*. Very often in his relationship with Selznick, they disagreed fundamentally on the cutting of the picture and practically everything else. Their goals weren't the same.

ROUBEN MAMOULIAN: In films there is really no precise demarcation between various functions of people. If you were to say, "What does a

producer do? What does a star do?" I couldn't answer that unless you told
me who was the producer, who was the director, who was the star. Because it is a personal equation. In some films the producer is the top authority. In others a star has a great deal to say. But in the ones that come
out the best, the director is in control. He is really the captain of the ship.

FRANK CAPRA: I was the enemy of the major studios and their producer
system. I believed in one man, one film. I believed that one man should
make the film, and I believed the director should be that man. One man
should do it, and I didn't give a damn who, but I thought the director had
the most to do with it. I just couldn't accept art as a committee. I could
only accept art as an extension of an individual. To me, film, theater, painting, editing, was the work of one man. And one man should govern it. His
ideas should prevail. Well, this was not taken very easily to begin with, believe me. At MGM, I was absolutely thought nuts, nuts, and they thought
Mr. Cohn was nuts, but he was *not* nuts. He found out my idea worked, and
then John Ford said to me, "How do you like being in charge?" And I said,
"John, come over here. Come over to Columbia. You can make any film
you want. Cohn, hell, he's a mouse." McCarey, Stevens, I brought all those
people to Columbia. All those major directors came, and they made their
best films there. Everyone loved it because it was one man making a film.
The only star at MGM was Leo the Lion. They had wonderful directors at
MGM, but you didn't know who they were. You never heard their names,
but you heard about me. I made my own film, and everybody knew it. You
stick your head out, of course, but what the hell. You either have it or you
haven't got it. I was really fortunate because I worked in a small place and
I became successful in a small place and I became much more important in
a small place than I would have in a great big place where there were a lot
of important people. So I was lucky, but I also worked. I worked like hell.
I was at that studio twenty-four hours a day. Film just absolutely amazed
me. I loved to be at the Moviola. I loved to feel that film. To me it was
sensual, that film. Actually, I fell in love with film. And once in a while I'd
stop, and here was this square, this rectangle, and it finally hits you that in
the molecules of that square is the whole life story of man, right there in
that funny little piece of stuff. There it was forever to be used today, next

year, a hundred years from now, and that's the magic: the appeal of limber plastic. So I worked like hell to get where I got, and I worked because I liked it, loved it, couldn't stay away from it. And I had this one idea that *one man* should make the film, and I still have that idea. A lot of people still don't agree with it.

ARTHUR KNIGHT: It was really one of the defects of the studio system, because as marvelous as those departments might be, each one of them was thinking of its own prestige, its own standing, its own skill, and not in relation to a particular film but rather in relation to their standing in the community at large.

FRANK CAPRA: As far as I was concerned, my main goal right from the very beginning was that I was in control of the story, the directing, the cameraman, the sound, the music. I wanted it to be mine 'cause I couldn't see how anybody could put music in it that I didn't like or I didn't want. Film is a director's medium.

NORMAN LLOYD: The director is telling the story. The writer may write it, but the way it is *told* is by the director. The great picture directors are storytellers. They can spellbind you.

DANIEL MANN: There was a great tradition of the very successful Hollywood director . . . William Wyler, George Stevens, Howard Hawks, John Ford . . . those great American directors who established this business. And this is a tradition to which all directors should aspire, because they were fine craftsmen, good businessmen, clever dealmakers, but what they really did was they made what has become known as the Hollywood picture. And those pictures can play still today.

Those men, all in their own way, knew how to make a deal. George Stevens once said, "Your picture is as good as you are at resisting the front office." Those guys knew how to deal with the front office. They were not sensitive fellows who let others do it. Today the business is no longer a studio business but a group of independents who make deals and bring packages forward, so they all have powerhouse agents or lawyers, whatever. But in the old days, the directors did those things themselves. They were very good at getting it done businesswise.

EDWARD DMYTRYK: If we had all known that they were going to be still running these pictures forty or fifty years later . . . and asking us to get up and talk to people about them . . . we probably would have shot them differently. As a matter of fact, we just made pictures. We thought the movie would go out and be run for a few weeks or a few months in the theater and then would be completely forgotten. We wanted a picture to be as good as it could be, but then we let it go. We weren't arrogant about it.

ROUBEN MAMOULIAN: Remember, those studios made fifty or sixty films a year, so they could take chances on some stories. They *would* take a chance if you came up with a very unusual, wonderful film idea.

FRANK CAPRA: The business in the old days had a system in place, but people got around it in ways that are typical in any kind of day-to-day business. Directors and producers had different goals, different levels of ambition. A producer was supposed to set up everything, get the budget, the cast, the story, whatever, and then work with all the necessary departments to prepare the way the film would look and tell its story and ultimately be sold to the public. That makes sense. It *was* a business, after all, but along the way, things could happen. A lazy producer, an incompetent producer, a studio head that considered *himself* the producer . . . actors who fought you over parts, both for and against . . . cinematographers who dominated a weak director . . . designers who wrecked your simple little love scene with fourteen eye-catching sequined bows on the girl's dress. It took a lot of people to make a movie, and each and every one of them wanted to make a statement.

There were two types of directors in the system. Some just wanted to do a good job for the studio and carry out what they were assigned to do. "House directors," I hear people call them today. There's nothing wrong about being a "house director." It took skill and commitment, and some very good films were made that way. But there was another type of director, difficult little guys like me. We wanted to make our own kind of films and own the look and tempo and attitude of what we made. My kind of director—those are the guys like my friend Ford and George Stevens and Willy Wyler and others—is someone who took over the role of producer as fast as possible. You had to prove yourself, but your goal was total control of your movie. And success freed you.

GEORGE FOLSEY: I worked with Frank Capra later in his career, on *State of the Union*, which starred Katharine Hepburn and Spencer Tracy. Working with Capra, you're with a man who's very important in the business, who's a very tolerant, accomplished director. You do what you can to do your job as good as you can. You bring to the job a certain technical excellence, let's say, and you do what you can do to make it worthwhile for him to have you there. I respected him, and I enjoyed my association with him. I was actually forced on him, so that made for an interesting introduction. I offered to be removed, since he hadn't chosen me, but he said he wouldn't accept that. I had no trouble with him at all. He was just a wonderful, wonderful man. As nice a man as you could know, really a nice man. His methods were a little unusual in that usually when you go from a long shot of a scene to a close-up or two-shot, you change the lens and the light to get better reactions from the individual actor, but he'd just play it right over again. But that was the way he worked, and we adjusted ourselves to it. I didn't feel it was always the perfect way to get the photography, but there are other things in pictures besides the photography. The thing is, Capra knew technically what he wanted. He didn't seem to pay an awful lot of attention to the camera, or at least as much as he did to the scene, which I think is right. I think the scene's more important than the camera position. Capra wanted spontaneity in the scene and a continuous flow of the immediacy of the scene, and I could understand that. We all went along with it. He'd cut in where he wanted to in the editing room. He put things together in the cutting room himself. He knew what he wanted and was clear about it. He was the master of technical filmmaking, actually, but remembered for his characters and stories.

ALLAN DWAN: I think Capra's name always rings out with me when I think of great directors—for a whole series of pictures. I think Capra came out better than most of them. I never saw a bad one of his.

LEO MCCAREY: I thought Frank Capra was the cleverest director in the business. He was my hero. I literally mean it. I ran everything he made, right from the beginning, before he had made a name for himself.

PETER BOGDANOVICH: I noted in *It's a Wonderful Life* that Capra had a Leo McCarey picture playing in the movie theater on the Bedford Falls main street set . . . in the background of the shot . . . and somebody asked him, "Why did you have *The Bells of St. Mary's* playing in the theater on the set?" and Capra said, "Because I think Leo McCarey's a great director. And he's an old friend."

LEO MCCAREY: Yes. Very good friends, yes. But I admired him even before I knew him. He understands movie directing.

FRANK CAPRA: I became a director at a small studio, Columbia on Gower Gulch on Poverty Row, making pictures for $20,000 each, making one every six weeks—two weeks to prepare it, two weeks to shoot it, and two weeks to finish. And nobody there said how to do it. You just had to figure it out. I thought the camera was something that should see life as it was, and I thought the microphone was something that should hear life as it was. That didn't mean you couldn't invent here and there, but I thought what you should see would be people as they would be under those circumstances, realism. And beyond that I didn't go in for fancy shooting. I stylized only one film, *The Bitter Tea of General Yen*. It's different from anything else I ever made, but it's a good film, some fine acting, but it has a kind of sheen over the whole thing that we put on it. Camera tricks. We used silk stockings over the lens at different places to give you a different effect. And where we wanted to see something clearly, we just put a hole in it with a cigarette and did all kinds of little things like that. But that's the only film I ever tried to become arty because I was trying to win an Academy Award. I complained once to Cohn about not winning for *Lady for a Day*, and he said, "Oh, you'll never win. They'll never vote for that comedy crap you make. They only vote for that arty shit." So I thought maybe I'd have to try one of these arty things.

JOHN BRAHM: Artiness is a stiffness. Artiness is a phoniness. Artiness is a deliberate and obvious exaggeration. It's phony and as such can be dismissed. You have to fight it, and luckily a director is not alone. There is a cameraman, an art director, and a lot of people to help you fight it. Of course, sometimes *they* can be the problem. A lot of people have to be constantly controlled on a movie, to ensure that the art director does not add things, that the cameraman doesn't do things that are phony, that an artiness does not creep in despite instructions. It can happen very easily. Some directors fall in love with themselves.

JOHN HUSTON: Hitchcock, a wonderful director, is always on the lookout for material that fits what *he* likes to talk about and tell, and he never steps out of that circle. I am not that way. When I make a film, it's only been because I was completely interested and fascinated by the material itself. I never went out looking for material to express a political faith or anything of that sort. Every picture is visually different so far as I'm concerned. I try and discover a new way of telling each story according to its own requirements, never to impose my own techniques. I'm not even aware of having any. I direct as little as possible. I think when I shoot, the camera is almost a physical presence. It's as though I am there. The camera is me, and I am there watching what fascinates me, fascinates the camera, and if it is sufficiently fascinating, I move up to it. Or if it's some moments when I want to stand back and watch the thing with complete and utter detachment and say, "This has nothing to do with me" or "I am God watching the behavior of people."

ROUBEN MAMOULIAN: Some people confuse style with mannerism. They say, "Well, let's shoot it all this way, and it will give the picture a style." It doesn't give it a style. It gives it a mannerism, and there is nothing more dull and annoying and irritating than mannerism. Sometimes even a good actor can become so used to acting that he has nothing but all the mannerisms left, but the soul has gone out of it. Style is your point of view in life on the human condition. It's the full expression of what you think, what you feel, and how you see this world. That's what is style.

FRANK CAPRA: I worked for very little money. This is important. I didn't give a damn how much they paid me. I never negotiated a contract with them. They came with a new contract, and I signed it. I didn't give a damn. All I wanted was the power. I would trade money for power. I could get much more money on the outside, but I couldn't get this power to make my own films, like I could at Columbia.

So I traded money for power to make the films that I wanted to make, and every film that I've made has my stamp on it. It looks like my film. It's me expressing myself. It gave me a means of expressing myself. That was important. It was more important than money because I knew that the money would roll in if I ever got really successful. It never really rolled in, but it kind of accumulated a little bit toward the end.

But I would never have reached where I got to if I didn't have that liberty that I got at Columbia to make the films I wanted to make, because I can't take orders. I just can't take orders. You tell me to do this, and I'll ask you, "Why?" and if you haven't got a good answer, I won't do it. So that's it. I just don't work well under superiors. The army was a tough place for me. But at Columbia I was my own boss, and that was very important to me. They didn't care. I was making them money and working very cheap for them, so we had a nice thing going there between us, and out of what we made there, Columbia grew into a major studio—much of it due to the pictures I was allowed to make for them.

GEORGE SEATON: You can't just say "producer" or "director" and have a reliable definition of the job. Frank Capra fought the system, and most everyone loved him and he got away with it. Ernst Lubitsch fit perfectly inside a studio, not only producing, directing, writing, but even becoming head of Paramount for a while. He made everything work the way he wanted it to. When you talk about great directors, I always think of Lubitsch. He was so subtle. He didn't have to use explicit sex. He could do more with a keyhole on a closed door and a butler with squeaky shoes walking down a hall than all of the "throw it in your face" directors. He told you everything that was going on inside a room . . . but from outside the door. He was a genius, in my opinion, and he represents the Hollywood director, system and all, at its functioning finest.

BILLY WILDER: This is what I learned from Lubitsch: Make it effective, but don't make it obvious. Make it clear to them, but don't spit it out like the audience is the bunch of idiots. Just slightly above their station. They're going to get it. They're going to add it up. You know, Lubitsch had a gift of involving the audience into writing the script with him as it was unfolding on the screen. In other words, he was not the kind of a director who kind of hammered it down and said, "Now, listen to me, you idiots. There now, put down the popcorn bag, I'm going to tell you something. Two and two is four." Big deal. Instead, he says, "And also three and one is four. And one and one and one and one is four." He says, "No, just give them two and two and let them add it up. They're going to do it for you. And they're going to have fun with it."

JOHN CROMWELL: Lubitsch used to frequent a health establishment on Wilshire Boulevard, and one of his favorite characters was the somewhat primitive little fellow that ran the place. He always gave Ernst his massage, during which a conversation was always in progress.

One day Ernst asked him why he had never married and ever after treasured his reply: "What should I get married for? You go with a girl. You fall in love. You get married, and right away, what happens? She has to have her teeth fixed."

BRONISLAU KAPER: I knew Lubitsch very well. As a matter of fact, I was at his house when England declared war on Germany. I'll tell you about Lubitsch. He loved to play piano. He just loved it. He played operettas, [Emmerich] Kálmán, [Franz] Lehár. He was possessed. But at a party, if I was there, he wouldn't sit down and play. He'd come to me and say, "Let's play four hands," and I would say, "All right." So I would let him sit in the center of the piano. Then I sat on his right side, and I played a little with him, and then gradually I evaporated. I moved and left him alone. Then he would play alone, and he just loved it.

Lubitsch was a fabulous man. And you know, when you say, "the Lubitsch touch," it is true. It existed. You don't know what it is. Some little touches . . . he wouldn't finish a joke. He would let you think, let you guess, let you enjoy it. The Lubitsch touch.

MELVYN DOUGLAS: His touch? It's handling things with such wit! *Ninotchka* with Garbo could have been called an anti-Communist film. But it was handled with such wit—which was largely Lubitsch's doing—that it made its points without the audience being made to feel they were having a message shoved down their throats. Comedy, when it is good and telling, is always a very effective "anti-instrument" in relation to anything. Yes, Lubitsch knew how to do comedy. He had the touch.

BILLY WILDER: The Lubitsch touch, yes. If I could explain it, you know, if I knew the formula, I would patent it, but nobody quite knows how to arrive at it. But the best illustration which I use when people ask me about the Lubitsch touch is from his version of *The Merry Widow*. There is a king and there is a queen. And there is a lieutenant. The king is played by George Barbier, a very opulent, fat actor in his sixties. The queen is Una Merkel. She was very pretty, and the agitator of the king, the lieutenant, is Maurice Chevalier. Now, the situation is that the queen is having an affair with the lieutenant, and the king finds out. Now, do it your way. Do it any way you want to. All the directors, writers, or students in the universe who are very good at comedy, very imaginative, would go out and come back a week later, and they would all have good solutions—amusing, maybe a little long, maybe a little too explicit, maybe too censorable—but nobody in the world could have come up with a better solution than Mr. Lubitsch.

Here's his solution: We open up in the bedroom of the king and the queen, and he's getting dressed. There is a little nose rubbing and tickling, and she is very nice to the king. Now he leaves the bedroom, and as he leaves the bedroom, we see that at the door with a sword, standing there and clicking his heels, is Maurice Chevalier. And he is watching the king as the king is going down some steps—it's a long staircase that leads down from the bedroom of that palace. Boom, boom, boom. Now we cut back to Mr. Chevalier, and he sees that the king is leaving, and he now enters the bedroom of the queen. The door's closed. You don't cut into the bedroom. Now, as the king is descending, he suddenly sees that he forgot his belt and his sword. He turns around, and he goes up the steps back into the bedroom. Now we have a situation going on. He opens the door, goes in, the door closes. We are still outside. We are never inside. Now the king comes out and he has got the belt, and he's got the sword, right, and he's smiling, and now he's going down the step, boom, boom, but it's not his belt! It's much too small for him. Back he goes again, and now he finds Chevalier under the bed. But you see how Lubitsch operates that thing. It's all done with a kind of à-côté, kind of throwing it away, he doesn't want to rub your nose in it. That is Lubitsch.

HENRY BLANKE: As I've said, I came to America with Lubitsch. I was his first assistant, his secretary, and also his cutter. Helping *him* cut, let me say. I learned all about cutting. Lubitsch was the most wonderful, imaginative editor. He cut his silent films all by himself. He never used many long shots, except if he needed it dramatically. Otherwise, he saved the actor the 150 feet of walking! . . . When we came to America, most of the silent pictures had 360 or 400 titles. Even in Germany that was true. In *The Marriage Circle*, Lubitsch used only 36. . . . Oh, I learned all about cutting . . . and producing. When I became a producer, I followed what I had learned from him. He would never take a script and photograph it or direct it if he wasn't active in the writing of it or in the ideas of it. Once the script was finished, he never looked at it. He knew exactly word for word what was written there. After I became a producer, I worked in a similar way. I always worked from the beginning of the treatment on, through the different versions of the script. When the final script was finished, then I watched over the whole production. This is the Lubitsch school.

BRONISLAU KAPER: Now, you might say that Lubitsch's pictures were not as commercial as Cecil B. DeMille's, but you could always recognize his style. "This could be a Lubitsch movie." Somehow certain people just create this halo around them. There was a good joke said by an Austrian writer, Anton Kuh, about a director: "He has a tremendous talent for genius." That was Lubitsch.

JACK BENNY: Lubitsch could direct anybody. He was probably—no, don't let me say probably, let me say definitely—the greatest comedy director that ever lived.

PETER BOGDANOVICH: I asked Jimmy Stewart if it was true that Lubitsch always acted out all the parts for his cast, and Stewart says, "Yeah. You couldn't understand him because he spoke with a very thick German accent, and then he mumbled on top of it so you couldn't even hear . . . and this was before I went deaf!"

GEORGE FOLSEY: Lubitsch was into everything. We had this dolly so you could be higher than it would be if you were on the straight, level way, and we had Lubitsch up on it and he was on a box, so he was higher yet, and the camera bumped into somebody or hit something, which stopped it very suddenly, and, of course, Lubitsch was propelled forward through the air, and Jimmy Goggles, who was this huge, big grip, just reached up and caught him in his arms, Lubitsch still smoking that cigar. He always had that cigar and never let it go . . . and he was a wonderful man. He saw comedy everywhere.

JACK BENNY: There was drama in the comedy I did with him, *To Be or Not to Be*. Lubitsch and I had been very good friends for a long time before we ever made this picture. Now, in those days, you know, I made a lot of pictures, and everybody thinks that I made only one lousy one, called *The Horn Blows at Midnight*, because that's the one that I talk about. They forget that I made the Lubitsch, plus *Charley's Aunt, Buck Benny Rides Again, George Washington Slept Here*, and a lot of big pictures that all made money, and most of them were good pictures. *To Be or Not to Be* was the best, I think, by far, and only because of Lubitsch. And Lubitsch, don't forget, not only directed it, but he wrote it with the writer. Now, in those days, let me tell you, it was very tough for any comedian to get a good director. It was almost impossible. Good directors did not want to direct comedians. Even when Bob Hope started making pictures and we were both at the same studio, we could not get the really great directors. They were afraid that we were going to put in our own jokes.

We could not get them. If I had had *To Be* as my own project and I asked for Lubitsch, a studio would never have given him to me. I couldn't have gotten him. I was just lucky that *he* had the picture and one day he called me up and said, "Jack," with that big accent of his, "I have a picture that I'd like to have you do." And I said, "Yes." He said, "Well, don't you want to read it?" And I said, "I say yes first, and then I'll read it."

Now, I have my own personal style of comedy performance, but Lubitsch would play every scene, every comedy scene, first ahead of me to show me how. Every comedy scene that I did, he played it for me first. And I'll tell you how badly he played it, but you knew by what he was doing exactly what he wanted. In the first place, before he was ever a director, he was a corny comedian in Germany, a real corny comic. Whatever he did, for some reason or other, whatever Lubitsch did, you got the point of it. He didn't mean for me to do it his way. He was showing me how he would have done it as an actor, not as a director. So he didn't want me to do it that way, but he knew that if I watched him play a whole scene, that I would know exactly what he wanted. And he did every single comedy scene ahead of me, and then I played it.

After he had asked me to be in the picture, he was a little bit embarrassed about it for some reason. He said, "I hate to ask you to do this, but would you please, could you make a little test, a short scene where you are playing a Nazi, imitating the Nazi?" And he was embarrassed to ask me. Imagine *Lubitsch* embarrassed to ask *me*. I would have played nine scenes for him if he had wanted me to. So I said, "Of course, I'll make the test, because if it isn't right for me I certainly don't want to do it." Miriam Hopkins was supposed to play the lead in it, and I wanted Carole Lombard. Now, I'm a guy who should be tickled to death that he was even asked to be in the picture, and I should have kept my mouth shut, but I just couldn't, because all I could see in this picture was Carole Lombard. And when I'd go to Alexander Korda, the producer, to say, "Why can't we get Lombard?" he would pass the buck to Lubitsch. So then I went over to Lubitsch, and I'd ask, "Why can't we get Lombard?" And he'd say, "Ask Korda." And this went on and on, and one night in New York, Mary [Livingston, Benny's wife] and I were out to dinner at the Stork Club, a late dinner with Alexander Korda and his wife, who was then Merle Oberon, and Korda was very drunk that night, and while he was drunk, I got him to wire Lubitsch to get Lombard. That's exactly how we got Carole Lombard. That was her last one, you know. She never lived to see it. There was a very sad line in that picture, too, by the way. I don't know if you got it, when Robert Stack wants to take Carole up in his plane, there's a line where she turns to her maid and says, "Do you think anything can happen to me in a plane going up that high?" It was very, very sad to hear. Her plane crashed when she was flying back to be on my radio show with Lubitsch so we could advertise and plug the picture. After that, we lost interest in the whole thing. The picture opened with no publicity. We did no comedy promotions on it. We did nothing. We just let the picture open cold. I didn't even go to see it until months after it had opened. None of us cared. That's how awful we felt about it.

GEORGE CUKOR: My experience with Lubitsch was not wonderful, although I have no doubt about his abilities. In my very earliest years in Hollywood, I was under contract to Paramount, and they assigned me to the movie *One Hour with You* because he was doing another picture, called *The Man I Killed*, I believe. I started it, and he was to produce. Now, even with the best intentions in the world, I could *not* do a Lubitsch picture, which was really what they wanted. That wonderful, starry-eyed, deadpan thing . . . no one could do it but him. . . . I didn't like Chevalier very much, and he didn't like me. Jeanette MacDonald was very nice, and subsequently we became very good friends, but it was a style I simply could not do. Mr. Schulberg was the head of the studio, and he didn't like the rushes. And then Lubitsch finished his picture and came on the sets. To all intents and purposes, I was directing, but I just sat there and did less and less . . . I don't know what the hell I did, really . . . and every day was a goddamned agony for me. I had to act as though I didn't mind. I finished the picture, but I didn't really direct it.

The way I would shoot a comedy was actually very different from him, not that I didn't admire what he did very much, but his was a sort of mechanical thing, highly stylized. Going through doors, mind you.

HENRY BLANKE: All the Lubitsch pictures were famous hits, and so were his German films. But I'll tell you the truth: he and I didn't know all about direction until we came here. We learned partly what we knew from Hollywood. They knew more about correct direction in America. We always wondered why our German films weren't as smooth as the American pictures . . . and when we talked to cutters here, we learned.

LEO MCCAREY: Lubitsch was all about good taste. I'd link him with Chaplin. I used to seek him out every chance I got. He could call me up at six o'clock, and I'd cancel everything to have dinner with him and talk about pictures. He spread himself too thin when he became production head at Paramount. We were great friends, and I told him not to take the job. Paramount was making fifty-two pictures a year! But you know, it appeals to everybody to be head of a thing.

BILLY WILDER: I wish I would have had more time and that I could have studied under him for a longer period, because he was just a great director. And as we all know, it's kind of like Chinese glassblowing . . . he took the secret . . . the touch . . . he took the secret of it with him to his grave. I only worked with him for two pictures. He just died so young.

LEO MCCAREY: He was a good inspiration. I designed the floral piece for his funeral. It was a beautiful piece, red and white carnations. The lettering was set against a background of white, and it read, "Auf Wiedersehen, Ernst." That's all.

JEANINE BASINGER: The personality of a director made a big difference in the old studio system. Many were contented just to do their jobs, and they did them to the highest level they were capable of. Men like Orson Welles, for instance, or Frank Capra, were men who wanted to make their *own* movies their *own* way. Orson ran into trouble, but Capra didn't. Both men were charmers, so it's a bit hard to understand. I used to love to hear Frank laugh. He would throw back his head and just laugh . . . it rolled out of him in an easy, flowing manner, unstoppable . . . and he had this big, beautiful smile. He laughed with easy confidence, a happy congeniality. I used to think this must have helped him enormously in dealing with men like Harry Cohn. And, of course, his strong record of critical and commercial success would have made any studio boss love him. Frank didn't need a studio man to tell him what to do, and he didn't need a producer, either. That's why he became his own producer so easily and why "Produced and Directed by Frank Capra" became his title card. His personality, by his own admission, was not one to work with a boss any more than Orson's was, but Frank got away with it.

RICHARD SCHICKEL: The directors the French dubbed *auteurs* were the men who, like a Frank Capra, just flat-out said they wanted control over their films and were willing to do what it took to get it. These men were those that I say were "the men who made the movies." Some of them took over producing for themselves. Some of them ran into problems with studio heads and producing controls, and some of them were perfectly comfortable working with a compatible producer. In that first category would be Orson Welles, and in the second, Vincente Minnelli, who worked happily at MGM with producer Arthur Freed for almost his entire career.

JOHN SEITZ: The great, great cinematographer Gregg Toland, who photographed *Citizen Kane*, told me that when he began working with Orson, who, after all, was only twenty-six and had not really made commercial movies before, he said to him, "You don't know the limitations in the movies." And Orson said, "There are no limitations."

CHARLTON HESTON: Orson is probably, I think surely, the most talented man I've ever met, which is not a caveat I often make. I'm not necessarily saying that he is the best director or the best actor I've ever worked with, but in terms of whatever that curious mix of creative capacities we call talent means, Orson has more of it than anyone I've ever known. I shy away from dealing with that utterly unreliable word *genius*. But in terms of gift, Orson has it. It's fashionable, and to a certain extent accurate, to say that Orson deserved better of the film industry than he got. I think that's true. It's probably also true to say that the film industry deserved better of Orson than it got. He's an extremely complicated, utterly charming, unpredictable, in some respects, I'm afraid I'd have to say, unreliable man. But I learned more from him about acting, I think, than from any director

I've ever worked for. Surely as much. And I learned as much about film-making, perhaps.

The film I made for him, *Touch of Evil*, is a flawed film. One of its most significant flaws is probably Orson didn't know me well enough when we undertook it to realize that he could trust me with the fact that his own role was the central role in the film. He felt constrained to attempt to disguise that fact from me by putting in one or two scenes and handling a couple of other scenes to advance the idea that my character, Vargas, is the central part. Of course, *Touch of Evil* is the story of the decline and fall of Captain Quinlan, Welles's character. And Vargas is a witness to that, to a certain extent a catalyst, but nonetheless, the picture is about Quinlan, and one of its virtues is Orson's performance. Orson likes to circulate the fiction that he hates acting. I really can't believe it. He is a very, very good actor.

The script was submitted to me by Universal, and it was a fairly routine police thriller. I said as much. "It's difficult to judge the script," I said. "It's all right. But this picture depends on who's going to direct it." And they said, "We don't know yet, but Orson Welles is going to do the heavy." And I said, "Well, why don't you have him direct it? He's a pretty good director." They reacted to this eminently reasonable proposal as though I'd suggested that my mother direct the film. They said, "Well, yes. Uh. We'll get back to you on that." I was amazed. I mean, there was *Citizen Kane* and *Magnificent Ambersons* and *Lady from Shanghai*. But they "considered" for maybe a week. I was up in Michigan at the time, sitting in the snow on vacation. And finally they got back to me—or my agent did—and they said, "Okay, fine, we'll have Orson direct it." I thought that was a great idea. I knew that he would rewrite the script totally, which he did in a week. A whole rewrite in a week. We were originally going to do it in Mexico, in one of the border towns, but Universal had understandable second thoughts, I think, about turning Orson loose so far from the paternal eye. Orson, with the resourcefulness that is one of the most significant characteristics of his talent, said, "Okay." He looked around a little bit, and he said, "Venice [California] is great for a Mexican border town." And, of course, it is. It's exactly right, just as good as any town we could have found in Mexico.

It was a very significant learning experience for me. At least one or two of the shots in the picture have become legends. The boom shot that opens the film is certainly among them. It's an incredible shot. It took us all night to make. Primarily, we had a marvelous boom grip, camera grip, on the Chapman. The shot really went very well, except we had a bit player playing one of the customs men who couldn't remember his line. I can understand this, because he would see this whole vast complex of filmmaking bearing down on him from about a quarter of a mile away, and when we got to him, he would freeze. Finally, Orson said to him, "Look, I don't care what you say, don't say anything. Just move your lips, but please don't say, 'Oh, God, I'm sorry, Mr. Welles.'" Finally, about five o'clock in the morning, just before first light, we got a printable take on it. It is, of course, a marvelous, marvelous shot. I think probably a more significant anecdote and an equally interesting shot is the scene when Quinlan comes into the apartment of the suspect and Joe Calleia conducts a search and "finds" the dynamite that is the incriminating evidence. The scene runs, I think, twelve or thirteen pages. In a normal A picture schedule, that's three days' work, and it was so scheduled. Orson rehearsed meticulously all the first morning on what it soon became evident was a master shot that encompassed the whole scene. They had to pull doors out and all kinds of stuff. The scene, aside from being twelve pages, had four or five speaking roles and a couple of extras coming in with coffee and things like that, and it had an insert of the dynamite, as well as action in three rooms. It was really very tricky. It was an unusual scene to consider doing in one, really, but Orson was determined to do it. We rehearsed all morning, and as you probably know, on every movie set, part of the production procedure is to report to the production office when you start rehearsing, when you start doing takes, and when you make a print on the first shot. They were prepared to do that on this take, except that we went through the whole morning and never turned on a camera. And so, after lunch, the executives began to arrive on the set, though they were not bold enough to approach Orson directly. He can be a somewhat formidable figure. But they huddled about in uneasy little groups in the back, talking to one another and shaking their heads, and we went on rehearsing. We never turned a camera on until nearly 5:30. Then we started doing takes, and of course it was difficult and things went wrong. Finally we got a print about 6:15 or 6:20, and Orson said, "Fine. That's a wrap.

We're two days ahead of schedule." He shot no coverage on the scene. That *was* the scene, and it works. Now, really, I think that is not the best way to do it. You really would want to have coverage on it, but Orson's purpose was a larger one: he wanted to demonstrate to the studio how fast he could work, and the studio, of course, was delighted. He never did it again in the whole picture, but they always thought he *might*. Now, if you can bring it off, it's a technique I recommend, but I warn you, it's very hard to do.

STANLEY CORTEZ: I've always said that when I stop learning, I will quit the business. I can always learn, and looking back, I realize I learned a great deal from Orson, as new as he was in the business at the time I shot *Magnificent Ambersons* with him. Orson brought from the radio world, from the world of theater, many innovative ideas to the cinema. That's the kind of person Orson was. And I think one of the greatest tragedies we have is the fact that Orson is no longer a director, that is, in the accepted sense. He's become an actor, and he's done many, many, many films, but this is a great and rare directorial talent, and I hope to God, and I really do, that someday Orson will come back as a director and really do the great things that he is so capable of doing.

ROBERT WISE: Orson's Hollywood story was not quite as simple as most people make it sound. He didn't come out to do *Citizen Kane*. He came out to do *Heart of Darkness*, and he made tests for *Heart of Darkness*, so he had been in and out and around the studio for, oh I guess, a year or so before he actually made *Kane*. As you know, I worked as editor on *Citizen Kane*. People always asked me how it was to work with Orson. Well, he had the capacity to aggravate you so damn much that you were ready to tell him one minute to shove it and go walking off the picture, and about that time he'd come up with some idea that was so brilliant you'd have your mouth gaping open and you'd stay. It was always like that.

I'm asked whether he let me function as an editor or whether he did everything or whether I could suggest things to him, and I *always* could. I find most of the time people with real talent are very receptive to listening to other people. They may not take the other guy's suggestions 90 percent of the time, but they'll listen. Orson had a reputation around Hollywood by those people who weren't working on the picture and didn't know him of considering himself the boy genius who wouldn't listen to anybody and wouldn't take anybody's suggestions or advice or points, and that I found in my own experience not to be true.

I learned certain things from Orson in editing. I think he was a master at sound, having come from radio and knowing mikes and knowing sound effects. I think I learned added extensions of the use of voice-over, sound effects, and how to deal with them.

STANLEY CORTEZ: There are so many myths about Orson, most of which cast him in a bad light. Never once was I interfered with by Orson Welles with regards to lighting. Never once. Now, many directors *do* interfere. If they have a constructive idea, I think it's great. Four eyes are better than two.

CHARLTON HESTON: Being an actor himself, Orson works very well with actors. He understands actors. I've had the good fortune to work with some very, very great directors, some, perhaps, better directors than Orson, although surely not many. But I don't think I've ever worked with a director who communicated better with actors. He could somehow persuade you that every set-up you did just happened to be the most important set-up in the picture, and then he would tell you why.

Now, I love acting for films, but even the best part in a film is going to have what? Three marvelous scenes in it? Four marvelous scenes? Five? That would be an incredible part if it had five marvelous scenes. Those five marvelous scenes are going to take up what? At most, 20 percent of the whole schedule. The rest is going to be maybe somebody else's marvelous scene or just getting in and out of cars and walking up and down stairs and things that are indeed essential to the structure of the film and can be very exciting from a directorial point of view—indeed, finally, must be exciting, or the whole picture is not going to work. But from a performance point of view, they really aren't all that much. Orson could persuade you that they were. And when the mood strikes him or the need occurs, he can charm the bloody birds out of the trees. He is a remarkable man, and I value and cherish his friendship and the chance I had to work for him. I would happily work for him again. Unhappily, *Touch of Evil* is the last film he made in America, and I think that's too bad. He has an undeserved reputation for being a profligate and wasteful director. It's true that he doesn't relate well with the studio executives who finally control his destiny, but Mike Nichols, for an offhand example, went further over budget in *Catch-22* than Orson has spent on all the films he's directed in his entire career. And Mike Nichols is still in great demand.

HENRY KING: I directed Orson in *Prince of Foxes*. I go on the set early, thinking I'm in way ahead of everyone. I walk in, and here's Orson Welles, at eight thirty in the morning, in full makeup and costume, and he's walking around the hall. I said, "What the hell are you doing here? You don't work until noon." He said, "Oh, Henry, you know I just love to get the atmosphere and the feeling. And I want to see how you work. I want to see how all this goes." You know that anytime he was called, Orson was always an hour or two hours ahead. Always. He was *totally* reliable.

MITCHELL LEISEN: Mr. Welles has always been a very boring person to me. *Citizen Kane* is probably the most interesting thing he ever did. But he's gross, and I found him a completely uninteresting personality from what I read about him. Never paid much attention to him.

GEORGE CUKOR: I was never infatuated with *Citizen Kane*. I never could understand what the whole thing was about. Was Kane a good boy or a bad boy or a villain? Also, it was rather distracting because Orson Welles looked different in every scene. He had different makeup. There were some extraordinary performances in it, Dorothy Comingore and others, but his was the least . . . although it *was* a fascinating picture. Just mannered. And it had a slightly hollow ring to it.

STANLEY CORTEZ: I must say that I feel deeply offended when certain people take it upon themselves to make certain statements about Orson. Some say he was impossible to get along with. I take exception to that. Orson was a great guy to work with. He really was.

RICHARD SCHICKEL: Orson Welles had a short run before he became controversial—actually no run at all, since his first film, *Citizen Kane*, was already a controversy. But he became labeled as unreliable or difficult. The story of what happened on *Magnificent Ambersons* is a classic Hollywood tale, which people try to make the norm rather than the aberration.

STANLEY CORTEZ: Well, the real problems for Orson began with *Magnificent Ambersons* in 1942. Today it's received as a classic throughout the entire world by so many people, both in the industry and outside it. But there is a peculiarity about the movie. Everyone has heard so many stories about it. There are articles, books, photographs, so many erroneous reports . . . well, in short, *Magnificent Ambersons* has become a controversial film. As great a film as it is now, it could have been monumentally great if you could see what was cut out. The amount that was cut out was around five thousand feet, and in that five thousand feet you would have drooled to see what you missed. Today the movie is used as an example of the horror and stupidity of Hollywood—cutting five thousand feet and ruining a masterpiece! Well, how often did that happen? It wasn't the plan of anyone in the business to wreck a movie. They were trying to make money but also trying to make good movies.

JEANINE BASINGER: There was no one example for the Hollywood studio system producer/director issue, and Vincente Minnelli and Arthur Freed are proof that the MGM model could work at a high level. Some directors, like Minnelli, whose movies were elaborately designed, welcomed producers to help pull his elements together. Minnelli was a less articulate man than either Capra or Welles, and he found a perfect producer in Freed at MGM, the studio that really was a producer's studio. Minnelli was a director who worked well with a producer, and Freed was a producer who worked well with directors.

GEORGE FOLSEY: Vincente Minnelli was a true collaborator, but he was never confused about his own ideas or decisions. He knew how to use what was good and bring it under his own control. Arthur Freed was the perfect producer for him.

VINCENTE MINNELLI: I came out here in 1941. I liked films, but I didn't particularly want to come out here, but Arthur Freed came to see me, and he had a wonderful idea, which was, would I come out here for a year without any title or anything and work with everybody. Any producer could use me to read a script or suggest ideas or do some shooting or work with writers. Well, I came, and it was the greatest year of my life, because there were a lot of people that I knew out here, Dorothy Parker and a lot of other people from New York. At the end of that year, I did my first full-length picture, which was *Cabin in the Sky*.

LESLIE CARON: Vincente Minnelli was a decorator on Broadway. He used to design the sets for Radio City Music Hall. From that he came out here and directed numbers in films. Then he started directing the whole film, mostly musicals but also comedies and some melodramas.

HARRY WARREN: Minnelli was a designer for the Balaban and Katz movie theaters in Chicago [for live pre-movie shows]. A very clever man, a quiet, gentlemanly man. Very artistic. Very nice, very polite. Never argues with anybody, never raises his voice. Doesn't want anybody to know he's the director of the picture sometimes. You can hardly hear him. He has a lot to do with the sets and stuff like that, how they're decorated, and he's very good at it.

IRENE SHARAFF: Vincente always knew what he wanted.

VINCENTE MINNELLI: I was a designer in New York, and you work under a great deal of pressure there. Well, the public library or the library print room becomes a haven for people, and I got into the habit of having my own boxes and boxes and boxes of sketches that I cut out of magazines and books and so forth. They became shortcuts to what I wanted. Sometimes I would use seventy-five to a hundred of those things and certain other things that I wanted, and I think that the background in clothes is terribly important to a picture. I think they show character, and they show the story. For instance, I would say that *Some Came Running* was like the inside of a jukebox, you know, and the clothes gave a style to the picture. It was cheap and gaudy. I believe all of those things are terribly important. I always had a strong hand on the design of my films.

GEORGE FOLSEY: Vincente Minnelli had the advantage over everyone in directing musicals because this was his field, this was what he did in New York, this is what he had come from—the theater and the big musical productions at the Roxy Theatre and the scale of the tremendous stage. Plus the fact that he was a painter and an artist and a decorator had to give him an advantage in that kind of thing.

VINCENTE MINNELLI: I never had much to do with the front office. Freed was a good buffer. I was generally involved with whatever group it was that I was taking pictures of at the time, some for Freed and some for other producers and different writers. Sometimes there were problems. I remember *Meet Me in St. Louis.* No one wanted to do that because they had read the script and they said, "There's nothing there." And on the face of it, there is, if you read it. And even Judy didn't want to do it. She thought it would ruin her career. She was told that she was trying to get away from that sort of thing. But Freed and I saw certain things in it, great nostalgia value and so forth, and so I ignored all those people, but Freed—his record with MGM was so good that L. B. Mayer, who was very, very close with him, said, "Well, let Freed make his folly"—but I must say that they all said afterwards that they loved it.

LESLIE CARON: I adored working with Vincente Minnelli. Vincente never gives you one goddamn piece of direction. I cannot remember one full sentence of direction that Vincente gave me. He puckers his lips and he starts stuttering, and then you have to guess what he wants to say. Then he moves on. He watches the swans or the lilies or the horse in the background. You have to work with antennae to guess if he wants it stronger or more comical or satirical. You keep trying until something seems to please him. But, you know when you have done it right. He never tells you, but you do sort of sense it. He usually tells you that the swans were great. I want talent in a director, and although Vincente didn't say much, he has talent. He is inarticulate, but he has talent.

ARTHUR FREED: The main thing I was looking for as a producer was always talent, real talent, and most of the pictures I made were with talented people that I brought in, people like Stanley Donen, Gene Kelly, and Vincente Minnelli.

HARRY WARREN: Arthur got along pretty well with the directors. In the first place, he assigned them to the picture, got them the job. So you can't fight with the guy who hired you. Working for Arthur was fine. Arthur was wonderful to work for. In fact, he paid me more money than any other producer ever paid me. At least, working with a man like that, you knew he knew something about songs. It was different than working with some producers, who knew nothing about songs.

BRONISLAU KAPER: I never worked with Arthur Freed, but I know from people who did that he was fantastic. And the greatest thing about Freed was that inasmuch as he had tremendous authority and power himself, he would not interfere. He engaged the most talented people, which already was the proof of good taste and judgment, and he let them work. He encouraged them always. He was never negative, always encouraging.

IRENE SHARAFF: Arthur had his opinions. He would like something, or he would dislike something, but everybody was in such d'accord in *An American in Paris* that, you know, it was really a constant love affair during the shooting and the designing of it. I think Arthur must be given a tremendous amount of credit for this. Arthur was somebody whose great desire was to do something that had a new dimension to it, a new visual form to it, and remember, Vincente was an art director. He designed scenery and costumes. Vincente himself is a *very* visual person. I suppose of all the people I know, Vincente and I speak the same language insofar as visual tastes go. Vincente was terribly excited about each department's contribution to the film. After all, as the director, he gets the credit for the finished collaboration.

HARRY WARREN: The Freed unit was *the* successful unit on the MGM lot. They had the best of it. They had a lot of talent. Arthur was not a fellow who did much talking, so you never knew what was on his mind unless he was talking about baseball or something else that had nothing to do with pictures. So it's hard to tell why he was so totally successful.

IRENE SHARAFF: The costumes were brilliant things in *An American in Paris*, but I must say the movie was Vincente's brainchild all the way. He knew what he wanted. I made one bright saffron yellow dress for it, just as a little present that I gave *An American in Paris*. It was done as a gift. I think Vincente and I talked about some costumes being done in very jewellike colors, very sharp prismatic colors, so that you got it as one sharp thing against another, compared to the subtleties of the ballet itself. You could talk with Vincente about these things. He was articulate about design.

PRESTON AMES: There was a scene in a little café, and Mr. Minnelli was very anxious to have a proscenium screen to frame the vignettes, and it was to actually be a framed mirror. He said, "I want to photograph this thing so it looks like the real thing . . . I want it to look as though we are photographing right into the mirror." I said, "Okay," because you never say no to this man. We ran into real difficulties if we went up to him and said, "Look, Vincente, I'm sorry, but we're going to try something else because what you are asking for is actually a physical impossibility." If you had a reasonable answer for him, that was fine, but if you didn't and just said, "I'm sorry, but I couldn't do it," then you were scum. "No" was a dirty word. We never used it. We never even knew how to spell it.

Shooting right into the mirror and not seeing ourselves was a terrible problem, although we solved it. But it was a challenge that was thrown at us: "Do it!" The typical Minnelli thing. You know: Why even ask? Why question it? Do it! This is why you loved Minnelli or hated him.

ARTHUR FREED: We just did it. Whatever it was. We all did it in those days. On *An American in Paris*, we shot the ballet in a couple of weeks, without a flaw. You've got to prepare. Then it's easy. My job was to facilitate the "prepare." Minnelli's was to just do it. We both did what we had to do because it was what we wanted to do.

PRESTON AMES: Arthur Freed was purring like a Cheshire cat because this thing which he had always wanted to do had come to life. It had happened. Minnelli made sure every tiny detail was right, and he could do that because Freed was there to back him up.

WILLIAM TUTTLE: Oh, the painstaking qualities of Vincente Minnelli! Many times I thought it was perhaps a waste of time to slow up production or to wait while something is being repaired or fixed according to Vincente Minnelli's direction. When you went to see the picture, the camera moved by it so fast, or it could have even been out of focus. But he still wanted it right, even if it wasn't in close-up. If it was twenty feet from the camera, it still had to be perfect. And I think that's typical of all his pictures. I recall once in *Brigadoon* they brought in some artificial big blocks of cheese. And he wouldn't sit still for it. They had to have real cheese. And he would never tolerate artificial flowers in a set dressing. It always had to be the real thing. I can't say that it improved the picture any, because you wouldn't know the difference, but I guess it just gave him that feeling of realism that he was looking for. And I recall one day we couldn't find anyone suitable to sit for the rendering that Toulouse-Lautrec did of Oscar Wilde. And it so happened that we had an assistant director on the lot [Al Raboch], a rather elderly man who at one time had been a fine painter and a famous illustrator. And I don't know how he had gravitated to the motion picture industry, but Minnelli had known him when he was an artist and always favored him and always had him on his pictures. I suggested him to pose for the Oscar Wilde thing because I thought he had the features that would be helpful. I enhanced them with some prosthetics to do the caricature of Oscar Wilde—he had rather almost a Cupid's-bow mouth, which I had simulated on this particular man. I came back to my department one day. I had been out on the lot. They said, "Mr. Minnelli is waiting for you on stage so-and-so." This was another characteristic of Vincente Minnelli, and I can't disagree with this, either, although it could be a little annoying at times: he always believed in going straight to headquarters, even though I had representatives on the set. Even though Cedric Gibbons had representatives on the set. Or the camera department there. So I met him, and he never seemed in any hurry to get on with the picture. He was just standing there waiting for Bill Tuttle. And I arrived, and I said, "Vincente, do you want to see me?" And he said, "Oh, yes, Bill." And he dragged out this little reproduction of the picture of Oscar Wilde. And he said, "Now, come here. Come over here. I think it needs to be just a little bit higher on this side."

I couldn't believe it, you know. And this is holding up production for fifteen or twenty minutes for my arrival so that I can raise a lip line. I guarantee you no one would know the difference. And I felt that I had it high enough already. But rather than argue about it, I raised it just a millimeter or something. I couldn't even measure it, you know. And he says, "That's better. Now we can go back and shoot." Then I went to see the dailies, and the camera went by so fast that it was a blur.

Jack Buchanan, who was a very well known British stage actor and had done a lot of musicals and had directed and produced and was a great man of the theater . . . he just couldn't stand Minnelli. He said, "You know, he gives you nothing to work with." He said, "I don't like his direction. I don't get what he's talking about."

VINCENTE MINNELLI: I made that character Jack Buchanan played in *The Band Wagon* and based him a little bit on me. I'm a very confusing person.

WILLIAM TUTTLE: Unfortunately, Vincente does not communicate very well. You know that he has very definite ideas, but he just doesn't seem to put them over with everyone. And yet some people seem to have an understanding with him, and they know what he wants. Gene Kelly worked very well with Minnelli and has the greatest respect for him and relied on him a great deal. And yet Gene is a very strong person. In movie work, the personality thing is so important . . . that you get along with people. It's something that's so difficult to explain, and it takes a while.

WALTER PLUNKETT: *Madame Bovary* was my first big experience with Minnelli, who is a most demanding, difficult perfectionist that I also got along with very well. Maybe I'm the same way. It was fun.

Vincente at least tries to show clothes. He takes advantage of anything he thinks is pictorial on his set. If you made a beautiful costume and there was something exquisite around the hem of the skirt, that calls attention to it, he'll find some way of having her sit so he is seeing the hem of her skirt. There were two or three directors at MGM that broke our hearts because they knew they were holding their jobs mostly by getting pictures in under schedule, ahead of time, and saving money. I would do costumes, but in order to get the shooting done, they'd say, "Let's just move in and do a close-up of her in this thing." You needn't have done more than just a neckline on it. That was the chief thing. Many of them just broke your hearts doing that. I would rather have a man like Minnelli, who knew what he wanted and had ideas. He wanted perfection in everything, and so did I. If you sort of married the director in ideas, great things could be done, and you both could be happy about doing them. And then if the cameraman also cared and worked to get the best angles and lighting for your costumes, it was a great joy.

VINCENTE MINNELLI: My cameraman on *Gigi*, Joseph Ruttenberg, was very worried about shooting on location at Maxim's in Paris, so he said, "Why don't we go for lunch one day and talk, because I have a few ideas." I said, "Fine." So we went there for lunch. He said, "You know, this ceiling is marvelous, this Tiffany ceiling," and he says, "but of course the mirrors, we can block those out," and so on and so on and so on. And finally I said, "Joe, you know, the whole quality of Maxim's are the low mirrors. They must be shown. They must reflect the entire room in them and somehow hide your lights." He said, "I was afraid you'd say that."

FRANK CAPRA: We directors can't all make the same kinds of films. You make the films that come out of you. If you have complete control over your films, every film that you make will be a chapter in your own autobiography, because your self will escape into it, and it should. If self doesn't escape into it, you'll have a conglomeration of stuff—you'll have too many minds in that one film, and you'll get a committee-made thing, and it's pretty hard to make art with a committee. You've got a chance of making a film that means something if one person guides it, one person makes it from beginning to end. One man, one film.

HAL WALLIS: Knowledge, capability, experience. That's what a director needs. For example, when I worked with Howard Hawks—he's very much an individual—and I made two or three pictures with him, and we got along fine, I followed my usual procedure, and I did the final editing, but during the shooting on the floor he was very much his own man, because he has his own style, and I was happy to see it on the screen.

IRVING RAPPER: If you haven't got heart, forget the whole picture. If you don't reflect heart or soul or whatever you want to call it, nobody will ever remember it. Technique alone is never enough. MGM used to be powerful with technique and sets and great glamour back in the thirties, but there's nothing there you will ever remember. And I would tell that to all the producers and all the writers I worked with. I said, "Where's the warmth? Where's warmth? What are you going to warm up to? Where are the people going to be touched? By the set?" My God, every time you saw an MGM set or a staircase leading up somewhere, you never saw the actor or actress. You were supposed to love the set.

RICHARD BROOKS: When I got ready to direct my first film, the cinematographer Karl Freund said, "I hear you are going to be a director." I said, "I hope so." He said, "I am going to give you the first lesson on how to direct a movie." I said, "That's great. What is it?" He said, "Tomorrow." The next day I came to the set, and he had two little brown bags with 16mm film, about four-hundred-foot rolls. He said, "Do you have a 16mm?" I said, "Yes." He said, "You look at these pictures. Lesson number one." I took them home and ran them. They were pornographic movies. You know, where they wore the socks and the long sideburns. The next day I came back with them in a brown paper bag, and I said, "Karl, they're terrific." He said, "I produced both of them. I write, I direct, I don't act, but everything else I do. My pictures. 1922." I said, "That's terrific. What's it got to do with directing?" He said, "Lesson number one. Many times you will be wondering, do you put the camera here or up here or down here?

Maybe you make the scene a little bigger, a little smaller. You say, 'What do I do?' Did you watch these pictures closely?" I said, "Yes." He said, "Okay. Lesson number one: Get to the fucking point."

RAY RENNAHAN: There were all kinds of directors, nice guys, tough guys, guys who cared about the camera, guys who didn't care. I worked with all kinds. John Ford was a peculiar director. He gave in to nobody, and that was it. His way. Good, bad, or indifferent. But I was the Technicolor camera representative. That meant a real specialization. He had to pay some attention. I remember when we were doing a picture called *Drums Along the Mohawk* for Ford away up north someplace. Well, it was a night shot one time—shooting under a backlight sky. It was just brutal, but luckily on that one picture we didn't have to worry about budget to get it right. And Ford didn't compose much of anything. He left it to me. When you see the picture, the result is very composed and painterly, but John Ford never interfered. I'd pick the compositions, and figure out the action and the color. It was a lot of glorious country up there, and you could get some great compositions, but Ford would say to me, "Do you want someone to come in or go out left or right?" They talk about directors' visual styles, but often they were actually leaving it to others on the set. John Ford was a great director of actors and not too involved with anything else. He would very seldom deviate from a given course, and he was murder on actors, especially women. He hated women in his pictures, and he hated a suggestion from anybody.

HENRY FONDA: Ford's kind of communication with actors is to chew you out to keep you from "acting." On *Grapes of Wrath*, there's a scene where the Joad family are aware of fifteen to twenty hungry children watching them eat. They are aware, and they are embarrassed by it. We came in to rehearse . . . and Ford picked on the character named "Unk." I wasn't looking at him, but evidently he had started to "act." Ford chewed him out in front of that whole company to such an extent that it just destroyed him. But then, when we shot it, he was numb—which was what we were all supposed to be: without emotion, drained of emotion. With Ford, I was known not to agree with a lot of things, and I even had an open disagreement a couple of times, but with Ford, let me say, you don't insist on having your way. Not with Ford I didn't. Not with Ford. Nobody does. And not with Otto Preminger, either. No.

GEORGE SEATON: Harry Carey was a very sweet guy, and Ollie Carey, his wife, was just a dear. They were very good friends of Jack Ford. Jack at that time was in the navy, stationed in Washington. He came up to see a stage show I directed with Harry Carey. I saw Ford, and I introduced myself. I didn't really know him at that time. I got him to his seat, and after the first act, he called me over and he said, "Where is the old son of a bitch dressing?" I said, "I can show you." So we went backstage, and Harry said, "Hi, Jack." Ford said, "Listen to me, you cowboy. You should never get off the saddle. You're ruining this man's play. You don't know what it's about. It's a beautiful, warm, tender play, and you're playing it like a goddamned cowboy." And he walked out of the room. After the second act he came back and bawled the hell out of him again. After the third act, we all went back to the hotel and sat around. Harry had a run-of-the-play contract. We wanted to replace him, but he refused to get out. Jack went after him again, and he said, "If you want to see this play succeed, get on a train and get back to Hollywood and get back on a horse." He was vicious. And then, changing quickly, he said, "Now that I've told you what I think, how are you, you old son of a gun?" Then they had a drink together. But Jack Ford had nailed his pal.

GERTRUDE ASTOR: When I was at Universal in the silent days, John Ford and his brother Francis were working there, too. . . . John Ford came from Maine, and he worked just like we did, you know, I mean as an extra for $10 a day. His name then was Feeney, the family name, you know, and he hadn't gotten to John Ford yet. Okay, I don't know whether he would like to hear that very much right now or not, but that was the truth.

He had vision, but he had brains, too, but he was always right and nobody else was ever right. He was right first, and you did what *he* wanted, John Ford wanted it the way he wanted it. And, boy, could he bawl you out if you didn't do it right. Um!

STANLEY CORTEZ: Many of the directors, the King Vidors, the John Fords, all of the great directors, believe me when I say this to you, they very seldom looked through the camera, very seldom if at all. Now, I did a picture with John Ford as an assistant cameraman. And John never looked through the camera. Never. He knew exactly what a lens would do, because he had a basic understanding of the cinema, of what this is all about. He knew exactly. I think Hitchcock is a great guy for this sort of a thing. He knows. These are all people who started a long time ago, and they have made it a point to learn.

GEORGE SEATON: Jack Ford always told me, and I think he's right, if you look at the Ford pictures, very seldom does the camera move. He has the movement towards the picture . . . and in picture after picture he directed, you can see where he just nails his camera down and things float *to* the camera and *away* from the camera. He doesn't move that camera unless there's a reason to move it. There's not just an arbitrary push-in. If a character is moving, fine, you move with the character. If somebody is going across a room, you pan with him. But you just don't pan from one character for no reason.

PETER BOGDANOVICH: John Ford gave me a very good piece of advice. He said, "Never rehearse action." I said, "Why not?" He said, "Somebody could get hurt." It's a cryptic remark, as all of Ford's remarks were, but it makes sense. What you do is discuss everything that can possibly happen and what you want and what you'll take if you don't get that, and then you do it. Usually you get elaborate pieces of action on the first take because nobody wants to do it again, and they all work like hell to get it right.

I was talking to Howard Hawks about the shot in *Red River* when the cloud comes in and covers the funeral. I said, "That's a hell of a shot." He said, "Well, you know, sometimes you get lucky and get one of those great Ford shots." I said, "Do you mean you thought of it as a Ford shot then?" He said, "Oh, sure. We all said, 'Let's get that Ford shot.'" I asked him if Ford had influenced his westerns, and he said, "Well, Jesus Christ, Peter, I don't see how you can make a western and not be influenced by John Ford!"

I learned from Ford, who said, "Just shoot what you need, kid, and don't give 'em anything they don't need and that you don't need." Ford was shooting *How Green Was My Valley*, and there's a great shot during the marriage scene. Maureen O'Hara's character is marrying someone she's not in love with, and they ride off in a carriage. It's a long shot, and the camera pans them off and holds on the minister, Walter Pidgeon, standing under a tree. This is the man she's really in love with. It's a long shot, and the cameraman said to Ford, "Jack, do you think we should grab a close-up of Walter under the tree?" Ford said, "Oh, no, Jesus—I mean, if you shoot it, they'll just use it!" He meant that the editor, who he had no control over, would use the shot just because it was there. Part of my training was to think only in terms of what is needed. The time to make up your mind about what the scene is about and how and where it should be played is on the set during filming and not in the cutting room. Otherwise you're wasting time shooting things you're not going to need.

IRVING RAPPER: I saw John Ford about half a dozen times before he passed away, and when I spoke to him, he said, "You direct by instinct, don't you?" and I said, "That's the only way I direct." And he said, "So do I. Come here. Let's have a bit of talk."

WILLIAM TUTTLE: When you're making movies, you're dealing with artistic people. Sometimes you're dealing with a purely practical person and sometimes not. Sometimes a great deal of importance is placed upon the makeup: sometimes more importance is placed upon the clothes. John Ford was a director who hated makeup and always said, "We'll do it with good acting." And if it was an age thing, "We'll do it with good acting and clothes." He just had a real aversion to makeup. And yet he was a great man, a great director. He certainly produced some great pictures. But if you stop to look at the pictures he did, they didn't require a lot of makeup to start with. He usually had a bunch of character actors working with him that looked the part already and required very little. That's what he liked, that's what he wanted. A kind of no-fuss naturalism.

LEO MCCAREY: Ford and I go way back. I got fired in the early days, a picture I made just got dropped, so I took it to another studio to try to get another job. And as I was sitting on the projection room steps waiting for the big boss to look at my picture, John Ford came along, and I told him what I was doing. He said, "Is your picture any good?" I said, "No." So he said, "Then your chances of getting a job are not very good. I've got an idea. I just made a good picture at Universal. We'll send for that and put your name on it." Well, in my rather wild career I've always regretted I didn't do it, because that's the perfect way to start as a director—with a bit of larceny. But I didn't do it. But John Ford knew the ropes.

ELIA KAZAN: Two directors I liked a lot when I first came here—and still do—were Jean Renoir and Jack Ford. And I used to hang around Ford a little bit and get his goddamned sour answers, which I adored. And I began to say, "I must learn from Ford. I must learn to hold the long shot and trust the long shot, not to cut into it." You know, the whole thing with a theater-trained person is to jump in and see the facial expression where sometimes the facial expression is more banal than if you leave it a mystery. So I think I began to feel that about that time, and I tried to do more of that, to tell a story by pictures, not by words. Like John Ford.

MERIAN C. COOPER: I made a deal with Jack Ford for him to direct *Stage to Lordsburg* [which became *Stagecoach*]. I was very high on Jack. I thought he was the very best director alive. Jack and I went up to Dave Selznick's house for dinner to tell him about the picture, but to my surprise, he was not impressed. He said we had no big-name stars and it was "just another western." He said we'd do better if we would do a classic like the Dickens book he had done at Metro, *David Copperfield*. Jack and I both jumped very hard on David for this. We both argued, and you know, Jack Ford can state a case as well as anybody who ever lived when he wants to take the time to do it. Anyway, we both stuck to our guns, and Walter Wanger ended up with *Stagecoach*, and Jack Ford and I formed our little company together, Argosy. You know, Jack Ford rides beautifully. He's a great natural athlete. Played golf or tennis like a champion. He was a great football player in high school. A helluva football player. A superbly coordinated human being.

NATALIE WOOD: Making *The Searchers* with John Ford and John Wayne was a very interesting experience for me. I was really a kid. I was about fifteen. And the whole cast was the Ford road company. They had been together for a long, long time. I really felt like an outsider and was. We were on an Indian reservation, and the crew lived in tents that were built for us. We had to conserve water. We could only take a bath every other day. That kind of thing. The conditions were very primitive, and there was nothing to do. There was a dining room, and there were a few rooms that were better built than just the planks. But for recreation you could walk to the dining room and back. That was it. And there was a piano in there. You could play the piano. I used to do that. They would play poker every night. Jeffrey Hunter and Pat Wayne were there, John's son Pat. Pat and I were about the same age, and we used to play Scrabble. My mother was there and my younger sister, who was then around eight or nine. So we'd get these Scrabble games going. That was the big excitement. We were there for about eight or nine weeks.

Ford was very terrifying to me, because I was there for about two weeks before I ever worked. Every day, they'd go out on location and they'd come back with these horror stories of somebody changing one word of dialogue, and "Pappy had put them in the barrel," is what they used to say. "So-and-So was in the barrel today." So I was terrified, because I had a tendency to change lines and thought I was going to get in the barrel. By the time I did work, it was a catastrophe because I had been lying in the sun and got this terrible, terrible sunburn, and that was the day before. I was finally going to work the next day. I got up and fell over. I was carried to my room and was being bandaged up. And Pat Wayne came and said, "Uncle John says you've got to go to the dining room to rehearse." And I said, "Well, how can I?" I was very irritable by this time. Two weeks playing Scrabble in the Monument Valley and hearing about everybody being in the barrel. I said, "I can't go there. It's impossible. I'm being bandaged up. Tell him to come here if he wants to rehearse." And then he came back again and said, "Well, I can't tell you what he said." And I said, "Well, what did he say?" He said, "Well, he just gave a terrible message." Well, the message was "Tell her to go shit in her hat." For amazing reasons, the doctor that they had on this very rugged location was a psychiatrist. And as he was bandaging me up, I was saying "Well, I don't want to be talked to that way, and screw him, and just put me on a plane and send me home. I hate it here. I hate my part. I hate the whole thing. I don't want to be in the barrel. Send me home." He was saying "Now, calm down, calm down." And at this point John Wayne and John Ford appeared in the doorway and saw that—I guess he thought I was faking or—I don't know what he thought. But when he saw that I was badly burned and the doctor was indeed wrapping me in bandages and all that, he couldn't have been nicer. He couldn't have been more kind and said, "Don't worry. Don't be silly. We wouldn't dream of making you work. We can easily shoot around you." So all of my threats and things were immediately obliterated, because he really was kind and understanding. And he was never mean to me. I never did get put in the barrel.

HENRY FONDA: Ford was and is a perverse Irish son-of-a-bitch genius who deliberately keeps everybody guessing. He doesn't let his assistant director, his production man, his script supervisor, or anybody know what he is going to do next. But they have all worked for him for years. His script supervisor was the same girl for every film I did with him. His assistant was always the same, his production men were always the same, and "Pappy" to them was *the man*, and that was what they expected and they put up with it. While Hitchcock, on the other hand, had everybody involved with him, from his production man, his first and second, his script supervisor and cameraman, all—everybody—was in on it. Ford, on the other hand, won't talk about your role with you. If you start to ask Ford questions about your part, he will turn you off. If you get too insistent, he will just take the page and tear it out of your script and there is nothing you can do. I've seen him do it. Now, why, I don't know. But it is so. Now, on the other hand, he's got a great instinct for things. In the "goodbye" scene, when Tom Joad says goodbye to his mother, for instance, in *The Grapes of Wrath*, it was a very emotional scene. Jane Darwell and I both recognized it for what it was, without talking about it. When we got ready to do that scene—it was fairly difficult technically, because the camera had to come out of the tent and then take Ma and Tom down the side of the tent until they finally sit down on a bench beside the outdoor dance floor. So just to get that movement—I mean, there was a pan and a dolly, I believe—it took an hour or more for the cameraman to set it up and be sure that he knew all the motions and could anticipate. We had rehearsed that movement a lot. Once we sat down on the bench, which was when the scene would start and the camera was in a position by then, Ford would cut. We never once rehearsed the dialogue of the scene when Tom says goodbye to his mother. Now, he didn't make a point of that, saying "Look, I don't want you to use it up," you know, "Leave your game in the locker room" kind of thing. He never talked about it. He just cut like he's got something else on his mind—to do something else—so after an hour or two hours of rehearsing it right up to that point, Jane Darwell and I were, you know, like a couple of frustrated racehorses chomping at the bit. And *he* knew that we knew our lines, *he* knew that we were ready. That is where Ford is like no other director—he will cast for what he knows he can expect from the actor. Well, I guess he knew what he could expect from Jane Darwell and me. He had worked with both of us before, and as a result, when everybody was finally ready and Darwell and I were *so ready* that when we got into that place both of us broke down with emotion so that we had to hold it back like this so as to not let go, and as a result we shot the scene and Ford just got up and walked away, we realized that by making us wait, he had gotten us ready.

JACK LEMMON: I tested for a John Ford picture called *The Long Gray Line* that Tyrone Power eventually played, and he ages to eighty-some-odd years old. God, for about a day and a half I sat up in makeup. They took all of these plaster casts and everything, with straws up my nose so that I could breathe, and it was murder. I had never experienced claustrophobia until then. I thought I was going to die. I thought they were trying to kill me. They resented New York actors, that's all I can tell you. Anyway, they got me back to a stage, and then we shot this test of me as an eighty-year-old Irishman. Ford, whom I had never met, kept saying, apparently to Jerry Wald, who was then at Columbia, and to Harry Cohn, "I am not going to look at any kid, for Christ's sake. I want Tyrone Power to play this part. I am not going to look at any kid." He never looked at the test, and he went ahead and made *The Long Gray Line* with Power. Then, one day, towards the end of the shooting of *The Long Gray Line*, when he was through with location and so forth at West Point and back at Columbia, Max, a friend of mine, who was a cutter, threw the test on at the end of Ford's picture. Ford said, "What's this?" Max said, "Oh, I don't know, it must have been in with the stuff." Afterwards, when the lights go up, Ford turns and says, "He makes a lousy old man, but he'd be a very good Ensign Pulver in *Mister Roberts*," and walks out. Pulver is twenty-one. And not only that, he didn't even know what I looked like without all that makeup.

ARTHUR KNIGHT: Some other directors [besides Ford] expressed their personal points of view in their movies, their ideas, their style.

FRED ZINNEMANN: I think Hitchcock is *the* great master—I don't know anybody else who can touch him—and I admire it, but that doesn't mean that one should try to imitate it.

ALFRED HITCHCOCK: Most of my creative work is done before the camera begins to roll. Yes, all of it. I don't understand why we have to experiment with film. Everything should be done on paper. A musician has to do it. A composer puts a lot of dots down, and beautiful music comes out. There is a rectangle up there and it has to be filled, but personally I never look through the camera. What for? To find out whether the camera is lying? I only consider the screen up there, and the whole film, to me, should be on paper from beginning to end—shot by shot, cut by cut—and each cut should mean something. . . . What is cinema? The assembly of pieces of film to create an idea . . . it's the only new art of the twentieth century, but it is essentially a visual art.

PETER BOGDANOVICH: Hitchcock had a great ability to jump from the subjective point of view of a character to an objective point of view. At times the audience is in the head of the character and at other times not. It's all done with camera angles and use of lenses and framing. Much of *Rear Window* is told from Jimmy Stewart's point of view as he looks out over at the buildings opposite. But at other times, at key moments, Hitchcock shifts to an objective point of view, where he purposely shows you that Stewart is asleep and clearly doesn't see certain things. It helps build the tension because the audience says, "Aha! He didn't see that!"

NORMAN LLOYD: I would say the distinguishing factor in Hitchcock's work is humor. That was his particular contribution. Above all, the irony and the humor. Well, of course, now he's older and he's calmed down a bit, but in the old days he was delicious to be somewhere with because of the devil in him. I have been in elevators with him. I remember we were in an elevator in the St. Regis Hotel in New York. He stopped at about the fourteenth floor going down and a nice old lady walked in, and Hitch shifted over to the other corner of the elevator. This lady is just standing there. Then, of course, I took this knife. There was nothing I could do but stab him in the back. And this lady's eyes went back and forth. He built up these whole things. It was his sense of fun, you know.

SHIRLEY MACLAINE: He said to me, "Murder can be fun."

BRUCE DERN: Hitchcock and I got along. A lot of actors are stood off by him. And rightly so. He is very tough to work for. But within the rigidity and within that form of his, you have more freedom than with any other director in the world. It's very simple: he wants to be entertained like anybody else. He comes to the set, and he sits there and wants to be entertained. He doesn't want to be bored. He wants you to turn him on.

JULIE ANDREWS: I'd heard that he was not particularly fond of actors. And that he had once said they were cattle. But when I was working with him, he was very sweet.

SHIRLEY MACLAINE: I didn't see him as cruel at all. I thought he was funny.

BRUCE DERN: He's a tremendous storyteller. He waits for just the right moment to slide in the punch line.

ALFRED HITCHCOCK: There's a thing called a tightrope which I walk. That's a tightrope between the commercial and the artistic. I think the main thing is, right in the opening, orient your audience to their locale. Get an audience wondering. In many films there is a great confusion, especially in my particular genre or work, between the words *mystery* and *suspense*, and the two things are absolutely miles apart. You see, mystery is an intellectual process like in a "Who done it?," and suspense is essentially an emotional process. I've only made one "Who done it?," and that was many, many years ago. When you get to the revelation, there is no emotion from the audience, just curiosity. The mystery has no particular appeal to me because it's just mystifying an audience, which I don't think is enough.

I often give a very, very simple childish example of what I mean. Four people are sitting around a table talking about baseball, whatever you like, five minutes of it, very dull, and suddenly a bomb goes off. Blows the people to smithereens. What does the audience have? Ten seconds of shock. Now take the same scene. Tell the audience there is a bomb under the table and it will go off in five minutes. Well, the whole emotion of the audience is different because you give them that information. Now the conversation about baseball becomes very vital, because the audience is thinking "Don't be ridiculous, stop talking about baseball, there is a bomb under there." You've got the audience working. And the bomb must never go off. However, you've got to do something. You've worked that audience into a state, and they will get angry if you don't provide them with any relief. And that is almost a must. So a foot touches the bomb, somebody looks down, says, "My God, a bomb," and throws it out the window. It does go off. Just in time. That is an example of how a director gives information to an audience and directs them. You can't expect them to go into any kind of emotion without the information.

To be honest, I am not interested in content at all. I don't give a damn what the film is about. I am more interested in how to handle the material to create an emotion in the audience. I find too many people are interested in content. Who cares? I don't care myself. But a lot of films, of course, live on content. I think one of the greatest problems we have in our business is the lack of people who can visualize.

GEORGE CUKOR: Of course, Mr. Hitchcock is so perverse. He would never tell you what he really thinks, never, never. He says everything in this very solemn way, and I have great respect for him, but he will not tell you anything. He's absolutely impassive. Extraordinarily, he's a very religious man. Would you know that? He's always going to church. You see, we don't know anything about him at all. It's marvelous. Yet he's fascinated by all kinds of ignoble things. I can't understand that. But you seldom know *really* why someone becomes a director.

GEORGE SEATON: Well, as a matter of fact, the only reason I became a director was to protect the material I wrote. I can't help you.

STANLEY KRAMER: Why do I keep directing? Because I'm arrogant and I've got an ego and I enjoy it.

RICHARD BROOKS: All I'm trying to do is tell a story.

VINCENT SHERMAN: I steal from good directors. We all steal from each other. When I realized that, I knew I could do it.

SAM FULLER: I think every director has his own way of shooting. And I've seen, let's say, two directors, one will go over a shot many times and try to correct it, another director will go over a shot many times and not even make a suggestion of a correction, would just say, "Once again." There's nothing wrong in that. It's the way he works. Nobody cares how you work or what you don't do. How do you use the camera? You use it. You just use it. I write with the camera. I write all my own stuff, but you can write with a camera. Your camera should be your typewriter. It should be your imagination. You can take any scene in the world and have the camera do what a writer does in a book. You've read books since you were kids. "Slowly, stealthily, he advanced toward the shadow that was only in his mind. He saw nothing." You can do that with a camera.

GEORGE CUKOR: As a director you've got to think of your own limitations. There are certain things you are sympathetic with, and there are certain things you say to yourself, "Well, I can do it because I'm perfectly com-

petent, but there's so many people who can do it much better than I can."
You've got to think in your heart, "I can do that a little better than somebody else." There are certain things you are antipathetic to, you're allergic
to. That shows on the screen. They asked me to do something about a
torch singer and gangsters . . . *Love Me or Leave Me* . . . and I said, "But I
can't do this with a straight face." I can only make funny gangsters, like I
did in *Pat and Mike*.

SAM FULLER: If they like Shirley Temple plots, you may not be capable of
giving them Shirley Temple plots because you may not be capable of writing a Shirley Temple plot. I'm not. I kidded with Zanuck about this when
I was twenty. He said to me, "Jesus, I'd give my right eyeball to have you
do a picture with Shirley Tinkle." I said, "Christ, I'd boil her up before the
title, right before the title."

GEORGE FOLSEY: Any cameraman like me—or, for that matter, any actor, art director, or whatever—learned that working with different directors meant adjusting to what they could do and what they couldn't do, or
maybe I should say adjusting to what they wanted to or didn't want to do.

JOHN SEITZ: For example, Preston Sturges . . . and I worked with him a
lot . . . once in a while made forty takes of a scene. And he loved to work
outside the studio on location, which was not common in his era.

HARRY WARREN: Preston Sturges is one of those mythical characters of
old Hollywood. He used to have a nice restaurant on Sunset Boulevard.
Now, when I was at Paramount, he was never around. I never saw him. I
didn't know him, although my granddaughter Julia married his son Solo-
mon Sturges . . . but they're divorced already. Sturges used to walk about
the lot with a retinue of ten people, like Cecil B. DeMille did. DeMille
looked like an English colonel about to review the regiment. Sturges did
the same thing. Big prizefighter as a bodyguard and what-have-you, all
kinds of people around him. Always. You never saw him alone. Lots of directors were like that . . . they needed their followers around, they needed

to play the role of Big Director Walks The Lot. Some of them were actors at heart.

GEORGE FOLSEY: Norman McLeod was so quiet that unless you kept the set extremely quiet, you couldn't hear him. He talked very quietly and very low, so the unit manager had a strict rule against jabbering and talking loud or making any noise at all. You'd come on Norman's set, and it was like a church. It was quiet . . . and he'd talk very quietly . . . and he'd walk very quietly . . . oh, he was a delightful man. Very appreciative of any suggestions or help that you could give him. We all loved him. Everybody loved Norman McLeod. . . . I can tell you about a lot of guys, all different. I worked with so many.

Victor Fleming was the kind of man you could not ignore. He was a big, strong, rawboned, fascinating-looking, lantern-jawed kind of fellow with no nonsense allowed. Very organized. He had been a taxi driver in Los Angeles, and he had a great big Pierce-Arrow roadster which he would take to location, and he'd just hop in this thing and take off over the hills and across the fields and everything else with that car. He'd pick a location and turn around and drive back, bumping over the landscape, and say, "Go over there. Get the stuff over in that direction." He was a doer. He was a challenging kind of man. He tested you. . . . Frank Borzage, well, gee, what a nice man. I think of him with the greatest affection, with a great deal of love. He was a beautiful, beautiful man and a doggone good director. He smoked. All the time. Incidentally, he was a very fine polo player. He was a scratch golfer. And he was, I think, a champion squash player and an excellent handball player. He won some California tournament. He was a fine athlete, a good horseman. What a guy. . . . Richard Thorpe never wasted a minute. He'd give you the scene and tell you what it was, and then he'd go back there out of the way. Then he would sit there and read the *Reporter* or whatever he had to read. I'd get everything ready and say, "All right," and he'd be up off his chair like that! Ready to come in and get the actors in and rehearse the scene and get ready to shoot. He was a very efficient man, and once I understood that he wanted to *move*, I enjoyed working with him because you knew what you were going to do and you did it. No fooling around. You just did it and got done with it and went on to the next scene.

And that's how you got through the day's work, and you got out of there and went home. I guess that Richard Thorpe would be the definition of what we call "house director." An MGM guy who kept the factory rolling.

WALTER REISCH: Mike Curtiz, of whom thousands of stories are told because he butchered the English language, was a genius in motion picture making. In his whole life, he never interfered with a script. Somebody read it to him, and he'd say, "Yes, I can make it" or "No, I cannot make it." He was not what they call today an *auteur*. He was a motion picture maker! He didn't ask questions. He was a man of the earth, of the soil, and he was some kind of miracle. How could he direct the background of a scene and keep it alive and make a scene have the breath of life? How could he direct Errol Flynn, Bette Davis, James Cagney, still without speaking the language any better than he did? He was unique. A mad Hungarian!

GEORGE FOLSEY: I had a lot of trouble working with Woody Van Dyke. He was a very cruel man. He was very quick as a director. He'd shoot it even if you couldn't hear it or see it right. He'd always shoot below the schedule, and then somebody would have to come in and give it a style and class and a quality that an MGM picture should have. But he was a great favorite at the studio because he was so very quick and they could point to Van Dyke as a good model. He'd do a picture in fourteen days, and the others would take thirty or whatever. "One-Take Van Dyke," they called him. I think that in his work, MGM found their formula for getting pictures out fast. He'd get the nucleus of the movie done quickly, and then somebody would come in and carefully do the things that had to be done to get the points over so they could release it. They didn't mind this formula, and I think he was kept there at MGM for that reason, plus the fact that he had an affinity with Eddie Mannix, who was a power in the studio. Mannix and Van Dyke had an association. I liked Mannix, a very honest, fine man, but I have to say I did not like Van Dyke. He was cruel and unreasonable. He would devise, in a sort of diabolical way, the most difficult, complicated shots to give what he considered his slow cameraman. What constitutes a slow cameraman? A careful cameraman. But Van Dyke thought guys like that ought to be made to earn their money, which I think is an absolutely idiotic premise. He was entirely without reason, and usually his ideas had nothing to do with good picture making. Only speed.

LESLIE CARON: You can observe a great deal on a set. Each director has a different way that he communicated with you. René Clair treated you like you were a moron. You would arrive on the set, and René . . . with a stopwatch . . . would do the part for you. To the absolute detail, he portrayed what he wants you to do. He has the precise turn of the head just as he wants it. And he does it all with a stopwatch. In Hollywood I found that most directors have no technique at all in terms of directing actors. They have a vague technique on how to make the camera work for them, and they know about action. They know right and left. They know how fast the horses should come. But they don't know how to talk to actors and get a good scene out of them. Raoul Walsh used to say, "Okay, honey, go ahead, but speed it up. Do it again faster."

GEORGE FOLSEY: In the sound era, there were almost no women, but I worked with Dorothy Arzner. For instance, she replaced Richard Boleslavsky on *The Bride Wore Red*. He was a great horseman, knew how to ride beautifully. But he'd had a dugout fall on him during World War I, and it had crushed him and he'd been sewn up too tightly around his heart . . . or something like that was what he told me. Anyway, he died, and I don't really know why they chose Dorothy to replace him. She had just done a few pictures, *Craig's Wife* with Rosalind Russell and some work with Katharine Hepburn. The picture was starring Joan Crawford, and Crawford was willing to work with a woman director. Contrary to today's beliefs, Crawford was flexible and cooperative.

I had first met Dorothy in New York when I had worked on a movie called *Honor Among Lovers* with Claudette Colbert and Melvyn Douglas. I had known her as a cutter at the old Realarts. Her nephew was a cameraman, and Dorothy was a woman director, which had become an unusual thing in the sound era. Dorothy was fine, fine, and early on she seemed very capable. She wasn't as capable, in my estimation, on *The Bride Wore Red*, because by that time she couldn't quite make up her mind what she wanted, as I just said. She used to drive us crazy. We always tried to help her, tried to find a way, because I liked her very much and wanted her to get on with it and make the decision and we'd just go with her decision. I had not had any such trouble with her in New York or at the very beginning. She was fine then and seemed very capable. People always ask me if she had trouble because she was a woman . . . did it make a difference to the technicians and the actors? It was only a little strange to have a woman director. After all, there had been many of them in the silent era. After a while, everyone just automatically accepted the fact that she was in charge and it was her job and she did it and no problem. No difficulty of any kind other than we weren't used to working with women by then. It made no difference. She was capable. She had come up from the cutting bench, and she had understanding about all the areas of filmmaking. The only problem I had working with her was just on the one film, *The Bride Wore Red*. For some reason, she was in an indefinite period of her life. She just couldn't decide things. It was frustrating. Joan Crawford did a lot to help her and to keep all the crews happy. She acted as a buffer for Dorothy and always supported her.

VINCENT SHERMAN: There is always a question about what power a director has. Who gets the final cut? There were many of the films that I saw where I felt the cutting was not as good as it could have been, not as smooth as it could have been. There were many things that were taken out of pictures that I think should have been in and vice versa.

I don't know if that battle will ever be won. In the final analysis I suppose that the man who puts the money up for the film should have the right to do the final editing. There has to be something worked out. It's not right that the man who is engaged to make the film, if he's good enough to be engaged to make the film and he makes it and shoots it in a certain way to get specific effect, then he should not be allowed to see that film through to the end. He also should have the right to not only make a first cut but to preview the cut that he wanted in front of an audience and then make changes after he sees the film. The only directors that ever got that, I suppose, were those who really reached the pinnacle. And I don't know to what extent even the biggest directors have had complete and full say over the final cut, but everyone was trying to express a point of view and have that power.

ELIA KAZAN: Now, the whole thing in art—and it's an ugly word, but it's a necessary word—is power, your own power. And it's very hard in a very expensive industry. You have to think, "I'm going to bend you to my will." However you disguise it, however you put gloves on, you're gripping his throat or her throat and saying sweetly, "My dear, this is the way it's going to be." When I first worked—my bad years in films—the worst experience I had was at Metro-Goldwyn-Mayer, and that was my own fault, but I had no power there and I was just "a director" and the whole thing then was for directors to have no power and I could explain it to anybody who's interested in why I had no power there—but I didn't really begin to make my own films until 1952, when I made *Viva Zapata!* That was the first film I made of my own. It said, "Produced by Darryl Zanuck," but he had nothing to do with it.

I had trouble with power financially because *America America* lost a fortune, *The Arrangement* lost a fortune. I would say most of my films except *Splendor in the Grass*, *On the Waterfront*, and *East of Eden* lost money. So they said, "If you leave him alone on his own, he's liable to lose you a bundle." *A Face in the Crowd* lost money. A tiny little film that I like a lot, *Baby Doll*, lost a lot of money, although it cost very little. But when all these films lose money, they rob you of power at the studios. So power interests me very much.

George Stevens had the only contract that ever has or ever will exist giving the director complete control over every aspect of his films. He was once asked which aspect he would give up if he had to give only one of the basic four away. The four aspects were: (1) selecting the material and working on it; (2) casting, sets, and costumes; (3) shooting it; (4) scoring, dubbing, and cutting. When asked which of those aspects he would give up, he said, "Directing the picture."

FRITZ LANG: I make a film at least five times before I actually make it. I make it when I cast it, when I go over it with an art director, when I go over it with the writer of the film and when I go over it with the assistant director and when I go over it with the cinematographer. And then I shoot it. By then I feel as if I've already made it and it's finished and all along the line, I've been in control . . . and then after it's done I lose control. No more power.

HENRY HATHAWAY: I think the director of a film, from the day he starts working till the day he finishes the film, contributes about 10 percent to the film's success. When I tell people that, they're shocked. Ten percent? You put yourself down for 10 percent? I say, *that* 10 percent is blood, sweat, and tears. That's a job like a carpenter. What makes a really good director is what he contributes to the other 90 percent. Some don't contribute anything to the 90 percent. Some contribute *all* to the 90 percent. Like in the early days of Frank Capra: he cast it, he set up everything, found the property he wanted to do, et cetera. One hundred percent. That was the old system. It was about balance, about power, about control, and no matter what the system says about how you're supposed to be doing it, a director can figure out how to do it *his* way.

FRANK CAPRA: Like I said, film is a director's medium.

STARS

RICHARD SCHICKEL: The men who made the movies were the directors. But for the average moviegoer, they pretty much didn't exist. For the people who put down the money for a ticket, Hollywood was always about stars. Stories, what we refer to as genres today, were important . . . but movie stars defined Hollywood for the public.

GORE VIDAL: You tell me somebody's favorite actor when they were ten years old, and I'll tell you who they are. Could Norman Mailer have existed without John Garfield? He's been playing Garfield ever since. And he doesn't really know it, but it's part of him. I've been doing George Arliss ever since. You know, you get hung up with an image. Now, it's interesting that your generation has come along and you've been brought up on ninety-second TV commercials. Now, what kind of images are going to come out of that I don't know. I can suddenly see twenty years from now some girl breaking down and really discovering that she's a Salem commercial at heart. Or a detergent.

BRONISLAU KAPER: The stars were really nothing holy to us. Judy Garland was like a studio child. We didn't even talk to her. I would sit in the office and see Garbo walking by and barely look up. I was at MGM, where there were, as their slogan said, "more stars than there are in the heavens." That was one of the great things about Louis B. Mayer. He had a fabulous talent, intelligence, and instinct about how to make stars. And he never lost faith in the possibility. When World War II started, all his big male stars enlisted: Clark Gable, Robert Taylor, Jimmy Stewart, Robert Montgomery. They all went to the navy, air force, marines. And the big female stars were getting older: Joan Crawford, Greta Garbo, whoever they were. Louis B. Mayer did not panic. Within one year he made June Allyson, Van Johnson, Van Heflin, Kathryn Grayson—all these people from nowhere. And he made stars out of them.

VINCENT SHERMAN: The studios had a nose for what the public seemed to want in actors. Sometimes they made mistakes, but they were efficient. They had a process for finding talent and polishing it and selling it to the public. The rest of us, working at our jobs with a million things on our minds, we didn't look at them with reverence or with any great halo of mystery about them. We worked with the actors the studios gave us, and the studios tried to keep a finger on the pulse of the public.

GEORGE FOLSEY: Cameramen and crew don't get much chance to fraternize with actors, because when they're working, you're watching, and when they finish a scene, you're busy with the next one and they're sitting back somewhere or learning lines or posing for stills. You don't get much of a chance to talk with them.

RICHARD SCHICKEL: If you go out and ask the general public who were around going to the movies in the thirties and forties and into the fifties what movies they remember, you're going to hear a lot about movie stars and very little about anything else. Maybe "I like westerns" or about a favorite book that was turned into a movie or what they saw on their first date. But movie stars were what sold the studio system product. Movie magazines were all about the stars, not the business. Even today, the idea of old Hollywood is defined by movie stars, the legends who still sell magazines, biographies, T-shirts, and the very same movies they starred in years ago. The stars *were* Hollywood. When people dreamed of going to Hollywood, it was to maybe meet a movie star. When people dreamed of working in Hollywood, it was about becoming a movie star.

JOHN CROMWELL: Hollywood emphasized the star system and the making of star names. With a star, you could make money.

HAL WALLIS: Stars were our insurance.

MERVYN LEROY: You knew the star was the draw. I'm talking about the star that you knew would really bring people into the theater. Today, actors won't bring anybody in unless the picture that they're in is really great. And that goes for anybody today. It's the way it is now, because the studios today . . . they don't make stars anymore.

   We used to have acting schools on the lot. We would take kids like Lana Turner and Judy Garland and have a school going, and we had a lot of things they don't have today to help them, groom them, teach them, and bring them along. We watched to see who the public responded to and wanted to see more of. It was a good system, because if you see a personality, a beautiful girl or an ugly girl that's got talent . . . it doesn't make any difference if they have talent . . . and you groom them, you are enhancing your business potential. The old star system kept the talent in front of the public, shaped a personality for them, created movie stories just for them, and kept their name and image out there in the movie magazines and newspapers. It was a whole different world back then.

ROBERT WAGNER: I went to Warner Bros. when I was sixteen years old. They went on a writers' strike, and I got bounced. Then I was signed by

Fox when I was eighteen, and I didn't really know very much about anything. They had teachers there to teach you drama. They had a test department. They had an opportunity for you to be in B pictures, C pictures, A pictures, whatever, to get screen acting experience.

NATALIE WOOD: And all sorts of things to learn, too. I mean, they taught you fencing, dancing—

ROBERT WAGNER: —riding, anything. I mean, all of that was open to you. When I was signed, there were 125 aspiring actors under contract at the studio. Metro had 250, I believe. And that was wonderful, because a lot of people who had real careers surfaced out of that. It's a different kind of thing, you know. I mean, Zanuck, when I was there, placed me. He started putting me in different pictures. I remember I was in a picture, *With a Song in My Heart*, which starred Susan Hayward, and I was in the film for about a minute and a half, and the people walked out of the theater, and they said, "Who was that guy?" And it started this whole thing with the fan magazines. This was a whole different kind of buildup.

NATALIE WOOD: And the fan mail departments, too, which no longer exist. In those days, the studios, the executives, used to take great note of the amount of fan mail that would come in from the public to figure out how popular someone really was. And now that's been abandoned.

RICHARD BROOKS: The old stars were taught how to act on camera. It's the toughest kind of acting there is in the world, much more difficult than on the stage, because on the stage you have a chance to build a character from beginning to end in three hours, or two hours and forty minutes if you have only one intermission. You can build. You can hear the audience. You have something to work with. You've had a chance to rehearse for four or five weeks. You know where all the jokes are. You know where the laughs come. You know where the silences are. You've built the character so you can build an emotional rise. But in film, you shoot for twenty seconds, thirty seconds, maybe a minute, two minutes. You have no audience to respond. The crew are busy doing their jobs. You perform your story out of sequence, with no continuity, and you do it perfectly, impeccably, but the take is spoiled by some technical thing and you have to do it over, maybe twenty times, finding the right tone and emotion time after time. And the roles are often tailored for who the public has decided you are because the studio told them that's who you were, and that's *not* who you are. It's a very hard kind of acting, and people are quick to dismiss it as not acting at all.

JOHN CROMWELL: Film acting is so completely different. It is a different kind of acting. In one way it is much more difficult to do. The first thing it does is require an entirely different kind of discipline of the actor.

The actor in the theater does a certain amount of prethinking, but when he comes to rehearsal, the thing that he is going to do grows slowly during the rehearsals. Gradually he accumulates momentum toward the thing that he wants to realize. Then his problems become quite different. In the theater the actor faces the rut of the long run and the repetition of this one performance over and over again.

The man in pictures has to do almost all of his creative work way ahead of the beginning of the picture. It all has to be in his mind, well gone over, because they may start the picture in the middle of the story. He has to be prepared to deliver what would be there as an accumulation of the story.

An actor's value in pictures was measured strictly by the amount and character of his fan mail and the reports from exhibitors throughout the country. This was a response to *personality* rather than a recognition of talent. If some technical facility went with it, then so much the better. These were the Gables, the Garbos, the Cagneys, the Crawfords, and the Davises. The legends.

WILLIAM TUTTLE: These stars in the old Hollywood were so distinctive. There was someone for everybody to love, all types, distinctive types. There were no two people who looked alike. Each was an entity on their own. There were no two Clark Gables. There were no two Spencer Tracys or Wally Beerys. They stood alone. And I think that's what gave them a certain charisma. Today you find so many similarities. I find it difficult to distinguish some actors that are on the screen today.

ADELA ROGERS ST. JOHNS: MGM had the big ones: Garbo, Gable, Rooney, Judy, Harlow, Crawford, Hepburn and Tracy, Jeanette MacDonald and Nelson Eddy, Hedy Lamarr, Greer Garson, Robert Taylor, Lana Turner, Wallace Beery, the Barrymores, Marie Dressler, Ava Gardner . . .

BRONISLAU KAPER: They had them, and they groomed them and waited for a chance. I don't recall the names of all of them, but do you know that Van Johnson became a star overnight? It was through a picture called *A Guy Named Joe*. Van Heflin became a star in one scene, in a movie called *Johnny Eager*. Of course, Mayer made Robert Taylor into a name also. I used to see Robert Taylor in the Commissary, and I'd say, "Who is that handsome young man?" and they'd say, "Oh, he's a stock player." Suddenly Robert Taylor was getting $250 a week, and he was a star.

HARRY WARREN: Everybody was there but the kitchen sink. MGM had absolutely everybody in the musical world. Didn't they bring in Frank Sinatra to sing "Old Man River"? It was *loaded* with musical talent, that lot was. It was just fantastic the amount of people they had there. Behind the scenes, of course, but they built up those musical stars: Garland, Gene Kelly, Fred Astaire after his RKO years, Jane Powell, Howard Keel, Cyd Charisse, Vera-Ellen, Mario Lanza, oh, boy, I am forgetting big names, because that's how many they had. These people were taken care of, believe me, because they were money at the box office.

VINCENT SHERMAN: Over at Warners they had Bette Davis and Olivia de Havilland and Ida Lupino and guys like Humphrey Bogart, Edward G. Robinson, George Raft, Jimmy Cagney, Errol Flynn. . . . Universal had horror film stars and made money with W. C. Fields, and Abbott and Costello earned them a fortune. Deanna Durbin saved them from bankruptcy.

HARRY WARREN: And at Fox, Betty Grable, Alice Faye, Gene Tierney, Dana Andrews, Cornel Wilde, Tyrone Power, Don Ameche . . . later came Marilyn Monroe . . . little Shirley Temple in the thirties . . .

JEAN LOUIS: . . . and Rita Hayworth was at Columbia, and they brought in Kim Novak . . . Paramount had both Bob Hope and Bing Crosby, plus Veronica Lake and Alan Ladd, Paulette Goddard, Ray Milland, Betty Hutton, Mae West, Marlene Dietrich, Carole Lombard.

PANDRO BERMAN: Astaire and Rogers were great draws at RKO in the thirties, and for a time, they had Irene Dunne under contract, and Orson Welles came in and they signed Robert Mitchum. Some stars went into a freelance sort of mode, such as Cary Grant after RKO, Barbara Stanwyck, and Claudette Colbert . . . and Selznick made money loaning out the stars he put under contract, people like Ingrid Bergman, Joseph Cotton, Farley Granger, the teenage Shirley Temple . . .

BRONISLAU KAPER: As I said, or MGM said, more stars than there were in the heavens. And closer, too, just up there on the screen in your neighborhood theater. For fifty cents.

STANLEY DONEN: These stars defined studio output, too. There was something unmistakable about an MGM musical, and it was partly Gene Kelly or Fred Astaire when they were both there. And besides the Freed unit making things like *Singin' in the Rain*, there was the Joe Pasternak unit there with someone like Jane Powell. You would never mistake any of those MGM musicals for a Fox musical, because if you were at a Fox musical, it would be flashy with its Technicolor, would have different choreography, but mostly it would have Betty Grable and Dan Dailey or June Haver and Carmen Miranda. The star shaped the vehicle. It had to be tailored around their talents and personalities. Betty Grable was Fox. Judy Garland was MGM. And behind them were art directors and cinematographers with specific styles, too. It all added up, but it had to be shaped around the star. The public went to see the star, really.

WILLIAM TUTTLE: There were so many things working for the star at that time. They never appeared badly in a picture. It was almost impossible. You didn't get that far, get under contract and be signed for a picture, and not have everything at your disposal for you to be able to do your absolute best. You were a studio investment, a "property." And I think that that's the reason for some of the people today who are commenting about the old pictures they see on television. They seem to enjoy them so much more because there wasn't a bad performance. There was just no such thing. It didn't exist. People who became stars were given the right parts. They were given things where they could excel. If the part didn't quite fit, if they brought a story and they planned to do this certain story and they were going to cast certain people in it, but they decided that this fellow couldn't read lines in a rapid-fire fashion, it was rewritten so that he *could*. Remember that MGM had a roster of directors, writers, cameramen, all under contract. You never had to go off the lot. What you needed was all right there. We had an acting roster from little children on up to men in their seventies and eighties: Lewis Stone, C. Aubrey Smith, and people like that. You know, in that age bracket. Then we had the young ones, the Bob Taylors, who were just starting in, right on down through the teen-agers, down to your Margaret O'Briens and people like that, that were babies practically. And if a part wasn't right, the director wasn't right, the cameraman wasn't right, it was changed so that it *was* right. I knew them to change cameramen three times on *A Guy Named Joe* with Irene Dunne. Three of the top cameramen in the business—one of them was Karl Freund, one was Ray June, and I think George Folsey—they were considered some of the best in the business, and they shot three different tests to be sure they had the person who would make Irene Dunne look her very best. And we had three different makeup artists test her look, her hairdos, and her clothes. Now, on *A Guy Named Joe*, Dunne was already a well-established star, but she wasn't an MGM star. She was borrowed from maybe RKO or some other studio, or maybe she was freelance or at least not on a long-term MGM contract, because they wanted the very best choice for this particular role and they thought it was her. So they gave her the full treatment anyway.

RICHARD SCHICKEL: The studios brought young people in and over a pe-riod of time developed them, hoping to create a career that would last for some length of time. Remember, people in the audience were taking these people into their lives in some way, hopefully for a long run. It was a pro-cess for the audience that's almost the same process as making friends. You know, we see them, meet them, first in a small role, and then we see them around another time, and then, you know, pretty soon they're our life's companion. The best star careers are those that don't burst upon people overnight. They build to some degree slowly. They insinuate themselves. But every star needs a moment where they really transcend themselves in some way. Otherwise they just stay on a kind of plateau. For example, I love the late Joel McCrea. He's a wonderful presence in movies. He was never a great star like John Wayne or anything because he never really had a *Stagecoach* kind of moment, which is that moment we focus in on him as a striking, powerful image. Being a movie star has a lot to do with their persona, which goes beyond their acting ability. Think of James Dean. The guy was in three films, and we still remember him. He had something that went beyond his acting ability. If James Dean had gone on and made twenty-seven movies, maybe he might not loom so large in people's lives. We don't know.

ARTHUR KNIGHT: The stars—actually, they called them actors and ac-tresses back then—were the people who sold the tickets. They probably had the least power of all the people working in the studios, except for the power they could exert by cajoling, threatening, referring to the size of their fan mail, marrying an executive or a director or a cinematographer or a designer or another star, whatever. Everyone outside the business revered them, but in the business, their significance came after everything else had been planned, designed, set up. The business was serious about the people we call movie stars, however, and they were constantly looking for potential candidates. And when they found someone, they spared no effort or ex-pense to develop them. They put them into their business system.

ANN RUTHERFORD: I am a classic example of this. I was brought in, given a screen test and a beginner's contract. I was taught everything, and so were all the other young people with me at that time. They spent time on you. When they figured you really *could* walk and talk, then they put the camera on you. Eventually, if you looked good—and they would have spent time experimenting on you with makeup, wigs, hair color, and clothes—the word would go out that it was time to fit you into a picture. If you were any good at all in that and showed any promise, they would have somebody write some special scenes for you. And if the public seemed to like you, you caught on in some way, you'd be moved to the next rung with good supporting roles.

I was put into a series of pictures called the Andy Hardy pictures. We made about seventeen or eighteen of them, I should say. After we had made, perhaps, three of them, they discovered that they had a blockbuster on their hands. They were big, big moneymakers. They made these things in four weeks, for peanuts. So Mr. Mayer thought, "Aaah, we will give it the A picture treatment." This doesn't happen today. It grieves me. I have seen so many young people in motion pictures flashing through, and I think, "Oh! If there was just a studio to bring them along further." That paternalistic thing is gone. To me, the big studios were never ogres. It was a passport to the world. It opened doors to me that in my lifetime would never have been opened. They gave me my career and taught me how to make it work.

MERVYN LEROY: In the old days they *made* stars. At Metro, they kept Nelson Eddy under contract for five years before he did anything, did *anything*, because he was clumsy. He didn't know how to handle his hands. They made stars. They don't make stars today. And when they *were* stars, they looked like stars and they acted like stars and they *were* stars. Cary Grant is still a star today, if he was ever in a picture. You know, it takes seven times around the world to make a star. Sometimes you say, "Oh, boy, is she great in this picture" or "Is he great in this picture." In America, it takes a long time to make a real star, penetrating around the world. It takes a long time to make a star that is a *real* star.

LUCILLE BALL: That's true. I was hanging around for a year as a showgirl, a year as a script girl, a year as a member of a studio stock company, just a contract player. Those are long years that you're talking about! They had things like publicity departments. They were a great, great help. You got to know a Howard Strickling, a Howard McClay, Papa Mayer, a Mr. Zanuck, Harry Cohn, Harry Cohn's assistant, the man who shot the pictures at RKO, Bachrach. You got to know maybe five or six people in the studio, but they were your friends, they were your mama and papa, and they took care of you. You don't have that now, and that's bad, I feel very sorry for today's kids. Seriously, I've talked to hundreds and hundreds and hundreds of kids that come around with tears in their eyes.

My story is pretty typical. I started from a small, dinky town—Jenkinstown, New York, a helluva town to be from. I always wanted to be in vaudeville. I didn't know it was dead. No one told me. And I arrived in New York City, and I was going to get into vaudeville because that's all I had ever seen. I had seen some pictures, and I had seen some Pearl White serials—you know, where they lay out on railroad tracks. I had seen that. But it never dawned on me to be in pictures. I wouldn't even dream of being in pictures. But to be in vaudeville, I could understand that. I had gotten into everything I could in high school and church and Sunday school and the Elks convention or whatever came along, I was playing there, dancing and singing and doing all the things I could do in my hometown. Vaudeville, that's what I wanted. So I kept looking for it, and no one told me it was dead, I didn't even know the Palace was closed! But anyway, I never got a job—never got near anybody—and finally I got so hungry I went into modeling. But the great thing is I kept my eye on showbiz, and I wasn't just going to run off and marry the first guy that asked me. I thought, I'll learn how to be a good model, because I have to learn how to do something well. I couldn't dance, I wasn't beautiful, nobody was yelling or screaming for anything I had. So I was walking down the street one day—this is a true story—a very hot July day, and a lady who had seen me in a fashion show saw me and said, "What are you doing here in July?" And I said, "What do you mean July? I'm working." So she said, "Nobody stays in town in July." She had just come from Sam Goldwyn's office, and they needed a showgirl for six weeks in an Eddie Cantor picture. And I said, "Anything to get out of town for six weeks. That would be marvelous." So I went, and in ten minutes I had a job. If I'd been tested, I probably never would've gotten it because I wasn't beautiful, *zaftig*, or any of the things the other girls were. The picture, instead of taking six weeks, took six months. After six months I knew I was in a kind of place where I could find a niche.

Now it became important to me to become part of the business. I loved it that much. I didn't care at all that I was a showgirl. I was learning. I felt a part of something, and I thought I could learn. So there came a time within the year that I went to Mr. Goldwyn and I said, "Mr. Goldwyn, now that I'm on the second line of the harem, could you allow me—I've been talking to some people, I know there's a stock company at Columbia—so could you—" "Yes," he said, before I finished. I went over and joined a stock company, and I learned a little by having a lot of seltzer water squirted in my face by the Three Stooges. Nice men, but. . . . But I learned a lot of things about comedy that I never want to do. And then, from that stock company, we all got let off one evening at six o'clock—boom. About thirty, thirty-five people were let out at six o'clock unexpectedly. The entire stock company. And we were just standing out in the street saying "What happened?" That was it. I didn't know where to turn. I had a date with some boy, and he arrived and I was crying and he said, "What's the matter?" "I lost my job! There was no reason. They just let us all out." He knew there was a showgirl call at RKO just down the street at nine o'clock. But I said, "I don't want to be a showgirl again." And he said, "What the hell have you been doing here that's so great?" So I said, "You're right." So I got the job, and I was there seven years.

Now, from that job within the studio, I only complained twice, and my complaints, I must say, gave me a step. Once I complained. I was playing in *The Three Musketeers*—one of the original ones with Walter Abel, God knows who else—and we were way out in Calabasas. It was very hot, and I was wearing four petticoats and a velvet thing and plumes, and I fainted. And there'd been a lot of cows around there. When I picked myself up, dusted myself off, I said, "Sir, get me a car, I'm going back to the studio, and I'm quitting." So they sent me back to the studio, I got out of the things, and I was called to the casting office. And Mr. Piazza said, "What's the matter?" And I said, "I'm not going on any more hot locations. I can't stand heat." That was my only complaint—I couldn't stand the heat. It wasn't that I minded being a showgirl. It was just the heat—I couldn't stay out there in those petticoats any longer. So he said, "Okay, okay, don't say you're going to quit." From then on I got better parts. The next time I complained, it was because of something physical. Some stupid director had not checked something. A man had read, "She dances out onto the soaped floor and goes into the splits and gets up, does a twirl, and twirls off." Well, the silly-ass propman soaped the floor. He really did, without asking anybody or discussing it. Who can do a split on a soaped floor without killing yourself? At that time I could do a split, so I twirled out and I did a split and I almost split right in half. When they picked me up, I said, "Get me out of here." Six months later, I was still ill. I had hurt myself very badly, but I never really complained. I was glad to be a part of the business.

There are certain things about making pictures. You make a picture now, and it comes out a year and a half later. You can get awful hungry in a year and a half. So there are other things that come up, perhaps things that are not as great as what you just did, the money isn't as great, and it's not all the big buildup. However, you'll be learning something, you'll be working with people, meeting someone, maybe out of thirty or forty people you'll meet one person who'll pop up a little later and be so damned important to you you don't realize it. That's the way I look at it. Yes, ma'am.

PANDRO BERMAN: My first recollection of Lucille Ball would be about 1934, when I used her, for the first time, I think, on the RKO lot as a model in *Roberta*. She's in there as one of the clotheshorses in one of the fashion shows. We had quite a little group of girls in there at that time. Lucille was a model along with about six very pretty girls. She was a very, very talented woman and is to this day. Just great. She was also very, *very* determined. She was ambitious. She *had* to make it. It would have killed her if she hadn't. I remember one instance when I tried to help her get started: George Kaufman was going to put on *Stage Door* in New York, and it occurred to me that Lucille Ball would have been awfully good in one of the roles, and I recommended her to Leland Hayward, who was sort of George's agent. And I got back a very frivolous reply, you know, because he didn't know her, and they obviously wanted someone else in the role. But when I subsequently made the picture, I put Lucille in the part, and that was really the beginning of her career. That was the first time she really had something to do.

JEANINE BASINGER: The goal of both the studio and the young person being groomed was to be put under contract. The studio signed the actor for years as a possible moneymaking asset, and the actor secured a guaranteed salary as well as publicity, protection, lessons in all sorts of things from diction to grooming to horseback riding, and the studio's help in fixing their teeth, providing a loan to buy a house, dealing with legal issues from parking tickets to drunken arrests. But in the long run, the contract for the star was a form of bondage and could even be detrimental to a career.

NATALIE WOOD: For whatever reason they might have, they could just say no to you. They wouldn't care. From the time I was at Warner Bros., the disadvantage was that you had absolutely no choice. You had to do things that you really maybe violently objected to, and you just had to do them, no matter what, or sometimes they would prevent you from doing something where you knew there was a good role for you. Oh, yes, they really owned you.

ROBERT WAGNER: They could suspend you.

NATALIE WOOD: I was suspended for eighteen months one time.

OLIVIA DE HAVILLAND: In my era, my first years at Warners and in Hollywood, if any of us wanted our own way about anything or wanted to influence anything regarding our careers, we had to find tricky ways of doing it. We couldn't do it outwardly. I had the following system: I soon learned that every script that was going to be made first came to the makeup department for a breakdown. The head of the makeup department would have to figure out how many makeup men he needed with wigs or certain makeup artists that knew how to put on beards, all that kind of thing, whether there had to be somebody who was good at making scars—an Errol Flynn film would certainly require scars, a scar specialist, and a blood specialist—so I would sneak the scripts out of the makeup department and take them home and read them overnight, and that's how I got *Strawberry Blonde*. I found out about it. I went to the producer, and I said, "I understand that you are making *Strawberry Blonde* and it isn't cast yet and I would like to play the part of Amy in it." He said, "You don't want to play the part of Amy." And I said, "Yes, I do want to play the part of Amy." He said, "But that's not the title role." And I said, "I don't care if it's not the title role. Let anybody else play the title role. The point is that that's a woman I understand, and I would like to play her. I just love her, and I want to play her." It was very tough getting that part, but I started it, I initiated it and, in a sense, chose it. Do you see what I mean?

JOHN CROMWELL: For an actor to try to break through or get roles they wanted, that took a hell of a lot of courage. In most cases it couldn't be done. Even the most popular actors of that time didn't really have the authority, didn't have the persuasiveness.

HOWARD HAWKS: Gable, Barrymore, Harlow, not one of those actors had a damn thing to say about the choice of stories. They did what they were told to do by very smart people. And they remade any portion of the picture that was bad. And they worked the star system so that if you went to see Gable, you knew that you were going to see a certain type of picture. You knew what he stood for. You knew if you were going to see Crawford, what kind of story it would be. When the day came that the stars decided themselves what they were going to do—holy smoke, what a mess they made. You know, because nobody was watching them then. There have been some awfully good people who failed miserably because they chose bad things. They were better off when the studios chose, but many of them wanted more freedom, less glamour.

LESLIE CARON: It wasn't all glamorous. It wasn't easy. It wasn't fun. You started, like, at $250, maybe $300 a week. Being a minor, part of my money was kept by the court. I had very little to actually live on. I lived in the motel behind the studio. And they put us automatically on suspension for twelve weeks of the year and didn't pay us.

OLIVIA DE HAVILLAND: Yes, those contracts allowed the studio to lay you off, you know, three months a year, without pay, and you couldn't earn any money from any other form of employment, because it was for exclusive personal services, that contract. So you would be perfectly willing *not* to do a film if you felt that you weren't going to do a good piece of work in it. You would prefer to be laid off without pay. And you would go to Jack [Warner] or go to somebody and, you know, somebody in a perhaps not as elevated a position as he but in a position of authority, and beg not to be put into such-and-such a film, saying "I know I can't do it. I can't do this piece of work. I just ask you to please lay me off, please just lay me off." Well, they wouldn't do that. They would threaten to suspend you or force you or threaten you into doing something you felt miserable about and also a film that you knew wasn't going to be a success, because you learned very soon that there would be a film, say, that wasn't very good but nonetheless was the kind of thing that would be a success. Well, you would be forgiven if it was a financial success, even if it weren't too good, because you would be identified with success. Then there would be a film that would be terribly good but maybe not too much of a success, but at least it would be terribly good, so that was all right. But if you were in a film that wasn't any good and wasn't a success, you would be identified with failure, and there was a fear of failure. It was considered a contagious disease, and you could get ostracized from being in a poor film that didn't make any money, and literally, if you made three in a row, finished, out, absolutely out. That was it. They dropped you. They figured actors weren't all that intelligent, and you had to fight that, too.

WALTER REISCH: On my first great ocean trip to America, at the same time the boat carried a young Viennese girl. I don't think I exaggerate when I say she was the most beautiful girl God ever sent down to Earth. She had on a gray tailor-made suit. She had just run away from her husband, who was the most powerful ammunitions tycoon in Europe—his name was Fritz Mandl. He had bullied and terrorized her with his jealousy and with good reason. That girl had had an incredible success in a picture called *Ecstasy*, in which I think she was the first actress to appear in her birthday outfit. Today that's no longer news, but imagine what it must have been like at the time of which we're speaking, September 1937. The picture, which was forbidden in every country, still found access to movie houses and was a big success. This girl was called Hedy Mandl and had been born Hedwig Kiesler. I was born in the same street of the same city as she—of course she was younger than I—her beauty was indescribable. L. B. Mayer had been in Europe and talked to her on the ship, immediately realizing that here was a potential motion picture star. He offered her a contract. She knew she was going to need money for a divorce. She knew she would have to make her own way somehow . . . and she had no idea that after she signed, MGM was going to run her life from then on.

Mayer, not a superstitious man at all, picked the last name of a dead silent star for her and said, "We are going to replace death with life." And he coined the name Hedy Lamarr. She had no idea that she was getting the name of a dead motion picture star, Barbara La Marr. And her name was changed without her knowledge or approval. This was common practice. Hedy, who was very superstitious and very feminine and naive, would have protested violently if she had known, I think. I would have protested if they had called *me* Lamarr, but it was a kind of publicity stunt. So the wires went to New York, advising them to expect a new motion picture star by the name of Hedy Lamarr, and as we arrived at Ellis Island—at that time every ship had still to dock at Ellis Island for immigration purposes—a girl more beautiful than any ever seen in America by the name of Hedy Lamarr came down the gangplank: not anybody's daughter, not anybody's sister or relative, and a star was born.

Her English was very good. She was a very educated girl, from a very good family. She had no problems at that time with kleptomania and those things of which she was accused later—rightly or wrongly, I don't know, I hope wrongly. She was a lovely girl but scared and terribly shy and terribly fearful that one day that guy with the whip—her husband—would reappear.

Now, when Louis B. Mayer took over the job of running the life of a personality, he did run it. Hedy had letters waiting in her hotel room which took care of everything, and five or six weeks later she landed in Hollywood, and here starts exactly the same Hollywood story as with all the others: for three years everybody admired her beauty, everybody had her to parties, she was the life of every party in Hollywood, in Santa Monica, in Malibu, in Catalina, on every yacht. But nobody gave her any parts—nobody, least of all MGM, which at that time had twenty-six active producers who each made three pictures a year, but she sat around getting photographed and publicized and told what to do until *they* decided what films she would be in. They owned her working life . . . and thus her future.

JOHN CROMWELL: I directed her in her first Hollywood picture, *Algiers*, with Charles Boyer. He was good looking, of course, but Hedy Lamarr just took your breath away. She was fine to work with, although early in the picture, I had a little set-to with her. She had gotten the MGM royal treatment, and she had a few days when she began to throw her weight around. I thought quickly to myself, and I said, "I'd better step on this fast." I said something in front of the whole crew. I did it deliberately, because I wanted to humiliate her and make her understand. She burst into hysterics and rushed from the set. I postponed the finish of what I was doing and went on to something else. About two or three hours later she came back, and I felt this peck on my neck. It was Hedy. She kissed me on the neck.

Stars were told what to do and stepped on if they didn't do it.

GEORGE FOLSEY: I was going to shoot her in *Lady of the Tropics*, and Louis B. Mayer came to me and said, "We want Miss Lamarr to look at least as good as she did in *Algiers*." He wanted her to look great. Well, when Louis B. Mayer tells you something like this, you know he's going to be watching that you do it, and I think I made her look pretty sensational. For her entrance into this huge club, gambling room–type thing, in Singapore, there were some slow revolving fans going around, and I had the good fortune of having her walk into it, and I saw the shadows of the fans come on her and I kept that effect on her in that particular part of the sequence. Very effective. She was a very, very beautiful woman to photograph—until she smiled. It was difficult for her to smile and be attractive. Incidentally, it was a lousy film.

WILLIAM TUTTLE: Well, one thing, Hedy Lamarr didn't have to undergo the scrutiny most new stars did for facial and figure flaws. It took two hours every day to see all the wardrobe and makeup tests that we shot on new contract players. They'd throw this out, throw that out. "Let's fix her eyelashes, they are too long" or "This is too much" or "That's too little" or "That dress doesn't look right," "I don't like the shoes" or "I don't like that hairdo." And there was somebody there taking notes on all this. So within a couple of hours after you got back to your office, you had a full report on what everyone liked and didn't like. And many times they'd say

"We're going to retest this" or "We're retesting this out." "This is going to be refitted" or "We like this hairstyle with maybe not quite so much curl." Or whatever. Most all of these people were really beautiful, but if we could change them for the better, that's what we were paid to do.

WALTER REISCH: This testing and "fixing" and planning for new potential stars was the usual thing with a major studio. They once had great plans for Joan Collins. Let's say that if, in the old days, Joan Collins had made a picture at MGM, she would have been as big a star as Joan Crawford, because MGM and Louis B. Mayer personally were greatly interested in creating female world stars, and he knew very well that this cannot be done without great promotion. But at 20th Century–Fox, where Collins was under contract, Zanuck was a great believer in male stars, and he was much more interested in George Sanders and that kind of actor than in their female counterparts. He didn't have real plans for Joan Collins.

GEORGE FOLSEY: John Carroll was one of the most interesting, absolutely fascinating characters I've ever met. I always felt that he should've been a far more successful leading man than he was. I think it was the way he was handled. I think if the people had tried and had understood him and had some more sympathy for John. . . . He was a crazy guy, but he was terribly funny and awfully good and had just enough good looks and style and quality to have . . . I think he could've been a big, big star. But he was not ever, I don't think, handled correctly.

For instance, we had a situation in *Rio Rita* at the very beginning of the picture. John was supposed to come in and get to certain places and hit his marks and so on as the boom followed him and did certain things. Well, John missed one of the marks somewhere in the middle of this scene very, very badly, and the operator wasn't prepared for this or expecting it, and it threw him off, and he stopped the boom shot. He said, "John missed the mark." Well, there was a room full of people in this crowded resort set or whatever it was, and nobody knew that this was one of John's sensitive points, and he felt humiliated in front of all these people. And I immediately saw that this was a very bad thing. It took us a whole morning to get him back to where we could shoot it again because he was so embarrassed and upset. His confidence was shot, and he felt sort of picked on and humiliated in front of a lot of people. Now, mostly, those people weren't even looking at him or didn't care. They never were listening. But this bothered him. I thought he was a fascinating guy, and I thought he should have been really a big, big star if they could've done something about taking that personality and producing it on the screen to his advantage.

JEAN LOUIS: Once they had made a star, they often tried to make a copy . . . for insurance. They always tried to revamp Rita Hayworth, but they never could do it. They could never find another one. They had some very pretty girl, Dolores Hart, and they tried to make her a Rita Hayworth, but she didn't have . . . well . . . she was not Rita Hayworth. And I never understood why they wanted to remake the same thing. There was another one, too, K. T. Stevens, who had the same face as Rita to a certain extent. Square. Angular. She was an angular Rita Hayworth.

ALLAN DWAN: There's no predicting stardom, really. A lot of money had to be spent trying people out. And there was no guarantee about people who were successful elsewhere working out in the movies. Remember Marilyn Miller? The big Broadway star? She was a great friend of mine. She was a big name in the 1920s theater in musicals, and she was brought out here as soon as sound came in. But she didn't do well out here. She was a sweet girl and a lovely girl and brilliant. A great dancer. Sang well. Charming. We all loved her in things like *Sally*—terrific. But she didn't become a big success in pictures. She did her own Broadway hits—two of them, I think. And they were all right. But it seemed unfashionable for an actress to do the thing she had already created in the theater. You must go to Hollywood and develop a picture personality. See, she wasn't a picture personality, and at that time you weren't accepted unless you had a big fan gathering. Fan clubs, you know. The public made *their* stars. They resented theater stars being shoved down their throats. They didn't want somebody brought in from the theater. They wanted their own people.

JOHN CROMWELL: The business was committed to the star system, and they all wanted to get their share of the loot. With a perfectly straight face,

Ben Schulberg told me this story: [George] Bancroft first evidenced his disregard for studio obligations by being late on the set. This was a serious enough infraction of the rules when it concerned only the principals of the cast. But when it involved several hundred extras, it was a cost that the studio could figure in dollars and cents.

Several talks with him availed nothing. Finally, Mrs. Bancroft was asked to come to the studio to talk about a solution. She tried to impress on the studio the *delicacy* of George's sensitive nature. "Why, gentlemen," she exclaimed, "when I go into George's room in the morning to wake him, I lay a slice of peach on his lips. If he eats it, he's ready to get up. If not, I must let him sleep."

When Ben and his wife decided to go abroad, Bancroft heard of it and promptly invited himself and his wife to go. There was nothing that Ben wanted less, but the head of the studio could never shirk catering to the whims of its most important star. Then he thought of something: Bancroft's contract was running out, and a renewal had to be negotiated. This seemed to be a heaven-sent opportunity to serve the company in an atmosphere of conviviality. Ben took every occasion to prepare the ground. In a crowded German beer hall with the strange guttural sounds assailing their ears, Ben observed, "You see, George, hardly any of these people understand English. When sound comes in, they won't understand you." Hardly pausing for breath, George replied, "When they see it's Bancroft, they'll learn English."

MERVYN LEROY: Yes, it's true that some stars became difficult. Not many. And we used to buy them clothes and do a lot of things with the girls and boys to dress them right. We treated them like kings and queens, but someone like Luise Rainer, who won two Academy Awards, asked for money and then became impossible. She was nuts. I made a picture with her. I didn't direct the picture, I produced. It was called *Dramatic School*. Irving Thalberg said, "Produce this picture. Look it over. We don't like it, but Luise Rainer likes it and we have one more picture with her, and we want to get rid of her." So I said, "Fine." So one day the director, Bob Sinclair, a New York director, called me on the set and said, "Come quickly," he said, "Miss Rainer has fainted." So I walked down on the set, and there she is, down on the floor, and everybody is looking at her. It was a hell of a mess. So I said, "What happened?" He said, "Well, she didn't like the scene and she ranted and raved and she fainted dead away." So I said, "Well, let's all go to lunch, and maybe she'll get up." I knew she hadn't fainted. I was positive she hadn't fainted, because she was acting. I knew it! So we all left the set, and we put the lights out. They put a pillow under her head, and then she came to, *quickly*! Believe me. Not many ever acted like that. She finished the picture, but I don't think anybody ever saw it.

ALLAN DWAN: Everybody wants to know: What makes a star? How do you define it?

GEORGE CUKOR: Ask me something difficult! Well, I think star quality is something that arrests you. That you see come alive on the screen. Big stars are fascinating. When they cross the screen, something exciting happens. Also, they have something else: Their faces move beautifully. They have very, very flexible faces. They have beautiful eyes.

ALLAN DWAN: It's someone who sells tickets. It's a business.

GEORGE CUKOR: There's something exciting about them when they're acting—a built-in excitement, but it's always a mystery. You never know why. What there is *in* them. Good looking—even though not all of them are good looking. There is a fascination about them. I remember in New York, *Mister Roberts*. I sat in the first row at this theater, and I could look down the aisle and see all of the people there. Then the footlights went on and cast a reflection light. I looked down, and one face jumped out at me. That was Garbo sitting there. The way her face took the light!

MITCHELL LEISEN: Sometimes it's maybe an unusual voice, like Jean Arthur's. And timing is so vitally important to stardom. It's a kind of instinct. If you have a sense of timing, it's wonderful. If you haven't got it, nobody can teach it to you. Jean Arthur had a fabulous sense of timing. Lombard had a fabulous sense of timing. MacMurray developed a wonderful sense of timing. Colbert had a beautiful sense of timing. Timing is knowing exactly when to come in, keep the rhythm flowing, cut into another line. When they had no sense of timing, you couldn't help them out. It's just impossible. So in addition to the predictable things of looks and personality, sometimes it's timing that can make a star.

IRVING RAPPER: Ginger Rogers once told me something so right about stardom. She said, "If somebody says to you, 'Oh, I just saw your picture, you're marvelous,' don't believe a word." But, she said, if years later they say, "Eight years ago I saw you in . . . ," you can believe *that*.

GEORGE FOLSEY: Marion Davies was absolutely the epitome of what you would consider a real motion picture star. She was surrounded by a great entourage of people. We always played her entrance music when she came onto the soundstage. They were playing this music for her all the time. We'd hear her music playing and we knew that she was on her way, and then we'd hear the dogs bark and she would arrive with a bunch of little dachshunds. Just a real motion picture star. And she loved to make tests at night of the costumes and so on, so we'd always have to stay. We always had a clue as to when we were going to make a test because some of her maids or somebody would come out with huge trays of sandwiches around five o'clock, and then we knew we were going to work that evening, making some tests of her. Now, I don't know whether it was just that she hated to go back to that Santa Monica castle, but we'd quite frequently have to make these tests because what she wanted, Hearst saw she got.

HENRY FONDA: I know I am a star because they put my name up there, but I don't *feel* like that. I just feel that I have been lucky over the years—that it all happened to me forty-some years ago—and that I am still able to work and they still ask me to work, so I've been successful. But I don't think about being a star. I mean, I was as difficult to get along with when I was struggling as an actor as I am today, I promise you.

I never had the adulation that becomes a problem, the kind that Robert Taylor had or Tyrone Power, Elizabeth Taylor, those people. I know what happens. Bob Redford today can't do anything normally. God, if I couldn't walk up and down Madison Avenue and do the galleries, it would become a problem for me, and I'm not sure how I'd face it. But it wasn't a problem for me. I never had that much. I'm recognized. It's not embarrassing. Very often it's quite moving. You know, when somebody comes up and says, "It just happens that I went to *Darrow* last night, Mr. Fonda," and he can't talk. I don't mind that. I never had a problem with it.

There are so many roles I can't do, that I'm not qualified to do. I regret it, but I am not ashamed of it. I'm from Omaha, Nebraska, and I never tried to become a continental type of actor with an accent. I would feel phony if I tried to do that.

CLINT EASTWOOD: I'm not going to play Hamlet. I have no interest in miscasting myself.

KATHARINE HEPBURN: Ethel Merman is not going to play Florence Nightingale. Everybody has their limitations.

HENRY FONDA: I came east from the Omaha Playhouse, and the first job I got was at the Cape Playhouse at Dennis, Massachusetts, which was in its second year as a stock company. It was one of the papas of the whole summer stock. Now, twenty-eight or thirty years later, it's still there under other management, and I wasn't interested in going there, but my daughter, Jane, wanted to be in their apprentice group, and I thought, Well, I don't know what that means. I later found out that what it meant was that she was keen on the stage manager, who was an undergraduate at Yale, and she'd met him and wanted to be closer to him. I'm telling this story because during that summer, when she was in the apprentice group, they prepared one act of a Restoration comedy. Now, to me, for a group of amateurs to do Restoration comedy is the silliest thing in the world, but this is the kind of theater it was, the kind of group it was, and I didn't know what it was they were up to. But anyway, eventually at the end of the summer they were going to do a performance of the one act of this Restoration comedy that they had been rehearsing, and all the friends of the apprentices, of course, could come. And I went. I think Peter went. I'm not sure. My sister was with me, I remember. And Jane was not playing a principal part at all. She was playing a maid with a little frilly apron, I remember, and the act had been on for maybe ten minutes before Jane made her first entrance. I remember it was on an empty stage—she just came on like that. Now, nobody knew who she was except my sister and I. Nobody else knew who she was, but you could literally feel or hear the audience react to this person—who didn't say anything, just came onstage. That's charisma. That's an electric something or other. There are all sorts of words for it: magnetism, you know. I just remember thinking you could hear the audience sort of straighten up or take a breath or something. There was a physical reaction that you were aware of—dear God, if she ever decides she wants to be an actress, she's got it going for her. She's got star quality. If you've got it, it's not something you can learn. It's not something you inherit. You're born with it, but you don't necessarily inherit it, because too many daughters and sons of charismatic actors are born without it, so I'm not taking credit. But Jane has got it. And if I've got it, thank you, it does help.

MERIAN C. COOPER: John Wayne is a star. He defines it. He's a *man*, and that's why people like him. A true masculine personality comes through on the screen. Wayne is just what he is in real life, the role he acts. He's a helluva fine human being, and he's got a great sense of humor about himself.

HOWARD HAWKS: Wayne will blow you right off the screen. Your only chance is to be quieter than he is. He doesn't do it purposely, but he can just do it. There's some quality that he's got.

ALLAN DWAN: Wayne's very simple and very plain, you know. That's a star. He says things in a certain way.

BRONISLAU KAPER: John Wayne has a speaking voice like Nelson Eddy has a singing voice.

HOWARD HAWKS: I always told Wayne, "I don't care if you murder the lines in the script, as long as you get the intent. And say it in your style." The first picture I made with him was *Red River*. We had a new boy, Montgomery Clift, and after the first scene, Wayne said, "This kid is all right," and he took an interest in him. He didn't mind working with him, and he didn't mind my changing Clift's character around and trying it a different way. Wayne would do anything to help make a better picture. He was one of the most helpful people that I know. Lots of times he doesn't know *what's* the matter, but when he starts kind of making faces to himself, I say, "What's bothering you?" And he says, "Something is wrong with this scene." And then you know to find out what's wrong. He doesn't know how to help, but he's awfully pleased when you do manage to find out what's wrong and fix it. This is the kind of stardom he was built for.

ALLAN DWAN: When I worked with him, it wasn't hard to get Wayne to agree that he wanted to do a picture. It was hard to get Wayne to go to Yates and say, "I *insist* on doing it." He didn't feel secure enough. It took him a long time to become a star. And then afterwards he was the kingpin—he'd go and tell him, "Mr. Yates, I like your office better than I do my dressing room. You go over in the dressing room, I'll take the office." He was a big shot by that time.

Directing Wayne was fine, very easy. He liked me, so everything went fine. The only trouble with Wayne in those days was he used to like to stay up at the bar quite late. He had a terrific capacity. But some of these young punks, these actors that were in the cast—fellows like John Agar—used to try to stay along with him, and they'd be a pathetic sight in the morning. Three or four times, I was having some difficulty getting some kids to do something or the kids weren't doing exactly what I wanted, and they were a little sulky about it, John Wayne says over my shoulder, "Goddamn it! Will you bastards do what he tells you!?" He yells over my shoulder at them! And they looked at him and then they did it fast. I said, "Thanks. That's fine."

MICHAEL WAYNE: I think that John Wayne, my father, has an image people like. But they also kid it and have good-natured fun with it. He's become kind of the symbol of the heroic American male.

I think he would have been a success at anything he did. He would have been an outstanding lawyer if he had been a lawyer. He would have been an outstanding politician, an outstanding anything, because he has that drive. He has charisma. It is just something you can't put your finger on. It is something that differentiates people. He has it. You can't say what it is, but my father has it.

GEORGE CUKOR: Gary Cooper is the supreme example of movie stardom. There is a story that Lewis Milestone used to tell. Gary Cooper was playing with Emil Jannings in a silent picture, and Milestone said to his assistant, "Shoot fifty feet of him just sitting there," and they never told Gary, who was asleep. Then they said, "Wake up," and Gary woke up. They cut this film into the movie, and when Jannings saw it, he said, "That young man should play Hamlet. He was born to be in movies."

It is a mysterious question, what makes them photogenic. I think it is very often the flesh quality. They're made so the light can come into their eyes and the face moves well. It's a very mysterious thing.

FRANK CAPRA: I think every actor is a star. And I treat every actor as a star even though the part is only that long. Ellen Corby had one scene in *It's a Wonderful Life*, one line. Jimmy Stewart is passing out money. "How much?" "Twenty bucks." The action's taking place. "No, I want twenty bucks." So I went up to her and I said, "You're asking too much. Ask for $17.50." So when she came to him, she said, "Can I have $17.50?" And Jimmy Stewart didn't know she was going to ask that, and he looked at her, and automatically he just grabbed her and just did the right thing. He kissed her, you see. But Ellen Corby on that just one line—she grabbed you.

ELIA KAZAN: I am not afraid to use anyone, because I was an actor and the fact that I was an actor makes me have less respect. I don't have a mystique about, oh, what an actor can contribute. Yeah, they can, they cannot, it depends. You can have damn good actors, and they can louse you up. But I don't have an awe of them, nor am I afraid of them. I know how rudimentary most of their training is, and I also know that many actors are trained badly. And one of the worst things you can do is get with an actor who has bad ideas. Now, what I try to do is to get to know them very well. People say that I take a walk with actors. But I do more than that. I take them to dinner. I talk to them. I meet their wives. I mean, I find out what the hell the human material is that I'm dealing with, so that by the time I take an unknown, he's not an unknown to me. I know the psychological makeup of his nature. I know a lot about him. And I can use it.

BILLY WILDER: I stay away from stars as far as possible. I never get too friendly, because it's just not good. It's just that other actors sense that there's a little clique. I remember that I was once making a picture with Marlene Dietrich and Jean Arthur, *Foreign Affair*, and I had known Marlene from Germany before I ever came to this country, when I was a newspaperman in Berlin, and we were very friendly. And in the middle of shooting, one midnight, the doorbell rang, and there was Jean Arthur, absolutely frenzied, with eyes bulging, and in back of her was her husband, Frank Ross, and I said, "What is it, Jean?" She says, "What did you do with my close-up?" I said, "What close-up?" She said, "The close-up where I look so beautiful." I said, "What do you mean, what did I do with it?" "You burned it. Marlene told you to burn that close-up. She does not want me to look good." This is typical, you know. It's a little insane asylum that is going on there, and they are all inmates.

The way I act with stars depends on what they will respond to, you know. I can become a masochist. I can become the Marquis de Sade. I can become a midwife. I can become Otto Preminger. I don't know what you do with an uncooperative actor. You kick him in the ass, I don't know. Or you say let's shoot the scene in two versions, yours and mine, and then you don't develop his version. How's that?

GEORGE CUKOR: I say, "How about you shutting up?" And then I'll try to say something very polite. Of course, it depends on who says it. Occasionally an actor has a good idea, and I always try to watch that very carefully. I don't try to relax them. Why should I? I don't want the actors to be too goddamn relaxed. Today you hear of "relaxation techniques." I don't know what that means. I know that Marilyn Monroe used to do this occasionally, and I wondered what the hell that was. I've seen actors be awfully pretentious and full of ideas, and a lot of it is just a waste of time. "How about you shutting up?" is a good idea.

STANLEY KRAMER: Problem actors? How do you resolve them? How do you resolve Frank Sinatra? You don't. You can't resolve him. I could never make any resolution. Frank had problems, always did. I made a couple of pictures with him. No resolution.

ADELA ROGERS ST. JOHNS: There's a wrongheaded idea about Louis B. Mayer and his relationship to stars. How he hated them. God knows he tried to save 'em, if only for the studio. He didn't want to lose Garland. He didn't want to lose Harlow. He would have done anything to protect them. That was his great genius, his great power, that he could produce them in there and keep them working every day. It was failure when bad things happened or when you lost a star to death or addiction or whatever. The studio had invested money in their success. He didn't want them to fail or get sick or lose confidence.

HARRY WARREN: Jack Warner was mean to stars, but not Louis B. Mayer. He wasn't. Warner used to lay off Bette Davis if she got fresh. Off the payroll she went. And he would have done it with Judy Garland, too. But L. B. Mayer wasn't that kind of man. When Garland reported sick, he used to send her flowers, try to win her over by being kind to her. But it didn't work with her. I worked with Judy on a lot of pictures, *The Harvey Girls, Summer Stock* . . . a lot of pictures. She was a strange girl. I was never intimate with Judy, except a "Hello" and stuff like that. Sometimes she'd pass you, wouldn't even say, "Hello."

Well, they had plenty of trouble with Judy Garland all the time she was on a picture. She got sick and disappeared. And they couldn't find her. Held up the company on every picture I was on with her. On *The Barkleys of Broadway*, they had to get Ginger Rogers to come in and do the picture because Garland took sick on that one. That's her whole history. Outside of that, I could say she was *great*. A great performer and great singer.

I think that the people—like [composer and arranger] Roger Edens and [entertainer, arranger, and vocal coach] Kay Thompson and those kinds of people—did a lot to hurt her, because they were always waiting on her hand and foot. The poor gal was so bewildered by it all, I guess. She was never alone. She was always surrounded by a lot of people. I know that

Mr. Mayer tried everything. I always said that if she worked for Jack Warner, you would never have heard of her. That's how different that story would have been. She did eventually go over to Warners, and they had a lot of trouble there, too.

JEAN LOUIS: Judy Garland was difficult for a costume designer. She was a marvelous person. I loved her. But she didn't have an easy figure to fit. She had no legs. She had a big bosom and very thin legs and a very high waist, too, and her weight would fluctuate. One day she was broader, and the other day she was thinner. If you're using the same dress for a long period of shooting, you had to take it in and let it out. And she didn't like to stand for fittings.

WALTER PLUNKETT: One day Garland did not show up, and the whole company was there and waiting. They waited and waited, then they got a phone call from her from somewhere down near San Diego at about noon, saying "I'm terribly sorry, and I'll turn around now and I'll come back as fast as I can." Eventually she arrived at the studio, and she was still shaking, and they told me to go to the dressing room. They said, "You seem to have a soothing influence on her, and can you stick around for a time?" and I said, "Judy, I just don't understand. You are one of the most loved people in the United States. You have a great following. People adore you. They say you are the greatest star in films, you have the most beautiful voice. They buy every record you make. People just love you and worship you. What is the thing with you?" She told me she actually had come to work on time, to be in the makeup department at eight o'clock. She looked at the sign that said METRO-GOLDWYN-MAYER, and to her it said, "Today they will find you out." And she looked again, and the letters said, "You are a fraud." She screamed and turned her car around without going onto the lot and started driving and ended up on her way to San Diego. She said, "Honestly, every day that I come to work, I know that I don't have a voice. And I know that it is all pushed and faked and I know that they're going to find it out, and the music department is going to come down and say, 'Let's stop this number because she can't sing, let's get somebody in to dub her number.' I know it will happen. I can't sing, I can't act, either." I was talking to her, and finally we got her dressed and got her calmed down and she went onto the set. I was starting to leave the stage as she was starting to shoot, and I got over to the door, and she just stopped shooting and said, "Hey, Walter, wait a minute. Wait a minute, Walter. Are you the best goddamned costume designer in the world?" I said, "Well, hardly." She said, "That's the way I feel, *hardly*. Don't *you* try to tell me how to have confidence in yourself." Then she got on with her number. Poor baby.

GEORGE CUKOR: Judy Garland was not just a musical star. She was an actress, too, and a very resourceful one. A very extraordinary actress with a great deal of originality. We had to do a scene in *Star Is Born* where her husband had killed himself and she was in a state of absolute depression. I don't believe in rehearsing the emotion of a scene, but you *can* rehearse the mechanics of a scene. In fact, I used to urge Rex Harrison, "Don't play it, don't play it, let it come out." Wise movie people go through all the mechanics and they just let it happen when the camera's turning. I'm talking of the generation before this one. Judy was sitting there, pre-occupied with it. I think we had talked it all out somehow, at least we both had an idea of what it should be. She was in a state of melancholia, depression, and I went up to her, and all I said to her, in a very quiet way, was, "You know what this is about, you know, you really do." She looked at me, thinking "Who does he mean, me, really to dig into myself, that I know all this?" She looked at me, and that was that. I'd never seen anybody in acute melancholia. If you remember the scene, a man comes to talk to her about how she feels and to urge her to attend a benefit per-formance that night. "Look here, you're just giving in to yourself. Why don't you come to this performance tonight?" He did this deliberately, and she lost her head. She got up and screamed like a human being out of all control, maniacal and terrifying. Some people have the talent of scaring people. It was so real. When Judy did this scene, there was no concern of what she looked like. It was absolutely terrifying, electric. The anger seemed to come up through the stage floor.

GEORGE FOLSEY: She was so good! She was a superb actress. A straight dramatic actress! Plus the fact that she could sing like the dickens and dance, and she was fun to be around because she'd play baseball during the lunch hour. She threw left-handed. She was a great person, but she often seemed to be distracted. She seemed to be living in another world. She could play the scene and then walk away from the scene and then become a kind of . . . somebody else, you know? Maybe not all there, you'd think. She was detached. I don't mean to imply that she was feebleminded, nothing of that kind, but she was detached. I don't know whether it was because she was ill or what.

STANLEY KRAMER: Montgomery Clift watched Judy Garland do a scene one day on *Judgment at Nuremberg,* and when she did it he was huddled in the corner like a puppy dog, to one side of the stage, and he wept. The tears were rolling down his cheeks while she did the scene. And when it was over, he came up and whispered to me, "She didn't do it right."

NORMAN TAUROG: In her early days, Judy would be there at seven thirty in the morning or seven o'clock in the morning. I had no problem whatsoever.

DON KNOX: Tell me more about Judy Garland. How does such a great talent, a person who is so highly thought of, destroy herself while she is still under contract with MGM? What happened there? Adela Rogers St. Johns tells one story. Mickey Rooney will tell another. You worked with her a lot. I don't want to get into any of the dirt of Judy. I just want to know how it was allowed to happen.

NORMAN TAUROG: How could MGM destroy her when she was in Chicago at the Blackstone hotel? How can Metro destroy her when she was doing a picture with me and she disappears for eight or nine days?

I think that everybody tried to talk with her. Mr. Mayer was kind enough on *Girl Crazy* to tell me that her hours would be from ten o'clock in the morning until five in the afternoon. She had insomnia, and she only slept in the latter part of the night. Instead of nine to six, she was working ten to five. Soon, instead of ten to five, it got to be eleven to five. Then she made up from eleven to twelve and then went to lunch. She would eat lunch until about one or one thirty. Then she would work until about four thirty. Everybody tried to help Judy. I happened to have been very fond of her. Some of the best pictures that I ever made in my life, I made with Judy. I was very fond of her and I liked her, but Judy was quite mixed up in her own mind. Metro couldn't mix her up. They were very good to Judy.

Look, MGM also had Deanna Durbin. They let Deanna Durbin go and kept Judy. They had them both at the same time. And Deanna did not ruin her life. I don't believe that there is any company in the world that can destroy you if you don't want to be destroyed. This is especially in a company where you work from nine to six. In between pictures you don't come near the studio. You are not there. Your time is your own. Why don't you straighten out in between? I think that Judy's mind was mixed up. She was as sweet a girl to work with as you could find. That was true as far as I was concerned. While working with her, I had no problem. It was getting her to work that was the problem.

WALTER PLUNKETT: The pressure on her was more than she could bear.

JEAN LOUIS: I don't think Judy Garland knew what she wanted. Once I saw her in the Hollywood Bowl when it was pouring rain. Nobody moved for three hours. It was sick, but nobody did. Because she had them so enraptured and captured that it was a sickness. But a kind of thing—like watching a snake come out of a basket—it's not necessarily a good thing, but you can't take your eyes off it. She murdered people around her. She would keep people up all night, calling them in the middle of the night. I was only making a film with her, but she'd call me in the middle of the night about the damndest succession of things and have her agent there and her business manager and a publicity man, keep them up all night. And everybody would be sick the next day, just couldn't operate. And Judy would go on like firecrackers, as though nothing happened at all. But of course near the end she couldn't sing anymore. And she disappointed a lot of people that way. But what's the story of Judy? I guess the story of Judy Garland, even as the camera slowly pans upward over the headstone, one must admit Louis B. Mayer is the villain. Because he was the father and she was the child. She was Judy Gumm, who was eleven years old, and he was Father Christmas. And he, Father Christmas, put her in four pictures a year: dieting, singing, dancing, personal appearances, everything. And she had a nervous breakdown at age fifteen. I don't know, you can't ever blame anybody for these things, really.

KATHARINE HEPBURN: . . . the whole Judy Garland incident . . . how much of it can you say the business is responsible for? Judy isn't the only person who has fallen apart in the business. It is a business that is fraught with troubled people. Human beings do that to themselves. I don't think that Dore Schary understood the wayward, tormented, wild sort of brilliance of Judy Garland . . . but I think Mayer did. I think he tried to understand the situation. He tried to give her as much help as he could, but without success. I don't think that anybody could have succeeded.

Mayer understood that an artist was something sacred. He understood that Judy Garland had something that he didn't entirely comprehend. Now there are terrible stories about what happened . . . when Judy began to fall apart. Mayer came to me. He said, "Do you know Judy Garland?" I said, "Vaguely. Not really at all." He said, "She is in a terribly bad way. She has made us millions of dollars. We should be able to help her. Do you feel you could do anything? Would you be willing to go and talk to her and see her?" I went and talked to her . . . I think she was an enormously complicated creature . . . if you are going to help anybody, this is not a two-hour job. . . . Could he really have prevented [her illness]? I don't know. I really don't know. I don't think that work ever really destroyed anybody.

GORE VIDAL: Movie actors should take the money and enjoy the glory and try not to let it go to their nerves. In the old days, they'd make three pictures a year, and it was hard work six days a week. A movie actor is essentially somebody passive. Ronald Reagan all his life has been told, "Sit there, go over there, move over there, here are your lines, read them off, look to the right, look to the left." And you're going to make him the president? No, I'd make his director the president. I must tell you that, plus, because a director's a hustler, he's a liar, he's a cheat. He knows how to run a country. But don't elect a professional screen actor to be president of the United States, no matter how nice or bright or whatever they are, because they've spent their entire life being moved about like a piece of furniture. They've been used. That's why all the men, almost without exception, become alcoholics, because it's just not in the male nature to be totally passive. And all the women stars take up needlepoint. The women come out much better. My God, eventually everything in their house is just covered. A major movie star has miles of tapestry by the time her career is over, and the man is drunk. It's a tough life.

ALLAN DWAN: A million-dollar star didn't always mean you'd get a million dollars at the box office.

GEORGE CUKOR: Well, stars changed as they moved forward and got famous and got tired. Some remained sensible, good mannered. I think that most of their demands, those from the really great stars, were, from all points of view, rather modest. They wanted nice dressing rooms and the privilege of having a manicure on the set. Or they wanted to be allowed to say a few things about the script. Most of those people were, on the face of it, just modest, proletarian kids. When you look at the careers of the Metro people in particular, you see fifteen, twenty years of stardom because they were produced very carefully. Their careers lasted because they were defined and guided by talented men who knew what they were doing.

KING VIDOR: Different actors, different ways. A psychiatrist friend of mine once spent the day on the set, and he said, "You're doing the same thing I am." But it was different things for different people. . . .

Jennifer Jones, you had to tell her the whole story every day from beginning to end. She did not see herself as a pro. She saw herself as a little girl and was scared to death about what she was doing. So you had to get her in the mood and tell her the fairy story about what was going on up to that point, and then she could do it, but you had to do it *every day*. I think just to be an actor always engenders a certain amount of fear, whether they can do it or not. I think every day they come on the stage all of them practically scared to death that they won't be able to do the job.

With [Spencer] Tracy, he was upset always, just staying on location, and he was threatening me always that he was going to go home and quit.

So I had to figure out that what had to be done was to have some attractive-looking woman sitting there admiring him and telling him how great he was. So we employed a woman to do that. In fact, we sent to Boise, Idaho, and got her clothes and everything, a whole wardrobe. He didn't know that. An attractive woman who was there, a vacationer or something, that was excited by watching him and all that. So that kept him out of threats, from saying he was going home and quit and all that sort of thing. So different people were different.

ELIA KAZAN: Stars *are* different. And that's sometimes what makes them into stars. And what happens to them in life shapes their image and sometimes how long they remain in our minds. Early death, for instance, or tragic death. I always get asked about James Dean. Gee, I hate to talk about Dean. I've talked about him so much, and it always ends up a little sour. I was casting *East of Eden*, and there he was, and I had one of these things—I had an intuition. I said, "This is Cal. This is the guy right here." He did a thing that always attracts me. He wasn't polite to me. And that always makes me feel he's not straining to butter me up or anything, that he has a real sense of himself. So then he—this sounds like a PR story, but it's true—he says, "I'll take you for a ride on my motorbike." It was very hard for him to talk, and riding me on the back of his motorbike—which I did like a damn fool around the streets of New York—was his way of communicating with me, saying "I hope you like me" or "Look at my skills" or whatever. So then I read him a lot, and he had—you've seen him—he had his own way. And I thought it was perfect for the part. I thought it was an extreme grotesque of a boy. I thought he was a twisted boy, twisted by the denial of love. And it turned out, as I got to know his father, as I got to know about his family, that he had been, in fact, twisted by the denial of love. I went to Jack Warner and told him that I wanted to use an absolutely unknown boy. And Jack was a crapshooter of the first water, and he said, "Go ahead," and that was the end of the conference. He wouldn't do that now. Nobody would do that now. Warner just was a peculiar guy. He would, as they say, bet the jockey, not the horse. Anyway, he said, "Go ahead." So I went back to New York, and I said to Jimmy, "We're going to California." So I said, "Be at my house at such-and-such a time," and I told a limousine to take us to the airport—a long, black limousine. Jimmy shows up with two packages wrapped in paper. He'd never been on an airplane before. So we get in this damn limousine, and we come out, and on the way from the airport to the studio where the guy was waiting to show us his room, he says, "Can we stop here a minute?" I said, "What's the matter?" He said, "My father lives in there." So we stopped, and he went in and got his father, and out comes a man who was as tense as Jimmy was and they hardly could relate. They hardly could look at each other. It was the goddamndest reaffirmation of the hunch that I had that I'd ever seen. They could hardly talk—they mumbled at each other. And Jimmy, I don't know what the hell he stopped to see him for, because in a few minutes he said, "Let's go." So he got in the car, and we went out. Then I got him fixed in his room, and I took him to the lot to shoot some wardrobe tests. So we started to shoot these wardrobe tests, and the crew couldn't believe it. They said, "Is that the stand-in?" I said, "No, he's going to play the part." And they couldn't believe it. But that was a good sign for me, because he looked real. He looked like an actual person. So then we started working, and he was good from the first day in fulfilling that part. With his first money he bought a palomino horse, so I had to tell him, "You can't ride the horse, Jimmy." He couldn't ride much anyway, but he was a farm boy. He started out as a farm boy. So he said, "Okay," rather resentfully. So the next thing was that he bought a motorbike. I said, "Jimmy, you can't ride the motorbike." Well, he got resentful about it. Then he got into problems with a girlfriend, so I moved him into a dressing room at the studio and I moved out of where I was and I was in a twin dressing room, so I only had a wall between us and I could hear him. Because I was anxious that he was going to do something terrible. He was nearsighted, which I didn't know when I hired him. He couldn't see at all, and I still think that one day he was riding in his Porsche and he did something at seventy or eighty miles an hour like rubbing his eyes or something—if he looked at the road without his glasses, he couldn't see what was happening—I'm convinced that something like that happened, because he was a good driver but he couldn't see. I had a scene where he had to jump and grab on to a train and climb on the train, and he almost got killed the first day because he missed the handle and the stairs on the side of a freight car. I had a lot of adventures with him. The unfortunate part of the story is that there's a saying that success is harder to take than failure, which is a rather shaky statement, but let's say that there's some truth in it, and success was sure hard for him to take.

NATALIE WOOD: Jimmy was introspective, but I wouldn't say he was a brooder. He was very thoughtful, and he was very helpful. He liked to talk about what we were going to do, and we did have a rehearsal period on *Rebel Without a Cause*. We rehearsed in the director's house over at the Chateau Marmont. Nick Ray was living there then. In fact, the set for Jimmy's parents' home actually was just Nick's living room. That's what it was. Jimmy worked a lot with improvisation, and so did Nick Ray. That was the first time I had ever done that in my life. I don't think James Dean was tortured the way people say. I had worked with him just prior to *Rebel*, in a television show, a GE Playhouse. It was a live television show based on a Sherwood Anderson short story called "I'm a Fool." And that was when I first got to know him. We used to go to lunch on his motor-cycle and all that. We were rehearsing in downtown Los Angeles in an old warehouse. At that time, he was very much in love with Pier Angeli, and the movie magazines were full of stories about that. I guess they had just split up, and he was very unhappy about it. He used to read those magazines a lot. It was the first time that he had ever had publicity . . . the first time he had lost his privacy or just to figure out what the balance was. What did it all mean, what they were writing about him? You know, that kind of thing. I think he did worry about that a great deal because he didn't want his individuality to be raped . . . at least that's what I thought.

CHARLES LEMAIRE: Whenever these star discussions come up, I think of Monroe. Marilyn Monroe. I was at 20th Century–Fox when they brought her in. I watched her evolution. In the beginning, she was one thing. At the end, another. Zanuck tested her for the part of the chorus girl in *All About Eve* who comes to the party with Gregory Ratoff and meets up with George Sanders. And he said, "Would you see to it that she has something really nice to wear for the test? I want to do it tomorrow." She came in that afternoon, and she said, "Hello, Mr. LeMaire, how are you?" And I said, "Fine." She says, "Please make me pretty so that I can get the part."

She tested, and she got the part. She was happy and grateful. She was put under a good contract, and one day she was standing outside in the foyer of 20th Century–Fox and Loretta Young came dancing in, and she said, "Good morning, good morning," to everyone, you know. And "How are you, dear?" and threw me a kiss and walked up to where she was being fitted for a nun's habit for *Come to the Stable*. Marilyn looked at her, and she said, "Oh, my. Isn't she nice to everyone." I said, "She's a star, Marilyn, that's a star, that's a star. That's a real, honest-to-God star. It's a real moving picture star, see how nice she is to everyone." She said, "Oh, my, if I ever get to be her . . . if I ever get to be a star, I want to be exactly like her. If I'm not, you just kick me in the backside."

Now move ahead just a few years to 1953, and Monroe is costarring in *How to Marry a Millionaire* with two huge names, Lauren Bacall and the box-office queen, Betty Grable. The costumes for the three women are being designed by the famous Travilla. So I'm the head of the costume department, and Billy Travilla calls me and says, "I'm having trouble with Marilyn. She won't wear the dress which is scheduled for the shoot day after tomorrow." And I said, "Why won't she wear it?" He said, "She's in a tantrum, and she's terrible." And I said, "Really?" And so I went in, and I said, "Hello, Marilyn." I said, "You know, now is the time for you to bend over, I'm about to kick you in the backside." And she said, "What do you mean!" And I said, "Do you remember when Loretta Young came in? You are not acting like a feature performer. I understand that you're giving Travilla trouble." And she said, "I'm not giving him trouble, I'm just telling him that I'm not going to wear that dress."

Try to imagine these three big stars and their outfits: Travilla and Bacall and Grable and Monroe and clothes. Bacall really wanted a straight-skirt dress in one scene. She felt that was necessary for her, and she had a great fashion sense. And Marilyn . . . this was still very young in her career . . . she wanted a very skinny skirt, very skinny. She always wanted tight skirts. Tight, yes. She was showing her butt. What to do? Betty Grable said, "I don't care. I really don't care. I've got enough other things to wear in the film that I like very much. I don't care about this. You can do anything you want." And Betty Grable was actually the biggest name of all three of them at that time. Then Bacall said she wouldn't mind if she wore a full skirt if it was full from way down below her waist. So in the first scene of the film, where the three girls first move into the apartment, Grable is wearing what is the least, to our taste today, the least attractive dress, with tons of fullness and many, many petticoats. There was already an issue of professionalism and cooperation with Marilyn. She didn't want anybody around her telling her what to wear. "I know how I want to look, and I can design my own clothes."

DAVID CHIERICHETTI: George Cukor had a terrible time with her. She wanted her way. Every dress had to be like the top of a bathing suit, with shoulder straps and a sort of fitted bra. She thought she knew. And that's what she insisted on wearing regardless.

CHARLES LEMAIRE: They got her into a beige suit at one point. She loved beige because she felt it matched her skin and she looked like she didn't have anything on, which was her pride and joy, not having anything on. Loved it. You know her answer to the guy who said, "What do you wear when you go to bed?" She said, "Chanel No. 5."

DAVID CHIERICHETTI: And "What did you have on when you posed for that calendar?" "I had the radio on."

CHARLES LEMAIRE: In her private life she never had any clothes done. She never dressed up. Where did she ever go? Never went anyplace. She'd come into the studio in the morning in a pair of dirty pajamas with bare feet. And hanging hair and no makeup and hair that had to be combed, hair that was hanging down. She looked awful when she came into the studio! Some of the fitters didn't like fitting her because they didn't like the uncleanliness of her look and her clothes. I had a terrible time with one of the fitters, one of the very best fitters, who did very well with things: "Well, if she doesn't come in with something clean on tomorrow morning, Mr. LeMaire, I'm not going to fit her." So we had to phone, tell some girl answering the phone, and had to say, "Would you please wear some clean underclothes tomorrow?"

I really don't go along with Marilyn too well. Marilyn to me was one of the great, great disappointments, the little girl who made good, you know? Everybody was rooting for her back in the days of *All About Eve*, and she just made them all feel like dirt, you know? Didn't want them around her. It started around the time of *Gentlemen Prefer Blondes* and *How to Marry a Millionaire* . . . when she became important.

JACK LEMMON: Marilyn was fascinating, but she had her devils. She might have covered it up, but she was tormented and very unhappy. I got along with her well and loved her very much as a person but at the same time was totally thrown by her. I could no more get close to her than fly to the moon. In a way she really wouldn't expose herself, although at that point in her life she had every reason to act that way. I still can't figure out her talent. I think she was absolutely brilliant, but I still don't know whether she knew how to act. She had a self-barometer, some built-in mechanism that knew when a scene was right for her. She only knew one way to work. I've never seen anything like it. She would just stop. She would never wait for the director to say, "Cut." She would just say, "Well . . ." and walk off, and we'd have to start again. You'd get trapped if you were saving yourself for a last-minute spurt, because there wasn't going to be any last-minute spurt. She just knew when it was going right for her. At times she acted *at* you instead of *with* you. It was selfish, but it was the only way she knew how to do it, and the scenes worked, there's no question of that.

NUNNALLY JOHNSON: I thought that Marilyn was, I don't know, the *most* obtuse woman. I just couldn't get to her or feel that I had established any kind of communication with her at all. There wasn't much opportunity. I didn't talk to her much. I worked with her early in her career, in *We're Not Married*. I went out on the set one day. Eddie Goulding was directing it. There she was with her baby in her arms, and you know you can legally only use a baby two minutes or something like that. She was standing there, and this baby was crying like hell, and Marilyn didn't even look down at the baby. I said to Eddie, "Now, look, don't you think that's a little unbelievable? Unless she's a complete idiot, a mother would look at her crying baby or would have some consideration." Eddie, who agreed with everything, said, "Quite true. Stop. Wait a minute." He went over and reminded her that this was *her* baby and that the baby was crying and perhaps it would be just as good to try to comfort the baby during the thing. Little things like that, I must say, made me dislike her. I cast her because . . . well, she was *there*. Later, she became huge and then a kind of legend.

Marilyn kept retreating farther and farther from reality. On her last unfinished film, *Something's Gotta Give*, she and George Cukor hated each other. I read that she'd been taken out of the picture and the picture called off. Unfortunately, that was the end of Marilyn. She never recovered. Marilyn just didn't know how to cope with life at all.

My conviction is she bored the hell out of everybody. She just didn't have the intelligence, but she was aware she didn't have it. When she married Arthur Miller—now, this is pure speculation—my guess is that she just wasn't interesting enough for Miller. Nobody finds it very difficult to talk before you get into the hay, but what do you say afterwards? Marilyn was like a child. She thought that a lay was the complete answer to everything. When Miller began to indicate that he was no longer devoted to her, she went out and had an affair. In each case, she thought that the solution was to make the man jealous, and that would win him back. When she died, she had nobody around. I was kind of ashamed of myself when there was some story in, I think it was *Esquire*, about six months later. It was full of quotes from, like, Cukor. I knew he loathed her, but "nothing but good about the dead." The only one who was quoted in several places as very critical of her, slanderous, was me. Of course, it had been said a long time ago. I'd said when I tried to talk to her, I felt as if I was trying to talk to somebody underwater. There didn't seem to be any real communication. Sometimes I couldn't understand whether she understood what I said. I remember talking to Olivier after he had played with her in that picture *The Prince and the Showgirl*. He was reported to have said, "Now, Marilyn, walk over to that chair, count three, and then sit down." After the first take, he went over to her and said, "Can't you count, either?" He was just outraged by her. He was directing the picture. He told me, "How could you help it? We'd line up a scene in a clinch, and here I am in her arms, right, face-to-face, and the fellow who would be handling the camera would say, 'Cut,' and she turned immediately to Arthur Miller." You know, not to Olivier. She was just downright rude in a kind of a stupid way.

BILLY WILDER: You want me to tell you about Marilyn Monroe? Everyone does. Whenever I do a motion picture event, usually it is my first question. The first question is always Marilyn Monroe, and I start with "No, she did not wear a brassiere." That sort of content. It was a very complex thing working with her because she had tremendous problems with herself. She was on edge at all times, on edge of deep depression inside, whatever you want to call it. It was always a kind of a question, you sweated it out: Is she going to show up? Is she going to show up on time? Is she going to live through that scene? Is she going to finish that picture? That is a very, very nerve-racking thing if you've got, like, $8 million in the enterprise so far. But when it's all done, it was well worth it. It's that old thing that I said, I don't know, four hundred years ago, that "Look, if I wanted somebody to be on time and to know the lines just perfectly, I've got an old aunt in Vienna. She's going to be there at five in the morning, never miss a word. But who wants to see her?"

GEORGE CUKOR: I love that today all sorts of people are coming out from back of the wallpaper having all sorts of theories about how Hollywood broke Marilyn's heart.

GAVIN LAMBERT: Yes, people with very little connection with Hollywood, never being here and knowing nothing about it.

BILLY WILDER: My God, I think there are more books on Marilyn Monroe than on World War II, and there's a great similarity.

GEORGE CUKOR: She was plenty tough. It may have been hard with her at first, but so is it tough on everybody. It's tough, getting a job for a pretty girl, I don't know what happens. I'll never forget, a beautiful friend of mine killed herself, and Zoe Akins said, "It was the only ending for her." I should think it was the only end for Marilyn.

She was very intelligent, she was tough minded, very appealing, but she had bad judgment about things. She adored and trusted the wrong people. She was very courageous when I directed her in *Let's Make Love*.

I knew that she was reckless, I knew that she was willful. I had no communication with her at all. She was very sweet, very nice, but you couldn't get at her. She was very concerned about a lot of things (she did a lot of shit-ass studying and all that), and I'd say, "Marilyn, you're so accomplished, you're doing things that are frightfully difficult to do." She could do, among other things, comedy. She had an absolute, unerring touch with comedy. She didn't seem funny in real life, but she was very observing, she had an unerring touch. She acted as if she didn't quite understand it. This was a perfectly natural function, and that was what made her very funny. She could also do low comedy, pratfalls and things like that.

I had very little influence on her. I made a climate that was agreeable for her, and I think every day was an agony of struggle for her, just to get there. It wasn't all willfulness. She was very shrewd in certain ways. I once heard her talk in her ordinary voice, which was a very unattractive, unappealing voice. She invented this appealing baby voice.

You very seldom saw her with her mouth closed because when she had her mouth closed, she had a very determined chin, quite a different face. She had a lovely face, but she wasn't all that pretty. The face moved in a wonderful way. It was a wonderful movie face. She could be very articulate—she knew what it was about, a great deal.

She had a lot of bad advice. I really didn't know her, but she was tough and ruthless. But in the beginning, she'd be very endearing, had beautiful manners. Marilyn either couldn't or wouldn't control herself. She was like a child. She wouldn't match things in a scene, you know, when you have a cigarette in one scene and you cut to the close-up, you can't not have the cigarette. But she simply either didn't have enough control of herself or wouldn't bother. Also, she couldn't sustain scenes. She'd do three lines or three words and forget it, then she'd do another line and forget it, so you'd have to do it piecemeal. But curiously enough, when you strung them together, it was all a complete scene. She never really did the same thing twice. She had, like all movie queens have, an excitement to her. I remember she had just come in late and ran across the stage in her high heels (she always wore high heels, they were very pretty), and just watching her cross the screen was exciting.

HARRY WARREN: Working in the movies could be tough on some of these actors. Take dancing, that's hard work. And someone like Fred Astaire had to choreograph his routines and rehearse them first, too, and then there would have to be . . . oh, I don't even know how many takes. Sometimes he or someone would make a mistake and they had to do it all over again. So nothing's easy for these so-called glamorous stars, but some of them seemed able to take it better than others. Fred had worked all his life and had been a big star before he ever got to the movies.

VINCENTE MINNELLI: He wanted everything to be carefully rehearsed, and he had to have everything *exactly* in his mind. He had to know every minute.

ROBERT WAGNER: He was a complete professional. And a perfectionist.

HARRY WARREN: Yes, Fred is a real perfectionist. But a very modest guy. He was always interesting to watch. But he didn't like people on the stage when he was rehearsing. He liked the gals who could dance better than he liked the gals who couldn't dance, because he had to teach them. And that's a bore, too, and tiresome. I think he liked Vera-Ellen when he worked with her, because she was a dancer. Orchestrating for him is kind of tough. He wants beats in certain places, to go with certain steps that he does. And he wants the music done in a certain way. Fred Astaire really knew music.

Fred was very polite. Gene Kelly was just the opposite. He was quite brusque: "I don't like that." But Fred was a very quiet man. He didn't talk much. At the meetings that we had on the pictures about scripts, he never said much.

PANDRO BERMAN: Fred Astaire and Ginger Rogers were the biggest stars that RKO ever had. Making the Astaire-Rogers pictures, we used to be able to get a Ginger Rogers picture in between the Astaire-Rogers pictures, while we couldn't get an Astaire picture in between because his work consisted of preparing dance numbers, which took quite a bit of time. So we were always looking for something to slide Ginger into. And one of the pictures that I liked very much that we did with Ginger was called *Bachelor Mother*, where we got a young man named David Niven on loan out from Sam Goldwyn. I happen to recall the salary, which was rather amusing in terms of what's happened since. We paid Samuel Goldwyn $5,000 for the picture for David Niven. Also at the time, I recall that Sam Goldwyn, who was a remarkable man and a great man and who also had the enormous gall of a Hitler, called me up one day after the first or second Astaire-Rogers hit and told me that he was going to do me a big favor and take Fred Astaire off my hands for a movie. Needless to say, he didn't get him! He wanted to borrow him at that time. And strangely enough, Astaire, who was very close socially with Sam and Frances Goldwyn as he was with quite a lot of other people in Hollywood, took a very perverse pleasure in the fact that they couldn't get him because, as he said to me one day, "You didn't know me and I didn't know you, and you gave me these marvelous opportunities." And he said, "All these fellows who are my friends, that I have known for years, none of them ever thought I was any good for films." So he was delighted when we could turn Sam Goldwyn down on him.

MERIAN C. COOPER: I put Fred Astaire under contract with RKO, but then I quit, you know. I wasn't going to run the studio any longer, but I'd seen him on the stage, and I thought he and his sister, Adele Astaire, were the greatest dancers in the world. She was more of a personality than he was at that time . . . but they were the best. I think he's the best dancer that ever lived right now. I got pictures that he did with Gene Kelly; Gene Kelly looks just like what he is, a hoofer. Astaire, even at his age, is a finished dancer, but when he was forty, he was a helluva dancer. So, from thirty to fifty, there wasn't anybody in his class. Now, [his sister] Adele was just as good a dancer, by the way.

PANDRO BERMAN: In 1934, RKO started the team of Ginger Rogers and Fred Astaire as a starring team. The two had worked together in *Flying Down to Rio*, which was made by someone other than myself at RKO, and they were playing in subordinate roles to Gene Raymond and Dolores del Rio. But they were so good that we immediately determined to star them as a team. And at that time I made a trip to Europe and to New York and searched for material and found two vehicles which I thought were suitable for them and bought them: *The Gay Divorcee* and *Roberta*. I bought those in 1933 and came back to the studio and started preparation and began to gather a group of people who were qualified to make musical pictures. And I was very fortunate. I got some really talented people in there ... Mark Sandrich, who had perhaps the greatest influence on those films as director and a pretty good musical organization all around. Composers like Cole Porter, Jerry Kern, Irving Berlin, the Gershwins, and then later George Stevens came in to direct one of them. We had a real good functioning musical organization. We made about two a year with Astaire and Rogers from then on for the next four or five years.

We were lucky that we were able to keep Fred and Ginger together. Not that he had anything against working with Ginger. He loved working with her, but he just wanted to be an individual. We overcame that little by little. Gradually he got to where he fought less about it, but it was a struggle.

Fred started out with 10 percent of the profits. It was one of the earlier deals of that type in the industry [predating Jimmy Stewart's 1950s deal on *Winchester '73*]. There were three of us that got it: myself, Fred, and Irving Berlin. That started the procedure. And perhaps that had some effect in keeping him working with Ginger, too, because as the profits began to roll in, he made some pretty good money!

HARRY WARREN: You know, Fred and Ginger were kind of uncommunicative people. They don't talk much. They come on the stage and do a scene and walk back into their dressing rooms. They have those dressing rooms on the stage—on wheels—and they don't mingle with people much. They don't talk. Fred never did. They'd stay polite, when you used to see them and talk to them, but that's about it.

IRVING RAPPER: Ginger Rogers had some star quality. I don't think she was Lynn Fontanne as an actress, by any means, but I do think she reflected the great glamour of Hollywood. She certainly carried it off with great style insofar as her personality allowed. I'll never forget, she asked me, "How shall I treat these people at Sardi's when they come in and look at me?" And I just said, "You just smell peasants." I think she liked that very much, yes. But she was a very good trouper and kept quite to herself. She became demanding in her later years.

RAY RENNAHAN: That was the star system. It led to "Make 'em pay."

IRVING RAPPER: But Fred never did. He was a hard worker.

RAY RENNAHAN: Well, Ginger became less professional. She would be due on the set at nine o'clock, and we were all ready to shoot at nine o'clock. We'd have the set all ready to go and everything, and she'd come in at eleven or eleven thirty, and then she wasn't in makeup and then she'd sit down on the bench and discuss the picture and then of course it was almost twelve and so they'd call lunch for the whole troupe and she'd go over and get her makeup and come back. So one of my boys started keeping track on the hours lost waiting for her, and it figured out at twenty-one days at eight hours a day. And she had a contract—I forget, but a tremendous penalty for overtime if we went over schedule—well, we ran weeks over schedule because of those twenty-one days.

HARRY WARREN: Fred liked to do special effects and all those things. He'd get in the studio at nine o'clock in the morning, and he'd be there all day. He was never late. He wouldn't leave the stage, even for lunch. He'd have it on the stage, all by himself, with a piano player. He figured out all his own routines. He's a polite worrier and an introvert, where Gene Kelly is just the opposite: he's an extrovert, and he doesn't worry. Different characters entirely.

Kelly had a way of talking that sometimes would grate against you. Some people found him difficult. Not with me, he wasn't. But I don't think he meant it. Sometimes if you're not used to a person, you don't know how to take them. Listen, I saw Fred one time tell Minnelli to come down off a boom on a ladder. He said, "If you don't come down, I'll come up there and pull you down." *Minnelli*. Who was his favorite director. These things happen in studios.

STANLEY DONEN: Fred Astaire absolutely flabbergasted me. When I saw him in movies as a child . . . I had just never realized anyone could dance like that. And I never lost that enthusiasm. He gave me this wild passion for, I guess, movies and dancing and feeling what his films gave me . . .

all his films. I came out to Los Angeles to get a job, and I auditioned at MGM. They had an audition for dancers, and I got chosen. And I ended up directing Fred Astaire! *And* Gene Kelly! People always ask me sort of silly questions about the difference between them. One is extremely athletic, and one is extremely delicate in his movements. And that's the big difference. The joy of seeing one is the joy of watching an acrobat and the other is like seeing a feather floating. And they both are incredible but quite different.

GEORGE FOLSEY: People like to compare Astaire and Kelly. I shot their only number together, "The Babbitt and the Bromide" in *Ziegfeld Follies*. It may be that I'm not very observing about things like that, but I wasn't cognizant of any difficulty between them. I only know that seeing Fred Astaire up there with anybody, I would always look at Astaire, because to me he always danced like a leaf blown by the breeze. He just looked like he was effervescent. Kelly is a much more acrobatic dancer, a very good dancer, but much more athletic, much more strenuous. Astaire does it with such absolute nonchalance and grace that whether he's with Rogers or whoever, I look at him. I just find myself looking at him. But Astaire and Kelly were respectful of one another.

GENE KELLY: We always disliked the fact that we were often thought of as a comparison. We dance completely differently. His style is intimate. Mine's broad. And when we worked together, we always had to accommodate each other. Our styles are not alike.

GEORGE SEATON: I directed Fred in *The Pleasure of His Company* in a nondancing role. Fred agreed that we shouldn't try to show his dancing abilities, because if we'd done that, then you're into a musical with Fred Astaire. But a funny thing happened one day when we were shooting a scene at a party. Fred and Lilli [Palmer] were just doing society dancing, and then I thought it might be funny if suddenly the orchestra changed to a mambo, without a moment's notice. Fred could then switch right into it and wheel her around the floor with her not quite knowing what he was doing. I said, "How about that?" Fred sort of looked very glum. He walked away, and I went over to him and said, "Fred, don't you think it's a funny idea?" He said, "I think it would be hilarious." Then he added rather sheepishly, "But I don't know how to mambo." So I said, "Don't worry about it, I'll get one of these young girl extras, and we'll go on another stage. We'll take a recording." We sneaked out. We went onto another stage, and, of course, in five minutes he could mambo better than anybody in the world. So we came back, and that was it.

GEORGE CUKOR: People always ask me questions: "What is Garbo like?" You see her on the screen? *That's* what she is like. People ask me questions about people, I tell them, "I get all of my gossiping information from *Silver Screen*." But I'll tell you, Garbo's extremely intelligent. Very practical. There were certain conditions in which she knew she could work. She was quite adamant about quitting at a certain time, and yet she was very flexible. At least I found her that. She was intelligent, and funny in a way. She was very nice and a professional, talented and magical. As for *Camille*, in which I directed her, that was an interesting thing, because it's the perfect meeting of the actress and the part. She was born to play that part. It was a very good part, with a long range to it. She did it with the most enormous gaiety, and it's a weepy, weepy thing.

HAL ROSSON: Garbo was different from anybody I ever met. I thought she was extremely beautiful. She had a very odd figure. Her figure was—I don't like to use the word *repulsive*—but there was a time when her figure was terribly repulsive to my way of thinking. Hedy Lamarr was a very, very beautiful woman, but Garbo, I can't emphasize too definitely, was more compelling or dynamic. When I walked on the stage, onto a stage that Garbo was on, I knew there was a power on that stage. I absolutely knew it. I felt it. I was certain of it. I never felt that way with anybody but Greta Garbo. Nobody else. There was electricity in the air.

SIDNEY FRANKLIN: Never got along with her at all. Well, I got along with every woman I ever worked with, and I could name quite a long list. All stars. But something about Garbo, I don't know. I didn't get along with her, and I don't want to say why.

TEETE CARLE: I remember her from the very beginning. The photographer Don Gillum called me up one day and said, "We have this little Swedish starlet out here, and we want to bring her out and get some shots. It's springtime, and [USC track coach] Dean Cromwell will be out with his athletes, and we want to bring her and put her in a tracksuit and shoot some pictures." So I said, "Fine," and they brought her out to USC, and there she was. She couldn't speak very much English. They treated her just like any other newcomer. They put her in a tracksuit. She stood under the high-jump bar, and a high jumper jumped over her. She also knelt down between hurdles and let hurdlers hurdle over her. I've got the pictures of her. She and Don started to leave, and someone said, "What was that little girl's name?" So I asked Don what was her name, and he said, "Garbo." I was never assigned as publicist to any Garbo pictures, and at no time during the four years that I was on the MGM lot every day did I see her even riding through the lot. She could have been a myth as far as I was concerned. She was *that*, really. Mysterious. But not so much at first.

HAL ROSSON: Garbo was always prepared. She knew all her dialogue, and she knew all the dialogue that you or any other actor was going to have to say to her. She was famous for the five o'clock quitting time, when her maid would come in and hand her her glass of water. She would drink a bit of the water, and then she'd just leave the set. Very definitely. I wouldn't say she never stayed beyond the five o'clock limit, but someone would have to talk her into it. If she was going to stay longer, there had to be some reason for it. And she had to give you the okay that she would do it. Otherwise she would not stay on that stage. A few stars got that arrangement for their working day, mostly because they just weren't going to do anything good otherwise. It was economical for the studio in the long run.

GEORGE CUKOR: She is very sensible and very practical. She says what she wants and is very fair, and these considerations are based on common sense. When she says something, she means it, she doesn't play tricks. For example, she quit at five o'clock, which seemed to be a great extravagance. I believe it took her that to go home, have her dinner, compose herself, and get some sleep. I think she was a bad sleeper always. She took that early quitting time, but on the other hand, she was never, never late, never wasted any time. There was no nonsense about her. She didn't fuss about things when she trusted people. She never saw the rushes, and I asked her why she didn't. "Well," she said, "I have some idea, some notion, of what I'm doing, and every time I see it, it falls so short that it throws me." She trusted the people she was working with. What she accomplished was by enormous concentration, relaxed concentration. I think she must have thought a great deal about what the part was. She had an image in her mind. Usually she would finish a scene and go to her dressing room. Very often when we were on the back lot, she would go to a little fenced-in, screened-off place, and she would take sunbathing. But on this picture she remained on the set and was very funny and sweet and very gay, and I think she was fairly happy.

With Garbo you must make a climate in which she trusts you. She doesn't tell one about herself. She makes jokes, she has a smoke screen. I tell you something, when we did *Camille*, in the very early part of the picture Irving Thalberg died, and he saw a couple of days' rushes and he said, "She's awfully good, she's never been this good." I said, "Irving, she's just sitting there." He said, "But she is relaxed, she's open."

MITCHELL LEISEN: I ran into her walking down the street one day as I was going toward the set. She was coming away from it. We just smiled politely to each other. On the set she was always completely surrounded by screens. Nobody could get anywhere near her to see her. Later I met her at a party at the [Samuel] Hoffensteins'. I sat at her feet and massaged her bare feet for hours. She was quite a gal. That's the only time I ever met her.

ROUBEN MAMOULIAN: After I signed the contract to do *Queen Christina* with her, I wanted to clear up some points that I had heard about. I had heard that Garbo, when she came to do an intimate scene, would go and have a sandwich and a cup of coffee. Then there would be screens put all around the set, and nobody was allowed to be there except the camera-man and the other actor. Then she would play this intimate scene, and after she had done it, the director would be invited to come back on the set. Well, I couldn't consider that. So I agreed to become my own producer, and now I could negotiate. I asked Miss Garbo, "Is this true about the scenes?" and she said, "Yes, I like to be alone when I am doing intimate scenes." I told her she had better get somebody else to direct her, but finally she agreed, and I thought everything was okay. We still had to work it out on the set, but that was working with Garbo. She was brilliant, of course, in the picture.

GORE VIDAL: Tennessee Williams met her and said he would do anything for her if she would come back to movies. "What would you like to play?" he asked. "What kind of part?" She said, "Don't make me a man. Don't make me a woman." The great androgyny.

GEORGE CUKOR: There was a scene in *Camille* where Garbo dropped her fan and she expected de Varville to pick it up and he wouldn't. He said, "Pick it up," and the way Garbo picked up that fan was the most wonderful thing. It was rather like a piece of sculpture coming to life. It was like the sorrowing Naomi. The tragedy, the beauty of the way she moved.

WALTER REISCH: They put Garbo in a comedy, but it was a Lubitsch comedy, so she was safe: *Ninotchka*. During the shooting, everybody said about the other cast members, "Felix Bressart will steal the picture" or "Ina Claire will steal the picture" or "The script will steal the picture." Well, I tell you, nobody steals a picture from Greta Garbo. And nobody did.

Ninotchka was the first picture in which Garbo really laughed. A short while after the picture *Ninotchka* was publicly released, with the whole advertising campaign revolving around the two words "Garbo Laughs," the following thing happened in Hollywood: Italy had declared war on the Western powers. There was no television in those days, and there were very few radios on the MGM lot because they had those newfangled elevators which killed practically every broadcast with their side effects. The only radio which really worked well was in the very far and remote office of Gottfried Reinhardt. One morning around eleven o'clock, everybody was assembled in that office because it was thought that Roosevelt would make a speech. It was the famous speech containing the words "The hand that held the dagger has struck it into its neighbor's back"—about

Italy attacking France. The door opened as we were all sitting there, and in came a lady in blue pants and an enormous straw hat. It was Garbo! Everybody got up, but she whispered, "Please, I just want to listen to the broadcast." There we sat, and she listened. As you remember, it was a classic and an historic speech, very touching. Strangely enough, everybody in that room—like Ben Hecht and S. N. Behrman and Michael Arlen and myself, and, more than anybody, Garbo—had many friends in France and also in Italy. When the speech was over, with the whole world and the papers advertising "Garbo Laughs!," Garbo cried.

BRONISLAU KAPER: You know, she was a mystery woman. It was part of the image. I heard that if someone took her home from a party, she wouldn't let him take her to the very house. He had to stop before, and she walked so he wouldn't know where she was living. The first time I was on the MGM lot, I looked through my office window, and I couldn't believe my eyes. I thought it was a vision, an apparition. It was Garbo. Garbo was more than a face. It was a symbol, an image, a fairy tale, really. Later I paid no attention because I worked there for years. But she was *the* star in Europe. You see, the other stars were more American. They were known, but there was something about Garbo. She was from *there*, from Sweden. And anyway, even here, there were stars who were much bigger money stars than Garbo, but there was a certain aura about her.

I did the music for Garbo's last film, *Two-Faced Woman*. It should be called "The Last Picture Show." It was her very last movie, and I must proudly say it was her worst. Absolutely the worst. With due respect to the people who made it, Gottfried Reinhardt, the producer, and George Cukor, with whom I love to work, with all his sometimes hysterical outbursts of temper . . . well, really, he's a fabulous man, a great artist, but this picture was a *miss*. Terrible. You cannot make a movie better if the story is basically a little foolish. Well, all that is analyzing, because some other pictures of Garbo's are also foolish and were still great movies. But they were constructed better. The whole idea of this alleged comedy was not funny. *Ninotchka* was crazy but had a fantastic idea and was funny. And if a picture is not funny and a woman who gets a little older, with an accent, tries to be funny, it becomes quite often pathetic.

RICHARD SCHICKEL: A lot of time is spent on the "What was So-and-So really like?" Sometimes not only does no one know, but the star doesn't know. Cary Grant understood the challenge of movie stardom. He said he gradually became "Cary Grant" and "Cary Grant" gradually became him, and the two men merged at some point, although not that early in his career.

GEORGE CUKOR: Well, Cary Grant wasn't really a trained actor. Cary Grant was in the theater, and then he had a lot of his training here. He was at first a rather wooden man, and then suddenly he discovered "I'm a comedian." He found a way to work.

JERRY LEWIS: You never saw him shift gears. That's what was so magnificent about him.

GREGORY PECK: People work in different ways, you know, and many ways are good. I've watched Cary Grant on a set with the camera going. I've watched him looking at actors already performing with the camera running, and he looks at the last few pages of the script, puts it down, and walks on right in the middle of the scene, and he's Cary Grant. He worked that way: walk on, and be your persona. He worked very, very well that way. But I enjoy preparation and study. And I come well prepared. Actors have different ways, and so do stars.

LEO MCCAREY: Cary Grant was impossible. He was nervous and uncertain and insecure. Hard to work with. I remember one day, I met him walking down the street at the corner of Vine and Melrose. He said, "Paramount let me go—I'm on the streets." I said, "And what do you think I'm doing? Paramount kicked me out, too!" We were two bums. The next year, we made *The Awful Truth*. He was worried about doing slapstick in it. He had no sound judgment. He wanted to get out of *Awful Truth* after we'd started it. He offered $5,000 to repay Harry Cohn for the expense Columbia had incurred. When I heard about it, I was so mad at him I wouldn't talk to him. I said, "Well, if five thousand dollars isn't enough, I'll put in five and make it ten." The studio had to convince him, and things were strained all the way through shooting. And he wasn't any easier in *My Favorite Wife* or *Once Upon a Honeymoon*. But years later, on *An Affair to Remember*, he was excellent. Cary Grant changed from the early times.

MITCHELL LEISEN: When I first worked with Cary Grant, he wasn't like he is today, I'll say that. He was a brash Cockney who thought he owned the world. We had a scene where a bomb hits the roof, and all the timbers and everything fall in. Well, I'd rehearsed that very carefully so that everybody had a place to go. Except Mr. Grant was off tap-dancing in a corner and wasn't paying much attention. It so happened that I had a switch in my hand that would set the explosion off, and it was open, but when the special effects department touched the wire to it, the thing went off. Since everybody had been rehearsed, they went to their proper place. Grant just stood there looking up and got it right in the face, and they had to send him to the hospital. He hadn't bothered to rehearse like everybody else had, but that prerehearsal of that scene saved everybody from a bad accident. They all dived into the spots where they were supposed to be automatically, except Mr. Grant. Cary Grant today is one of the most charming people you could possibly know, a very good friend of mine. I was out at Universal one day eating lunch by myself, and all of a sudden I felt a hand on my shoulder. I looked up, and it was Cary. He'd seen me and had come clear across the room to be sure to say hello. He's different now. He pays attention.

PANDRO BERMAN: We made a deal at RKO with Cary Grant. We got Cary from the freelance market after he had been dropped by Paramount. Paramount had had him for quite some time under contract, and they let him go because they had been using him in the wrong way, as a straight leading man, and I guess they were somewhat dissatisfied. So when they dropped him, we made a deal, I think, for about five pictures over a period of years. Something like that. He wouldn't sign an exclusive term contract. And we put him in a picture called *Sylvia Scarlett*, which was an abysmal failure as a film but which had some lovely things in it, especially for Cary, who played comedy for the first time. Played a Cockney and really had a ball. And his talent flowered in that role under George Cukor. It was as a result of *Sylvia Scarlett* that we knew we wanted to use him and use him to the hilt, and one thing we had that we were able to do it with was *Gunga Din*.

GEORGE CUKOR: Cary has a native intelligence. Mind you, he's better when he's well directed.

GAVIN LAMBERT: Who isn't?

HOWARD HAWKS: We were doing *I Was a Male War Bride* with Cary Grant. We had a scene where Cary, as a French captain, had to answer questions from an American sergeant that would usually be asked of a little French girl who is marrying a GI, such questions as "You ever had female trouble?" and "Have you ever been pregnant?" and all kinds of ridiculous questions. We looked forward to making the scene. We got up to making it, and it wasn't funny at all. We didn't know what was the matter. And Cary said, "It's falling flat, isn't it?" And I said, "It certainly is." I don't know where the suggestion came from that a man like Cary Grant would be amused at the sergeant having to ask him these silly questions: "Oh, sergeant, female troubles? I've had them all." All of a sudden: "We can do that, we can do that," and he got over in the corner with the sergeant who was asking, and in two or three minutes the scene became very, very funny because the sergeant was embarrassed and Cary was having fun with him. We made an entirely different scene. Cary was flexible. And he grew to be a totally professional actor.

MAXIMILIAN SCHELL: Spencer Tracy was, for me, the most professional actor I ever met and the most human and the best. It's just that simple. Although he had his tricks, too. He had his clichés, too, but they were just so good and not yet used by others that he could use them over and over again. And he was aware of them. He always had a certain vanity, like every actor, but he was so simple. And his whole life, he conducted so beautifully and so dignified that he was just a great human being, as well as a great actor. I think the film camera captures the personality of a human being and a film actor much more than the theater. In the theater, you can just be theatrical. You can be very affective, but it has nothing to do with your soul. But a film has to deal with your soul. And Spence had just attained an individual moment of his wonderful late work in *Judgment at Nuremberg*. He had two lunch hours, from one to three, and he could quit at five. And of course, like every movie company, when they had a shot on him and it was a quarter to five, everybody started very quietly to work and set it up and hoping he forgets about the time. And at five, he just left. And one time when I had my last speech, he came to me and said, "Max, do you want me for the speech, off camera?" And I said, "Spence, it's five o'clock." And he said, "Well, do you want me?" "If you are asking me, yes." So he just stayed, waited for the shot. It became 5:10. Everybody said, "Spence, it's five o'clock." And he said, "No, no, Max needs me. For him, I'll stay." So that shows you what a great human being. Because it's for an actor, especially for a young guy. I wasn't known at that time. And Katharine Hepburn gave up years of her life just to be with him, and he was just a great human being.

HOWARD HAWKS: Bogart was a joy to work with. He is one of the finest actors we've ever had. He is capable of doing any kind of scene that you can think of, and he was really awfully good to work with. I had a lot of fun with him because we were working on a story and we got an idea—no matter what you wrote, he was insolent. So he said, "Well, let's make a girl insolent." We started to work, and we worked out the part. And I said to Bogart, "As long as it doesn't come as a surprise to you, we're going to make the girl more insolent than you are." Well, he said, "You've got a fat chance in doing that." I said, "I don't know, I think we've got a pretty good chance. I'll tell you one thing, every scene that we make with her, she is going to walk out and leave you with egg on your face." He just looked at me, and I said, "After all, I'm the director."

VINCENT SHERMAN: Bogie was always a skeptic. One of his favorite phrases all the time was "Let's cut the crap." He was a no-bullshit guy. He was very down to earth, very realistic, and somewhat embittered. And for good reason. He had been a good stage actor. He made a big hit in *The Petrified Forest*, and he came to Warners, and he was just thrown a bunch of lousy parts. Everybody regarded him just as another heavy. Amongst the directors when I first started directing, they didn't think too much of him. That's the honest truth. Cagney was the big man at Warners, and Flynn and Robinson. But nobody paid too much attention to Bogart. He had to work a decade to become a star.

RANALD MACDOUGALL: Bogie was a very private fellow, you know, he was so amazingly untouched by acting. He would do a marvelous scene and then pick up his chess game right where he left off. He was an infinitely painstaking craftsman. He would cut things away—Spencer Tracy was another one who cut things away. You would never catch Spencer Tracy or Bogart overacting. Never. They would cut everything away. It was their schooling and their marvelous reality as human beings and performers.

He once told me, "Movie acting is not a profession for a grown-up man." Dressing up and the makeup and all the rest of it, that's part of the feminine mystique, and for a man to put on makeup and pretty himself up and get ready for the camera, he said, "That's not for grown-up men. You have to be a child to do that at all well." And his point of view was valid, and particularly for him. Conversely, Eddie Robinson was a thorough actor. Bogie would tell you—and probably half of it was perhaps just Bogie talking—but he'd say, "Well, I'm in it for the money. They pay me, and that's it. I don't care what I do." He did care, and it wasn't just money, but that was his attitude. He was a tough fellow, and that wasn't for him. Robinson, on the other hand, he was a thorough actor. It didn't matter what he did, he would give everything to it.

VINCENT SHERMAN: He always seemed to be somewhat detached from the circumstances and the situation around him in a picture's plot. He had a sense of doubt about the problem and also seemed to be somewhat in control. There is no question that he was enormously effective. As we look back now, we can see he was certainly one of our better screen performers.

RANALD MACDOUGALL: Bogie became ill, in the historical sense. He had his operation for cancer, and I knew, I think, about four or five months before it actually happened, that he was terminally ill—not from him, nor from Betty Bacall. And one of the reasons I think—I thought so before, and this simply confirmed it for all time that I thought Betty was an extraordinary woman—was the way that she took care of Bogart during that time, because she never babied him or nursed him or anything of the sort. That is, she just carried right on as though everything was fine. I'd go there and see him, and he'd be in bed and she'd bring him a drink of scotch. On one occasion he got about three of them, and I finally gave her a look—and later on she said, "There isn't anything in it, it's just weak." But Bogie's whole attitude was that nothing had happened and never would and "We're going to make the picture," and so, I say, I spent three or four months keeping up the pretense with him that we were going to go ahead with it and do it and so on and so forth. He kept saying, for one reason or another, "Well, when the hell are we going to start?" And I'd say, "Bogie, I can't get the boat yet. I'll let you know the minute I do." You know, that sort of thing. We were both playacting, and that was sad.

HARRY WARREN: One of the top box-office stars for nearly two decades was Bing Crosby. People think of him as a recording artist or partner with Bob Hope in the Road comedies, but Bing was a top box-office star, in the top five, for decades. I worked with him. It came out of the blue. At six o'clock in the morning my phone rang, and a voice is on the phone that I recognized right away as that of Bing Crosby. He says, "Are you working?" I said, "No." He said, "Would you like to do a picture for me?" So I said, "Sure, but what happened to Burke and Van Heusen [a songwriting team]?" He said, "They're busy," or something. The title of the picture was *Just for You.*

He rode a bicycle onto the stage. He said "Hello" to everybody, one quick "Hello," and then he recorded and he left. He never talked to anybody . . . or . . . there's no camaraderie or fun, or anything like that. Same with most of them. They're all like that. I think they all copied Crosby. They all found out how Crosby acted, and so they all have that "ten-foot invisible pole" between you and them. I think you have to be very intimate with him to have a conversation with him. I was never intimate with him. The same thing with Martin and Lewis. Dean Martin didn't talk at all. He wouldn't talk to anybody. And Lewis did all the talking. And he bossed everybody around until you'd have to leave. You got tired of listening to it. And the other guy wouldn't talk at all. Jerry was producer, director, cameraman, and everything. He did all the talking, and Dean Martin just sat there and looked at him. The only thing that would stop Jerry Lewis was an elephant gun. You could see that this thing was coming to a boil all the time, that they were going to split.

Crosby always was aloof, though. He never was friendly. Yeah, with Jimmy Van Heusen and Johnny Burke. He was friendly with them but never friendly with me. The same with Sinatra. He was never friendly with me. He'd say "Hello" to me or something, but that's it. But it's funny, I don't think I can remember ever having been told, by a producer or an artist or an actor, that they didn't like a song. I remember playing a whole score for Bing that I did with Leo Robin. We just sat there and played it, one after the other. He said, "Fine," and walked out. That's all he said, though—no conversation, "How are you?" "Haven't seen you in a long time." Nothing.

RAY RENNAHAN: Crosby came to LA and sang at the Cocoanut Grove and became very popular there. Then Mack Sennett made a little series of short sound films with Bing, and it made a star out of him. He had plenty for motion pictures. He's one of the greatest stars we've ever had.

RANALD MACDOUGALL: Bing Crosby was marvelous to work with, just marvelous. He has his own way of doing things, you know. Casualness is Bing Crosby's natural tempo. He's a low-pressure fellow. He's that way about life, too. He'll live to be a thousand as a result of it. I am sure he must have had a fiery ranting and raving in his youth, but that has long since burned away. He is very calm, a very private man. I always felt that he had about two inches of glass all around him. You couldn't get too close to him.

KARL STRUSS: I did most of Bing Crosby's films at Paramount. At a certain angle, whether Bing looks right or left of the camera, that didn't make any difference, it was as much as possible necessary not to show his ears. They stuck out a little bit more, we'll say, than normal. And I know that before I started to photograph him, that I was told that he would even tape them down.

GEORGE SEATON: Bing is not the kind of person who uses the Method or anything of that sort. But there's one short scene [in *Little Boy Lost*] where he gets off a little bus. He's going to the train station. He's leaving the boy. He has a suitcase in his hand. He walks from the bus to the train platform. Now, while we were lining up the shot, somebody came out from the hotel to deliver mail to him, and he sat there reading a letter. I said, "Bing, we're ready." He did the scene, and the whole crew started to cry. In his walk, he had the whole weight of the world on his shoulders. I went up to him afterwards, and I said, "Bing, my God, it's just a walk, but I tell you, the tragedy in that walk was something." It fit the part completely, because he was leaving this little boy. He turned to me, held the letter up, and said, "Dixie has cancer." That's when he first knew that Dixie [his wife] had cancer.

LEO McCAREY: Bing Crosby could do no wrong as an actor.

GEORGE SEATON: When I asked Bing to do *The Country Girl*, he felt that he just couldn't do it. I coaxed and coaxed, tried to give him as much confidence as possible, but he said, "Look, I'm a crooner, I'm no actor." I kept fighting with him all the time, and finally he said, "All right, I'll do it." We had the advantage of having the three principals on a run of the film contract. We went down to Palm Springs, and I hired a hall and we laid out the sets with tape and we rehearsed for two weeks with [William] Holden and Grace and Bing, so that they could really play long scenes and we wouldn't have to do it in little twenty-foot takes. But Bing was still not convinced that he could do it. He was so frightened of it. Now, we came to the first day of shooting. We were all there at nine in the morning, but no Crosby. Nine thirty and no Crosby. Ten o'clock, no Crosby. Ten thirty and no Crosby, and I'm calling all over town to find him. Finally at about eleven o'clock Wally Westmore, who was head of the makeup department, said, "You've got trouble, you'd better come up here." Now, Bing and I had talked about a toupee for him, something that made him look his age. We had selected one, and it was just right. I ran up to his dressing room, and there he was wearing his *College Humor* wig, a wavy, marcelled thing, one that he had worn in all of those Paramount musicals twenty years earlier. He said, "This is what I'm going to wear." I said, "Bing, it's ridiculous, you know you can't wear that." He said, "I've got my fans to think of, and I'm not going to go out there with a toupee with a little bald spot on the top." Then I got an inspiration. I said, "Bing, you're absolutely right, you're *so* right, because this character is a vain, horrible son of a bitch. So you wear this wig, but the only thing I ask you is that in one scene in the dressing room, peel it off. This will make the character, because it will show what a horrible, stupid old man he is." He said, "No! I'm not going to take it off." Then I said, "Well, Bing, then you have to wear the other wig." After a long silence I added, "Bing, I know why you're putting up this defense at the moment: you're frightened." He started to cry. He said, "I'm so frightened you can't imagine. I can't do this part." I said, "Bing, I'm frightened, too. So let's go on the set and be frightened together." So he took my hand and went on the set, and after that there was no problem whatsoever. When people congratulated him on the rushes, it helped him a lot. He's a dear, dear man, and I think he gave an exceptional performance.

His mother came on the set one day and came to talk to me. She said, "I don't like Harry"—she still called him Harry—"I don't like Harry to play a drunk. He had problems as a boy." I said, "He's not playing a drunk, he's playing a reformed drunk. He doesn't drink in this, except later he has some cough syrup." So she said, "All right, but I don't want him to drink in this picture." I invited her to come on the set anytime she wanted.

Now comes the day of the scene in Boston where he downs a couple of bottles of cough syrup and goes on a bender because he hasn't got confidence in himself. The day before, I had said to [producer William] Perlberg, "Keep him out all night long. And Bing, I don't want you to shave. And I want you to get loaded." He said, "George, oh, no, I—" And I said, "You don't have to get loaded." He said, "All right." So Perlberg kept him up all night long, and he came into the studio the next day, and I tell you, there was blood running out of his eyes. He looked simply awful but just great for the scene in jail. Well, this is the day that Mrs. Crosby decided to come on the set, and she came in and she took one look at him and she said, "Harry! You've been drinking!" And turned right around and left.

NORMAN TAUROG: Stars that lasted were always smarter than you might think. They might not have big educations, but they learned on the job . . .

and they were shrewd, and they knew they had to survive. Some of the women knew more about lighting than you do or the cameraman did. They always knew which was their best side and which wasn't their best side . . . or what kind of dress worked for them. . . . They were always trying to look out for themselves. They had to. And you are not trusted, believe me. They had learned that the hard way.

HARRY WARREN: They watched out for themselves. They did their jobs no matter what, but sometimes there could be two actors working in a picture who didn't talk to each other. That was tricky, because they had to talk to each other in the scene.

JEAN LOUIS: Constance Bennett and Lana Turner were both in the 1966 *Madame X*. It was all okay until we came to a scene where they were both supposed to wear a fur coat, Lana in a white mink and Constance in a sable. Lana said, "I don't want that white mink coat. Look, I am blond. I want to wear sable. Let *her* wear the white mink. I want the sable coat." I said, "All right, we'll see what we can do." So I go to the other one. And she said, "I don't want to wear the white mink coat. *I* am the sable girl! I don't want to." So Ross Hunter, the film's producer, came, and he made peace by saying firmly, "*You* wear the white mink coat" to Lana "and give the sable to Constance." Lana was the star, but it had been designed for her to wear white, to offset her blond hair. Sable was the more expensive fur. She wanted it. But, you see, stars didn't always get their way. Lana wore the white like she was told. She was, really, a cooperative girl.

BETTE DAVIS: Well, you know, there's a great misunderstanding that any time two women work together, there's automatically going to be a terrific feud. The press did everything in the world to see that Joan Crawford and I had a big fight. Well, in the first place we didn't have any time. We made *Whatever Happened to Baby Jane?* in three weeks, so we didn't have any time for a feud. It was absolutely impossible. I have often said that if it was three months I don't know what would have happened, but anyway, in three weeks nothing happened, because we are both professionals. Actually, the men have bigger feuds than the women. It's an old wives' tale that women can't get along, you know. It truthfully is. It's just absurd.

RIDGEWAY CALLOW: You know, some of those big stars—it's amazing, their impatience and their annoyance. I remember one time I was working with Bette Davis, whom I adore, I think she's marvelous, but she can be bitchy on the set, very bitchy. At the end-of-the-picture party, I said to her—I'm very fond of Bette—I said, "Bette, how is it that such a marvelous person as you is so goddamn bitchy at times?" She said, "I'll tell you a story: In the old days, every time a script was sent to some of these dames around here and they refused to do it, the front office would say, 'Oh, what the hell, give it to Bette Davis, she'll do it.' And then an assistant director would say, 'Oh, give her a nine thirty call. We don't give a damn when we get around to Bette Davis, let her wait.' After years of this I got bitchy. Now if an assistant director feels he's not going to get around to me by nine o'clock, he gives me a ten o'clock call. Now the studios say, 'Please, would you read this script, Miss Davis, to see if you'd like to do it?' That's why we get bitchy." Jean Arthur said the same thing to me.

VINCENT SHERMAN: If you want to talk about big stars, Bette Davis was a *very* big star. Recently she was interviewed by David Frost. They were talking about the various roles that she had played over her career, and they were mostly neurotic and offbeat characters. She said, "The truth is that I am really not like that at all." He asked her if she had ever played anything that was close to her as a human being. She said that she thought the closest thing that had come to her as a person was the part in *Old Acquaintance*. I directed her in that, and I think that is true. I told her that I thought she should just play herself for a change. The woman was intelligent, was a highly sophisticated human being, was talented, knew what was going on, had a great sense of humor about herself and about other people. It doesn't reveal all of the facets of her as a human being. Very few parts do. But as an intelligent, sensitive, sophisticated, humorous human being, I think it was close to her.

RANALD MACDOUGALL: Well, quite frankly, I think Bette Davis is more talented as a performer than Bette Davis herself has ever thought.

She always had a terrible, to me, insecurity about her performances, so she had to style. Everything was stylized, everything was compartmented, everything was planned, everything was—there was no such thing as an ad-lib situation or a loose, relaxed situation or "let's see how this works out" situation. It was cut into marble. And anyone who has to have that kind of rigidity about what they do, to me, has an insecurity. Eventually an iron door descended between me and Bette Davis, and it was four feet thick. I never existed after that. Literally, she didn't talk to me again for fifteen years. She never talked to me for fifteen years, and at the end of that time—you know, I would have cheerfully talked to her at any time, because I thought she was, and I still think she is, a fascinating person. But I was definitely not on her list of human beings.

IRVING RAPPER: Bette would be the first one to tell you of her tremendous differences with directors, and she always admits she's a very difficult lady. A lot of directors couldn't get along with her very well. She didn't get along with them. When I was first going to direct her, I was sitting in the lunchroom one day, and William Wyler, who was her favorite director and my favorite director, passed me in the lunchroom, and I said, "Oh, Willy, I'm so glad you came by. What is Bette Davis like to direct?" And he smiled and he said, "Well, Irving, when she is good, she is an angel in Heaven, and when she is bad, you want to give up the entire business."

JOHN CROMWELL: I directed her in *Of Human Bondage*, which really made her a name. She was only a contract girl then, and her studio was only too delighted to loan her out. They liked having some of her time picked up and paid for by another studio. Also, somebody undoubtedly read the script and saw the promise in the part. They immediately said, "Of course. Let her do it. They may make her into a star for us," which is what we did. That often happened back then. I'll never forget the interview I had with her because of what Bette said. What she said was so indicative of her character then and throughout her career. She said that she liked the script, and then rather fearfully we asked if she'd like to play a bad woman like that, and she gave the answer "Yes. Under one condition." And what was it? "No compromises." It was so typical then to alter a character to make her more sympathetic or to change the conclusion of a story to a happy ending, but she wanted to play an evil woman with "no compromises." I never saw anybody go about her job with greater singleness of purpose. She realized this was the chance that she had been looking for, and she was determined to make the most of it.

RAOUL WALSH: I directed some twenty or thirty movies without credit, probably. You know, people get in trouble and the director gets sick, or he'd leave or do something—have a fight with the star. The last one that I remember was with Bette Davis. John Huston was directing her in *In This Our Life,* and they had a fight just before the ending of this thing about how the picture was going to end. She wanted it to end one way, and he wanted it to end the other way. So he took a walk. So Warner called me in, and he said, "Raoul, this is a tough dame, and I think you can handle her." That was the way he approached it. So he said, "Will you go over to Pasadena and make this ending so we can get this thing done and get this dame out of the studio." Nice girl, but really tough: she'd demand this, that, and the other thing. But she was all right. So I got in a car with Bette. We were to work over in Pasadena, and we stopped for dinner. The unit manager, while we were at Eaton's, which used to be at that time a place where the society folks and elderly people came from Pasadena and gathered in this huge dining room, so while we were having a drink there and getting ready to have some dinner, the unit manager came in and handed me the script, the new ending. So I said, "Bette, this will probably interest you," and passed it over. She read it, and you never heard such a volley of oaths in your life. The ceiling went off from her screaming and yelling. People started to get up. But I finally talked her into it after a couple of shots of laughing water.

IRVING RAPPER: To advise Bette and to direct her are actually two different things. She liked to argue with the director. If a visitor came on the set, they'd say, "Oh, my God, this is the last day of the director and the actress working together." But it seemed to me that Bette would always probe during her rehearsals with the director to see which way she should carry a character. I think she is terribly insecure. I think she'll admit it herself.

She always tried to influence everything on the set every day. Every day. There's always something she wants to emphasize in different scenes, and she never gives up, which I love. She's a perfectionist, you see. And she definitely knows what she wants from a director.

BETTE DAVIS: Oh, I want the world.

IRVING RAPPER: When Bette Davis and I worked together, say on *Now, Voyager*, nobody dared interfere because they'd either hear a yell from me or a yell such as you've never heard from her. I had to get used to her. I thought she gave, on the whole, rather restrained performances in my films. We always think of Miss Davis in terms of histrionics and, I mean, of overacting, of course, histrionics. A good term. But she was remarkably restrained in the first two pictures I did with her. There's a great drama in the poignancy of Bette Davis. She can be quite vulnerable. She always thinks she needs dialogue. She doesn't. Like Marlon Brando or Spencer Tracy—three actors who do not need dialogue—but try to tell her that on the stage. I always told Bette, "Bette, you are more dramatic when you say nothing." But she always feels she has to give and give, and she doesn't have to. She's so powerful. Her mere presence is enough. When she comes to a party, when she comes on TV, her presence stuns everybody. She must realize this, but she needs to be reminded because she's too gifted and brilliant an actress to overdo things. She feels she needs to exert herself.

BETTE DAVIS: I struggled in my early years, and I never forgot it. George Arliss was really the man who saved my life, because I had been fired after a year at Universal. They were happy to have me go, and I was rather happy to go, too, in a funny way, because the pictures had been pretty grim. And the phone rang—literally, I was packed and ready to go back to the theater—and this beautiful voice said, "I'd like to speak to Miss Davis," and I said, "This is Miss Davis." And he said, "This is Mr. George Arliss." And thinking, George Arliss calling me? You know, I was just in awe of this great actor. So, thinking that some friend was ribbing me, I said, "Ooooh, Mr. Arliss, how lovely of you to call me!" So this went on three or four times, you see, and he just kept calmly and coolly saying "Miss Davis, this is Mr. Arliss." So then I knew it was, and he asked me to come out to Warners immediately for an interview. Well, I couldn't believe it. I don't know what speeding records I broke driving out there. And he interviewed me for a part in his next film, *The Man Who Played God*, and he asked me how long I had been in the theater, because he never worked with anyone who hadn't been in the theater—he would not take on anybody—so he asked me how long I'd been in the theater, and I said, "About three years," and he said, "Just enough to rub the edges off," which I thought was a beautiful, beautiful remark. So he cast me as the leading lady in *The Man Who Played God*. We were going to start very, very soon, and I'll never forget going up to the wardrobe department, and I was just jumping up and down, saying "Oh, I've got a part with Mr. Arliss!" They thought I was a lunatic. But of course, then I stayed at Warners eighteen years after that, so he was the man who played God to me and the most beautiful man, beautiful, wonderful.

At Warners I had to play many parts I loathed. Oh, many. In the beginning I did. Terrible things. You know, *Parachute Jumper*, *Housewife*. *The Golden Arrow* was a dilly. Of course, I hated them, but I was in no position to fight them at that time. I was an unknown actress, and they had a right to have me do them. That's why I finally knew I was getting nowhere— because of these ridiculous scripts. *Three on a Match*. You can't imagine. They were dreadful scripts, dreadful, although I learned a lot. You learn a lot more, really, in the beginning from doing things you don't like. Often today, I think, with no contract system and with complete choice of scripts, that actors are apt to pick the things that they want to do and like to do most and not progress as much.

But those contracts we had back then were lifetime contracts with suspensions. And it could be fifty years if you signed for five unless you did everything they said. I broke away, went to London, brought a lawsuit, and in a way, I won. I lost, but in a way I won, because after that it was the beginning of getting directors like Willy Wyler and better parts.

JOHN CROMWELL: There were decades of autocratic rule by the studios. There was exploitation of talent and personality. Stars were invariably underpaid, while they brought in huge profits. In the last analysis, the organization of the motion picture producers was strong enough to hold together and prevent a star from walking out of his contract. They banded together and held strong.

IRVING RAPPER: Bette had great power. She had great power to create and destroy. A tremendous, overpowering personality. She couldn't write her own ticket at Warners, nobody could, but she couldn't stop herself. She always came in like a gust of wind and electrified you. One never goes to see Bette because of beauty. They go to see a great performance, and they really get it. But she *always* posed a challenge to *every* director. And Jack Warner.

BETTE DAVIS: People ask me about myself. I can only answer as an actress. Somebody asked Claude Rains once—one of my idolized actors, one of the greatest actors I worked with—and somebody asked him what his method was, and Claude Rains said, "I learn the lines and pray to God." And I am basically in that category.

RIDGEWAY CALLOW: In a way, I don't blame those women for fighting. In the old days, particularly, new girls would come into the studio. They'd kick 'em around, give them lousy little parts, let them sit on their ass until late afternoon. Then all of a sudden they'd get a break. So when they got breaks and got to the top, some of them go to the other extreme and give the studio a hard time. But, you know, I've never seen a temperamental *great* star in my life. Because the minute you treat them like a star, you've lost the battle. Dore Schary told me to treat Grace Kelly like a star because she'd just won the Oscar for *The Country Girl.* I was the assistant director on her next film, and I was told, "I want Grace Kelly treated like a star." I told him I didn't know how to do that, and he told me to do the best I could. Well, we gave her a dog's life on the picture, and she loved every minute of it.

JOHN CROMWELL: A great deal is said about people who were difficult. Most of us remember very little of that. But what prompted any such behavior in most instances was a real sincerity and a real desire to do better

things. That was Bette Davis. Also Maggie Sullavan, who had a little reputation. It was nothing but a revolt against shoddy material for both of
them. Everyone's gotten interested in the old stars now, and they want to
hear about bad behavior, sexual affairs, or box-office poison stories.

GEORGE CUKOR: You know, that "box-office poison" thing was nothing
but a mean article in a fan magazine that labeled a few great stars that way:
Hepburn, Crawford, Dietrich, all the legends. One article by a hack. Now
it's treated like government statistics.

RANALD MACDOUGALL: When I did *Mildred Pierce,* which I wrote, Joan
Crawford was supposed to be box-office poison. She had left Metro, her
home studio all her career. Of course, she was a monumental performer
and personality, and all she needed was a change of scene and a change of
direction, and she was off and running again.

GEORGE FOLSEY: Joan Crawford was a real star. She was very obedient,
very cooperative, a good coworker, very capable, and very knowledgeable about the business. She was the opposite of what some people think.
Evidently she was a great actress, because people believe she was the roles
she played.

VINCENT SHERMAN: I would say that Joan Crawford was one of the easiest people that I ever worked with in films in terms of taking direction
and being able to achieve what you wanted to achieve. She takes direction magnificently. There are certain characteristics and mannerisms that
she has, although not as many as most of the top stars. She has physical
trademarks. The full mouth. The broad shoulders. Certain things are part
and parcel of her character that she has carried along over the years, and
some people like them and some people don't. She was very good in script
conferences. She knew instinctively the things that she could do well. She
was a collaborator in working to achieve a total effect. She was the kind of
person that you could talk to about the way you wanted to shoot the thing,
the background, the cutting. She was conscious of everything that went
on set. That was her experience. Her whole life was dedicated to making

pictures. She had some outside interests, but I would say that 95 percent of her life was involved in making films. Her career attests to her ability and her devotedness to this industry. Like all of us, she had a great loyalty and devotion to the business, and like all of us now and then would get very disgusted with some of the things that would happen in the town. But she was an indefatigable worker.

RANALD MACDOUGALL: She's not demanding. She really is not demanding. She's very meticulous but not demanding, and there is a difference. In connection with making *Possessed*, Curtis Bernhardt and I and Jerry Wald went to Joan Crawford's house to have a conference with her about the script, and in Joan's house, which was up there a ways, she had two drawing rooms. That is the only description for them. One was on one side of the foyer and was very feminine, with ruffles and organdy flounces and, I don't know, very, very feminine, a lovely room, and the other one was masculine. It had a bar in it. It had leather-paneled walls and was definitely masculine. And when we came in, we were ushered into— it was the first time I had been to her house—and we were ushered into the male one. We were men. If we had been women, we would have gone to the other one, I assume. At any rate, we went into that one, and we were sitting around waiting for Joan, which was not very long, and we were looking and I said, "Good God, leather, that's real leather on the walls!" And I turned to Jerry Wald, and I said, "You know, Jerry, that is real leather. It must be like living in a wallet." Joan knew what being a star was all about.

BRONISLAU KAPER: I met Joan Crawford when she was at the top of MGM. And I just want to show you how stupid a man can be. That's me. I wanted to be very nice to her when I met her. I wanted to pay her a great compliment. So I said, "Oh, Miss Crawford, already as a little boy in Poland I was a great fan of yours," which aged her about twenty years. Now, she didn't believe that anybody could be that stupid. She thought it was a joke. So she laughed at the joke. She had a good sense of humor. Later we became very good friends. But if she were not as nice, our relation would have been finished from there on.

VINCENT SHERMAN: She was very easy to work with. She was very picture wise. You didn't have to tell her where to stand or how to move to get the best light on her.

IRVING RAPPER: I liked Joan Crawford very much, and she was extremely nice to me and most considerate and helpful. She was terribly charming and sweet, and I enjoyed working with her and I always wanted to work with her.

RANALD MACDOUGALL: Joan, like all great stars, and particularly her, because she really works at it, would take a while to get ready and to get made up. She was in at six o'clock in the morning to start getting made up. Makeup at six thirty. And I would make a point of coming in at six thirty myself because I wasn't asking anybody to do anything I wasn't willing to do. I would come in at six thirty, visit with her and talk about what we were going to do and what we had done, things like that. And whenever the cameraman got there, why, we would start lining up the day's work, and then we would shoot. But then once in a while a break would come, when we would have to break a sequence, at which point in time Joan would get comfortable. She would get into slacks or something of that sort, and she would come down and rehearse that way. And the crew, being very knowledgeable, knew it was going to take her at least an hour and a half to get ready to shoot again, and they would get very slow, you see. She'd rehearse in slacks, and the crew would—well, of course, I was anxious to get on with it. I was anxious to keep the tempo and the dramatic tempo. So she did this about three or four times, and the graph of activity would immediately go way down. Then she'd come back, and then it would take another hour to get steamed up again and get moving. So one morning—it was a constant thing—so one morning I went to her, and I said, "Joanie, the company is getting very slack. They are kind of letting down. They are not working as hard as you and I are, and you know how I am, I simply cannot bawl people out. It's not my way of doing things. I cannot raise my voice or holler, it's not my style, but would you mind very much if I bawled you out today?" She said, "What do you mean?" I said, "Well, something will happen—I don't know, but it will be something trivial, Joan. What I'll do is I'll bawl you out. I'll just let myself go, if you don't mind, and bawl you out, and the crew will hear that and they'll snap to, because they won't want it to rub off on me and it won't bother you, and then I'll get it out of my system." She said, "Fine. Okay. When are you going to do it?" I said, "I don't know. It can happen anytime. Who knows?" So the next time she came down on the set with slacks on, I lit into her. I said, "Miss Crawford, I've known you for I don't know how many years, and you are one of the hardest-working people I know, but how *dare* you, with all these good people standing around here waiting to make you important and do everything they can for you, how *dare* you come down and pay so little respect to their work that you appear to rehearse a scene in slacks and without makeup?" Oh, I laid it out. And behind me I can hear, I can feel, people really congealing, waiting for Joan Crawford to say that she is not going to take this from any living human being. They are waiting for the atomic explosion to reoccur, and I got all through in a *rage*—a lot of it was tension, too, you know, I wasn't entirely acting—and I got all through, and Joan said to me, "You are absolutely right, sir. I'll never do it again." She was meek and mild and sweet and lovely, and the whole crew went "Aaahaaa," and then we went back to work and she never did it again, but interestingly enough, at the end of the day, I walked back to her dressing room with her, because then she would take off her makeup and go home, and on the way back she looked at me sidelong and she said, "You think you are pretty smart, don't you?" She was a real star—the work came first.

LESLIE CARON: Joan Crawford is not a great actress. She is a great star.

GEORGE CUKOR: Actually, she's a very accomplished actress. I felt her two performances in my films *A Woman's Face* and *Susan and God* were extremely good, and then she went and did *Mildred Pierce* and won the Academy Award. You know, people forget how very popular she was with moviegoers.

GEORGE FOLSEY: Oh, Crawford was box-office gold. They took very good care of her. I had a very fortunate situation with her. Clarence Brown, one of her directors, didn't like the way she was being photographed, and he had seen some of my work and arranged to get me for *Chained*, which costarred her with Gable. Crawford wore lovely gowns and very ornate things. In one scene, she had a lace collar, very beautiful, and up in the rafters was an electric light, a stage light, there for illumination for the stage, and that was the only light that was on, and it came down and hit Crawford right on, and looking at her, standing there, she looked beautiful, so lovely, and the quality of light was great. So I lit her that way for the scene. She was one of the most beautiful women in the film business.

JEAN LOUIS: Joan Crawford was willing to stand for hours for a clothing designer, which many of the women were not. At MGM, she was one of the great fashion icons. Adrian made her clothes. She had the perfect, angular body for his work. Her shoulders were naturally square, and she didn't need pads. She had a very good figure. Very good. Her shoulders were broad. And she had that phobia about ankle-strap shoes. She had to have all ankle straps, and they were not in fashion at the time I worked with her on *Harriet Craig*. She told me she couldn't stand regular heels because they wouldn't stay on her feet. She had very small feet, and they'd slip out of the shoes. People always say she insisted on her shoulder pads. That's a joke. She had no shoulder pads, I'm telling you. Her shoulders were broad, and she had a perfect body to hang clothes on. Broad shoulders, small waist. Oh, but those ankle strap shoes.

VINCENT SHERMAN: I had been invited several times to Miss Crawford's house. I had had lunch with her and dinner several times. I found that there are certain things that definitely relate to Miss Crawford. Her home was elegantly and properly kept, and she was very demanding of certain things in her home. She had to have the right dishes and the right piece of furniture for this and the right towel for that bathroom. She wanted certain formalities to be observed. For example, the man must open the door for the woman when she gets out of the car. The man must pull out the seat for her when she sits at the dinner table. Some of these things were very important to her. I imagine that in her background she didn't have these things, and therefore they became symbolic to her.

RANALD MACDOUGALL: Joan never forgot where she came from and how lucky she was, she felt, to have her stardom. She was the definition of Movie Star . . . but she never forgot that once she needed help. For instance, for *Mildred Pierce*, she came into the studio herself to do a test with Ann Blyth, to help her get the role of Mildred's daughter. It was practically unheard of for a star of her caliber to do any kind of test, much less with an unknown trying for a supporting part. But she knew it mattered for her own performance who would play her daughter, and she also knew it would help Ann Blyth. They remained friends for life. Crawford was a loyal friend, and, believe me, crews loved her. She never made trouble for anyone, but I think what I remember most is how she showed up to make that test with Ann.

IRVING RAPPER: I was always in the Bette Davis camp, but I have to say that once she was asked to make a test with a new actor who might play the young man opposite her in *The Corn Is Green*, and she said no.

FRANK CAPRA: Barbara Stanwyck was an interesting case, because when I got her, she was very young and very inexperienced and she put out all she had in her first scene and then could not repeat it, that is, could not repeat it with the same kind of enthusiasm and fervor she had in her first scene. Well, I found this out very early, and that created some very difficult problems because I had to go and shoot her close-ups, scenes that I wanted to use in the picture, first, and I couldn't rehearse her with other actors because she'd start giving out, you know, instead of just talking, instead of just rehearsing as most people rehearse until they get the thing going fine and they save their best performance for the time when the camera's turning. She'd give her best performance in rehearsal, and this did create some problems. And later on, I ran into another person with the same problem: Frank Sinatra. The reason Frank Sinatra had so much difficulty with directors is they never got on to this thing, he could not reproduce a scene.

ALLAN DWAN: Stanwyck was a very remarkable girl. Good worker. Terrific worker. And a great friend to the workingmen on the crew. She was a real mixer. She helped everybody.

CHARLES LEMAIRE: She was probably the most professional of all the big stars, which is why her career lasted so long.

RICHARD SCHICKEL: Barbara Stanwyck is always my choice of the older women stars. I think she's a truly fabulous screen character. A star's career is a drama. To my knowledge there were sort of four separate Barbara Stanwyck careers. One: a career in which she came out here very much as a girl who had been in the choruses of various, not particularly grand, Broadway productions and in a couple of Broadway straight dramas. She came out here and was treated as if she were kind of a female James Cagney. She represented a new strain in American cinema at that time, that of a rather hard, distinctly urban character, female version. She was the first of those, really, in a way, although I suppose you could say Clara Bow had a little of that aspect to her. Second: Frank Capra found something else in Stanwyck, and he gave her that character who tended to pretend to be tough but was really misunderstood, particularly by middle-class and upper-class people, who viewed her as a threat to their young males. Capra gave her a voice to speak back to their hypocrisy, which was a big step for her. Then came her comedy career, her great screwball efforts, and I like showing her adorableness. And, of course, she has lasted beyond any female star, maturing into effective dramatic roles and representing the American woman who endures. And her career has endured. She has stayed at the top all the way.

TAY GARNETT: The Hollywood of the 1930s, 1940s was a world of glamorous female stars. They called them glamour girls. Women like Jean Harlow, Carole Lombard, Lana Turner . . .

HAL ROSSON: Carole was fantastic. She was more of a worldly person than Jean Harlow [Rosson was Harlow's third husband]. Carole was a very, very professional person. Jeannie was very professional, too, but a different type of personality. Carole was more aggressive, a different type. My association with Jean Harlow—well, I always attempted, and I believe I was very successful in always being able to divorce our working day from our personal life. Completely. She brought her work home with her as far as

I was concerned. We could talk about camerawork or something, but we at all times—"we" meaning Jean and myself—we attempted at all times to keep our workmanship together completely divorced from our social life. Business was discussed very little. Very little. I worried sometimes about the way she spent her money. She spent a lot of money, but she made a lot, too. I'm sure that she enjoyed having money, what it could do for her and helping her family. She was very close to her mother. Very. And as I think back, she thoroughly enjoyed her stepfather. But she wouldn't have permitted him to be unpleasant to her. Nobody could be unpleasant to Jean. If Jean could help you, she would do so. That was the girl's nature, and she didn't do it to have a story told in the fan mags. That came from her heart. Everybody called her "baby." I can assure you that if I've heard the word "baby" applied to Jean on one occasion, I've heard it five thousand times. Her mother constantly always called her "baby." It's evidently an association that grew up in that family between the mother and the daughter. Of that I'm sure. She wasn't like her screen image. I don't think that particular girl knew the meaning of the word "bad tempered." She was a charming person, a nice person. She was a favorite at the studio, universally liked at MGM.

ADELA ROGERS ST. JOHNS: Jean Harlow was a beautifully educated, beautifully bred girl. She came from one of the finest families I've ever known. And I knew her grandmother and grandfather. She went to the best finishing school . . . and she was highly intelligent.

TAY GARNETT: Everybody liked Harlow. She was very popular with the people she worked with. She was popular with the crew. She was popular with everybody.

RIDGEWAY CALLOW: On the other hand, it was impossible to get any sort of scene out of Jean Harlow in her early years. She was one of the world's worst actresses, in my opinion.

HAL ROSSON: Jean was a very interesting woman. She supported her family. She wasn't dependent, but she relied on the studio to assign her work.

She was very different from the roles she played. On-screen, if Gable gave her a hard time, she knew how to retaliate, but in real life, that wasn't her nature. She was not at all a person who retaliated. I think she would have been ashamed of herself had she done so.

RIDGEWAY CALLOW: Carole Lombard was so different. People describe her as earthy, but to describe Carole as earthy is putting it mildly. She had a great sense of humor, but it leaned towards the risqué, or I should say "dirty." But when she uttered certain taboo four-letter words, they sounded like poetry. And she was a remarkable girl. She'd be playing a dramatic scene, and she'd start to tell you a dirty story—loved to tell dirty stories—she'd be right in the middle of the story, and she'd be called to go on the set and do a scene. She'd go in and do the dramatic scene and come out and then immediately resume with, "Now, as I was saying, the man, et cetera, et cetera." Yes, she was a real person and one of the finest—if not *the* finest—ladies I have met and worked with in my long career.

JOHN CROMWELL: I remember well the first time I ever saw Carole Lombard. I was in the anteroom next to the stage where auditions were being held. Suddenly the door from the stage opened, and through it came a lovely blonde. I judged that she was all of seventeen. She was crying her heart out as she slammed the door shut and leaned on it, sobbing in bitter disappointment.

She was quite plump, I would almost say fat. That tended to arouse my sympathy for her. I knew that she hadn't seen me, and I kept very still so she wouldn't have further embarrassment. She finally became aware of me, and she dashed across the room and out of the door, her emotion reaching a last desperate climax.

After she was a star, I came to admire Carole Lombard almost as much as anyone that I had ever met. Perhaps this was because a large part of her brain worked like a man's. She was utterly devoid of those coquetries which almost every woman uses more or less at times most innocently or instinctively in her relationship with the opposite sex.

In the motion picture business, these instincts were so much a part of the equipment for success both on film and off that it is remarkable that it was a great relief to work with such a girl when your concentration on the job was never complicated by the consciousness of a game that many thought to be maintained for workable relationships.

At the same time, any man would be pretty dull who couldn't relish and be stimulated by Carole's quick, keen brain, which was always well oiled by an impish kind of humor. She was intrigued by the business of making pictures. She was also the most profane woman that I have ever known. I never did find out where she acquired this amazing habit. Her swearing was absolutely devastating in its effect as it rolled out of her almost fragile beauty

During our first movie, she was married to William Powell, a most competent and admired actor, not only with the public but with his co-workers. There was a great deal of exactness and precision in Bill's work, which only his intimate friends knew he carried over from his personal habits.

Carole used to regale us with stories of her meticulous husband preparing to go out in the evening. In such matters Carole was the woman to delight most men's hearts because she could get ready to go anywhere in a half an hour. She would laugh uproariously at the picture of herself as the impatient wife, waiting while Bill painstakingly arranged a handkerchief, adjusted a coat, or fiddled for the umpteenth time with an already well arranged tie.

A few years later, when she and Bill most amicably agreed that they had made a mistake, she married Clark Gable and became a dedicated sportswoman, which pleased him. She learned as though it were a new profession to cast a fly, shoot a gun, and rough it in the woods and mountains to fulfill his idea of an ideal companion.

LEO MCCAREY: The one to watch out for was Mae West. When she'd get mad, she would hum all of the time, like a rattlesnake before it strikes.

MITCHELL LEISEN: Mae West! Nobody wanted to work with her. I didn't want to work with her. She was a very independent person. She wanted to write her own scripts and play her own part.

ARTHUR KNIGHT: Many of the stars of the studio system often came from poor backgrounds, and they had suffered, particularly the women. Their climb to the top was difficult and took time. They reacted to it differently, but most of them worked hard to stay on top and keep in good favor. So many of them didn't really have self-confidence. An exception was Katharine Hepburn.

WILLIAM TUTTLE: She just had confidence in herself. As a makeup man, I can't think of any player who is just going to walk in with no makeup in front of a director or producer, except for Katie Hepburn, who was always pretty natural anyway. The makeup artist is really the only person who sees them as they are. You know their innermost secrets, and they must have a certain trust in you that you're not going to go out and say, "Well, you ought to get a load of them without makeup." But if you were working with Katharine Hepburn, you could forget all of that because she could care less whether she looks perfect. A person who is like that, as self-assured as she is, doesn't have much respect for someone they feel is not qualified to do their makeup. And they would very quickly tell them. Very outspoken about it. You had to build up respect with the female stars, but Hepburn just had confidence and assumed she was going to be all right no matter who or what.

TEETE CARLE: I think from the very beginning Katharine Hepburn just always wanted to do things differently.

KATHARINE HEPBURN: I wanted to be a star. That was my object. What's the matter with being a star?

PANDRO BERMAN: David Selznick, when he became head of RKO, brought in Katharine Hepburn. He signed her to a studio contract, not a term contract, which was the general form in those days. Leland Hayward, her agent, was a little too smart for that. David was able to sign her to a series of films exclusively for RKO but with a limited period during which she was paid a flat sum for each film. And if the film ran overtime in shooting, she was able to collect additional salary. As a result, Hepburn had a little better deal than was prevalent in the industry. She wasn't on a weekly contract. They couldn't shove her into just anything, you know. I produced her film *Morning Glory*. It was directed by Lowell Sherman, and he did a stunning job, and he got her rolling so that she won her first Academy Award in *Morning Glory*.

MERIAN C. COOPER: She was always a brilliant actress. They made the great mistake with her when I left RKO of trying to cast her as Amelia Earhart in *Christopher Strong*. It's just awful. A horrible picture, but you see, Hepburn is a hard person to cast, and they didn't yet quite know what to do with her. You have to cast her a little on the masculine side and very much on the feminine side. You have to put them both in there. Now, *Mary Queen of Scots*, which John Ford directed, was a complete bust because they cast her as Mary, Queen of Scots. She ought to have been playing Queen Elizabeth. She'd have made the greatest Queen Elizabeth that would have been on the screen, you know. She made a lousy Mary, Queen of Scots.

GEORGE CUKOR: She didn't quite find herself at first. She was a little too mannered. Her career could have gone one way or the other. She could have become a great glamour girl, but she's too human for that. In fact, in *Christopher Strong*, her second picture, she wore very tight, glittering dresses and was about to become a glamour girl. But in spite of everything, her humanity asserted itself, and her humor. She is a human being, the humanity of her emerged.

JOHN CROMWELL: Katharine Hepburn was the most glamorous star at RKO. She was made so much of that it was to her credit that she wasn't completely spoiled. When she first arrived in Hollywood, she had recently left the New York stage after much too brief a stay. She made an astonishing hit in her first picture, *A Bill of Divorcement*, with John Barrymore, but to me her finest performance was while she was still at RKO in *Alice Adams*. I was so attracted by her work that I followed her career closely. I always felt that she never lived up to the potential of her talent. It may have been due to her upbringing, or it may have been a philosophy in living that she had worked out for herself, perhaps too early.

She came from an aristocratic family of more than comfortable means. She was always used to having pretty much what she wanted. I don't mean spoiled. She was much too intelligent for that. But she was certainly born under a most rewarding star. She was not really beautiful, but the combination of a well-sculpted face and features and a generous mouth was constantly pleasing and attractive. Her eyes reflected the brightness of her mind. She had an almost mindless energy. She was an astonishing athlete with the kind of bodily coordination which made her excel in any sport that attracted her. Above all, she possessed great strength of character. She made up her mind at an early age what she wanted to do, and as far as I know she never deviated from that plan.

She had all of the self-confidence in the world. Everything that she did was calculated for its effect. The minute she got out to Hollywood, instead of doing the type of things that a newcomer did, she bought an old, broken-down, secondhand station wagon. She went around in blue jeans and a sweatshirt practically all of the time, unless she went someplace for dinner, of course. All of this was calculated to be different. Anything that she did was well thought out. Perhaps this enforced self-confidence was such that it would never allow her to think for a moment that she couldn't do anything that was handed to her, no matter what it was.

She was instinctively a very good actress. She had never taken the trouble to learn more about the business. She had had only a short experience in the theater when she came to Hollywood. When she arrived here, she immediately became a star.

GEORGE CUKOR: Oh, yes. She started strong but had a lean period. She'd been a big star, and then things hadn't gone so well, and people said, "Box-office poison." I should think that's libelous. She certainly rehabilitated herself. It was the kind of stupid, graceless thing that was said in fan magazines and by some exhibitors. Anyway, she did this play in New York, *The Philadelphia Story*, and then she had a contract that she was to do the movie. Now, all the picture companies were trying to buy it, but she had control of it. She was very clever about it. She's somebody who has a great deal of intelligence and taste and everything, but she also has common sense, a sense of reality.

She chose the vehicle for her own return. She had the money—some say from her family, others say from Howard Hughes—to purchase the rights. Her background was not one of poverty and no education.

GEORGE FOLSEY: I had to make a test cold of Katharine Hepburn when she replaced Claudette Colbert in *State of the Union*. A very charming, delightful person. Just wonderful. During the time I'm making the test, she said, "Now make me fat. Make me fat!" She didn't want to be gaunt and thin, she wanted to be nice and round and fat. And I said, "Miss Hepburn, I've been trying to make myself fat for years." She said, "Don't give a damn about you, just make me fat!" Talked like a rubber band at you. What a charming, delightful, wonderful person she is. And, of course, she was an excellent person to photograph as long as you, as *she* says, "Don't show my chicken neck."

ARTHUR KNIGHT: Stars expressed themselves, but carefully, often through humor. Most of them behaved impeccably on the set, around the lot. The ones you hear about who were truly crazy and nobody knew what to do about it were the Marx Brothers.

LEO MCCAREY: Over at Paramount, I found myself directing the Marx Brothers in *Duck Soup*. The amazing thing about that movie was that I succeeded in not going crazy. They were completely mad. I enjoyed shooting several scenes in the picture, though. My experience in silent films influences me very much, and so usually I preferred Harpo. But it wasn't the ideal movie for me. In fact it's the only time in my career that I based the humor on dialogue, because with Groucho it was the only humor you could get. Four or five writers furnished him with gags and lines. Groucho thought he was the most creative, but to my mind, Harpo was. He was the most responsive and the funniest.

BRONISLAU KAPER: When they came to MGM, you couldn't escape them. They were all over the studio. There were three of them, and the fourth one was always following them. This was Zeppo, their agent.

Groucho was biting, the quick wit, insulting people. Very fast! You had the feeling that he was answering you before you asked him. He still does the same thing. He's always ahead of you. Even at his age now, he's one step ahead of you.

Harpo was an image, a legend. Harpo was idolized by the high intellectual and artistic set of New York and the United States as a kind of a genius. He was a very talented man, but they made a little more out of him, maybe because in movies he didn't talk. And that makes him more interesting. You couldn't put your finger on him. He never said anything stupid. And also his grin, his eyes, that twinkling in his eyes. You always had a chance to believe that there is something much more behind this than what you see. He was in a circle with Alexander Woollcott and a bunch of great writers. This was a whole group of high-class people, and he was the scapegoat. They made him a genius.

Now, Chico was the simplest and the sweetest. He didn't pretend to be funny, he didn't pretend to be witty. No genius. He was just there, sweet, with this funny Italian accent. And whenever I saw a Marx Brothers movie, I always loved him, because he never insulted anybody, he never hit anybody. He was the most lovable of them all.

I watched Harpo playing harp. He was in this respect unbelievable. I understand he never took a lesson. He played everything by ear. So did Chico. Harpo played everything by ear, and the imagination, the tricks he did on the harp, the harmonies, improvisations, everything.

I never heard Groucho play guitar, but supposedly he did. I heard Chico and Harpo because they had offices on the lot and I used to come to them when we worked on the harp, the piano. Not that I had to show them anything, don't get me wrong, they did everything. I never thought, even when I wrote something for them, to tell them how to do it. They had their own style, which should not have been touched.

Groucho asked me once to play for him one of the first Irving Berlin songs. And he said to me, "You know, I sang this song for Irving Berlin. When I finished, Irving said to me, 'Groucho, if you ever have a strong urge to do this song again, call me, and I will give you ten dollars not to do it.'"

GEORGE SEATON: Groucho was a good judge of his material. If an ad-lib was good, it stayed in. If not, out it went. I learned one thing about comedy from him, which I think was very valuable. I remember it every time I'm writing comedy. Do you recall the famous line "Either he's dead, or my watch has stopped" while Groucho was taking Harpo's pulse? It was first a question: "Is he dead, or has my watch stopped?" Well, it was nothing. We were trying to analyze it, and Groucho said, "A question demands an answer. The audience is waiting for the answer. It's the same as 'Why does a chicken cross the road?' That's not the joke. The joke is 'To get to the other side.' They're waiting for the answer. Let me make it a statement." So he went out the next performance and said, "Either he's dead, or my watch has stopped." Then, *boom*, the whole roof went off. So that's something in comedy. It's the answer that has to be funny.

It would be easy to make up stories about the Marx Brothers, but in their case you didn't have to. These guys did amazing things. They rode a horse into Thalberg's bungalow. Harpo rode the horse in there, and the other Marx Brothers ran in with him. But this was part of their act. Everybody should have an act.

At one time someone came onto the set and said to the set designer or to them something about "Entrances and Exits" and they said "Exits" and they all left. They did all those things you hear about.

GEORGE FOLSEY: I was on their first film, *The Cocoanuts*. The movie director was Robert Florey. He had just come from France, where he had done French tragedies, and he was projected into America to do a director's picture with the Marx Brothers. It was an insane decision, because in the first place, he didn't have the remotest idea who they were or what they were or whether it was funny. Their humor is so completely zany. I liked Florey very much. He was a good director, but he couldn't handle them. They absolutely floored him. He should not have been the one to direct them. The minute the Marx Brothers got through with a scene, they'd all disappear. One would go one place and one another, and it would take a long time to round them up because the studio was a heck of a big place.

The only one who was around that we could find was Zeppo. He was always on the stage. Well, the scenes only revolved a little bit around Zeppo, and the main ones were Groucho, Chico, and Harpo, but eventually we got to kind of know where to find them. We'd find Groucho on the telephone . . . with his broker . . . Harpo in the main projection room playing his harp, and Chico up in the dressing rooms . . . up in the top of the stages, away up in the top of the building . . . and we used to have two or three assistants, and they'd all go to an appointed place and corral their particular man and bring him back.

GEORGE SEATON: Groucho was a very serious man. I think you will find that most comics who rely on jokes and dialogue are very serious, because it's a serious business. Harpo was one of the sweetest guys you'll ever know. He was a dear, dear man. He was quite eloquent. Harpo became the darling of the Algonquin Round Table. Alexander Woollcott thought he was just as funny as Chaplin. I'm not one to disagree with that, because I think Harpo was a genius. Harpo began to take Woollcott's estimation of his talents very seriously. So when they were doing a picture at Paramount with Herman Mankiewicz producing, I think it was *Duck Soup*, Harpo came in. He had read the script, and he came in to Herman and rather, almost pontifically, said, "What is my character?" Herman Mankiewicz, who had a tongue like a razor blade, said, "You're a middle-aged Jew who picks up spit. That's your character." That was the end of that.

PANDRO BERMAN: I tested a young fellow once that I thought was very attractive, and I wanted to put him into *Sylvia Scarlett* in the role Brian Aherne eventually played. But I had a problem with Katharine Hepburn about it. She raised such hell against him and was so anxious to have Aherne that I abandoned the whole concept. The young man's name was Errol Flynn.

RAOUL WALSH: Warners had Cagney and Bogart, and in those days, they were the only two stars you could kill in a picture. You couldn't kill Flynn. You couldn't kill Gable. You couldn't kill Cooper or any of those fellows. The exhibitors wouldn't even play the picture. No one wanted to see Flynn killed, but with *They Died with Their Boots On*, he played Custer, so I couldn't change history. Flynn didn't mind dying, as long as he got paid for it.

HENRY KING: Errol Flynn was a lot better actor than people ever give him credit for being, I'll tell you. Errol Flynn was a good actor.

BETTE DAVIS: Well, Errol was one of the most charming people in the world, but he did not have an ambition to become a great actor. He loved all the other parts of it. And in his marvelous adventure films he was divine. He was probably the most beautiful-looking thing I've ever seen in my life. But he and I didn't approach work in the same way, you know. He used to think I was ridiculous, and I felt sorry that he didn't love the actual work more. He was perfectly horrid about me in his book—that I scratched his face with my rings—of course it's all ridiculous. I did no such thing. Those are the little things that helped my career as a monster. But anyway, I must say in *The Private Lives of Elizabeth and Essex* I almost did not do it because of Errol, because he was not up to playing it, because the script was almost blank verse, you know. And I must say that every time the throne room doors opened, I just sat there and closed my eyes and pretended it was Olivier.

IRVING RAPPER: He was not Olivier.

VINCENT SHERMAN: Errol was a very complex man, much more complex than most people think. In general, I think that the world has an image of him as being an irresponsible playboy. He *was* that, too, in many ways. There was a certain immaturity about him. But I think that he was perhaps a very deeply unhappy man in many ways. He enjoyed the success that he had and the fame that he achieved, naturally. But I think that he would have preferred to have people think of him as a good actor. He felt that nobody thought of him as a good actor. The first week that we were shooting on *The Adventures of Don Juan*, he was on time on the set, ready to shoot. He was there at 6:00 a.m. Everything was going beautifully. In about the middle of the second week, he had made a film that had just opened in New York. He got roasted terribly in it. I didn't think that he deserved it. He was always trying to get away from doing costume drama and action films and westerns. He wanted to be an actor. He wanted to prove that he was an actor. Every time that he went for something else, he got clobbered. It got to the point where people would say, "He's great if he's sitting on a horse and if he's got a sword in his hand." But as an actor he didn't win much acclaim and he didn't get much respect.

As I said, he had been behaving just beautifully for the first week or ten days of the shooting. I was in his dressing room one morning, and he said, "Did you see these reviews?" I had seen some of them, but I said, "No." I didn't tell him that I had. I said, "How are they? Good?" He said, "They really let me have it." And he laughed. But that afternoon he started drinking. I felt very sorry for him. He wouldn't talk about it, because he wasn't the kind of guy to say, "It makes me unhappy." He just didn't tell anybody. He drank. From that time on, he never really was the same in the picture. He was also having some marital difficulties at the time.

He was a strange character in other ways. He was a very warm guy, very charming. At the end of the first week of shooting, he came up to me one afternoon. He threw an arm around my shoulder and said, "You little bastard, I really love you." I said, "I love you, too, Errol." He said, "You know what I mean. I can love a guy. But I can't a woman."

I discovered many things about him subsequently. He disliked his mother, whom I never met and never knew. He hated her. He was the first man who I ever heard refer in awful, awful terms about his mother. He loved his father and hated his mother. There is no question in my mind there were some problems that stemmed from his relationship with his mother that carried over in his relationship to other women. There were things that he said and did during the nine months that I was associated with him that led me to believe that he had a certain contempt for women. He didn't trust them. He felt that they were all basically untrustworthy. It was sad for him to feel that way.

When I got to know him better, I asked him a few stories about his early life. He told me some very amusing stories about the days when he was in Australia and out of a job and how he used to pass a restaurant and see a blue-plate special. He thought, "If the day ever comes that I can afford a blue-plate special in some restaurant!"

There is no question, too, that while he had contempt for costume films and he didn't consider them a great asset, they were. He knew how to handle a sword. He knew how to wear a costume. He looked at ease in it. Perhaps he should have been born in a period when they lived that way, when they dressed that way. Perhaps he would have been more comfortable in that kind of period. Everything seemed to fit him in that era.

One day we were doing a scene in which I was planning to have Errol come into [Robert] Douglas's office, where he was summoned for some reason. Errol was going to show his disdain and lack of fear of this powerful man by walking around the office casually and nonchalantly.

What happened was that Errol was so loaded that day that he couldn't walk around. So I changed the whole thing, and I had Errol sit down and had Douglas stroll around him. I am not sure that it wasn't a better scene that way than the one I originally conceived.

What had happened was that Errol's poise and security was demonstrated by just sitting still. His attitude came through very well that way. It turned out to be a very good scene. But every day some kind of adjustment had to be made to get the production going and keep it going after he started drinking.

Up until about five or five thirty, he would be fine. But then he would begin to take a drink. So it was a difficult situation. And twice during the making of the picture, he became ill. He became ill the first time after we had been shooting for five or six weeks. He went home, and they said that his heart was bad and he had to take a rest. We stopped shooting for, like, four weeks. Many of the cast still had to be paid.

Then we worked another few weeks, and then we had to stop again. He was sick again. I heard subsequently that he wasn't ill. He went down to Laguna to photograph the mating of the whales with his father, who was a marine biologist.

Errol's health was really not good. I don't know whether it was from drinking or what. I don't know. His heart was not really good, except that he abused himself a great deal. He was able to duel for, like, fifteen seconds, and then he would be huffing and puffing and almost black in the face. Then I would have to use the double. But he was so skillful at what he did that he could give the illusion that he was tireless and that he fought every moment of the fight. But most of the work, really, was done by [fencing master] Freddie Cavens and his son. It was tedious work. I was not always able to do what I wanted to do. It was sad he died so young. Age fifty.

HENRY KING: Tyrone Power was a very sweet, wonderful person.

JOHN CROMWELL: Marvelous, wonderful, generous, hardworking, no-nonsense, ideal, and lovely.

HENRY KING: I gave Ty the first part he was ever in. Ty was always just as simple at the end as he was when he started. He was just a simple, honest person. He wanted to be a good actor more than anybody I ever saw in my life. He came from a distinguished acting family, you know. But he tried so hard and was so charming that he could get around with directors, and they would let him overact. He had a tendency to sort of push things a little bit. But it was because he wanted to be good, really good, and not just rely on his looks.

RANALD MACDOUGALL: Gary Cooper was an amazing man to watch work. It was quite a lesson, an amazing thing. Down through the years, many people have commented about something that happens in front of a camera, and to me the best illustration of that is the difference between Gary Cooper and John Garfield. Now, when Garfield was doing an emotional scene, in one way or another all of the writers who could would arrange to get there and watch, because Garfield had such power and command and force and presence that it was like watching the world's greatest performer. No matter what he was doing, he was just marvelous to watch, but only a small fraction of that came over on the film. What you saw on film never measured up to what Garfield had given and done. Conversely, to watch Cooper was a revelation . . . there was a whole performance you hadn't even seen going on.

HENRY HATHAWAY: Gary Cooper could play anything from Mr. Deeds to Sergeant York.

FRANK CAPRA: Mr. Cooper is a much better actor than anybody gives him credit for, always has been.

JOHN CROMWELL: It isn't a matter of whether Gary is a great actor or what his shortcomings might have been. As a matter of fact, he might have been damned good. But the problem is that the audience identifies him only and always as Gary Cooper. When you do the story of Abe Lincoln, you want to do it as he was. The audience just accepts this without doing anything about it. But immediately to them if Gary Cooper plays it, Abe Lincoln is Gary Cooper. You put in any well-known name, and it becomes that, and your character goes out the window. This was one of the amusing things about Hollywood.

HENRY HATHAWAY: I want to tell you the story of the reporter who came to interview me about Cooper. He was convinced that Cooper did not really know what he was doing on the screen, that he was not a thinking actor, because he was always asleep on the set. As a matter of fact, while we were having the interview, Cooper was sitting in a chair, asleep. The guy looked at him and said, "You can't tell me that man knows what he's doing." So I said, "I *know* that he knows what he's doing! He can't do a scene unless he knows what he's doing, because I've had to explain it to him too many times!"

RICHARD SCHICKEL: Gary Cooper settled very quickly into a real star persona, which he did not do a great deal to avoid. When you are talking about stars, maintaining a star persona over a period of, let's say, well, some of these careers are forty years or so, in order to do that, be Gary Cooper on-screen for that long, you require variants on the theme in order to stay viable. Cooper was one of the very best at doing this. He didn't just play Gary Cooper as a cowboy. It's surprising that when we think "Gary Cooper," we think "cowboy," because probably not more than a quarter of his sound films were, in fact, westerns. He could do a variant. He seemed a very American figure, so Lubitsch could put him in a European context as "the American," as in *Bluebeard's Eighth Wife* or *Design for Living*. And *Ball of Fire* makes a wonderful variant on him because he plays an innocent schmuck and he's so funny. He could do naive perfectly. Surprisingly, he played a number of college professors in his career . . . he was far more varied than is remembered, but he can maintain his "Gary Cooper" throughout. It's amazing, but it's even more amazing if you remember that he was quite different off-screen. Yes, he could ride very well and was from Montana, but he was fashionably dressed, maintained a beautiful home, very elegant, and was a notorious womanizer. An agreeable man that everyone liked, of course, but still . . . not really that specific persona.

IRVING RAPPER: John Garfield was a *fantastic* personality. He was the only actor that I knew who played behind the eight ball but with tremendous heart. He could never play an evil person that you wouldn't sympathize with, because he played right from his heart, always. You always sympathized with Johnny. All other actors play themselves and slough it off. This fellow, no matter how evil the character was, he always touched you with his heart.

TAY GARNETT: Garfield was a wonderful, simple, unaffected, very simple boy. When I say simple, I don't mean simpleminded. He was a highly intelligent boy, but no affectations, no artificiality. His early death was something we had more or less expected. He knew he had a weak ticker. He told me about it, but there was nothing he could do. He said, "I'm not going to live for my heart the rest of my life. I'm going to live for me." And he did just that. If he wanted to play handball, he played handball. None of the doctors in town could make him stop.

IRVING RAPPER: And he hated the old order in Hollywood. He was very rebellious. He was a natural rebel, really. He was professional enough not to air his opinions out loud, but he hated half the stars. He thought they were terrible, like Errol Flynn, for instance. "When is he going to learn to act?" he'd say.

JOHN CROMWELL: William Powell was a very satisfactory fellow to work with. He was a very accomplished actor. He had no pretense at all but was rather fastidious about everything that he did. He was very meticulous and a hell of a good worker. That was something that you certainly appreciated. There was always a fine sense of character in anything that he did. It may not have had a great deal of depth, but it was usually very good.

HENRY HATHAWAY: The men were sometimes less confident than the women. Marlene Dietrich always thought she knew more than anybody else, including von Sternberg. She was intelligent and she understood, but she's so strong. There's some women that have got balls, and she's one of 'em. On the other hand, she's a complete domestic. She was always bringing lunch on the set for somebody or having them over to dinner. Then she was the tough sex dame. It don't match.

MITCHELL LEISEN: Dietrich knew every light on every set. She knew exactly where her cue lights were. If she had to turn, the guy on the dimmer system would switch the key light, and she would say, "That was no good. My nose got in the light." She knew more about photography than anyone else. She still does. She was a rather fat little German hausfrau when she came over here. She wore slack suits all the time, pants. Marlene knew exactly where the camera was, where the key lights were. She was a better photographer than the cameraman, usually. Carole Lombard would cut a take. I'd say, "What's the matter?" "I turned my head too far. Didn't you see that light hitting my nose?" Those two were very hep as to what the lights were doing to them.

Carole was so beautiful that it didn't make much difference what you did to her. She could be photographed from any angle. She wasn't like Claudette Colbert, who had only one side to her face. I used to go around slapping myself on the left cheek all the time because that was the side I had to photograph.

TAY GARNETT: Dietrich looked like no other woman you had seen in your life. She had a masculine kind of loyalty to anyone she liked. She was almost aggressively loyal. She was so generous. She should be one of the wealthiest women in the world today, and I think she's still working for a living. I don't think she has anything outside of what she makes. She just gave it away. Like someone said years ago of Joe Schenck, if you were a friend of his, it gave you a license to put your hands in his pocket. That was the way it was with Dietrich. If any friend of hers got in trouble, "What do you need?" If she had it, you had it. She was wonderful to work with. We had a magnificent cameraman on the picture, Rudy Maté, and she liked him and had faith in him. But once in a while she'd say, "Rudy, honey, I think it should be that one instead of that one." She knew how to light herself better than ninety-nine out of a hundred fine cameramen.

HAL MOHR: She was wonderful. She walked right into her key light every time. When I was lighting one of the sets for *Destry Rides Again*, Marlene got up on the grid with me when I was lighting it, and she'd say, "Leave this light up here." She started to light the set with me and got herself so involved, putting the wrong lights in the wrong places, that she forgot to get ready for her scene. She had learned a great deal from Joe [von Sternberg]. She thinks he's the best photographer that ever lived, and I think in many respects she's quite right. He was one director who knew lighting. Marlene is a wonderful woman, a lovely woman. We were very sympatico to each other because I knew what she needed in lighting and I lit accordingly. Of course, I had no control of her makeup, and she felt she had to wear a foot and a half of makeup. She thought she needed it, but she always looked very well. But she understood lighting.

GEORGE FOLSEY: Oh, the women stars and their lighting and their makeup. Claudette Colbert was famous for having to have certain specific treatments from her cameraman. She always saw to it that she got what she felt she needed. She would go to the projection room and look at the film when it came in from the lab. She checked on things but was cooperative about it. She was sharp about the business.

JEAN LOUIS: And about clothes, too. Claudette was so fussy. I've never seen anybody as fussy as Claudette at that time. Maybe she changed since, but she knew a lot about clothes, more than anyone. I had a marvelous tailor, and we made her a houndstooth-patterned black-and-white suit. Tiny little checks. A quarter-of-an-inch plaid houndstooth. As we fit that suit on her, she says, "That shoulder is higher than this one." I said, "No." And the tailor said, "Miss Colbert, you know everybody has a shoulder a little bit higher." She was adamant, "No. This shoulder is bigger than the other one." We said, "No," and forgot about it. We were three hours in the fitting room with that suit. We leave, and she said she was going to get dressed. At twelve o'clock we go back to the fitting room, and she was still there, sitting on the floor and counting the checks on both shoulders. And after a few minutes, she cries, "I am right! There's one more check on this side than the other!" That's the way she was, but she knew clothes.

Otherwise, she was wonderful to work with. Claudette went home at six o'clock, come hell or high water—she just said, "Six o'clock, good-bye." You might as well quit shooting, unless you had something else you could do without her. But on *Arise, My Love*, she had a long speech, and she thought Brackett had done a fantastically beautiful job writing that speech, and she kept almost crying because she wasn't getting it right. I kept saying "Come on, honey, let's go. Let's do it tomorrow morning." "No, I'm not going to let this lick me." I think it was nine o'clock, and she was wringing wet. She was fighting to get that scene the way she thought Brackett had intended it. She cared about doing a good job.

RAY RENNAHAN: Well, if you wanted an easy day lighting a female, get Shirley Temple. No kidding. She had a beautiful little face, and all you had to do was get the exposure on it. It was always clean, smooth light, no strong contrast from either side was needed. Nothing to hide. No little lines. And she was easy. Once on her birthday the propman brought in this big box of candy and gave it to her. We all assumed it was a birthday present for her, but she came up and she gave each and every one of us a piece. She passed it around for the whole group, and we each got a candy.

ALLAN DWAN: You couldn't describe her. Just absolutely marvelous little girl. Greatest in the world. She was fun all the time. I created a little police department for her, and she was the chief of police. I had some badges made. I was only captain. And everybody around her had to wear a badge and salute the chief, and the chief had to keep discipline. And so because she had to keep everything straight, she behaved herself. I'd say to her, "Chief, the electricians are pretty slow today," and she'd go and bawl them out, and they'd speed up. Once when I was going to get a speeding ticket, I flashed my badge at the cop, and he took it and looked: "Shirley Temple, Police Chief," it said, and he said, "My God, where did you get this?" and I said, "I'm the captain. Would you like to have it?" And naturally he said, "Sure. Go ahead. Drive on. My kid will go crazy about this." So I got out of a ticket with that badge. That was the power of stardom in those days.

JOHN SEITZ: I did five pictures with Shirley. She was quite bright. She had a great memory even before she could read. It was an amazing thing. Mrs. Temple got very mad at Carole Lombard because Shirley did a picture with her, and, you know, Carole was quick with the swear words. So Mrs. Temple took Shirley off the stage. Shirley was also trying to help Carole out when she couldn't remember her lines, and Carole didn't like that. The child knew everybody's lines, including her own. It was an amazing thing about her.

If she had to cry, we did the usual thing. We'd say, if she had trouble crying—if she'd been playing hard and it wasn't easy for her to get into the mood of crying—you'd simply say to her, "Now, Shirley, I want you to think that you'll never see your mother again. She's gone. She's going away and she's gone, and you're not going to see her anymore. Now, just think of that." And boy, would those tears roll!

RICHARD SCHICKEL: The glamour girl stars were never thought of as actresses, but they were movie stars *because* they were movie actresses. They were not just playing themselves, the way many people thought. They came into the business young and worked hard and became popular with masses of people who remained lifetime fans. That has to count for something, your Betty Grables and Lana Turners.

GEORGE SEATON: Grable was an amazing gal, because she would come on the set and have a frown on her face. I wouldn't say that she looked awful, but it was just the whole demeanor. Then somebody would say, "Action," and it was exactly as if you turned on all the lights in the studio. Suddenly the smile came on, and this personality just jumped at you. Betty readily admitted she was not the greatest actress in the world, but she knew what she *could* do. I guess that photograph of her—that World War II pinup in the white bathing suit—was seen more around the world than anything Marilyn Monroe ever did. Every collection of pictures from the forties always includes that one. I think the trick with Betty was to show her personality and give her an opportunity to be Betty Grable, because that's what the people wanted. They didn't want to see Betty Grable trying to be something else. I made a mistake when I put her in a long-dress period costume film, *The Shocking Miss Pilgrim*, and didn't show her legs. Well, anybody who doesn't show Betty Grable's legs has to be a little bit insane.

TAY GARNETT: Lana Turner was a hard worker. She tried. She's beautiful, and she has some very effective vocal tones. With a very thin voice, she still has some truly effective vocal tones, and when you put her in a hushed voice, she can sound very dramatic. And she is highly intelligent. She did understand storywise what was going on. Why she was saying the things. There was never any compromise in her mind. When she thought of something or read it, it was *that* specific thing. There was no deviation, there was no substitute. There was no second place, second choice. You couldn't say to her, "If you don't get that, what do you want?" Because if you said that, she'd say, "I want that. I don't want anything else." And she very quickly latched on to the character in *The Postman Always Rings Twice*. I think perhaps—and I don't have any justification for saying this—but I think perhaps a lot of that girl is Lana.

GEORGE CUKOR: She was interesting because she's a perfectly charming girl to work with, very amenable, very good mannered. She said something that's so interesting: "Honey, if I can understand it, I can do it," which is very important. She was starlike in a rather innocent way. Although she was perfectly modest and good mannered and she'd been at the studio as almost a child, a very young girl, she was very, very polite. For instance, there was a script girl she liked who was no longer young, and Lana would never ask the woman to come to her. She would always go over to the woman.

RICHARD SCHICKEL: There were some electrifying personalities, and they weren't all glamour girls. Think of Jimmy Cagney, Mickey Rooney . . .

IRVING RAPPER: Cagney was a very spontaneous actor, a very electrical actor. You cannot get on the seventh take or the fiftieth take what you get on the first take with Jimmy. He's like Bette Davis. They are very similar with their electrical appeal to audiences, and there's hardly a take that isn't good from them unless it's a wrong camera move or mistake or something.

HARRY WARREN: I met Mickey Rooney at Warner Bros. when he was a little kid, when he appeared in *A Midsummer Night's Dream.* He's a clever guy who can do anything: plays piano, sings, dances, acts. He does anything. Very clever. He was easy to work with. He's very businesslike when he works. He's a quick study, too. He loved doing musicals. He's also a songwriter. And a good golfer, too. And he's a good actor. That guy was amazing, but he's had his ups and downs.

TAY GARNETT: I knew him for years. I liked him. I felt very sorry for the little guy. He never had a normal childhood. He had been a star from the time he was about nine or ten years old. He had never been to school . . . his only schooling was on the studio lots, which was no real schooling at all. He had no normal life with other kids at all.

ANN RUTHERFORD: Mickey Rooney was the prime motivating factor in the success of the Andy Hardy pictures, one of MGM's most lucrative series of films, and he wasn't really the original focus. It was Judge Hardy, but Andy took over, that is, Mickey. He was so creative, so instinctive. If he saw a throw rug on the floor, he would pick it up, and you would see him going down a cellar. It became a cellar door. He was marvelously creative. He was totally responsible for the success of those pictures. You see, an actor *can* contribute something.

GEORGE CUKOR: Especially a talent like Mickey Rooney.

ANN RUTHERFORD: Oh, brilliant! A total genius!

TAY GARNETT: But when you think about it, Rooney has kept going. He'll work till the day he dies. Some of the stars just can't sustain it, either professionally or personally.

GEORGE SEATON: I think Montgomery Clift had one of the most promising careers of any young actor, but things happened to him. It just didn't work the way it should have.

STANLEY KRAMER: Monty Clift in his youth was the most beautiful looking actor on the New York stage. He was truly beautiful, and he was a matinee idol, a true matinee idol. He was the juvenile of all time. But he had a bad automobile accident which scarred him, and it influenced him and affected him and he was drinking and he had big, big problems and always had a death wish of one kind or another. He became unreliable. And he needed someone to tell him he was wonderful or "I know that you're having a little problem and you don't remember the lines, but what's the difference? You're wonderful." But you can't do that all day, every day.

OLIVIA DE HAVILLAND: Well, we did *The Heiress*, and the one thing I liked about Monty—what was difficult first of all, and then I'll say what I liked about him—what was difficult working with him was the fact that he had a very talented woman on the set with him. She was a sort of coach for him, and he would play a scene and then look up to see what she had to say at the back of the set. She would signal him as to whether it was okay or not. So that was really rather trying. You had to work under this. He was playing it as he had worked it out with her, very meticulously. But what I liked about him was the fact that he *cared* so much, that he cared enough to have a dialogue coach hidden behind the set, you know, signaling him—*that* I liked. He was not selfish in the way that Ralph Richardson was, and he wasn't out blatantly, in an exhibitionistic way. He was just tremendously interested in caring about his work, and that I liked.

HOWARD HAWKS: He had something you see rarely today. He was somebody who really wanted to work. He went out for two weeks with a lunch and a cowboy, and they didn't come back all day. They'd come in for dinner, and at the end of that two weeks he could ride a horse. He could handle a gun, and he could even make a special little mount to get into the saddle. He worked like the devil.

GEORGE SEATON: I think Montgomery Clift had one of the most promising careers of any young actor. I think he was tremendously talented but he wasn't sure of it. When I directed him in *The Big Lift*, he had with him a Russian woman who was much older. I was informed that she was his secretary. The first incident occurred an hour after they arrived in postwar Berlin, the location. Housing at that time was terribly short, but we managed to get an apartment for Monty and his secretary. We had things sent from Paris, some drapes and a carpet, trying to make the place as attractive as possible. I and my family lived in a house that had a bomb hole in the roof ten feet in diameter. The city was practically destroyed. So Monty came in, and I said, "This is it. We've got these drapes from Paris, and we fixed this and that. I hope you enjoy it." He said, "I visualized something with a garden." I said, "Monty, you don't realize how hard it was to get this place." He said, rather curtly, "I'm sorry, I visualized something with a garden." I knew he would get on the next plane and go back, so I went to General [Lucius] Clay and told him my problem. General Clay had to take a colonel and his family out of a house and put Clift in. Well, that didn't sit too well with me, but after all, we had to work together, so I tried to forget it. Now, the first day of work, another unfortunate thing happened. I would say, "Print," when the take was all right, and Monty would say, "I think I can do a better one." Well, anytime an actor says he can do a better one, I'm on his side. So then he would do another take, which I wouldn't like, and he would say, "I think that was fine."

Then my producer-partner, Bill Perlberg, tapped me on the shoulder and said, "Do it again, but just before you say 'Cut,' turn around and look at the secretary back there." So I did, and she was shaking her head. I knew that she was okaying takes for Monty. So I shut down shooting that day, and I said, "Monty, I'd like to talk to you." I picked him up at his house, and we were walking around Zehlendorf, where we both lived. It was a suburb of Berlin, a district, rather. I said, "Monty, please let me know what this gal does for you. Is she your coach? If she's your coach, that's splendid, because my wife is probably the best dramatic coach in the business, so I understand. The three of us should sit down ahead of the scene, discuss it, and then decide what we're going to do with it. On the set I have to be the boss. I don't want her okaying takes, I don't want her signaling to you. I want her way in the background if she's going to be there." Rather haltingly, the way he always talked, he said, "George, you don't realize. You hired Montgomery Clift. I am not Montgomery Clift, *she* is Montgomery Clift." So I said, "All right, then, let's go over to your house. I'd like to talk to Montgomery Clift." We went over, and I talked to this woman and explained the whole situation, and she said, "No, I'm not his coach, I help him to find the truth." Well, that kind of nonsense is something up with which I would not put, as Mr. Churchill would say. So it became a little hard because of a strained relationship. I insisted that if she were on the set, she had to stay in the background.

Now Mr. Paul Douglas arrives. He's to be Monty's costar. Mr. Douglas got off the plane and said to me, "I hear this guy is a miserable little punk. Duke Wayne told me that." I said, "No, he's a wonderful fellow. I've talked to him, everything is fine." So Mrs. Seaton had arranged for a dinner so that the two boys could meet, and the "secretary" was along. Paul had had a couple of drinks, and he passed a remark about her, I forget what it was, it was something Freudian—I want to forget. But as we left the dining room, Monty sort of good-naturedly slapped Paul on the back, just a pat on the back, and Paul wheeled around, grabbed him by his shirtfront and lifted him off his feet, and said, "Don't you ever hit me, or I'll knock your goddamn teeth right down your throat."

With that friendly beginning, the next day we started to shoot with the two men. Now, Monty had a habit of leaning in scenes. Whether it was deliberate or whether it was a lack of technique for films, I can't say, but he always leaned upstage a little in a two-shot so that the other person had to turn his head a bit away from the camera. Well, he did that a couple of times in a rehearsal, and then he did it in a take. Paul Douglas took his heel and came right down on Monty's toes and said, "Don't ever try to upstage me, I'll break your foot the next time." That was the kind of relationship they had throughout the whole picture. So it wasn't a happy occasion, but we managed to get through. And I wasn't the only one who had trouble with those two guys, especially Clift.

RIDGEWAY CALLOW: Marlon Brando was not self-indulgent the way the press said. When we were in Tahiti making *Mutiny on the Bounty*, the remake, Marlon Brando didn't go around to the bars. Very occasionally he'd drop in, maybe at night, but usually he'd go out to his house, which was seventeen kilometers from where we were working. He was always extolling the virtues of Tahiti, and I said to him, "You sound like an Air France travel guide, for God's sake, Marlon." He turned solemn. "Well," he said, "look, I love it down here because I can be myself. I, not Marlon Brando, the star. I'm Marlon Brando, a man. I can go around barefoot, stripped to the waist, wear anything I want, and nobody pays any attention. You're just as important down here as I am as far as the people are concerned. Here a human being is judged by local standards. That's why I love it." Brando was another one of those guys from Omaha.

STANLEY KRAMER: As a young man, Marlon Brando was the most exciting thing that ever hit celluloid. He was dynamite. He just came on, man, and the electricity happened.

RIDGEWAY CALLOW: Marlon was blamed in a magazine article for insisting on a house in Tahiti which he was only in a few days but which cost the company eight thousand dollars. It was also said that the house was about fifty kilometers away. Now, the reverse was the actual truth. In the first place, the house was only five minutes from the location at Matavai Bay, and it was an old, old house. It was in terrible shape, and we actually did spend eight thousand dollars in fixing it up to make it livable for Marlon. He was there only a few days—that was correct—but what they didn't state was that after he moved into the house, MGM suddenly decided to move the Pitcairn sequence back to the studio and not shoot it in Tahiti. We were scheduled to be in Tahiti a much longer time.

He would come to me every night and say, "What are we doing tomorrow?" Then he would come in the next morning and know the script as well as the director. He was an immense help to any director. He was full of ideas. He was also great for morale, as he had a great sense of humor—when things would get rough, he'd wisecrack and tell funny stories. One time he told a story to a group of Tahitians about Omaha. Every time he said "Omaha," they would laugh. Later we found out that *omaha* in Tahitian means "going to the bathroom."

Brando came up with some odd ideas. One was the velvet dressing gown with the nightcap. It was a creation of Brando's. I once said to him, "I don't know whether you're playing Fletcher Christian, Little Lord Fauntleroy, or the Scarlet Pimpernel," and he looked at me, laughed, and said, "Well, I'll be damned if I know, either."

There's a very interesting story about Marlon's approach to the death scene. He came to me the day we were to shoot and said, "Get me a couple of hundred pounds of cracked ice." I said, "What for, Marlon?" He said, "Don't worry about it, just get the ice. Get it in the bags, spread it out, and throw a sheet over it." So who am I to argue? I got the ice, and he took all his clothes off excepting his shorts and laid down on the ice just before the scene started. Then he put his clothes on quickly and got in front of the camera. He was petrified. He had lain down on that ice for forty-five minutes. He said, "I wanted to get the death tremors," and that's how he did it. He was lying, supposedly dying, and looking up into Tarita's face. The camera was shooting over the back of her head, and he's supposed to murmur a couple of words in Tahitian, as he dies, but he couldn't remember the words. So we got a grease pencil and wrote the words on her forehead. There he was looking up at her forehead with the camera behind her shooting, and that's how we got it. When he finished the scene, we had to drag him and give him a hot shower. Then we lost three days' work because he got a cold.

A little later, the English cast had gone back to England, and we still had to shoot the scene where Brando was supposed to come ashore and dance with the native girls in a sort of drunken orgy. So that morning Brando arrived on the stage with a couple of bottles of Jack Daniel's under his arm. He came to me and said, "Everybody says I'm supposed to be a Method actor. Well, by God, I'm supposed to be drunk today, and I'm going to be drunk. And so is everybody else." I notified the production office immediately, and they called me back and said, "We won't interfere, do the best you can." So Marlon was passing these bottles around, and everybody was getting crocked. He came over to me and insisted that I have a drink with them. I tried to fake it by gurgling and giving the bottle back, but he said, "No, you can't fool me that way, you swallow it." So I swallowed a little. Meanwhile, they were getting drunker and drunker. We had four set-ups to do, and I tried to get a close-up of Marlon. He was wobbling around, and we tried to hold him up. He really was an unpredictable actor.

GEORGE SEATON: I know that Marlon has been criticized, but I can tell you honestly, I've never known anyone who worked harder, who was more professional. He was the first one on the set in the morning, the last one to leave. He knew every word. He never argued for one second. He didn't sulk, he just did his job. What they figured would take twenty-three days, we did in eight, mainly because of Marlon's complete cooperation. I think he's been bad-mouthed tremendously. About *Mutiny on the Bounty*, he certainly didn't want to play it the way it had been played before, because there would have been odious comparisons, because the first version was just magnificent. He wanted to play it as a British fop, which was an interesting characterization if it had been consistent, but they never could make up their minds. Brando has been terribly maligned. I'm sure other people have had other experiences, but I can only tell you my experience with him, which was a happy one. He was one of the new breed of stars, not like a Clark Gable, who was in the original *Mutiny*.

TAY GARNETT: Clark Gable was magnificent. You know, he would do a scene where he had to be something other than just a big, strong guy, where he had to have some emotions—and he'd be going pretty good, and he'd be almost through it, and he'd stop and say, "That stinks!" So we'd do it again, and he'd be a little better. And I'd say, "Look, would you like to try it again?" and he'd say, "I know I'm stinking it up, but if you're willing, I think I could beat that." Now, he was never quite as bad as he thought he was. He downgraded himself terribly. He was always striving for something he never quite hit.

He had great modesty. He was not a great actor. He was a great personality. And he had a lot of wonderful qualities, generous qualities, warm, human qualities, and I think a lot of that shone through. It's tough to fool a camera.

MITCHELL LEISEN: You could get some real challenges. W. C. Fields was the most obstinate, ornery son of a bitch I ever tried to work with. Really. If he found that you had made an opening in your plot for one of his routines, he'd say, "Well, I think I'd better go down and rehearse my dialogue." He would come back two hours later slightly swacked and say, "I've decided I'm not going to do that routine at all. I changed my mind. I'm going to do this one instead." Just to louse you up.

IRVING RAPPER: I always have had a nice word for all the great actors who played small parts on the screen. Let's not forget them. They formed a background and a support system for the stars that was absolutely reliable and fortified every movie. I'm thinking of Laura Hope Crews, Dudley Digges . . . I remember particularly people like Ian Wolfe and Franklin Pangborn, who was so very, very funny. And Lee Patrick, Helen Westley . . .

RANALD MACDOUGALL: . . . Clifton Webb, who came to Hollywood at the height of his powers and was a very elegant, polished man, a delight in his own very particular way . . .

IRVING RAPPER: . . . and Joseph Schildkraut, who brought his stage greatness over to films.

GEORGE FOLSEY: And Dame May Whitty. She was a very accomplished woman. Said her lines, did all the things she was required to do. British people like C. Aubrey Smith and Gladys Cooper, as well as Dame May. They all speak English so beautifully. Aubrey Smith was a great, charming man . . . he was genuinely a very, very, very old man, not just made up to look older but really old, but also a very distinguished man . . . in his eighties and still acting. Gladys Cooper was a very charming woman. She must've been a really beautiful woman when she was young. She was still just beautiful. Great charm.

JOHN BRAHM: Marjorie Main was absolutely unique. She had something nobody else had. She's a personality all on her own. She's so weird that when you look at her, you don't know whether you should smile or not. And she's an excellent actress. She means what she says, and the way she reads a line is just wonderful. And she knows how to create a mood for a scene.

IRVING RAPPER: Eve Arden made every line funnier than it actually was.

JOHN BRAHM: And that horrible-looking guy, Marc Lawrence. His face was pockmarked. His awful heavy-looking presence made him a perfect villain.

ALLAN DWAN: Walter Brennan! A three-time Oscar winner. A very good actor. Very sensitive, too. I mean, he was always very eager to do it well. And he was never happy or satisfied with what he did. But if you encourage him a little bit, he'll go all over the place. He'll do anything for you. I had him play a general in one of my pictures—I've forgotten which one—in which he had to deliver a long instruction to a class of flyers and tell them what they had to do. I believe it was in the B-29 story, *The Wild Blue Yonder*. But at any rate, he had to get up and deliver a long tirade on behavior of that day, where they were to fly and what they would do, and point out on a map "We'll go to here," and this and that. Stuff that only a general would know what it meant, anyway. And he battled with that and memorized it and he got up and delivered it, but he'd get stuck every once in a while. And boy, the suffering he'd go through when he couldn't get it! And he'd hate himself. He'd go "What the hell's the matter with me? I'm an idiot." *Nobody* could have learned those lines. So I would encourage him and say, "You're going great, and it's amazing that you remembered that much. Now, let's pick it up and get along with the rest of it." And he got through it fine. He did it just beautifully. And toward the end of it, when he began to get tired, he began changing into that Walter Brennan "old guy" character, the way people think of him. The general got awful old before the scene was over!

He used to love to work without his teeth. If he had the slightest excuse, he'd take those falsies out. He loved to be old Gramps, the old flirtatious guy who was on the make.

GEORGE FOLSEY: You want to talk scene stealers? S. Z. "Cuddles" Sakall. Absolutely fascinating man. Never saw a man so cute as he was. He was an absolute doll. He would sit in his dressing room. He had a language problem. He didn't speak English very well, but you would never know. I don't say that you would not fully know, because you could listen to him, and he obviously had a very definite accent, but he handled it masterfully. He would sit in his dressing room with a little abacus, and he would say the lines for the scene that he was going to play once, and then he'd move the abacus over. And he would say them again, and he'd move the bead over, and he'd say them again. And all he did, all day long, was to say the lines and move the bead over until he had said them, sometimes, five hundred times.

MITCHELL LEISEN: Character actors were stars in their own way. Many of them had fan clubs. They are not the same thing as what we called "dress extras." Those were a colony unto themselves, actors who made a living playing the extras in scenes at any studio in any film. A dress extra in those days was only getting peanuts for pay next to what they get today. So there was no big hassle about that. Sometimes you'd have them bring two sets of clothes. If they were supposed to be in specialized costumes, we outfitted them, but they had to furnish their own wardrobes for street clothes or evening gowns. They supplied their own wardrobes for that. One picture I did, Betty Hutton in *Dream Girl*, we bought all the extras' wardrobes, dressed all the extras, rented all the fur coats for them. I wanted a certain class about it and wasn't trusting the extras to have the right wardrobe. They'd all come to me and say, "Can't we wear our mink coats to lunch?" I said, "Go ahead."

Of course, some leading stars also became supporting actors or character actors later in their careers, people like Claude Rains or John Barrymore or Marie Dressler. Barrymore was sheer heaven! Fantastic! Just fantastic. I had to have his last wife in a picture to keep him sober. She was on the set every minute. Maybe I shouldn't say this, but I will. I was sitting next to him at the old Trocadero bar one night while we were working on the picture, and somebody said to him, "John, how did you ever happen to marry Elaine Barrie?" And he said, "My boy, that broad has six sailors in her throat, all going, 'Yo de ho.'" I fell right off the stool. He was quite a character. By the time we finished with a set that was a patio where they have breakfast, it was smelling like an old toilet, because John would never go to the toilet. He would just go behind the bush. There was no stopping him.

TEETE CARLE: Charles Laughton was also from the stage, and he had a theory. He was a character actor, you know. A Gary Cooper walks in with that shy manner of his, and you know he's going to capture the audience almost from the very first picture he comes into, because he's a personality. Charles Laughton was going to have to depend on being a great actor, and he *was* a great actor, and I imagine he had read and knew of a lot of other cases where personalities like him had gone to Hollywood and they hadn't been accepted. A great many stage people had that view. So Laughton really refused to be publicized . . . he just wouldn't do it. He wanted to be unknown as an off-screen person so he could be a character on-screen.

GEORGE CUKOR: What is extraordinary about Marie Dressler—she was *the* biggest, biggest star of her time. She was sort of a low comedian and hokeypokey, too. She ruled in musical comedy, low comedy. As the time went on, she herself acquired a kind of distinction, a kind of magnificence. She was a law unto herself, you know. She'd mug and carry on, and when she came on, she had such aplomb, such effect. She very much could get the audience's attention.

GEORGE FOLSEY: Well, maybe the supporting actress of all time was Margaret Dumont, who had to support the three Marx Brothers without really understanding what her role was. Margaret Dumont was always a mixed-up woman. She never really quite knew what was going on. Not really. Well, she knew, of course, but she either played the dumb grande dame to the hilt or she *was* that way. I couldn't tell, because later on we got to know her quite well. We used to go to dinner with her at the old

Ivar House here in town, and we'd meet her there sometimes by accident, sometimes we'd take her there . . . and she was not unlike the same person in the play, you know.

Dumont was a dear woman. She could take it. She had innate dignity. Whatever those crazy Marx Brothers did to kid her around, she'd always say, "Oh, you funny boys, don't do that." She didn't have a hair on her head. She was absolutely bald. She wore a wig which Harpo used to steal. When we were on tour, she'd have to get off the train with a little turban that said PULLMAN on it! She was great, she was really the fourth Marx brother. Her dignity, they'd play against that dignity, she never tried to get laughs on her own. She was absolutely superb. Years later, after her time with the Marx Brothers, when I was directing my first picture, *Billy Rose's Diamond Horseshoe*, there was a scene in which Betty Grable has a dream. She goes to meet Mrs. Richbitch (I forget what the name really was). She walks up a tremendous flight of stairs, wearing a beautiful mink coat, and at the top is the grande dame. All the character had to say was, "Good evening, my dear, so good of you to come." When I started to think about casting it, I said, "Maggie Dumont." I knew she was still alive, because every afternoon she would have tea at the Knickerbocker Hotel. So I called her, and I said, "Maggie, I'm doing a film. There's a small part, not very much, but if you'd like to do a favor for me—" "Oh, my dear boy, of course, of course. But send me a script, I want to see if I'm right for the part." So I sent her the script. Now, literally, all she said was "So good of you to come, my dear." So she called me and said, "Yes, George, I think the part is quite suitable. Who will design my clothes?" I thought, Here's my chance to make her "Lady For A Day." I got hold of Charlie LeMaire. He was the head designer at Fox. Of course, Charlie had worked with her, so he said, "Oh, George, this is wonderful. Let's go all the way. I've got a few outfits in stock, but I'll do sketches of them, and we'll submit sketches." So we went down to tea, and we submitted these sketches. Of course, they were on the rack already. She said, "Dear Charles, I think this suits the character better than this one." "Oh, yes, Maggie, of course." Now, she came for a fitting, and she said, "Now, I see this woman wearing very expensive jewels." I said, "Maggie, you're absolutely right. Don't worry, we'll get Krouch." He was the big jeweler here in those days. He had fantastic jewels. Well, everything was set, and now we came to shoot the picture. I tipped Betty Grable off. I said, "Betty, this is probably the last thing Margaret will ever do. Let's make it memorable for her." She said, "She's a wonderful woman. Let's go all the way." So I got the biggest dressing room you've ever seen. Bigger than Betty's, right next to Betty's, with a star on it, MARGARET DUMONT. I sent roses, and Bill Perlberg sent roses. She had more flowers in there than Forest Lawn Cemetery. Of course, Charlie LeMaire was there personally to supervise the final fitting. Any little thing, he'd call a seamstress over, and they'd fix this or that. So Betty came in, and she said, "Oh, Miss Dumont, I'm so pleased to know you, I've admired you for so many years." Now came the fellows from Krouch. There were two guards with .45s, and they had trays and trays of diamonds, emeralds, and rubies. I said, "Maggie, you know this character better than I do, so you pick what you think is right." She picked a diamond tiara. Now, when we came to start the scene, and Maggie in the first rehearsal said to Betty, "My dear, I think it would be better if you stood about eight inches back." Betty said, "Oh, yes, madame, oh, yes." She really was dear about it. We did one take, we did two takes, we did three takes. She was finished, so she said, "Which take are you going to use?" I said, "I haven't decided, I have to see it on the screen first, Maggie. My guess is number two. I think that's the best." "Well," she said, "I sort of like number three." So I said, "You come to see the rushes, and if you like number three, by all means, we'll use number three." When the rushes came through, she saw them. She studied them, and she wanted to run them a second time, a third time. Finally she said, "My dear boy, I think you're right. Number two is better than number three." I said, "Well, thank you, Maggie, I think you capture the character more completely in take two." So she had her day, and it was just magnificent.

About three weeks later, I was at a party with Groucho. I told Groucho the whole story, and Groucho practically cried. He said, "You know, it's wonderful for you to have done that. She hasn't worked since the last Marx Brothers picture. What am I saying? *I* haven't worked since the last Marx Brothers picture!"

ARTHUR KNIGHT: The old star system doesn't exist anymore.

RICHARD SCHICKEL: Movie stars now are, in fact, well-trained theatrical actors. It's a whole difference in movie stardom between now and Barbara Stanwyck coming out of the chorus or Myrna Loy walking around the corner or Gary Cooper being spotted sitting on a horse as an extra. Back then it was because somebody spotted them, noticed them. And their relationship to today's business system is different.

TEETE CARLE: A great change took place when companies began giving stars a percentage of their pictures. Then it became very important for a star to have his picture be a financial success—not for prestige, not to build a fan base, but actually for the dough that he's going to get. If he's got 10 percent, as Gable used to get, or 10 percent of the gross, like Cary Grant—you had people like Cary Grant, who was living a very smug life and didn't really have to help with publicity—he suddenly finds that it's very interesting for him to get out and go traipsing across the country and do television interviews and appearances. But that makes them feel that they are in charge of everything. Cooperation takes a hit.

PETER BOGDANOVICH: Somebody asked me what I thought about salaries for stars, and I said I thought that they ought to be paid a million bucks, but if the picture didn't gross that kind of money that they ought to return what they didn't get, you know, 'cause after all you're paying them because supposedly they can bring that amount of people into the box office, and if they don't, then they ought to return the money.

ALLAN DWAN: It reduces the business to an affair in which you participate and have the honor of being associated with some big-name actor. And you do all the work so that actor can get all that money, and you're honored by being associated with him, 'cause that's the kind of a business it is. It's a stupid business, and it's heading for rocks on that basis.

MERVYN LEROY: There are no stars today. Redford, I think, is a great actor and possibly a star. But there are no real stars like Clark Gable and Spencer

Tracy and Cary Grant. There are no real Garbos and those kinds of people, because there aren't any. They don't exist.

RANALD MACDOUGALL: A gulf exists between actors in the old generation and this one. I could go on for days and tell you the depths of the pettiness of some of the so-called stars of today. They are killers, you know. They kill people. Ulcers. And they have very little talent. . . . All the people from old Hollywood were professionals. They were *professionals*. They came in in the morning, they learned their lines, they knew what they were doing, and if they had any questions, they would ask you, and they would be glad—with one or two exceptions like Bette Davis—they would be very glad to have your opinion, and if you couldn't give them anything, it was okay, but they would ask, and they would invite your participation. They were secure. They knew what they were, and they knew what they were doing, and they had expertise.

MERVYN LEROY: Well, as I said, there are no stars today.

GEORGE CUKOR: All those stars! Those rosters of stars. And supporting actors. Those assets. And they *were* assets, because the studios "owned" them. When you think of all those famous names, many still revered today, it's staggering!

CHAPTER 9

THE PRODUCT

FRANK CAPRA: What's remarkable is how many of our old pictures can be played today. Think of the names of some of them, and you'll see what I mean. I'm happy to say that *It Happened One Night* and *It's a Wonderful Life* are among them. But think of the vehicles created for the stars that were the famous Hollywood movies that everyone talks about and writes about. *Casablanca, Stagecoach, Mrs. Miniver, The Awful Truth, High Noon,* and *Shane, My Man Godfrey, How Green Was My Valley, Rebecca* . . .

RICHARD SCHICKEL: . . . *The Adventures of Robin Hood, White Heat, Public Enemy, Cover Girl, Top Hat, Swing Time* . . .

ROBERT WISE: . . . I like to think *West Side Story* and *The Sound of Music* will endure . . .

VINCENT SHERMAN: . . . *Now, Voyager, Mildred Pierce* . . .

GEORGE CUKOR: . . . *Camille* . . .

VINCENT PRICE: . . . *Dracula, Frankenstein, The Invisible Man* . . .

ARTHUR KNIGHT: . . . *Singin' in the Rain, Some Like It Hot, Double Indemnity* . . .

ROBERT WISE: . . . *Citizen Kane, The Cat People* . . .

MERVYN LEROY: . . . *The Wizard of Oz* . . .

OLIVIA DE HAVILLAND: . . . Oh, so many, so many, and let's not forget *Gone with the Wind.*

FRANK CAPRA: The Hollywood Product. Made to make money and last for one season. Still alive and being watched and respected today. Old Hollywood: America's definition of itself.

MERVYN LEROY: Oh, don't get me started! We all remember the pictures we made, the successes and the failures! It was our life . . .

MITCHELL LEISEN: . . . all the things that happened on set and the ups and downs, the big plans that went to hell and the poor little project that caught on.

HAL MOHR: I remember every minute of it, and I would be ready to do it all over again right now. It was a great life, and the films were great, the memories even better.

I. A. L. DIAMOND: Everybody can quote half a dozen good lines from *Casablanca*, from *Ninotchka*, from *The Maltese Falcon* and any number of other pictures. Now, the two big laughs in *Shampoo*, as far as seeing it in the theater, were "I want to suck his cock" and "Do you want to fuck?"

BILLY WILDER: Now, having got that off our chests . . . I'm kind of surprised that you used such language.

I. A. L. DIAMOND: I'm just quoting.

KATHARINE HEPBURN: Sex, pornography, and obscenity have always sold better than anything else. Now you make it respectable and you make it sort of an art form. . . . [Sam Peckinpah] knew better than to make *Straw*

Dogs. This is the rottenest piece of work that I ever saw . . . it's laughable and cheap. It is brutality . . . I think it's phony. I think *A Clockwork Orange* is phony. I think that *Sunday Bloody Sunday* is phony. I think they are just pathetic. I just go and laugh and throw up.

MERVYN LEROY: *The Wizard of Oz* is my favorite subject. I had wanted to do it since I was a kid—and it took me a long time to sell it, a long, long time, because people thought I was crazy making a fairy story just for kids, you know. But it *wasn't* just for kids! MGM wanted to star Shirley Temple in it, but I had seen Judy Garland in a picture called *Pigskin Parade* that was made at 20th Century–Fox. And she was so great that I just couldn't get over her.

HAL ROSSON: *The Wizard of Oz* was a huge gamble because it's an unbelievable story and fantasy doesn't always come off well on the screen. Seldom. Very seldom. At the studio preshowings there was a huge gathering of studio personnel there, and of course everybody was naturally hoping and praying that they had a big hit on their hands.

It was a sneak preview in San Bernardino. In fact, it was the first time the picture had ever been shown to the public in general. There was a lot of excitement there. Is it going to go over, or is it not going to go over? Is it going to go over big or only small? The lights go down, and the picture is on. And the excitement, I can assure you, is huge! The primary reason we were there and why they wanted us to make comments was to help in the editing, in the final true editing of the picture. And there was a big discussion as to whether or not the picture was going to go over. We talked about "Over the Rainbow." I liked it.

MERVYN LEROY: They actually discussed taking it out. Can you imagine?

HAL ROSSON: *Oz* was an instantaneous hit. I know because I was there at the big premiere at Grauman's Chinese Theatre, and the picture was very well received. I think that *The Wizard of Oz* was really years ahead of its time because we had such a wide variety of characterizations in that. For instance, the flying monkeys had appliances very similar to what *Planet of* *the Apes* uses. They were a little more stylized type in makeup than *Planet of the Apes*, but nevertheless the same type of appliances were used. The makeups were fantastic, but they were uncomfortable and couldn't be worn too long.

KING VIDOR: Victor Fleming was the official director of *The Wizard of Oz*, and he and I were good friends. Our offices were right across the hall. He said he would take over *Gone with the Wind* if someone would take *Oz* over. Then he'd do *Gone with the Wind*. I was so damn glad to get out of doing *Gone with the Wind* that I said, "Sure, I'll take over *The Wizard of Oz* instead." I went over Monday morning and sat on the set all Monday and late that afternoon, ran all the stuff that they'd shot up until then. Next morning, Fleming was over at *Gone with the Wind*, and I carried on with *The Wizard of Oz*. I shot three weeks of *Wizard*, and I shot the "Somewhere over the Rainbow" song when Victor went off and took over *Gone with the Wind* from George Cukor. I went on to fill that out for him, but I didn't want screen credit for it because he had cast the picture and approved the sets and had been in on all the preliminary conferences, and I didn't believe that anyone who walks in with everything already established deserved split credits, and neither did the Directors Guild of America. They ran the whole picture for the committee and they gave second-unit credits to the second unit, and my name isn't on *The Wizard of Oz*. I wouldn't permit it. In the old days, when people were under contract, you might take over when someone was ill or walked off the set or was pulled for another assignment. The work was considered to be the studio's, and they could assign you or reassign you, and most of us understood that. If we didn't do the whole picture, we didn't feel we needed credit, necessarily. We were making a living.

RANALD MACDOUGALL: For me, *Mildred Pierce* was a great experience. Making the picture was a marvelous working environment, very stimulating, the best the studio system could give you. It was over at Warner Bros. Jerry Wald had called me one day and said he had a picture for Joan Crawford, a script she was supposed to do called *Mildred Pierce*. Did I know the James Cain novel? he wanted to know. It was the worst of the

James Cain novels, you know. The others were infinitely better . . . this was not one of his best works. [The screenplay I read] was much too long. It was about half a pound too much script . . . and it was tedious. It took a long while, as in the novel, for the characters to develop, mature, and get involved with each other . . . *and* . . . there was no murder in it. I came up with the murder. I said, "You start with a murder, *bang, bang*, it adds something daring for its time." I suggested that the shots ring out the murder before the titles.

Jerry said, "I want you to have a meeting with myself and Mike Curtiz," and I didn't know Mike at all. Knew him by reputation and a lot of funny stories, all of which were true. All I knew was that he was a mad Hungarian, wore puttees—very colorful—and had odd sex habits during lunchtime. Everybody else was a lunch bum. Mike had his own lunch idea.

He had a reputation for not getting along with writers, which I was perfectly conscious of. His English was, to say the least, atrocious, very often highly amusing. After I had worked with him awhile, it became perfectly comprehensible to me. He would always call a woman "he." At one time he was describing what he wanted in the way of a scene, and this is precisely what he said. He said, "He's in love on her, she's in love on him, the old man smells a rot. You fix?" And I said, "I fix." Mike was a very good motion picture director because he was outer motivated. The image of what people did, the external, meant a great deal to him.

Crawford played Mildred Pierce perfectly. She approached everything very professionally. She was very cooperative. And incidentally, she was much too nice a person to give people trouble. I never saw her, in all the time I worked with her on this and other pictures, to put her foot down and take a stand and say, "I've got to do this," or anything like that. She is not like that. She doesn't make big adamant scenes. I never saw her do it. She's such a marvelous woman, really.

Mildred Pierce was a great success because of her performance, and, of course, the excellent pace and tempo of the picture was Mike's. He was great at keeping track of tempo.

Mildred Pierce was an example of what the studio system could do, the kind of collaboration and the way time was spent writing and rewriting and the way people could accept each other and work together. But the rumor system! Crawford and her shoulder pads and all that nonsense. A real Hollywood picture in every possible way. And still being shown today.

RICHARD SCHICKEL: *High Noon* marks a shift in westerns. The Anthony Mann–directed westerns with Jimmy Stewart—*Winchester '73*, *The Naked Spur*, et al.—they gave us the antihero western guy, but *High Noon* is the politicalization of the 1950s, or postwar, western. *High Noon* is of interest in retrospect. It was a postwar movie developed by an independent partnership, to be released by United Artists, and thus not a big studio film. Yet it was nominated for seven Academy Awards, including Best Picture, and it won four, including Best Actor for Gary Cooper. Its theme song became a hit, so the usage of a theme song became a staple of the genre. It doesn't rely on beautiful western locations . . . it's set in a crummy-looking little town . . . and it introduced Grace Kelly to the public in a significant way. In a sense, it was an example of a new Hollywood product: cheaper, on limited location, more political and downbeat, showing the established stars as aging and introducing a newer one, and produced by an independent entity and released by United Artists. It was not a product from one of the big studios like MGM or Paramount or Warners. It represents a Hollywood movie that points toward the future. And it's one of the most rewatched and generally known movies of its era.

FRED ZINNEMANN: Our concept in *High Noon* was one of, first of all, the unity of time and place. The unity of time was the idea of our screenwriter, Carl Foreman—the idea that screen time would be identical with the running time of the film—about an hour and a half, but also wanting to confine the whole thing to the village itself to show the menace, the threat, only in static shots of the railroad tracks, as against the constant motion of the man who is looking for help and finding none.

FLOYD CROSBY: The budget for *High Noon* was only about $750,000. We shot the picture in about thirty-four days, and we did one sequence we didn't even use. It was where the sheriff had two deputies, and we shot a sequence to show why one of the deputies wasn't there when he was needed. He was out to catch a criminal when they had a fight, and then he gets involved with a little Mexican girl in a cantina and gets drunk and doesn't get back in time for this thing. And that whole sequence—the other deputy—was thrown out completely, about three days of work. So actually, of what was used in the picture, I think we shot thirty-one or thirty-two days. And the only high-priced actor in it was Gary Cooper. The girl . . . what was her name? . . . Grace Kelly . . . wasn't high priced then. This was only the second picture she'd ever been in. She was not a name at all.

STANLEY KRAMER: I will tell you a little story about *High Noon*, which I produced. Dimitri Tiomkin did the score, and Dimitri Tiomkin is, of course, a very shy, retiring fellow who never makes any fusses or noises— *not much*. But he wrote a ballad, and I thought it wasn't any good. And it wasn't. So he wrote another one. And to show him what kind of ballad I thought it should be, I took an old Burl Ives recording of some folk thing, and I put it on the picture and ran it for Tiomkin, you know, for mood. He got it, and the next thing he came up with was "Do Not Forsake Me, Oh My Darlin'." So I got the song, and everybody felt it to be a wonderful thing, and it fit, and I used it in the film.

Now, everybody knows that every time Gary Cooper took a walk, the song came on, lyrically, which for those days was very much out of line. Using singing—using bridges—in this thing is crazy. Well, we used them because it was a new idea. It went to preview in Inglewood, California. And I had eleven bridges through the film of this song. On the fifth use the entire audience broke into giggles and laughter. Now, I am sitting there, knowing six more are coming. So you can imagine what a preview that was. I mean, it was a disaster area. I'm telling you, if anybody had anything decent to say about the picture—the cards that they wrote. They even stopped using dirty words on the cards and just said, "Get that lousy song out of there." Well, I took it out by stages. Finally I took out seven of those renditions, not including what was at the beginning and the end. The beginning had the whole song, and the end reprised it. But there were four bridges in between, and I tell you, that song had a good deal to do with a lot of the aura around *High Noon*, as well as the action.

FLOYD CROSBY: *High Noon* was a kind of landmark picture. It was memorable for so many reasons, but those of us who worked on it felt we were in a newer, freer environment off the studio lot. And it was just such a huge success. It grossed $12 million.

ROBERT WISE: *The Magnificent Ambersons* is often used as a classic example of how films were ruined by Hollywood . . . how genius was crushed . . . and a picture was cut down and ruined. Well, I was the editor on that project, and I can tell you what happened on *Magnificent Ambersons* was not a typical studio system story at all.

When war was declared, the first thing that happened was that Orson got a bid from the government to go to South America. He had a date on which he had to report to Washington for a briefing before he left, and my memory is that was the latter part of February, early March, something like that—we're now talking early December, mid-December. So Orson in his own inimitable way started thinking about his future and the whole thing, and he decided that maybe it would be a good time to clean up a lot of things that were loose. He owed RKO one more picture on his contract. He thought it would be a lovely thing if he could get that picture out of the way and be done and finish all his commitments to RKO before he had to leave to go to South America.

He had the script to *Journey into Fear*, which he had had around for some time and never gotten off the ground, so he decided that the thing to do was to make *Journey into Fear*. He couldn't find anybody to play the Turkish general, so he decided to play it himself. Now, he's already directing *Ambersons*, and he's also doing the Lady Esther radio show once a week. So from the middle of December to the end of February or early March, Orson was finishing the directing on *Ambersons*, he was taping about a dozen hour shows for Lady Esther ahead because he had that commitment, he was producing and acting in *Journey into Fear*, most of which was being shot at night.

This was kind of typical for Orson.

In the final release, very much what Orson set out to do in the film was, I think, there. From a purely artistic point of view, it was obviously a finer piece of work and a better film in his original version. I wouldn't defend what happened to it for anything in terms of the artistic level, but when you're faced at a given point with the need to get a film out that will somehow play with an audience, things happen. Unfortunately, a print of Orson's version, the long version, doesn't exist because it was the work print. The negative was never cut on that version, so it was never a print existent. All of the things that were cut out were just put in a vault in a bin at RKO and eventually destroyed, so there's never any possibility of that original version of Orson's ever coming to life.

My memory of it was that there wasn't any particular different application in the editing in the before and after of the film, just whatever is expressed there primarily was probably reflected in his script, his screenplay, and his development of it. But my recollection at this point is that there wasn't any special changed treatment.

I think there were about, as I recall, four or five bridge scenes, because in having to cut out as much film as we did, we just had places where we had to bridge over and make work. That's a bad way for a film to finish. The director ought to always be there to do whatever's necessary in the editing and to make whatever retakes are necessary, and normally Orson would have been there under any circumstances. He just literally was unable to come up and be involved in it, and yet the studio couldn't sit and wait for him to come back from South America, where he had gone. It was just a bad bit of timing. But normally your director would be there, and he would be at the previews. He would have his own suggestions and solutions to the problems expressed at the preview and be involved in the writing of and development of the bridge scenes and directing them himself, so it would still, you know, be his baby.

When Orson left *Ambersons*, RKO had to get it finished and released for financial reasons. The business of filmmaking rolled on, but it was nobody's intent to destroy *Ambersons*, just to get the money back. Obviously, his original would have been what we'd all rather have had.

RIDGEWAY CALLOW: William Wyler was [the first one] assigned to direct *The Sound of Music*. As a matter of fact, he went to Austria, had scouted and selected the locations, came back to the studio, worked on the script for a while, and to the best of my knowledge and belief, he turned the story down, feeling there wasn't a picture in it. So Fox asked Bob Wise to do *Sound of Music* after Wyler had rejected it.

Bob merely did the picture as a favor to Fox. It's ironic. He did a favor for Fox and made himself a multimillionaire. He went to Europe, but before he left he told me he did not like any of the locations that Willie Wyler had selected, feeling they were too pretentious. He chose his own.

I remember when we did the openings scene with Maria singing on top of the mountain, which was photographed from a helicopter. We used to call the location "Maria's mountain." It was in Bavaria, over the border from Austria, and it was on the top of a hill. The grass was beautiful—nice and long—and when the wind hit it, it waved beautifully. We had to change our schedule for various reasons, so we did not get around to the top of the mountain until late in shooting. One day our production manager went 'round to check the location, and to his horror he found that the owner had cut all the grass! But fortunately we didn't get to the sequence for another two or three weeks, so it had grown in the meantime. But when we did get the opening scene, it rained constantly, and there was quite a steep slope going to the top of the mountain. We practically had to crawl up there on our hands and knees—even the four-wheel drives couldn't get up the mountain. They were slipping in the soft mud. So we found an old ox there, and I'll never forget one day sending down for Julie to come up to the top of the mountain. We felt this rain was going to break, and she came up, sitting on the oxcart drawn by an old ox, with a mink coat on and a huge umbrella over her. It was one of the funniest sights I have ever seen. But Julie took it in great fun. We huddled at the top of the hill, and when the sun broke out, which it did finally, we got the shot. I think it is a beautiful shot.

ROBERT WISE: You always have those films you look back on and feel you turned a corner in your career, that you got more recognition after you did them. As a piece of work, to whatever degree it might be called an artistic thing, *The Sound of Music* doesn't compare to *West Side Story* in terms of its textures, feelings, but I think, given the property and what we did with it, I feel very satisfied the way we treated it, and there is a satisfaction certainly, if not from the critics, from knowing the millions of people around the world that loved the film in all countries. This gives you a good feeling, not the same kind of feeling you get out of the recognition of a *West Side Story* or something like that.

By the time of *Sound of Music*, we were working in situations completely different from those we had when I started out at RKO editing *Citizen Kane*. We were out in the open on location in Austria and dealing with different kinds of problems, such as wind, mown grass, rain, and language misunderstandings. And everything was changing: tastes, audiences, competition, costs, new technology. It wasn't like we were making *Gone with the Wind*.

RAY RENNAHAN: *Gone with the Wind*? That's quite a story. That thing.

RICHARD SCHICKEL: *Gone with the Wind* is considered by some people to be the high point of the studio system . . . 1939 is called the greatest year in Hollywood history because so many famous movies were made and released in that time frame. But *GWTW*, as they call it, is boring and dated and politically offensive in some ways. And it was made by David O. Selznick with his independent company, although released in a famous deal with Metro-Goldwyn-Mayer. It's a product made in the studio way, and it's huge and famous, but it's not the best of Hollywood. It's just a great representation of how all the forces in Hollywood could be brought together to make an epic film. In that regard, it's a high point of *one* kind. It represents what the studio system was all about: producer cinema, with great movie stars, maximally using a great army of superb technicians, artists, and specialists, shot within the relatively new technology of Technicolor, and released, sold, promoted, and ballyhooed as much as any movie in history.

PANDRO BERMAN: You're speaking of *Gone with the Wind*? Well, *Gone with the Wind* was perhaps the most kicked-about property before it was finally purchased of any property that ever came to California, and I was one of the people who had a hand in kicking it around. I shouldn't have missed out on it because I was told about the property in its early stages, when it was first sent around in galley proof, by three women who all said that it was the greatest. One was Mervyn LeRoy's wife, Doris Warner LeRoy. One was Katherine Brown, who, at that time, was working for David

Selznick but who had previously worked for me. And the third one was Lillie Messinger, who was our story editor. And all three of those women, under different circumstances, came to me and asked me to buy it. Doris had been thrown out when she proposed it to Jack Warner. Katherine Brown had been thrown out when she proposed it to David Selznick. And Lillie Messinger, who was working for me, had urged me to buy it.

Later, after the book was published and became a success, everybody tried to buy it from David. And Warner Bros. made a big offer to David to come over there and make the picture for them. And Louis B. Mayer, I guess, had what David wanted most, which was Clark Gable. And that's how it came to Metro. David was financing his own films at that period and could have made it himself, but he felt that it was too expensive a project, I guess, to make without Gable. So that was how Metro came to get their hands on it. Metro had turned it down originally also. These maneuvers were typical of the picture business at that time.

ADELA ROGERS ST. JOHNS: Everybody—readers, moviegoers, people in the business—all said, "Don't make *Gone with the Wind* unless Clark Gable's going to play Rhett Butler." And nobody ever thought of making it without him. You just couldn't. I believe somebody had suggested somebody else, and, I mean, the shriek went up. You could hear it. The Clark Gable thing was definite. You couldn't, just couldn't, not cast him as Rhett. There was no way from the minute you picked up *Gone with the Wind*. We were a generation that had watched Mr. Gable on the screen, and we were absolutely mad about him. He was the one man in the world as far as people were concerned—both men and women. Gable had charisma. *There he was.* And nobody has ever found any other man to come anywhere near him.

I go back and see *Gone with the Wind* every time it's released, and *there he is*. And he's still to me the most attractive man I ever saw, the most joy of life that made you feel that life was worth living, had the most in it, the most excitement. And it's interesting because Margaret Mitchell had never seen him. No, Peggy had never seen him. So . . . there it was: you *had* to cast Gable. So Mr. Selznick took himself over to his father-in-law, Louis B. Mayer, who wasn't speaking to him but who had Gable under contract, and said, "All right, let's make a deal."

RAY RENNAHAN: *Gone with the Wind* was a merry-go-round of cinematographers and directors. I was there because I was the official Technicolor photography representative. They had to have me. Selznick wanted a certain type of photography, and Lee Garmes was put on it, and Ernie Haller and several other people. No one was on that picture from beginning to end. No one. Selznick just kept changing. And then, of course, the directors: George Cukor and King Vidor and Sam Wood and Victor Fleming . . . and William Cameron Menzies, the production designer, doing a lot of directing, I think . . . and Breezy Eason did some second unit. What a circus! Fleming did probably 40, 45 percent of the picture. Cukor probably did 5 percent. Bill Menzies did a big bulk of it because he was the art director, and all the stuff leading up to the middle of the show, to the intermission, Menzies did that.

RIDGEWAY CALLOW: No, George Cukor started it, and then he was taken off the picture after two or three weeks and replaced by Victor Fleming. Then Victor Fleming got sick and Sam Wood came on the picture, and then Victor Fleming came back. We split the picture into two units. Sam Wood directed one, and Victor Fleming directed the other. Wood directed the Reconstruction sequences—the rebuilding of Atlanta—in its entirety. Selznick says that Wood did three edited reels, which would be thirty-three minutes in the finished film, or at least that much. They say that the famous big pullback shot of the wounded Confederate soldiers at the depot was Fleming's, but I give the credit for that to Bill Menzies, the production designer. He devised and created the shot, and it was his suggestion that we use an oil derrick crane in order to pull the camera back to such a high position. I think Menzies was one of the few geniuses I ever met in the picture business. He was a great art director, a great designer, a great creator, but a lousy director. When he tried to direct, he flopped.

Menzies was very charming, had a great sense of humor, and he loved to tell stories—dirty stories. And he was a great drinker. For lunch he'd have five martinis and wouldn't eat anything. Then at night, he'd really start to drink.

RAY RENNAHAN: Fleming directed the dialogue and most of the action stuff was directed by someone else. And Cukor directed some dialogue. Cukor was fired.

GEORGE CUKOR: You know how to harm, saying that. It's a boring goddamn subject, and I don't give a shit why I was replaced. I *was* replaced. David Selznick was a friend of mine, and I still really don't know. Gable, if it was Gable, thought that I couldn't handle him, that I only knew how to handle ingenues. I thought it was rather stupid. I prepared the whole picture, and I was there when it started. I shot for about a month or two. And behind the scenes, I did some black market coaching for nothing.

But I will say this: it *was* a blow, but I survived.

RIDGEWAY CALLOW: Cukor could never have shot all of *Gone with the Wind*, in my opinion. He was a great woman's director, but he's not a physical director. He couldn't have done the battle scenes or the evacuation of Atlanta. *Gone with the Wind* was essentially a man's picture, despite Vivien. On any woman's picture, Cukor's the greatest.

I think Gable wanted Victor Fleming all along. He had made several pictures with him and liked Fleming. Gable worked well with everybody, but the crew didn't like him. I know at MGM they said the crews were crazy about him, but they were not as crazy about him as Selznick. He was very aloof on that picture.

Then there was Victor Fleming. When he first came on the set, he said to [Assistant Director Eric G.] Stacey and myself, "They tell me that you're supposed to be the best team in the picture business. But I'm going to put both of you in the hospital before this picture is over." That was his greeting to us. Instead, *he* went to the hospital and *we* didn't. Before the picture ended, he said to me one day, "What are you going to do at the end of this picture, Reggie? Why don't you come out to MGM? We have a big studio. They can use a man like you." I called Victor Fleming up six times while waiting for *Rebecca* to start and couldn't even get him on the phone. That's typical Hollywood.

OLIVIA DE HAVILLAND: When George Cukor left, Vivien and I were absolutely desperate. We got the news, we were on the set of the bazaar sequence. We were both dressed in black, if you remember, because Scarlett has lost her husband and I have lost my brother. When we got this news, we immediately went to visit David. We left the set, and we went to see David Selznick, and we spent three hours in his office *beseeching* him. We *cried*, we pulled out our handkerchiefs, and they had black borders—you should have seen the poor man. He went over to his window seat—he had a marvelous window seat—and he just sat there. The windows were open, and when those handkerchiefs came out, I thought he was going to go straight over the sill. But he was strong. I don't think he had ever had a tougher test than that he received that day in his office with these two women in black beseeching him to keep George Cukor. And he didn't—he was very strong. That evening, encouragement came to me from a very strange source. I went out to dinner with Howard Hughes. We never thought back then that all of these extraordinary things were going to happen to Howard Hughes, though he *was* an extraordinary man. But that night he took me out to dinner, and I told him how anguished I was by this change. I was sure that I couldn't relate, you know, that the characterization would escape me with anyone else on the set, in spite of the costumes and hair, and Vivien had the same terror, too, so Hughes helped me. It was the most extraordinary thing. You would never think that a man like that would have quite that degree of sensitivity and insight, but he did have it, and he gave me one of the nicest gifts that any human being has ever given me by the reassurance that he offered that night. He said, "With George and Victor"—Victor Fleming was the one coming on the film—"it's the same talent, but Victor's is strained through a coarser sieve." Those were his exact words. And I therefore was able to start to work with Victor Fleming with a positive and receptive viewpoint. And, of course, that's very necessary.

We had to adjust to Sam Wood, too, because eventually Victor had a sort of nervous breakdown and he had to leave the film. And Sam Wood began, but by this time I had a certain amount of confidence. I thought, If we can make the transition from George to Victor successfully, and we did, I think that perhaps I can make it from Victor to Sam. In the end, when Victor returned, Sam continued, so that in the morning you would do a scene on one set with Victor Fleming, then complete it and go off to Sam Wood in the afternoon on another set while Victor went on shooting with another set of actors. It was an extraordinary experience but a unified force, of course, which David Selznick held together.

And there's a naughty thing I have to tell you, and that is the following: Sometimes just the same I would get uncertain about a scene, preparing it over the weekend, and I would call up George Cukor and ask if I could see him. And he would say, "Of course." So I went up to see him, and he would say, "Well, now, I think we should do it—I see her doing it this way." And I would say, "I understand. Yes, I see it," you know, and he would do one or two lines, and I'd say, "Oh, yes, now I know. Thank you very much." And then I would go ahead and play it that way. Well, I had to keep it a secret, you know, because it was the most unorthodox thing to be doing, but of course I felt sort of guilty toward Vivien. Then, when the film was over, I found out that Vivien was doing exactly the same thing.

WALTER PLUNKETT: I had to dress all the actresses who tested for the part of Scarlett. Norma Shearer made a test. Everybody made a test. Unknowns like Susan Hayward. Everybody. And I think Miriam Hopkins was strongly considered because she was actually a southern girl. The most important test was Paulette Goddard. Selznick really wanted Paulette to do it. But then there was a long letter signed by the Daughters of the Confederacy saying that it was well known that Paulette Goddard was living in sin with Charles Chaplin and no girl of the South, no daughter of the Confederacy, would do such a thing as that and they would boycott the film if Paulette Goddard did it. I know, because I was in the office at the time, that Paulette Goddard was told to come in for the contract but to bring her marriage license. She and Chaplin went to China, I think, the very next day and said they got married on the ship. Selznick thought she was the best bet at that time, before Vivien.

Some people say Katharine Hepburn made a test, but Katharine never did make a test. I know she talked about the part. I've heard a lot of reports saying that she was brokenhearted about not getting it, that she wanted very much to do it. I have never believed that, and I understand that recently on *The Dick Cavett Show* she talked about it. I had always remembered that she told Selznick that she didn't think she was right for it. I understood that she said her voice was pure Yankee and nothing you could do would make it right for a southern girl. However, she did say on the Cavett show that she had told Selznick that if at the last moment he had not found anybody and wanted to start shooting, she would try. Vivien was perfect, of course.

RIDGEWAY CALLOW: There was some talk at the time that Leslie Howard wasn't always prepared in his lines during *Gone with the Wind*, but that is not true. I've never known him not to have his lines. You know, Leslie Howard had a lot of trouble. His wife weighed about three hundred pounds. She didn't come with him from England, but he had a very lovely French "secretary" named Violette Cunnington who was with him all the time. She later was blown to pieces in an air raid in London during the war.

RAY RENNAHAN: Oh, there were so many problems on *GWTW*. You know, Thomas Mitchell, who played Scarlett's father, couldn't sit on a horse, couldn't ride a foot, and we had to practically lift him on and off, but we made him look like quite a horseman. It wasn't him that did the famous on-screen ride across the meadow . . . it was a stand-in. Everything that Mitchell did was done with close-ups of him getting on or off. For the rest of it, he couldn't ride as well as I could, and I can't ride at all, but he looked like a tremendous horseman in the shot. And we made Scarlett's eyes green. Vivien's eyes were blue. That was tricky. There's nothing you could do intensely on that, because if you threw any green on her face, it would change the whole color, so it just had to be handled very carefully. People who met Vivien later were often astonished to discover that her eyes were pale blue, not green. And, of course, another problem was that we ran out of money on *GWTW*. We had to stop production because Selznick was completely out of money. He was over budget, which was only originally in the low millions. And then MGM came in and took over the picture by putting up enough money to finish it. That's how they got more control of things . . . the whole control was theirs after that. But Selznick knew what he wanted and was not afraid to spend money. There were very few with his ability for making good pictures.

RIDGEWAY CALLOW: And he knew who to hire, like Menzies. They had these old exterior sets on the back lot of Selznick International that they had to tear down in order to build Atlanta and Tara. So Menzies conceived the idea to burn the old sets down with controlled fire. They put some false fronts up—very cheap false fronts—and set fire to it all, because when it's burning you don't know whether it's a western street or whether it's Atlanta or what it is.

WALTER PLUNKETT: One trouble for me as designer was that Margaret Mitchell described every dress Scarlett wore as being a green dress. Read the book. It was one green dress after another, with the exception of her black mourning things and the one red dress. It was always green. I was corresponding with Margaret at the time, and I wrote and said, "Dear, I'm doing a little editing of your book and Scarlett will wear a couple of other colors but green." She laughed about it. She never realized. She didn't set out in her mind to put Scarlett in green and didn't realize how often she had said it.

Clark Gable was sweet, and I liked him very much. We got on well except that he had an idea that he wanted Eddie Schmidt, his personal tailor in Beverly Hills, to make his clothes, and we had already arranged to have a studio costume tailor do them. Actually, the costume tailor was not as good a tailor, but I insisted that if we went to Eddie Schmidt that I be at every fitting and that Eddie Schmidt not push his modern ideas into it. I had to compromise. Eddie Schmidt wanted the great broad-padded shoulders of the 1930s period, and I had to fight with him on it. However, I did compromise and I did allow in some padding of the shoulders, and I'm very glad I did because it put Gable apart. It separated him from the appearance of the rest of the people, and this was right for the script.

Leslie Howard, you almost had to watch him to make sure he put his costume on that day. He hated the part, he hated being in it, he refused to learn his lines. He arrived on the set, and he said, "There's plenty of time for me to learn my lines while they're setting up the camera." He could deliberately walk into the camera with his coat unbuttoned, and the wardrobe man would have to rush in and make sure that it buttoned. He just was determined that he was going to walk through the part and give it nothing, which again was quite all right for the picture because Ashley was nothing, it didn't matter! All the accidental things came out as excellent.

Every Selznick picture was a tension-racked thing. Every morning on your desk would be this note from Selznick. Sometimes it would be absolutely insulting, it would be so rude, and at the top of the thing, it would say, "Copies to," and you read the list of the people who had copies. It was everybody from every other department. It would say, "What's the matter with Walter Plunkett that he can't design anything? The dress I saw on her yesterday was a hideous concoction, and very likely we're going to have to redo the whole sequence because of it. . . ."

I remember once that they did have to go to an earlier sequence with Scarlett after shooting for quite a long while, and Vivien was very tired and run-down. I don't think the dress mattered, but Selznick came on the set and bawled her out for looking tired and for the bags under her eyes. He said, "You're supposed to look like a young virgin in this sequence. Why don't you take care of yourself?" and yelling and screaming at her. In the meantime, because he was afraid of scandal, he had sent Larry Olivier off to New York to do a play so that Hollywood would never realize that the two of them were happily having an affair. Selznick was leaving, and he bawled her out. He got clear across the stage when Vivien yelled at him, "You know goddamn well what's wrong with me and why I'm looking the way I do. Just let Larry come back and give me a good lay, and my face will look all right again!" That shocked a few members of the crew.

ARTHUR KNIGHT: And in the end, for all the replacements, problems, chaos, *Gone with the Wind* became possibly the most famous movie ever made in Hollywood. And it won eight Academy Awards, including the first ever for a Black actor. Hattie McDaniel won Best Supporting Actress for her portrait of Mammy. Despite many modern objections to its portraits of slaves, *Gone with the Wind* is still shown regularly today.

BILLY WILDER: Well, we all have a lot of stories because we made a lot of movies. In the olden days, a studio like Paramount made forty pictures a year and Warner Bros. made, like, fifty, MGM made sixty, then there was RKO, then there was Universal. Now if a studio makes six pictures a year, this is a major thing. The men that now run the business are sitting, thinking, Shall we? Shall we not? Shall we put it in turnaround? Shall we go half and half with a group of financiers from Tunisia? Then, when you start shooting, they look over your shoulder.

PANDRO BERMAN: These corporation men are not the old storytelling studio heads of the past. They loved making pictures, and that's why a lot of people think those old films were better than the films we're getting now. On the other hand, there's the school of thought that thinks these films were all sentimental hogwash or hack jobs and that the motion picture of today is the really good motion picture, the ones today being based on the work of one writer, one director, or a combination of a director-writer. And there's no question that there's something to be said for both sides.

FRED ZINNEMANN: Well, back then, we directors were taught that we had the total obligation of pleasing the audience, and never mind how we felt about it. You will find a great many actors, some of the greatest today, you talk to any of the great English actors, Peggy Ashcroft, for instance, I asked her once—we were talking about the Method, you know, the acting Method—"Do you have to cry in order to make the audience cry? Do you have to feel the emotion at all to be able to get the audience to share it?" "Not at all," she said. "I feel it's my own private business. My job is to make the audience feel an emotion—that's my work, that's what I do. I don't have to cry to do it." Now, applying this to picture makers, some of us would feel that our vocation is to entertain the audience, to bring something to them that's worthwhile—in terms of an emotional experience, let's say. And others would say, "Well, to hell with the audience. I want to put on film what I feel, and if they don't like it, the hell with them." You know. It's probably perfectly valid, and it would be very interesting, because it's really the number one question of our time when it comes to artists.

MERVYN LEROY: You know what's wrong now with the studios? You take them a script that you feel is great, and they have twenty people read it to see whether they like it or not. Well, you can't please twenty people. You can't please eighteen of them. But that didn't happen in the old days.

You only had Irving Thalberg or Mr. Mayer or Mr. Warner or Mr. Selznick or Mr. Goldwyn or any of them. They would have maybe one reading with somebody. But you give a script to twenty people, you might as well forget it. You have to believe in yourself and fight for it! It's just like *The Wizard of Oz*. I mean, no one believed that it should have been made, and I mean *no one* at Metro, but I said, "*I* want to see it. I've wanted to see it since I was a kid."

There's only one thing that a filmmaker needs to realize: you don't photograph the money, you photograph the story. There's a lot of "geniuses" around in our business today who think you photograph the money.

CHAPTER 10

THE END OF THE SYSTEM

GEORGE CUKOR: The studios were amazing. They had to keep it all going. It's heroic, the work that they did. And the problems they faced and solved. It bores me when little nincompoops today say, "Oh, well, the studio system was nothing. What did they do at the studio that was worth anything?" Well, they did a hell of a lot. A hell of a lot.

JEANINE BASINGER: The studio system in Hollywood really *did* do a hell of a lot. No matter what problems arose, no matter what tensions, arguments, and mistakes or flops were made among the generally productive and positive studio set-up, Hollywood plowed ever onward. What a business! So we have to think about this: If the studio system worked so well and had so many talented people dedicated to it who could set aside their differences and egos to have a sense of fun, family, and flexibility— what happened? Why did the old system disappear? What killed it? Well, the seeds of its ultimate downfall were present right from the beginning, buried under the howling success and the excitement over the glamorous new art form that was also a business. The problems were built in, systemic, and ultimately came to the surface. By the midsixties, the old system was, for all practical purposes, gone with the wind. The problems included censorship, the formation of unions, the government forcing the studios to sell their theater chains and stop their practices of block booking . . .

SAM WASSON: . . . the House Un-American Activities Committee, the defections of stars after the de Havilland decision that disallowed suspensions of contracts, the threats of competition from both television and new material from international markets . . .

JEANINE BASINGER: . . . and the one that still, to this day, plagues the industry, the lack of inclusiveness and diversity. It was a lot . . .

SAM WASSON: . . . and taken together, it slowly changed the business from the old studio system into a new Hollywood that really had no organized system at all.

PANDRO BERMAN: One of Hollywood's earliest problems was censorship. It is looser now, but are films better? It was such an issue in the old days. Back when my father was involved, there were different state censor boards throughout the country. As you can imagine, the problems of *that* were enormous because every picture was reedited to suit the requirements of each individual censorship board.

RAY RENNAHAN: Censorship happened *after* the picture was made. The individual censors in the individual states had their own laws, and they were all so varied at the time. One scene could be shown as it was made in New York, say, but not in Massachusetts. Or neither state would show it, or both would alter the film but not in the same way. It was a hodgepodge of things. And, of course, in the business itself, any producer or production department did anything they wanted. They were their own masters.

HENRY BLANKE: You never recognized the picture you had made from one state to another. It was terrible. Studios became willing to cooperate so that the states would more or less leave a picture alone after it was finished and there could be uniformity for the picture you released across the country.

PANDRO BERMAN: The states, of course, were responding to the complaints of their citizens, their voters. The public raised a lot of mischief about some of the movies, so it was obvious *something* should be done. And the motion picture code came into being, first under [Motion Picture Producers and Distributors of America president] Will Hays and then later under Joe Breen.

JEANINE BASINGER: Under social and political pressure, the studios realized that rather than having to make movies that tried to cope with inconsistent state laws, they would be better off if they agreed to some sort of Motion Picture code they could live with. A set of guidelines had more or less been emerging from about 1922 onward . . .

SAM WASSON: . . . and a list of "dos" and "don'ts" had begun to emerge . . .

JEANINE BASINGER: . . . and the Motion Picture Producers and Distributors of America, under Will Hays, passed a list of "don'ts" and "be carefuls" on June 29, 1927, a form of censorship code. The studios officially adopted it on March 31, 1930.

SAM WASSON: It's sometimes just called "the Hays code."

JEANINE BASINGER: The studios adopted it, yes, but they "enforced" it to suit their own needs. It was self-regulation. One wag referred to this agreement by the studios to censor themselves as like "hiring Jack the Ripper to judge a beauty contest."

SAM WASSON: The "don'ts" included, among others, profanity, nudity, white slavery, miscegenation, and "willful offense to any nation, color or creed."

JEANINE BASINGER: The "be carefuls" left room for interpretation, because it was suggested that some topics be handled in "good taste." "Good taste" was a slippery area. It included "use of the flag, international relations, arson, the handling of firearms, brutality, and possible gruesomeness such as hanging, or a woman selling her virtue, rape, men and women in bed together, and the use of drugs."

SAM WASSON: It was also suggested that pictures should "be careful" about presenting the institution of marriage. This put arson, marriage, brutality, and firearms on a par.

JEANINE BASINGER: Pictures made from 1930 to 1934 are now known as "pre-code," which designates sound pictures made during the studios' loosely applied period of censorship. On June 13, 1934, a strict enforcement began, with the adoption of the Production Code Administration, an amendment to the original Code. During the period of 1934 to 1954, the Code was under Breen, the man Hays appointed to do the enforcing. The studios followed the Code to nearly the end of the 1950s, at which time its influence began to weaken, and in 1968 it was replaced by the MPAA film rating system.

PANDRO BERMAN: At first, because the studios were self-censoring, we began to get a period when there was a certain amount of freedom. Not freedom as there is today, but a little bit rougher treatment of some subjects, particularly at Warner Bros. and at MGM. Irving Thalberg got a little bit on the fast side with some of his lady stars, like Crawford and Garbo and Shearer, making pictures like *The Divorcee* and others. And Warner Bros. got pretty rough with their comedy. The studios got away with lenience from about 1930 to 1934, but then a tougher application of the Code came into play, and that was what we lived with for many, many years. In general, this Code authority worked extremely well, except it put a great hardship on those of us who wished to do anything realistic. It was fine for the studios. It kept them out of trouble, but the individuals who wanted to make a real story were handicapped because the basic concept of the Code really was that you must be punished for everything you did wrong. If a girl had an illegitimate child, there had to be a punishment for that. Or whatever happened. And as a result, you were very often frustrated!

MITCHELL LEISEN: Most of us never paid much attention to the Production Code.

GENE KELLY: You'd find a way to outwit them.

BILLY WILDER: There are times when I wish we still had it because the fun has gone out of it, the game that you played with them. We had to be clever. In order to say, "You son of a bitch," you had to say, "If you had a mother, she'd bark."

RAY RENNAHAN: We never saw censors while a film was being shot. They stayed pretty well in the background.

MITCHELL LEISEN: I guess I was the first one to openly challenge the tougher censor laws with *Murder at the Vanities*. The gals were really naked in that. I used the Earl Carroll girls, and they didn't mind. They had a few spangles and a bead in the middle of their navels, and that was about it. It was released in 1934, just before the Hays office brought out the new, tougher code.

We had this statue of Venus with the apple, and one bosom is bare. The stupid censor came out and said, "You've got to cover it up." I said, "Look, I am terribly afraid that I'm not going to mess with Praxiteles's best work. This is a classic, and, boy, it's going to stay that way. I'm not going to have any part of that." And then, just to tease him, I deliberately had the butler walk by and scratch a match on it. In *Murder at the Vanities*, the opening number with all the jewel boxes, the lid of the powder box opens, and reflected in the lid is this girl and she's about as naked as she could possibly be.

I. A. L. DIAMOND: I think nudity hurts laughs. I mean, if you're watching somebody's boobs, you're not listening to the dialogue. I don't think that any of the Lubitsch pictures or, say, *Philadelphia Story* would be any better or funnier if you saw Cary Grant and Katharine Hepburn in the nude.

BILLY WILDER: Hepburn? Big laugh.

CARL FOREMAN: As writers, we were driven crazy. Just for the fun of it, I always used to put some red herrings in my scripts, a little bit of misdirection, you know. I'd always write something like a scene where I'd say "Int: Kitchen—Day, Mabel, stark naked, comes into the kitchen and goes to the refrigerator." Back a letter would come: "You can't have that!" Then we'd have a big fight, and then finally I'd give it up very gracefully. *Finally* give it up, you see. Because I'd scared them, and they'd forget to look for anything else, we'd get to keep "Oh, hell" or something. Big deal we got to keep "Oh, hell."

ALLAN DWAN: I don't think censorship ever retarded anything. It stimulated us into inventing something that would get by.

GEORGE CUKOR: Here's how you got away with eroticism: the uncensored thought. Here's how you got past the censorship code: an audience *thinks* what you inspired them to think or picture in their minds. Actors—and directors—knew how to get an audience terribly excited, and it would be as sexy as anything they could imagine.

STANLEY KRAMER: In those days, film censors were a little different than they are now. They censored your *theme*. We could do certain things on film if there was also a parallel good which came from it—in other words, if the criminal got paid off in the end. If crime doesn't pay, you can show the criminal and his work. We always had that compensating virtue for every ill we could . . . and did . . . show. Which isn't too realistic, is it? But we could make it work.

HENRY BLANKE: More people should read the motion picture code of the 1930s and 1940s. In the old days, a lot of people got away with things [because it was open to interpretation]. Censorship was always a problem, but it was as the world changed after World War II that it became a business issue. Audiences wanted more realistic stories. And foreign films—with a more natural world—became competition.

RICHARD SCHICKEL: Censorship played out over time. History took care of it. Hollywood has always had a curious relationship with history. It was always dancing to a different beat, starting with the Depression, when at first it didn't feel the collapse the way other businesses did.

JOHN CROMWELL: The Depression ultimately *did* bring about an important change in Hollywood, however: the formation of the guilds [unionization].

RUDY BEHLMER: Studio employees in the 1930s had long, long hours, six-day weeks, little or no overtime pay. They would be coming home early in the morning after finishing late at night, et cetera. This applied to players as well as crew. There was a significant change immediately after the formation of the guilds in the whole structure of the business.

RIDGEWAY CALLOW: Yes, it came immediately. Conditions were better right away. The exploitation ended, and I have to thank the actors for a great deal of that. The Screen Actors Guild stipulated that the members wouldn't work Saturdays anymore, and if they did work Saturday, they got double time, which is quite a bit of money. If the studios had been reasonably fair, maybe there wouldn't have been any unions, but unionization cost the studios in profitability.

JOHN CROMWELL: Every department formed a guild, and unionization changed the working day of the studio system to a degree that was significant for salaries and hours put in by the average employee.

TEETE CARLE: The guilds were trade unions. Their first concern was to get better conditions. For instance, there was Sunday after Sunday that I would have to go to the railroad station to meet somebody arriving on the train. I'd have to leave my family, you know. And we would work nights. The Screen Publicists Guild was organized in 1937. I was a charter member, and those were the days—in 1937—when *all* the crafts were being organized. The actors, the cameramen, the electricians, the stage technicians, they had gotten organized as the A.F. of L. under IATSE [International Alliance of Theatrical Stage Employees] . . . but the writers weren't organized. The publicists weren't organized. The directors had no organization, no guild. The producers had, naturally, no guild.

JOHN CROMWELL: The formation of the Directors Guild was not a simple matter. It brought out the deep-seated convictions of a few who felt that it was undignified. They felt that creative people like directors had no place in organizations for protection. Led by Cecil B. DeMille, the die-hards tried in vain to stop the movement.

ROBERT ALDRICH: Ten directors got into a room in 1935 and said that the major companies were exploiting them and they thought they needed a collective bargaining instrument. They tried for the next four years to be recognized as a collective bargaining agent. They weren't until March 13, 1939.

GEORGE SEATON: The Directors Guild is not quite as volatile as some of the guilds, although they have accomplished great things. Now we have preparation time. Before, they just threw a script at a director and said, "You start shooting on Monday!" The poor guy didn't know where he was. Now there is a two-week preparation time. All the guilds meant a blow to the studio system, because guild negotiations always cost them more of their profits.

ROBERT ALDRICH: [The Directors Guild] was unsuccessful for many, many years, but now it exists for its members and it does protect them. It's really a legal blocking mechanism, a divide that has evolved over the years that has really guaranteed the director certain basic creative rights. Those creative rights have been improved every year so that nobody can touch the film until the director has finished his first cut.

PANDRO BERMAN: I think the first negotiations that I entered into as a representative of the producers with the representatives of the Directors Guild took place around 1937 or '8. The producers at no time demanded bargaining power or were anxious to get it, because they felt there was a certain justification in the ruling that made them part of management. However, they did manage to occasionally get a bone thrown to them in regard to negotiations with other guilds—which delayed somewhat the stripping of the producer in his authority. Needless to say, it didn't succeed in its purpose, and the industry changed in spite of the Producers Guild. Whether the producers were able to slow down the process to any degree is a question of doubt. By 1970, the directors had achieved what they wanted to achieve in 1950. The business was drastically changed both creatively and financially by the emergence of and strengthening of all the various guilds. The studios lost power . . . and profits. . . .

JOHN CROMWELL: . . . but when World War II arrived on December 7, 1941, and the entire industry focused on the war effort . . .

TEETE CARLE: . . . Hollywood had an all-out war effort. . . . We were all on committees, doing things. . . .

JOHN CROMWELL: . . . In fact, the great effort of the motion picture industry to the war was appreciated by the government, which used its facilities and its talents whenever possible in all kinds of ways.

TEETE CARLE: We directed all our efforts to trying to sell war bonds. People were in the auxiliary police and the air wardens and the Red Cross . . . all the guilds pitched in.

World War II was the golden era of motion pictures—I think the grosses were greater during World War II than ever, just unbelievable, they'd never been that way before. These were what caused the long runs—a picture like *Going My Way* played ten weeks or twelve weeks at the Paramount Theatre, and there was a backlog of pictures. Pictures could be two years getting onto the screen. And a lot of publicity would go out, and then the picture would go into limbo, into a hiatus period, and just lie there waiting to get into a theater.

During that hiatus, you didn't want people to get the idea it had already been released because they had read something about it a year before. They'd say, "Gee, that picture's been released, and I didn't see it." By the time [the picture was in the theater], your stars and your personnel are in Timbuktu or some are dead.

MITCHELL LEISEN: Instead of running two weeks, movies were running six months. They were piling up on us. Movies were such a popular form of entertainment. Cheap. Available. We did a fashion show at the end of one picture. After the picture was finished, I gave a party and had all the press and all the fashion editors, and we put the whole show on of all the clothes. Then the picture was held up for two years before they finally released it. I finally went in and started screaming bloody murder. "Look, this was high style when we did it. It will be old-fashioned by the time we get it out." The pompadour had already gone down. The whole hairstyle had changed.

SIDNEY SHELDON: During World War II, almost no picture lost money. People would go to see anything because they were so desperate for entertainment. There was a great curtailment of necessities. You couldn't get much gas. There was rationing. You couldn't drive. You really couldn't get entertained very easily, so all movies made money.

MITCHELL LEISEN: All kinds of little problems cropped up for the business [during the war], but we cooperated fully.

WALTER REISCH: We couldn't shoot any outside locations. It all had to be inside the studio. You couldn't even shoot outside [on the lot], because there was a curfew on lights in California then. No spotlights were permitted on the back lot.

FRANK CAPRA: There were restrictions on what you could spend for new materials and shortages of things you needed, and stars were gone to war. So old stuff was refurbished, old costumes were redesigned, and new stars were created.

HARRY WARREN: Directors like John Brahm had to be indoors by eight o'clock at night. He had to observe a curfew because he was a German citizen. They took him off a picture. The only reason they let him go—he was a good director—was because they had night shots to do and he couldn't work at night. He had to be indoors by eight.

MERVYN LEROY: Directors left town to make films for the government: Capra, George Stevens, John Huston, many others. Some of our best. Actors went into service: Jimmy Stewart, Clark Gable, Tyrone Power, Victor

Mature, Douglas Fairbanks, Jr., Wayne Morris, and others. I worked for Nelson Rockefeller making little films on how to put fires out and how to comb your hair nice for the army. I did everything that wasn't interesting, how to put the bombs out and all those things, how to keep the bathrooms clean. But we were doing it for a reason.

FRANK CAPRA: As I said before, I hated the army. Always hated having to answer to authority. But I was proud and happy to serve my country. Hollywood put everything on hold for World War II. Everything was more or less suspended. Popular old pictures were reissued to satisfy the demand, and almost anything was a success. And then it was over, and everyone came home to enjoy the victory and the prosperity that was waiting . . . and to face the problems that had not gone away and were also waiting. Or the new problems that were waiting . . .

OLIVIA DE HAVILLAND: Well, yes, there were problems for the studios. I had created one of them. I am the de Havilland of the legal de Havilland decision, which actually changed the course of the motion picture industry, certainly as regarding ownership of star contracts. You know, in the film industry at that time—back in the studio system—you just wanted to be honest with your work and do a piece of work that you could feel proud of so that you felt you deserved the money that you earned. And you wanted to be treated with respect. Some stars were fine with the fame and the money, of course, but some of us fought things. Like Bette [Davis] and Jimmy [Cagney] and, of course, me. I am the one who finally took it all on [after] Bette Davis went to London in the mid-1930s and tried to sue Warners over this issue.

BETTE DAVIS: Well, I lost it totally. But wouldn't you know it would take two women to break those studio men down? Olivia and I were sitting in the greenroom at Warners together not too many years ago, and we were thinking back to our days together there. We were remembering and looking at the place all those beautiful people had once been and so many had already gone, and she looked at me and said, "Wouldn't you know we'd both still be alive?"

OLIVIA DE HAVILLAND: For me it was an historic legal battle. Let's say it started back when I went to Jack Warner about *Gone with the Wind* and I said that I very much wanted to play Melanie. It would mean a great deal to me if he would lend me out. My contract was with Warners, you see, and I could make no decisions on my own. I was under contract to them, and Jack had never loaned me out before. And he said, "Well, you don't want to be in that picture. It's going to be the biggest bust in town." I said, "I don't care if it is the biggest bust in town, I want to be in the picture. Can't you lend me? Won't you lend me out?" "Well," he said, "you'll go out there and you'll come back, and you'll be *difficult*." And I said, "I won't be difficult, I promise you. I give you my word of honor that I won't be difficult." I remembered that promise later, of course, and look what he did to me *then*, that naughty man! Eventually, he loaned me out, but of course it was a business exchange that made that possible. David Selznick held a one-picture commitment with Jimmy Stewart for the services of Jimmy Stewart at Metro, and Jack wanted to use Jimmy for *No Time for Comedy* with Rosalind Russell. So in exchange for this one-picture commitment with Jimmy Stewart, Jack let me go over to David Selznick for *Gone with the Wind*. Now, the day I finished shooting in that film, Jack called me back. I had been in many films with Errol Flynn as his leading lady. Jack said he had cast me in *The Private Lives of Elizabeth and Essex*, but this time Bette Davis was Errol's leading lady, and I was Bette's lady-in-waiting. He put my name below the title. How do you like that? But he was provoking me. Do you see that? He was provoking me to break my word to him and be just what he said I would be, which was *difficult*.

He also let me know he had some other parts to assign me that were not good, and I thought, Well, I can't keep on doing it anymore when it involves this kind of penalization. So I took a suspension. And that was really something that people were frightened of in those days. A suspension was this: studios could suspend an employee's contract for the period of time it took to make any film that you refused to do and add it to the end of the contract. It could be two and a half months, however long. Then you went past that period of time to the end of the contract. There was a big difference between layoff and suspension. He didn't put me on layoff. Well, I took the suspension, and then he assigned me to [another film], which I knew was going to be a disaster, but he was now going to capitalize cheaply, really cheaply, off the success I had made of my part in *Gone with the Wind* instead of doing something responsible and intelligent with me in a good film of his own. I then took any number of suspensions.

I didn't see my contract ever ending with Jack Warner. At that moment, I met Martin Gang, a lawyer. He told me that there was a seven-year law, a law in California which forbade an employer from enforcing a contract against an employee for more than seven years. He said that in order to take advantage of it—I asked to read it, by the way—it was only two paragraphs long, I think—and it seemed to mean *calendar* years. You see, a year can mean many different things. The real question was, was it a year of work, you know, a year of labor? What did "year" mean? From reading the law, it seemed to me to mean a calendar year and it seemed to be quite clear, so he said that we would have to ask the court for a declaratory release, that is to say, an interpretation of that law as it applied to an actor's contract. And nobody had ever dared to do that before. He said, "You could lose in the first court, I have to warn you about that, because there is only a single judge who presides over the first court and Warners will try to influence the judge by saying that you are just a fractious, irresponsible, spoiled movie actress and you are willful and temperamental and just difficult—all from Jack's point of view." He said, "You could very well lose, but then in the appellate court there are three judges and nobody's put on a witness stand. There is no question of influence, the two lawyers file their briefs, and the judges consider the case from the point of view of pure law." And he said, "We could appeal to the Supreme Court."

Well, we went in to the superior court, that was November 5, 1943, and one of Warner's lawyers did put me on the witness stand, and he was very ferocious with me, and he kept saying, you know, "Isn't it true that you *refused* . . . ?" and he got terribly melodramatic and violent—he was something—and there I was on the witness stand, and he was trying to get a rise out of me, too, so that I would strike back and be temperamental, you know, and appear fractious. And the press, I must tell you, were very mean to me, and I couldn't understand it. After all, we were all union members, and I could understand a journalist sitting up there, and they tried to depict me as a small, vexatious movie actress. Oh, I was really upset when

I read the newspapers the next day. And somebody told me, "Don't be naive about it, don't you realize that those newspapers depend on Warner Bros. for advertising? You don't think they are going to present your side of the case favorably, do you?" I won the case, and Jack immediately appealed it and enjoined, I think, 150 studios, ten of which had been defunct for fifteen years. He enjoined them from employing me, and nobody did employ me, so then we went to the appellate court—that was September 10 of 1944, almost a year later, and it was just as he told me it would be, three judges and the lawyers filed their briefs, and I went—I just appeared at the back of the courtroom and listened to the argument. There was a little bit of fireworks then, and there was one judge—I thought, Oh, no, no way. He's not going to vote for me, I can see that! Well, he did. It was a unanimous decision. For me, it was thrilling. Jack appealed the case and enjoined every studio in town from employing me all over again.

During all this, going on two years nearly, I couldn't work at anything, not at anything. Well, wait a minute, radio, I think I did a few radio shows for *Lux Radio Theatre*, I think I did do that, yes. Finally, on February 3, 1945, the attorney called me and said that the Supreme Court of California had ruled that there wasn't any reason to review the case. Two favorable decisions in the appellate court—no more need. I won!

SIDNEY SHELDON: Remember. A lot of factors contributed to the decline of the motion picture business. But there were serious legal issues that went against the studios and affected their profit margins: the de Havilland decision and the antitrust decrees that forced the studios to sell their movie chains and stop their practice of block booking.

During the 1930s and through World War II, almost every studio had its own chain of theaters. Before a camera turned, those pictures were automatically booked into the whole chain. There was no television then, so that wasn't a competitive factor. Then the distributors got unhappy and said that the studios were forcing them to buy everything. If they wanted one good picture with Clark Gable, they had to take four bad ones from the studios. It was called block booking. They had to buy a package of five. If they didn't want to take the five, they couldn't get the Gable picture. Finally they filed an antitrust suit and won. Then television came in. The movie business got worse, lost customers, and the grosses started going down. The foreign market became a competitor instead of an automatic sale. It was a series of things.

SAM ARKOFF: At the beginning of the fifties, the television era really started in earnest. The older people, the middle-aged and older people, were moving out to the suburbs. They were sitting in before their television set all night instead of going to the movies. Now, you couple that with the fact that the motion picture companies had been reeling since the late forties, when the antitrust decrees forced the distribution and exhibition combines to split up. Before these antitrust decrees, a motion picture company—let's take Metro, which was owned by Loew's—was an exhibitor and a big chain. So Metro would make fifty pictures a year, and it would know that it was going to be able to sell fifty pictures before the season even started. That was block booking. If you wanted Metro pictures, you bought *all* of their pictures. You might have a right to cancel out one or two, but those MGM pictures would play in Loew's theaters. Warners pictures would play in Warners theaters. And this, of course, was the subject of the antitrust action. Now, the minute that the divorcement came around, they had to then sell each picture separately. Then the companies couldn't be sure that they could sell fifty pictures a year that they had a ready market for.

This was really an unfortunate situation for the studios, because it permitted many stars, of course, to set up their own companies, which has led to some degree, indirectly at least, to the current status, where the flies have taken over the flypaper. But, of course, it did more than that: it disbanded the training ground, because when a company was going to do fifty pictures a year, it could afford to start people in, for example, as apprentice editors, and then as editors and from editors conceivably to directing short subjects, because they made short subjects in those days, too, because they were filming a whole program, and so on. So this was the state in the fifties, and it looked okay on the surface. The studios were still in business, but the seeds of disaster were growing.

JEANINE BASINGER: Hollywood was hit hard by the case known as the Paramount Consent Decrees. It's probably the main factor that brought about the end of the old studio system, not television as most people tend to believe. It was an antitrust case brought against Paramount. Paramount was the primary defender because it was thought at that time to be the largest studio, but all the studios were involved and affected by it. Well, it was simple enough . . . the major film studios owned the theaters that they showed their movies in . . . and since they also made the pictures . . . and had all the creative personnel under contract . . . and owned the film processing labs and distributed into their own theaters, they were in monopolistic violation, in illegal trade practice. This case had been around since the late 1930s, about 1938, but it finally got to the Supreme Court in 1948. The Court decided against the studios, and they had to divest themselves of their theaters and stop block booking. It was the end of the original Hollywood studio business system, although, of course, Hollywood did not collapse overnight. It continued in production, and most people didn't know the difference.

FLOYD CROSBY: And then suddenly, in addition to everything else going on, there was this whole political thing, the witch hunt. It had started in '47. The first hearing that called all the Hollywood people was in '47. I was blacklisted from '47 to '54. I don't know when they made up this list. I just know, for instance, this sort of thing would happen. My agent would say, "I'm pretty sure I've got you a job at RKO on a picture." And then a couple of days later, he'd say, "Well, they say now they've got one of their contract men who is out of work and they're going to use him." Well, it wasn't that way at all. It was that they looked me up and saw I was on the list. I don't know when this list was [first] made of organizations that were considered subversive. I think it was a very cruel and unfair thing. I never became a party member, but I was interested. I used to go to some of the groups that were trying to find out about Communism. And because people were interested in finding out about another system, to blacklist them and not let them work was completely the action of reactionaries who had a big financial investment in this system, even though it was working badly. They were scared to death of anything else happening.

RANALD MACDOUGALL: The House Un-American Activities Committee was then chaired by J. Parnell Thomas, and it culminated some years later with the McCarthy era. J. Parnell Thomas ultimately went to the same prison occupied by some of the "Unfriendly Ten." Nowadays that whole era is called the McCarthy era, but I am being very explicit because it was divided into two parts, and the real fervent, sometimes hysterical, preoccupation with the politics of writers, real or imaginary, began, really, about 1946 and 1947 with J. Parnell Thomas and was continued later on in other areas by McCarthy, although the writing fraternity was not free of it during the interim. It didn't wax and wane, it simply started and grew and grew very onerous, as history shows.

CARL FOREMAN: I call those years the so-called McCarthy period because McCarthy himself was not involved in it. *His* committee was not involved in it. And, in fact, McCarthy really started afterward. Today we call it "McCarthy." We give that generic name to the whole thing. I think it's better just to say "the blacklist," period. It was the Un-American Activities Committee. What happened was, he saw how marvelous it was for headlines, that's all.

RANALD MACDOUGALL: I was a member of the board of the Screen Writers Guild. The Screen Writers Guild at that time really was made up only of screenwriters. During my time on the board we went into radio writing and began organizing, in a union sense, radio writers as well. Ultimately, television writing came in, but that was years later.

When I was on the Screen Writers board at that time I was quite well aware that there were Communist-oriented members in the guild. I think that in almost any organization there will be a fairly representative spectrum of political thought from the far left, if you will, to the far right. At any rate, Parnell's committee achieved the happy notion, or came to the happy conclusion, that they would get a lot of publicity by going after Hollywood, and I can't characterize it in any other way. It was blatant. You could get headlines by doing that, and they got the headlines, and they did it. And they started their intensive hearings, and it was very shortly apparent they had struck gold, because they were getting a lot more headlines than they should have had. And a lot of people—good intentions, some of them, bad intentions, others—went to Washington and made all sorts of testimony which led to the conclusion that the motion picture industry was absolutely a hotbed of Communism and filled with writers whose only purpose and intent in life was to breed Communist dogma, whatever the hell it might be on that particular day, to the screen and force it down the throats of the American public, thereby corrupting them, as though an idea could corrupt anybody.

And among many others, I was named before HUAC by a writer who is now deceased. I had never met him. I didn't know anything about this particular man at all. I hate to particularize on myself, but this is what we are talking about, but what I say with regard to myself applies much more stringently and in worse effect to many, many others. I didn't suffer as badly as many of them, but I am indicating that I did get hurt . . . I felt the indignation of it. It was overwhelming to me. So I wrote a letter and sent a telegram, pointing out to them that I wanted to testify, that I was not a Communist and never had been and so on and so forth, and I never got a reply. . . . They never called. They were not taking answers, they were only taking accusations. They weren't interested in answers. They were interested in accusations.

The result of all this was a blacklist, a mutual blacklist among the production companies, an agreement, if you will, that they would consult with each other and if someone were found to be persona non grata by some measuring scale *they* would devise, he or she would not be employed by any of them. That was the basis of the blacklist. Later on, not much more was known about it, very little. And no publicity, of course. It was a secret conspiracy, as such things had to be, and that started at that point. Time, of course, as it can be depended upon to do, went by, and the blacklist—it took many of us quite a while to realize that there was such a thing, that it was in operation, and that it had ramifications and dimensions that were completely unknown to us, but becoming huge—a lot of people who were on that list, the blacklist or the graylist, didn't even know it. They just knew that things were changing for them.

JOHN CROMWELL: This sad period of our history has been well documented. If one looks for some sort of explanation, it might be found in the sudden release from a concentrated discipline of nerves during the four-year war period.

CARL FOREMAN: From 1952, I found myself living in England as a result of the Hollywood blacklist, and I got by in one way or another and I was always looking, since I was surviving and so forth, and writing under assumed names, or whatever, to avoid the blacklist. Because the blacklist followed people everywhere, I felt inhibited about writing something original. That was one of the penalties of being blacklisted, at least as far as I was concerned.

Without exception, every blacklisted Hollywood writer went through a severe period, a period when he or she could not write. Now, some recovered from it, and some never did recover from it. There are guys and girls around today who have never been able to write anything past "Fade in" since that day. They're into something else now. It was very difficult. And I had it very bad. When I sat down to the typewriter, instead of writing "Fade in" or "Scene I" or whatever, I would find myself writing to the editor of the *Times* and saying, "Dear Sir, You know what they're doing to me?" You see, I was full of rage and anger and self-pity and whatever the shock was that we had all gone through. In any event, I was working on a screenplay, and it just was no good. I had a conference with this producer, very nice guy, very sympathetic, and he said to me, the gist of what he was talking about was the political situation was affecting my work, you see? And in a terribly well-meaning way he was saying to me, "Look, why don't you forget all this stuff? Why don't you make peace with those people over there? Do what they want you to do. Name a few names. Get yourself off the blacklist, and get that weight off your shoulder."

What he didn't know was about six months before, they had pulled my passport. And I wasn't telling that to anybody because there was no point in spreading this around. It was bad enough to have them do that, and I was suffering the consequences of that, which meant that I couldn't travel. When we parted that night and I went upstairs to bed, I literally didn't sleep all night long. I was awake constantly, and I was scared. I knew fear, real fear. And I hadn't written a good script, either.

RANALD MACDOUGALL: It's a shaming thing to have to justify one's own life. It's like being in a sewer.

CARL FOREMAN: Obviously it was unthinkable for me to be an informer. It was rigged anyway. The whole thing was a performance. The committee knew in advance who its cooperative witnesses were, and they had been well rehearsed prior to the appearance, and so it was just a question of going out and saying what they had been told to say. Whereas, on the other hand, if you didn't cooperate with the committee, the minute you said, "I refuse to answer," for whatever reason, your head was chopped off. You were just walked down to the guillotine, and you were finished.

ROBERT ALDRICH: I was invited to do a picture that was a nineteen-day marvel called *The Big League*. It brought Edward G. Robinson out of the graylist. Now, everybody knows what blacklisting is. Graylisting was when you may or you may not have been a Communist. You probably were, but you never had a card, you couldn't go in and say you were sorry. You couldn't say you were sorry for anything, because you didn't belong, but nobody would give you any jobs. It was more serious than blacklisting. The blacklisting, if you elected to, you could say, "I once was a Communist, and I'm sorry." Of course, those with more integrity said, "I'm not going to say anything." But a guy on the graylist never had a chance to say anything. Robinson was on the graylist because his wife was a Communist, and he wasn't. He couldn't get a job. Bert Allenberg, who was then president of William Morris, convinced Metro that he really should be employable. As an act of conscience, I guess, they gave him a job playing a baseball manager in this nineteen-day epic. Eddie Robinson is a marvelous actor and a brilliant man, but he is about as physically coordinated as a spastic. So I would sit back on the other side of the field with a ten-inch lens and photograph him in close-up. He thought we were doing the long shot, because if he knew, he would trip over himself. He would walk to first base and trip over home plate. It was a picture about the training camp of the New York Giants, and they opened it in Brooklyn, so you can imagine how good a picture it was.

HOWARD KOCH: I was one of the ones that Warners even protected [from the blacklist] for quite a long while, not for any personal reasons, but my pictures had made money. I mean, it was just like that.

ABRAHAM POLONSKY: The whole thing was a fraud from beginning to end. It didn't prove anything. It was just PR, because these were Hollywood names. I don't know important persons whose careers were ruined, anyone who was an informant. Do you? Who was valuable to the industry, I mean. Or had some value to the industry. Do you know of any? I don't know of one name who was an informer, who was ruined, who was of any use to the industry. I don't know of one. Not one.

When I got back [from testifying to HUAC], [producer] Sol Siegel said to me, "Well, work at home for a while. And see what happens." I worked at home, and almost every day, the *Hollywood Reporter* said, "How come Polonsky's still working?" So finally, Sol said, "They're putting too much pressure on us. We're going to have to let you go." So okay. That was the end of that, but they tried to keep me working. They gave me two weeks' salary. They were very nice. Fox acted very well. When they heard I was subpoenaed, they called me in and they said, "Look, why don't you just give them a few names and stay here?" But that wasn't because of political reasons. They just thought that would make it easier for everybody. They wanted me to stay, I suppose. After all, I had just done a hit picture for them.

RANALD MACDOUGALL: The natural inertia of a highly successful enterprise lulled the business for a long time. The motion pictures made money during the war years. They made an enormous amount of money [during the Depression and World War II] without too much planning or too much worrying or even too much decision-making. We would sit down and dream up something, and two or three days later I would be working on it and the project would be underway. After the war, there were suddenly other forms of entertainment available—readily available—and other problems and challenges emerged. The business had to pull itself together and start responding to a harder market situation. They looked for new stars, new ideas, new kinds of stories—to a degree. What they really started thinking about was new gimmicks . . . technology . . . that would draw customers into the theaters. After all, it had worked with sound . . .

RAY RENNAHAN: . . . and with color . . .

MITCHELL LEISEN: . . . and with all kinds of specially developed effects, like snow falling all over the place . . . we used untoasted corn flakes. They're very light and very white. And sometimes we used feathers, but they blew all over the place . . .

RAY RENNAHAN: . . . and then we got snow machines and tons and tons of ice, and they'd grind it and blow it all over the stage . . . and then we learned to manufacture a facsimile snow . . . and we sprayed it . . .

FRANK CAPRA: . . . and we shot in icehouses, and the cameras froze up and so did all of us . . .

JOHN SEITZ: Well, we developed wonderful effects, and audiences loved them. And after sound, color became the big thing, and audiences loved it. It was expensive, but it drew people, but when you shot a film in color in the early days, you had a lot to cope with. Natalie Kalmus was always given credit on those films as a Technicolor adviser, but that was just a formality. She wasn't there for the shooting. She was the wife of the owner of the Technicolor patent. It was a good job for her. Why not keep it? She hardly ever came on the set. Dr. Kalmus, her husband, was quite a guy—and quite a salesman. His continual cry was "We don't live in a black-and-white world!" We don't. And we don't live in a two-dimensional one, either.

RAY RENNAHAN: Natalie Kalmus was listed in everything that Technicolor made up to the time of her divorce from Dr. Kalmus, I think. Natalie was an employee, the same as I was, but she was the president's wife. She had nothing to do with lighting, only set dressing and color costumes. Not even on makeup. She had no real function.

NORMAN TAUROG: Those Technicolor people were sharp businesspeople. They made us use their own cameras. They had their own patent, their own everything. They had the world by the tail. We had to rent Technicolor cameras, and they only had so many. They couldn't make them fast enough. They cost around $30,000 or $40,000 each. You had to hire people who worked for Technicolor to shoot, too. They knew the Technicolor camera and had been trained on it. But you also had to use your own head cameraman and then one of *their* head cameramen. You could use your own operator or their operator, but you had to use their loader.

HOWARD SCHWARTZ: You had to have a commitment with Technicolor a year or two years in advance to get the cameras. They only had so many cameras. If you were doing a low-budget picture, then forget it.

RAY RENNAHAN: It's a detailed story. First there was the two-color camera, and those were hard to work with. We took them into the lab every night, and the machine shop worked on them to get them ready to shoot again the next day. But the three-color Technicolor camera was Mitchell manufactured, and they were precision cameras. If they were properly threaded up, there was no problem at all with the three-color.

NORMAN TAUROG: That goddamn thing would give you a hernia every time you moved it.

WILLIAM TUTTLE: We had to get a completely different system of makeup.

RAY RENNAHAN: . . . and you might have to change the color of a dress or repaint a wall or something or keep one department from putting a strong color in that would depart from a given scene.

GEORGE FOLSEY: And then you got Monopack, and then studios started developing their own color systems. Warnercolor is just Eastmancolor developed by Warner Bros. laboratory, as was Metrocolor developed by Metro's laboratory. In essence, it's all Eastmancolor and Eastman's formula unless you make some technical changes or handle it expertly and do it well or whatever.

ROBERT WISE: Color was still special and drawing customers after the war years, but it began to be commonplace, and other technical devices were looked for and used to stimulate the box office. Zanuck's idea was that CinemaScope was going to be a great time and money saver for films, but also a great moneymaker at the box office. I was at Warner Bros. preparing a film when he gave his first demonstration of it at Fox. Anybody who had worked at Fox was invited over to see this demonstration.

Zanuck had in mind to simply shoot everything right out in front. You had a three-page scene with five actors, and you'd stage it and your camera would be there, and that would be all. No coverage, no alternate angles, nothing. You'd just shoot the sequence and go on to the next one. He thought you could then make pictures in ten or twelve days. This demonstration was at a time when the impact of television on the box office began to be noticeably felt. Everybody was getting desperate to find something to combat TV with—not only what would draw people in, but "How are we going to get our costs down?" CinemaScope at first was a tool primarily intended to get the cost down, but it didn't work out that way.

MILTON KRASNER: I did *How the West Was Won* in Cinerama. It was another invention that was supposed to put the movies back on top.

GEORGE FOLSEY: CinemaScope was a fascinating format, very exciting, very interesting, and because it was big, big, and wide, it seemed a good challenge to TV. The business suddenly went—*Bingo!*—over into that direction. It was a technical problem and took a little getting accustomed to for us photographers. It took some thinking about how to frame and compose the picture and so on, but it had so many advantages, just the same as when sound first came in. 'Scope gave a bigger look to the whole thing. I think it was an exciting period and wonderful. It changed a lot of concepts.

VINCENT SHERMAN: In CinemaScope you had to cut a little bit differently. You had to sustain scenes a little bit longer. You couldn't have as many quick cuts. You also had to be careful about shooting one person against a light background if the other was against a dark one. We all suddenly were rethinking our shooting plans for new technology. Films got slower and started having longer running times.

JAMES WONG HOWE: CinemaScope is long and narrow, like a Band-Aid.

ROBERT WISE: It's lousy in terms of depth of field, and at first there was a problem with distortion in the faces.

RANALD MACDOUGALL: I think it was William Wyler who said that it was a marvelous way to photograph a snake. Or maybe it was Wyler who called it the mailbox, the letter box slot. I was trying to write for it. The difficulty I had with it, really, was no greater than anybody else was having with it. It was just one more idiocy in an effort to get people to go out to the movies instead of staying home to watch TV. The studios were falling behind. Things were changing. I must say, I was at Metro at that point, and it really seemed to me to be a dinosaur. It was really a dinosaur, sinking into the mud. I had the feeling they had been left behind by about forty years. We tried to make everything interesting.

HOWARD SCHWARTZ: One of the reasons that Fox came out with Cinema-Scope at that time, besides Zanuck's idea of shooting it like a stage play and saving money, was the fact that 3D was becoming a big thing. Everybody was thinking, Oh, this is it!

JAMES WONG HOWE: The industry needed something at that time to stimulate interest in film, like 3D. But CinemaScope killed 3D off. Fox had made this 'Scope picture, *The Robe*, to introduce the process. It cost them a lot of money, and 3D interfered with the box office of CinemaScope. Fox went out and advertised CinemaScope so strong . . . and the people who made 3D were a small independent company. They had these cheap glasses with paper frames, and they'd break and all that . . . that couldn't compete with Fox and 'Scope. I think if they had done it right and then pursued it further . . .

ARTHUR KNIGHT: The business scrambled. Technology was tried. Every effort was made to make movies new and important and competitive to offset the loss of block booking and theater ownership and stars going independent and all that.

CARL FOREMAN: And they started to vary and change the content to a degree. As the 1950s progressed, unthinkable issues started cropping up more in the stories: questions of race, sex, approaches to religion, and politics. It was a kind of revolution.

GEORGE SEATON: Well, you see, the audience had changed. For Hollywood movies, there was a problem. The GIs came back and went to school [on the GI Bill]. There was a postwar baby boom and a housing shortage and the atom bomb and the Cold War . . . and race riots . . . and women being pushed out of their wartime jobs.

RICHARD SCHICKEL: Hollywood was a big moneymaking industry, set in its ways. It was trying to keep its audience through new technology and trying to keep up with the times with movies like *Blackboard Jungle* and *Island in the Sun* and *Intruder in the Dust* and *Caged* and all kinds of things, but as liberal as it thought it was trying to be, it wasn't keeping up with the changing times. And it was failing to look at what a White man's business it had become.

BETTE DAVIS: In my era, it was a good period for women and women's films. One actor once complained to me by saying, "The only thing that the leading man in a film has to be sure of is that his haircut in the back is in perfect shape." He wasn't going to be facing the camera, you see. Yes, there were women's pictures for all those years. And it's now been men's films for many years. It changes with the world, doesn't it?

ELIA KAZAN: My wife, Barbara Loden, directed a terrific film, *Wanda*. She's now getting ready to make another picture on the same scale. Low budget, a crew of four, and it was all small and handmade and all made on real locations. I think she did a terrific job on that picture, and she's also one of the best actresses within her range in the country today, maybe the best in that range. But see, she makes *Wanda* and gets excellent notices, but it dies everywhere. Nobody goes to see it. She doesn't get any offers, and now she still hasn't gotten backing on this new picture that she's been promoting for a year and a half. She's running around scrounging this afternoon. Well, it makes you feel very bad. Something's wrong, and I don't know what to do about it. You are dealing in power here, and at the moment she's trying to get enough power together to make another picture.

KING VIDOR: I made *Hallelujah*, an all-Black film, in 1929 [for MGM]. Well, it was a big fight to do that picture. I didn't care whether it made any money or not. It was a thing I wanted to do. I wanted to dedicate it to a Black woman that I knew, who sort of raised my sister. That's the reason I did the film. It seemed like such a good idea to me, but it took about three years to get it done. I kept saying I wanted to make a film with all Blacks, and they kept turning me down. When sound came in, I thought, with the singing and dancing I planned, this will cinch it. Louis B. Mayer and Thalberg had been turning me down, so I went to Nicholas Schenck, who was actually the president of MGM, the head, the moneyman, and I talked to him about sound and told him the list of all the things we could have in the picture. He still refused. And finally I said—I was under contract, getting quite a large sum of money per picture—so I said, "I'm willing to put my salary into it alongside your dollars and not draw any salary," and that did it. When I said that, they said okay. They said, "We'll let you make a picture about whores if that's the way you feel." But really, my films made money, and I used to work on something to keep my box-office reputation up, and so they'd figure there would be money coming in, and then I'd take a big chance and they'd let me do something I wanted to do, like *Hallelujah*! It was one of those . . . and it was an all-Black film . . . there was plenty of talent to hire. I found Nina Mae McKinney in a musical show in New York. She was in the chorus, third from the end. We made some tests of her, and she showed up right away. There wasn't much argument about it. She had it, that's all. She really had it. And for the male lead, we got Dan Haynes, who was the understudy in *Show Boat*.

But I never thought no one else would not be making Black stories or using Black actors in important roles for decades in Hollywood.

SIDNEY POITIER: When I first walked on the 20th Century–Fox lot, the only other Black person there was the shoeshine boy. I worked at Columbia Pictures when there wasn't another Black person to be seen. Today it's different. I'm a believer in history, and where you are sitting now would have been paradise for those who went before us. In the early days there was a man named Oscar Micheaux, a Black moviemaker at a time when it's impossible to conceive of there having been a Black moviemaker. He did not ask permission for what to make. He did not get a collective democratic point of view on what he should do. He made his pictures, and you know what he did? He put them in the back of a car and traveled the country. If there's anything useful that I can tell today's young filmmakers, it's that story. That's what you have to do. Not necessarily put your films in the back of your car, but you have to be true to your own vision and make those pictures that you want to make.

PAUL MAZURSKY: You know, I was in *Blackboard Jungle* with Sidney in 1954. And the cast all stayed at the motel in Culver City, and Sidney had to stay at a hotel on Adams, because he couldn't stay at our hotel. He'll tell you it's changed, but it's still terrible. It's changed a little bit, but it's still terrible. It won't change by magic. You know, it's like digging a hole. You toss the dirt out. Just when you think you've tossed it all, more comes sliding back in. You've got to dig faster and faster.

ANTHONY QUINN: People ask me how I prepared to play the role of a Mexican in *The Children of Sanchez*. Well, in the first place, I'm Mexican.

I have tremendous source material within me. I lived it. I lived in a barrio, I lived in the *vecindad*, and I've known the Sanchez family—I mean, not the book family, although I met them, but I mean, I've known them all over my community. I knew them in Mexico, I knew them in Juárez, I knew them in El Paso. I lived in a community very much like this in El Paso and then in San Antonio. I was brought up in the east side of Los Angeles, and that's a kind of *vecindad* in a larger way, but all these questions were strange to me. But then I was reminded that I've made over 120 Hollywood movies, and I've played everything from Native Americans to Greeks to rajahs and Samoans and anything that people thought looked dark skinned. Hollywood had a habit of casting white people as Asians and Jeanne Crain as Pinky.

DIAHANN CARROLL: I think you have to operate on a double standard when you're a Black actress. I believe it's absolutely necessary for you to understand that the industry is not yet dealing with me as an actress. This will be, I hope, the beginning of all Black actresses and actors thought of as *people*. I think it's a bigger adjustment from the point of view of the audience than it is for me. I just don't think people think of me as having come out of a community with a welfare family around the corner. As I said the other day, I think most people think I was born in a wealthy White home and raised in Beverly Hills. But that's not true. I was born in New York in a section called Harlem, which my mother reluctantly calls Harlem. She calls it something else, like "upper Manhattan."

RANALD MACDOUGALL: In 1956, I wrote what was supposed to be a liberal new approach in movies, *Island in the Sun*, to star Harry Belafonte, a Black man, as a romantic lead. But did we really break through with anything? Was Hollywood and the White world ready to change and go forward? I said, "He's a great singer. I've admired him in concert, and I don't know if he can act his way out of a paper bag. . . . He's never done a dramatic picture before." And I said, "But there's one all-essential risk here, and the answer to the question I'm about to ask you really is the answer to the film." I said, "Can he kiss the girl?" Well, at that point Sol [Siegel] picked up his sunglasses off the desk and put them on. You know, I had worked with Sol many, many years, and I knew that when he was going to not tell you anything directly, he would hide his eyes from you one way or another, either by looking out the window or, in this case, putting on his sunglasses. I should have taken more heed, because he said, "Well, you'll have to write it as you feel it, and then we'll see what develops." I said, "Sol, that's the problem of the picture. You cannot do this picture honestly unless he has a full relationship with that girl, and it's a White girl, and it's a White man who comes into it." And I said, "The contest is then rather more meaningful than simply two men fighting for the woman." I said, "All that flows from that is impaled in the answer to that question. If he can kiss the girl, I will do the picture, with all the risks involved." And he said, "Well, you have to do it your way." I said, "Okay." And I went to work on it, and, you know, that question was not answered. It was evaded. Nobody was really ready for an honest change.

DIAHANN CARROLL: There was a period in which some [studio] movies were made that were supposed to be about Black people. *Hurry Sundown*! I adore Otto Preminger, the director, as a social human being. He has a great sense of humor. And he's a fantastic host, and he's a really groovy man. I mean, if you go to his home to have dinner, you're going to have a great time. Okay. But those movies—*Carmen Jones* and *Porgy and Bess* and *Hurry Sundown* are not Black movies. Otto is from Austria. I mean, Otto is *really* from Austria. I was in *Carmen Jones*, which takes place in the South, written by a White man. *Carmen Jones* made money. Dorothy Dandridge was alive and extremely beautiful. They gathered together an array of Black stars, Belafonte, Dandridge, and I think Brock Peters. It was just a wonderful little group of us there. And none of us really wanted to make the film, to tell the truth. But we all wanted to be in moving pictures, so we made it. We found things hadn't changed a great deal for us. Then they called around again and said, "Guess what, gang? You've got another chance. We're going to do *Porgy and Bess*. And we're going to give Otto another chance, too." So we all got excited again, because we were going to Hollywood and we were going to make another moving picture. And we all came out and made fools of ourselves again. And we made this thing called *Porgy and Bess*. And *Hurry Sundown*? I don't even know what to say about *Hurry Sundown*. What I know is that there's been a long, long time in Hollywood where equity hasn't happened. Maybe it will. Maybe.

JOHN BRAHM: Filmmaking during the fifties in Hollywood was the time when everything went to pieces. All the problems came to the surface.

GEORGE CUKOR: You know, there's an awful lot of crap written, this literature about Hollywood in the past, that people want to know, and for the most part, I think it's a waste of time. They're all stories, and I know. I've read certain books—books written about Katharine Hepburn—they ought to shoot the man who wrote it, because he didn't know anything about it, and I think it's just a moneymaking scheme and a lot of them are stupid and detestable.

We all look back and remember the old days. Today it's different. You can't just telephone and have the foreign department send this up and clear all the rights to this and get all this and get it over here. You're all on your own, which is, in a sense, a very good thing, but it's a different kind of thing. One was pampered back then, and now you haven't got everything at your fingertips and you have to fend for yourself. Some of that can be very stimulating, but I tell you what is sad. There were the most wonderful, wonderful technicians here in the studios, wonderful. They had seventy-five years of absolute technical perfection. Well, these people have retired and died. I'm sure there are all kinds of new ones, but the old guys were of a dazzling brilliance. They were just great. And also they had something in their spirit which was wonderful. They had a stake in the picture. They wanted the picture to be right, and they were with you all the time. The studio technicians were dazzling and wonderful men, wonderful men. And they're gone. That's the sad thing.

BILLY WILDER: Oh, yes, Hollywood is totally different now. Totally different. When I was making pictures like *Sunset Boulevard*, which was, after all, about Hollywood, in those days there were designated, well-known, and advertised enemies. Or fortresses to take. Warner Bros. Paramount. MGM. Harry Cohn. Louis B. Mayer. Darryl Zanuck. Today you'd never know which studio is still going to be there next Monday or who's going to be the head of what studio. Whose ass are you to lick that is not going to be there? How can you wage a war against Coca-Cola? It's a whole different game.

It was a whole different spirit, it was a whole different kind of competition. We all *talked* together about movies. We talked about "What are you doing? What's the picture about? What's the scene? What are you going to have in it?" Now they talk about "What kind of a deal did you get? What kind of a percentage? Is it on the gross? Is it in turnaround? Is it a set deal? Is it negative pickup?" All of those things. We never heard of those things before. We just made movies.

SIDNEY FRANKLIN: You felt you were offering something to the world and it was going to help people, do some good for people or something. You didn't make it just for the sake of making a picture and getting a salary and for the money and all, you made it because you also thought that you were going to do some good. Now I think pictures are mostly made just for money. They were always made for money, don't misunderstand me, but I myself—as long as you're talking to me—I made pictures a great deal of the time knowing or thinking they were going to help the audience, not just entertain them.

BILLY WILDER: The community that was Hollywood is gone. Now, if you want to make your picture, you write it at home. You rent some stages someplace, you shoot, and a week later, you walk out of it. It's like going to the Ramada Inn. You don't live in the studio anymore. There's nothing.

ALLAN DWAN: You don't see anybody. You can go for years out here now and see nobody that you know. None of the old crowd, you know. They're busy over in that part of town, and you're busy in this part of town. Socially everything's busted up. They're all in little cliques now. And if you don't happen to run socially or care about socially going out—I don't like mixing. I don't like it at all. I'm a loner.

PAUL IVANO: Our days are gone, but those were the pioneer days of the motion picture industry.

JOHN CROMWELL: Our days were the early days of the greatest profession in this country, the greatest profession that this country has ever known. The one form of entertainment that most people could afford was the movies. And no matter what, the business went on. It's a resilient business.

JEANINE BASINGER: In fact, it's still going on—but there *is* a big divide between the old Hollywood—the studio system years that lasted up until about 1960—and the so-called New Hollywood that started in about 1970. In between, from 1960 to 1970, there's a limbo period in which both systems are rattling around. One is dying, and one is trying to be born. The studio buildings remained. The names on them remained. But what went on inside them . . .

CHAPTER 11

IDENTITY CRISIS

SAM WASSON: People in old Hollywood always talked about "the movies"—that was the business they were all in, making the movies. After 1960 the conversation began to change. They talked about "a movie," as they struggled to get one made. There was now the question of power. Where once it rested entirely and unquestionably with the studios—with the production chiefs at the top of the industry—power in the burgeoning Hollywood began to shift.

MICHAEL OVITZ: It started happening in the late fifties and early sixties.

JEANINE BASINGER: The first generation of studio heads was disappearing. Louis B. Mayer died in 1957 and Harry Cohn a year later. Paramount's Adolph Zukor was already eighty-seven years old in 1960 and Darryl F. Zanuck left Fox in 1956 to become an independent producer in France.

PHILLIP DUNNE: Zanuck started telling me how much money [producer] Frank Ross had made and kept on *The Robe*. Because he got a capital gain on the whole thing, because he'd developed the project and sold it. And Zanuck had figured out that on this one picture Frank had made and kept as much money as Zanuck had made and kept in ten years. Made and kept is the thing. He said, "Well, I'm in the wrong business." I had always had the feeling he resented this very much, and was beginning to feel trapped. And I think he was tired. He never would admit it, and he would never look it. But I think he was just kind of tired. I think at the rate he had gone, he had to burn himself out sometime. Creatively, he had to burn out. You would notice it in the meetings. He'd begin to lose a little bit of that enthusiasm. There were doubts. There were moments that you would go in and sit there in silence for long periods. You know, he just wasn't sparking. I think he was frankly just bored with the whole thing and getting a little bit tired and not able to drive himself as he had in the beginning. You see, he was very, very young when he started. He was now old, middle age was creeping up. And so the genius of the studio, and I'm using it in its old sense, was dim now. Suddenly political things were given priority. These were always the first things that were brought up, you know. They'd read a script, and you'd go in for a conference, and instead of talking about the story, they'd say, "Can we get into any legal trouble over this?" That was the emphasis. This knocks you down.

MICHAEL OVITZ: Buddy Adler replaced Zanuck . . .

NUNNALLY JOHNSON: Buddy Adler . . . I'm afraid that was like working with nobody . . .

I called Buddy, and I said, "I'd like to see you about one of your [script] notes, which is rather important." I went up to his office, and I said, "You say here in the notes that the fellow shouldn't have thrown the girl out. I've read this over, and I don't see any hint that he was throwing her out. On the contrary, he was begging her to remain with him and wanted her to stay with him." He said, "Well, that was my understanding of it." I said, "All right, let me read this to you. Let me read the speech that you're talking about." He said, "All right." I read the speech, a speech about that long, and I said, "Is there anything in there about him throwing the girl out?" He said, "No." "Well, actually," he said, "I never read those long speeches." Now, this was the head of the studio. He didn't have to read any of them if he didn't want to. It's perfectly possible to turn it over to somebody else who is better qualified. Christ, Harry Cohn did. You can't think for one second that Jack Warner read all these scripts or anything like that, but they at least turned the script over to somebody who's qualified to pass judgment or to recommend to him whether it should be done.

PHILLIP DUNNE: It was 1959 and 1960. I went to see Dick Zanuck [Darryl's son]. I remember, it now comes back to me, I went to see Dick, and I said, "Does your father know what's going on here?"

NUNNALLY JOHNSON: After Buddy, I think Bob Goldstein became head of the studio.

PHILLIP DUNNE: Goldstein issued a dictum that all pictures should have shooting schedules of either twenty-one or thirty-five days. This is like saying everyone's got to wear a number 8 or a number 10 shoe.

NUNNALLY JOHNSON: In 1962, I was doing *Mr. Hobbs Takes a Vacation*, and Goldstein called me up in London and wanted me to do *Cleopatra*. I said, "I don't think that I'm the man for that. Somebody else has already started on it." There'd been two or three scripts. I said, "I'm already at work on a script." But there was great pressure involved in *Cleopatra*. At that time Walter Wanger was the producer and Rouben Mamoulian was the director, and Goldstein insisted that I should drop the other thing and go to work on *Cleopatra*. Now, they'd already spent about a million dollars on sets in England which they couldn't use. I said I'd have a go at it if they were serious about it. Anyway, I went down to the Dominion Theatre one night, which was the only film theater in London that had Todd-AO, with Wanger to look at the stuff Mamoulian had done. When I finished looking at it, I told Wanger, "I don't think this fellow is ever going to shoot this picture." He said, "Why not?" I said, "He's testing fabrics. A man is really desperate when he begins testing fabrics. He's afraid to come to bat." I told Walter, "I'll bet you a pound, just a pound, that he never starts it." About a month later, I got an envelope from Walter. It just contained a pound note. That's the way I heard that Mamoulian was off the picture. That's when they brought in Joe Mankiewicz, and that's where they dropped me.

SAM WASSON: The ongoing debacle of *Cleopatra*—shut down in England when Elizabeth Taylor fell ill only to change directors (Mamoulian to Mankiewicz) and resume in Italy to frantic rewrites and further crises—baffled everyone. Huge stars, top writers and directors, and a cast-of-thousands production—for years, this had been a Hollywood specialty. What had changed?

PHILLIP DUNNE: Elizabeth Taylor was always the number one problem, headache. When they got the five thousand extras lined up, they didn't have her. She was taking the day off.

RANALD MACDOUGALL: At any rate, it was a wild, mad time. By now the studio, which is very nearly deserted by that time . . .

SAM WASSON: . . . layoffs, liquidations, like an emergency garage sale . . .

RANALD MACDOUGALL: They were pouring resources into *Cleopatra*, and they were closing down—they only had one gate open and all that sort of thing, and people were leaving in droves. There were very few people left except myself and Wanger and Molly, Zanuck's secretary. I think Molly understood quicker what was happening more than anybody else.

PHILLIP DUNNE: Joe Mankiewicz, who is an extremely talented picture maker who needs a producer, was totally on his own, was carrying a burden no man should carry: he was trying to write at night and shoot during the daytime. Joe was a wreck, but it was partly of his own making, because he had insisted on all these radical changes that only he could carry out and he didn't take the time to do them. They were trying to expedite the unexpeditable.

RANALD MACDOUGALL: Of course, you know, all of the things you have ever heard about the picture in terms of cost were all true—all true, and more, probably, than has ever been admitted. . . . In any case, that is the situation in which I found them, and Mankiewicz had gone dry as a writer. . . . I went out to the studio, and I saw the five hours of cut film they had, and it was as turgid a piece as you can possibly imagine. The scenes went on for twenty pages, you know, the obligatory scenes. The ones that were connectives, he had enlarged into philosophical discourse. He had also fallen into many traps of the pure inventor, as opposed to the fellow who goes to the facts: he invented things. He had a scene where the dancing girls came out of the water and everybody was horrified because there was violence of some kind, and I pointed out to him that, at that time in history, women and men did not mingle like at a cocktail party in Beverly Hills.

PHILLIP DUNNE: And then, of course, when Zanuck came back and applied the cure, the cure was to spend another $5 million. There's Zanuck's boldness, *toujours l'audace*. He came back, and—he was right. The only way to save it was to pour money into it.

The bad thing was, of course, the old saying "Is it on the screen?" And half of that $37 million, or whatever it was, is not on the screen. It was false starts and paying off actors and paying off directors and sets that were never used. What they've got on the screen is not a $37 million picture but a $15 million picture.

SHERRILL CORWIN: No exhibitor ever asks how much a picture cost to make. No exhibitor! He couldn't care less. Does it sell *tickets*?

MICHAEL OVITZ: It was feast or famine at Fox. *Cleopatra* is a disaster but *The Sound of Music*—another massively expensive production—is an enormous, enormous hit.

SAM WASSON: But the equally massive *Star!*—a musical re-teaming of *The Sound of Music*'s Julie Andrews and director Robert Wise—was an enormous flop.

GORDON STULBERG: You take *Star!*, and you put Julie Andrews together with Bobby Wise and a musical, and you have to say, going in, you've got to have a winner. But people wouldn't recommend it if they saw it. The word of mouth on the picture was dreadful.

ROGER CORMAN: The majors were putting too much faith in what *Sound of Music* did.

MARTIN SCORSESE: The mega-flops were coming in.

JOSEPH E. LEVINE: In 1966, we made five family pictures. Even my own family didn't go and see them!

JEANINE BASINGER: It was hard to see what was actually happening. All the issues of block booking and theater ownership and the things that brought the old system down had happened, but Hollywood still had gigantic old-fashioned hit movies going on in the 1960s: *West Side Story*, *The Sound of Music*, *The Longest Day*. They diverted attention from warning signs, disasters like *Cleopatra* and *Star!*

JULIA PHILLIPS: When I first started in the movie business at Paramount, what they were releasing that year was *The Molly Maguires* for $22 million that nobody went to see, *The Brotherhood* for $10 million that no one went to see, *Paint Your Wagon* for $22 million with Lee Marvin singing. They had been sitting on *Darling Lili* for two years, and they decided that it had been such a bad year, they figured, "What the hell. This is the year for it."

DAVID BROWN: *Hello, Dolly!* as a stage show had done $40 million box-office gross in the United States. When we previewed the film in Phoenix, we had a sparse turnout. We had tremendous internal showings among the executives. We were all hugging each other at those. Once again, we had saved Fox. And everybody was certain that this was going to be our *Sound of Music*. The picture was great. Barbra Streisand. Walter Matthau. It worked beautifully. Well, we took it to Phoenix. To our astonishment, despite having announcements on the air that *Hello, Dolly!* was to be shown, there was half a house there. We became desperate. Richard [Zanuck] and I both took various highways that were leading to this shopping area and stopped cars and said, "Wait a minute, *Hello, Dolly!* is playing." Then we got on the public address system, and we were begging people to come to the theater. We should've known then we were in trouble.

BARBRA STREISAND: I had no interest in playing *Hello, Dolly!* I don't know how it happened, even. Some people's publicity runs away. Sometimes somebody will say, "Well, she's going to play *Hello, Dolly!*" It was like a jolt to me. At that time I really didn't know why I did it. It was like somebody announced me for it, and all of a sudden—I forget why I did it. It was a mistake, though, because I remember my first meeting with Gene Kelly. I said, "Well, what is your concept? I mean, how are you going to do it? Are you going to shoot through lace, or is it going to be Victorian?" And he just looked at me. I don't know. I hated that movie.

MICHAEL OVITZ: *Hello, Dolly!* was a huge disaster. I mean, it cost $25 million. That would be like three or four hundred million bucks today. I mean, it almost sank the company. The reaction to that was swift and pioneered by Ned Tanen at Universal: he went antithetical to everyone else. He put together a whole series of low-budget movies. They were all done on $1 million budgets.

The business didn't know what it was anymore.

A.D. MURPHY: If somebody hits with a certain type of film, then everyone wants to make one on the not unlikely assumption that "Oh, I guess a lot of people out there are interested in seeing this." So everybody will make them. And the public will go to see it, until the public stops going to see it. But one thing that doesn't change is that the top ten films at any one time do half of the available business and all the rest are fighting for the other half. That is always true. The public gravitates toward the hits. The hits are like magnets.

MICHAEL OVITZ: The film business is bifurcated in two directional movements. One is when the film business is ahead of its time from a standpoint of predicting things and the other is when the film business is reactive to itself. In other words, when a film comes out and gains acceptance, it stimulates, albeit two years after inception, a whole round of films like it.

PHILLIP DUNNE: We can look now and say, "This was really the time of Commodus or something, the Roman Empire had begun to fall." Not only the old studio falling apart, but the whole motion picture business as it had been was falling apart at the same time. . . . So all we saw was a stupid man in the front office [Spyros Skouras] and ridiculous scheduling, but maybe these are just symptomatic of the great disease of what was destroying Hollywood.

NUNNALLY JOHNSON: Skouras didn't want to make *The Diary of Anne Frank*. George Stevens told me that he said, "I don't think we ought to make this picture." George said, "Why not?" He said, "It's anti-Semitic." George said something like "Whoever said a thing like that?" He said, "Bernie Gimbel told me." I thought, My God, who's making the pictures now, department store owners?

PHILLIP DUNNE: Zanuck was succeeded by an inadequate man and then by a disaster. So you couldn't hold the studio together. It was impossible. Then there were signs all around. They sold off all this real estate, and Skouras gave it to Alcoa.

MICHAEL OVITZ: That's Century City. I came to Fox right after that.

PHILLIP DUNNE: The Century City thing was a giveaway to get money to pay off the stockholders. That was basically the idea, so they could declare a dividend. Well, this is selling your birthright for a mess of pottage. The best real estate in town was given away so it would continue to look like a profitable organization. But it happened all over. Metro went under at the same time. Perhaps it started even earlier, with the death of Thalberg . . . Warners in some sense survived because Jack Warner, for all his faults, had certain administrative talents. He could hold it together. And Universal got a little bit ahead of the game and jumped into major television production first of all, and so did Columbia before the other big studios got into it. And that's basically what Universal is now, it's a television studio. They try to keep the picture thing going, because that's the prestige, but it doesn't amount to much.

SAM WASSON: And with fewer movies being made and made more expensively, it was often more convenient for studios to distribute films made outside the system—films made by independent filmmakers.

JOHN CASSAVETES: So I got a place. And I said, "I know all these producers now and casting agents and people in the business, directors and writers." So I took a loft in New York on 48th Street and invited all my friends to come, and I said, "Look, just put on your shows and I'll force them to come down here. I'll grab them down here." And then no one showed up. So I had this place for a year. I took an ad in the paper and invited anyone to come in and act, because I didn't want to just let it go to waste. It was a beautiful stage and a place to work, and no one wanted to do it.

So the next day, maybe a hundred people came in off the streets: cops and pickpockets and college kids and I don't know what, guys from the sanitation department, you know. They all said, "I'll be an actor!" I started work on the stage with these people. So we started working on improvisation and integrating it with the written word. We'd take a script, a formal script or a classic, and then I'd send people up on the stage. So that's the way it got started. I made this film called *Edge of the City*, and this guy Jean Shepherd had a radio program called *The Night People*, and I went on Jean's show, and I said, "Wouldn't it be terrific if just people could make movies, instead of all these Hollywood bigwigs who are only interested in business and how much the picture was going to gross and everything?" The next day, $52,000 in dollar bills came in. Not only that. Shirley Clarke, who was working in those days as one of the few independent filmmakers, had the only equipment in town, so she brought it down and said, "Go ahead, take it. I'm not doing anything for six months. Take the equipment." So when it was finished, we didn't have enough money to print the sound. It was improvised, the whole picture was improvised. There was no dialogue, so every take was different. So we looked at it and said, "What the hell are we going to print here? I don't know what they're saying!"

So we got lip readers. They read everything, and it took us about a year. We had a wonderful time, though. We knew a liquor store down the street, we were drunk all the time, happy. It was a happy experience.

Over a period of three years we worked on this film, *Shadows*. And none of us knew what to do. I mean, we didn't know anything about film-making at all.

A. D. MURPHY: The question comes out, "Why don't theaters play some good independently made films?" The answer is that every truly independent producer, let's say Samuel Goldwyn, David Selznick, somebody who really can raise his own money, he can't keep a theater alive fifty-two weeks a year. So the exhibitor, naturally, looks to people who will have something next week and next month and next year. It is not anything malicious against somebody who has a good film.

SHERRILL CORWIN: There are just the physical problems: getting your prints distributed and inspected, keeping orderly bookings. It really is quite impossible. Cassavetes just takes his pictures and gets on the telephone and calls up exhibitors all over the country and he books them.

JOHN CASSAVETES: A couple of press agents were [at an early screening of *Shadows*], and they said, "We want to handle this picture." They were guys who were just, like, off the street. They said, "We're press agents, we charge twenty-five percent." So I said, "Twenty-five percent of what? Let's look at the picture." So we all looked at the picture. The first ten feet came, it was all shot in 16[mm], it was three years, and it was brittle. And within two seconds, the film ripped, and it just ripped for the next twenty-five minutes. And we'd go back and patch it. So [United Artists executive] Max Youngstein left, and he called me after about four hours, and he said, "Look, I don't care what the picture's like. You're in such trouble with this movie that there's only one thing to do. I'll give you five thousand dollars and get you off the hook, we'll bury the picture and forget about it. I can write it off for the company." He said, "Please, take it, that's all you'll ever get for it."

So we said, "Aw, I don't know, Max. Jesus, it's nice of you to offer, but we have [been working] three years! If I started dividing five thousand dollars amongst all of us, it's three hundred or four hundred dollars, and it really doesn't seem worth it to sell it for that. I'd rather keep it on the shelf." And at that screening was a guy named Albert Johnson. He ran the San Francisco [International Film] Festival. And he wrote for *Film Quarterly*. I never had heard of it. So he wrote a review on it, and it was a terrific review. But a year went by, and I was broke, out of work, and I couldn't get a job as an actor, and nothing was going well. So I went out in the daytime and went to bars and played football and did anything that I could do, and I got a phone call. And my wife was seven months pregnant, nine months pregnant at that time. And I went to Europe and did a picture, because I was broke. I did a picture in Ireland which was never released. And while I was over there, this guy who ran the National Film Theatre said to me, "I read this beautiful review by Albert Johnson in *Film Quarterly*." This is now a year later or a year and a half later, and the film's just been sitting there. I forgot we made it. So I read this review, I didn't know what it was about, it was a really startling review. I said, "Jesus, is that our picture? It's fantastic." Anyway, the guy said, "We're having a festival called 'Beat, Square and Cool,' and we'd like *Shadows* to be in it," and I said, "Fine," and then I forgot it immediately. And I get a phone call from [actor] Seymour Cassel. He said, "John, you've got to send the film here. We don't know what to do. These people are all going to be there, and we've got to have the film." So we sent the film, and he writes me back, "It's a smash. The picture's a smash over here, you can't believe the notices. I mean, they're going crazy, they're jumping up and down. The London *Times*, the Manchester *Guardian*, they're all going crazy, you've got to come over."

PETER FALK: If I was just starting [again], I'd just get the people that I'd like, and I'd go out and make a film. I wouldn't try and beat that other thing. I think that's too tough. I would say it's more fun to get together with yourselves and make something and work that way.

BUCK HENRY: The crew didn't have the foggiest notion what John was doing, because I think he likes to start and keep people in a kind of state of slight nervous suspension. He's got an idea, and he's going to work toward it his way. And it's great to look at the script girl because she has this crazed look.

JOHN CASSAVETES: None of us knew what we were doing. When lighting a scene, we didn't know what we were doing.

SAM WASSON: Others would learn—at film school.

JOSEPH E. LEVINE: Years ago, what the hell did college students care about a cinematographer?

GEORGE LUCAS: What I really wanted to do was go down to the ArtCenter in Los Angeles and become an illustrator. But my father said, "Well, you could do that, but you're going to pay for it yourself"—and it was a very expensive school. He knew I wasn't going to go out and work my way through school. Basically, I'm a lazy person. So the plan was to go to San Francisco State. A friend of mine who I'd grown up with and known ever since I was, like, three years old, from the neighborhood, was going to USC, and he was going to become a business major. And so he talked me into going up to Stockton to take the entrance exams and even to the point of applying to the school. And I said, "Well, what am I going to do down there? Do they have an anthropology department?" And they said, "No, but they have photography." And lo and behold, I got accepted. I never expected to get accepted down there. What I didn't know is that the film school was desperate for students. They only had about 200 students, and if they dropped below, like, 150 or something, they were going to lose their accreditation and be kicked off campus. So they were desperate to get kids in there.

Nobody wanted to be a film student. There was no point in it, because you couldn't get a job in the industry. The most you could hope for was to be a ticket taker at Disneyland or working for Lockheed making industrial films. So I went down there and discovered that it wasn't a school of photography at all, it was a school of cinematography. And I had no idea there was such a thing as a school where you learned how to make movies. I thought it was rather strange, but my close friend said, "Well, don't worry about it. You know, I've heard it's easier than PE, and you'll get through, and you like photography." And so I said, "Okay."

My first semester there, I took a history class and a beginning cinema class—which is basically very rudimentary, mostly still photography. And then an animation class, which was an advanced animation class I was able to get into. And once I was there for about a month, I realized that this was it. I fell in love with it immediately. I realized that it was very easy for me to do. I started feeling confident.

They gave me one minute worth of film to test a camera with, an animation camera, and instead of testing it, I made a movie out of it, a one-minute movie, and put a soundtrack to it. It won lots and lots of film festivals, and suddenly I was, like, a rising star at the school. And then I said, "You know, I can really do this." It was just the first time I really found something that I was good at. And from then on, I was completely obsessed with movies. I lived, ate, slept movies. I lived on chocolate bars and coffee and worked day and night and didn't think about anything else.

PAUL SCHRADER: I ran into Pauline [Kael] through someone I had met in a bar. It's that simple. And she became, you know, a patron, and she got me into UCLA, and that's how I started going.

GEORGE LUCAS: You know, there was no DVD, there was no VHS, there was no nothing. So if you wanted to see *Citizen Kane*, you literally had to wait for it. You had to check the paper every day, you had to check Arthur Knight's class, you had to check UCLA, you had to just really be on top of things. And of course, 150 other students are doing the same thing. So as soon as something would come up, everybody would say, "They're going to show this or that" or "They're showing *Gone with the Wind*. It'll probably be the last time we'll ever get to see it." Just because you couldn't get it anywhere. That was the big challenge. But we would see movies every single day. I was seeing, like, ten or fifteen movies a week during that period.

MARK CANTON: UCLA at that time was so radical, that with the exception of a few of us, nobody would even say the word *studio*.

GORDON STULBERG: When AFI came into being, it was perhaps the most significant indication of the ultimate disappearance of the old order. The men that were still around when I was breaking my eyeteeth on the business as an executive would have been horrified at the thought that there could be a place where young men and women who really wanted this as a career would come and study and learn and ultimately be fed in.

MARTIN SCORSESE: At the New York University that I attended in 1962 to '65, there was no School of the Arts. It was a Washington Square college. It was a liberal arts college. You just took film. You took a history course in the beginning, and third year, we were able to do a short film and maybe the fourth year a short film. It was really nice, because we had thirty-two students, finally, in the senior year, that was it. But I had never taken any acting courses. I had no idea how to talk to an actor. In fact, the first young man I put in a short film I did called *What's a Nice Girl Like You Doing in a Place Like This?*, I was about twenty years old, maybe actually in my mind eleven years old, really, but it was kind of a combination of quick cuts and Mel Brooks's routines and Sid Caesar and Ernie Kovacs and the French New Wave, the Italian New Wave.

SPIKE LEE: But getting into those schools at that time, you had to get an astronomical score on a GRE. Lucky for me, at NYU, they understood that standardized testing should not determine whether you should be admitted into NYU film school. So it all worked out.

MARTIN SCORSESE: I didn't have enough money to buy even an 8mm camera. I used to draw all my pictures. My first movies were all drawn, like storyboards, when I was a kid. Steve Spielberg used to have his own 8mm camera, used to do a lot of his own 8mm stuff. I couldn't do that. Eventually, I borrowed my friend Joey's camera, one of the characters in *Mean Streets*, and I shot some 8mm stuff. But the only way—the university was the place that got me the money, got me the chance to make the pictures.

TOM POLLOCK: I figured out that the best entertainment clients would be these students at the film school. And so I started recruiting them and said, "When you get out of here, and you get in the industry, I'll be your lawyer." And they said, "How will we pay you?" And I said, "You don't have to pay, we'll take five percent of your income." They thought this was great.

GEORGE LUCAS: I mean, the one great thing about being at USC at that particular moment in time is there was no prejudice about film. Everybody there loved everything. I had a friend that loved the Beach Party movies, another one that liked Kurosawa, another one liked Godard, another one liked John Ford, but nobody put each other down.

MARDIK MARTIN: The first thing that Marty [Scorsese] and I did together, a short called *It's Not Just You, Murray!*, was actually edited in [NYU professor Haig Manoogian's] home. He was living in a large home, and we actually did it there. He was more than just a teacher. He put his whole soul into his students. We took the Moviola from NYU and went into his home over a holiday weekend, because I was living in a room the size of a postage stamp.

MIKE FRANKOVICH: It's the same thing as Francis Ford Coppola when he was at UCLA. I remember lecturing there. He made some pictures for AIP. I remember when he was taken to Ireland. He wanted to get a job on a picture that he heard AIP was going to make in Ireland, and AIP was going to spend $200,000 on the picture. They were looking for a soundman, so he went and talked to the producer, Roger Corman. Corman said, "I need a soundman." He says, "I'm a soundman." So Corman says, "Fine, if you will work for such-and-such money"—very low scale, $100 a week or something—"you can come down and be the soundman." So he goes home, and he calls up a soundman he knows, and they spend the whole night briefing him. He gets some books, and Coppola goes to—Coppola will tell you this—goes to Ireland as a soundman on that picture. While he's there [Corman] had about sixty thousand feet of film in raw stock left. So Coppola went to him as they finished the picture, and he said, "Why don't we use this sixty thousand feet and make another picture?" And he says, "Well, we need a script." He says, "I've got one." Well, he didn't. This was on a Friday, and on Monday morning he came in with a script. They shot a script, and that little picture they sold to AIP as well, so that started Coppola.

MICHAEL OVITZ: That's when all the young executives stepped up.

JOHN SCHLESINGER: Some reader at MGM suggested Elvis Presley would be good for *Midnight Cowboy* if it was turned into a musical. And someone at United Artists, for whom I did the picture, seriously said, "Make Ratzo Sammy Davis, Jr., and you have a hit."

GEORGE LUCAS: Suddenly everybody was, you know, ninety years old.

PETER GUBER: The actors playing teenagers were fifty-three years old. I was young and sitting around the table at Columbia Pictures. There were forty White men. The average age was sixty-five years old. I was twenty-five.

JOHN LANDIS: I went to Fox. I had to cut my hair and wear a tie and show up in the mail room. "Good morning, sir."

BERNARDO BERTOLUCCI: I think in the sixties there weren't a lot of young American directors. Also, there wasn't a very interesting American cinema during the sixties.

AL RUDDY: And I would say that the Europeans were so far ahead of the American producers. There were no majors in these countries, so you saw Carlo Ponti, Dino De Laurentiis, who were very enterprising people and who learned very quickly that they could pick up a phone and sell MGM in the United States for *X* number of dollars.

GORDON STULBERG: I got to know foreign distribution operations quite well, and it was quite clear that if you had Steve McQueen, for example, or Clint Eastwood or Barbra Streisand, that the guarantees that were payable in Australia and Japan and South Africa and Italy and Germany— just the guarantees that you'd get whether the picture performed or not—would be three or four times the salary you paid the actor for the whole picture.

SHERRILL CORWIN: That's a new way of selling film and a very effective way.

AL RUDDY: I mean, strip it off, just like pieces of a banana. You may decide you want to keep certain territories for yourself, but you, in a sense, control the distribution of the various pieces of the film that constitute its total financing.

ARNOLD KOPELSON: And you take those contracts, with a completion guarantee that's issued by an insurance company, and you take it to a bank, and you borrow the total cost of making the movie. And generally, your contracts are for more than the budget of the movie, more than the anticipated negative cost plus interest. And generally you can come in with a profit before you start your first day of photography.

MIKE MEDAVOY: Joseph E. Levine went out, paid X number of dollars for a script, paid X number of dollars for the stars, and in effect, really, financed the picture himself. He then went to territorial sales, he sold some countries. Then he came to the United States, and he made deals with exhibitors, who bought out X number of dollars. And I don't want to even tell you what the numbers are, but they are fairly substantial.

JOSEPH E. LEVINE: Let's take *8 1/2*, which was a three-way coproduction. Columbia Pictures took the whole world except for Italy. Italy was taken by [Angelo] Rizzoli, a man who used to produce pictures in Italy, and I was the coproducer for the United States and Canada. The picture did nothing in Italy, a very famous art picture, *8 1/2*, probably one of the most famous. I never understood it, to tell you the truth, but we promoted the hell out of that picture. You know what we did? We had over a hundred screenings for different egghead types, and it became a cocktail, what I call a cocktail picture. "Have you seen *8 1/2*? You must see it." It became the thing to do and we did a hell of a business [in the United States] with the picture. I remember months later, I owned a theater on 57th Street, and Fellini wanted to see *8 1/2*. It was still running, it ran a year, and he wanted to see it, he wanted to look at an actor he had used. He was in

New York, and we went to see it. We sat in the theater, and there was nobody in there, and we had come to about the middle of the picture, and I said, "Federico, I never knew—what the hell does that mean?" He said, "I don't know."

WILLIAM FRIEDKIN: This is art expression. There's no limit. My God, look, here's a film called *Breathless* by Jean-Luc Godard. This is incredible. This is blowing me away. Fellini, *8 1/2*. You ever seen that? Does it mean anything to you? You know what it meant to us? I mean, when I saw *8 1/2* twenty-five years ago, the style, the technique, what he was trying to express about society, about human nature, human behavior, and then just forget the editing and photography and brilliant characterization and all of this stuff that was being done back then.

GEORGE LUCAS: This was the time of an incredible array of great European films being distributed in the United States.

SAM WASSON: A debate arose amongst the new, young generation of filmmakers. Who were the world's greatest directors?

STEVEN SPIELBERG: My generation and the one now coming up are completely different, because the generation now coming up is full of people who were raised even more on movies than I was. I discovered movies fairly late in life, but all my friends who are just beginning to make movies are incredibly well read. They are almost film historians. They can talk circles around me about who did what and who was the editor of Max Ophuls's films.

WILLIAM FRIEDKIN: As young filmmakers we're looking at, *boom*, every week something from Fellini, Bergman, Kurosawa, Antonioni, Godard, Resnais, Satyajit Ray, the greatest filmmakers in the world, and the arguments we were having in coffeehouses in the streets as filmmakers were, you know, what's going to win out? The formalism and the kind of dreamscape of Fellini or the improvisational quality of Godard? The argument was between Fellini and Godard!

FRANÇOIS TRUFFAUT: Virtually every first film from our group, if you can call it a group, was well received. The problem always came with the second film.

GEORGE LUCAS: I was a huge fan of Godard because I was an editor and experimental filmmaker and he was pushing the boundaries. When it came to how to tell a story, Fellini was everything to me, as was Kurosawa. With Kurosawa especially, an American audience was being made to explore a radically new but fascinating foreign culture. What did any of us know about the history of medieval Japan? We were really being dumped into an alien environment. I loved being thrown into the middle of something with no explanation. I assume it's the same for someone who grew up in a village in China. They would look at a western and say, "What is going on here? What is this place?"

WILLIAM FRIEDKIN: In the sixties, it was experimental, it was alive, it was vibrant. And young filmmakers were really turned on by this stuff.

PAUL MAZURSKY: We wanted to be them, work like they did.

CONRAD HALL: Sven Nykvist and Ingmar Bergman have been making pictures together for twenty-five years. They care about each other. It's not a studio system where somebody's telling you about not enough light on the faces or anything. It's a total rapport with somebody who's helping you on.

JANE FONDA: Sven told me while working with Bergman, they would go away for months before they would start a film and decide what kind of effects they wanted and how they were going to film it. We don't do that here, because you'd have to pay all this money, whereas they would just go off and do it. For weeks, just the two of them.

GORDON STULBERG: What we face when you're trying to imitate Fellini and Bergman is the puritan ethic that's ingrained in the people who are picture makers in our society, who come out of generation after generation in which sexuality has been so forbidden, so covert, so tied up with something that was immoral and illegal and wrong. There are creative people in our environment today, when they attempt to bring it to the screen in the same context that a European does, somehow or other, it gets dirty. Somehow or other it's artificial.

PETER BOGDANOVICH: I think something that has hurt American cinema is that younger filmmakers have gone after Antonioni and Fellini. Such pretension! Where's Raoul Walsh when we need him?

Film culture in New York in the fifties and sixties was a vibrant one, and there were a lot of opportunities to see rare films back then. People were starting to take film very seriously. . . . I worked for Dan Talbot for a couple of years at the New Yorker Theater on the Upper West Side, which could hold something like a thousand people. Dan was the first person to show classic American films rather than foreign films, which the Thalia and most of the art houses were doing. He was following the *Cahiers du Cinéma* lead. For them, Hawks was a greater director than Fred Zinnemann and Hitchcock was greater than David Lean. The idea, as stated by various French New Wave critics like Truffaut, Godard, Chabrol, and Rohmer, was that despite the impositions of the studio system, the personality of certain directors would show through no matter who wrote it, who shot it, or who was in it. Their points of view triumphed over the multiplicity of restrictions that might have existed.

MEL BROOKS: I think the word should be *author*, I'm not sure, but if the French want to say *auteur*, let's not quarrel with them. They're okay.

ANDREW SARRIS: In 1943, two movies came out in America, *Casablanca* and *Watch on the Rhine*. Now, *Casablanca* was based on some ridiculous play. It was called something funny, *Everybody Comes to Rick's*, and it was Warners' two very sharp, very clever scriptwriters—the Epsteins worked on it. Michael Curtiz took over the direction, and it was rather an interesting, unusual bit of casting, Humphrey Bogart and Ingrid Bergman were costarred, and it was the kind of movie that they were making jokes at while it was going on. No one took it very seriously. It opened in New York at the end of 1942 and opened the rest of the country the beginning of 1943, and it was a smash hit. I mean, the public made it a hit. Critics, you know, gave it so-so reviews. The other funny thing, when the Academy Awards came along, it won the Academy Award for Best Picture. The picture that won the New York Film Critics Award was *Watch on the Rhine*. Now, *Watch on the Rhine* was a Lillian Hellman, very ideological play, a thesis play, very dull and stiff, Paul Lukas repeating his stage performance, Bette Davis taking a minor role so Paul Lukas could do the screen performance for Warners. Very ideological left wing, you know, not romantic at all. Full of propaganda and rather stiffly directed. All of the New York intelligentsia felt that *Watch on the Rhine* was a serious movie and *Casablanca* was idiotic. It was typical of Hollywood to make a picture like that. Now, today, any serious critic, I don't care whether *auteur* or not, looking at those two movies, will find *Casablanca* more interesting, much more interesting—a much more important movie, a much more significant movie, much more important artistically, mythically, by any level, as compared to *Watch on the Rhine*, and the exact opposite was true in 1943.

GORE VIDAL: The laughter that went through this town when the French— who are always wrong—remember that! Whenever the French have a theory, you must begin by saying "It's incorrect." It's a nation devoted to the false hypothesis. On that they build marvelously logical structures, but the hypothesis is always wrong. They suddenly decided that all these hacks that we'd been laughing at for years were great creators.

PETER BOGDANOVICH: According to these critics, Zinnemann and Lean made films without much of their own personality in them. For them, clearly Hawks, Hitchcock, Ford, and others were the governing force behind the films they put their name to as director.

SAM FULLER: Motion pictures is really a one-man outcry.

MARDIK MARTIN: You can do a scene that says one thing on paper, and if I give it to each one of you, that same scene, each one of you is probably going to do it differently. Am I right?

HOWARD W. KOCH: The great directors get more than the script. That's the difference.

CHARLTON HESTON: It's clear to me that the medium really does belong to the director.

ELEANOR PERRY: Granted, we can argue about it.

DAVID LEAN: Alec Guinness always said I was trying to make him be like me and that sort of thing, and I don't know how one's to avoid this. One's bound to bring up certain facets of oneself almost unconsciously.

VITTORIO STORARO: The moment you select from the natural world this space to tell this story, no doubt you're making your own choice, even consciously or unconsciously, you're telling something very different from any other person.

ELEANOR PERRY: I just think that it's gone too far, this whole thing. The author of the film is certainly not the director. Does anybody agree with me?

CLINT EASTWOOD: I believe that *auteur* crap is exactly that. I mean, it's an ensemble.

ELEANOR PERRY: If you're going to have an *auteur*, what about the producer who gets the idea, finds the writer, puts the package together? He's just as much the *auteur*.

BOB RAFELSON: Somebody once started to talk to me about *auteurism*, which I really don't know very much about. I decided that I would open up every picture with a solid color. Years later they can say, "Ah, now we recognize that all these pictures were made by the same person."

WILLIAM FRIEDKIN: It's true that one intelligence can and does generally inform a project, but the fulfillment of that vision requires a great many talents.

SAM WASSON: One such intelligence was emerging independent American International Pictures. In the midsixties, AIP picked up the baton dropped by the major studios—and passed it on to the upcoming generation of new talent looking to break into the movie race.

JEANINE BASINGER: Of course, there had always been independents in Hollywood. During the studio system, there was Chaplin, Sam Goldwyn, David O. Selznick became an independent, Best Picture winner *Marty* was independently made. . . .

SAM WASSON: But the difference was that here the independently made film became a staple of the post-studio era . . .

DENNIS HOPPER: AIP is American International Pictures. And American International Pictures was really devised to fill a void by some very intelligent men who realized that there were drive-in movies. Roger Corman and Arkoff—Sam Arkoff—and Jim Nicholson, no relation to Jack Nicholson. And they started AIP, and they made movies primarily for drive-in movies. At that time, drive-in movies were big everywhere.

SAM ARKOFF: You'll still hear from old people complaining about the kind of pictures made today. "Where is the family picture from yesteryear?" That's unmitigated fecal matter. Because frankly, as soon as I was able to go to picture shows by myself, I never went with my parents again. And that's really true of most of us. So the so-called family picture really is Mom and/or Dad taking the little kiddies to see the Disney pictures. That's really what it amounted to, the family picture.

By the late fifties, American youth wasn't prepared to take that sort of sop. And so we began to make pictures like *Hot Rod Girl*, *Dragstrip Girl*, and so on, which really didn't deal with the parents, only dealt with the kids. And ultimately, in the very early sixties, we started the Beach Party series with Frankie Avalon and Annette Funicello, which have today become high camp but were taken seriously enough in those days. The only adults we had at all were stick figures like Don Rickles, Buddy Hackett, Morey Amsterdam, you know, people like that, who were figures of ridicule but who were not either parents or that sort. And so the kids worked out their own destinies without the preaching that was so inevitable in youth pictures that had been made prior to that time. They weren't successful because they were about surfing. Most of the country didn't know about surfing. That was just an attractive background, the beach. The fact really was that the young people wanted to be recognized as being individuals.

Now, those were the early sixties. As the sixties progressed, you got into a different time, you began to get into more of an alienation, where kids left home and went to not only Haight-Ashbury and Greenwich Village but just left their own homes and worked in their own towns, for example. We used to have twenty, or at times we'd have fifteen or twenty, kids in an audience who would have moved out of their houses working at Baskin-Robbins or in a fast-food shop. In the meantime, the other companies were completely oblivious to all of this sort of thing. But in the middle sixties, AIP made pictures like *The Wild Angels*, which starred Peter Fonda and Nancy Sinatra. We followed it up with about twelve more motorcycle pictures. We always thought one good picture deserved five more. In those days, we were turning out twenty, twenty-two pictures a year, and so we needed pictures. So if you opened up a vein of not even gold but even copper, you just kept mining that vein until you ran out of ore.

Jim [Nicholson], who used to like to drink after six o'clock, would finish a bottle of whiskey and by two o'clock in the morning would have some of the damnedest titles: *I Was a Teenage Werewolf, The Amazing Colossal Man.* . . . And from the title, we would then figure out the graphic, the artwork for the ad. We did everything bass-ackwards, really. And when we had that ad, then we would call in one of the writers. My late brother-in-law probably wrote forty or fifty of the scripts. And because he knew budgets, he would write to a budget.

So in the early days, we used to make pictures for anywhere between $75,000 to $100,000, two hundred and a quarter. Black-and-white pictures shot in two weeks of six-day weeks. We made *I Was a Teenage Werewolf*, for example, which starred Mike Landon, for about $125,000. It's a million-dollar title, really. So we set up a four-picture deal for Roger [Corman] and we were off and running.

BRUCE DERN: Corman was the first guy to let any of us in our generation have starring kinds of roles in B movies.

ROGER CORMAN: I was giving them an opportunity to make their first film, which hopefully I would make a profit from, and hopefully their career would take off.

JACK NICHOLSON: It was *The Cry Baby Killer*, which was my first movie. I thought, This is it. Two months in the business, and I got the lead in the movie.

I read for that movie about a half a dozen times, actually. They read everybody in the city for that movie, which is good. Very few movies read people or interview them at all. It's a nerve-racking experience. I was yelling and screaming, a raving maniac to get this part. I did think this was it. I said, "This is a change in my life. I'm going to be a movie star." After I did it, I didn't work for years.

It's sort of a blinding glare, that movie. I was completely into it. I started studying, so I used every single thing religiously that I had ever learned in class. I was constantly preparing and writing all over my script. It was just a mess. Then I saw it, and I thought it was terrible. It just drove me nuts. I thought, What is this? It took a lot of time to come out of it. You always meet good people on these things, though. That's where I met Roger. I worked cheap enough for him, and so I started working with him as a result of this. The great thing about Roger's movies is that you do play different things: costume stuff, which I do as badly as possibly can be done, gangster pictures. In those days, there were a lot of insane murders being done, which I've always been partial to. That was great. . . .

I always knew what was bad about them, but I always also knew what was good about them. Roger and [director] Monte [Hellman] and all the people that I've worked with are totally free. They can't afford creative pretension or bullshit. They just don't have the time for it. It just can't go wild. It can't be done. They're really trying to make the best with what they have. If you're making a horror movie for AIP, there's no need to get upset if you've got to do some weird screaming or have a lot of blood all over you.

ROGER CORMAN: I started as a writer and sold a screenplay for Writers Guild minimum, which, I think, was $3,000 at the time. I tried to get more from the producer, so we compromised, and he agreed to give me an associate producer credit and another $3,000. On the basis that I had $6,000 in my hand and I was an official associate producer, I raised $5,000 more, which made $11,000. I felt if I could get a total of $15,000, I'd make the film. A fellow came in to direct it because I wasn't directing at that time. This was around 1954. He asked me how much I would pay him, and I said, "If you can raise four thousand dollars more, you can direct this picture." He did, and we made the picture for $15,000 in cash and a series of deferments. We shot it in six days, all on natural locations, including Malibu. If you look closely, you can see trucks moving down the Pacific Coast Highway as the voice-over says, "Deep in the uncharted jungle of South America . . ." It was a science fiction film that I called *It Stalked the Ocean Floor*. We made a deal with Robert Lippert, who had a small distribution company at the time. He felt that was too arty a title and said, "You're going for the high-class market, kid, and *It Stalked the Ocean Floor* won't do it." So he changed the title to *Monster from the Ocean Floor*. He said, "You've got to tell them what the picture is about." He may well have been right, because the picture did reasonably well and we went from there. Then it was simply a matter of taking profits from that one and putting them into another picture.

BRUCE DERN: You knew you were going to be ripped off by everybody. The gaffers knew it, and the prop people knew it, and the electricians knew it, and everybody knew it. Transportation knew it. Roger knew it. But he'd say, "We're making movies." He knew what he was doing. He was making movies.

ROGER CORMAN: It's an even trade on the first film. [The first-time director] gets a small amount of money and makes his film. I get the profit off the film, and he gets the opportunity to start his career.

SAM ARKOFF: I think there will always be a market for the ingenious young filmmaker who has a really bright idea who can call on all his friends.

ROGER CORMAN: Generally, I'll pick the subject matter. I'll say, "Okay, we'll go with the bike picture" or "I think we need a contemporary horror story." Then I'll turn it over to the guy to see what he can come up with.

DENNIS HOPPER: Corman, if he trusted you, would give you a film and let you go out and shoot on weekends, second-unit stuff. He wouldn't pay you, but he'd give you the camera.

ROGER CORMAN: When I backed Francis Coppola, he had been my assistant for something like eight or ten months and already learned what was necessary.

BRUCE DERN: Corman was the champion of the good actor and the good writer and the good director.

DENNIS HOPPER: That was a big thing for us, man.

I had starred in a picture called *The Glory Stompers*. And Jack Nicholson had starred in a picture called *Hells Angels on Wheels*. And Peter [Fonda] was the big star. He had made one called *The Wild Angels*, and he was big, man.

ROGER CORMAN: Most of my controls are before the shooting and afterwards. For instance, I'll check out the script very carefully, the production staff, the casting, and so forth, and then I'll probably have some sort of control over the cutting. During the actual shooting itself, on most of the films that I've backed, I never even go to the set. I really feel it's best on the basis that I say, "Okay, I'll back this man as a director. He should have the opportunity to simply go and direct his film." The only time I'll generally step in is when I'm looking at the rushes, when I see something that really causes me to jump out of my chair looking at the rushes, I may have words with him about that.

PETER BOGDANOVICH: I came out here about 1965, having written articles for *Esquire* and so on and so forth, and I went to a movie called *Baby Angels*, which has nothing whatsoever to do with the story. But sitting behind me was a fellow named Roger Corman. And I was introduced to him by somebody who was living with us. And he said, "Hello," and I said, "Hello," and that was it. And then about a week later, he called me up and he said, "You write for *Esquire*?" I said, "I do, yeah." He said, "Would you be interested in writing for movies?" I said, "Sure." I don't think I said, "Sure." I think I said, "Are you kidding?" And he said, "Well, I'm interested in a script. I'd like to do a picture, sort of like a cross between *Lawrence of Arabia* and *The Bridge on the River Kwai*, but cheap." So I said, "I can do that."

So [Polly Platt and I] started to work on a story. And then we never did get completely done on that. And Roger called up and said, "I'm starting another movie called *The Wild Angels* and the script hasn't come in yet, but it's coming in soon. Would you like to work on it as well?" "What would I do?" "Well, would you sort of be my assistant?" I said, "Okay, what do I do?" He said, "Well, just come up, hang around. I'm doing this picture very quickly, I need somebody to hang around." So I went in. I'm starting to work, and I said, "How much and how long do I work?" "It'll be about three, four, maybe five weeks preproduction and three weeks shooting, and that's it." Well, I worked on the picture twenty-two weeks, and I just did everything you could do on a picture.

ROGER CORMAN: I feel that any script can be made for any budget. You can make *Doctor Zhivago* in six days for $50,000, but it's going to look different than David Lean's version.

PETER BOGDANOVICH: Roger said, "Be sure you know before you get the set-up where your next shot is, because the minute you have to think, the crew will fall apart. Don't think—just go! When you finish a shot, just turn to them and say, 'Okay, we're over here.' Even if you don't know where the hell you're going, just pretend. It keeps everybody on their toes and keeps morale up."

JACK NICHOLSON: *The Little Shop of Horrors* was the low-budget production of all time. Roger had the sets all ready. He went in a couple of days over the weekend and lit them. He had an old-time cameraman, Archie

Dalzell, who prelit the sets so that when they wanted to shoot, they just went over and put all these plugs in. Then he said, "All right, action.". . .

Roger never much directs the actors. He'll tell you if you're doing something too cute or too much. I never forgave him: I did *The Raven*, [Peter] Lorre and [Boris] Karloff and [Vincent] Price, and I wanted to be as funny as they were. It was too many funny people in one movie. This is the kind of direction, here it is: "You can't be as funny as they are." That's my interpretation of the role from Roger.

PETER BOGDANOVICH: With Roger there were practical lessons. He sort of learned how to move fast, down and dirty, and get in and get out. And that's great. It served me, that knowledge and that way of working, that somewhat informal, guerrilla kind of filmmaking. You steal, you cheat, you lie, you do anything you can.

It was a lot of fun. I learned a lot about cutting, of course, being thrown into the lion's den—and Roger liked the picture. And so then he asked me to make another. He asked me if I'd like to make my own picture. That's really how I got started. He says, "Boris Karloff owes me two days. I made a picture with Boris called *The Terror*—it wasn't much of a picture—with Jack Nicholson. And what I want you to do is to take twenty minutes of Karloff's footage out of *The Terror*, then shoot twenty minutes with Karloff in two days—that's forty minutes. Now you got forty minutes of Karloff. You following me?" I said, "Yes, sir." He says, "Now get some other actors and shoot another forty minutes with those actors in ten days, and now we've got an eighty-minute Karloff picture. Can you do that?" I said, "I can try."

ROGER CORMAN: Knowing exactly what you're going to do in advance is one of the greatest advantages to shooting a low-budget film. On the other hand, after having planned that much in preproduction, you must stay flexible enough so that if it doesn't work, you throw it out.

PETER BOGDANOVICH: We had to kill Karloff off about halfway through the picture because I only had him for two days. I showed the outline to Sam Fuller, and he said, "Why did you kill Karloff off in the middle of the picture, kid?" I said, "I've only got him for two days." "Don't think about that! Ignore that! He's the star of the picture. You can't kill him off in the middle." I said, "But Roger won't give me the time." "Ignore that!" he said. "Write the script like you got him for the whole picture. Never worry about anything practical when you're writing a picture. When you're directing it, that's another problem, but right now you're writing it." In three hours, Sam proceeded to rewrite it, quite brilliantly. After I looked at the changes, I said, "But Sammy, this is a complete rewrite. I've got to give you credit." He said, "Naw. If you give me credit, they'll just think I wrote the whole thing."

FRANK MARSHALL: And we shot *Targets* for, I think, it's twenty-nine days here in Los Angeles. And I think the budget was $125,000, which was a lot—it was 1967. But I got to do everything: I helped build the sets, I did props, I acted in it, I shot some of it, I rented the cars, I drove the cars, I found the locations, just anything they needed doing to help the film I did, and I just fell in love with making movies.

PETER BOGDANOVICH: So we had a lot of fun, and when the picture was finished, every studio turned it down. There wasn't one studio that didn't. And for a long time, nobody would buy it because of the subject. I think they probably didn't think it was very good, you know? Or maybe they thought it was too wild. God knows what they thought. They just didn't like it. They weren't interested in it, except for Paramount, which sort of liked it but not enough to put up any money. Roger wanted all his money back from all the hundred and thirty [thousand] that he put out. He didn't want to take a chance, he wanted to have that back, you know. So I took a chance. And I was running it down at Arthur Knight's cinema class [at USC]. And we invited the trade press there from the *Hollywood Reporter* and *Variety*, and I said to them, "You like it or if you don't like it, review it." Well, they happened to like it. So they wrote reviews in the trades, and the next day, Paramount calls and says, "We're still interested. Have you sold it yet?" I said, "Yeah, we have a deal at AIP. But maybe we can get it back from them. The deal isn't closed yet." So he says, "What's the deal for?" I said, "A hundred thirty." He says, "We'll make it a hundred fifty," and they bought it. . . . And then it was a big internal struggle. I must admit, Bob Evans and Charlie Bluhdorn were the ones who really liked it. And almost nobody else at the studio did. And whenever there's an internal struggle like that, particularly over a picture that didn't cost much, the people [who actually] have to go on the line and sell the picture are the ones that prevail. And so it was not well sold.

ROGER CORMAN: They did nothing. They opened it up in New York and got, as you may know, sensational reviews. It just got magnificent reviews and didn't do any business.

PETER BOGDANOVICH: And nobody saw it.

JEANINE BASINGER: Just as Bogdanovich had worked with Karloff, the new generation of filmmakers arrived in time to cross paths with their predecessors, many of their heroes, as they were making their way out.

STEVEN SPIELBERG: I did my first show, *Night Gallery*, with Joan Crawford. It was frightening because I hadn't met the crew before I came on the set, and [I was so young] they thought it was a joke. They really thought it was a publicity stunt, and I really couldn't get anybody to take me seriously for two days. It was very embarrassing.

She's a very nice woman, Joan Crawford. I mean, Joan could have been the real crisis on the project. Instead, Joan was the only person on the crew who treated me like I had been working fifty years. I mean, Joan was just sensational. She understood that I shouldn't have been there making that particular show, I should have been making something out of my imagination, and she was very compassionate, and we worked very closely together. Joan was a total refreshment.

The other icy refreshment was the prevailing temperature on the soundstage. Joan always works with the air conditioners blowing. This was inside in January.

QUENTIN TARANTINO: I would like to have worked [then]. It's for all the groovy actors that I could have worked with in their prime and some of the cool actors from the fifties and sixties that were still around. I mean, I could still work with Bette Davis. That would have been fucking awesome.

RON HOWARD: Bette Davis was very dubious about my directing [her in the TV movie *Skyward*], but she really liked the project and wanted to go ahead with it. She kept calling me "Mr. Howard" on the phone, and I said, "Well, Miss Davis, please call me Ron." And she said, "No, I'll call you 'Mr. Howard' until I decide whether I like you or not." And so I was a little concerned about that. I went to work the first day, and she was very cordial, if somewhat distant. And, well, it was 106 degrees. And I had a sport coat on, because I was trying to, you know, look like an adult or something. And I went up to her in the cockpit of this plane, this little mock-up, we're working with out in Texas, and as I was approaching her, she kind of was like, "Oh, oh, my God." And then, for the whole benefit of the crew, who fortunately, I had worked with once before, she said, "Oh, my God, I saw this child walking up to me. And I had no idea who this child could possibly be," and then laughed and got a big laugh from the crew. And I laughed, and so then I leaned in, and I gave her the direction. And she did it.

And when the day's shooting was over, I said, "Well, Miss Davis, you're through, you go on back to the hotel now, I'll see you in the morning." And she said, "Okay, Ron, see you in the morning," and kind of patted me on the ass and went back to the hotel.

WILLIAM FRIEDKIN: I did the last *Alfred Hitchcock Hour* ever made. My contact with Hitchcock consisted of him coming on the set on my first day of shooting to film his introduction. I was really terrified, because he was this great director. He came up to me and stared. He said, "Mr. Friedkin, you're not wearing a tie. Usually our directors wear ties." I thought he was putting me on, but he was absolutely straight. That's all he ever said to me.

DENNIS HOPPER: Yeah. Well, like, when I first started, with the exception of Kazan and Nick Ray and George Stevens, I must say, most directors at that time were like schoolmarms. They were full dictators, they were screamers, they were yellers, they were to be feared. But these guys knew what they wanted, and it was quite amazing.

CHARLTON HESTON: The closest analogy to a film company I know of is a military operation. I'm not talking about everyone having his shoes shined and lining up in formation. I'm talking about preoccupation with logistics, the importance of weather, food, fatigue, transport, supplies, communication, morale, and authority. Good command is vital. I spent a good while in the army, and that's why it's not an idly chosen phrase.

JANE FONDA: It never occurred to me to ask a director to be consulted on style or content. I remember halfway through my career, I'd been an actress for twelve years, and I made *They Shoot Horses, Don't They?* It was the first time that a director other than my husband had asked me what I thought and discussed the script with me, the story, changes that needed to be made. I couldn't believe it. It was Sydney Pollack.

MICHAEL OVITZ: This was the new way of doing things.

CONRAD HALL: Now that we have reflex cameras and we have directors that operate on improvisational scenes, who, in an improvisational scene, is going to determine what material is going to be used?

SAM WASSON: That was the question, not just on the set or in cutting rooms but in the front offices: Who controlled poststudio Hollywood? The studios didn't own the talent anymore. Did that mean the talent owned the studios?

DUSTIN HOFFMAN: Why can't you be a producer-actor? Why can't you say to a director, "This is my film, will you help me make it?"

JON PETERS: People like Michael Douglas, Jane Fonda, Barbra, myself, various people who succeed set up their own umbrella, set up their own situation.

BARBRA STREISAND: At the end of *Funny Girl*, Willie [Wyler] gave me a megaphone that said "DGA" on it. He really thought I should direct.

JANE FONDA: I auditioned for Kazan, for Natalie Wood's role in *Splendor in the Grass*. And when the audition was over, Kazan called me down to the footlights, and he said, "Are you ambitious?" I said, "No!" Oh, the minute I said it, I—you know, I knew . . . I mean, who wants to hire some young girl that's not ambitious? But, looking back, I know where it came from: good girls weren't ambitious . . . then. I couldn't . . . *own* it! I couldn't own it.

CLINT EASTWOOD: I think it's a logical step unless you're satisfied to wait in the trailer between shots. I've always liked film. I enjoy watching movies. I enjoy the process of making them and felt that I wasn't satisfied [just acting], so I had to give it a try.

BARBRA STREISAND: For too long, I had given in, even though I knew intuitively that I shouldn't. I had heard people say that Barbra Streisand is difficult to work with because she always wanted to control things. Actually, that's not true. I've never really had control, and that's the reason I formed my own company, was to begin having control.

JANE FONDA: So much of who I was had to do with activism. I was organizing, I was not in Hollywood. I was on military bases, I was in VA hospitals. I was in Detroit going to union organizing meetings. I was talking to people near toxic dumps. I was organizing. And I was very conscious of the fact that my celebrity separated me from people. And my career was not what came first. And I considered leaving the business. And when I was in Detroit, I met a guy, his name was Ken Cockrel, he was a Black lawyer. He eventually became mayor of Detroit. And he said to me, "Jane, organizers are a dime a dozen. The movement doesn't have movie stars. Your career is really important." Whoa. That completely transformed the way I thought about acting and about my career. Suddenly it was important for me to have a career, and I had to be intentional about it, which meant I also had to start paying attention to what I was making movies about. And I started to want to make my own movies.

CHAPTER 12

NEW HOLLYWOOD

SAM WASSON: Opportunity knocked. In the decentralized New Hollywood, the gold rush zest and chaos of the silent era returned to the movie business . . .

JEANINE BASINGER: The disintegration of the studios impacted not just the business of making movies, but the culture of the community at large . . .

SAM WASSON: Who went to the commissaries anymore? Who crossed paths on the back lots and enthusiastically exchanged ideas about this script or that actor?

JEANINE BASINGER: In this Hollywood, you almost had to go out to find work. What if your phone never rang? Networking—social interaction with an eye to dealmaking—became compulsory for the freelance filmmaker.

WARREN BEATTY: I think of being at my first big Hollywood party. It was upstairs at Romanoff's, and I crossed the room dancing, and I saw Rita Hayworth. I was stunned. She was dancing with a guy who seemed to have kind of floppy shoes. And I was just staring at her and staring at her, and I couldn't get over it that I was looking at Rita Hayworth. And, and, uh, she danced over close, and then she looked at me! And I said, "Well, excuse me, I'm sorry, but you're Rita Hayworth." And she said, "Yes." She said, "And you're Warren Beatty." And I said, "How would you know that?" And she said, "Well, he told me." And the guy—and I said, "Oh, how do you do?" I said, "What is your name?" And he said, "Well, I'm Clifford Odets." And I thought, You're Clifford Odets? I said, "Could I talk to you?" You could have airbrushed Rita Hayworth out of the picture at that point. And he said, "Well, you can come to my house tonight, after this party." And I said, "Really? Fine." So we went over to Beverly Drive, and I walked in. He introduced me to a group of people, and I said, "Hi." Now, I tell you this story because it's about how dumb I was about movies. I said, "Who's the kinda heavy guy over there?" He says, "Well, that's Jean Renoir." And I said—this is how much I knew about movies—I said, "Really?" I said, "Renoir? Is that any relation to the painter?" He said, "Well, yes. He's his son." And I said, "Really? What does he do?" He said, "What does he *do*?" I said, "Yeah." He said, "Well, he's a director." I said, "Well, what has he done?" And he said, "Well, he did a little picture called *Grand Illusion*. He did something called *Rules of the Game*." And I said, "Is that right?" I said, "Any good?" He said, "Well, I—I think you really should see them." And so to my credit, I went and I got 16mm prints of both of those movies, and I thought, These are the best movies that I had ever seen. And I became quite friendly with Jean, who lived over here in Benedict Canyon. And I felt he was at that point not appreciated. Well, he hadn't been appreciated by me.

JANE FONDA: You know, Warren and I became friends, and I remember after we both started acting in Hollywood, I remember hearing that he'd made a list of the directors that he was willing to work with, which absolutely *floored* me.

WARREN BEATTY: I was interested in making a movie about Édith Piaf, and I arranged a meeting with Truffaut in Paris. I don't think Truffaut found me very interesting. He might have, I don't think so. But he suggested that I talk to [screenwriters] Bob Benton and David Newman about a script that he had worked on about Bonnie and Clyde. It had also been worked on by Godard. Godard came and visited Arthur Penn and me when we were making *Mickey One* in Chicago. And Truffaut suggested that I call them, which I did when I went back to New York. And I went over to pick up the script from Bob Benton, and I read the script, and I called him back and said, "I like it. I'd like to do it."

It's almost invariable for me that when I read material that I like, I don't see myself in it. I didn't see myself playing Clyde Barrow—I sort of saw Bob Dylan, who I kinda knew, and I thought he kinda looked like Clyde.

The ballast of *Bonnie and Clyde* is really a matter of the socioeconomic travails of the 1930s and the approach to dealing with the acquiring of a kind of fame on the part of Bonnie and Clyde and the romanticizing of what they engaged in, in robbing banks, in speaking for the little guy, the people who had been dispossessed. And so you have to wind up saying "Well, gee whiz, I'm going to have to be a little funny about this." You know, when Stanley Kubrick and [producer] Jimmy Harris were going to do *Dr. Strangelove*, they started with a book called *Red Alert*, which was a very serious story about nuclear catastrophe. And they wound up saying "Well, this is just preposterous." And they wound up making one of the great comedies.

ARTHUR PENN: The way the film originally ended was with the deputies gathered in the bushes waiting for them. We cut between Bonnie and Clyde, who are getting closer, and the deputies waiting. There was kind of raw comic dialogue, things like "Man, it's cold. I wish I was home with my wife." "I wish I was home with your wife, too"—that kind of country talk. Then Bonnie and Clyde arrive, and at the moment the shooting starts comes a blackout. Now, these are people I'd read about in the newspaper in the early thirties, practically the first identifiable personalities I remember as a kid. I felt we couldn't end the story like that. I thought we had to turn them into legends, move from reality into a new degree of experience. In a certain sense it's the same reason why we didn't do it in black and white. It was to say that this is not a document of what happened. It leaps forward in time and brings it up to the present, which is where the idea of changing rhythms in the final scene came from. I wanted the final scene to say, "We're moving out of this kind of time and this kind of place into another experience."

PETER BOGDANOVICH: I think, in fact, the argument for *Bonnie and Clyde* is that you did feel their deaths.

WARREN BEATTY: When I made *Bonnie and Clyde*, pretty boys didn't really produce pictures so much or maybe certainly not at that age. Kirk [Douglas] had produced very well, Burt Lancaster was involved in producing [through Hecht-Hill-Lancaster], and of course Orson, but he passed through the pretty-boy stage early. Anyway, I was a little bit derided. "You're not going to call yourself a producer, are you?"

ARTHUR PENN: Warren isn't the easiest guy to work with. He's a very insistent and extremely intelligent guy who'll make you defend what you say until either you make it very clear to him or completely abandon your position. In the case of *Mickey One* we were working on a fairly obscure piece of material, and I got to the point of saying "Warren, shut up and do it my way. I can't discuss it with you anymore." What that did was deprive us of a certain kind of interchange, something we [later] enjoyed enormously on *Bonnie and Clyde*, where Warren would say to me, "I'm going to question you and quarrel with you anytime I want to. And you can tell me to shut up or quarrel back with me. But you always finally have the right to say, 'Look, I said everything I have to say about it. I'm directing the picture and you're acting in it, so do it my way.' But I want to be able to talk to you about it." So that was the way we worked, and it worked just fine. We had some very raw exchanges, and often the crew would think we were fighting, but in point of fact we were really just engaging and trying to kind of irritate each other. It was "No, goddammit! I don't want to see that cold, dead, handsome face show up on the screen one more damn time. I'm sick of it. It's not enough just to deliver that good-looking body. Go to work!" A lot of Warren's best acting comes out of that state of mind.

WARREN BEATTY: It was the first picture that I had produced. Arthur had been having a bad time on a couple of movies, and he didn't even want to make another movie. And then this was Gene Hackman's first good shot and Faye and Gene Wilder's first movie. It was Dean Tavoularis's first movie as a production designer and Theadora Van Runkle's first as a costume designer.

ARTHUR PENN: When we finished *Bonnie and Clyde*, the film was characterized rather elegantly by one of the leading Warner executives as "a piece of shit." It went downhill from there.

CHARLTON HESTON: The phrase that's tossed around often—I really think it's lost all currency and most of its meaning—is the "antihero." I really don't know what the hell it means apart from someone who obviously is not a hero. You find the phrase "great man" put in quotes more often than not. I reject that.

WARREN BEATTY: *Bonnie and Clyde* was criticized by the older moralists, who felt that they were commissioned with defending the morality of the country, certain elderly critics.

SAM WASSON: Namely Bosley Crowther, chief film critic for the *New York Times*. His famous pan of *Bonnie and Clyde*, followed by Pauline Kael's equally famous rave in *The New Yorker* sparked a fierce debate, and clearly established a divergence of eras old and new.

JEANINE BASINGER: Not only that: it raised the profile of the film critic in Hollywood.

DAVID ANSEN: I mean, in the old days newspaper attitudes about critics was, anybody's a movie critic, you know, take somebody out of the sports pages, say they went to the movies for a while. And that kind of all started changing in the sixties and seventies.

JOHN BRAHM: We never took any notice of what critics said in the old days. I never knew what they said. I was not aware of it.

ALLAN DWAN: I don't remember ever paying any attention to what it did at the box office or what critics said.

CHARLES CHAMPLIN: The audience that now exists for motion pictures is probably more attuned to the critics than film audiences have ever been. I think you find that a lot of the films that do very well at the box office will also have done well in top-ten lists across the country. I don't think that means the critics have sold out to popular taste. The critics haven't gone soft. It's because the audience is very different from that automatic-habit-formed audience of the past.

GORDON STULBERG: I'm staggered that people should think that it's only for want of a certain kind of product that we've lost this enormous audience. The fact of the matter is that what we've lost is a habit, and having lost the habit, the habit is really never going to return. . . .

STEVEN SPIELBERG: Every Wednesday a new film would come in, and they would all be entertaining, and you'd go to the movies constantly.

DAVID PICKER: I didn't give a damn what was playing, I just went to the movies on Saturdays. Other people went three times a week. Today you don't do that.

MICHAEL OVITZ: Every Saturday at nine o'clock in the morning, we were dropped off at the movie theater. Two movies, two cartoons and a serial and a raffle. And it was all kids. And we were there from nine to two every Saturday come hell or high water.

BILLY WILDER: The critics have become important because today's business doesn't know what it's doing. They need somebody to tell them.

SAM WASSON: Pauline Kael told them in *The New Yorker*. Andrew Sarris told them in *The Village Voice*. In the *Los Angeles Times*, Charles Champlin told them, and in the *New York Times*, it was Vincent Canby. As never before, these and others had what no critics ever had in Hollywood: power. Swaying the public, they could sway the box office.

RICHARD BROOKS: There are some directors today who get close to the press. I don't know if they go to bed with Pauline Kael or what the hell they do. I'm not sure. They show her a script. They take her out to a location. Or they bring them here and run a rough cut for them and explain all the things it ought to have in it or ought not to have in it or whatever. I take that back about going to bed. I don't know if they go to bed. Maybe they should. Maybe every director should. I don't know. Somehow they get them close and let them read part of a script. They tell them the idea. They ask them, "Do you think it ought to be four hours long, or do you think that's three hours and two minutes and twenty-one seconds too long?" Or whatever. I can't function that way. I don't function that way. No one did in old Hollywood.

Most of the time the critics today—very often, I shouldn't say most of the time—they're reviewing one another. They talk about another critic's review. And you're caught somewhere in the middle, and you don't know what they mean, so they're going to break your heart. When you've finished it and the studio sees it for the first time, they'll break your heart, because they'll say that four minutes and thirty-one seconds ought to be taken out of there, and you'll say, "Why four minutes and thirty-one seconds?" Well, it's a good, round number, I guess. I don't know how the hell they decided. "Take six minutes out, and it'll be terrific." "How do you know six? How about seven? How about three and a half? How about nine and a quarter?" "Well, I don't know, I just have a feel." Well, they're full of shit. They don't have a feel about anything. They'd just like to get one more running in a day. Instead of five they'd rather have six. If it's a hit, they have that many more runnings. So they'll break your heart. And when your picture opens, maybe the audience will break your heart. So it's going to be rough on you. But if you love it, your real reward is in the making of the picture, not in getting in that big fucking black limousine and going out there for opening night, where they will applaud for you and some critic will write that you're a genius. Forget the critics.

PAUL SCHRADER: There were quite a number of us who really were satellites of Pauline's planetary view. And it was myself and Roger Ebert, Manny Farber, David Denby, Gary Arnold. We would check in with great regularity with her, and then the phone would ring. And she would say, you know, "This film, we've got to get behind it, we got to support it." And one of the great things about being a critic at that time was that criticism was part of the movement.

When you were a critic, you were carrying the message, you were bringing the banner of Godard, you were carrying the message of *Masculin Feminin* and *La Chinoise*. When I was writing for the LA *Free Press* every week, which was a very radical publication, you were part of the countercultural movement and you felt a genuine sense of social belonging as a critic.

BRUCE DERN: Now, some pictures will build. Some pictures you can tool with, like they did with *Bonnie and Clyde*. It wasn't successful and they revived the campaign, but that took only because Beatty is a tremendous producer.

STAN KAMEN: Warren Beatty had 40 percent of the profits of *Bonnie and Clyde*, and he has seen over $7.5 million for his 40 percent of profits.

If a picture is doing really well, then at some point the lawyers and the artists' representatives audit the studio. There are auditors in New York who are experts. I don't think that there is a lot of cheating or anything like that. The chances of profits meaning anything when a picture just about breaks even are very dim, but if a picture is really a huge hit, you just can't hide all that money—there's just no way to do it, and the person is going to see profits. The profits can be enormous, because sometimes the percentage of gross that an actor or director might have is a lesser percentage because it's gross instead of net. But sometimes if a picture is a huge success, if you have a larger percentage of profits, you'll do better than if you have 10 percent of the gross. Warren Beatty in that situation came off much better than if he had had 10 percent of the gross.

WARREN BEATTY: Well, what's somebody's concept of what's going to sell is not somebody else's concept of what's going to sell. I remember Jack

Warner writing a letter, which is in that archive at Warner Bros., which was very critical of a very nice man named Walter McEwen who decided to make *Bonnie and Clyde*. And I liked Jack Warner but he said in the letter, "Walter, I don't know why you've decided to make this picture *Bonnie and Clyde*, these things went out with Jimmy Cagney. You're going to lose all of the money that we're going to make on *Kaleidoscope*."

BUCK HENRY: None of us thought *The Graduate* was going to be either a runaway hit or a kind of mass cult film. I don't think anyone ever thinks that.

MIKE NICHOLS: I was in Hollywood, and I was at a party at Jane Fonda's, a big party in a tent, with a tree and a band. And there was a very funny guy under one of the trees. And he said, "So how do you like Hollywood?" And I said, "Well, here under the shadow of this great tree, I have found peace." And we laughed for a while, and that was Buck Henry. And right then and there, we got to be friends and spent most of the evening bull-shitting and laughing. And after a few days I thought, You know what? I bet he could write *The Graduate*, because he had been an improv comic like I was. And we had a fantastic time working on it for months and months.

And then my brother sent me a record of these young guys. And I would play it in the morning when I got up to go shoot *The Graduate*. At a certain point I thought, Schmuck! This is your score.

BUCK HENRY: I've never, ever liked songs about people wearing flowers. I liked the sixties, just aspects of it—more about that later.

MIKE NICHOLS: And it took me quite a long time of hearing it every morning to realize that it was this thing that I think is very important to movies, the "happy accident," the found thing. And once they start to come, they come like, like meteorites. They keep coming at you, these coincidental things. So we'd already shot a lot of the montage, and [editor Sam] O'Steen and I just dropped in Simon and Garfunkel. And that was quite amazing what happened. They were, in some ways, the voice of Benjamin.

NED TANEN: You're always dealing with the mood of the public at the moment you put that picture out. Does anyone really think that in 1978 *Easy Rider* would be a hit movie? I don't presume to know what a general feeling in America is. I don't presume to know what a general feeling in my office is.

BUCK HENRY: I had no feeling. I never have a feeling. I have a slight feeling of doom every time.

MIKE NICHOLS: We were stunned. We had no idea.

WARREN BEATTY: And it related to certain things that were so undeniable, like the situation in Vietnam.

BUCK HENRY: Sometimes people say that the film causes the change. Well, of course it doesn't. Film reflects changes that are already going on. And it would have perhaps been more difficult, even a year before, to do the story of a guy who has an affair with his girlfriend-to-be's mother. Is that syntactically coherent?

MEL BROOKS: After Mike Nichols had done *The Graduate*, I said, "If Mike Nichols could have gone to Joe Levine and said, "I want to do *The Green Awning*." "The what?" "*The Green Awning*." "What is it?" "It's a movie about a green awning." "Does any famous star walk under the green awning?" "No, all unknowns." "Are there any naked women near the green awning?" "No, no naked women." "Are people talking and eating sandwiches and scrambled eggs in outdoor tables under the green awning?" "No, it's just a green awning. Panavision. Just a green awning. It doesn't move." "How long would it be?" "Two hours. Two hours, nothing but a green awning on-screen. No talking, no dialogue, nothing." "All right, what the hell, we'll do it."

LARRY TURMAN: It's a bit of a guessing game. There's a lot of insecurity.

DENNIS HOPPER: Anyway, so *Easy Rider*.

PETER BOGDANOVICH: Peter [Fonda] and Dennis Hopper came to Roger Corman and asked if he wanted to make *Easy Rider*, but Roger turned it down because they wanted half a million dollars.

DENNIS HOPPER: It's very complicated. We were all at AIP now. We all, I mean, Jack Nicholson was writing screenplays and acting. Peter Fonda was the big star at AIP.

ROGER CORMAN: On the bike thing, I just wanted to make one picture. I wanted to make what was eventually called *The Wild Angels*. And I didn't make a second [motorcycle picture] because I said that I didn't want to get into the same trap that I did on the [Edgar Allan] Poe pictures [*House of Usher, The Pit and the Pendulum, Tales of Terror, The Premature Burial, The Raven, The Tomb of Ligeia, The Masque of the Red Death*], so I said what I'd do, I'd be executive producer, whatever that means, on another bike picture, and Danny Haller directed that, and it was called *Devil's Angels*. It did well, and all these other ones came along, and I figured, Okay, I've started the damn cycle, maybe I'll end it, so I backed Bruce Clark with *Naked Angels*, and that was successful, and I'd begin to think they'd go forever.

PETER BOGDANOVICH: *Easy Rider* really began with *The Wild Angels*. Peter Fonda basically plays the same character in both films. Brando in *The Wild One* hadn't done well, and *The Wild Angels* was the first really successful biker picture. It started a whole genre, and without it there would be no *Easy Rider*.

DENNIS HOPPER: So we promised that we'd never make a motorcycle picture. Because what we were becoming were these, like, you know, if we had a guitar, we'd be singing motorcycle guys, you know? I mean, we could see ourselves becoming these singing cowboys. It was sort of a nightmare scenario. So we promised that we wanted to make a movie but we'd never make a motorcycle picture. So we went around, Peter went around, with *The Last Movie* and tried to get it made and tried to do this and tried to do that. And nothing ever happened. So finally, he calls me from Canada, and he's with Sam Arkoff and James Nicholson, and they're selling *The Trip* or something up in Canada. And he calls me and wakes me up in the middle of the night and he says, "Look, man, Hoppy," he says, "they're going to give us the money to make a movie. And they're going to let you direct and they're going to let us both act in the picture, and I'm going to produce it. The only one drawback is, it is a motorcycle picture. But, like, you know, I got this great idea. See, we smuggle all these drugs, and then, like, we get on these gleaming bikes. We sell the drugs, and we get on these big bikes, and we go to Mardi Gras. And then, like, a couple of duck hunters shoot us in Florida." He said, "What do you think about that as an idea?" And I said, "Peter, are you sure you have the money?" And he said, "Yeah, I got the money." I said, "It sounds like a hell of an idea to me." So that was the beginning of *Easy Rider*.

PETER BOGDANOVICH: The deal was about to go through, but AIP got skittish about Hopper directing. So Dennis went to Bert and Bob.

DENNIS HOPPER: Since Bert Schneider and Bob Rafelson [of BBS Productions], who were old friends, had just made *The Monkees* series and were about to do their film *Head*, which is about the rise and fall of the Monkees, I knew they'd have a lot of bread.

BOB RAFELSON: The Monkees were all over the world, so they thought we were some sort of experts in the youth market. Columbia figured we knew something.

BRUCE DERN: They had a set-up at Columbia that was very good. Bert Schneider was the first B in BBS, and his brother Stanley was the president of Columbia Pictures, and their father, Abe, was the chairman of the board of directors. They had a very good set-up. It wasn't that they were wired, but they had carte blanche. Any picture they made, as long as it stayed at a million dollars, they never had to show a foot of film to anybody. When it came time to put it out, they got the money they needed for publicity and everything else. So they weren't shucked.

DENNIS HOPPER: Bert's sitting there and Rafelson's sitting there, and I think Jack Nicholson came in at one point and is sitting there. Because Jack Nicholson is now producing with Bob Rafelson and writing *Head*, see. Bob says, "Call Bert tonight at home." So I call Bert. Now, this is the son of Abe Schneider, who was there the day I told Harry Cohn to go fuck himself. Abe Schneider is now chairman of the board. Harry Cohn is dead. And this is Columbia Pictures. And Bert's brother was then head of production. And Bert had been, at twenty-five, treasurer of Columbia Pictures. So anyway, I call him at home, and he says, "I don't care if you act and direct in this movie if you want to do this movie with us." So anyway, that was the beginning of it.

BOB RAFELSON: *Easy Rider* was nonunion. That picture cost about $300,000, and Bert and I financed it. It was a little bit like taking all the money we made on the Monkees and putting it on red. There wasn't even a fifty-fifty chance. I just felt very strongly that Dennis could make this film and that it was important for him to make it.

NED TANEN: The only thing you can ever go on, doing this, is a gut reaction. All the research in the world won't help you, and the basics don't change: people are isolated, people are lonely, people want involvement, people want to feel something.

BOB RAFELSON: I always believed there was the possibility in Hollywood and in America for directors to make pictures with some autonomy. We discussed this as a concept, and Bert felt that was true. I guess the first person to join the company and make a picture was Dennis Hopper, who is no easy kitten. Neither Bert nor myself, to give you an idea of the company, ever visited the set of a picture that was made for BBS. The directors made the pictures on location and came back.

LÁSZLÓ KOVÁCS: I'm happy filming a location [as on *Easy Rider*], practical location shooting. It's very difficult and it creates a lot of compromise, but it also gives you something, something I can't really explain. Some kind of an atmosphere, some freshness, that you can't really get on a soundstage.

You walk into a big soundstage, and you start to be slick and you're putting lights where it doesn't really belong, over the head. It's a different kind of a thing. If it's possible to do something on location and there is a choice and they ask me, "Which way would you rather go?" I would say, "Let's go to the location," because you get something. You get something through the window, if you just see one seagull flying by.

DONN CAMBERN: At that time, *Easy Rider* seemed like an enormous amount of film. It was actually only about 135,000, 150,000 feet of film, but at that time it seemed like it would never stop. Excluding, of course, the film for the trip [to Mardi Gras], which had been shot prior to even beginning production on the film. The previous February, Dennis and Peter and company went down to New Orleans and shot in 16mm, shot close to 30,000 feet of—they were stoned out of their minds. They shot everything they could point the camera at. So we'd been working on the picture for about eleven months. We'd gone through several stages. The first cut was four hours.

FRANK PIERSON: Excuse me, editing for eleven months, or does that include the shooting?

DONN CAMBERN: That included the shooting as well, which was about ten weeks. The first cut on the movie was, like, four hours and forty minutes. Dennis just wanted everything, so we tried everything. We went through a whole period of time where we were compressing the picture very, very slowly. We moved, we had started editing the picture off the lot, and then Bert wanted us on the studio lot at Columbia, so we were editing right there at Columbia. After a period of time it became apparent that Dennis was not going to let go of any more of the picture and it was still way long and it was unwieldy. There were—different people would come in and help. Jack Nicholson would come in and look at it. Dennis, of course. Peter would look at it and critique. Henry Jaglom would come in—this was an ongoing process. But Dennis, being the director, would not let go. He simply would not let go. So Bert at one point said to everybody, "I want everyone to leave," and he said to Dennis, "Donn and I are just going to work for about three weeks. I want you to completely stay away, and then we'll run it for you when you come back, and if something really disturbs you, we'll talk it out and we'll put it back. But this can't just keep going on." So we did, and at that time we had, by that time we probably sat down with a two-and-a-half-hour movie, and in terms of length we brought it down to somewhere in the midnineties, which is just about where it is today. Dennis came back. He was disturbed by a couple of things, but basically we had the movie. And during the whole course of this, we kept bringing in albums of music and trying different songs, different pieces against all the different montages, looking and looking, and finally we settled on the songs and these choices and started to license them. Finally we got the whole thing put together and had a running for Columbia Pictures, and I must tell you that while we were working on the lot, because of the way we looked, we all had hair down to our shoulders, everybody gave us a wide berth. Nobody would really come close to us. They didn't know what the hell we were going to do.

FRANK PIERSON: This was in the days when the producers on the lots still wore suits and ties.

DONN CAMBERN: That's right. And editors wore suits and ties. Cameramen, everybody wore them. So we finally come to this day, it was on a Friday. At that time the man who was the head of physical production at Columbia, his name was John Veitch, and John's office was in the front of the studio. As you walked in the entrance and walked through this maze that was Columbia at that time, you passed these windowed offices, and that's where John Veitch worked.

FRANK PIERSON: And talk about a suit, he's the ultimate.

DONN CAMBERN: The ultimate, absolutely. Absolutely. And on this particular Friday afternoon, we ran the picture for three people. There was Leo Jaffe, who was at that time was president of Columbia, Stanley Schneider, who was vice president and Bert's oldest brother, and a man named Robert Ferguson, who was their marketing man. And it was just Bert and myself and my assistant at this running in the one large screening room at the old Columbia studios. And we ran this picture with the music—it was not dubbed, the music was in, and it was in very, very good shape to the ear. Leo Jaffe was sitting in the second row by himself. Stanley Schneider was sitting about two rows back in the corner. Ferguson was sitting on the other side a couple of rows back, and Bert was sitting in front of me, and I was sitting by the console so I could ride the gain [adjust the volume] on the movie as we went through. We played the whole movie, and it ended, it was quiet, everyone was waiting for Jaffe, and there was a pause—it seemed like a year. Jaffe, who at that time was in his late sixties, stood up, turned around, and he looked at Bert, then he looked at Stanley and at Ferguson and me, and he said—this is a quote—he said, "I don't know what the fuck this picture means, but I know we're going to make a fuck of a lot of money." And we're all elated. I walk out, I go to the editing room, I get my jacket or something and I'm walking out, now, past John Veitch's office, who flies out of his office, puts his arm around me, and says, "Donn, I understand we got ourselves a movie." And I thought, Here we are. This is Hollywood.

SAM ARKOFF: Now, you've never been to one of those exhibitor conventions, God spare you. But in any event, we had this audience [for *Easy Rider*] of about a thousand exhibitors and their wives. And there was a stream of exits by these people as the picture wore on, and finally at that orgy scene in the church, the rest of the audience just filed out. As they came out, they said, "Sam, we know the picture will do well, but you can't play in my theaters." And I'll tell you, we were really thinking we might get barred out of theaters. So we opened up in a number of theaters and crocked them.

GORDON STULBERG: The picture opened in a theater in Boston which nobody could find. It was a Walter Reade theater that hadn't done $6,000 a week since it opened. The picture opened at $40,000.

DONN CAMBERN: And of course it did turn out to be enormously successful. It played in many venues, it played for twenty-four hours a day for weeks on end.

DENNIS HOPPER: I won Best New Director at Cannes . . .

JOYCE SELZNICK: . . . And Jack Nicholson . . .

DUSTIN HOFFMAN: . . . I love Jack Nicholson's work in *Easy Rider*. I love that performance . . .

SAM ARKOFF: And lo and behold, the exhibitors who had walked out and said they wouldn't play the picture were all criticizing us for having sold it away from them. But the point about that picture was that in the last scene, when they buried their comrade and you hear the police sirens in the background and the other chap says to Fonda, "We have to get away, the police are coming," or words to that effect, and Fonda says, "There's no place to go," this was the prevailing attitude in that part of the sixties, by a good many of the young people.

FRANK PIERSON: And for all of those people, this was the first movie that had come through the pipeline in any big way that gave voice to those feelings. And it was an astounding event. It really opened up so many doors for so many people so quickly. There's never been quite that kind of, in my experience, in Hollywood.

DONN CAMBERN: No, mine, either.

SAM ARKOFF: I think we picked up something because we were aware of it. And we were aware of it in part because we needed to be aware of it. We didn't have stars.

JEANINE BASINGER: No stars, a loose script, a modest budget, a first-time director. Overnight, the studios decided the *Easy Rider* formula was the new brass ring—the box-office answer to their identity crisis.

A. D. MURPHY: Film companies, distributors, and exhibitors woke up to the fact that people don't go to films, they go to see a *specific* film. It's an impulse purchase. There have been many studies. People make up their mind to see a film about six hours before, and they go that day. It's literally an impulse purchase. It's not like getting seats for a rock concert next month or something like that, it's an impulse purchase, and when people want to go to see a film, they will pay the going rate. It's the psyche of the impulse purchase: "I want it, and I want it now." It's only when you come out and don't like it that you look at the price tag and bitch when we didn't like it. But when we wanted it, we would have paid any price. It's like a junkie that needs a fix—whatever the going rate is.

BOB RAFELSON: I've even read quite recently, for example, that some of the directors who are now among the younger generation of directors— and I don't consider myself a part of that generation—say that we somehow single-handedly set out to destroy Hollywood. I think what they are saying is that there was a sort of pretentiousness involved with our concern, or our self-concern. We were accused of making nonentertainment movies and personal statement movies, a sort of perverse *auteur* approach to the Hollywood industry. Now, of course, immediately after a film like *Easy Rider* came out, hundreds of similar films were made by the studios in an effort to capture the youth market, as they called it. I would not say, in this particular instance, that flattery was a high form of sincerity or whatever they call that when you copy somebody. It was just rip-off time.

MICHAEL OVITZ: Here's something to think about: Steven Spielberg did *Duel* in 1971 for the ABC Movie of the Week. That was a watershed moment for the entertainment business. The whole concept of making theatrical grade movies for a million or under was the absolute rampage of the time. The reaction to that was swift and pioneered by Ned Tanen at Universal. He went antithetical to everyone else. He put films together like *Two-Lane Blacktop* and a whole series of low-budget movies. They were all done on $1 million budgets.

BOB RAFELSON: Everybody was going out and trying to make an *Easy Rider* or a road movie or something like that. Then I think people really began to resent the fact that ours possibly succeeded and theirs didn't. They couldn't quite copy the impulse from which these pictures emanated. Basically, they emanated from the fact that Dennis Hopper was a crazed artist. You can't just hire somebody to be that.

FRANK PIERSON: A lot of us had been at Screen Gems across the street. Screen Gems was the television adjunct of Columbia. It was Jack and myself and Paul Mazursky and Bert, Bob Rafelson, John Cassavetes, and a whole bunch of people, Bob Altman, and we were all over there trying to make television pilots, and we had just made our move across the street to Columbia.

DONN CAMBERN: On Friday afternoon we would run the picture at Columbia just amongst ourselves. The grass would come out and everybody would get high, and then we'd go on and have a long conversation in Bert Schneider's office. Bob Rafelson, Jack, myself, Dennis, Peter, and those would go on for hours. And the next morning I couldn't remember what the hell had gone on.

That's another interesting note, and I must make note of it. In those days, the late sixties, there was a lot of innocence surrounding dope. Not like it has developed into. And as a result of that, there was a lot of dope in our editing room.

SAM FULLER: These kids liked to smoke.

SAM ARKOFF: There was a time when if I heard "Do our thing" or "Do my thing" one more time, I would have regurgitated in front of them.

SAM FULLER: Today, they're leaning toward a flavor of ad-lib quality.

SAM WASSON: It was an aesthetic tendency born of political and technological changes. Improvising lines, whole scenes, camera moves, and taking collaboration to new extremes, the New Hollywood made a profound—some would even say destructive—break with a formal sensibility that many would regard as classical.

DAVID BROWN: Mr. Hitchcock told us that he would no more improvise during shooting than the conductor of the New York Philharmonic would improvise while conducting. He believes the time to improvise is when you're working with paper—not film.

RICHARD RUSH: There was very little improvisational work being done on film because of the necessity of duplicating the performance for coverage. And we started doing improvisational work and working out coverage techniques to really go in and get the necessary stuff off of what was good that had happened.

SYDNEY POLLACK: Curiously, what you want in a film is a confused actor, a slightly unsettled actor, someone who's not quite certain about things.

PETER BOGDANOVICH: You have to rehearse to the point where nobody knows exactly what they're going to do but they think they know approximately what they're going to do. Then it's time to shoot.

WARREN BEATTY: It's the director's job to be in control. It's the actor's job to be out of control—and, but somehow, as a professional, to be in control slightly of being out of control. And if you're a good director, you don't want to be in total control. Everything will be boring, it'll be planned, and there'll be no spontaneity, so as a good director, you want to be slightly out of control of being in control. So you're a guy at the same time being out of control of being in control and being in control of being out of control. And in this way lies certain institutions that you can be sent to.

ROBERT ALTMAN: When I cast a film, most of my creative work is done. I have to be there to turn the switch on and give them encouragement as a father figure, but they do all the work. If an actor comes to me and asks, "What exactly should I do when I come in that door?" I'll say, "Have you thought about wearing cowboy boots instead of those slippers?" I'll say anything except answer their question directly, because the minute I've narrowed the 360-degree possibility down, they're not creating things themselves, and I'm doing the work. I want to see them do the work.

WARREN BEATTY: Bob Altman, God bless him, would be the first to tell you that *McCabe & Mrs. Miller* was created as we went along. We really got to the script as we were shooting.

ROBERT ALTMAN: I'm more interested in the impression of a character and the atmosphere than what actually happens.

PETER BOGDANOVICH: I asked James Cagney at a dinner party, "What's a good director to you?" He said, "Kid, I've only worked with five." I said, "How many directors have you worked with in your life?" "Eighty-five. But only five are really directors." So I said, "What does a real director do?" He said, "A director to me is a man who, if I don't know what the hell to do, can get up and show me."

ROBERT ALTMAN: How can I tell them what I want them to do when what I want to see is something I've never seen before?

JOHN CASSAVETES: What I try to do is to try to make myself as little important as a director while we're shooting as is possible to the point where, you know, it drove Peter [Falk] crazy a lot of times, because he'd say, "Listen, this is a very simple problem. Tell me what I'm doing here, and I'll be able to get out of it." You can't tell them, Peter.

PETER FALK: Yeah, John doesn't tell you. He really doesn't tell you. Not saying nuthin'.

HAL ASHBY: I just go in there and wing it.

JANE FONDA: Hal came from an editing room, and he would do forty takes and print them all.

HAL ASHBY: Shit, yes.

JANE FONDA: And, and then he would go into his editing room and create—and mold, like, a sculpture.

WARREN BEATTY: This is what I would say about Hal Ashby [directing *Shampoo*]: he really was entertained by actors. He never said anything much. Whenever he said something, he was right. And he was constantly amused. And if you were stupid, you thought he wasn't doing anything. But he was. He was not an egotist. He just was the most lovable, trustworthy, witty, sensitive—

JEROME HELLMAN: Ashby's a man who is always very open to discovery, to surprise. He loves that spontaneous part of the process.

ROBERT ALTMAN: Well, I don't have much to do with the actor's performance.

JOHN CASSAVETES: It's not really interesting to me, at least, to set up a camera angle.

ROBERT ALTMAN: I wasn't concerned about the shots being composed well.

PETER FALK: I dislike very, very much when I walk onto a set and I know that the director has an idea ahead of time, where he wants that camera to go and where he wants the scene to go.

JOHN CASSAVETES: Everything is a choice. And it seems to me I don't really have to direct anyone or write down that somebody's getting drunk. All I have to do is say [in the script for *Husbands*] that there's a bottle there and put a bottle there and then they're going to get drunk. I didn't have to tell [Victor Kemper, director of photography] anything on the close-ups in the bar. He just shot everything by himself, worked out his own camera, and the only thing I said to him was, "Feeling."

IRWIN WINKLER: When we came along, maybe because we weren't trained in the Hollywood tradition, we shot in the streets. We thought that real locations would be more appreciated by the audience, that they would give a sense of reality that we felt was necessary for a good story.

RICHARD SYLBERT: In those days, New York was about our own form of neorealism. It's in the tradition of the Italian street film. In other words, what we wanted was a poetic realism that was not done in Hollywood.

ROBERT ROSEN: I mean, one may be shooting in Italy, immediately after the war, and obviously have difficulties getting hold of soundstages and good film stock and a range of other things. You're shooting in a way that's quick and dirty. And you have that grainy quality to the film. Here, the logic of production led to a particular product. But then that particular product becomes emblematic for a certain kind of reality. And so, then, we've changed our film language. And now one strives for, for example, some of those quick-and-dirty techniques and that grainy look as a way to convey the meaning of a certain kind of realism—the dialectic between industrial conditions and a change in [film] language.

KEN ADAM: The designer's function has changed. He can still be as important as when he had to create a picture in a studio from nothing. But the cameraman has become much more important.

HOWARD W. KOCH: A Panaflex camera is really something. If you ever saw the cameras when I was first out in the business, you couldn't carry them, you know.

CONRAD HALL: I hate the perfection of film.

GEORGE ROY HILL: Nobody can beat Connie [Hall] outside. He's a fussbudget inside. He was when I worked with him. He had not yet mastered the technique of studio lighting, and he became very restive and very impatient and very fussy inside.

CONRAD HALL: Basically, I like it to be not perfect. My eyes aren't perfect. I don't know if any viewer's are, but I don't see everything perfectly, and I like it stressed.

ROBERT ALTMAN: I just cover it as if it were actually happening. We just have a little more control. I can say, "Let's do it once again!"

JEFF GOLDBLUM: [Working with Altman] was a very kind of communal thing.

FRANK PIERSON: The main thing [about BBS] is that within that community of filmmakers, directors, writers, actors, editors, everybody, there was a tremendous collegial spirit, and we were all looking at each other's pictures and one thing or another . . . Peter Bogdanovich was working over there—

PETER BOGDANOVICH: Larry [McMurty] and I were writing a script. And it was a lot of fun.

FRANK PIERSON: I can remember going to *Five Easy Pieces* when Bob [Rafelson] wanted to know what was wrong with his first cut and Mike Nichols had been invited in and Bogdanovich and a whole bunch, and afterwards everybody sat down and tore the picture apart and there was no ego, seemingly, involved in it.

DONN CAMBERN: I remember sitting in the projection room for the first-cut screening of *The Last Picture Show* with Peter and Bob and Bert, and there was quite a bunch of us. And it was exactly that same sense, you know? It was "Let's see what we got, and then let's go in and see how we can make it better." And it was an amazing time. It was a very open time. Very, very open about your work. It was all open amongst ourselves, but the studio was still the enemy.

DAVID CHASMAN: A studio is very like a royal court. There is usually one decision maker. The titles vary from studio to studio, but the things to watch for are "number one" and "number two"—number one being the chief executive officer and number two being the chief operating officer. And around are layers of counselors, advisers, people with limited authority.

LYNNE LITTMAN: They're all vice presidents of something.

JULIA PHILLIPS: There's usually a guy that's called the head of production, but there is also a president, and sometimes—oh, it's just as well to talk to the person that's the highest you can.

JEANINE BASINGER: In many ways it sounded like the same old system that existed before the 1960s. But it wasn't the same.

ERIC WEISSMANN: Now, what happened in the studio is this—I can only talk about Warner Bros.—

JULIA PHILLIPS: Warner Bros. for a time was like Haight-Ashbury.

ERIC WEISSMANN: Each studio has a different way of operating, but they may be more or less comparable. Every Monday, Wednesday, and Friday we [at Warner Bros.] had a production meeting that was attended by Ted Ashley, who was the chairman, Frank Wells, who was the president, John Calley, who was the head of production—

MICHAEL OVITZ: John was a man of taste, a wonderful guy. He was a studio man but also a talent-centric man.

ERIC WEISSMANN: —Dick Shepherd, who was cohead of production, the head of casting, the head of the story department, the head of physical production, Charles Greenlaw, and myself and my assistant, who were the business affairs guys.

At Warner Bros. we had a very good situation, which in those days gave us a real advantage over other studios. We had no board of directors to report to. We had complete autonomy, and we had what seemed to be unlimited funds. There may have been a discussion that we had $13 million or $14 million or whatever it was to spend that year, but I must tell you that I never heard that mentioned, and I never heard the fact mentioned that we didn't have enough money. And we were able to make decisions instantly. We didn't have to call the parent company. We didn't have to call anyone. And it enabled us to get a submission in the morning—and incidentally, if there was a rush, we would call a special meeting, we didn't have to say, "Well, we have to wait until Wednesday's meeting," I mean, there were things that were bought just instantly.

DAVID CHASMAN: What we [studio executives] do for a living is we perceive talent—if we have the wit to do that. We cultivate talent—if we have the ability to do that. And we pursue and woo talent—if we have the charm to do that.

HAL ASHBY: I don't like to go and sit and bullshit with those guys, because they've got nothing to say. So it's your natural instinct to stay away from it, because they're a negative force. They're negative. They put negative energy, whatever the hell you want to call it, into what you're doing. Every goddamn time. I've never sat around with any of them that gave me an idea that was worth a goddamn. Strangely enough, the only one that I ever got anything out of was [Paramount head of production] Bobby Evans. And Bobby Evans is as slick as they come. But I'll tell you, there's something in the man. He cares.

ROBERT EVANS: We've been an unusually successful film company.

HAL ASHBY: When I got down into the editing process of *Harold and Maude*, when he started to look at the film, he remembered the film from the dailies. He's the only one that talked to me about what was going on in the film. He said, "I remember such-and-such." That's always exciting. Anybody that does that.

BLAKE EDWARDS: Evans had something to do with *The Godfather*, so he's made some right decisions. He just didn't make them with me, that's all.

HAL ASHBY: He also knew how to work with a filmmaker. And he was great, because he was the one that kept telling me to hire Ruth Gordon [to play Maude]. Every time I talked to the man, he talked about Ruth. He said, "She's the only one to do it." I said, "What the hell are you talking about?" He said, "Well, I just saw *Where's Poppa?*, and I didn't like it." I said, "Well, I went to see it, and I liked it." I saw it after that, after he said that. But it was one of those funny changes. But I loved him for that, too, because I saw his point of view.

They originally started talking about making it for $800,000. The budget we were talking about was $1.25 million at that time, and there was this whole big thing about it going on. I remember Bob at one point, with all these production people and the attorneys and everybody from Paramount around this big table, and he said, "Jesus, Hal, when we first started talking about it, we were talking about eight hundred thousand." I said, "Well, Bobby, I guess that was just a dream. It was my dream." He said, "You said we could do it." I said, "Well, it's my dream." He said, "Well, your dreams are my ass." It was one of those wild things that went on like that for about a half hour. And at one point, I remember, I said, "Bobby, I don't know what the hell we're talking about. We've been talking about $1.2 million for the last six weeks." He said, "No, we haven't." I said, "We have. I sat right here in this office and told you when Chuck [Mulvehill] went through it, it was going to be around $1.2 million." And Bobby took a long while. He took a long thought about it.

ROBERT EVANS: Really, your basic element is what's on paper, and then the elements that you attract to that at least give you the opportunity of going to the next step to make the film.

HAL ASHBY: I saw his mind clicking over, and he said, "You're absolutely right, and I apologize." In front of all of them. And that you don't find too often. Oh, boy, oh boy, that you really don't find very often, let me tell you. And he said, "Excuse us just a minute." He took Stanley Jaffe outside and came back and said, "Make the picture."

JULIA PHILLIPS: Universal is like the Pentagon.

GORDON STULBERG: When you get a Lew Wasserman at Universal and a Disney sort of situation, the management is so firmly in control that the board of directors, which legally represents the interests of stockholders and which legally supposedly runs the corporation at law, doesn't monitor extensively the activities of the company. The company is dominated by its chief executive officer and the chief operating officer.

DAVID PICKER: Well, when you're talking about Lew Wasserman, you're dealing with one of the greatest brains this business has ever had, if not the single greatest.

AL RUDDY: Now, this is how well run Universal is. We turned in a script at five o'clock in the evening. By nine the next morning, there were three production managers, boards, and budgets in the office. Literally, the whole goddamn thing was ready to start going. It was madness, like throwing it in a machine and seeing hot dogs come out the back. They are amazing.

STEVEN SPIELBERG: I thought Universal was the prime rib of movie studios. I kept remembering Orson Welles's famous line that a movie studio was the best toy a boy could ever have, and I began to function at Universal as if it were a giant sandbox.

ROBERT EVANS: Universal is the only company that has a huge television program, so everybody they sign, they use in television. And then they have picture commitments with them at Universal's option. When you have fifteen hours of television in a week, you have a lot of people you can use who try and break in. I would do that, too, if I were Universal. We don't have that, though.

GORDON STULBERG: When I arrived at Fox, it's hard to believe this, but Fox had a philosophy of not renting the studio to outsiders. The studio as late as 1971, when I came in, still thought that the studio was an adjunct of the feature division. Now, I don't think there is a soul in this room who could conceive of a studio making enough feature pictures, studio-based, to occupy the stages, even with its television activity, to keep that studio operating. So I brought in, within two months after I got there, the fellow who had run the lot for me at Columbia, a young man by the name of Bernie Barron, and I said, "What you're going to do now is take the studio and make a profit center out of it. You rent to anybody and everybody, and if the feature division of Fox needs a stage and there are no stages available, we'll go out and rent. But we're not going to keep stages empty and available for the feature division. The company is swimming in red ink from unabsorbed studio overhead."

ERIC PLESKOW: United Artists is not in television. We don't have television production. Our business is motion pictures, so we think differently from others.

MIKE MEDAVOY: We don't own a studio.

ERIC PLESKOW: We never did own a studio.

JULIA PHILLIPS: United Artists likes to see themselves as a bank. You know, "We're just giving you the money, and you go and make the picture."

ERIC PLESKOW: Okay, we work as a team at UA. There is no one person who makes this decision alone. Mike [Medavoy], out here, he has a very able assistant, Marcia Nasatir. They read the material, and we have readers, of course. Now it gets to them in New York, Arthur Krim and Bob Benjamin and myself read it, so there's about five people who read it. Obviously it's a very rare instance where all five of us agree it's terrific. There are a lot of arguments that go on, and you win some and you lose some, even within the group. But in the overall, we come to some kind of a consensus, and then it gets made.

MIKE MEDAVOY: At UA we work quite differently from other companies, I think, and that is that we have a tradition of having to let the director or filmmakers make their pictures and we stay out of it.

GARETH WIGAN: I was the agent for John Schlesinger and Jerry Hellman when [UA] made *Midnight Cowboy*, and I was based in London, and I saw *Midnight Cowboy* three times before David Picker, who was the head of production at United Artists, saw anything—he saw no stills, he saw no

dailies, he saw nothing. Nobody at United Artists saw that picture or anything on it at all until John and Jerry were ready to show it to them.

JEROME HELLMAN: We said no to the R [on *Midnight Cowboy*]. We felt
that we would be more comfortable as filmmakers if the ratings council
gave us an X. We took the X. The rating cost United Artists money, because there were places that wouldn't play an X-rated film. But the management supported us.

WALDO SALT: David Picker basically said, "Do it," and stood by.

JEROME HELLMAN: "You're filmmakers," they said. "You're the guys
whose feelings have to be trusted." Even with the X rating, the film was
very successful, of course. After we had won the Academy Awards and
after films had been released with R ratings that were much more explicit, the code administration called and asked if we wanted to resubmit
the film. "We'll resubmit the film," we said, "but we will not change one
frame." They looked at it again, and they gave us an R.

MIKE MEDAVOY: You know, different companies—

ERIC PLESKOW: —think differently. You know, to think alike is an antitrust violation in this country. We don't even talk about what we think. We
don't even think about what we think.

SUE MENGERS: I think you've got to remember that the people in the studios are salaried employees, they are not owners. They are people who
are employed by boards of directors, the heads of the company, and they
get a salary, and they're scared, too. I always think the ideal in those jobs—
it's just my own theory, and it could be totally fallacious—is that those are
the jobs that should only belong to rich people, because if you run a studio
when you're scared and you're worried about your own job and getting
your own salary, you make decisions out of tension and fear, while when
you were Louis B. Mayer, who made a fortune because the tax structure
in those days was such, plus he had ownership, they were able to go more

with their instincts. I just think there is a lot of fear within the studio structure among the studio people. How often do we pick up the trades, and a studio executive has left for "indie prod"?

JULIA PHILLIPS: It changes from studio to studio. It changes from six-month period to six-month period. The most insecure job in the world is that of an executive.

ERIC PLESKOW: We have a fiscal responsibility to the stockholders of the company and to the banks. But we are not, in fact, makers of movies. We're not producers, we're not directors, we're not actors.

DAVID CHASMAN: The general rule at each studio is that there is a stratum of executives who have the authority to initiate development. That is to say, they can authorize the payment for the development of a script. Then, when it comes in, that script has to be assessed to see if it can attract elements justifying a final approval for production: what is known in the jargon of the trade as a "green light." Those are few and far between.

ROBERT EVANS: My job as head of production is to look at things that are presented to me.

ERIC PLESKOW: We're not creators. Mike [Medavoy] and I don't create movies. We select projects.

NED TANEN: We're all in the business of trying to find material. There is no big secret about it.

RICHARD ZANUCK: You've got to hustle with the literary people. You've got to get the material. Because without material, you're just you.

DANIEL MELNICK: I've never had a time in my adult life, since I've been in this business, when I haven't felt depressed by the amount of reading. And it's always like I was back in school and it's Sunday night and Monday's the test and I haven't done my homework. One of my fantasies when I stopped running a studio was "Now I'll be able to read fiction or nonfiction for pleasure." And there's just no way. Somebody asked me about a recipe the other day, and I heard myself saying "I'll get some coverage for you."

MIKE MEDAVOY: I mean, everything you can think of comes in: one-page outlines, ten-page outlines, hundred-page outlines, books, treatments, screenplays, projects brought in by a director, projects brought in by an actor, projects brought in by a producer, projects brought in by an agent. At the present moment, I think we have ten [people reading material].

The kind of thing they do is, they do a one-sheet summary of the plot, a half a sheet to a sheet, depending on how many comments they may have, on the plot, and then they do about a ten-page breakdown of the script, almost scene by scene, in other words, explaining what happens in each scene. Based on that, one can eliminate, I would say, a good 65 to 75 percent of material that comes in. Because the subject matter usually is something that will turn you off. It's either following a trend, or the characters of the piece are uncastable. And there will be reasons why you could easily say, "Hey, this couldn't work."

NED TANEN: To a large degree, the whole movie business is research and development. And if you're lucky, one out of every six or seven [projects] that you develop gets made. At the end of the year, there's that terrible moment of truth when you suddenly say, "How the hell did we spend four and a half million dollars this year in pictures that didn't get made?" It's that wonderful moment when everybody hates everybody else because "You didn't make my masterpiece" and "How dare you write this piece of garbage?" That's the game. It's really who you're in business with, what material, and whether somebody who works with you really believes in that material and why. I can't define it more than that. I get into a lot of pictures I don't believe in. But nobody is a genius in the movie business. Nobody. And anyone who thinks he is is a damn fool or a liar.

SUE MENGERS: I mean, I know what's bad, but I don't know what's good. Do you know what I mean?

NED TANEN: I don't know who's a genius and who isn't. And I take a lot of meetings.

SAM WASSON: Once studios manufactured stars. But the contract days of scrupulous trial and error were over. In the New Hollywood, where actors worked freelance controlling their own careers and personae, filmmakers cast them praying, not knowing, if they would become stars.

JOHN SCHLESINGER: *Midnight Cowboy* was a case in point. Jon Voight's photograph failed to elicit one bit of enthusiasm for the producer, Jerome Hellman, and me to even meet him, and it was only due to the forceful personality of the casting director that we met him and read him in one scene. Then we were bowled over.

JOYCE SELZNICK: I was worldwide head of talent for Paramount, and I sat and looked at this [low-budget film] in the projection room, and all I could see was this fellow on the screen that knocked me out. And at the end of this showing, I said "Who *is* he?" And two days later, Jack Nicholson came in my office. And he sat there, and it was kind of fascinating. He had been around a long time. Typical old Hollywood story. He had done everything from directing to producing and he [was] really ready to throw in the towel. He said, "I'm giving it three more months, and I'm getting out because I've got a family and I just cannot make a living in this business." And I did try to sign Jack Nicholson to Paramount Pictures. And I did not get very far, that is true. But true to his word, three months later he ended up in *Easy Rider*.

MIKE NICHOLS: And when I was casting *Carnal Knowledge*, I said, "I have to have that guy." I hadn't even met him. So then I met him, and then I thought, Oh, my God, this is the guy.

NESSA HYAMS: Gene Hackman is another example. He was nowhere until *The French Connection*. I mean, he worked constantly, but he was not a big star, and he just got a role that worked.

STAN KAMEN: Billy [Friedkin] really felt very strongly about Gene Hackman. He had to fight like hell to get him.

NESSA HYAMS: Gene was the last person they wanted for the part. They didn't want him. I mean, they tested Jimmy Breslin.

LYNN STALMASTER: You have so little control [as an actor].

GEORGE CLOONEY: The first agency I was with was a small agency, and they mostly represented you if you were Mexican or—so I would go up for only Mexican roles, which, you know, I'm from Kentucky—

BRUCE DERN: Find some person that you know who's working on the lot a certain day you want to go there. Call him up and just say, "Look, can I stop by? I'm coming to see you." Just find a way—I hate to say this, bullshit them. Just tell the guy at the gate that, you know, you have a script in your hand, and say to him, "I'd like to deliver this to so forth and so on. I know he's working on such-and-such." The guard at the gate will say, "Sure." Just say, "I just want to get him the script, and the agent couldn't make it." Basically, they are going to say, "Okay," especially if you have your picture book with you and something like that. You've got to do that on every single lot. Then when you're on that lot, you've got to go berserk. You've got to hit every single person that casts. You've got to hit every television show. On top of that, you go up to the producer of that show. You go up to his office. It you can't see him, see the secretary. You say, "Look, I went down to the casting office. I know what you're going to tell me, that I should do it through the casting office, but could you please give Mr. Berg this picture and the credits, so that when Lane Allen calls, or whoever, I'll know I'm getting the best possible shot at him. Even though he may never call me, at least I'll know the producer of this series and the casting director will know who I am." You just have to repeat that and repeat that, and finally out of frustration—you just assume that you're right for something.

MERYL STREEP: Juliet Taylor was the casting director for Woody Allen's movies, and she's a fixture in New York—great, great, imaginative casting director. She would go to all the shows, and she saw me in a production of an Arthur Miller one-act on the same bill with a Tennessee Williams one-act, and I had gotten some good reviews for that. So she asked me if I would like to fly to London and meet Fred Zinnemann [who was casting *Julia*]. And I was really stunned, because it was to audition for the part of Julia. At that time, they weren't sure if it was going to be a star or they wanted to get an unknown opposite Jane Fonda. So I flew and met Fred Zinnemann, and he said as I walked in, "Well, I've already decided to cast Vanessa Redgrave." I said, "Well, you know what, that's fine. That's fine. I mean, I completely understand." He said, "Would you take a smaller role?" And so that's how I got my first job.

LYNN STALMASTER: There's no explanation for so many things that happen in our business.

NESSA HYAMS: Luck.

STAN KAMEN: Luck is a lot of it.

JEANINE BASINGER: It's usually about luck. You couldn't always predict what an audience was going to go for. In any year, what captures an audience's attention?

MICHAEL OVITZ: Okay, here's what came out in 1971: *A Clockwork Orange, The French Connection, The Last Picture Show, Straw Dogs, Harold and Maude*—all tiny budgets. Nineteen seventy-two: same thing but budgets started to creep up a little more. Nineteen seventy-three: a little more than that . . .

JOSEPH E. LEVINE: Years ago, if you made a film about China, you did it on a back lot at Paramount. You can't get away with that kind of a thing today. If you're going to make a film about China, you've got to shoot it in China. You can't do those kinds of things. People are wise to that, they know.

KEN ADAM: In the past fifteen to twenty years, the majority of films have been made on location.

PAUL MAZURSKY: That's why so many movies go over [budget]. When they get there, they're not prepared. You can't do it. It's very easy to do it inside a room. You can do anything inside a room, but not outside.

ROGER CORMAN: You can prepare faster when you're in the studio, because it's simply a matter of building the sets and working off of that.

FRANK YABLANS: You can light it better [in a studio]. You've got flexibility. You've got mobility. It's also cheaper.

ROBERT ZEMECKIS: Just put up some banana plants.

PETER BOGDANOVICH: On *What's Up, Doc?* I never saw a budget. I never knew what the budget was until it was all over. The only thing I've ever heard on *Doc* was John Calley called me up. We were shooting up in San Francisco. He called me up, he says, "You know, Peter, the chase is very expensive." I said, "It is?" He said, "It's going to cost a million dollars." I said, "Well, that's an expensive chase." He said, "Is there anything you can do to make it cheaper? I don't know how, you know? When cars go down the street, they got to go into the glass and the Chinese dragon. I don't know what to do. They're all good jokes. I don't know what to cut out." He says, "You haven't got any ideas?" I say, "No. I think it's important to have the chase, don't you?" "Yep—well, I just thought I'd ask." That was the whole conversation.

ERIC WEISSMANN: Incidentally, at Warner Bros., we had a weekly report of budget, how much on, over, or under we were—but on *The Exorcist* that sheet never was distributed.

POLLY PLATT: On *A Star Is Born* [1976] I went in and I said, "I need five hundred thousand dollars for this movie," and Howard Pine, who was the production manager, said, "Well, that's ridiculous, we don't have that kind of money for this film." And so I said, "Well, how much money do you have?" "Well, I'll tell you that after you revise your budget." Well, I mean, this went on and on and on. I never found out. It's called money. It costs money to achieve style.

SAM WASSON: Designers had to reinvent the wheel every time out . . .

JEANINE BASINGER: All the people you needed to make a movie were no longer on the payroll. It wasn't like it was in the days of the old studio system when people were available day to day to work on any movie.

SAM WASSON: In the old days, most everything was done in-house. It was easier to apply cost control and budget realistically.

ANTHEA SYLBERT: Now, let's take *Shampoo*, for instance. It is about [late-1960s Beverly Hills], a very specific place at a very specific time historically. It is almost more difficult when it is that close to you and you have lived through it than something which is more divorced from you, because you start wanting to deny certain things that you yourself did. You say, "I didn't wear my skirts that short. I never could have done such a terrible thing." Then you start looking at photographs of yourself and your friends and people who were not your friends, and you discover what it is that you did and you no longer can deny it: there it is in black and white. Men did, in fact, open their shirts down to here and hang seven thousand things around their necks, started to become the peacocks, started in a funny way to become the sex object. I mean, Warren Beatty in that movie is, in fact, the sex object. None of the women are. So now you say to yourself, "What do I do about that that is both real and works dramatically?" So you say, "Okay, if I'm going to put him in a leather jacket, I want it to be the softest leather jacket that ever happened. When you touch it, it should almost be a sexual experience. I don't want a heavy leather jacket anymore." So I have eliminated a whole category of things that are not possible, and it is that process of elimination which, I think, has to happen in all areas, whether it be art direction, costume designing, cinematography . . .

Now, when I first do the sketch, I make a mistake. I have put zippers on the jacket. And we start to make it, and I see the zippers, and I start to think to myself, Zippers are not really sexy, because they have made something rigid about it, and they are keeping me from seeing his body as well as I want to see it. So instead, we started from scratch and we laced it and had all the things hanging, so there was even a kind of movement when he wears it. Even the jeans. We started off by just buying jeans. After all, jeans are jeans. Well, you couldn't see his body well enough in just the jeans, so we even custom made the jeans. His shirts were silk. So everything you touched and he touched became sexual, even to the scarf. I mean, everything that he wore had some kind of sexuality to it, and more time was spent on his sexuality than on any of the females'. Are you beginning to understand what I mean? Now we get into the area of color. Pale blue is one of those things that is very hard to photograph, so the shirt, which was blue, and the jeans, which were blue, were all overdyed in brown so that it brought it down one shade, not so that you could tell once it is photographed. Once it is photographed, it looks like it does in real life, whereas if you leave it alone and you photograph it, it takes on a strength and a life that it doesn't have when you're just looking at it with the naked eye, because somehow the camera does something that I don't understand to that color. Even skies. For instance, someone like Gordon Willis would prefer that the sky were white or gray than on those days when it's blue, because it just takes over.

RICHARD SYLBERT: You say to yourself, "Okay, *Chinatown* is about a drought, so all the colors in this picture are going to be related to the idea of a drought. And the only time you're going to see green is when somebody has water for the grass." It's about a drought in 1937 in southern California. All the buildings in this picture will be Spanish except one. And they'll all be white. The reason they're white is that the heat bounces off them. And not only will they all be white, they'll be above the eye level of the private eye. Above eye level means, for the private eye, that he has to walk uphill. It is always harder emotionally to walk uphill. You then decide what the colors are going to be and why they're going to be that way and what the range should be, let's say, from burnt grass, which is a terrific color, to white, which you know you're already going to deal with, to umber. Umber is interesting, because it's the color of a shadow. And in a movie like this, the more shadowy the better. You use the layers, the planes, use everything you can. All these things are available to you to structure a movie. Even opaque glass. You know what's interesting about opaque glass in a mystery? You can't quite see who's behind it, and it looks like frozen water. And in a picture where they're talking about water, it's an interesting object to get involved with. And you just keep doing that wherever you can.

POLLY PLATT: I always find directors talking to me about how they want a "look" like Vermeer and Rembrandt, and all of a sudden we start shooting and they don't remember anything, all of a sudden they forgot the whole thing. Or the cinematographer wants a diffused, gray tone to the film. He says, "We won't shoot on a sunny day. Never. We want it gloomy, dark, and we don't want any contrast in this film." Then a sunny day will arrive and we'll have nothing to shoot, and all of a sudden, we're shooting.

KEN ADAM: But I'm always hoping—and it is not just for selfish reasons, because I like to design—that there will be a return to a studio environment. Because I think one can, in many instances, give more of a heightened reality to a scene in a studio environment than by shooting actual locations. I've proved it on a number of pictures. You saw *Strangelove*. The war room was a complete fabrication.

RICHARD SYLBERT: The game is making choices. You make those choices because you're solving problems with them: dramatic problems, not technical problems. There are millions of good technicians in Hollywood that can solve your technical problems. But if you haven't got a good idea, you can't make a choice.

ANTHEA SYLBERT: Any choice is better than no choice at all.

POLLY PLATT: We're all sort of struggling to make it the best, but in order to make it the best, eventually there needs to be somebody who wants the best and who's given the power to get it the best.

CHARLTON HESTON: If van Gogh had been a film director, he would be unknown, because if you construct an analog for that, his brother, Theo, would've been a studio head and would've financed one, maybe two films, which would not have been successful, and that would have been the end of his career.

ROBERT TOWNE: [When we made *Chinatown*] no head of a studio would dream of suggesting that an ending of a picture should be changed because an audience might not like it. You'd look at the guy as if he were crazy.

ROBERT EVANS: I don't star fuck. I writer fuck. I director fuck.

ROBERT TOWNE: I grew up believing you could do interesting films within the mainstream of Hollywood, and in that time, you could. I mean, *Taxi Driver* was a mainstream movie. *Chinatown* was a mainstream movie.

ALEX LASKER: I don't want to bring this subject up if it's a sore point, but you seemed to mention you go over budget quite a bit.

ROMAN POLANSKI: Yes.

ALEX LASKER: Obviously, because you are a perfectionist, you won't settle for anything until you find just what you want.

ROMAN POLANSKI: Yes.

ALEX LASKER: Don't you get in trouble with getting money for the next one?

ROMAN POLANSKI: Well, yes, I do.

ALEX LASKER: Why don't you just add extra money to it or extra days when you know you are going to go over and not pay the penalty?

ROMAN POLANSKI: Yes, but then they won't let you do the picture, so you see, it's always the same story. You see, at the beginning of every film, you do the budget, and this budget is usually a realistic one, the one you are going to end up with anyway, and then [the studio executives] start cutting it down and there is no picture, so you accept the cuts and you go over the budget to reach the figure which you came up with in the first place anyway. But often, also, it is as difficult to anticipate what the cost is going to be. I understand that when they are building houses they go over the budget. Yet it's easy to establish how many bricks you need and how many working days you need and so on. With films, every film is a new adventure, it's a discovery of a new continent, and you don't know exactly what the difficulties are going to be. . . .

It depends also on how good the people you have around you.

HAL ASHBY: I was so loaded on *Harold and Maude*, I could hardly walk. You want to talk about profundity? I was lucky I didn't fall in the bay.

DONN CAMBERN: So we had a lot of fun in those days.

PETER BOGDANOVICH: All of it was fun.

MIKE NICHOLS: There are many funny stories about making *The Day of the Dolphin*. And I won't tell any of them.

ANTHEA SYLBERT: We worked hard, and we had fun.

GEORGE LUCAS: That's basically what happened in the seventies.

FRANK PIERSON: That kind of overnight change in the whole atmosphere and opportunities that opened up for a whole new generation of people—

MICHAEL OVITZ: But going forward, the million-dollar movies became $3 million movies, and film budgets started to rise. What happened was, in 1974 and '75, you had *One Flew over the Cuckoo's Nest, Three Days of the Condor, Jaws, Barry Lyndon, Dog Day Afternoon*—these were what I call transitional movies because the budgets started to creep up.

CHAPTER 13

THE CREEP UP

GEORGE LUCAS: I'd gotten this scholarship, it's called the Sam Warner Scholarship, which was to work at Warner Bros. for six months. Traditionally, what a student did is go there, and he could choose what department he wanted to be in. You know, the editorial department, script department, whatever.

The day I arrived was the last day that Jack Warner was there. He left that day. The company had been sold to Seven Arts. They were doing one Seven Arts movie on the back lot, *Finian's Rainbow* [directed by Coppola], and the rest of the studio was completely empty. So my choices of what I was going to do were extremely limited. So they put me on watching *Finian's Rainbow*. They were the only people on the lot. And I watched it for about a week, and I said, "Look, I've just [observed the making of *Mackenna's Gold*] for six weeks out in the desert. I have no interest in Hollywood movies. I have no interest in watching these people do this stuff, it doesn't interest me." And I went back to the production department and said, "Could I possibly get assigned to the animation department?"

I'd gone on a tour, and I realized there was only one guy in the animation department, he was sort of the caretaker, sort of just sat there and watched after things. But they had all these cameras and they had short ends and all kinds of stuff, so I said, "Well, if I can get in there, I can probably make a movie." And then somebody told Francis that I was trying to get off his movie, and we were the only people on the crew that were under sixty years old. We were both film students, we both had beards, and he said, "Why do you want to get off my movie?" And I said, "Well, 'cause it's boring and, uh, there's nothing to do." And he said, "Look, stick around, and I'll give you something to do. Come up with one good idea every day," and so I did. I went around with a Polaroid and picked angles and hung out in the editing rooms. That really was my strength, editing picture. Francis's strength was working with actors and writing, and so, in the end, we became a good match.

And then Carl Foreman offered me the opportunity to make a feature out of *THX*, because it had just won the National Student Film Festival. Francis heard about that, he said, "Don't go over there and work for them. I'll get you a job to do it over here." So I said, "Well, okay." 'Cause I'd spent a little more time with Francis, so I said, "Okay, we'll do it here." And so he got me a deal to write a screenplay. At the same time he said, "You'll come along on *The Rain People*. I'm gonna make this little tiny movie with about fifteen people. You can be the assistant art director, the assistant director, the assistant camera, and the assistant everything, and you can write your script, and you'll get paid to write your script if you can work from four to six in the morning. We're just gonna travel around the country and torch some cars." So I thought that was a great idea.

And then we finished that movie and Francis said, "You know, if we can shoot here and have a studio here in the middle of Nebraska, we can make a studio anywhere, we don't have to go back to Hollywood." And I said, "I agree," and I told him about [independent filmmaker] John Korty and about how he had a little studio out on Stinson Beach, right on the beach, and he had a Steenbeck [editing table] and a screening room, and he made these little, soulful independent movies. And Francis says, "That's it! That's what we should do!" And so we drove from Nebraska to San Francisco and visited with John and decided that's what we were going to do, was move to San Francisco. We rented a little old warehouse down in the south of Market area and set up American Zoetrope.

So when Francis told me to write the script for *THX 1138*, I said, "I can't write, I'm not a writer." And he said, "Well, if you're ever gonna be a director, you've got to become a writer." So I worked on the screenplay.

When we finished *The Rain People*, I showed it to him, and he said, "You're right, you're a terrible writer." So we hired a very, very good playwright, and he wrote a script, but it was nothing like what I wanted. It was more like a play than a movie, and it definitely wasn't pure cinema. And so by the time we finished *The Rain People*—and I brought my friend Walter Murch up to do the sound on *The Rain People*—Walter and I, we were very close friends at USC, we were in sync, he helped write the script for the first [USC student film version] *THX*. And I said, "Let's try to see if we can together sit down and make a movie that we feel works." And so we did. We sat down and wrote the screenplay together, 'cause we think very much alike. And we came up with a script that we loved. Francis didn't quite understand it, but he said, "Come on, we'll get this thing made."

The Kinney Corporation had bought Warner Bros. from Seven Arts. And so Francis said, "Well, we've got to wait a while until these people show up for work." So the day that John Calley and Ted Ashley and those guys showed up for work, Francis sent them a telegram saying "We're in the middle of production here, you've got to tell us what's going on. Either shape up or ship out." And they didn't know what was going on. And he went down there and convinced them that they needed to do this picture, that we were going to do sort of *Easy Rider*–type pictures, you know, youth pictures, you know, avant-garde kinds of films that would appeal to the youth market. And he made a deal for seven movies. One was *THX*. I had been working on another film with John Milius, *Apocalypse Now*. Francis had been working on *The Conversation*.

STEVEN SPIELBERG: The great thing about young filmmakers who have made it is that this gives the big studios blind confidence in the other guys waiting in the wings. Ten years ago, they wouldn't have hired anybody under thirty to make a picture, and now most of the life support for our business is coming from young people.

CHARLTON HESTON: I call directors "Sir" even though I'm now at a point where at least half of them are younger than I am and make a hell of a lot less money.

GEORGE LUCAS: When I made *THX*, I was sheltered by Francis. We believed very much in the art of cinema. We wanted to push the envelope of movies, and I was a young kid, you know, right out of college, and I knew that this was a one-shot deal, that I would never get a chance to do a movie like this again. I mean, I was aware of that. And, and I knew that once we finished it, I'd probably never get to work in the industry again. But at that point I didn't really care 'cause I really wanted to be a cameraman and make documentary films, so I didn't really care. I said, "Well, this is great. I got this opportunity, I'll just take it. But I'm certainly not going to try to conform to something that I'm not. This is the movie I want to make, and I'm going to see what I can do with it, and it'll be fun to work in a bigger medium and see if it goes into a theater and all that sort of stuff." So it was a big experiment for me, just making a feature film. But I didn't feel that I had to bend my vision, uh, for any commercial ideas, 'cause I knew Warners wasn't looking at the movie. They hadn't read the script, they weren't seeing the dailies, and obviously, I mean, when you saw dailies, you couldn't figure out what was going on. It was a completely obtuse movie, you know, and they were busy with other things. This was such a low-budget picture that it was way off their radar. And we were up here in San Francisco, and nobody bothered to come up and see what we were doing.

In those days, Francis was very much emboldened by his youth, is one way to put it. But he loved to jump off cliffs. I would sort of stand at the cliff and say, "You're going to die," and he'd say, "Oh, you're crazy," and he'd always land on his feet and say, "Come on down." One of the cliffs he jumped off was to . . . say, "We're going to make all these movies [at American Zoetrope], they're gonna be great," and the studio had not seen a thing, so when we finally finished the movie, we took the film itself down to Hollywood. It was on a Thursday. But Francis also took a box—as it happened, a black box—full of scripts. We had six scripts that went down there with it. And the studio looked at the movie, and they were in shock. I mean, they just—they had no idea what they were looking at, it was just way out there in terms of— well, they couldn't believe what had happened. Then they were furious with Francis for not, you know, taking a stronger hand and making it more into a commercial film. And they read the scripts. They said, "Well, we don't want to have to do anything to do with it, Francis, and these scripts are no good anyway." You know, they threw away *The Conversation* and *Apocalypse Now*, among others. And they were really very angry about the whole thing. And they said, "Francis, you have to pay back all the money you've spent. The deal's off, and we don't want to have anything to do with you anymore." And I think we had spent about $300,000 that somehow Francis had to pay back, but he had nothing at that point. We lost everything.

They came back and tried to recut *THX 1138* and that was a drama, and I was furious with them and indignant and all the things a young filmmaker is when the studio starts stirring up your creative vision. And then Francis had to worry about how he's going to make the money to pay this back and what was he going to do for a living and how was he going to pay the rent on Zoetrope.

Paramount offered him this, you know, potboiler of a gangster movie that nobody wanted to direct. And he asked me, "Well, what should I do? Should I take this job?" And I said, "Francis, we're broke. I'm going to have to go and get my own job, and you're in debt, so if I were you, I'd take this movie." Well, he said, "But I don't want to do other people's movies." But he took it.

MARIO PUZO: When I wrote the novel, I didn't even think about the movies. Somewhere along the line, Paramount saw part of the novel and gave me an option. But that was like having a rich uncle slip you a few bucks. It didn't affect my writing the novel.

ROBERT EVANS: Mario Puzo, who was an inveterate gambler, needed money, and he had thirty pages of an outline for something called *The Mafia*, which was eventually changed to *The Godfather*. And we supported him for three years, worked with him while he was writing his manuscript. That's what I call a house project, not buying a bestseller. That was a big difference.

FRANK YABLANS: You've got to understand a studio's mentality. They're investing so many dollars in a project, and when they make that commitment, they have to look to recoup that money. If you're working off a novel that the audience knows about, you already have that much of a selling tool, you're that much ahead.

ROBERT EVANS: [Frank Yablans] is basically in charge of distribution, advertising, because it's handled out of New York. He goes to all the functions, the president's meetings. I don't go to anything. The only thing I've come to in a long time is right here today.

WARREN BEATTY: And Charlie Bluhdorn, who ran the company that owned Paramount, which was called Gulf + Western, liked my work, he liked *Bonnie and Clyde* very much, and he wanted to send me a book that he had commissioned. It was called *The Godfather*. He commissioned it to be written for $24,000. Did you know that? $24,000. He sent me the book and said, "Do whatever you want: you can direct it, produce it, act and everything." I read it and I said, "Charlie, I just don't think this is going to work."

AL RUDDY: I was offered a lot of money to write a book about what really happened during the making of *The Godfather*. I told this guy, "Look, let me tell you something. Your offer is very, very generous. However, I promise you that I would never live to spend that money. That's out. I am never going to discuss all the politics and the intrigue and the subterfuge that was involved in the making of that film."

MARIO PUZO: I think all you guys realize that the director is more important than the writer by this time. Does anybody think different? Francis rewrote me and I rewrote him. That's the way it worked. Same thing on *The Godfather II*: I did first draft, then he did second draft, then we'd get together and I'd do third draft. I think it worked fairly well.

ROBERT EVANS: Before the making of the film, Francis had tremendous pressure on him, because he was both writing the script and directing the film, and he had budget problems. There was a lot of pressure on him from the various [crime] families of New York not to shoot the picture in New York. We almost moved the picture one time to Kansas City or St. Louis because of the tremendous pressure there was in New York not to make it there. And Francis was a nervous wreck from it. There was actually a conspiracy against Francis on the production side of the picture to keep Francis from making the film.

MARTIN SCORSESE: I brought *Mean Streets* to Francis. He said he was going to read it but never did. He couldn't read it. He was in the middle of *The Godfather*, going crazy.

AL RUDDY: I've always said that the great thing that happened in *The Godfather* was that every guy that was making that movie, literally every guy, needed a winner. I certainly had never done anything like that. Francis needed a monster. Brando was in trouble. Al Pacino, you know, Jimmy Caan and Bobby Duvall, they were nobody.

AL PACINO: I was Francis Coppola's choice from the start. And he had this image, and I was the one. One of the reasons is, he had seen me in a Broadway show. He wanted me to be in his movie that he was doing in San Francisco called *Love Story*, of all names. It never was done. It was a very good movie, well written. And he was going to direct it, and he wanted me to star in it as a college professor who falls in love with a young student. Well, Warner Bros. at the time said, "What? Who is this person? This Pakino, Papino, what is his name? And he's short, for one thing."

They turned Francis down. And I remember at the time, I went to San Francisco, and Francis and I spent a few days together. And we got to know each other. That was it, that was the reason, because a year later he called me to tell me that he was directing *The Godfather*. Well, I congratulated him. I said, "They're smart to use you," and he says, "Yeah. And uh, guess what? I want you to play Michael Corleone." I thought, This guy's got a thing with me or something. What's the matter with him? I mean, is he crazy? I thought, Well, gee. I had read the book. And I thought, My God. I mean, of all the parts. I mean, I'm not right for Michael Corleone. I thought, Gee, he's off there, too. So I humored him, you know. And then after a while, it was reality. I was up for the part, as was a hundred thousand other actors. But he wanted me, you know. And you can't lose when the director really wants you.

ROBERT EVANS: Francis wanted to use Al Pacino. I did not. He was right, and I was wrong. We tested a lot of people for the part, and Al Pacino didn't even make a good screen test on it. It's strange, he just didn't.

AL PACINO: He wanted me, and he fought for me. And he fought for Marlon. And—and they wanted neither of us, really.

DIANE KEATON: I was overwhelmed by *Godfather*. I just really did feel like the outsider.

AL PACINO: My first meeting with Marlon, I remember meeting with him in Harlem—an Italian restaurant in Harlem, I think it was Patsy's. And Francis Coppola got us all together, sitting around this table: Jimmy Caan, Duvall, myself, the late John Cazale. And we sat around the table with Marlon having Italian dinner. And the odd thing was, each one of us became the character we're going to be in the movie. We sort of went to that—at least, I went to it because of my shyness and my inability to articulate. But at the same time, Marlon, too, had an image. And he projected this larger-than-life thing that he also used in his own way. And he was a prankster, too, so he would lay it on sometimes. But I got close with him for a while there on the picture.

MARIO PUZO: Now, I have to say that Bob Evans over at Paramount, his function on *The Godfather* was that he would listen to Francis and he would listen to me and, as much as he could, go with us. The big incident on that was that he didn't want to film the Sicilian sequences in *The Godfather*. They wanted to leave all that out because the picture was finished, and they had to go to Sicily and shoot that. Everybody's opinion was asked, and Francis and I said it was an absolute essential. The studio didn't want to do it, but Evans went ahead with us and went our way.

ROBERT EVANS: Well, you never know until you see the totality of it. You have to see everything before you can pass judgment on it.

AL PACINO: When I saw it, I thought, How could you do that? He just—he kept it a secret, let's say. And Gordon Willis, of course, who shot it, the two of them together and Brando. It was one of those—I'm still wondering if I dreamt it.

JEANINE BASINGER: Published in March 1969, Puzo's novel was a smash, spending over a year on the *New York Times* bestseller list. In an unprecedented move, Paramount, knowing it had a hit on its hands, opened the picture wide and fast, fanning the flames of the popular interest, saturating the public with *Godfather, Godfather, Godfather.*

DAVID BROWN: The old idea was to take a class film and open it first in New York, probably at an East Side house, then in Westwood, and then let the media percolate to the peasants of the world the word that it's a great hit. *The Godfather* broke that pattern because of the urgency to see it. When Paramount released *The Godfather*, it released it simultaneously in many houses that previously had never played anything but single, exclusive engagements.

JOSEPH E. LEVINE: Nobody would think that a cigarette company wouldn't launch a cigarette and spend $5 million to advertise it and not have it available in every drug and grocery store in the country. That was the thing we used to miss in the picture business.

DAVID BROWN: It has now become apparent to the distributors today that they can get their money back faster and satisfy the urgency to see a film by adopting a broader release pattern.

ROBERT EVANS: Good distribution can make a picture very successful, while bad distribution can make it just another picture.

SAM WASSON: But *The Godfather* was a startling example of *smart* distribution, *blockbuster* distribution, an essential element in the burgeoning equation of how to assemble, manufacture, and sell not just a movie, but a giant hit.

A. D. MURPHY: You've got to remember that no enduring business lacks the middle element of distribution. It's called *wholesaling.* Let's imagine that one of you has invented something or come up with an idea, and it's so good that somebody says, "Would you make one for me?" So you make one, and people come back. "Would you make one for me?" And pretty soon the creator or the manufacturer is making more and more. All of a sudden there is a public demand for the idea. Pretty soon the maker cannot keep up the quality anymore because he's too busy out on the front lawn collecting bad checks and stuff like that. The only way that business can survive is if someone comes along and says, "Look, pal, you go back and do what you do best. You make it, but I will undertake the responsibility for financing you making it. I will also undertake the responsibility of marketing it to the public—either the stores or the retail buying public— and I will collect from them." That is the distributor. That is the wholesaling function, and when you don't have a healthy middle element there, you don't have a healthy business.

ROBERT EVANS: It's never happened in the motion picture business in the last twenty years where a company has owned 84 percent of the profits of a film and no gross participation given away. And this happened to be the biggest picture ever made, which is *The Godfather*. It is a totally house-controlled project. We developed the book with Mario Puzo, we developed the script, we hired the producer, we hired the director. It was a totally studio-oriented project. So when a picture like that does $150,000,000 and you own 84 percent of it, it's like hitting a very big gusher.

NED TANEN: The only way to get *American Graffiti* made was to put Francis's name on it, because *The Godfather* had exploded two days earlier, and he was no longer an imbecile, he was now a genius, which is the history of this ridiculous community we live in.

GEORGE LUCAS: Then *American Graffiti* came out. It was a giant hit.

STEVEN SPIELBERG: I'm sure that this has happened to all of you sometime. You say, "Wouldn't it be great to do a film about this?" And you get some kind of a notion that you don't have the wherewithal to make the movie yet, and somebody else comes along and makes it, and it's *American Graffiti*, and it makes all this money and it's about your childhood and you were those characters, and you wanted to make that movie, but George made it instead.

GEORGE LUCAS: But my feeling was that I'd just been really lucky and it wouldn't happen again.

MARTIN SCORSESE: When I did *Mean Streets*, it was after *The Godfather*—it was about Italian Americans—it may have helped because of *Godfather I*.

STAN KAMEN: *Mean Streets* was independently financed.

AL RUDDY: If you say, "Hey, look, I'm bringing in the financing, it's my film, I'm going to give you the film to distribute," now you're talking to them as distributor, not as financier. That's the best way to go. The majors are the majors for a specific reason. They are big organizations and generally very professionally staffed. You pay for that size. You pay for that organization. If you feel that you want to do it yourself, you can do it for less money, a lot of times with greater enjoyment.

JOHN PTAK: The studios used to totally finance their own pictures, but in the last fifteen years, studios have become more involved in cofinancing, negative pickup deals, and outright purchases. Cofinancing is where a studio puts up, say, a million dollars, and a private financier puts up another million. To make the case easier, when someone like Dino De Laurentiis puts up a million dollars and Paramount puts up a million dollars, Paramount might get US and Canada, Australia and Great Britain, your principal English-speaking countries. For De Laurentiis's million, he would get the rest of the world to do with whatever he pleases. Studios more recently have entered into cofinancing situations with each other.

MARTIN SCORSESE: Roger Corman was the first [producer in Hollywood] I brought *Mean Streets* to. His readers loved it. I said, "Can we do it?" And Roger said, "Marty, I understand we got a script from you, and everybody here says it's one of the best scripts we've received. However, I'd like to ask you one thing." He said, "I haven't read it. Has it got gangsters?" I said, "Yes, it's got gangsters." He said, "Has it got guns?" I said, "Yes, it's got guns." He said, "Has it got violence? Has it got sex?" I said, "Yes." He said, "My brother just made a picture called *Cool Breeze*, which is the first time that my brother, Gene, is making money. It's making a lot of money." He said, "Now, if you're willing to swing a little, I can give you a hundred fifty thousand dollars, and you can shoot it all with a nonunion student crew in New York. The only thing is, I'd like [the cast] to be Black." I said, "Roger . . ." Goes to show you how much I wanted to make the picture. I said, "I'll think about it." So I walked out knowing that I couldn't do it. Then that same week, a good friend of mine, his name is Jay Cocks, his wife was out here doing *Old Times*, a Harold Pinter play, with Faye Dunaway—his wife is Verna Bloom, and she was out here alone and wanted to have dinner with me. She said, "This young guy just came into town, his name is Jonathan Taplin, he used to be a road manager for Bob Dylan and the Band, he wants to get into movies, he's twenty-six years old." I said, "Fine, we'll go for dinner." So at dinner he says, "What script do you have?" I say, "Well, I'll just scare this guy away," so I say, "I've got this script—" So what happened was that he read the script and called me up and told me that he liked the script, which I couldn't believe. I said, "Oh, really? Well, wait till you see the pictures." So he saw *Who's That Knocking* [*at My Door?*], and he saw *It's Not Just You, Murray!*, and he saw *The Big Shave*. And he called up and said, "I like your pictures." This was all in the space of one week. I said, "Okay, Sunday night we're having a preview of *Boxcar Bertha* at the Pantages. Sam Arkoff hates it. Roger Corman likes it, but everybody else at AIP hates the picture." So I said, "Come to the preview with us." And I figure we'll blow it right there. If the audience doesn't like it, we're dead. So we got to the premiere at the Pantages, and it was the best preview they'd had since *Wild Angels*. And Arkoff was outside, and he told me, "It's almost good now." He smiled. He wouldn't give it all to me, but he liked it. And then afterward, Jon and Sandy [Weintraub] and I and some other people went to the Chianti restaurant, where this whole thing started, and we had a few drinks, and he said, "If Roger can get me a letter saying he'll distribute the film, I can get you money to make it in Cleveland." So I said, "Okay, fine." So we went to Roger. Roger said, "Okay, you've got the letter." We walked out, and I was stunned. I said,

"We've got the letter, which means we can probably get the money." He said, "Yeah." So he went to Cleveland, and he called me back a few days later, and he said, "Terrific news. They got the letter, and they want to go ahead." I said, "How much are you going for?" He said, "Three hundred thousand dollars." I said, "Terrific." Then what happened next is a little shady—not shady in the sense of the dealings, a little shady in my own mind, because I'm not sure exactly what happened. What happened was that he got the money from a guy named E. Lee Perry, who's got executive producer credit on the picture—a young guy, he was about twenty-four years old at the time and had just inherited a lot of money at the time—we got the money from him, and for about three weeks we were going strong. To make money, I was editing a picture for Roger that was directed by Vernon Zimmerman called *The Unholy Rollers*, and I was also editing *Elvis on Tour* at the same time. So I was doing two pictures at once, and we were also doing rewrites on the script, building up the girl's character, doing all kinds of things. And then he called one day and said, "The money fell through." And I said, "Well, that's it."

So anyway, what eventually happened, this guy Perry came back into town, and we had dinner with him. It was him and his wife and Taplin and his girlfriend and me and Sandy. And it was very relaxed, because I knew that the guy wasn't giving us any money, so I didn't have to worry. We just told a lot of funny stories and had a good time, and the next thing I know, we've got the money back. Because what had happened was that the kid's family had called up Jon's family and said, "Your son is trying to swindle our son." That kind of thing, you know. But we got the money.

Mean Streets was done in twenty-seven days. We had to finish when we finished, and that was that. You know, I kept adding scenes. I added the backroom scene, the long improvisation. I added a scene in front of the gun shop in New York. I added the scene where they steal the bread in front of his uncle's shop. All that stuff. I added a lot of stuff like that. And I kept pushing the limits of the budget and drove everybody crazy, you know. But that was the only thing we could do, because the more we got down there, the more fun we had and the more we realized the atmosphere we wanted to get. A lot of my old friends are in the film, a lot of guys who are just hanging around are there in the picture as extras. But where we really went over budget was in the music. The music killed us.

The Rolling Stones came to $15,000. Each. First it was $7,500 each, and then they doubled it.

The music was very important, because you can [walk down the street in New York] and hear the march from "Aida," and as you walk by another room, you can hear "Handy Man" . . . and then in another place you hear Eric Clapton, and then in another place you hear an old Italian folk song, and you keep going and there's Chinese music. Especially in the summertime, it was incredible. I don't know if anybody here ever lived in tenements in the summer, but in one building it was all one house, all the doors open, everybody would go in each other's houses, everybody would eat whatever everybody else had, and there were always fights in the streets. There's something extra-violent about New York.

But that was my own energy, though.

SAM WASSON: You needed that kind of energy. In post-studio Hollywood, the path from script to screen, formerly a straight line, grew longer and twistier than ever.

PAUL SCHRADER: I was doing a review of the film De Palma had done, *Sisters*, and I was interviewing Brian, and it turned out that Brian was a chess player. He was looking for a chess partner. So I started playing chess with him. And I told him about the script *Taxi Driver*, and he was living on the beach.

JULIA PHILLIPS: And this was the time of the Boris Spassky–Bobby Fischer chess match, I forget what year that was. So all of a sudden, Nicholas Beach got crazed with chess. I used to play chess with Brian all the time, and we became friends. And there was a guy following Brian around him writing for a film magazine. Paul Schrader was like his little puppy dog. And he mumbled, and he kept his eyes on the ground, and he dressed in rags, and he was really quite a character.

PAUL SCHRADER: In Japan, if a man cracks up, he closes the window and kills himself. In America, if a man cracks up, he opens the window to kill somebody else. And that's what's happening in *Taxi Driver*.

MICHAEL PHILLIPS: At that time, in the early seventies, Julia and I were living out at the beach, and Brian De Palma was living next door to us with Margot Kidder.

PAUL SCHRADER: Michael and Julia Phillips had just done *The Sting*.

TOM POLLOCK: [It was] a very small community.

JOHN PTAK: It's a village.

JOSEPH E. LEVINE: My son, who's now thirty-two, used to play on the floor with Sophia [Loren] when he was fifteen. Imagine rolling around the floor with her. It could happen to you.

JOHN PTAK: It's a business that relies very much on association.

MICHAEL PHILLIPS: And this is the way that things always seem to happen. Things don't come through the formal sources of agents, but they come through friends and tips like that. Anyway, I read *Taxi Driver*, and I loved it. And we tried to sell it.

JULIA PHILLIPS: *Taxi Driver* took four years from the time that we first met Paul Schrader at the beach, and he had not gotten his self-confidence yet and he was speaking into his armpit when he spoke at all, and that screenplay had been around, as they say. It had been around to every studio. We optioned it probably six to nine months after it had been around.

PAUL SCHRADER: And then Julia and I saw a rough cut of *Mean Streets*. And we said, "Well, you know, who really should do this is Marty and Bobby, you know, they're perfect for this." So then we sort of made a pact to do it: Phillipses and Scorsese and De Niro and myself.

MICHAEL PHILLIPS: And they agreed. They had no other offers for anything. And then we went around, and we found we still had nobody willing to make this movie until we just finally lied about how much it would cost and waited for *Mean Streets* to come out.

MARTIN SCORSESE: I showed the answer print to Francis Coppola. He hired De Niro that night. He called him the next morning for *Godfather II*.

ERIC WEISSMANN: Now, in the case of a picture such as *Mean Streets* being sold to Warner Bros., what will happen is to try to get the seller to commit himself first. The guy will say, "I'll sell the picture," and the buyer will say, "I'll buy it. What do you want for it?" And the seller will say, "What do you want to pay for it?" And then you dance around that a little bit. The seller may ultimately say, "I want a million dollars for the picture." And then the buyer will say, "Why? On what basis?" And the seller will say, "Well, that's what it cost." And the buyer will say, "Can you prove it?" And the seller will say, "Yes," or he may say, "It's none of your business what this picture cost. You've seen the picture. Do you want to buy it or not?" You'll talk more elegantly, because you may be friends with each other. Sometimes they don't talk more elegantly. Now, your problem is that the chairman of the board is calling you every fifteen minutes, saying "Did you make the deal?" and it's kind of hard to make a stand under those kinds of pressures. Sometimes there is a difference in the price of pictures because there is a difference in the cost of pictures, and a person who has spent $500,000 in doing a picture is not going to sell it for $300,000.

The whole technique of negotiation depends on what your philosophy is. If you want each time around to make the best possible deal, you're going to blow at least half your deals. Also, you're not operating in a vacuum, you're operating in a context of future negotiations. The reason I was able to say to the person who wanted to sell *Mean Streets*, "I'll only deal with you if you'll deal with me and with me only," was because, first of all, he had confidence in Warner Bros., and secondly, he had confidence in me, because he knew that chances are if I wanted to make a deal, which I wanted to, he was going to be able to strike a fair deal.

MARTIN SCORSESE: Jonathan [Taplin] wanted to open the film in twenty-five cities, just like *The Last Picture Show* and *Five Easy Pieces*. And he went to Bert Schneider and talked to him, and he said, "Do it, because there's nothing opening in October except *The Way We Were*, and that isn't going to make a cent." Famous last words . . .

I had no idea how we were going to sell that kind of picture. How are you going to sell it? As the gang that couldn't shoot straight? That was our first concept—guys running around with shorts on with guns and hats. Because Johnny Boy takes off his pants at one point. And it would have looked like a comedy. And next thing I know, we opened in LA, got nice reviews, did two weeks' business, and that was that. Everyplace else, the same thing. And at the same time *The Exorcist* was coming in. And that was $14 million, and it was [the same] company [Warner Bros.], whose whole life depended on *The Exorcist* at that time, because *Mame* they were a little shaky about. So naturally, they're not going to worry about *Mean Streets*, a picture they paid $750,000 for and they didn't make anyway. They're not going to cover that, and why should they? As they say, "Why throw good money after bad?" In fact, they want us to buy back the foreign rights, and we're in the process of doing that now. In fact, I'm trying to get them to rerelease it in LA, but they want to wait. At least they should show the damn picture in Los Angeles, you know. Because the only people that have seen it are in the Bel Air circuits and the Beverly Hills circuits, in people's houses. That's the only place they screen it. So in a sense, it's not all their fault, and it's probably our fault. It's inexperience, and it's a damned hard picture to sell. How do you sell a picture like that? I remember we had two ads, one with a gun in it and one with a dead body in it. And [distributor/ exhibitor] Don Rugoff said to me in New York, "The ads that don't sell are the ads that have guns and dead bodies." And those were our two ads.

ERIC WEISSMANN: Sometimes you have a movie like *Mean Streets* where [Warner Bros. head of distribution] Leo Greenfield said, "Despite the spectacular reviews it got, we should show this in New York forever, run it one year in New York before we show it anywhere else, and eventually the word of mouth and the buildup will be so enormous that people will have to see the movie." Well, we got drunk with the reviews and we showed it everywhere at the same time and nobody went to see it.

And then you try to change the advertising campaign and appeal to a leather jacket crowd instead of an art crowd and show it in Detroit, and that doesn't work, either. You know, sometimes the people don't want to see a picture no matter what you do with it.

JULIA PHILLIPS: On the day that *Mean Streets*, I think, opened the New York Film Festival and got all those rave reviews, John Calley called me from Warner Bros. and offered me $650,000 to make *Taxi Driver*, on account of Marty was such a good filmmaker, and we went into actual serious negotiations on that.

PAUL SCHRADER: And *The Sting* came out.

MICHAEL OVITZ: The picture was huge.

PAUL SCHRADER: And then, all of a sudden, that bargain package of *Taxi Driver* sort of looked more like a bargain.

MICHAEL PHILLIPS: But then Scorsese was unavailable and De Niro in the interim did *Godfather II* and he won an Oscar.

JULIA PHILLIPS: Everybody stuck together, but both Marty and Bobby were getting noticed from *Mean Streets*. Bobby went off with Bertolucci to do *1900*, and Marty went off to Marlon Brando, theoretically to do a picture about Wounded Knee, which put Marty in the hospital and made him immobile for months and unable to breathe. Bobby came back.

PAUL SCHRADER: So there's a hiatus period of a year or two, and there was a way at one point to get it made with Jeff Bridges. And we just said, "No, let's hang in there on this one. Let's just pay the price. If we don't get it made, we don't get it made," which in retrospect was very high minded. Although when you're in the middle of these things, they don't seem so high minded. It's really the arrogance of youth more than anything else.

JULIA PHILLIPS: We had set up a deal with David Begelman at Columbia, who had just then taken over the studio, and he needed product and he needed some prestige, I think, and Steven [Spielberg] and Michael and I had made a deal there at that time . . .

MICHAEL PHILLIPS: We had brought them *Close Encounters*. And Begelman was really happy about that, because he snatched it away from 20th Century–Fox, where we were starting to set it up.

STEVEN SPIELBERG: I had thought a film about the UFO phenomena treated realistically, up to a point, would be a big hit.

JULIA PHILLIPS: You could make six *Taxi Driver*s for what it cost to make *Close Encounters*.

STEVEN SPIELBERG: My father woke me up out of a sound sleep when I was about six or seven years old, threw me in a car in the middle of the night, and took me out to a field somewhere where there were about a hundred people looking at the sky. It frightened the hell out of me, but it was a meteor shower.

KATHLEEN KENNEDY: Steven has this ability to bring about an idea and then really open it up for discussion. It doesn't matter who's involved in the process. If they have a good idea, he's going to listen to it and he's going to add on it. When people are in an environment, a creative environment like that, and they realize that that isn't closed off to them, then I think people begin to get very creative and they begin to get very alive in terms of ideas. And he's very good at creating an atmosphere like that, and I think, consequently, it shows in his films.

STEVEN SPIELBERG: I had an imaginary friend when I was eight years old who was from space. He was my spaceman friend. And I used to, you know, really imagine him. I was kind of a weird kid. Anyway, even at eight I was a pretty weird kid. I didn't have a lot of friends, and I had this little spaceman friend.

JOHN WILLIAMS: I met Steven Spielberg at Universal Studios when he was a very young man. I think he was about, maybe, twenty-three years old, twenty-four years old. One of the executives there, Jennings Lang, said, "I want you to meet a young director who has a film called *Sugarland Express*. Would you like to have lunch with him?" I'd never heard of Steven Spielberg.

Okay, so Mr. Lang's office arranged a lunch at a very fancy restaurant in Beverly Hills, and I was five minutes or so late to the restaurant. And I went over to the table, and here was this kid, he looked like he was seventeen years old. He stood up, and he said, "I'm Steven Spielberg." And I felt like an elder, more or less immediately. "Oh!" And he was dressed like a very young person might. And the wine list came over. He looked at it, and I could see—I don't think he'd ever held a wine list in his hand before. And we had lunch and spoke about his film. I had no idea what he had done before, some television, I think. But I discovered five minutes into the conversation that this young gentleman knew as much or more than I did about film music. He started singing the themes of films that I'd written, subthemes, you know, that I'd forgotten about, and everything of Max Steiner or anyone else you wanna pick. He was really quite a scholar, an erudite, almost, in this area. Much more than I. And I loved that about him, of course, instantly. And we could sit and dish about film music, ones that I'd played for, the ones I liked, didn't like: "Well, why didn't you like it?" "Why do you like this?" An insatiable capacity to learn. A glistening intellect, obviously, in the first meeting with this kid.

STEVEN SPIELBERG: I began at about fourteen, making little films. I began editing in the camera, and then I began splicing because white flashes would show on the film when you stopped the camera. So I edited the flashes out, and that led me to primitive revelations that if you put two pieces of film together with two people, one looking right and the other looking left, you have created conversation. This is how I began, and the films grew larger and larger until one day I made a feature that ran all of two and a half hours, and I had the Eastman Lab apply a sound strip, and I rented a machine called a Bolex Sonorizer that is now out of date— collector's item—and then postsynced the whole film. The actors came in and watched their lips move and went through one or two rehearsals before they spoke to themselves on the white screen sheet. It was my first feature, a science fiction picture, and I get a kick out of seeing it every now and again.

It cost $500, and that was it. But it took a year to make. I had to go to school, so I could only shoot on Saturday and Sunday. But this is what hurts: all the films I made never helped me. They helped me to grow as a filmmaker, but they never helped me get a job.

RICHARD ZANUCK: Steven Spielberg literally used to climb over the studio gates—I mean, until the guards were so accustomed to seeing him on the lot that they thought he was working there.

STEVEN SPIELBERG: I used to tote these reels about, attempting to show them to anyone, but I could not get an audience. I found it impossible to get anyone to spend five minutes in a screening room looking at my pictures.

RICHARD ZANUCK: David [Brown] and I both received the manuscript of *Jaws* along with a few other people in the business at the same time very early in the game. It was right off [Peter] Benchley's typewriter. David was in New York, I was in Los Angeles, and we read it immediately. We had some advance word on it that it was something special and hot. And independently, as we were reading it, we both decided that it was highly commercial, very unique, and something that would interest us as producers. Within twenty-four hours, we were well into the negotiations on that project. We found ourselves in the middle of a fierce bidding contest with some other very important people. We did everything. We got down on bended knee. We tried to sell Benchley through his agent, because we didn't know Peter at that time, that we were the best men to make the picture. And that's all we had to go on, because the other people had as much money and financial resources as we did.

SUE MENGERS: You know, one studio will pay $1.1 million, then another will pay $1.15 million.

RICHARD ZANUCK: It got down to who's going to make the better picture. And we convinced him that it was us.

STEVEN SPIELBERG: Actually, what happened was, they offered me a film called *MacArthur*, but I didn't want to do it because that's two years out of your life, working in ten countries, a garden variety of dysentery in each one of them. So they said, "What do you have that you'd like to do?" And they had a book called *Jaws* that I was very interested in, and I said, "I'd like to do this, I'd like to develop it from its raw state."

VERNA FIELDS: Steve is the kind of director that gets ideas from ideas.

KATHLEEN KENNEDY: I think working with him, myself included—but I include everybody who works with him because his movies require hundreds of people to make them successful—he has a unique ability to inspire people to do much more than they think they're capable of doing.

VERNA FIELDS: He can get on a set and see something that the art director did. It'll bring forth a million great ideas.

STEVEN SPIELBERG: When I first read the *Jaws* galleys, I was amazed that I was so captivated with the ocean. I don't know anything about the ocean. Why suddenly did a shark attacking three men in a boat appeal to me?

FRANK YABLANS: It's judgment! Nobody really knows!

STEVEN SPIELBERG: I was able to make some artistic justification in knowing that I was about to make my first commercial sellout movie going in. I had to do something to justify why I was making *Jaws*, because people were critical.

FRANK YABLANS: I bring the property in, and Alan Ladd [Jr.] says, "Gee, Frank, I don't know, a picture about a shark? You can't make any money!"

GEORGE LUCAS: I thought it might be interesting.

FRANK YABLANS: You've got to be crazy!

AL RUDDY: I just want to tell you one story. It's my average-guy story. I went to the School of Architecture of USC, and Frank Lloyd Wright used to come down once a year. He told a story that I love to tell about our business, because it's exactly the same. The two architects are designing a building, and they are sketching and sketching, and finally it's 3:00 a.m. They're arguing about "This is better, that is better, mine's better, yours is better." One guy says, "Hold it. You and I are very sophisticated people. As architects, we both went to school for years, been designing for years. We both agree that both designs are good, but we can't agree on which one is better. But we do know one thing: we are building this building for the average guy. Let's get that old guy out in the hall, who's mopping the hall, and we'll let him tell us. Whichever one he likes, we agree to go with." They go out in the hall. The guy's out there mopping the hall, and they say, "Would you come in my office for a second? We'd like to ask you something." The guy says, "Oh, yeah, man, I'm coming." He brings the pail and mop and comes into the office. The two architects are there, and one guy says, "Look, we would like to ask you something. These are two designs for two buildings. We would like you to tell us which one of these designs you like the best." "Oh, yeah, man, sure." He looks at one, then he looks at the other, then says, "I'll tell you, baby, I like this one here, but the average guy is probably going to like that other one." So trying to find the elusive average man is very difficult.

STEVEN SPIELBERG: The book hadn't even been released at that time. It was in galley form when I said I'd direct it, and it didn't become a best-seller for months after that.

FRANK YABLANS: It's my judgment versus your judgment. It's Alan Ladd's judgment versus my judgment.

STEVEN SPIELBERG: What happened was, Benchley did three drafts of the script and then Peter and I were agreeing on most everything, except Peter really had had it, because he hated to fly, he hated flying out to Los

Angeles. He would only write in his New Jersey home. So we didn't have much communication except for the several times we'd meet here in LA and talk about the script. And he told me about a book he was writing called *The Deep*. It wasn't called *The Deep* then, but he wanted to go off and do that, so he sort of volunteered his exit. And then I hired Howard Sackler, not because he wrote *The Great White Hope* but because he was a diver and a good friend of David Brown's. And David suggested I talk to him. We had a meeting, and Howard came up with some simply marvelous ideas, one after the other, and together we rewrote the script in about three weeks—totally.

I'm never really satisfied with anything. I'm always changing, and I needed somebody on the set every day with me to change the things I wanted to change. I sort of needed a short-order cook, so I hired Carl [Gottlieb], who was a friend of mine for seven or eight years. And the humor was there before Carl got involved. Howard's draft was hilarious. As a matter of fact, after Carl got involved, we began to cut down some of the humor. Though Carl's mostly known for his comedy writing, that wasn't the function he performed on Martha's Vineyard when he was writing for me. Carl was there for about five weeks only, and Zanuck and Brown decided that they had paid him enough money and sent him back to Los Angeles. So for five, probably four and a half months, we were left to our own devices. And the actors, along with myself, would sit in a room together just about every night and refine the dialogue and think of new moments and pieces of business. And the movie kind of took shape as we went along. But the structure was there from the fourth draft.

It's probably a terrible thing to say, but I so enjoyed making *Duel* that I felt that there were so many similarities between *Duel* and *Jaws*. I felt it would be the sequel to *Duel* in disguise. And there were so many things I couldn't do in *Duel*, because I only had sixteen days and only three weeks to cut it and put it on television, that I felt I could take all of the other ideas that were sort of leftovers and, you know, quick-heat them up in the microwave oven and stick them in *Jaws*. Which is what I did throughout the picture.

You know, your eyes are larger than your appetite. Mine always are.

A typical day on *Jaws* would be "Okay, we'll get forty pages in one day! We're going to finish this movie on Tuesday! I know we've got four more months, but I'm going to be done tomorrow! I'm going to do forty pages!" And sometimes I'd actually believe that, because we all got kind of crazy on the island. And I'd take the whole crew out there, and I'd plan a lot from the storyboard. I'd say, "Today, we're going to get all these shots." We'd put them all up on the, on the cork board . . . and all of a sudden it's five o'clock, and we're still waiting for the first shot of the boat coming toward the camera. And that was a typical day. It was planning everything and getting nothing. And for 155 days of that until the movie was done from a 55-day schedule.

VERNA FIELDS: Steve sent me out [on second unit] to get a barrel away [from the boat]. That's all. Took four days to get that one shot.

GEORGE LUCAS: Steven Spielberg and I used to have contests to see who could shoot most in the fewest number of days.

STEVEN SPIELBERG: The reason there are so many smiles when the people are running out of the water, away from the shark, is because the AD was saying "It has big teeth, and it's going to kill you! There's blood everywhere! People are being torn apart! The shark is coming! The shark is there! Run for your lives!" You hear that, and after a while, the results are pathetic.

DAVID BROWN: We now like to recall those days. [At the time,] we even considered suspending production to gather our strength and return in the fall. However, experience told us always to press on. And at no time was there an airlift of executives from the MCA/Universal black tower. At no time was there an ultimatum given to us: "What are you doing with that fish?" At no time did they say, "Shoot it in Griffith Park Lake." If there is a lake in Griffith Park.

RICHARD ZANUCK: There is one on the back lot, though.

DAVID BROWN: *Jaws* is an example of studio trust. It goes beyond trust. And it is an example of what producers can do with their much-battered credibility. Because there were times, I'm sure, when they thought we were insane, and there were times when we thought we were, too.

VERNA FIELDS: My favorite story about the cutting of *Jaws* is that each time I wanted to cut, I didn't, so that it would have an anticipatory feeling. And it worked.

STEVEN SPIELBERG: When I showed John [Williams] a cut of *Jaws*, I think it was probably in 1974. I'd finished making the movie, it was going to come out in summer, I had put temp music into the picture, and I used one of John's own movie scores from his Robert Altman collaboration, a movie called *Images*. And because I felt that that music was viable and was disturbing and it would make the shark like an intellectual. I was always, with *Jaws*, trying to make something greater and more important than it was ever supposed to be.

JOHN WILLIAMS: And I said, "Well, I've got this idea of doing this kind of *thump-thump* thing."

STEVEN SPIELBERG: John called me, having seen the cut. "Oh, darling boy, no, no, no, no, no. It's a pirate movie. It's a shark and it's survivors, and oh, no, *Images* is not the right sound for this. Let me work something up, and I'll present it to you when I've found the music."

JOHN WILLIAMS: I started to play thump. *Thump-thump.*

STEVEN SPIELBERG: I came back a few weeks later, and John invited me over to his house, and he took me into his living room and he sat at the piano.

JOHN WILLIAMS: *Thump-thump-thump-thump-thump . . .*

STEVEN SPIELBERG: He took two fingers like chopsticks . . .

JOHN WILLIAMS: He said, "What is that?"

STEVEN SPIELBERG: And he waited. And I tried to smile, because of course John has a great sense of humor. And then he added a little bit of—he went *dun*-dun . . . *dun*-dun and waited. And I started getting nervous in my heart. And then he went *dun dun dun dun dun dun dun dun dun dun dun*. And from then on my heart's really beating fast and I'm getting flopsweat.

JOHN WILLIAMS: *Jaws* is a very good example of how making films might be something like cooking. First of all, it takes ingredients that you've selected. It takes time. You can't cook something that takes two hours in an hour. And also, no matter how much and how experienced you are, you're not going to be sure exactly what the result will be of this particular alchemy. I said to Steven, "Well, maybe when the orchestra with the cellos and basses do this, it might be a dramatic device that will work." "Well, if you think so, let's try it. Why do you think it will work?"

SAM WASSON: In the old days, of course, the studio was the kitchen . . . and the cupboards were stocked with ingredients . . .

STEVEN SPIELBERG: I have absolute trust and faith that John is right when he sees my movie for the first time.

JOHN WILLIAMS: I said, "Well, I'm not sure it will, but it can be done very softly, or it can be done definitely loud if you want the full orchestra pounding these notes, add a few notes to it as we go. Or it can go slowly and speed up and speed up and speed up, giving us a sense that the shark is getting closer to us, even though we don't see it."

RICHARD ZANUCK: *Jaws* was going to be a major and massive release with a very intensive initial television exposure campaign, probably the biggest, I would say, of all time.

STEVEN SPIELBERG: I fought Universal because they wanted to release *Jaws* in a thousand-plus on one day and just take the money and run. And

I was saying "God, you got to go out in two hundred fifty theaters maximum." And we fought back and forth, and they told me that I was wrong, and they said in effect, "Who are you to tell us how to market the picture? Go make your movies, we'll market them."

JOYCE SELZNICK: It's not easy to put movies together. But it's harder to sell them once they're made.

ERIC WEISSMANN: Do you open it with a luxury one-theater showing in New York to try to build word of mouth and get good critical reviews, or do you know that the picture is going to be hated by the critics and you want to open it as broadly as possible before anybody finds out how bad it is?

NED TANEN: One of the toughest things that any of us have to contend with in this business is how to market a movie. It has become an increasingly difficult area of the business, and it may be the most difficult area of the business. Since people who go to movies generally are not people who read newspapers, there is an enormous amount of wasted money in newspaper advertising. Television advertising for movies is so extraordinarily expensive that you can spend three or four million dollars on television advertising, cash, so fast that you will not know what even happened to the money. And it's obviously only good for a certain kind of movie, which is the *Towering Inferno* kind of movie, where you can show something in a fifteen-second spot that will at least get somebody's attention.

ERIC PLESKOW: Obviously, you do not do *Cuckoo's Nest* on television because you will not get who you are trying to get.

GORDON STULBERG: The purpose of TV and radio is to be strong and dramatic enough to make you aware of the picture, not necessarily to get you to go see it, because generally when you see it on TV or you hear it on radio, you're not going to the movies at that moment, so you've got to have something dramatic enough to impinge on the subconscious of the person seeing or hearing, and that's a very difficult trick.

DAVID CHASMAN: Some of them require less effort than others because of what they are. If you have a marquee that says "Robert Redford and Barbra Streisand in *The Way We Were*," 50 percent of your promotion has been done for you. When you have a more fragile commodity, a picture without stars that must succeed by virtue of its art and its content, that calls for a certain amount of ingenuity in terms of screenings for critics, screenings for what are called "opinion makers."

HARRY UFLAND: If you say it's the greatest thing that ever happened, people are going to come in and not like it. They're going to feel let down. If you don't hype it enough, nobody will come. It's a real problem.

DEDE ALLEN: And these marketing people are extremely smart. They know what weekend to put it in, how to play it. That's an art. That's a real art in itself: how to present a picture.

JEANINE BASINGER: This new kind of marketing was a major shift from the simpler system of old Hollywood where movies were sold by genre and star.

DANIEL MELNICK: When you go to find a time to release a picture, it becomes very confusing, because you look for a time when the competitive factors seem to be ideal, and there's always either another very big picture like your picture coming out or there's the World Series or the NBA playoffs, you know, things, Olympics, elections. I mean, when you look for a quiet time, it's very, very hard.

ERIC PLESKOW: September is a murderous month, so you handle movies differently in September and October than you would in June, July, and August.

ERIC WEISSMANN: We would cover whether we had enough pictures to be in release for each particular month, and if we didn't, then the plea would come: "Jesus, you've got to get us a picture for May a year from now, because we've got nothing." And then people would say, "Well, I think you'll have that picture, because I think the Kubrick picture which is going to open in February is going to be so big that it'll keep you going through May."

A. D. MURPHY: Contrary to a lot of attitudes and beliefs and myths, you can almost week by week predict the number of people who are willing to come out and see a film, and over the course of the year it looks like an electrocardiogram in an intensive care unit. After Christmas and New Year's, people go back to school, they're broke or whatever, the holiday is over. Attendance can tumble two-thirds in a week. It thrashes around at the bottom. Then Washington's Birthday holiday weekend, any holiday weekend, comes up a bit relative to where it was before. Then after the holiday it goes back again. Then Easter and spring vacation, and it's up a little bit higher than it was at Washington's Birthday. Then it goes back in the doldrums again. Then it comes up again for Memorial Day weekend, but then it doesn't go down because schools are letting out. It keeps going up through June, and from June until Labor Day it is as high as it sat anytime during the year. Then right after Labor Day, school begins, a new TV season, so forth, it comes downhill and kind of levels off in October and November, up a bit at Thanksgiving, drops, and just before Christmas are the two worst weeks of the year, the first two weeks of December, and then along about December 20, the business will quadruple for two weeks and start all over again.

DANIEL MELNICK: I think we're all convinced that people go to the movies mostly at Christmastime, so we release our big pictures at Christmastime and advertise them heavily, thereby creating a situation where people are going to the movies.

A. D. MURPHY: But there are times of the year you couldn't get people out at gunpoint, so the business is continually expanding and contracting.

ERIC WEISSMANN: There was a picture called *The Long Goodbye* which did very badly in Los Angeles. It got wonderful reviews in New York. They showed it again in LA with excerpts from the New York reviews, with a big

TV advertising campaign—and they still didn't want to see it. I mean, they just didn't want to see that picture.

JULIA PHILLIPS: All this money is spent making a picture. Then they take two weeks to come up with an ad concept, they book it into a couple of theaters, and they send it out there. It's as if you sent your four-year-old off to nursery school for first day and didn't kiss him goodbye and didn't give him breakfast. It's crazy.

DAVID BROWN: When you have a film like *Jaws*, where there is apparently a great deal of interest in wanting to see it, why wait? Why make them wait six months or a year? Why make them stand in line with no hope of getting in and then go away, perhaps never to return?

NED TANEN: If you're buying television time for that kind of extravaganza, for lack of a better word, you had better be able to maximize your return quickly. You can't release it in six cities and be spending $4 million on television advertising. So you better be out everywhere.

DAVID PICKER: If Universal couldn't get the terms they wanted from the best theater in town, then they took the worst theater in town, because they wanted to open at a certain time.

NED TANEN: Universal is a company that handles distribution of films—I would say "tougher," but what I really mean to say is "better"—than other companies.

DAVID BROWN: Well, Lew Wasserman, who is chairman and chief executive officer of MCA, Sid Sheinberg, MCA president, and Henry H. Martin, president of Universal, actually created the master plan for *Jaws*. They consulted with us all the way, and we agreed with them.

DAVID PICKER: Let me ask you a question: Why did it work on *Jaws* and not on *The Great Waldo Pepper*? You know, Bob Redford is a giant star. One picture had it, and the other didn't. I think they chose to distribute in a way that got the most out of the picture in the case of *Jaws*. I think the way they distributed it was wonderful. But if they did the same thing with another picture?

ALJEAN HARMETZ: *Jaws* became the largest box-office hit of all time.

DAVID ANSEN: The other thing that *Jaws* did, it also invented the whole concept of summer movie. The summer blockbuster really didn't exist before that.

PAUL SCHRADER: We are in a commercial business. Film is predicated on an audience of millions of people. And if you are not comfortable with that fact, you should get out of it. There are a lot of ways to express yourself in this world, and only a few of them cost this much. If you want to be a rocket scientist, you have to accept the fact you have to work for the United States or Russia—you know, you're not going to be a rocket scientist for Warner Bros.

GORDON STULBERG: It's not like a painting to be hung in a museum. If you desire to have the financial wherewithal to express your creative sense in the sense of film for public acceptance, if you desire to have entrepreneurial capital put up for it, and that's where it comes from—if you're not looking for that, you apply to a foundation and get a grant and do the work of an author, do a film that may wind up at the Museum of Modern Art in New York. But if you come into this business—and essentially it is still a business, it is a venture capital enterprise with stockholders that put up their money—you do have an obligation, an obligation to do a film once you have accepted their money, that appeals to the widest possible audience consistent with what your desire is with respect to the film. Not to subvert your desire to do a fine film, a film that meets what you want to see on the screen, but the recognition that for what the investor puts up, you've got to reach the widest possible audience.

ARTHUR KNIGHT: It's not like a book of poems that you keep on your shelf and you read occasionally. It's something that has to be seen by a great number of people at any one time, and those people are the art patrons of this particular form. And I think that this is a very basic element in understanding what film is all about.

DALTON TRUMBO: I've written pamphlets. I have total freedom with the pamphlets. They can be published for fifteen cents, given away, or sold. Total freedom.

PAUL SCHRADER: You do an album that sells a hundred thousand copies, you have at least met the needs of your commercial base. You write a book that sells twenty-five thousand copies, you've met those needs at least. You make a movie, two or three million people have to see it. Otherwise, you're in the wrong business. That doesn't mean every film is going to be a success, and that doesn't mean that a failure should stop you from working, but that should be part of your ongoing consciousness, that I am in a mass audience art form and until they figure a way to do it cheaper, I will either acknowledge or not acknowledge that fact.

JULIA PHILLIPS: David Begelman [at Columbia] hated the *Taxi Driver* script. I begged him in a lunch. That was in the stage when I could still throw myself at people's ankles, and I begged him to read the script again, which he did on a plane, and he called me and said, "I still hate it, but I'll give you nine hundred thousand dollars to make the picture," and we said, "Absolutely, of course we can make the picture for nine hundred thousand dollars," and from that point we inched them upward.

MICHAEL PHILLIPS: We ultimately had a budget of a million and a half.

MICHAEL OVITZ: They're creeping up . . .

PAUL SCHRADER: These prices are not a function of greed. They're a function of power.

JULIA PHILLIPS: You know, Bobby got hotter, Marty got hotter. They still had no product, but [Columbia] had had the success of *Shampoo*, which maybe encouraged them, you know, in supporting such an offbeat enterprise.

PAUL SCHRADER: It was one of those serendipities, you know.

MICHAEL PHILLIPS: I see it all the time that any job working on a film in any capacity is worth it. You can't always see how A leads to B, but somebody who you work with will think of you when he or she is in another position a year from now. And I see these networks of people rising. People change hats. It's wonderful, wonderful mobility.

Anyway, but with Scorsese and De Niro, that package just acquired value over time, and they hung in there, particularly De Niro. He hung in there at his old price, he agreed. He got $35,000 to make that movie, and we all hung in there on original price.

JULIA PHILLIPS: We went from $900,000 to $1.1 million to $1.25 million. I think we were finally approved at $1.35 million. To make a long story short, we ended up at $2 million, which in this day and age—I think with that quality of picture—is a miracle. And for this they harassed and hounded us to the point where both of us were surviving mainly on drugs. Michael went back to smoking, for which I will never forgive him. Marty has asthma all the time, and at one point he said that the solution to the problem was that he was going to buy a gun from John Milius—a very small gun. He was a very small person—and he was going to shoot a certain number of people who shall remain nameless but we all know and recognize.

MICHAEL PHILLIPS: The total above the line of the movie producers, writer, director, and star was about $150,000 or $160,000. And I think that's why the movie was made. It was a bargain.

STEVEN SPIELBERG: Marty Scorsese called me. I was over at Universal, and he was scoring *Taxi Driver* at Warners. Marty said, "You got to get over here. The score is brilliant. You got to just drive over here!" So I got in my car, and I drove over to Warners and went into the recording session and went into the booth and sat with Marty for an hour listening to *Taxi*

Driver. Benny [Herrmann] was sitting on the floor, smoking a big cigar. He was covered in ash—his stomach went out to here. And Marty said during a break, "Okay, you got to come meet Bernard Herrmann." So he brings me out by the hand, and he parks me in front of Benny Herrmann. And he said, "Benny, this is my friend, Steven Spielberg." And I said, "Oh, Mr. Herrmann, I'm such an admirer of your work. You're such an amazing genius." He looked at me, said, "So why do you always hire John Williams?" And he actually passed away that evening. That was the last day of his life. I got to meet him on the last day of his life. He unexpectedly died asleep that night, at the hotel.

SHERRILL CORWIN: How *Taxi Driver* got away with an R, I'll never know. I'm talking like a typical exhibitor now. You know those ads that say "See it with someone you love"? I wouldn't want to see *Taxi Driver* with someone I loved. She'd slap me in the face! Anyway, exhibitors don't want to show X films. They will if it will sell tickets. If it'll make a buck, they'll show a Z!

PAUL MAZURSKY: There are no rules. It's a game without rules.

JULIA PHILLIPS: What I think is a miracle is that we've gotten movies made at all.

CHAPTER 14

THE DEAL

ABBY MANN: It's a funny thing, when a star likes a script, all of a sudden, the number of people who like it becomes amazing.

KENNETH TURAN: Nobody wants to be the first person to step back and say, "You know, we're not going to pay this much."

AL PACINO: I remember Mario Puzo came to me. I met him at the Ginger Man in New York, and he says, "I have a script for you, *Godfather II*," he said. "Just so you know, it's bad." I said, "Thanks, Mario." He says, "It's bad, but you know." "You should know that," I said, and it was. And so I thought, Uh, well, okay, I'm not doing *Godfather II*. And then what happened is the offers got higher each time. First it started at a hundred thousand, and two hundred, then three hundred, and it kept going up.

MEL BROOKS: I don't want to give twenty-five points to a star. For what? They're only there for three weeks. I'm there for two years.

HOWARD W. KOCH: You get caught in that thing, and it starts to get up, and everything accelerates from it. Because Redford's getting $3 million and what's-his-name $1 million, the shellfish won't work for scale.

JON PETERS: And getting over the initial common denominator that all of us, especially at the studios, have, which is absolute, total fear, because a wrong decision is millions and millions and millions of dollars. And it's not like we're talking about the old days, where you make a movie for $1 million or $800,000.

MIKE FRANKOVICH: The budget on *Lawrence of Arabia* was a million dollars.

DAVID PICKER: So the escalation of the competitive marketplace, based on the need for success and the need to prove yourself, that you're in the market and can attract filmmakers, caused problems for a lot of companies.

HOWARD W. KOCH: I personally would love to go back to the days of MGM if there was a way to do it. You know, get a stock company, because everybody at MGM was on a contract. Nobody owned a piece of a picture. There were no entrepreneurs.

SUE MENGERS: Very few stars can command enormous participation, like gross from the first dollar. The best participation is if you can get gross from every box-office dollar. The next best is gross after breakeven, which means when the picture has paid back its negative cost and its advertising. After that, profits. But Joe Levine, who is getting criticized for the prices he is paying, also is not giving participation. So if you're a Robert Redford, you may get $2 million for doing it, but what if suddenly the picture turns out to be *Jaws*, and had you had your normal deal, which in Redford's case would be gross from the first dollar, he could have walked away from it with untold sums of money. So the producer has to make that choice: if they don't want to give up participation, they have to give more front money.

JON PETERS: It's a frightening situation.

SUE MENGERS: No one is forcing the studios to pay these prices. No one. I have seen things where it's absolutely reprehensible, the competitiveness between the studios, where they're absolutely convinced that if they don't pay a certain star that price that someone else will, and that only com-pounds the problem. I'm delighted to say to my clients, "Hey, they just won't pay it." But I'm not going to say it if they're going to pay it to a ri-val's client. I just won't. And as long as they're dumb enough to pay these prices—I mean, Gene Hackman did not want to do *Lucky Lady*. I mean, he did not want to do it, and they kept offering him more and more and more money. Well, everyone has their price. I mean, it wasn't as though he was being asked to exterminate people, he was being asked to play in a movie, and finally these people came up with the kind of money that it was almost obscene for him not to do the film.

DAVID PICKER: During the years at UA we were very steady, but now you get a *Jaws*, you get an *Exorcist*, and everybody wants to know why we don't have an *Exorcist*, so the pressures are much different.

STEVEN SPIELBERG: It's changed. It really has.

SUE MENGERS: I think the studios are too nervous to keep on putting all their money, to keep on rolling the dice on two or three pictures, and, God forbid, if they don't have a *Jaws* or whatever, they're in a lot of trouble.

DAVID PICKER: You know, *The Exorcist* didn't have stars, *Jaws* didn't have stars, *American Graffiti* didn't have stars.

SUE MENGERS: The guys in *Jaws*, nobody knows who they are outside our industry, and they're getting paid outrageous sums of money. So again the acceleration starts. "Wait a minute. The guys in *Jaws* are getting five hun-dred or six hundred thousand dollars a picture. What does a McQueen get?"

DUSTIN HOFFMAN: I mean, it's a terrible business. What other art form is like this? I don't know of any other. I mean, it's like having a palette with paints on it that are worth a fortune.

DENNIS HOPPER: When I was in *Giant*, when I was eighteen years old, *Giant* was the most expensive movie ever made. It cost $14 million. And they thought that was incredible. I've seen it so many times. And it's huge gambles. I mean, if you spend $200 million on a movie, you've got to make $400 million before you break into profits. That's, like, *whew*.

SAM WASSON: After *Jaws*, Hollywood decided elaborate marketing strategies could act as an insurance policy against its swelling budgets. But of course, a smart campaign cost money too.

JOYCE SELZNICK: It probably costs more money to sell a picture today than it costs to make.

ERIC PLESKOW: Take *Rocky*, for example. It cost us 66 percent of the budget to find out whether we were right on *Rocky*. And I assure you, it didn't open "smash." It had to build, and it had to be nurtured. In the end, we will spend about four times the budget in advertising alone, in the US and Canada, just to exploit the film.

CONRAD HALL: Profit margins increase and the quality margins decrease.

GORDON STULBERG: It's turning turds into Shinola, if you please, because there's a way to market a certain product, and audiences will buy it and enjoy it and say that they haven't had a bad evening.

FRANK YABLANS: I mean, there's no windfall like a movie. It's the biggest crap game in the world! You put down $2 million, and you take back $100 million. You put down $10 million, and you can take back $200 million. It's incredible! The numbers are staggering. Nobody's going to walk away from that. You'd have to get me to Las Vegas first, because it's a great gambler's business, which is why we're all here. We're all loonies.

GEORGE LUCAS: When you make a film, you're dealing with the largest group of psychotic, neurotic, difficult people you could ever imagine.

JON PETERS: This is a business where every morning, if you read the trades, you read about only the successful people. And if you're not successful, or even if you are, it is so debilitating to read about everybody doing everything, it could kill you.

PAUL MAZURSKY: When they read the trades, they go, "Oh, they bombed! Isn't that terrible?" But they're all laughing.

STEVEN SPIELBERG: It's a very competitive business. As close as we [Lucas, Coppola, Spielberg] all are to each other, I'm one of the few moviemakers that will admit that there's a great deal of competition between all of the directors and writers.

ERIC WEISSMANN: You can never really act with reckless abandon because tomorrow the wheel may turn.

FRANK YABLANS: It's a romantic notion, the rags-to-riches idea, but you have to understand that you're living in beautiful Beverly Hills, which is a Mecca of failure!

MORGAN FREEMAN: A lot of people come here with a dream, and you can see them, they're still here. But no dream.

FRANK YABLANS: When you consider that basically, one out of five or six films is successful, then you have to understand that one out of five people is successful and that the others are all failures.

JON PETERS: It could eat your guts out, you could throw up, you could go into the painting or aluminum siding business, or whatever.

AL RUDDY: Look, you have to be obsessed. I'm totally convinced that you can never get anything done in this business unless you're totally obsessed. I had a guy from the *Wall Street Journal* come down once to do an interview on show business, right? He says, "What do you think it takes to make it in this business?" He's writing away with his pencil. I said, "A total neurotic." Screech! The point breaks! He says, "No, seriously." I said, "I am very serious. I think you've got to be insane, obsessed, or neurotic to make it in this business. What other business demands that you gamble the most important thing that you have in your life, your time? When you're young, that time is crucial, because if you don't make it at a certain point, you're not going to work as a junior executive at General Motors. Along that way, your chances of what we call a normal life are also very difficult, because of your anxiety, worrying about whether you are going to make it. You don't have any money, there's very little opportunity to start working, so you must sustain that fantasy that you have. That's two. And number three—and this is the most horrendous part of it—even if you're willing to suffer the anxieties, even if you're willing to give up the things other people want, the chances of making it are still one in a thousand. You wouldn't play odds like that in Las Vegas, would you? Who else but a totally obsessed neurotic is going to go one, two, three on that deal?"

GEORGE LUCAS: This is not a good thing to do if you actually want to earn a living.

DAVID PUTTNAM: Real estate's a much better business if you're really interested in money.

GEORGE LUCAS: If you want to make money, I suggest you go into the stock market. The people who come in wanting to be famous and make money are misguided, because this is a bad job. It's terrible. Really it is. There are many easier ways to make money and become famous.

You know, I *barely* created Yoda.

STEVEN SPIELBERG: George came to Mobile to visit me on *Close Encounters* and complained for five days.

GEORGE LUCAS: I had this project, this space adventure, it was at United Artists. So I said, "Okay, I'm ready to do this now," and they said, "We won't have anything to do with it. We don't want it." So then I was also obligated to take it to Universal. I took it to them.

NED TANEN: There is no secret about the fact that my company thought that *American Graffiti* was an unreleasable television show which we had in the can at that point, and I literally could not get permission to spend $25,000 for the *Star Wars* screenplay.

DAVID CHASMAN: Possibly one of the most misleading terms ever applied to the phenomenon of films and their exhibition is the word *industry*. It implies a repetitive industrial pattern. It implies criteria which the Wharton School of Business reveres: quality control and cost control. Well, you can get everybody in the world to agree on what constitutes quality in a ball bearing. You can't get two people to agree on what constitutes quality in a film.

GEORGE LUCAS: Then Alan Ladd, Jr. [at Fox], who had seen a screening of *American Graffiti* and liked it, said, "Look, I don't understand the [*Star Wars*] story. I don't understand what you're pitching, but I think you're a talented guy. I'm not going to bet on this movie, because it's too weird. But I am going to bet on you." That's how I got it. I found somebody who was interested in me, not in the project itself. That said, I had only $10 million to make the film. For what we were trying to put on-screen, it really was a low-budget production.

When Fox decided to go with *Star Wars*, I negotiated with them. I wrote a little deal memo that was two or three pages about how much money I was going to get, how we would split the profits, all that stuff. They ended up just handing over their boilerplate contract, which I never signed, because it took me a year to come up with my first draft of the script. During that time we were working on the contract, trying to make a deal. In the meantime, I had ended up with a screenplay for *Star Wars* that was nearly two hundred pages long. I said, "Okay, I can't film two hundred pages, so what I'm going to do is take the first act of the script and make the movie from that." I knew I wanted to make the other two movies at some point and didn't want the studio to be able to stand in my way. My assumption was that the first film wouldn't do very well and the studio would bury it, just like the other two, and I'd never be able to continue working on the story because they would end up owning the rights. Once *Graffiti* was a hit, I said, "I'm not going to change the deal. I'll leave it all exactly the same. The money's the same, everything is the same. But the one thing I want in the contract is the sequel rights." They were looking at it from a very pragmatic point of view, which corporations do, and said to themselves, "We can pay this kid a million dollars now and take the sequel rights, or we can give him the fifty thousand dollars he's asking for plus the sequel rights to a movie that may not be worth anything. Since most movies aren't worth anything, let's just not worry about it." So they signed away the sequel rights. It was the same thing with the merchandise-licensing rights.

NED TANEN: I can say that Fox did not really know what they had on their hands, and we've done the same thing, so that is not a criticism.

GEORGE LUCAS: I wasn't a born director.

RON HOWARD: George Lucas can't talk to actors. I mean, he's just afraid, he doesn't really know what to tell them.

GEORGE LUCAS: Part of my problem is that over the years I've dreamt up things that couldn't be put on-screen unless I moved the state of the art and technology forward. Science fiction is great on paper, but it's much harder when it comes to cinema, because for at least a brief moment you have to make it appear to be real. It's really determined by available technology, and for many years those hurdles were impossible to overcome. The connection here is actually that all art is technology, whether it's picking up a charred stick and drawing pictures on a wall or creating the Death Star. When we finally finished *Star Wars*, I don't think anybody, you know, understood that it would go anywhere

ALJEAN HARMETZ: They showed a 20th Century–Fox film early, you know, a month early, and before all the publicity or anything had come out. And as we drove over from our house to MGM, where they were showing this, actually, my husband said, "What's this about?" And I said, "Well, the director, George Lucas, said he made it for twelve-year-olds." And Dick said, "Well, let's go home." And I said, "No, we should go because we liked *American Graffiti* so much." So that was the first public screening of *Star Wars*. Nobody who walked into that theater knew what to expect. And when it was over, I saw something that I had never seen before and have never seen since, which is an audience of about four hundred jaded Hollywood people and members of the press standing and screaming and applauding. Once the movie got out into the theaters and was overpraised, the people who went to see it two months later said, "What's all this fuss about?" But when we walked out of the theater that night, I said jokingly, "We should buy 20th Century–Fox stock," which of course I couldn't do because I was on the staff of the *New York Times* and I could not own any movie stuff. And so I would not have, but it turned out that at least half a dozen people who were in the theater that night did exactly that and made a considerable amount of money.

GEORGE LUCAS: The executives cried in the screening, which I couldn't believe. I mean, I just couldn't believe it. I mean, it's, you know, it's even unthinkable that an executive would see your movie and break down in tears. But that's what happened.

STEVEN SPIELBERG: George was so anxious that *Star Wars* would be the biggest flop in his personal history that he went to Hawaii to get away. I met him in Hawaii the day the film opened.

GEORGE LUCAS: We were building sandcastles, and he was musing about how what he really wanted to do was a James Bond film. He'd gone to the producers and asked them if he could do it and said he would only do it if he could bring Sean Connery back. They didn't want to do that, so Steve backed off. I turned to him and said, "I have the perfect film for you. It's basically James Bond." I told him the story of *Raiders of the Lost Ark*.

STEVEN SPIELBERG: George likes to talk about everything. I mean, everything. He has little histories. He'll talk about something a character does, and then he'll give you the whole history of how the character and his life to that point.

GEORGE LUCAS: Steven and I work in a funny way, because he'll come up with something, and I'll say, "Oh, I don't like that idea, you know. But it's your movie, and you can do whatever you want." He'll say, "No, no, no, no, it's not my movie, it's your movie, we'll do whatever you want." So with that, we never really have arguments. We sit down, and we say, "Well, what's best for the movie?" Regardless of this is my idea or your idea or this is the way I want it to be or you want it to be, what actually works in the context, and we usually come to an agreement about what actually is the best route to follow.

JON PETERS: Fox opened *Star Wars* in a very small pattern, because nobody knew what they had.

GEORGE LUCAS: I had no idea that absolutely everyone would want to buy shirts and pillowcases and toys.

A. D. MURPHY: 20th Century–Fox was not blind to what they had in *Star Wars*. Months before the film opened, there was a lot of promotion in college campus areas, and there was a paperback book beforehand, but they couldn't drag Carrie Fisher around to interviews because nobody in the media knew or cared about Carrie, Harrison Ford, or Mark Hamill. But beyond Fox's wildest hopes, there were a lot of people who got a vibration: "I want this, I want this." And by 3:00 p.m., by the end of the first show on May 25, 1977, the thirty-five or forty theaters all over the country were calling in extra crews of ushers. They knew then.

NED TANEN: The three kids in *Star Wars* nobody ever heard of, including their parents, and the movie opened the same day in twenty-three places around this country, including Grand Rapids, Iowa, and it opened a hit in Grand Rapids, Iowa, and it opened a hit in New York and LA. And that's what it always comes down to. There was something about that movie that made it work before it ever opened. It is something with people, with an audience. It has nothing to do with *Time* magazine or Pauline Kael saying it's a masterpiece. It really doesn't.

ERIC PLESKOW: *Star Wars*, in this country, outgrossed *Jaws*.

NED TANEN: Do you want to look at De Niro's picture on the cover of *Time* and *Newsweek* about *New York, New York*? I can give you a couple of my own beauties, including one with James Taylor [*Two-Lane Blacktop*] that I don't even want to think of at this moment. That is not going to do the job.

JON PETERS: So there are no answers.

GEORGE LUCAS: I got lucky, but I'm one in a million.

NED TANEN: *Star Wars* is the biggest phenomenon in the history of the business.

BEN BENJAMIN: We have 10 percent of George Lucas's percentage on *Star Wars*. So it's lovely. Oh, George had about 30 percent, a little over 30 percent, of the gross.

SAM ARKOFF: Lucas looks at pictures as what they are: part art and a lot of business.

GEORGE LUCAS: After *Star Wars*, I built a place in the woods. Mostly what creative people do is think, and I realized we needed a place to do that. It's not a race-around-and-do-things kind of house. I wanted a place full of the most advanced technology where we could sit, see the trees, and think about things. Skywalker Ranch, if anything, is devoted to giving people a chance to work in a beautiful environment and then go out and sit on a stoop for a few minutes and watch the birds fly by. Another reason for the ranch is my interest in architecture. It speaks directly to my love of building things.

And so when the toy thing came along, I thought, Well, this is great, because that's what play is. Play is being able to take something like *Star Wars* that you see in the theater and then come home and play with it and use your imagination to tell other stories and to come up with other ideas and to have other adventures, but your own that you make up yourself.

I had complete control over merchandising, but split the revenue with Fox for a period of time. Of course, the merchandising of the film became huge.

STEVEN SPIELBERG: You know, I wish I had a piece of the *Jaws* business in T-shirts. I could have made a fortune.

SAM ARKOFF: *Star Wars* gets about as close as you can get, really, but if you try to be all things to all men and women, you're likely to fall between the cracks and not please anybody

BUCK HENRY: That's what democracy is all about. More McDonald's hamburgers are inevitably going to be eaten than filet mignons.

DAVID PICKER: Everybody is reaching for the golden ring, right? That golden ring has gotten more golden over the last few years. And people go to fewer movies than they used to, but they go to the ones they go to more than they used to. The middle-bracket movie has almost disappeared.

SUE MENGERS: Well, a very few are making a lot of money. . . . But there isn't enough work to sustain an entire industry today, because if a studio does two $12 million movies, that's their budget for the year.

NED TANEN: Every movie now is a little conglomerate.

GORDON STULBERG: If a picture doesn't do well, it doesn't merely lose the negative cost. It can also lose its prints, its advertising, the so-called distribution fees on that picture. And four or five pictures of an average of $8 million or $9 million each plus prints and advertising can be totally destructive to a company.

JOHN PTAK: Needless to say, studios have turned to spreading their risks to other areas to cover down years.

DAVID PICKER: Well, the reason that the conglomerates moved in was that for the most part the movie companies couldn't make it on their own. The business is too erratic and too volatile, too cyclical.

SAM WASSON: Corporations started swallowing up flailing studios in the identity-crisis years of late sixties, but it wasn't until the late seventies, on the heels of the incredible, eye-opening windfall of *Star Wars*, that they started running those studios like subsidiaries of large parent companies, which is, after all, what they had become.

JOHN PTAK: Columbia is one of the last studios to be taken over and run by corporate thinking. The rest of the studios are really very large corporations that are in many businesses, especially Universal, which even owns a savings and loan.

SUE MENGERS: Therefore they're not as adventurous as they were when they were going through their youth syndrome.

JOHN PTAK: In 1936, Warner Bros. made sixty pictures. In 1940, they made forty-five. In 1950, they made twenty-eight. And in the last twelve years, it's vacillated between thirteen and twenty-two.

DAVID PUTTNAM: And I see the day when a lot of the things that I treasured as a kid have ceased to exist, because they don't make any economic sense in a worldwide corporate environment.

GARETH WIGAN: The more money that gets involved and the more potential for making money, the more people are going to be involved, unfortunately.

DAVID PICKER: The business used to run on somebody's word, and that isn't true anymore, sadly. In the days when Lew Wasserman and Abe Lastfogel were running their agencies, if you made a deal, you could shoot the picture and never have a piece of paper that was signed. Today I wouldn't suggest to anybody that they spend a nickel until that paper was signed.

DANIEL MELNICK: Somebody said about politics that "Today what you have to go through, all the deals you have to make to get elected to high office in America, preclude, virtually preclude, anybody of quality entering the process." And unfortunately, I think the movie business becomes more and more like that.

SAM WASSON: There were always agents in Hollywood, but with rare exception—among them Jules Stein, Lew Wasserman, Leland Hayward, Swifty Lazar—agents were at best expert negotiators, at worst, functionaries, just "doing the deals."

SUE MENGERS: Slowly now the image of the agent is returning to one of much more importance, much more respect.

SAM WASSON: Now that the talent, no longer bound by studio contracts, was working freelance—and in a blockbuster economy that could pay out better than ever—the deal itself, and by extension, the agent, assumed new importance in Hollywood and the locus of power shifted yet again.

BEN BENJAMIN: If Olivier gets $1 million, we get $100,000.

MICHAEL OVITZ: I have no clue where 10 percent comes from. I don't think anybody knows. It's just always been the number that's been in existence for a hundred years.

SUE MENGERS: So basically what I look for is earning potential. Who is going to be successful and therefore make money?

TOM POLLOCK: That's why the key job of the agent in representing you is to figure out which executive at which studio needs your movie, who will go and fight for it.

SUE MENGERS: Yes, you go to a studio, and what you try to do is at least once a month get brought up to date by the head of the studio, the head of production, as to what the schedule is: "What films have you bought? What books have you bought?" Then you try to sell them [screenwriters] for the books: "What screenplays have you bought?"

BEN BENJAMIN: I had a call from a studio executive at Universal, Jennings Lang, and he said, "Do you have a bright young writer that I could use on such-and-such a project?" I said, "I've got the greatest guy in the world."

SUE MENGERS: An agent's dream is a writer-director. That's the dream, to have the hyphenate, because that's someone who can create their own material and is not sitting there saying "Get me a job."

STEVEN SPIELBERG: Mike Medavoy contacted me, and we talked, and I signed with Mike when he was at CMA.

SAM WASSON: CMA—Creative Management Associates. In 1975, they merged with International Famous Agency to form International Creative Management, or ICM. Creative Artists Agency, or CAA, formed that same year. The sheer size of these agencies led clients to consider whether they would be vulnerable to internal conflicts of interest or benefit from the agencies growing power.

SIDNEY SHELDON: The advantage of going with a small agent is that they don't have that kind of client list to worry about.

LEE ROSENBERG: In the large agencies, there is an agent/client division. This agent has thirty-five clients. Now, to convey his enthusiasm to another agent in that agency is a waste of energy and creative activity for that agent, because that other agent also has his thirty-five clients. He is interested in picking up a paycheck regularly, so his performance for his people is much more important to him than his performance for that agent's people. So you have that problem.

SUE MENGERS: It's like the agents who have their own agencies and are totally dependent upon their clients for the commission. You sometimes might find yourself recommending something to a client because you want that client to go to work so you can make some money, while if you're with a large agency and you have a contract and you know you're going to get paid whether your client works that year or not, you're able to be much more objective about what they should or shouldn't do.

ERIC WEISSMANN: I remember somebody talking about Lee [Rosenberg] as an agent, saying that he was interested in two of his clients, one who was very expensive, on whom the agent could have made a big commission, and another one who was not expensive, and the agent said, "I think for your project I would recommend this particular client, the less expensive client." Now, in a way the agent may have done a disservice to his more expensive client, but maybe he felt that the more expensive client was going to get a job anyway. And the agent did himself a great service because that particular buyer raved about him. He said, "My God, he saved my project. He gave me wonderful advice, it was unselfish advice, it wasn't just to get the biggest commission."

BRUCE DERN: Fred Specktor called me on the phone. He was an agent at William Morris who had never represented me and was never interested. He said to me, "I think that you have been sold wrong for the past few years. I think that you should stop television, shouldn't play villains, and you should sit and wait till we can get you into the leading-man category. You can be a viable commodity in this industry. You have the potential to do it all, to be a superstar, but it's going to take a lot of patience." It was scary. I had to borrow money from my wife that she wasn't thrilled to give me. . . . I went to William Morris, and Fred Specktor supported me and my wife for eight months. He gave me what amounted to $800, $900 a month to make it through that period of time where we took no work. . . . But he supported me for about eight months, and we hung in there. Actually, sixteen months without work. But it took that kind of commitment.

SIDNEY POITIER: Actors do what their agents say, not in terms of what parts they will play but how they behave in terms of their fees, their remunerations. To give you an example: I was in a group called First Artists with Steve McQueen, Paul Newman, and Barbra Streisand. Dustin Hoffman came in later. I thought we had a perfect union. Each of us would get a $150,000 fee as an actor. We would get 10 percent of the gross as a part of our fee. We would own 50 percent of the profits of the film. I did four films for First Artists, Newman made three, Barbra made three, Steve made three, Dustin made a couple. We made twenty-eight movies. Agents and the studios destroyed that union, because McQueen's agents knew they could get $5 million up front instead of working on a picture for our group. Barbra was being offered huge sums, Paul was being offered huge sums. So between the offers from the studios and the agents who are maneuvering on behalf of the actors, the studios and the agents won, and First Artists never got beyond twenty-eight films. It's not easy to pinpoint the bad guys, because everyone has a right to look out for their best interests.

SUE MENGERS: You know, what used to drive us crazy is that you would work very hard to help put a picture together and really slave on it and work hand in hand with the producer in trying to make the right deal, and then the picture would be finished and there would be a preview and you'd hear about the preview and you would be told that there were no agents allowed. You know, like those signs: "No soliciting." And only recently has that kind of stopped because some of us said, "The hell with you." I mean, how dare you? We made as much of a contribution to this film as the studio.

BRUCE DERN: The agent has a life to live himself. He believes in his clients to a certain extent, but he's got other clients. He's never going to go to the wall for you.

JANE FONDA: You have to make them really want to fight for you.

SIDNEY SHELDON: It may take fifty phone calls to sell you.

THOMAS RICKMAN: I've found that agents, particularly if you're a writer, are good at getting you jobs you might not want to do but you might want to make some money at. If there's something you want to do, they're no good at all. That is because most agents like to package things. If you go in and say, "I'm going to write this script, and I'm going to direct it," that robs them of one element. If, however, you say, "I want to make a lot of money," then they'll call you fifty times a day with stuff to do.

GORDON STULBERG: I've had many clients come in and ask for advice about how to approach a studio with a project, and, as simplistic as it sounds, my answer is "Give them as little to think about as possible, as little to worry about as possible. If you've got a good script, for Christ's sake see if you can attract a player."

JOHN PTAK: They really don't have the time. They've got to look over twenty or thirty projects that are developing, and so any one studio executive simply doesn't have the time to be the father to one particular project and that's all. He's the father to fifteen or twenty projects.

SIDNEY SHELDON: There's good news and bad news. The good news is that [the big agencies] handle all the stars and directors in the business. They can take your story and give it to Steve McQueen and say, "We like this, we think you should do it." That's a lot of power. The bad news is that they are usually too busy to do this.

ERIC WEISSMANN: Some agents may be a little bit more shady, and there you may need a lawyer to protect you.

HAL ASHBY: Attorneys I don't need. Agents can be very, very good, because they can find material for you.

JOSEPH LOSEY: I've given up agents, they've never done anything for me. From now on, I work with lawyers.

ERIC WEISSMANN: Since lawyers are not so much in the forefront of selling and being in the marketplace—part of what an agent does is that he has to puff and lie a little bit. He's a salesman, he has to tell you that this car has only been driven in Pasadena by an old lady who had a heart attack twenty years ago, so it only has five thousand miles on it. That's kind of his job—the lawyer's job is not quite that. But you have a problem of conflict all the time.

BEN BENJAMIN: I should say there are quite a few lawyers who assume the role of an agent—which they have no right to do, but they do. As agents, we are not permitted to practice law. We cannot draw a contract. We cannot defend a client in court. All we can do is serve as a witness and look at their contract.

ERIC WEISSMANN: Now, let me touch on the forms of contracts. The two major ones when we have deals for more than one picture would be an option contract, where the employer is entitled to your services—let's say you're the director—for one picture a year for up to seven years. I'm not committed to use you, but each time a year passes that I don't employ you, if that ever happens, then the contract terminates and you're free to go. The other thing is that I just pay you a salary of $1,000 or $2,000 a week or whatever it is, and I pay you whether you work or don't work, and I have the right to continue doing this year after year. I have the option, maybe exercisable thirty days prior to the end of the particular year, to keep on doing this for the next year. Now, there may be escalations, and furthermore there may be various credits. For example, I made a deal with a director at Universal on a term basis pursuant to which Universal guaranteed him, let's say, two years employment and then had options on a year-to-year basis for a total of seven years, and let us say the guarantee was $60,000 a year. However, for each service the director performed, he would be credited a certain amount of compensation. If he did a pilot for a half-hour movie, he would get a certain credit. If he did a two-hour movie for television, he would get a certain credit. If he did a motion picture that was released theatrically, he would get a certain credit. So there was a chance that he would get more than the original guaranteed compensation, which, in my example, was $60,000.

But then what the studio can do to you is that they'll say, "We will exercise the next option but only if you give us an amendment to the deal. We'll let you direct a major picture, which might entitle you to a $100,000 credit, but we don't want to give you the $100,000 credit. Will you give us a waiver on your deal and let us have you direct this picture, and we'll only pay you $60,000 for that?" The director may say, "Yes," because he's so anxious to direct the picture, and he doesn't dream it's going to make $60 million. I don't know if I've answered your question.

Let me just mention one more thing. In the situation where a director is employed on an option basis, as distinguished from a term contract, you have a preempt procedure. Now, what that means is this director says, "Until I know that I'm employed by you, I can't sit around waiting for you to make up your mind what to give me, so if I get another offer, I want to have a chance to do that." The studio says, "Yes, but the problem with that is that your offer may come one day before we're ready to go with our picture, so we want a chance, since we really gave you the first job and you gave us the option agreement, to use you." So the preempt procedure has been worked out, which means that the director gives the studio a notice saying "I've got a chance to direct a picture for United Artists." And Universal has thirty days or fifteen days or five days, whatever you negotiate, to say, "No, you can't do the picture for United Artists, you've got to do it for us." But at that time Universal is committed to employ him, at least to pay him, and they are also committed to start his services, to start the compensation within a certain outside period, so that the director doesn't give up the United Artists deal for a picture starting in April and then not work under the Universal deal until next December.

Now that becomes even more sophisticated. Sometimes directors will say, "A studio cannot preempt and must have a specific picture for which to use the director." Because what the studio may do to prevent the director from doing a picture for a competing studio, it may be worthwhile to them to preempt it and to pay him and knock that other studio out of the box. I was in a situation once where a director had an option agreement with a producer client as a result of the director doing a movie for a producer-director, and the director wanted to do another photoplay elsewhere, and he did not send the preempt notice to his client. Meanwhile, the producer exercised the option and there was a great bluffing contest because the director did not know whether the producer had a picture or didn't have a picture, and he didn't even know whether the producer didn't have the picture, if he had the money with which to pay the director. But the producer won the bluff because he knew that the director could not afford not to do the other picture. He was very, very interested in doing that picture, and the way that was settled was that the director had to buy his way out of that contract. This producer, in fact, made a lot of money on a couple option deals by forcing the people to buy their way out. Generally, when it works well—and it generally does work well—the agent and the lawyer and the business manager work together. Now, the business manager can say, "Hey, I've got a desperate cash-flow problem and we've got to get this guy a job, and we can't let him say anymore that he doesn't want to do it unless it's a surefire Academy Award." He may give us the tip-off, saying "We've got to get the guy a job." Or the business manager may say, "You know, there's so much money around that I don't care whether he gets $200,000 or $100,000 on the next picture. If he wants to take a piece of the gross instead of cash and if that makes your deal more easy, go ahead and do it." So we all kind of guide each other.

Now, that gets us into the whole area of clout, credibility, inside information, and the function of a lawyer, the function of an agent, and how they can help or hurt each other. I had a situation where a client was made an offer for a picture and the agent was requesting cash and a percentage of the picture's profits, and we couldn't make headway. The head of business affairs for the particular studio is a personal friend of mine. We went to high school together and we are close friends to this day, and I have always been very lucky, in having a dialogue with him, where there is a point where we will absolutely level with each other. You know, we won't do that all the time, but when it gets a little risky, we will. And he called me and said, "Look, we offered seventy-five thousand dollars. I think you can get a hundred thousand dollars, and if you do a lot of huffing and puffing, there will be a great tearing of hair, but you can get a twenty-five-thousand-dollar deferment, too." He says, "However, there is no way that you can get a percentage of the profits, and these are the reasons, and I just wanted you to be guided accordingly." Well, I was able to tell the client, "It's unfair that you don't get a piece of the profits, but there is no point in complaining. It's the lay of the land. I think we should do the picture. I think we should accept the offer." And I at least went to bed that night confident that we got the best offer there was available for us, and the client was convinced by that, too. Then I was able to give the agent instructions, and the agent was able to go through the dance with the other guy, and ultimately, after much moaning and groaning, he got $100,000 and so on. It's like a fixed horse race in a way, like a wrestling match.

BEN BENJAMIN: There is a new agency now, CAA, it's a spin-off, really, of William Morris, where about five young fellows defected from the Morris agency [William Haber, Ron Meyer, Michael Ovitz, Rowland Perkins, Michael S. Rosenfeld] and set up their own agency. And then there was a strong, independent agent, Marty Baum, who used to be with our company, who joined forces with them. And they are the most competitive, I think, to us of anybody in the business right now. They're just doing a wonderful, wonderful job.

DUSTIN HOFFMAN: Ovitz.

TOM POLLOCK: Michael Ovitz.

MARTIN SCORSESE: Mike Ovitz coming up to me after making *The Color of Money* and tapping me on the shoulder and saying "You know, you can get paid for this."

MICHAEL OVITZ: I grew up in the valley four blocks from the RKO studio. That's where I learned. That's where I became totally enraptured with the business.

I would sneak in. This was the fifties. There was no security. We'd sneak in under the fence and go watch them shoot these black-and-white television shows like *Ramar of the Jungle*. I can remember watching a group of human beings create an environment that came out of someone's head, that wasn't real but *became* real. And when they said, "Action!" it was as real as can be. And when they said, "Cut!" it was just all chaotic. And it was such a mesmerizing experience, because they had people in costume and they had prop masters and they had makeup people and hair people and continuity people, and sitting there as a kid, a nine-, ten-year-old kid, watching this was such a privilege. At the age of ten, I'm watching product being made.

The concept of seeing a group of people all pulling together to get two minutes of usable footage in a twelve-hour day—and that's all they get, two minutes in a twelve-hour day. And I would sit and be mesmerized, and no one had to tell anybody what to do. No one said to the makeup person, "Go dab the nose." No one said to the prop master, "That glass is one foot from where it was, there's no continuity." Everyone was an expert in their field. And by the way, I didn't know what I was knowing then. But I'll tell you what. I fell in love with it. The process.

I worked for Universal when I was sixteen. I gave the tours. I was a tour guide. I can't tell you how much I loved it. There were five guys then, and I was one of them. And I see men walking around the lot in suits, getting treated like God, and then walking up to Lee J. Cobb, Lana Turner, Alfred Hitchcock, Michael Caine, and being well received and hugged. I said, "Who are they?" "Well, they're agents." "Where are they from?" When I went into the commissary, it was the agents who were populating it, having lunch with the filmmakers. I witnessed agents doing things the executives wouldn't do. They took care of every need that the talent had.

I got a job in the William Morris mailroom in 1969. Well, there were two kinds of agents at the agency. There were those that worked their tails off. Like Stan Kamen worked twelve, fourteen hours a day and then worked at night. But then there were agents like Joe Rivkin, who was a former MGM executive who was there because Abe Lastfogel owed him. There was another agent there named Benny Thau. Benny did nothing. He just sat and read the newspaper every day. Those guys' time had passed them by.

It was really weird. They would put TV shows together, but their idea of packaging was not mine. Their idea of packaging was only in television, not in movies. And that's an important distinction. They would package around a producer. And it became very clear to me that was not the way to do it. The way to do it was to package around the performer, the writer, or director. Period. So I said to the company, "What are we doing here?" Their point of view was I was twenty-six, what did I know?

The other thing I did that no one did was, I read all these books. I read Frank Capra, *The Name Above the Title*. I read *Memo from David O. Selznick*. I went to the bookstore. I'll never forget this. There was a place called Brentano's bookstore in Beverly Hills. I ordered every book that was a coffee-table picture book, the history of MGM, 20th Century–Fox, Universal, and I studied this stuff like I was going to college. I had a context like no one else.

I'm twenty-one years old, I'm trying to get ahead [in the Morris office], and there's no such thing as the internet, right? Everything's on paper. And I'm delivering all this paper. And I said to myself, "Okay, what's the most important thing for me right now? There are two things and two things only: one, to be recognized by senior executives that I'm an up-and-comer, and two, I better learn what they already know." So I went and bought a woman's scarf—I'll never forget this—for, like, eighty bucks at Saks Fifth Avenue, and I brought it to a woman named Mary [a secretary at the Morris office], who had a chain with a key to the file room around her neck. I wanted that key. I brought her the scarf. I was in.

She had a key made for me. So every night and all weekend, I just sat there, starting at 8:00 a.m. I read every deal, every authorization paper, every piece of publicity. I read stuff about Omar Sharif that I shouldn't have. I read personal correspondence that was filed away. Everything was filed. You weren't allowed to throw paper out. Everything got filed because you had to keep it for litigation. So I read everything. And I did it in three months.

Those deals were weird. I learned so much. Mostly front-loaded deals, almost no back ends. No one thought [back-end deals] were worth anything. Studios just resisted it. It just took forever. But what I learned by looking at the files was supply and demand.

CAA, in my head, was born in early 1970 in the file room at William Morris Agency. I saw all of it. I saw the future of the business. Didn't know what to do about it. Didn't have a clue, because I was on a track at William Morris to get ahead, so I couldn't put myself in the position of taking myself off that track. But I knew what the company should look like. And that's why I left.

The Ann Miller thing was the straw that broke the camel's back. We're all sitting at the William Morris conference table. And every guy sitting around the table was a senior executive. And then sitting behind them were a bunch of guys sitting in chairs, which were the midlevel guys. And then the rest of us were in the peanut gallery sitting against the wall. And I was the assistant to the president, Sam Weisbord. And Sam announces this amazing news that he's signed Ann Miller. The reality is that Ron Meyer and I looked at each other and Bill Haber, and we go, "I beg your pardon?" And Ron, to his credit, stands up and says, "Great lady but, like, who cares? Let's re-sign Steve McQueen. Let's sign George Roy Hill. Let's sign serious people." The company was completely focused on television and Vegas. It was old school.

This is why CAA killed it. We made a decision in 1978 that I was going to go into the movie business from scratch and build a business. And that's all I was going to do: movies. William Morris never made that decision. The head of William Morris was the lead television agent. At the end of the day, the man or woman carrying the flag at CAA to this day has to be a motion picture agent. They have to be. Because it's still the Rolls-Royce of the business. Long-form celluloid trumps everything else. It just does.

JANE FONDA: I said, "I'm tired of paying all this money to agents that not only don't get me jobs but don't give me particularly cogent advice." There have been some exceptions, of course. But for five years I had no agent. And then I went in and interviewed Ron Meyer and Mike Ovitz at CAA. I felt like I was talking to people who knew how to give me real advice and could make things happen on the studio level. They know what's going on. They're very hip politically. They all come in and throw ideas around, and this is what they did with me. Out of one of those kinds of meetings I actually bought two novels to make into movies. No agency ever did that for me before. I never had access to any group of young, exciting heads all getting together to try to service my needs as a company.

MICHAEL OVITZ: What I figured out was that you pull together as a team, that if we're going to handle Dustin Hoffman, five of us better be working for him, not one. And that was the core of CAA. I said, "We're going to kill everybody with a simple thesis: if we have a client and he's only got one agent, there is more likely than not the chance that he will have a conflict with that one agent at some given point in time. But if he's got five agents working for him, he can move past one to pick up the other."

SAM WASSON: As large agencies grew their client lists, they grew in power. After all, they were selling what the studios were buying. But what then was a studio?

ARTHUR PENN: I don't believe studios have a genuine function and see no reason for them to exist today. If they weren't so well placed in terms of real estate, they would have been consumed a long time ago. Century City is what really saved 20th Century–Fox.

SIDNEY SHELDON: Major studios today are really distributors and a source of money for independent producers.

JACK VALENTI: Today they are mostly distribution organizations, renters of studio space, financiers and buyers of properties which have been put together by mostly independent people.

TONI VELLANI: This is the basic difference between now and the past, when they had producers on contract.

JOHN PTAK: The producers are all out there looking for jobs, basically.

A. D. MURPHY: In the old days at a studio, they would be carefully brought along. If it didn't work this time, try again. Now everybody is really on the dime to be a success or fail. And the same thing with producers.

NED TANEN: There are really very few people left who are professional as producers. Even forgetting the great producers, the professional movie producer really, to a very large degree, doesn't exist anymore. It was an invaluable service because it was the buffer zone between the financing and distribution of a movie and studio input, which is sometimes valid and a great deal of the time not valid, and a director who fancies himself an *auteur* and is off just spending money as though he's printing it in the back room.

A. D. MURPHY: Everybody's a freelancer.

NED TANEN: Somebody literally bought a paperback and it exploded and suddenly it's a hot property, and guess who your producer is? It's a guy who was a butcher last week who has really no interest in the film business, who has no background, no understanding of the physical problems of making a movie, and is of no help to the director and the film itself and who ends up to a very large degree being a producer.

MIKE NICHOLS: Many movies have a guy who paid $1,500 for the rights and spends the rest of the movie saying "Why wasn't my name in the *Variety* article?" That's what a producer is.

DAVID PICKER: There is the producer who has come up through the ranks, through the making of the film, through the crafts, fellows who have been ADs or production managers who have now gotten enough experience and who have been lucky enough to find a relationship or a project that somebody will package and finance. And then there are the producers who are kind of throwbacks to the producers of the 1930s and '40s, who were salaried by the studios but who were responsible for the development of the script, working with the director, the casting of the movie, and I consider myself in that bracket, along with a bunch of other people who are totally involved in every aspect of the films they make and whose influence is felt and seen. There is the agent-turned-producer whose business it is to package a picture and get somebody to buy it and take his fee and run away, and that's a very common kind of producer today. There is the producer who's also something else, like a director or a writer who gets pictures put together because he has a secondary talent which people want, or a primary talent which people want, and who therefore also has the muscle to produce his own film. In some instances they are terrific. In some instances I think they shouldn't do it because it affects their work.

BILLY WILDER: These producers come to you and ask, "What is the theme of your picture?" They're very proud to have a theme. It's kind of a joke among us writers. You tell him, "The theme? Don't you know? The theme of this is 'War is hell!'" He says, "That's terrific."

"What is the theme of this picture?" I say, "The theme of this picture is 'You can't eat soup with a fork!'" That's it, and he is very happy. "No man is an island" works magic, I think. Just give them that. In the old days, we were just telling good stories, and producers knew what could help that happen.

PETER GUBER: Show me a producer everybody in the whole town hates, everybody hates, loathes, makes fun of him. If he's got a great script, you go make the picture. Show me somebody that everyone loves, is endearing and gracious, not a bad word said about him, he's wonderful, he's kind, but he's got a bad script. Know what they say? "Pass."

BRIAN GRAZER: I remember somebody saying to me, "You have no money, you have no leverage, you have nothing, the only thing you can do is write ideas down and try to sell them, create a currency that way."

LAWRENCE GORDON: It's the only business I know of where you can start with a yellow pad and an idea or your computer and an idea and make millions of dollars and become famous and have a career. Okay, think about that. If you want to open a restaurant, you got to have some money. If you want to have anything to do with Silicon Valley, you have to have some money. We don't have to have any money.

SAM WASSON: If anyone who had a script could be a producer, anyone who owned paper and pen could be a screenwriter.

MICHAEL PHILLIPS: There's a wide-open door to Hollywood today, and that's the original screenplay. That is the only really wide-open chance, because if that script knocks somebody out in Hollywood, just one person, you're the director, you're the producer, or you're the writer, whatever you want to be, all you have to do is be involved with that.

WALDO SALT: You know, there is a whole industry that is developing that's related to attempting to find ways of formulaising writing, particularly for the screen.

PAUL SCHRADER: I'm now teaching full-time at UCLA, and one of the courses is in screenwriting.

SCOTT ALEXANDER: Okay, so in the old days, children, people did not write screenplays in college.

ELEANOR PERRY: Well, you know, in the first act you set up the problem and the characters and so forth, and in the second act it's that old sawbuck that you get them up a tree, you know, the conflict begins, and at the end of the second act—roughly, the end of the second act—is where it seems like an insolvable, suspensable, impossible situation, and then in the third act it's resolved.

FRANK DARABONT: Moses did not come down from the mountain with a tablet that says "Write a three-act structure, or you'll go to Hell."

BOB RAFELSON: I am sometimes unfollowable—if, indeed, you're looking for a story to follow.

JOHN MCTIERNAN: Could you talk about the pitfalls in that approach?

BOB RAFELSON: Nobody goes to see the movie. That's the major pitfall.

SAM ARKOFF: I'll give you one great example: Mr. Cimino.

MICHAEL OVITZ: *Heaven's Gate.* Believe it or not, that was all very helpful to me. This is how it happened . . .

SAM ARKOFF: Mr. Cimino won an Academy Award. I'm not going to talk about how good a picture he made, *The Deer Hunter*. Okay, it was a pretty good picture, all things considered. All of a sudden he's out making *Heaven's Gate*, what is nothing more, really, than a western.

ISTVÁN POÓR: When you finished the script of *Heaven's Gate*, what was the first reaction of the studio?

MICHAEL CIMINO: Well, they never saw a script. I presented it. I just talked it through. It took me two hours. It was an oral presentation, which is kind of difficult to do. I sat in a room with half a dozen people and told them the story. And they committed to making it based on that presentation.

SAM ARKOFF: Now, westerns have not been particularly successful in recent years. The old western legend is really gone. Kids don't grow up with guns as much today as they do with spaceships. But the fact still remains that with a budget of somewhere in the neighborhood of $10 or $12 million, Mr. Cimino is now over $30 million. Now, you know, this is utter nonsense. I don't care what you think about the creative rights and so on and so forth. That's absolute nonsense. . . . I don't think anybody will question Michelangelo was a great artist, but when the pope hired him to paint the ceiling of the Sistine Chapel, the pope told him what he was going pay him. And he didn't tell him to cover all the walls and the floor and this and that. He told him, "Paint the ceiling."

MICHAEL CIMINO: We began preparing the film before we ever had the script. I mean, the physical preparation.

MARTIN SCORSESE: Well, it all comes down to power at some point. How much muscle do you have, and what will they put up with?

MICHAEL CIMINO: It was just a tremendous physical job. And just the sheer size of it. I mean, just to deal with eighty teams of horses. The amount of wranglers that one needs for that.

MARTIN SCORSESE: Obviously I'm going to try to get for myself as much freedom to do what I want to do as the situation will bear.

JOHN LANDIS: Hollywood's become so fragmented, the superstructure is broken down in terms of the studios. So what happens is, once a director is hired, he is basically the producer of the movie.

GARETH WIGAN: I think the producer is being squeezed out, not only by the studio wanting to take charge but, in a funny way, also by the studio abdicating some of the take-charge things—say, "We want this star, we want this director, so we will give them the power."

A. D. MURPHY: Say that the director wants the big scene. The studio says, "Oh, well, what the hell, let him do it." It's going to come out of their participation anyway. There is nobody there to say, "Wait a minute." But a good producer would be there to say, "Wait a minute."

MICHAEL CIMINO: The movie opens with a commencement scene. Now, there are eight hundred people in that scene. Now, they all have to be dressed. All of those people had to be cast. In other words, nobody was just put in. Every person who was there was Polaroided. There was a Polaroid taken of every person. Each face was selected. Those people were then dressed. I then reviewed those people, and we made adjustments in each of their wardrobe, change hats, change coats, whatever. Everybody was altered, you know, if trousers didn't fit right, if shirts didn't fit right. Now, another Polaroid was then taken, so that you wind up with eight hundred Polaroids all precisely numbered.

LAURA ZISKIN: You hire the directors. My friend Bob Garland says it's the only business in the world where you hire someone who becomes your boss.

FRANK MARSHALL: The final decision is the director's in every area and doesn't stop with directing actors. You got to direct the wardrobe guy, you got to direct the propman, you got to direct the transportation guy, you got to direct the marketing people. It never ends.

MICHAEL CIMINO: Now, also, we have a street. There are a thousand people on a street, and you've got eighty teams of horses and a train. You're dressing certain people that you know you want a certain look at the railroad station, a certain look of people on the streets. Nobody will see it, but there's a group of masons walking down a street. And so you begin, simply, "Okay, take this face here and this face." And then you begin composing the street. And we took one full day to arrange it. You can't have several thousand people wandering around not knowing where they go.

GEORGE LUCAS: There's an individual called the line producer. And he is the one I would call the real producer. Some people wouldn't say that, but I would say that. He's the guy that manages the movie. He's the guy that is the business manager for movies. Basically, he hires people, he fires the people, he scheduled the movie he needs to have done on time. He's the real nuts-and-bolts guy. He's the guy that sees to it the checks are cut and people get paid and, as they got hired in the field, comes in on budget. And he's there to help the director achieve his vision economically and resourcefully and creatively. It's a very creative job. it's just creative in a very different way.

MICHAEL MANN: It's like being a janitor for a high-rise.

DUSTIN HOFFMAN: What a silly art form, what a wonderfully silly art form to give you a budget, based on something they know nothing about. We got a scene here to do, and they're telling you it's got one lighting set-up, three actors on a stage, a reverse shot with the crowd out there, it should take you no more than a half a day or a day. What happens if we don't cook? What happens if something's wrong and we're not getting it? Can we stay here another day?

MICHAEL OVITZ: The incredible failure of *Heaven's Gate* left a hole in the system. It left the studios gun shy. So what we at CAA did was step in. It was the best thing in the world for us. I woke up one day, and I said, "My God, this is a godsend."

Life in the movie business started to change. What began to happen is that one movie out of ten pops—*Superman* in 1978—but only one. And then nine little ones behind it, *Raiders of the Lost Ark* and then everything behind it. So each year the split between the big movies and the little movies narrows. It goes from one and nine to two and eight, four and six, five and five, and then, when you get into the mideighties, everything goes big again and all the seventies stuff dissipates.

CHAPTER 15

PACKAGING

MARTIN SCORSESE: By the time we finished *Raging Bull* and it was released, the whole industry had changed.

TOM POLLOCK: Basically what's happened is that the studios abdicate the creative initiative for a film to outside talent, whether it is an independent producer with an idea, a director with an idea, or a writer who with his agent comes in and says, "I'd like to develop this idea."

SUE MENGERS: Agents have more power than the studios. They need the agents, because the agents at the moment are the major suppliers of talent and material.

MICHAEL OVITZ: The studios were just banks.

GORDON STULBERG: The more you can package outside the studio, the better the chance you have of having it considered at the top level of the studio and getting a fast answer, yea or nay, a fast answer.

JOHN PTAK: I mean, the most common package is really a writer-producer or a writer-director.

JULIA PHILLIPS: I think that's why there are so many bad movies: too many good packages.

MICHAEL OVITZ: CAA packaged three hundred films in fifteen years. Everything we did was a package. The economy was so flush that if you pitched me an idea, I knew if I could get financing or not. So I could say to the writer or director, "It's a go." And the writer or director would look at me and say, "What do you mean, it's a go?" And I'd say, "We're going to get it paid for." That's what I would say. And I was never wrong. Neither were the other agents in the building, because (a) we were culturally attuned, (b) we knew what the schedules were of each company, (c) we basically programmed two of the six studios, Christmas and summer movies. There wasn't a year in ten years that Columbia didn't have a CAA package.

MERYL STREEP: [Sam Cohn at ICM] wasn't interested in me doing *Sophie's Choice* because he didn't handle [Alan] Pakula or [William] Styron.

SAM ARKOFF: Now, agents don't know anything about making pictures. All they know is the fact they learn their craft, or what they know about the business, by representing clients. Now, they don't know anything about production itself. So the problem is, they want to be nice guys. Agents always want to be nice guys. And that's no time for a nice guy. Not, after all, as long as this is a business, which has, as one of its purposes, at least making enough money so that you can continue to do business next year.

MICHAEL OVITZ: *Tootsie* was a passion project of Dustin Hoffman's, and it was our goal to package the elements around him. Bill [Murray] was my client and my friend, and so was Dusty [Hoffman], so was Sydney [Pollack]. I had to get all of them to agree to work with each other as a package. We did.

Dustin cast the love interest for *Tootsie* in our office. Two hundred women came in to read for both parts [Jessica Lange's and Teri Garr's]. Now, I will say selfishly, I didn't talk Dustin out of casting at CAA for another reason: it made CAA look like we were omnipotent. A giant movie is casting out of the CAA building? And the agents of these women are sending their clients to CAA for an assignment? I knew exactly what I was doing.

We were always a step ahead. The staff meetings at our competition started at 9:30. I started ours at eight. We *finished* at 9:30 with all that information. Like if you came to the table, you're an agent, and you said, "There is this book. I've read it over the weekend. It's phenomenal, and it's great for Gene Hackman." "Great. We don't represent Gene Hackman." "Not a problem. Let's call him." Nine thirty, get out of the meeting. One of the agents calls Gene Hackman, says, "We're sending you this book. It's perfect for you." His agent gets out of their meeting at eleven. Gene Hackman's already put a call in to him. CAA's already given him a book that he read that he's interested in. We're always a step ahead. We're just always a step ahead.

We put together big movies. We packaged them around talent. That's what we did.

ROBERT EVANS: Blockbusters . . .

JANE FONDA: Whatever happened to trying to deal with the broader community?

A. D. MURPHY: The attitude right now is "Enough, enough, I've had enough." Some of the films in the sixties, and the plays and the books, were antagonizing the very people that they were trying to reach. And as soon as Vietnam ended, I think in this country and a lot of countries, people said, "Enough. We're going to stop right here and kind of let everything settle down before we move along."

DAVID ANSEN: I went back, and I looked at what the summer movies were in the summer of '71. And it was a whole different world. I mean, you got movies like *McCabe & Mrs. Miller* and *Panic in Needle Park*, which nobody, *nobody* would think of as a summer movie. And even the sort of more popular things like *Billy Jack* had a definite sort of counterculture edge. Because one of the things that happened was the counterculture sort of ceased to exist and there was just one culture.

ALJEAN HARMETZ: What was very interesting about the movies of the seventies was that movies that were essentially downbeat, movies that didn't have happy endings, movies that were ambiguous had a mass audience. People were willing to accept that. And that lasted through '77.

MICHAEL OVITZ: 1980.

MARTIN SCORSESE: I think things changed from 1981 on.

CHARLES CHAMPLIN: For a time, when the movies had this new freedom, they began to get into hard-edged things and social realism, exploiting the new freedom of the screen in a positive way rather than a negative way. But as Vietnam wore on, as the economy continued to fall apart, there was this continual erosion of confidence in the processes of government. I think people found it harder and harder to go out and experience yet more psychic pain in the movie theaters, this despondent view of the human condition.

SAM ARKOFF: And once it was over, there wasn't very much left of it, except a few gold beads on middle-aged men. But while it lasted, it was one hell of a decade.

JULIA PHILLIPS: Now every studio has a very big, very expensive picture, and if some of them happen to be science fiction, it would be because of the special effects. It's getting very expensive to make a movie.

NIRA BARAB: Is that going to change?

JULIA PHILLIPS: How is it going to change? How is it going to go back?

NIRA BARAB: I don't know. Isn't something—

JULIA PHILLIPS: Well, when it all goes into the toilet and some other person comes along with something that's like an *Easy Rider* that was made for no money independently, then everybody who's twenty-two with a light meter around his neck is going to be a director again.

DAVID CHASMAN: There are recurring cycles in popularity. Today, people keep assuring me that westerns don't work. They point to the failure very recently of a number of expensive westerns or pictures perceived to be westerns. My answer to that is a trade ad taken out in 1935 by a cowboy star named Ken Maynard: a picture of Ken Maynard with two guns, looking very grim, an inset of his horse (whose name was Tarzan), and the legend "Westerns are not dead!" So in 1935, westerns were dead, too.

JULIA PHILLIPS: Well, the cycle used to be, somebody told me, seven years, but I think that since we live in fast times, it's about five. Pretty soon it will be three. But they're going to run out of money.

MICHAEL OVITZ: At that time in the business there was a balance between big budgets and small budgets which allowed young talent to break in.

SAM ARKOFF: If you want to really get into the system, you almost have to go out of the system.

GEORGE LUCAS: I didn't want to have to listen to the studios and make films on their terms, and, fortunately, *Star Wars* gave me an opportunity to become independent of the studio system.

JOSEPH E. LEVINE: I used to make pictures for MGM, I made pictures for Paramount, never made a quarter, unless the picture makes so much money or unless you can be like that wonderful new independent from San Francisco. What's his name?

STEVEN SPIELBERG: George.

JOSEPH E. LEVINE: There's a guy! I never met him, but I love him. He's young. He snubbed his nose at Hollywood. I love Hollywood, but he has quit the Writers Guild, which is *farkakte* anyway, and the other guild, and he said to them go to hell. And *he* distributes a picture. I mean, the company distributes the picture. But they don't make a nickel on that picture, because *he* controls it. *He* paid for it. And he's able to dictate, and that's what we're talking about, strength. We're talking about his strength versus your strength. You have to remain strong. You remain the hammer instead of the anvil. I've always been the hammer. This picture I'm the anvil. They're hitting me on the head, they're hitting me on the head. But this guy from San Francisco, this kid, he's wonderful. He makes these marvelous pictures. Greatest pictures I ever saw. Raiders of the lost something. I saw it three times! It's terrific! It's a real show-business picture! Real hold 'em! It's terrific! And the first hundred million dollars, Paramount doesn't get a quarter. It's an exercise in futility for them, but this picture will go to a hundred million more, so they'll make money, unfortunately. But this guy's got the right idea. Lucas! You watch his career and do what he does, and you'll be all right. Even do what I did, and you'll be all right! And I'm not Lucas. Anyway, that's the whole secret of this business, and now I'll go.

NED TANEN: It has gone, strange enough, a little bit back toward a family audience. No one quite knows why. But it does almost stop dead at about age thirty-seven.

SHERRILL CORWIN: Because people over thirty have more to do, other things to do. They have children to take care of. I don't think you're ever going to get that big bulk audience except on very rare movies like *The Sound of Music* or *Jaws*.

STEVEN SPIELBERG: I mean, I never planned for those films to be popular. I didn't make *E.T.* to be popular. I didn't make *Close Encounters* to be popular. We made *Raiders* to be popular, but I didn't make *The Color Purple* to be popular. It's sort of interesting how that all works. And I've been as surprised as everybody else when the results are more popular than I ever dreamed possible. So much so that there becomes a backlash at a certain point where people start to suspect your intentions because these films are so wildly popular, all my big megahits, so to speak, like *Jaws* and *E.T.* It's always been everybody loves the movies for the first few months, and then, when they start breaking records, they say, "Well, wait a second, there must be a trick here. This is some kind of an evil seduction afoot, and I don't trust that Spielberg, he's manipulating me now. I know I had a great time, I enjoyed that movie, I saw it four times, but that little fucker manipulated it."

ALJEAN HARMETZ: What happened in the eighties is that all the movies—an exaggeration, not all the movies but a great number of movies—were aimed at adolescents. And the teenagers took over the movie theaters, basically, between 1978 and 1984. Nobody was even making movies for adults, nobody wanted adults, because not only could they get a great deal of money from teenagers, they would go see a movie two, three, or four times. That was the other thing about *Jaws*: it was a movie that kids want to go back to over and over again. Of course, the same thing was true of the *Star Wars* series, the Indiana Jones series, all of them big merchandising bonanzas and movies that adolescents went to half a dozen times.

DAVID NEWMAN: When I was working on *Sheena: Queen of the Jungle*, I was sitting with a producer and he introduced me to a guy at Columbia who was the liaison between the toy manufacturers and the movies. They're talking about Sheena dolls, and Sheena lunchboxes and Sheena bathing suits—all the merchandise. I thought what business are we in man, the toy business?

TOM POLLOCK: It's easier to sell to younger kids because they haven't yet developed the sense of self-awareness to know that they can choose what it is that they can do. They tend to be really, really more influenced by peer pressure.

JOEL SILVER: I was very fond of the young male demographic, which I thought was a very loyal demographic.

DON SIMPSON: I suppose when and if [Jerry Bruckheimer and I] both become adults, we might make different movies with different points of view. I hope it never happens. I mean, I have no desire to become an adult. None.

JOEL SILVER: Forget about the fact that the summers weren't full of action films, there *weren't* action films! I mean, I went to work for Larry [Gordon] because he had made them when he was at AIP. You know, except for the Bond films and the Dirty Harrys, there was nothing out there. There was no one making these kind of movies. And I thought, Well, I want to do this, this is what I want to do.

MARIO PUZO: Well, we have to face it, this is kid stuff, *Superman*, for me, anyway. It's not serious.

A. D. MURPHY: After *Superman* and *Star Wars* and *Close Encounters*, the public now is used to some very sharp-looking special effects. The public's taste is always rising. You could fake it ten years ago, you know, Godzilla, the tabletop, and the cheap miniatures. You can't get away with that anymore.

GEORGE LUCAS: I made *Star Wars* the same way I made my student films. It was about saying "Okay, I've got this amount of limited resources, but I'm going to do four times as much as the other guy." The script was carefully written in terms of what could be done with special effects at the time. In the midseventies, just panning the camera around a spaceship was tough enough.

GALE ANN HURD: One of the reasons that movie budgets are so high is because *they're* doing the research and development. Because up until that film proves it can be done, no one knows for sure whether it can be done, and someone has to pay for that research and development. And generally it's the budget of the film that pays.

DAVID PICKER: In the history of the motion picture business, the majors have been the last people to spend a nickel or a dime on research and development, and there's a very good reason for it, and the reason is that that money is a long-range investment and what movie companies are looking for are short-range returns. So they haven't felt that they have been able to afford research and development. So all the really interesting technical advances have come from lunatics in basements or documentary filmmakers or people like [Robert] Gottschalk who invent cameras and lenses or Dolby sound systems or whatever it is. But almost never through a major.

GEORGE LUCAS: With *The Empire Strikes Back* it was a case of creating a two-foot-high green creature with big ears and a walking stick and making him seem alive. Believe me, that was really pushing the technology at the time. I knew I couldn't go to Coruscant or have Yoda fight with a lightsaber and all the other things about Jedis and pod racing I had written into the backstory. I didn't even consider that at the time. The first thing I wanted was to be able to edit digitally on a computer. This was back in 1980.

OWEN ROIZMAN: Well, of course, with special effects, you really aren't doing it. I mean, special-effects people are doing it. I know Irvin Kershner. When he did *The Empire Strikes Back*, he told me that he sort of felt lost at times, because he would do things on the stage. And actually, nothing was happening behind the people. It was all going to be done later. And he found it very frustrating and very mechanical.

ARTHUR PENN: What I also believe is that the criteria for verisimilitude which is obtained in American films—not least of which is pride in the high degree of technology—are essentially an inhibiting factor.

JIM HENSON: It seems like everything is going to end up electronic. I think everyone expected that high-resolution TV would be utilized widely by now. To be working in films sometimes feels very archaic. It feels like you're using really old techniques, especially when you have to do these opticals in a laborious process, compared with what you can do on video. The optical image manipulations that you can do with the new video boards are enormous and wonderful.

WILLIAM FRIEDKIN: In the old days, when they wanted breath to show in a room, they used to build a stage in the Glendale Ice House. Well, the Glendale Ice House doesn't exist anymore.

SAM WASSON: Neither did the concept of the autonomous studio head, working independently of the board of directors, green-lighting movies without the input of the marketing people or those in neighboring industries looking to make the parent corporation a bigger profit on ancillary sales—toys, T-shirts, lunchboxes, boardgames . . .

PETER GUBER: The interdisciplinary philosophy is really useful in the businesses the way it's evolved today.

GEORGE LUCAS: This whole magic thing of licensing came into being which didn't exist when I did the first [*Star Wars*] film, but it started to become a very lucrative way to finance the films. *Return of the Jedi* wasn't financed just with the revenues from the movie. Half of it was financed from the revenues of the licensing products.

JON PETERS: *A Star Is Born* [1976] sold eight, almost nine million albums at $9.98. So actually, the album grossed almost as much as the film.

GORDON STULBERG: It boggled my imagination that 20th Century–Fox didn't have a record label in the [1970s]. It subcontracted its tracks to ABC Dunhill, and on the occasion where it picked up a copyright, that went to ABC Dunhill, and when you looked at the record—I mean, it wasn't as though it would be novel for Fox to go into the record business when you looked at Warners and you realized how much of Warners' income came from its record labels. It was just incredible that Fox hadn't been in it.

JON PETERS: To have a hit record or to have a score that you can play on the radio is very helpful to a film in relation to the public becoming aware.

GARETH WIGAN: I don't think the studio is the right way to pursue a career if you want to pursue a career in filmmaking as opposed to marketing.

TOM POLLOCK: In very few cases is there a studio executive today who says, "I'd like to do a film about this."

MICHAEL OVITZ: On *Rain Man*, CAA did it all. We packaged all the elements and even did the marketing. At the time we did all the marketing for Coca-Cola so we were set up to do films. Originally, people asked, what do we know about advertising? We weren't in the ad business, but we had a sense of what people wanted to watch. We were culture mavens. We knew the audience. We proved ourselves with the success of the Coke campaign. We also proved ourselves by knowing that Dustin Hoffman should make a movie about an autistic guy with Tom Cruise as the brother.

And the studios didn't have a lot of choice, because of the fifty top-grossing directors, for example, in 1990, CAA represented, like, forty-five of them. So you couldn't say no to us.

We provided services and support to the clients. At the end of the day, that movie was made by Dustin Hoffman, Barry Levinson, Mark Johnson, Tom Cruise, and Ron Bass, all CAA clients.

JOHN PTAK: What we're saying is that the studios are not just in the film business.

TOM POLLOCK: They just aren't making those kinds of decisions. That's the real change in the film business in the last ten years.

JOHN PTAK: It would be foolish from an investment standpoint to put all their money into films. They could end up with a total disaster and out of business in two years, which is what almost happened to Columbia. Of course, MGM has the Grand Hotel in Las Vegas, where they get most of their income.

DAVID PICKER: I mean, these people are not moviegoers. No way. They don't know anything about movies.

TOM POLLOCK: All you really need is the ability to judge what is an attractive package.

SAM WASSON: Hollywood had fought—and triumphed—over television before. But with the entrance of cable and home video came the question, once again: Would one medium devour the other?

GARRY MARSHALL: TV people have a way of working not better, necessarily, but faster.

WILLIAM FRIEDKIN: How many pages did you shoot today?

SUE MENGERS: I don't understand the mentality.

WILLIAM FRIEDKIN: In television, page count is the most important thing. It's like body count in the Vietnam War.

GORDON STULBERG: There is going to become a point, and it won't be too far in the future, when pay television, instead of having to drink at the trough of posttheatrical release, is going to have enough money to go out and finance features on its own, and when it does it's going to raise hell at the major studios in terms of traditional forms of distribution and the opportunity of motion picture theaters to attract income.

ROGER CORMAN: You see, the real problem with television is, you can't have a hit on television. You've sold it in advance.

BUCK HENRY: I'm willing to write it for enough money, but I'm not willing to look at it.

WALDO SALT: I think television took over the aesthetic of radio and completely skipped over the aesthetic of film.

PETER BOGDANOVICH: Hitchcock said most pictures are simply pictures of people talking, and that's become more and more the case.

WILLIAM FRIEDKIN: You're watching TV, you know the way they're going to cut the thing. You know what the next shot is. So then you're so bored figuring out what the next shot is, you start figuring out what the words are going to be.

VERNA FIELDS: I've been very lucky, I haven't really cut for television. But I'm told that you really have to go establish and move in fast and get your close-up so that they can see it on a little screen. And things like that.

LEONARD ROSENMAN: I remember years ago I used to read the newspaper while I was watching television, because you didn't have to look at the set to know what was going on. Everyone was saying everything you needed to know. Then one day they played John Ford's *The Informer* on TV, and of course I had to actually look at the screen because the thing is [by comparison] silent. Isn't that the name of the game?

LARRY GELBART: It was William Paley who called television "the best cigarette-vending machine that was ever invented."

NED TANEN: That's all they care about.

SAM WASSON: Television executives began to infiltrate the movie business as never before.

PAUL MAZURSKY: You're not dealing with people who are not meant to be patrons of the arts, they're businessmen. They care about money. They're not all villains. Some of them are very educated. And they're very liberal, and they give to causes, many of them.

WILLIAM FRIEDKIN: Young executives from television who took over the movie companies and agents don't know anything but the bottom line.

JOHN PTAK: The studios have begun to lean more towards their executives being administrators rather than producer filmmakers.

MICHAEL OVITZ: Wall Street guys and lawyers.

NED TANEN: And they make a bloody fortune. It's one of the great businesses one could ever be in.

JOSEPH E. LEVINE: It's a tremendous business. And they're going to use up pictures. You'll never be able to make enough pictures.

GORDON STULBERG: Between the installation of cable and the hitch-hiking of pay television, certainly at the height of all of your careers you're going to find that the economics of this business is going to change in a fashion that was never anticipated. It isn't anticipated now and certainly wasn't thought of twenty years ago. The ability to milk a paying audience in the home has absolutely indescribable financial dimensions, and there will come a time . . . that's why, if you read the trades, you see an increasing preoccupation, which is long overdue, with the ultimate rules that will govern the relationships among free television, pay television, and theatrical release. It's going to render asunder the traditional forms of release as we know it.

Little by little, we are wiring America.

ROBERT ALTMAN: The release of the film is a trailer for the video sales.

STEVEN SPIELBERG: What terrifies me is the idea that TV screens will get larger in the home, sound systems will get better and better, and people will no longer go out. They will only share the mystery with their immediate friends and family. And that's sad, because movies are theater.

JON PETERS: I think also what's happening is as the cities and the big cities deteriorate and as this country expands, the situation as we know it today, the cost of parking, the cost of food, the cost of movies, the cost of a babysitter is becoming so prohibitive that people will be at home with their own entertainment center, where they can literally do this. I think it's around the corner. I think it's really coming. Which is great for everybody, right?

DON SIMPSON: Having run production at Paramount for eight years and having had to make seventeen movies a year, I saw that it's impossible to make movies you love at a studio, because your job is to make money purely and simply—which is okay, that's your mandate, but there's no way you can be specific about it. And it's a death-defying task. Studio executives have by far the hardest job in the world, which is why they're the most hated individuals, because you turn into one, you really do. You can't do the job and be a good person. I don't care what the press says, it's impossible. What you find is in trying to spread yourself so thin, you eat yourself and everybody else alive, which is why the half-life of most serious studio executives is about two years. It's either that or cancer. I mean, it's just awful.

HARRY UFLAND: A case in point: We were at the Cannes festival this year, and every single day in the newspaper Alan Ladd, Jr., was being fired. Every single day. It was embarrassing. It was tough on him and his wife. There was an article in the paper every single day. *The Omen* came out, and really, whatever you want to say, a stroke of luck and catching lightning, right? The picture goes out and does $50 million, and Laddie and everybody else gets promoted. And in a three-day period, there he was fired and promoted. So, you know, they don't know.

DAVID PUTTNAM: It's much more interesting for me to come and talk with you than go and talk to the board of Universal Pictures. I don't expect anything from them other than the kind of lowest common denominator of what they feel is required to keep their stock at the level they find acceptable.

NED TANEN: I have to go to a management meeting tomorrow in Santa Barbara with all of our people in the company, and I had to have a meeting with several people who are going to lecture to us tomorrow about "Why can't you really computerize filmmaking?" They are people from the Harvard Business School whom I have these meetings with about every six months, and they are obligatory, and it's always "We can do them about a boy and his dog, there's no way you can miss." And you end up in these meetings, and you really do come out of them with a very, very strained attitude, because you're not communicating at all that you're dealing in one of the last custom-made businesses. It is an art form, and the terrible problem is that it's an art form bucking up against "Are we going to make any money?" Because if we don't make any money, it ain't going to be an art form because it ain't going to exist.

HAL ASHBY: Those guys don't have a fucking clue of what goes on in my heart, in my head, and what I'm thinking about. They don't know. And they're sitting back there in those production offices, and they say, "Well, if he shoots tonight, that's going to cost twenty thousand dollars, for Christ's sake." So what! And in the end they're wrong, because they're not even there.

A. D. MURPHY: As for dealmakers—we've got them all over the place, but they can't produce. They can't look at dailies. They can't say, "We're beginning to slip here, should we rewrite?"

ARTHUR PENN: They watch the dailies, even though they don't really know what the dailies relate to. They barely remember the script they originally read because they made the deal a year ago. They're sitting in this screening room at Warner Bros., and three minutes of film comes on from this picture and three minutes of film comes on from that picture. What happens, of course, is that some executive jumps up and says, "Aha! A cloud! Who's the cameraman on that picture? Get him out of here!"

ALAN PAKULA: Every time you move, they're all there in back of you, all with questions, waiting for you to give an answer. That's why, when you get in the editing room, it's all so wonderful. Suddenly there's a kind of medieval cell, this monastery where you can work in peace on your film. I just love being in the editing room, and it's very hard to get me out.

JACK NICHOLSON: You know, if you took "faster" and "clearer" out of the patois of everybody who isn't a director or an actor in Hollywood, they would have nothing to say at the meeting. Nothing to say, period. There's no other real grasp. And "likable." Those three things. In fact, you could just turn that on, and you'll be right up to speed at any meeting they have lately.

DAVID LYNCH: Executives have a lot of problems of their own, because they have to make money, and that's the scary part. When they listen to things they can't get a handle on, they become afraid.

MICHAEL CIMINO: If you put yourself in their place and imagine yourself making the sort of decisions that they have to make, handing over the sums of money that they do to people to make movies, it's pretty awesome to turn over X millions of dollars every year and hope that something comes back. It takes a lot. It takes a certain kind of personality to do that.

DAVID LYNCH: But I've had good lunches with these people.

RICHARD LAGRAVENESE: What I learned is to listen to the spirit of the note, not the detail of it. In other words, they're having a problem with something, and they're going to give you a solution for it. Forget the solution, but listen to what they're having a problem with and see if it resonates, because sometimes they're absolutely wrong and you have to be confident and fight for it and will make it stronger.

KENNETH TURAN: What really happens with Hollywood movies [today] is that the more movies cost, the more the studios are desperate to have every single person in America see it, because they need to recoup their investment. And the best way to have every single person in America see it is to make the movie as dumb as possible so that it won't be over anyone's head.

JAMES CAMERON: I think to do it correctly, you have to test-market the cut of the picture in two or three different places so you get a good, broad demographic baseline, and then whenever you make a change, you have to go back to those same or equivalent demographics and do it again to be able to track your results.

ERIC PLESKOW: I don't think it works. It doesn't work. We've tried it a few times. You see, the trouble, what I've always been saying, is this is a wonderful country. It's been built on an individualistic basis. And I think in the next twenty or thirty years it will be destroyed by computer and market research people and Harvard Business School graduates. They're going to have everything on charts and graphs to such a degree that you won't be able to do anything unless it's on a chart. And that's not what this country's about, and that's not what your leisure time is about, you know.

TOM POLLOCK: Movies are made for all the wrong reasons. They cost way too much money. And when I say all the wrong reasons, I've been there and I've been part of it. So this is part of my own personal twelve-step program: "My name is Tom Pollock, and I have filmed a concept rather than a movie."

STEVEN SPIELBERG: It's the concept first that the audience goes to see. Well, *Jaws* is a concept picture.

TOM POLLOCK: And by concept, I do not mean story. Please understand, there's a big difference between concept and story. *Concept* is a marketing term. And a good concept is something you can sell. That's what concept is about. Concept isn't about "Gee, is that a really interesting idea for a movie!" It's about "Can I sell this movie after I make it?"

DON SIMPSON: *Flashdance* was booked in the theaters prior to us even finishing the screenplay.

JERRY BRUCKHEIMER: All we had was a title, which was *Flashdance*, and we didn't know what flash dancing was. If you see the picture, you still don't know what it is. We finally decided we never would know, so screw it.

ADRIAN LYNE: Simpson is like a child. Very, very enthusiastic. Very erratic, but very, very enthusiastic and excited.

DON SIMPSON: My office is a sea of debris. I read periodicals like a maniac for ideas and stuff, so it's just, like, packed with newspapers. Jerry's is basically very well designed and clean and precise, as is emblematic of our personalities. And you know, we'll bounce ideas back and forth. Jerry will turn to his phone, I'll turn to mine, we have four TV sets in the room. I'm an inveterate television watcher. I love it, and they're up on banks and I'll watch TV over here. Jerry will listen to music over here. So you've got an overlay of images and sound and magazines here and the pristine element here, and we'll throw stuff up in the air and see where it sticks. We have about thirty-one projects in development at the moment. Each one of them is an original idea of ours.

ADRIAN LYNE: And he's good. Good in terms of tub-thumping *Rocky*-esque, that sort of thing.

DON SIMPSON: The things that were important to me when I was fifteen, except for a new car which I have, are the same things that are important to me today, relatively speaking, in dramatic terms. I still want to see the same things. I still am attracted to the same things.

ADRIAN LYNE: These movies are the same if you look at them.

DON SIMPSON: The honest answer is, we always have the movie laid out before we hire the director, when we know the movie we want to make, we know the story we want to tell, we see the frame, we see the point of view. And that's how we know what director to look for. We're not asking for a director to come to us and tell us what movie we're going to make. We already know that. We're looking for a director who understands the movie *we* want to make.

We like to take directors when they're down, because that's the point in time when they are most amenable to guidance.

If you're a director and you want to work with us and you have another vision of the movie, go make another movie. We're not interested, you know? Make your own movie, then. We're hiring you to make the movie that we can see.

I went into business with Jerry, since he knew how to make movies and I knew how to get movies made. *Top Gun* we had release dates prior to starting filming.

NESSA HYAMS: If you can cast a star, the script may not be so terrific and the director may not be the greatest, but they have this movie star in it, so let's make the movie.

DON SIMPSON: Usually our pictures are time constraints for us.

JON FAVREAU: And there's a whole new thing that you have to learn about: interacting with people who've achieved the status whereby which they are causing the movie to happen.

DAVID O. RUSSELL: That's the card you have to play ultimately with any actor. They have you by the balls as long as you have to have them.

HOWARD W. KOCH: You're not going to take Barbra Streisand out of a picture, so you spend most of your life being a diplomat. Or she calls you at night and you talk to her all night on the phone. She says, "Shouldn't we do this? Don't you like my hair this way?" And you keep cajoling and working, and you have seventy-five days of madness, and your wife says, "Listen, it's either Barbra Streisand or me."

BLAKE EDWARDS: Yeah. Peter [Sellers], to say the least, was very much into the occult, had long conversations with his deceased mother.

LYNDA OBST: What actors do is, they announce their eccentricities to you early on and then they push the envelope.

DON SIMPSON: *Beverly Hills Cop* was always designed as a drama-comedy, always, and it was always designed for Eddie Murphy, with the exception of the first actor we hired, Mickey Rourke. Mickey Rourke was the original Beverly Hills Cop. Jerry and I went to lunch with him. We wanted to hire him prior to that. We knew him.

JERRY BRUCKHEIMER: And we paid for lunch, too.

DON SIMPSON: And we also had to make it one, two, three in the afternoon because he didn't get up till 2:45. And he came to lunch with a beer in his hand, so we knew we were in good shape. And what happened was Mickey said, "So tell me about the movie." And I had really written a story for *Beverly Hills Cop* about four years prior to that, and I kind of made up a lot of new elements on the spot. And Mickey said, "I love it, I'll do it." So we made a deal with Mickey, and we started off in the screenplay from that perspective, and it was always with comedic overtones. Matter of fact, the original character that Mickey Rourke was going to play was a cop who was kind of addicted to gambling. He'd stop every half a day to call his bookie on the pay phone. He was a cop from East LA, not from Detroit. He was partly Hispanic. I mean, we had this whole thing designed. And what happened in the interim was I'd hired Eddie for *48 Hrs.* Next, he popped in our office and said, "What are you guys doing?" We told him the story of *Beverly Hills Cop*. He went crazy. "So why haven't I heard about this?" The reason he hadn't heard about it is because the guys I used to work with, Eisner and Katzenberg, hadn't told him about it! They didn't want him to do the movie!

We then started writing it for Eddie without telling anybody. We finished the script, Paramount gets it, and they call us and say, "Great news, guys! Big surprise! Your movie's a go, and we already cast it!" Now, this has never happened to us. We say, "What do you mean you already cast it?" "Sylvester Stallone committed to it." We went, "What?" I mean, we like Sly as a human being and as an actor, but it's, like, *what?* Turns out they had a pay or play deal for $3.5 million with Sly, and they had a window by which time they had to give him a movie or they had to pay him the money.

JERRY BRUCKHEIMER: We were the sacrificial lamb.

DON SIMPSON: We were the sacrificial lamb, as it were. Now, what happens is we met Sly, you know, and we get along well. Sly, however, wants to do a rewrite and we say, "Fine, no problem." Sly goes away to Germany for eleven days, does a complete rewrite, honest to God *complete* rewrite, and I'm here to tell you it was brilliant. The quality of that work in eleven days was as good as I've seen in twenty years in Hollywood. The screenplay popped. It was, however, a $40 million different movie. I mean, it was *Cobra*. What he did is, he went out and wrote *Cobra*, and he changed the name of the character from Axel Foley to Axel Cobretti. And he drove a car that had a cobra on the back of it. This was not the *Beverly Hills Cop* we had envisioned. So what Jerry and I did quickly was say, "Well, what do you do when you have a movie that's different than you want to make? I know! You budget it." So we budgeted. And when you budget a script like that, you know it's going to—we came out at thirty-seven point five. The studio freaked out. They called us—this is what's interesting about studio guys—they said, "How could you guys let this happen?" We said, "Wait a minute, who put Stallone in the movie?" They said, "Well, we did. Who told him he can do the rewrite?" "Well, we did. Who's got the thirty seven and a half million dollars?" "Well, we do." "Well, fuck you." So what happened was, they freaked out and they said, "What are we going to do?" We said, "You guys made all the decisions." They called a meeting with Jerry, myself, and [director] Marty Brest, and Marty Brest was great. He was like a human top spinning around with "What am I going to do? It's a different movie! I got Sly!" I said, "Calm down, calm down." This is where the studio experience came into play. We made sure that the proper players were in the room, and in this case it's [Michael Eisner, Jeffrey Katzenberg, and] Barry Diller, because Barry Diller had always loved the original vision of the movie, and he was not happy about Sly Stallone as Axel Cobretti. And he was pacing the room in his pinstripe suit just pulling madly on a Marlboro. "How the fuck did this happen? I can't believe—Michael! What—" Finally he turns to Jerry, he turns to me, and says, "What are you guys gonna do about it?" Jerry looks at me. I said, "We're gonna cast Eddie Murphy." There was silence. Cigarette is put down. Diller says, "That's the best idea I've heard today. Do it." On the spot, Jerry turns to me, I turn to Marty, we get up and leave the room. Leave the room! And I hear Diller telling Katzenberg and Eisner that they have to go to Sly's house that night and tell him he's fired. So we fly to New York to talk to Eddie. Now, what Mr. Diller doesn't know is, we've already given the script to Eddie the day before, and he's already said yes. So we already had Eddie in our back pocket. We didn't even need to go to New York. We took the free trip, landed at JFK, called Eddie, said, "We're here," he said, "Great, turn around," we went back. You know? We had Eddie in our pocket, and they made a deal with Sly whereby Sly could take what he had written and do what he wanted, and he moved into Warners and made *Cobra*.

LAWRENCE GORDON: Michael Eisner was a president of Paramount at the time. And he got in a fight with somebody on the phone with me sitting there. He had to pay off Nick Nolte a million dollars. And they had owed him for a movie they canceled. And he was screaming and yelling at the agent, "Fuck you! Fuck you! Fuck you!" And he hung up. And he turned to me like a madman. And he said, "You have anything for Nick Nolte?" "Well," I said, "I've got this one thing about a cop. He has to get a convict out of jail for forty-eight hours." He said, "You have a script?" I said, "Yeah, I do," and *boom*, we're making a movie. Well, that sounds funny. But that's the way it happened.

Do not think that movies get made because a bunch of very intelligent creative people are sitting behind a desk, saying "Oh, my God, do I love this script. Oh, God. Oh, my God, we have to have to see this on the screen. Oh, my God." No, that's not what it is. "Do we have anything for October? What are we going to do? We have a commitment with Sean Penn. We can't, we have nothing for him. What are we going to do?"

NEIL JORDAN: The person who is the authority is the person who gets the largest fee—it's probably your principal actor. And if Arnold Schwarzenegger is being paid $20 million and you, as a director, get paid two, there's no doubt where the power lies, really, is there? I don't think you can make a film coherently without the power to actually rule the set. Does that make sense?

KATHLEEN KENNEDY: I hesitate to say that it's out of control. You know, if Kevin Costner can open a movie like *The Bodyguard* with the kind of money it did, is he not worth it?

ARNOLD KOPELSON: There are only, literally, about ten stars that make a difference.

SAM WASSON: But if their box-office power translated to creative control, what then was the job of the director? Who was making the movie really? The star?

GEORGE ROY HILL: Newman will talk a scene to death before he gets up to do it, and you learn eventually to just sit through his talking because it has nothing to do with what he's going to do. It's his security blanket. He likes to talk. He likes to approach it intellectually. But when he gets up, and particularly when Paul opens up and starts sailing, he's pure instinct, and it just comes out marvelously. Redford goes crazy if you talk to him about a scene. He will not talk.

SYDNEY POLLACK: Although Redford had formal training, he hates rehearsals and is a very instinctive actor who doesn't like to talk about things.

BRUCE DERN: I can tell you this: when we were in the hotel room in *The Great Gatsby* and I looked at Robert Redford, I told him he was nothing. He knew what I was talking about. I wasn't talking about Jay Gatsby. He was a good friend of mine. He knew I was talking to him on a level about his work at a certain stage in his career. It got through to him. And afterward he said, "You know, that's not acting to me." He said, "That's not what it's about, if it's got to be that personal." I said, "Hey, Bob, that's the only thing that makes it an art, when it's that personal."

SYDNEY POLLACK: There's something very American about him. He has a much darker inside than what one sees on the outside. He's prototypically American in that sense. America has this glamorous exterior and a rather troubled, dark interior. Redford has that.

BARBRA STREISAND: Well, I mean, there's Robert Redford climbing on top of you, you know? You don't have to act, you know?

PETER BOGDANOVICH: I could tell you stories, but they're too dirty to tell, about Barbra.

JANE FONDA: I don't know how it is for other actors, but my relationship to who I am has always been really important to my being able to act. If I'm not happy, I just can't do it.

BOB GAZZALE: Of all the film debuts, you are in a scene with Jane Fonda [in *Julia*]. How do you walk into the set that day?

MERYL STREEP: Oh, I was so—

BOB GAZZALE: I had nerves for you.

MERYL STREEP: I still am in awe of people who can just walk into a movie that's already been shooting and shoot their one day and be confident—no, I was in flops sweats. I didn't know anything, I didn't know . . . how to *begin*. I didn't know, you know, "Action!" I thought maybe that was someone else that was supposed to do something when they said that. I really didn't know anything. And Jane really took me under her wing completely, and she said, "You know, that little line on the floor that you're not supposed—don't—don't look at it, that's where your toes are supposed to be. And that way you'll be in the movie. If you're not, you won't be in the movie." So she was so funny. And I wish that we had, you know, I wish that I had tape of the improvisation that we did at the bar, because she just completely cracked me up, we had so much fun. And then when I saw the movie, of course they, for the purposes of plot, took the dialogue from the first scene and put it on the back of my head for the second scene. And that was a great education in how movies are made and what happens. It was a very heady experience to go off to England and shoot this film with Vanessa Redgrave and Jane Fonda.

JANE FONDA: Our first scene together was in Sardi's after the triumphant opening of *The Little Foxes*. And Lillian Hellman walks across the floor of Sardi's, and everyone's applauding. And Anne Marie, played in black wig by Meryl Streep, is following her. And the camera's taking both of us. And then I walk off camera and Meryl walks into camera and the camera stays on her. And I remember the next day I went to see rushes, I was by myself. And I saw this actress do something with her hands and her mouth . . . that told a whole story in one gesture, and my hair stood on end.

MERYL STREEP: You just don't know what the other actor is going to do. You can have all these ideas about what you're going to do with your little character, and then the guy can just reach out and touch you in a moment when you didn't expect anybody to touch you and your whole thing falls apart, so it's not, for me, valuable to make too many decisions or to analyze.

ARTHUR PENN: Dustin Hoffman does this kind of thing constantly. He's always asking other actors to do it to him, not to play the scene but to try and break him up, unseat him. He wants to be caught unaware.

DUSTIN HOFFMAN: Now we get into the restaurant [in *Kramer vs. Kramer*], the scene doesn't work. The scene *does not work*. It was very simple. Meryl had a big speech. Eight sentences into that speech, she told me she wanted the kid back. And I'm sitting and I'm sitting and I'm sitting and I've been playing a character now for four or five weeks. So I have a sense of him, you know, and I'm sitting, I'm saying "Why am I sitting here? Why am I sitting? Why don't I leave? What am I talking to her for?" And the director says, "What's the matter?" And I said, "I don't know what I'm sitting here for." And Meryl is getting upset, she thinks I'm not interacting with her. I said, "I'm not *not* interacting with you! Why am I here?" And she starts telling me why I should [interact with her]. I said, "Don't tell me why I should!" You know, we're *working*, we're *raw*, you know, we're separated people and getting a divorce. So we're using ourselves, you know, we're not on speaking terms half the time, you know—we are and we aren't, you know? So we walked out. We weren't speaking to each other. I wasn't able to *match* her. I wanted to match her. I wanted to get back at her emotionally, and it wasn't in the writing. So somehow we did a take. And after the take, I didn't even plan it, but I didn't want to leave. You know, it's like an actor that doesn't want to get off. And I was so upset that she had had more stuff to work with. I just took a glass and I just *boom*, and it went up against the wall in shards. [Director Robert] Benton loved it, and they wanted to reset the cameras. It's in the movie. Meryl wanted my heart. She had glass shards in her hair. She said, "What are you *doing*? You could have *blinded* me!" I mean, she was furious. She hated me.

MERYL STREEP: I never really could figure out how you got your satisfaction, how you got your rocks off in the movies. I understood how to do that on stage for this big effort that's completely consummated at the end of the night and then you go out and drink. In films you have just this long dragged out—every day, there's a new problem, there's a new thing. And then you just leave it and go away. And a year later, somebody shows you what it is that they've made. And that's a long time to wait for satisfaction. And I couldn't really understand it, how to enjoy it.

MICHAEL CIMINO: When Bobby [De Niro] and I were preparing *The Deer Hunter*, I don't think we were ever on a plane or a bus or a train or wherever the hell we were that we weren't going over the script line by line. "What does this mean? What does this mean? What did you have in mind with this? What do you think about that?" It was just constant, constant, constant questioning, a constant process of clarification.

MERYL STREEP: Well, Robert De Niro . . . I mean, talk about exhausting the possibilities. You know, he really likes to rehearse, and I'm, like, done on take four, let's say, and he wants to go twenty-two times, and he keeps coming up with different weird things and surprising us and himself.

MICHAEL CIMINO: Bob is a wonderful example of that as an actor, because he feels that if we just keep working, we'll find it, somehow we'll find it. And you do.

MERYL STREEP: That's Cimino. You know, he listened. He's good. Everybody hates him. I don't know why.

PAUL THOMAS ANDERSON: What I've learned about Tom Cruise is that whatever you've seen him do in a movie is clearly exactly what the director has asked him to do, because he's that kind of an actor. It's just like, "Can you do it standing on your head and backwards?" "Yeah, sure."

JJ ABRAMS: No one works harder than he does.

CAMERON CROWE: He does control his image. He controls his image in ads and in trailers, so he definitely sees all that stuff. A lot of it was sent off to England, where he was doing his movie with Stanley Kubrick. I mean, he was fully involved in each one of these trailers that they put together for *Jerry Maguire*. I wondered how he was able to produce *Mission: Impossible* while he was making *Jerry Maguire*. I guess he just finds the time to do it, because he went over little cuts on some of the trailers and improved them quite a bit. What he would say is the thing you long to hear as a director. He said, "You know, guys"—and believe me, he'll call every one of the people involved at the studio on the making of these trailers, all of them, and say— "You know, guys, this is a better-quality movie than you're giving it credit for. This is a Kmart movie, the way you're selling it. This should be dealt with with more class." And in fact, he upgraded the whole presentation of *Jerry Maguire* in a way that he could only do because he had the control.

MIKE NICHOLS: And I . . . how do you describe Jack?

JACK NICHOLSON: I'm a director's actor.

MIKE NICHOLS: Well, luckily, everybody knows Jack.

JACK NICHOLSON: I considered myself—and do consider myself—the greatest improvisational actor working in films. I say that because I write well on my feet within these strictures.

MIKE NICHOLS: Jack is such a force for the positive. And I understood from watching him what lifted him, because he was connected to every single person on the set, the wardrobe ladies in the third row of vehicles in the wardrobe trailers—to them, to everybody beyond, to the greens man. He had a relationship with everyone. And so when he started a scene, everybody's love just lifted him. I'd never seen anybody quite so gifted at using whatever was around to do what he needed. And he was hilarious when he had to be naked. He'd say, "All right, everybody, 'Steve is coming out, don't be too depressed,'" and he would just turn it into a terrific number. And he had the crew in stitches.

GEORGE CLOONEY: But also remember that actors are very vulnerable, right? Because the goods that they're selling is themselves. I've been in love scenes with a director, like, "Cut, no." And you're like, "No, that's my, that's my go-to. That's my, that's my thing, man. No, what the fuck, I'm two times the sexiest man alive! Fuck you!"

DAVID PICKER: There are dozens of movies that are very successful that don't have these guys in them or these women. And even these guys and those women make pictures that nobody goes to see.

SAM WASSON: At least nobody in America, maybe.

ARNOLD KOPELSON: If I have a star, in the foreign market, you don't need to be a good director. If you have a major star that is going to commit to a project or lend his name to a project, you'll be able to sell it.

MICHAEL OVITZ: Hollywood always was a global business, but when I started, foreign [box office] was 10 percent of the gross. Getting to the nineties, it was 40 percent. So increasingly, when you make something you're making it for a worldwide audience.

NED TANEN: One of the reasons companies make sequels is because they are films that you know there is a base for an international market in.

AL RUDDY: Foreign is staggering because the only truly international film today is the American film.

LAURA ZISKIN: It's a more international business than it's ever been, and I think that will just become increasingly more so. But you know, you end up doing what you like. I can't think like someone who—I can't think like the Japanese audience. You know, I may share some things, some frame of reference with the Japanese audience, but not all of it. So I can't, unless I go and study that audience, I can't say, "I'm going to make a movie for Japan."

DAVID BROWN: The problem with non-English-speaking films is that we rarely can reciprocate in patronage what they can export to us. India produces more films than Hollywood, and yet Indian films are so unappealing in this country that trade barriers are frequently raised. A hit English-speaking film with lots of action is popular the world over whether subtitled or dubbed. But the national film, even the French and Italian film, has a demonstrably limited audience. I wish that were not so.

WILLIAM FRIEDKIN: Since *Star Wars* came out, that kind of film or a variation of it is what commercial cinema is all about, not just in America but everywhere in the world.

JOEL SILVER: When I worked for Larry Gordon, Larry had worked at AIP for years, and he had kind of tested this thing. It's kind of like old Jews passing down this kind of thing. It wasn't really complicated. It was every ten minutes, every reel of a movie, there has to be an action beat, because the audience wants to have action, wants to feel a charge, so you have to fill the picture with elements that can be kind of played as action beats, and then, in between, that notion of the zinger, these are all phrases they're putting on from television, which was a kind of a funny button on the end of the scene, which, you know, we give these to Schwarzenegger, they built their careers on these things, but the idea was a funny line and action beats and just, you know, this was commercial filmmaking.

DAVID ANSEN: What's depressing is that in a sense, Hollywood is creating the audience it deserves.

CHAPTER 16

EVERYBODY'S BUSINESS

SAM WASSON: The increase in blockbuster-budgeted movies and subsequent decrease in production transformed a once prolific Hollywood into a risk-adverse industry, economically and artistically terrified of saying yes to filmmakers.

KENNETH TURAN: The way the movie business works, people make a film every three years. People don't have much of a track record anymore.

SIDNEY SHELDON: Years ago, once you got into a studio, you would be able to stay for years and years and years.

ARTHUR HILLER: When I finish a picture totally, I think, "Okay, am I going to be hired again? Is anybody going to want me?"

LEE GRANT: And while you're waiting for the phone to ring, there are long, vast, empty spaces in which your talent is totally unused.

BRIAN GRAZER: But you know what? Can I interrupt? So the way I was able to do it . . . I didn't learn how to story tell. I was able to sell these ideas because I have an extreme, an amazing, amount of energy and passion, and that somehow translated to something.

KATHLEEN KENNEDY: Passion helps a lot, because, like anything that you do, if you really like it and you're not really thinking about the hours you're putting in because it's fun and you like the people and, like I said, have a strong passion for the material, you can do just about anything.

PAUL MAZURSKY: Only your passion will carry it through.

BRIAN GRAZER: So seldom do you ever hear the word yes. You're always hearing no.

PAUL MAZURSKY: You only need one yes, even if you get forty-nine nos. And if you have the passion to make something, you get the one yes.

LAWRENCE GORDON: You know the Sinatra song, you pick yourself up and get back in the race? Yes, that's what you do.

BRIAN GRAZER: So all of a sudden somebody's going "Yes, we'll make your movie." And then you're just crazy. You want to do that. But then there are all these contingencies. "Can you get this actor? Can you get that actor?" And you start jumping through hoops that you shouldn't be jumping through, many times.

PAUL MAZURSKY: But nos are normal.

TOM POLLOCK: You have to overcome the studios' natural reluctance to trust you with a million dollars.

LAWRENCE GORDON: Anybody says no to me when I'm trying to sell them, something's wrong. *They're* wrong. And if you don't think like that, *you* will be wrong.

JULIA PHILLIPS: *Patton* took twenty years for that guy to make, twenty years for Frank McCarthy to make. And he went through a lot of other pictures in between, and every time he'd pull it out of his bag and flog it until somebody finally went with it.

JOEL SILVER: The process of crawling your way up in this town is so painful. I mean, it's just hard. It's just hard because people don't want you to get in, so you have to kind of fight through it. You got to fight through it.

JOHN SINGLETON: I wrote *Boyz N the Hood* in the late summer, early fall of 1989. And I was a first-semester senior in college and going to USC, which was costing me $20,000 a year. And I was trying to figure out what I was going to do when I got out of school. You know, I knew very well that I wasn't gonna get a job working in the film business. So I kind of, like, planned to take this test in the LA school district and become an elementary school teacher. In the meantime, I'll write my screenplays and try to figure out a way to get in, and if I couldn't get in, I'd, you know, raise the money myself and mine the relationships that I had.

And I started doing an internship with a company at Columbia Pictures, and my job was to read the scripts and do coverage. The woman who hired me for the internship program, her name is Karen Teicher, and she read the two screenplays I had written up to that time. One screenplay was called *Twilight Time*, and the other one was *Boyz N the Hood*. And she said, "You know, this is a good screenplay. I know a few agents—one agent at William Morris and a couple agents at CAA. So let me take your scripts around and talk to some people and see what comes of it." And I said, "Cool." I really didn't seriously consider the studio system to be a viable option, you know, for me as a filmmaker. Nevertheless, she took my scripts, and she went to the two agencies, and she set up two meetings with me, one with William Morris, and then one with CAA. And the CAA meeting came first. So I was, like, maybe something will come of this! But I did take it with kind of a grain of salt.

So I go into my meeting [with CAA] and I'm, like, like, so skeptical about these people doing anything for me because they've never met anybody like me. They don't know, you know, my kind of vibe. So I'm like, "Okay, well, tell me what's going on here." And [agent Brad Smith] opens up and says, "I've worked at the Yale Repertory, I worked on Broadway, with August Wilson and Lloyd Richards on *Fences*, and I'd just like to say, we want to sign you. I read your material. I think you have that flavor. It reminds me very much of August Wilson." And anyone that really knows me knows that August Wilson is, like, my idol. I was just real cool. I was like, "Oh, that's good." But inside I was like, "Yes! Yes! Yes!" But I didn't want to give it up.

I went down the street to a pay phone, and I called up Karen. "CAA wants to sign me! They want to sign me!" She was like, "Great, great!" And so it was really great for me, because here I am a senior in college, and I'm signed with the biggest agency in Hollywood. And up to that time, you know, I went to film school, I was one of only twenty Black people in a program that had two thousand people in it. And I always felt, like, under siege because, you know, here were these kids, and some of them had families in the business. It was not anything really blatant, but it was like an implied thing, like, like, people would look at me almost like, "What are you doing here?" You know?

It made me kind of, like, not so much angry, but it made me more, like, thick-skinned. So after a while, instead of being, like, trying to be cool with everybody, I was like, "Fuck all y'all," excuse my French. So getting signed by CAA was, like, the shackles are off! So it was, like, it's, like, there's nothing y'all could tell me now! There's nothing that cannot be accomplished that I cannot do.

So fine. I get signed by an agency now. So what am I gonna do? I don't have a job anymore. Because I started, like, getting awards for my screenplays to pay my tuition so I could get a little bit of money here and there. But I wasn't working. And so I said to my agent, "I'm not eating right. I mean, you gotta give me a job or something." He says, "Well, I'll tell you what I'll do. I'll schedule meetings with people. I'll try to get you to as many meetings a week as possible, and preferably, we'll try to make them lunch meetings so you'll eat." I'm like, "That's cool, 'cause I only need one meal a day." What really sparked things was, I had a meeting with a guy named Stan Lathan, who was working for Russell Simmons. And Russell Simmons was putting together an entertainment company, he was thinking about getting a deal with Columbia Pictures, and Stan read [*Boyz N the Hood*]. He loved the script. But I think he wanted to direct it himself. So he gave it to Russell. And

Russell and I had breakfast at the Mondrian. And I was like, "Another free meal!" So we're sitting across the table and he's like, "You're supposed to pitch me the story." I said, "I don't need to pitch this story. This is not *Krush Groove*, you know, this is about growing up where you hear helicopters over your house and you hear automatic gunfire in the distance and stuff and, you know, it's about LA." So he got on, like, the MGM Grand [jet] that existed at the time, and he read the script and he called down from the plane to, like, the people he was negotiating with at Columbia, and he says, "I just read the script, and it's the greatest script I've ever read in my life! I swear! This is the first movie I want to produce!" So here's Russell Simmons, who has a company that pulls in at least $15 to $20 million a year on his own, through Sony, and he's making a film deal for this great script by a [former] intern.

BRIAN GRAZER: It is truly a function of energy that gets things done.

JJ ABRAMS: I was in my senior year of college, and I was back in Los Angeles wandering around. I grew up here, and I was wandering, going Christmas shopping, and I was leaving the Century City mall. I was going down the escalator, and this woman I knew, Jill Mazursky, was going up. "Jill, what's going on?" And we started talking, and she had written and sold some screenplays. I knew I needed to figure out what the fuck I was going to do. You know, the day was coming where I needed to figure it out. So Jill had sold stuff and she had an agent and she was living the life that I thought, God that's amazing. So I said, "Let's write something together." She said okay, and we got together that week and we came up with an idea that was a comedy that we wrote a treatment for. And I went back to Sarah Lawrence to finish my senior year. And I got a call a week later that Jill had shown it to her father, who's the director Paul Mazursky. Paul had shown it to Jeffrey Katzenberg, who at the time was head of Disney. Jeffrey Katzenberg said, "I want to buy it." And he did.

MICHAEL OVITZ: It's timing and passion.

STEVEN SPIELBERG: It doesn't take much gall. It takes desire to really do it. To really be a moviemaker or a writer or whatever you want to be, it just takes a blind faith that overcomes all fear.

JOHN SCHLESINGER: It's the energy for the fight. You have to fight constantly.

LYNNE LITTMAN: It was a question of my own steam, it was real clear. I mean, I was calling up people and saying "Hello, I need $250,000 in two weeks." People I didn't know.

JOHN SCHLESINGER: I think one of the problems about getting older in this business is that it isn't that you lose your talent or your vision or even your energy, just the energy to deal with rejection and people looking at you with that kind of Christian Science smile on their faces.

CLINT EASTWOOD: I don't think in the immediate future, but some day, I'm going to look in the mirror and say, "Clint, you don't look too good."

WILLIAM FRIEDKIN: The life expectancy of a director is probably less than that of a professional football player. A director has seven or eight years where he's really giving the public what they want. It isn't easy. One of the reasons it isn't easy is because you do a successful picture, make a lot of money, and buy a house in Beverly Hills. The only people you ever see are your butler and cook and the guy who drives you to the studio. You leave an air-conditioned house and get into an air-conditioned car to go into an air-conditioned office from which you go to an air-conditioned screening room. You never touch a dog on the street or talk to a guy in a bar or on a subway or know what the hell he wants. That's why a lot of guys don't know who their audience is.

GEORGE LUCAS: After I finished *Return of the Jedi*, I went through a divorce and determined at that point that raising my daughter was the most important thing in my life. I figured I could produce a few films with some friends just to help them out, but my main focus was really raising my kids. I ended up adopting a second daughter and then a son, and I knew I couldn't direct and raise these kids at the same time. A director goes to work at six in the morning and doesn't get home until ten at night. He isn't free to go to parent-teacher conferences. So I said, "Well, I'll be a producer. I can take days off when I need them and basically focus on raising my kids."

SHERRY LANSING: I don't know what a man feels like in the job. So I'm just supposing that. But I don't feel the pressures of being a woman or being young. Do you know? I don't feel that. I feel the pressures of trying to find fifteen movies that I want to make, that I feel committed to, that I feel a passion about. That's the pressure.

KATHRYN BIGELOW: I don't think filmmaking is gender specific.

POLLY PLATT: I don't think that I would have gotten anywhere if I had been a yes-girl. And I don't think I have to work harder than anybody else to make it, a man or a woman.

SUE MENGERS: I don't think an unknown woman has any better shot than an unknown man. I think it's equal.

VERNA FIELDS: "What has she done?" Which is a normal question which they would have asked about anybody.

POLLY PLATT: I consider myself an artist first. Sex is second.

DYAN CANNON: I really don't look at it as a male or female thing. I look at it as talent. If you're talented, I want you around.

MARCIA NASATIR: I was brought up on strong woman actresses. *Kitty Foyle* [1940, starring Ginger Rogers], which was probably my all-time favorite movie. I would have dressed in that favorite style. I mean, those black dresses with the white collars and cuffs is the most vivid image of what I thought the working woman was. She dressed in that outfit. And these were very strong women, they were terrific.

KATHLEEN KENNEDY: Part of it is, I probably didn't even think about it. Because l just remember being so focused on what I wanted to do that it never occurred to me that somebody wasn't going to let me.

JULIA PHILLIPS: I stood at the doorway at the head of distribution's office. I said, "I'm a pregnant woman, I have flown three thousand miles, I'm in my seventh month, and if you don't give us more theaters, I'm going to cry." I mean, I got an IOU, with my trembling hand actually carrying it back on the plane. Anything, anything. And you can have no pride about these things, either.

JANE FONDA: Problem people, troublemakers, are going to have a hard time getting work. But to say, "Look, I'm a woman, and I know that a big part of the audience is going to be women, and you're going to serve the film better if we find a way to say this so that it is not titillating," that will be respected.

JOAN TEWKESBURY: I hate the idea of a "woman's viewpoint." More than anything I hate it—not because I'm a woman, I love being a woman, but a viewpoint is a viewpoint is a viewpoint. It's colored by more things than just what sex you are or what color you are. It's colored by where you grew up, who you spend time with, who you talk to, who you loved, and when that was good, and when it was rotten. All of that stuff forms a viewpoint.

LEE GRANT: I don't consider just doing films about females or with a female point of view. I've been through a lot in my life, and I really think of myself as a humanist, not just as a feminist, although l think women should be feminists. The topics I'm attracted to are varied and, in a lot of cases, quite political. And the sensibility that I bring to it is a female sensibility, because I am female. But if it's a woman's story that I really want to have told, then there has to be a reason for it beyond the fact that it's a woman's story

PAUL MAZURSKY: You know, they didn't want to do my movie because it's Jewish. And I'm Jewish. And the ones who turned it down were Jewish, probably. So what?

JOHN PTAK: Why should one lean towards a first-time director as opposed to someone else?

PENNY MARSHALL: It wasn't a problem, and I wasn't asking them. It happened. I mean, I came in through the back door. So it wasn't like I was knocking on their door, saying "Please hire me."

LEE GRANT: I think that people in this town respond to success. And they don't care who does it if it's really high-concept material and the work is good and the money comes in at the box office. Penny Marshall and Martha Coolidge and Amy Heckerling, all these people who had a real sense of the youth market and brought that to the studios, really opened the door for the rest of us.

PENNY MARSHALL: They also felt that I was responsible. Larry [Gordon] and Joel [Silver] were both at Paramount when I was there doing *Laverne & Shirley*, so they knew the late hours I had to work, the stamina. I also went down the river, the Grand Canyon, with Jeffrey Katzenberg because somebody backed out. I went, and they saw that I could paddle and walk up nine miles. That's part of directing, stamina. And also, I require very little sleep.

DEDE ALLEN: You know, there's an awful lot of competition on a film, and that's something you have to be very careful about. In many ways, I think [being an editor is] harder on a man than on a woman, because women are used to playing more of a supportive role, in my generation at least, than a man. And therefore it becomes competitive for an editor because very often what you do best you can't talk about.

PAULA WAGNER: I think it's tough for men, too, you know. This world is tough for all of us. And so I've always had this kind of empathic feeling for people and never got too caught up in "I'm a woman," although I certainly burned my bra, believe me, a number of times in the seventies and had consciousness-raising groups and all of that. But it's tough for all of us. My partner is a man, and I have a son, and, you know, we're all in this together, so I'm kind of at that place where the world you make for yourself and you embrace people.

JANE FONDA: I haven't felt any resentment because I'm a woman. Crews have said to me they can't wait to work with me because they like the idea of a woman running around. And I want to wear short skirts and do the whole thing, too.

LYNNE LITTMAN: I mean, nobody [on my crew] had ever worked with a woman, which I didn't even think about, you know, it's funny and all of this stuff. I mean, when you finally are in there, you never even think that people are going to look at you funny. But they did. So in a sense, I had to prove to them that I knew more about this whole deal than I did on some level—maybe not on their level but on some level—which was going to carry the film, which had carried it for a year and was going to carry it for another year. And they better come on my carousel. So they did.

SHERRY LANSING: Once the walls start to be broken down, then it becomes natural to hire the best person for the job, be that a man or a woman. And I think, that is, when we have true equality, you won't say, "There are more women being hired now." It will just be accepted. It will just be natural. The important thing is that we get to a point where it is simply that you are judged on your qualifications for the job, period.

SIDNEY POITIER: I've had difficulties making certain films but really never had any difficulties because of race. That's not to say I haven't had an enormously long-running relationship with racism.

LEE ROSENBERG: Let me say this: there is no line as far as I know, and as far as I'm concerned, there is no criterion that would exclude a Black man or woman. In fact, we wanted a woman to work with us. It would be advantageous, tremendously advantageous, because there would be a high visibility. It would be an exclusive, in a peculiar way. For venal reasons and access and so on and so forth, I would say it would have been marvelous if a Black man had come to us and said, "I'd like to work for you" and it had worked out. Other than that, I can't identify any more reasons why there aren't any more Black people or women in the agency business.

SIDNEY POITIER: I have never met a producer who was not interested in my particular concept of the "Blackness" of a script. I sought to present as forceful an image as I could in order to counter the prevalent one. The prevalent image in those days was that Negroes were lazy and shiftless. So in my pictures I was cool and hardworking. If you look at the films, you'll see that I tried to present that which was most lacking: a guy with a job other than the usual menial ones. I played doctors and lawyers. I played a psychiatrist for Stanley Kramer. Of course, some of those films are heavily dated today, but I believe in the historical evolution of things. You and I are in this room partly because of that history.

TOM POLLOCK: What do we end up reading? The scripts that we've commissioned, because we've already liked the ideas, the ones written by people whom we worked with before or whose work we know. So that means that the new voices are read by people who don't have any power within the system.

SIDNEY POITIER: The fact is that most of the scripts I did were written by Whites, which is to say that to require you to write only for Whites makes no sense. To require me or this gentleman to write only for Blacks also makes no sense. A writer has a point of view on something and with his script speaks to that point of view.

ELLA TAYLOR: I knew that when Carl Franklin made *One False Move*, a terrific, small movie, nobody knew that he was Black originally. And I think that in a way that almost worked to his advantage that he could make the film and that he wasn't typecast.

CAMILLE TUCKER: We don't want to be stereotyped. We don't want to do all the "girls in the hood" stories. Maybe some of our stories will have girls in the hood, you know, in them. But just because it has a girl in the hood, it doesn't mean that, you know, it's going to be something that we're going to really relate to.

MARK CANTON: I mean, no one who's financing any of this entertainment is going to want to put up tens of millions of dollars, you know, in order to fail. So they're really responding to material. Nobody gives a fuck who anyone is. What they do care about, ultimately, is: Do you have a piece of material that they respond to?

HARRY UFLAND: You don't know where a script is going to come from. You don't know where the next big director is going to come from.

JJ ABRAMS: I mean, now the equipment exists that is readily available to all of us to actually make the stuff. But it's an amazing and significant difference where the idea for a story or film or short doesn't need to be theoretical anymore. It can be actualized. And you can do it yourself. And you can do it tonight if you want to. And that, to me, is one of the most amazing things, that you could go to a friend and borrow [a camera] or go to a relative or a store and rent any of the equipment you need and get [results] that look often as good as they do using the same equipment that the professionals are using.

PAUL FEIG: Tape costs nothing.

RICHARD LAGRAVENESE: I had just gotten married, and I kind of wanted my life to start, and I started writing *The Fisher King* in my spare time. And over a period of maybe, like, a year and a half, I'd put it down for five months, I'd pick it up. For six months I wouldn't look at it. And my wife was supporting us.

WALDO SALT: I live cheap.

RICHARD LAGRAVENESE: Really, I would not have finished it or completed it if it wasn't for my wife, because she'd come home from work and I'd do the dishes and she'd read and she told me, she said, "There's something here. Keep going." I had no idea what I was doing. And then when I finished it, it was the worst writers' strike ever. Nobody could read. It was the '88 writers' strike, and nobody could read and nobody could buy and so more time went by, and then when the writers' strike ended two weeks later, it got bought.

SCOTT ALEXANDER: The spec market was sort of created by the Writers Guild strike in the late eighties. And before that, you didn't really break in with a spec script. [Larry Karaszewski and I] wrote a whole script on my Kaypro. And we were so proud of ourselves, and all our friends thought we were crazy. Literally no one at USC had ever written a whole script.

LARRY KARASZEWSKI: So we had an office at Fox, like, literally a month after we graduated from undergraduate school!

SCOTT ALEXANDER: I was twenty-two!

RICHARD LAGRAVENESE: The executive at the studio called and said, "You know, we thought during this period, everyone was thinking, that left to their own devices, writers would write that story they've always been dying to write." He said, "You can't believe how many cop movies we've got." And so that, to me, was always a lesson about not writing for the marketplace.

WILLIAM FRIEDKIN: Anybody can do it today.

JJ ABRAMS: The excuses are gone, too, the rules are gone, so are the excuses.

WILLIAM FRIEDKIN: It's a wide-open ball game.

ARTHUR PENN: The question is, how much of the so-called film industry is, to borrow a phrase, genuinely the only game in town? Does one definitely have to work within the system? Is the establishment the only way to go? My sense is that increasingly it's not the way to go.

ROGER CORMAN: I would say the majority of films in the art houses in New York City are probably not handled by the majors. So right there, you know, in the art house circuits, the art house method of distribution, you don't need the majors at all.

ARTHUR PENN: One does not have to go through the studios.

STEPHEN WOOLLEY: You have to look at what they won't do. Simple as that: What won't the studio do? What is it that Columbia or Paramount or Warners won't do? What areas don't they go into?

CALDECOT CHUBB: [Joe Roth said,] "At 20th Century–Fox, we make movies that can be advertised on television. That's what we do. And everything else is independent filmmaking."

MARIE CANTIN: Why don't we start off with just trying to define what we think we mean by the words *independent film.*

EDWARD PRESSMAN: Independent films are all those films not fully financed and distributed by the seven major studios.

NESSA HYAMS: There are a lot of people around who want to invest in movies for tax purposes. There is a lot of independent money around.

STAN KAMEN: People for whom it's glamorous. They may be in the oil business or some other business. You find that they fall in and out quite quickly. None of those independent financiers stay in very long because they do one or two that just die and don't do any business and they've lost everything, and even though they've got a tax write-off, they're not very pleased about it.

EDWARD PRESSMAN: I remember making *Badlands*, and we had one investor who delivered his money in ten-dollar bills.

JOHN PTAK: Outside money is not always concerned with our time schedules, and although it takes time to get the money together, you can only keep your elements together for so long. It can be precarious. The money can pull out. The job is enormous and takes very often a disproportionate amount of the time.

JAMES IVORY: We just assume that we will be able to raise all of it by the time that we need it.

Heat and Dust was a Universal picture. Universal loved that film, they wanted it, they took it for distribution in this country and Canada. And then what happened was, they no sooner got it than everybody at Universal was fired or left. And then the film was in a kind of limbo, and you couldn't even get anybody on the telephone to talk to you about it. It was impossible to discuss any further ad campaign or play dates at all. There was nothing we could do.

CHARLES BURNETT: In the eighties, no matter how great the film was, you weren't going to get distribution, most likely, you know, it just wasn't set up for that. Now the whole system has changed drastically.

SAM WASSON: By the end of the eighties, the Sundance Film Festival had grown from a local phenomenon to the premier independent film festival in America. The simultaneous growth of independent distributors, like Miramax Films, mutually enhanced their visibility and prestige. In unofficial collaboration, Sundance and Miramax launched the careers of many new filmmakers, and with them, a new era of independent film in and out of Hollywood.

ALJEAN HARMETZ: All of us who were at Sundance in '89 saw a dripping wet print of *sex, lies, and videotape*. I mean, nobody had heard of this filmmaker, nobody had heard of the film. And within the first screening of this film, it was all over the festival.

CHARLES BURNETT: Park City is very good to launch a film.

STEVEN SODERBERGH: I think it's bad to give people this inbuilt prejudice about who they're going to make their movies for. The point is, are they going to get to make *their* movie? It doesn't matter who pays for it, is it going to be theirs? And that's all I worry about.

JON FAVREAU: The big goal was Sundance.

CHARLES BURNETT: It was just a small, independent, quaint, you know, festival with no agents or anyone hardly, you know, just a few reporters.

CAMILLE TUCKER: The exposure, which I'm sure you all know, it's just so important, to try to get your film in as many film festivals as you can.

JON FAVREAU: And you wanted to get the buzz going, because back then you could actually have a small movie, get it picked up, and then build an audience.

ALAN RUDOLPH: See, the thing is, when you make all these films, just stitching together the financing, you're not guaranteed anybody will release them.

CAMILLE TUCKER: I think Sundance was really crucial for us, and the big premiere that we had [brought] a lot of people in the community behind us. The steam just kind of started rolling.

DAVID LYNCH: Ben Baronholtz for Libra Films distributed *Eraserhead*, and he started midnight films with *El Topo*. And so he thought *Eraserhead* was the perfect midnight film, and he was willing to go with it. They don't put any money into the film, they just put it into a theater, and if word of mouth is good, everything's fine. It survives. It'll go up and down, but in the big picture it'll always be growing. But if word of mouth is bad, that's the end of it.

TOM POLLOCK: The profits of all the studios come from their big hits. They don't come from the movies that turn out a small profit every year.

LAWRENCE BENDER: There's not that many people distributing independent movies, you know, a handful: Miramax, Goldwyn, New Line.

STEPHEN WOOLLEY: I had a script [of *The Crying Game*] for Cannes in '91, and I thought that every American distributor and every financier in the world would fall over themselves to try and put money into the movie, and quite the reverse happened. They all hated it. They just hated it. Every American distributor, every American distributor, man and woman, rejected the script. Nobody liked it. No one liked it. I promised [writer-director] Neil [Jordan] I'd get it made in the summer, and he was very upset with me. I was saying, "Well, I think we can get some money from here, some money from there," I'm trying to pull all the little bits and pieces, pockets of finance from European distributors. It just didn't amount to very much, and in the end I kept pushing the film back month by month. And, of course, Stephen Rea and Miranda Richardson, Forest Whitaker, who were the people we really wanted for the film. This is a small film with not very big fees—they were getting more and more upset, more worried that they were passing on other projects, until Neil just said, "Well, look, I may as well go up and finish my book or do something else, 'cause obviously the film isn't going to get made." And then I realized the only way we could possibly make it was to rule out the American financing and just say that we will have no money from the US. And I approached all the cast and the crew and asked them to defer 30 percent of their fees, which would cover roughly what you would expect from an American distribution deal on a British production, which is about 30 percent of the budget. They all agreed to do that, which was great. We managed then to start shooting the film in November, which is very cold in Britain. So we were shooting all these cricket scenes and all these scenes by the sea, supposedly in the middle of the summer, but it's actually November. We were actually blessed because we just got all this incredible winter sunlight.

NEIL JORDAN: Then we showed the picture to the same distributors and they loved it.

JASON BLUM: I actually did acquisitions for Miramax in the nineties. And I was one of the people who passed on *Blair Witch*, sad to say, but I lived through that experience. And what I learned from that experience was, I wasn't alone, most people did pass. And even when it was screened at Sundance, there wasn't a big bidding war for it. The company that bought it was kind of a second-tier company. And the thing that I internalized from that experience was—and I'm sure you've heard a million people say this, but really—no one knows what's going to work. And if you think it's going to work, stick with it.

LAWRENCE BENDER: What we were going to do with *Reservoir Dogs* was create a project that you can do for a small amount of money, which means few locations, few actors, a few special effects. And, you know, use your creativity and come up with something that takes place in a room or whatever it is, but come up with something interesting and creative and different that happens in a contained situation, and then go out and make it. Shoot it on Super 8. That's what Sam Raimi did for years. That's what Scott Spiegel did. That's what Quentin and I were going to do. . . .

He and I were going to pool our money and borrow some money, we were going to make it for $30,000, and that's the truth. [But first] he gave me two months to go try to find money.

NEIL JORDAN: You go where the money is.

LAWRENCE BENDER: We had a Canadian guy who was going to give us a half million dollars to make the movie, which was, for us, an amazing amount of money, if we would consider making Mr. Blonde a woman, which was his girlfriend, and this is a true story, this is not a made-up story. You hear about this stuff all the time, but when it really happens to you, it takes you by surprise. It was so out of left field that we went home and thought about it for an hour. And we had another person who's gonna give us a million and a half, and he saw the movie as a comedy and we saw the movie as a comedy. We didn't realize he thought about it more like a comedy like the Coen brothers' *Raising Arizona*, which is a very different kind of comedy than we saw. And it's very hard to sit in that office when someone finally, *finally*, is offering you money and they want to completely change your vision. And what do you do? It's a difficult decision to make. What gave us the power in our own minds to turn down those offers was, in our mind, we knew we were making the movie. In the end, if everyone came out and said, "We're not going to give you the money," we were still going to make the movie with our own money. So we had our own basis of power, where we were coming from, even in that position where we looked like we had no power.

QUENTIN TARANTINO: I think it's obvious, I don't come from that whole Robert McKee, Syd Field kind of thing, where the dialogue, everything, is kind of moving everything forward, and everything is some Chinese box, every sequence and every dialogue is put in place and moving this whole apparatus forward and forward and forward.

GEORGE CLOONEY: I did audition for *Reservoir Dogs*. I would have done a better job if I'd known Quentin was going to be such a talented director.

HARVEY KEITEL: Well, a woman colleague of mine from the Actors Studio called me one day and said, "I have a script, Harvey, I think that you're gonna like." And knowing her and her work, which is very good, I asked her to send it over. I got the script, and I was aware of something *other* on the page. And I called Quentin to tell him I wanted to make the film.

LAWRENCE BENDER: Harvey Keitel gave us our credibility for *Reservoir Dogs*. You know, as soon as you get a cast member that has some credibility, it also gives you credibility as a filmmaker, because "Wow, this actor wants to work with this guy." Well, if this person, this actor, who has done a lot of work, respects the filmmaker, that gives me some pause to think maybe I should, too. And that helps quite a bit.

CALDECOT CHUBB: You go to Miramax, you'll definitely have a fight. Doesn't matter about what.

LAWRENCE BENDER: I think you're right. I mean, they wanted to make some changes in *Reservoir Dogs* about the ear scene, and we didn't make them.

ANTHONY MINGHELLA: Yeah, Miramax had a lot to say about *Cold Mountain*, particularly in postproduction. And I felt that they were entitled to have a lot to say.

SAM WASSON: Throughout the 1990s, Miramax kept bringing in the Oscars, giving the major studios a run for their money.

MICHAEL OVITZ: As a matter of fact, if you look at the pictures over the years that have been nominated for awards, increasingly, more of them are tiny little independent pictures.

SAM WASSON: But the ascension of the independent film—its infiltration into the mainstream—was a double-edge sword.

KATHLEEN KENNEDY: Part of that is that movies are getting so expensive, the marketing of movies is getting so expensive, that even the independent world is consolidating into big business. It's a different kind of big business, but in essence, it's just a lot of different banks.

LAURA ZISKIN: Movies are now a contest every weekend. It's really sad. I think it's the tragedy of entertainment news that has created this appetite in the audience to know the score, you know, "Who won the weekend?"

A. D. MURPHY: The motion picture industry [was originally] very, very intent on keeping its [financial] secrets to itself, which is at cross purposes with what [*Variety*'s] mission has always been . . . [but] the motion picture business is now being run by professional managers. The good side of professional management is that they are new. They don't have any sacred cows, and rather than have a lot of gossip that may be worse than it really is, their answer is "What the hell, everybody knows if we have a success or not." So it's a lot easier now finding out what the film rentals are and what costs are.

ROBERT TOWNE: And I remember I was driving my daughter to school, and she was in the sixth grade, and she started telling me the grosses on the movies for the weekend. And I realized that the crossover had come that way. I never knew what the grosses were on movies in the seventies. Never. Even when I had a piece of the movie.

DENISE DI NOVI: It's a strange thing what's happened in the last few years, where the average moviegoer partially bases their decision to go to the movie on, you know, seeing the grosses on *Entertainment Tonight* or in the paper the next day, or . . . I mean, people have a right to know, but does that really reflect anything? I don't think so.

DAVID PICKER: My grandfather would always say, everybody has two businesses. Their own and the movie business.

ROBERT TOWNE: And since we are a nation—a statistical-loving nation— much of our love of statistics has sort of moved from baseball, where you'd know Joe DiMaggio's batting average or Ty Cobb's or Mickey Mantle's or somebody else, into the grosses of the fucking movies.

SAM WASSON: Heeding the statistics, Disney bought Miramax in 1994, beginning the slow end to what once seemed a new future—an alternative to Blockbuster Hollywood.

CHAPTER 17

MONSTERS

GEORGE LUCAS: The move from celluloid and the photochemical process to the digital process has pulled the cinematic arts in a new and very exciting direction. Artistic revolutions have always gone hand in hand with technological ones. Artists aren't doing their jobs properly if they aren't banging up against the technological ceiling.

JOHN LASSETER: Before I started working with the medium, it was quite interesting that the [digital] tools were only in the hands of a very few people. The tools were in the hands of the people at universities and companies who basically created the tools. And at the time, it was very similar to the feeling like if all the paintings in the world were created by the chemists who mixed up the paint at the lab, you know, and they made all the paintings. It had that kind of feeling to where these tools were incredible, but let's get them into the hands of the artists and filmmakers. And so I focused myself on the filmmaking side of it, what I knew and brought to this medium, working way back from a knowledge of traditional animation principles, and I just, like, went ahead and applied them directly to what I was doing. And we produced a number of short films. And in about 1989, we [at Pixar] had just finished our short film called *Knick Knack*. And it was our first short film. We won an Oscar.

And so we felt like we were ready. And so we started doing television commercials at that time, just to build up our staff to get some production experience out in the real world. And it was in February of 1991 I pitched the idea of *Toy Story* to Jeffrey Katzenberg, Peter Schneider, and Tom Schumacher in a 7:00 a.m. meeting at Disney, and everybody told me, "Man, that's prime Jeffrey time, you are so lucky. He must think a lot of you."

TOM HANKS: When Jeffrey Katzenberg called me and said, "Would you be interested in doing a voice for a new project we have?" I said, "Sure, I'll do it." "So come on by, and we'll talk about it." And what they were doing is talking about *Toy Story*. They said, "Well, we want to show you what it is first." So, okay, fine, you can show me. But I don't care what it is! What they had done was, they had taken a line or a snippet of dialogue from *Turner & Hooch* and animated it to the Woody character, just on a blue screen, but—but Woody *moves*. Because this is not a cartoon, it's computer generated.

FRANK DARABONT: Hanks is king. He's God. He rules. You know, he's one of those guys who just shows up on a set and you need twenty takes? "Great, no problem. Tell me what you need. Do you need two? That's all you need? Great. Call me when you're ready for the next thing." You know, he's really remarkable.

MICHAEL OVITZ: When Michael Crichton pitched me *Jurassic Park* after two years of not writing anything, my first response to him is my son Chris loves dinosaurs. He was ten. I love dinosaurs, and my dad, may he rest in peace, loved dinosaurs. Everyone loves dinosaurs. And there is only one human being on the planet that can make this movie, only one. So I said, "Michael, it's binary. We either get Spielberg to make it or there's no movie. I don't have a second choice."

GEORGE LUCAS: The goal was to create a digital character that looked like an actual character. There were testing grounds for the special effects we were working on, like *The Young Indiana Jones Chronicles*, and eventually we arrived at the stage where we said, "Why don't we try to do a digital dinosaur?" We had thought about doing *Jurassic Park* with puppet animation, but when the tests came back, we nearly had tears in our eyes. We were looking at the screen and saw this *Tyrannosaurus rex* running. It was the Holy Grail of digital animation.

KATHLEEN KENNEDY: I mean, all of us just sit in there giggling 'cause we can't believe that the technology has gotten to this point. We're even doing stampedes.

GARY RYDSTROM: I really would make the case that a lot of the best sounds we found recording stuff for *Jurassic Park* were from very nonexotic sources. My dog, Buster, who is a great source of stuff—when the *T. rex* decides to shake a *Gallimimus* to death, Buster's growl with a rope toy worked pretty well.

GEORGE LUCAS: You might compare it to the invention of the light bulb or the first telephone call. For me, it really was that momentous.

SAM WASSON: Special effects, shifting the emphasis of moviemaking to postproduction, are often done in a crunch. Delays so late in the process can play havoc with release dates, which can play havoc with terms supposedly guaranteed in contracts.

JAMES CAMERON: We've got this big picture, there's a lot of public scrutiny over budget—*Titanic*—and we're scrambling to try to take time out of the picture. And now we're cutting in a frenzy. And we're running out of time. And it looks like because of the way the visual effects are streaming in that we're probably not going to be able to have it done before somewhere around August 6. And it's going to be a nightmare to get to that. Anybody that's been through the editing process knows that if you want to take time out of something, that's admirable and improves the pace, improves the flow of ideas, but you have to sweat it out, you can't just cut it out, it comes up two frames here and ten frames there.

So Paramount wanted Fox to make the decision [to postpone the release of *Titanic*] so they could sue them, and Fox wanted to make the decision so they could sue them. Nobody wanted to postpone the movie.

And I'm sure that they thought, Well, that's up to the wacko filmmaker to postpone the movie, because he's powerful. So at a certain point, I realized they were waiting for *me*. So I called [Fox chairman] Peter Chernin and said, "You know what, we got to postpone this movie. And I think it's going to be to our benefit in the long run." And the thinking at the time was, we'll have more time to edit the picture properly, and we've got a huge investment and everybody knows it. So let's at least make it the best possible movie that it can be . . . and we got the worst possible press of any film since *Waterworld*.

TOM POLLOCK: *Waterworld* didn't cost $100 million, which is what it was supposed to cost. Had it cost $100 million, the studio would have made $100 million on the movie. As it is, it cost $170 million. It went $70 million over its budget, 70 percent more. The studio ended up breaking even on the movie, which doesn't say much for that because, in fact, it worked all over the world. Now, whether it was good or not, that's something else. *Waterworld* was a movie whose concept was filmed, as opposed to a screenplay. There was no screenplay. As a matter of fact, there were two screenplays, both were filmed on the set: the director's and the producer-star's screenplay. It's a very long story that I won't go into.

JON LANDAU: Movies make release dates. Release dates don't make movies.

JAMES CAMERON: Nobody's tried to release a mainstream picture over three hours in a long time since *Dances with Wolves*. But that's what we did. And so for a while, you know, I was kind of the villain on that. But [delaying the movie] turned out to be strategically a brilliant move that I could take credit for after the fact, except that it was mostly luck. But the other thing is: always take credit for things, whether they're lucky or not. That's fundamental.

JON LANDAU: Someone once said to me, "Nobody remembers a bad movie that came in under budget."

ARNOLD KOPELSON: But you're talking budgets of 50, 60, 70, or $100 million, so it's not only return cash flow, it's the interest on that money, which mounts up. And more importantly, it's earnings per share for the public companies. They want to show their stockholders that they're making a lot of money. And it's also capturing the market. They want to be number one in the marketplace. So you have all these considerations working against your making the best possible film. So you do work seven days a week, and it never ends, and you try to do the best job you can. And there's always that lingering doubt: Could I have made it a little better? . . .

Sometimes you're having two and three previews within a week and a half, and they're recutting all night long to make the changes.

SYDNEY POLLACK: Often you realize that a single close-up means you can do away with a whole page of dialogue.

JOEL COX: Now that we have the Avid [editing software], we just save *everything*.

DEDE ALLEN: The question is: Do you have time to think?

ANNE V. COATES: One of the other dangers of cutting digitally is the loss of what we call "thinking time." An editor needs time to think. Certain things strike you only after a period of time. There is often no way you can think of certain things under pressure. An editor often needs that space. Of course, now with things digital, the studios think you can do it all very quickly. I have never learned to be absolutely magical with my fingers, because I want to have the time to think that I used to have when I was hanging up film and rewinding on a flatbed editing machine.

DEDE ALLEN: Do you have time to sit back when something is wrong?

MICHAEL MANN: I mean, there are some situations where studios, because of the cost of money, shorten their postproduction. You got twelve reels, you got twelve editors, get the movie done in two weeks. It's just—

BARRIE OSBORNE: Most of my information is secondhand, but I'll tell you what I know. A long time ago, Saul Zaentz thought that he'd liked to option the books, and he did, from Tolkien. And then along the way, he agreed to allow Ralph Bakshi to make the animated *Hobbit*. Then further along, more recent history, Peter Jackson was going to do *King Kong* at Universal. Universal had just gone through a battle with Fox between *Dante's Peak* and *Volcano*, and they felt that they had made a tremendous mistake trying to beat the other studio. Both studios wasted a lot of money trying to be the first volcano picture into the theater. And they felt their pictures suffered and they had wasted more money on it than they otherwise would have liked to, just trying to get out first. So they had that in mind when they were going to make *King Kong*, they realized that Disney was making *Mighty Joe Young* and Sony was about to make *Godzilla* with Jan de Bont. And so they called Peter and said, "We're not going to do this. We just went through this race. We're not going to be the big monster picture in the theater."

And so they put *King Kong* on hold. Peter had done *Heavenly Creatures* with Miramax, and he had a first-look deal with Miramax, so as soon as it was in the trades that *King Kong* was on hold, Harvey [Weinstein] called Peter and said, "What do you want to do, Peter?" and Peter said, "I want to do *Lord of the Rings*." Now, Harvey had just bailed out Saul Zaentz on *The English Patient* and made it possible for Saul, whose financing was falling apart, to do *The English Patient*. So in a way, maybe Saul owed him a favor. And so when Harvey called Saul and said, "I'd like to do *Lord of the Rings*," he got the go-ahead. And that's kind of what I know.

MARK CANTON: A perfect example, again, of all the geniuses that run Hollywood: Peter Jackson makes *Lord of the Rings*. Nobody wanted to make a movie with Peter Jackson.

BARRIE OSBORNE: Miramax had originally said to Peter, "We'll make two movies, you should write the trilogy in two films," and he and Fran [Walsh] sat down and did that, and then Miramax, as it got closer to their start date, Miramax said, "Well, we've changed our mind, we'll only make one movie. And we want you to tell a trilogy in one film." And Peter said,

"That's impossible. I can't do that." And they said, "Well, we'll find some-one that can." And so that was the end of the production for Peter, except his agent, Stan Kamen, worked out a deal with Harvey that allowed Peter a month to try to set the film up elsewhere.

MARK CANTON: He had twenty days to go and set it up.

BARRIE OSBORNE: And he went in to New Line, and Bob Shaye said, "What? You only want to make two films here? What's wrong with you? You should make *three*."

MARK CANTON: And then everybody said, "Well, that's going to be the end of New Line."

BARRIE OSBORNE: And then when I sat down and started to plot out how to make three films, the production was easy enough—overwhelming, but easy enough to figure out. It's just like making one huge movie, fif-teen months of production, 274 shooting days, with sometimes as many as three main shooting units and two main second units, a scenic unit, an aerial unit, a battle unit, a blue screen unit, four miniature units. And interestingly enough, each movie had more [visual effects shots] than the last movie. I think we started out with four or five hundred in *Fellowship*, which was a much easier story, and something like eight or nine hundred in *Two Tow-ers* and fourteen or fifteen [hundred] in *Return of the King*.

PETER BOGDANOVICH: Today special effects are getting so good that who knows what's real?

BARRIE OSBORNE: The editor on *Return of the King* worked five years on the cut. So he had a lot of time to look at a lot of different versions of the film. But we, particularly Peter, had the benefit of looking at the film. We would have a fine cut of the movie each year in September of the prior year before release, and then that fine cut would sit on the shelf as a preview cut, really, that would sit on the shelf. Peter could look at the film with fresh eyes in January and come up with a plan to address issues in the film.

GORDON STULBERG: If you do the sequel at the right price, you know, it's money in the bank.

KATHLEEN KENNEDY: I find that the most difficult thing in this town is how everybody wants to do what somebody else already did.

TOM POLLOCK: I mean, there's an old sort of line that what sells in Hollywood is the same as everything else, only different, and I'm not sure what that means except they want original material that's not too original.

BARRY LEVINSON: I kind of look at modern movies in a sense the same way like as if you're going down the highway and you get hungry and you want to eat. You're going down the highway. "What is that, Dolores?" "I don't know. I don't know. I never heard of it. I don't know." You see another place, a little Chinese. "Should we head for Chinese?" "I don't know. I'm not sure." And then you see McDonald's. "Oh, the hell with it, let's go to McDonald's."

JAMES CAMERON: *Terminator 2* came together very, very quickly because, in a sense, it had a preapproved story line because Arnold already knew the idea, and [producer] Mario [Kassar] said, "You and Arnold already have something worked out, *right*?" and I said, "Yeah," and I asked him if he wanted to know what it was, and he said, "No, no, as long as you're happy with it." Okay. Eighty-million-dollar movie, and he didn't even want to know what it was about.

STEVEN SPIELBERG: I think sequels, in a way, can be very dangerous because they compromise your status or your self-esteem as an artist.

TOM POLLOCK: Everybody's scared to lose their jobs.

ISMAIL MERCHANT: Today there is this executive, tomorrow that executive . . . There is no personal commitment.

MICHAEL OVITZ: We used to get the best of the best in Hollywood. In the fall we had, as I used to term it, the fall crop. You get ten thousand wannabes coming to the city, and they take jobs as waiters and seamstresses and coffee runners on sets—anything they can get to get into the business. I could tell by '94 or '95 that the people coming to our mail room were less qualified as people. I could see it. They didn't know the history. They weren't interested in old movies.

JJ ABRAMS: I love *Star Wars*. I mean, you know, it wasn't, like, "Okay, I want to make a *Star Wars* movie." But in fact, I actually was more intimidated and nervous about it. Because *Star Wars*, especially the last three films, they've done everything: they've done every alien, every weather system, every planet design, every ship, every weapon, anything that can be done, they've done. So you look at a guy doing a space movie, like, how do you do an alien that wasn't in Scene *X* of that movie?

JOEL SILVER: We opened *The Matrix Reloaded* in almost twenty thousand screens at the exact instant all over the world. I think only *The Matrix* can do that. I don't know if you can do that with *The Cat in the Hat* or you can do that with, you know, maybe *Lord of the Rings*, but I mean, you need the right movie to have that kind of reach. I mean, this movie was the largest-grossing in the history of Russia, I mean, it opened in China, it sold every theater in India.

GEORGE CLOONEY: We're doing the Berlin Film Festival, and they put us in a room, and, you know, you sit at a table of thirty people, you do six sessions of this, and of the thirty people, three people from Japan are like, "Matt Damon doesn't have a mustache, does he?" Or "No, no, no mustache," and you go with it, you're selling to each one of these people. You're selling like a door-to-door salesman.

STACEY SNIDER: You know, at the big studio, there is room for distinct voices, iconoclastic directors, and you see that in the release schedule, right now, directors like Alexander Payne and Spike Jones and David Russell. I mean, there are definite *auteur* pieces that get funded by the studios, but, you know, the studio is, by and large, their apparatus, their infrastructure, is geared toward wide release. That's what they know how to do. That's what we excel at: 1,500 to 3,000 to 3,000-plus wide releases with marketing support behind it. It doesn't mean that they shouldn't strive for quality, it doesn't mean that they shouldn't strive for good story-telling, good casting, good production value, good directing, but it's going to be an entertainment aimed at a wider audience.

KENNETH TURAN: Jim Cameron made an obvious point that I think is a good one. He says the only constant worldwide is actually good guys and bad guys. Ideas of beauty vary from culture to culture, ideas of comedy vary from culture to culture. The essence of a violent film can sell everywhere around the world. And I think the more that Hollywood is dependent on worldwide revenue for its money, the more that's going to predominate.

TOM HANKS: By and large, most studio comedies now are about college kids trying to get laid.

STACEY SNIDER: We had, you know, *American Pie, Bring It On, Fast & Furious* . . .

JON FAVREAU: There's only two types of movies that are going to be making money, I think, in this era of piracy. One is a big tentpole event film, where you have to go to the theater, like an *Avatar*, and the other is a semi-low-budget-ish comedy that can break $100 million. But those are really the only two genres that people are going to want to pour money into right now. Everything else is slowly disappearing and migrating to the internet, migrating to television.

GORDON STULBERG: The disaster film gives you the opportunity to put up on the screen a combination of absorbing elements that the medium at home cannot touch.

MARK CANTON: It used to be, the sequels will do half or three-quarters of the original. Now they can far exceed the original because that's the impact of DVD and home video.

ANNE V. COATES: Now that we're digital, you can do all sorts of different versions, but I don't.

MICHAEL MANN: Shooting in digital on *Collateral* affected how I worked with the actors a lot. In the sense that it wasn't four-hundred-foot loads or thousand-foot magazines, it was, you know, an hour tape. Both Tom [Cruise] and Jamie [Foxx] are very disciplined, very well prepared actors, so we would roll through a four- or five-page scene, and maybe the first part was really good, and I wouldn't cut at the end of the scene, I would say, "Roll me back to—" and I'd give them a starting point about a third of the way into the scene. And we would just keep going. So our takes were eighteen-minute, twenty-minute takes. And I use multiple cameras so that I'm getting it all. If there's a moment where it all just kind of catches fire, and it's wonderful, I have all the coverage. So in that sense, it became a very interesting style to be able to do a whole scene and then not stop and do a pickup but just within the context of the same take, just roll right back into it. And so you got into kind of a rhythm for the actors and myself, a rhythm of performance that was really good. It was good for these two actors. As I'm saying it, I don't know that, for example, it would be right for Russell Crowe. He approached things a little bit differently.

WARREN BEATTY: Now I feel that there's a more casual approach to what acting is all about. I think that has to do with the technology that you can shoot all of this tape, you can go on and on with digital stuff. And you don't have to get it right away.

DUSTIN HOFFMAN: It's a shame that maybe in the twenty-first century, in your century with digital and everything, that you will find more and more a way to get away from having to get it right the first time.

PAUL FEIG: But anybody who wants to be a cinematographer here knows, you know, cross shooting is, like, the thing you hate to do. And every cinematographer just hates it, but I can't do this kind of comedy without cross shooting. Amazing improv happens. And I got one side of it, and trying to re-create it, it's never the same. It's like capturing lightning in a bottle.

JON FAVREAU: I like improv. And I work with people who know how to improvise. I don't hire people who just make shit up, I hire people who know where the scene has the beginning, the middle, and the end. They have to do certain things. It's not a comedian trying to score.

PAUL FEIG: We always had a couple of writers with us on *Bridesmaids* who would, you know, kind of be doing stuff. Annie Mumalo was always on set. And so literally, it's kind of either be, like, "Let's give me ten versions of this joke" or "this ending," because, you know, we want to top this or this one's not working, or they're getting ideas, too.

OREN PELI: After we had the cut of *Paranormal Activity*, we would be like, "It would be really nice if we had an extra scene," and I would call him up and say, "Hey, what are you doing this weekend? Come over, we'll shoot something."

STEVEN SPIELBERG: I think it's dangerous, as a matter of fact, letting an actor run off with an idea.

MICHAEL CAINE: It's very well to improvise when someone says, "You come into a restaurant and everyone says, 'Good evening, Charlie,' and you say, 'Hello, Harry,'" and that sort of thing. But to actually improvise emotions means that you're improvising your own emotions, don't you think? It's the supreme example of playing yourself, which, if you happen to do, you can get very bad reviews for.

STEVEN SPIELBERG: That's where you have six-hour first cuts.

PAUL FEIG: YouTube has changed everything, because you see everybody, the funniest stuff you're seeing out there is real stuff that's happening that's caught on tape, or it's people just thinking they're funny on tape.

JON FAVREAU: Back then [in the midnineties], you could actually have a small movie, get it picked up, and then build an audience. Now the center of gravity is moved to the internet—not press outlets—and blogs and

Comic-Con and Twitter, and the power isn't necessarily just in the hands of the critics or just in the hands of the distributors anymore. If you've got a turkey, the word gets out, and you see sharper declines and inclines [in box office]. There's immediate biofeedback from the audience.

JEFFREY KATZENBERG: So if you're between twenty-five and thirty-five years old today, between seven in the morning and seven at night, those twelve hours, you're spending over five hours [on your smartphone], you're communicating, collaborating, you're on social media, you are playing casual games, and right now today you're watching seventy minutes of YouTube, Facebook, Instagram, Snapchat—

PAUL FEIG: The internet is such a game changer for everything. First of all for filmmakers, because you have instant distribution. When has that ever existed? Now that you can do a $2 movie and somebody in an agency can see it or a studio, and suddenly they call you in for a meeting. So there's no excuse not to be doing stuff.

JASON BLUM: Steven [Schneider] is the one who identified *Paranormal Activity*. The movie was sent to him by CAA. And he saw it, and he came into my office like, "You got to see, this movie is the coolest movie ever."

OREN PELI: Someone said something along the lines of like, "Sound is seventy percent of what you see." And I think this movie is even more because you don't really see almost anything, but the sound kind of lets you know what's going on and builds up your anxiety.

JASON BLUM: Everyone saw it, and everyone passed, multiple, multiple, every distributor passed multiple, multiple times. And we finally got a decision maker in a room with an audience to see the movie. And because the movie was around on DVD, everyone had seen it on DVD. And that's what they had passed on.

OREN PELI: There were no rehearsals for *Paranormal Activity*, but I kind of made sure that they hung out together and spend some time so they become familiar with it, though in retrospect, I don't know how necessary it was from the very first callback.

LAWRENCE GORDON: The fact that you go out and make [*The Blair Witch Project* or *Paranormal Activity*] for $30,000 and be making number five or whatever it is, to me that's just startling. You should be so encouraged by that. That there is now a possibility. It's been done. It's been *done*. You can go out and make *Paranormal Activity* for whatever, I think I read $30,000, and it goes hundreds of millions of dollars. The fact that you can do that . . . you couldn't do that before.

SEAN BAKER: So I thought, Okay, cool. All right, we might not be the first iPhone movie, but we'll be the first iPhone movie shot in 'Scope. And then it happened to be that there was an app called FiLMiC Pro that sort of locks all the settings and allows a higher compression, a higher-quality compression rate. So it actually messes with the way the phone captures video, and so you get a higher-quality output. And those two tools together really kind of convinced me that it could be done . . . if you had seen us from across the street on Santa Monica, the only giveaway that we were a professional shoot was the sound.

AMY HECKERLING: Forget the big screen. That's dinosaur shit now.

PAUL FEIG: Most people work in a job, they come home, and they go, "I want to watch a sitcom, I want to just laugh." And so I kind of embrace that.

WILLIAM FRIEDKIN: All this stuff is sitcom. It's all comes out of sitcom. And the guys that are making the calls, they made sitcom. Because the way you make television shows, they have testing. People sit, they test, if a character comes on the screen, people push a button, they don't like this character, *boom*, they write him out—or her, you know—and the whole thing is homogenized. And that's the way they want the movies today.

JACK NICHOLSON: Anybody who had a pancake at the International House of Pancakes on Sunset when it first opened and then goes there today understands why conglomeration deteriorates the quality of the product.

DAVID PUTTNAM: It upsets me that our street-corner restaurants have become McDonald's. Not because I've got any objection to McDonald's but because there's a kind of hegemony going on which is not political hegemony, it's a kind of cultural hegemony.

WILLIAM FRIEDKIN: People are going to films today not to be turned on by ideas. They're going to films because they want to turn off.

MIKE NICHOLS: Nowadays, the only plot they want is *Cinderella* or *Rocky*.

KENNETH TURAN: A movie that cost $60 million can't be that sophisticated.

HAL ASHBY: Who in the hell wants to aim a film down the middle? Is that what the fuck they make a film for? For the middle of the road? I mean, what the hell is that? You don't make your films for that. You know, you make your films for a reason.

DAVID NEWMAN: It used to be that the business and the movies were one and the same. When you read those wonderful anecdotal film books about Hollywood in the forties, you think, well, it was all part and parcel . . . the craft and the art and the people. It isn't the same now. It's not pleasant.

LUCY FISHER: The higher up I got, the further away I got from actually making movies. And the more I got to see making movies was only, you know, "Get the budget," "Get the deal." I was constantly in a meeting that I didn't want to be in. I was constantly in a room I didn't want to be in with people saying no all the time, and with all these business guys saying why they didn't want to make a movie instead of being in the room with the creative, excellent talent saying why they *did* want to make a movie. So that's why I stopped, for just my own personal fulfillment.

ROB REINER: But my philosophy has always been, there are four kinds of pictures: there are good movies that make a lot of money. There are good movies that make no money. There are shitty movies that make a lot of money. And there are shitty movies that make no money. So my feeling is, make only good movies or what you think are good movies. Some will make money, some won't make money, and you'll wind up doing okay because the worst thing you can do is make something you don't think is too good and then it doesn't make money. You feel like an idiot. You feel like a real idiot.

TOM POLLOCK: There's no reason for marketing costs to go down. I see hundreds and hundreds of millions of dollars of losses in the moviemaking business leading to, probably, further collapse, further consolidation. And probably at the end of the day, you'll have four big companies running everything, all vertically integrated from publishing the book to owning the server on the internet whereby you get video on demand.

I don't mean to sound Marxist here. But it won't be until the system collapses that anything different can come out of it. But it will, it will collapse. And better, more and better, movies will come out of it. In the meantime, this has happened, by the way, in Hollywood every, oh gosh, every twenty-five years or so. So it's not like this hasn't happened before. It happened in the seventies. And it happened in the fifties.

MARK CANTON: The whole globalization of the industry has made it colder. And the simple fact is, the movie business is no longer a business that you can handle on a stand-alone basis. In 1980, when I joined Warner Bros., we were like a mom-and-pop shop compared to what Warners is today.

SAM ARKOFF: There is no way of pleasing 200-plus million people.

JON FAVREAU: I got bad news for you: it's not Rotten Tomatoes, man, it's how much money your movie makes. Look at who's working! Look who's at the top of the list! But am I in a position because of *Iron Man 2*?

Am I chasing something? Am I chasing a false idol? This might be the last chance ever to make a small movie on *film*. I can make an awards movie on film, you know, or make my passion project where they let me do that. So I make something else where things blow up.

HARLAN ELLISON: Anyway, about selling out—

WARREN BEATTY: In so many cases, the person who is in show business makes the public the parent. And so to win the public, to lose the public, to flirt with the public, to hate the public, to love the public becomes a never-ending and exhausting and ultimately debilitating task. And in these days, where the fame is so quickly gained and so quickly lost—

HARLAN ELLISON: You can go through your whole life and think you are a good person and a moral person and an ethical person and sell out a million times and never even recognize it, because there is always a way to rationalize it.

If at some time in your life you are lucky enough to be put against the wall in that corner where you cannot escape, where you must make the decisions, where you must risk something utterly, utterly true and irreplaceable to you, your life, love, *real* love, something valuable, every cent you ever had, your reputation, something, whatever it is that makes you function, whatever it is that is absolutely valuable to you, and you are willing to say, "Fuck it. I must do this even if I lose that," then you find that you have done something courageous, and the next time you have to do it, it's easier. And the next time easier and the next time easier, and pretty soon you do it automatically.

If you are willing to go for broke and shoot it all and risk it all, you will find that when you come out of it, you'll be a vastly different person and no one can kill you.

PAUL SCHRADER: Am I being honest and true to myself?

WILLIAM FRIEDKIN: I came into the business believing that it was a medium of expression, that it was an art form. I no longer believe that. I no longer believe it. The evidence of my experience, in my eyes, tells me that that's not true. It's a money thing. It's about pumping out dollars.

DAVID PUTTNAM: Corporations don't exist without people. Somehow they've managed to perpetrate a terrific confidence trick, where you have been convinced that you need them. In the end they need you. And the more gifted among you, they need desperately.

JORDAN PEELE: I couldn't wrap my head around how a producer would give me money for a film where the Black man kills a White family at the end and we're cheering for him. I didn't give the industry the credit.

[Working with Blumhouse Productions] was perfect for this process, because [Jason Blum] works with these microbudgets, so, you know, I got to make my movie. He didn't come in and meddle. I had nobody telling me anything had to happen. I got some great notes from his team. I got some notes that weren't great, and I got to not use them.

MICHAEL OVITZ: I sat on the phone this morning with two young development executives, and they were very sweet, but they couldn't tell you who Frank Capra was. It's a whole different world. Try talking to Steven Spielberg or Stanley Kubrick without any film knowledge. You can kiss your ass goodbye. And they're so poorly trained now. Even at my old company.

Two thousand five, I got out. You could tell it was over. You could just tell it was over. Attendance was down. People were less interested in film. The internet was kicking in big time. People were distracted with their phones. You could just feel it. You could smell it. There was no interest in movie stars. It wasn't the same business. It just wasn't. People started going up to the internet, and it started to suck the talent out of the system. People used to go to two places to make money: Hollywood and Wall Street. And all of a sudden Hollywood started to take a back seat to everything. Look around the business right now. Today, who are the big personalities? Where's Barry Diller? Where's Terry Semel? Where is Freddie Fields? Where's Sue Mengers? Where the hell are these people? Name me a studio head right now who's an old-time Harry Cohn. Gimme

Harry Cohn. Gimme Jack Warner, Louis B. Mayer. There's nobody. These are *talent* guys. Harry Cohn really gave a shit. When I started in the agency business, I could go see John Calley, and he'd say, "Let's do a deal." *Deal.* Frank Wells. He'd make the deal. He could see the movie right there, just like Thalberg. These guys just don't exist anymore.

What happened? Tech. Guys up north start creating Netflix. So the movie business did what they always do. They see tech blow up, and they ignore it. When the dot-com bubble burst, the entertainment business did not take advantage of the moment to go in and fix what was digitally wrong with the business. And once you saw what was going on with iPods and mobile phones, you couldn't help but say to yourself, "This is the future."

Small movies have always been an alternative to the big system, but then when streaming started, there was absolutely no differentiation. Next thing you know, there is no movie business in Hollywood.

ALEXANDER PAYNE: I was doing a Q&A in London for something called the Script Factory a week ago, in fact, and they were asking me about the hegemony of American films, you know, economically and culturally around the world, and how you can be in any country in the world and thirteen out of fifteen screens are showing shit American movies, and how did I feel about that? I said, "Yeah, it's awful." And I hate the way, well, I'll name names, people like Jack Valenti would go around trying to crush national cinemas in favor of just this capitalist machine that drives our cinema. But what I said was, "You have to understand that in the United States, we suffer from the same problem. We ourselves also do not have a national cinema about ourselves, where we can see American experience realistically reflected on-screen."

DAVID PUTTNAM: We inhabit a culture which has been carried away by the fun and the spectacular dispersal of unreality. It's a culture that's been encouraged to separate such things from the damage that goes with them. As I see it, there's an unfortunate complicity here, a complicity between the financier, the filmmaker, and the audience. All of us are caught up in a cycle which none of us entirely controls. And yet its effect, its tragic effect, is to reduce all of us, because it undermines the value of the medium, which unquestionably, unquestionably possesses the power to affirm and to reaffirm our common humanity.

MICHAEL OVITZ: We've trained the audience to consume differently. This is our own fault.

GEORGE LUCAS: It doesn't matter what medium you're working in. The cinematic experience is the same.

VITTORIO STORARO: In a sense there is always a need for us to get in a large amniotic sac, so to speak, a large theater, to see big romance—stories that are connected with space cannot be contained on a small screen. They need to be seen by a large audience.

SHIRLEY CLARKE: Films are meant to be seen by an audience in a darkened room on a large screen. They are carefully planned to be seen that way.

RICHARD GLADSTEIN: And do you do research screenings?

PAUL THOMAS ANDERSON: No.

BRAIN GRAZER: If it was science, then every movie would be great.

MICHAEL OVITZ: Look at these later movies that won Best Picture— *Green Book, Parasite, Moonlight, Spotlight, Birdman, 12 Years a Slave, The Artist, Nomadland*—and people ask, "Why is the movie business in trouble?" No one saw any of these movies. Think about *Titanic, Forrest Gump, Gladiator*—people went to see them! But *The Artist*? It's a beautiful little film, it's not Best Picture! Best Picture is a movie people go to see and love, as well as being extraordinarily well-crafted.

JJ ABRAMS: You know, the great thing about the business is that there are no rules. There are fewer rules now than ever. I mean, I would have said there were no rules, you know, ten, fifteen years ago, but you know, whatever, you know, what vague poser rules there were have since disappeared. So now there's like nothing.

HARRY UFLAND: Nobody can come and say, "This is the way to do it," because it changes every minute, every day. You don't know. There are a lot of ways to do it. There's no one way to do it

JOHN SINGLETON: The coverage from Orion says I have no talent. It says that the dialogue was bland, it just really degrades the whole script. And from Columbia the coverage says, "We're in the hands of a good director, this could be a very great film."

LAWRENCE GORDON: People are frightened. If you run a studio, you got to understand something: You sit behind a big desk and an office is big, and you got people, a thousand people, working for you. And you sit there and somebody comes in, tries to sell you a movie, and you have to make a decision: Are we going to make that movie or not? It's almost like President Obama sitting there with a red button. Because when you press that button, you may blow something up, and it may be you. You may blow up your ass.

ROBERT ZEMECKIS: The movies that I made that failed at the box office, I didn't do anything from where I stood as a filmmaker different than I did for the ones that were very successful. So my explanation for it all is, to quote, you know, William Goldman, which is "Nobody knows anything."

MICHAEL OVITZ: It's Bill Goldman's line.

KATHLEEN KENNEDY: I'm not the first one to say this, I think Bill Goldman said this, but it's true, absolutely true. No one knows.

LAURA ZISKIN: It's like roulette or something.

GEORGE LUCAS: You're all professional gamblers. That's what you do for a living.

DAVID BROWN: All generalities are false.

DANIEL MELNICK: There are no rules.

MIKE MEDAVOY: There are no rules. We don't have any rules.

PETER GUBER: There are no rules in this business, but you break them at your peril.

SIDNEY SHELDON: The one thing I have learned, being an expert in this business, is that the experts don't know anything. Nothing. And if you rely on the experts, you are in big trouble.

JOHN LANDIS: Who the hell knows? Certainly not me.

DON SIMPSON: We have no idea.

SAUL ZAENTZ: I don't know what they want to see.

JOEL SILVER: You never know what's going to work.

LAURA ZISKIN: I don't know any better than anybody else.

MIKE MEDAVOY: I'm going to beat this out of you guys this afternoon. There are no rules.

CURTIS HARRINGTON: There are three cardinal rules of filmmaking, according to Curtis Harrington. I want you all to remember these. One is: Never make a film with animals. Number two is: Never make a film with children. And number three is: Never make a film with Shelley Winters.

DAVID PICKER: There is no correlation to whatever reality is because there is no reality in our business. I mean, it is a fantasy business, and it's what people *think* is good, because nobody knows. I get asked all the time, "What kind of movies do you want to make?" Or "What kind of movies do people want to see?" Nobody knows the answer to that. Do you know what you want to see next year? That's when the films I'm developing will be made, and then they'll be released nine months after that. All you can say is "I'd like to see something good" or "I want to see something I want to see." I don't know what I want to see. You don't know what you want to see.

WARREN BEATTY: Nobody knows. As Bill Goldman says—

IRWIN WINKLER: Nobody really does know anything. It's just this wild guessing game.

KATHLEEN KENNEDY: You never know. So it's the luck of the draw: you try to tell a good story, you try to make it the best way you can, and then there's a big unknown. Believe me, nobody knows. That's why, when you go into this business, don't be afraid of the mystique, 'cause there's a lot of mystique and there's a lot of people who spend a lot of time trying to convince you they know. Nobody knows.

ERIC PLESKOW: I tell you this: anybody who tells you that they can, today, put this business onto computers and run it that way and modifications of it, whether it's the research of material or the marketing of the film, they, in my view, are absolutely wrong, and I will fight them to the death, actually, to their own death, I guess. It's an instinctive business: you go by your own instincts and by your own tastes.

ERIC WEISSMANN: *Blazing Saddles*, a picture where an Indian tells Jewish jokes. Who could ever think that that's going to be a success in Kansas City? I must tell you, I was one of the first thirty people who saw that picture. I saw it with Mel Brooks, and Mel Brooks was sick because no one in the audience laughed.

LAWRENCE GORDON: And I remember once when I had my financing company come in, and my chief financial officer said, "Let me run some numbers." He came back, and he said, "The worst that can happen is that we would make four million dollars, that's the worst that can happen." So I said, "Great, let's make it." We lost $90 million.

SAM ARKOFF: You just have to go by your gut feel. This is a business, fundamentally, where you fly by the seat of your pants, feeling your gut.

FRANK YABLANS: There are no mavens. We're all pretty much the same, struggling, scared as hell, mortgaged out!

ERIC WEISSMANN: It's a strange thing, you know, our business has a very bad reputation in a way, and on the other hand it's a very nice one to work in.

FAY KANIN: We still have a puritan streak in our country which says that anything that's entertaining has got to be the work of the Devil.

NED TANEN: This is Sodom and Gomorrah, folks. You know, there are things one loves and things one hates. You love your mother and apple pie, and you hate the movie business, because it's dirty and we know about all those people in Hollywood.

LAWRENCE WEINGARTEN: I'll say 80 percent of the critics are the people who came to Hollywood and couldn't make it.

DAVID PUTTNAM: They refer to Hollywood as "Tinseltown," as if somehow it didn't really matter.

SAM MARX: I say this about people who talk like this: There were trains leaving every day. There were boats leaving. They could have taken roller skates or a bicycle. They could have walked. Nobody was holding them here. I suppose you know that S. N. Behrman made that kind of a crack where he talked about the slavery and all of that. He said, "What do you get for it? Just a lousy fortune."

PETER BOGDANOVICH: Hollywood is a little town that has two studios, and there's another studio in Burbank, there's another studio in Culver

City. They've made some very, very bad movies, and they've also made some very, very good movies, and if you make a list of all the very good movies they made and all the very good movies made in Europe, you will find the very good movies made in Hollywood or in America, there are more of them. "I don't like Hollywood"—it's such a cliché. Why don't you say "Burbank"?

DAVID ANSEN: Sometimes I get very fed up with the sort of provincial attitude that New York has about Hollywood and LA. The media's cynicism about Hollywood is as glib and as cynical as they're accusing Hollywood of being often.

BRONISLAU KAPER: Look, you're a famous New York reporter. You don't come to Hollywood to praise. It doesn't make any sense. You come from New York to Hollywood to criticize Hollywood. Wherever you come from to Hollywood, you have to criticize Hollywood, because that's the standard thing to do, the big cliché.

JULIA PHILLIPS: You know, there's a battleground atmosphere in New York that makes you feel that it's reality.

PENNY MARSHALL: I was cold in New York.

MARIO PUZO: And the sun is shining out here. Why would I have contempt?

WARREN BEATTY: When I was a kid in Virginia, they'd say, "Well, those movie stars, they're not really good looking. They make 'em good looking for the movies." And I thought, Oh, well, that makes sense. And so when I came to Hollywood, I couldn't believe how good looking the people were.

DAVID PUTTNAM: One of the most exciting moments of my life was arriving by air in 1963 for the first time in America. I actually felt I was coming home, to the font of all my hopes and aspirations. My dreams had been shaped here in Los Angeles, five and a half thousand miles from my childhood home.

HARLAN ELLISON: Yes, there's no denying that if you happen to be somebody's brother-in-law, you can probably get financed a hell of a lot sooner.

MICHAEL PHILLIPS: The most important thing is to rub elbows with film-makers.

JAMES CAMERON: Just get out there and shoot some film, really.

BOB RAFELSON: I know it sounds a little facetious, but steal the money, make the film, and then pay them back or explain it later.

MICHAEL OVITZ: You can put an independent movie together if you wanted to. You can get a bunch of friends together and get money to finance a movie. You could probably make it for three to five million dollars. There are multiple ways to get the money. You might even be able to use crypto.

AL RUDDY: Anyone can do it.

HARLAN ELLISON: If you've got talent, you don't have to worry about the rest. They will find you.

MEL BROOKS: I started life as a drummer. I'm sorry I stopped, because it was the best and the loudest way of calling attention to myself.

BEN BENJAMIN: Coming from a small mining town and not ever having had the slightest training or experience in showbiz, as we say, I found, early on when I went in the business, it's being a salesman, really. It's selling. And I sold men's clothes, and I sold other things. So I felt that I was a good salesman.

JOSEPH E. LEVINE: I had everything stacked against me. If you want me to tell you how poor I was, you'll cry. I don't want to make you cry.

GREGORY PECK: It's true that I slept in Central Park, but those were, relatively speaking, crime-free days.

SIDNEY POITIER: I was equipped to do nothing but work with my hands.

SHERRY LANSING: I was a schoolteacher.

PENNY MARSHALL: Veterinarian. I wanted to be. I wanted to just get married and have twenty-two children. I wanted to be a cowgirl. I never wanted to do this.

SAM FULLER: Well, I was a reporter for about eight, nine years. I was only in the infantry for three.

KATHARINE HEPBURN: Having a college education is totally worthless in our business.

MARK CANTON: You need a haircut? Jon Peters still carries his scissors around with him.

JIM HENSON: I started in this business knowing absolutely nothing about puppetry. I actually went to a library and got a book on puppetry to figure out how to build puppets.

DAVID LEAN: I said, "I'll do anything, carry tea, anything."

BRIAN GRAZER: I got a job as a law clerk.

NED TANEN: I used to sell used cars.

SHERRY LANSING: I was teaching math and English in Los Angeles. And I taught math for three and a half years. And I enjoyed it very much. At the time I was married and then going through a divorce. And when I realized I was getting divorced, I thought that I really wanted to be with adults rather than with high school students. And I didn't know what I wanted to do. And I knew that I had to earn money. And I wasn't quite sure how to do it. And I wanted a lot of free time. So, now, that wasn't what I decided to do. No, I was a photographic model when I was in college. I went back to doing that. And then was cast in commercials. And then in films. I was a terrible actress. I can honestly tell you all this. I have great respect for all of you, because I found it so difficult and so painful to do. When I walked onto my first set, I must say that I looked around that set and got fascinated by what everybody else was doing, and that led me into the production area two years later. And I started out as a reader. I read scripts, looked for good writing, and looked for people to develop ideas with. And then worked up within the studio system.

AL RUDDY: It's how much you work. There's no one in this room who can't do it if you want it.

GEORGE LUCAS: Any good director—Steve Spielberg, anybody you're gonna find—bottom line is, they love movies. Is Steven a human? Course he is. You know, he's got seven kids, he's got a life, but at the same time, there isn't a second in the day—you know the way it works? They say about men there isn't a second in the day that goes by that they don't think about sex. Well, a filmmaker, there isn't a second of the day that goes by you don't think about film. You know, that's all you think about. I mean, you're with your kids, you're doing your stuff, and you're living your life, and, you know, you're having sex, but you're basically thinking about film. And that's your life. And if that's you, then you're going to make it.

DAVID CHASMAN: Movies have shaped us. They have made us what we are as a society. Movies have made us what we are as individuals. I don't know if this is—no, this is not a digression—in the Gordon Liddy book, that some of you may have read—much was made of his holding his hand over a flame, and when somebody said, "What's the trick?" he said, "The trick is in not minding." That anecdote was used in *All the President's Men*, if any of you saw that. You will find that anecdote—word for word—in the first five minutes of *Lawrence of Arabia*. Peter O'Toole burns a match down to his fingers. The sergeant tries it and says, "Ouch. What's the trick? It hurts." And O'Toole says, "The trick is in not minding if it hurts." A movie shaped Gordon Liddy's idea of heroic behavior. All of our notions of manly behavior, of womanly behavior, of social behavior, of societal interdependence or societal antipathy derive, for good or ill, from movies, which is why I think they are important.

It is Clark Gable taking off his shirt, being seen not to be wearing an undershirt, and undershirt sales immediately plummeting. And it's more than that. It is Vivien Leigh wearing a snood, a Civil War hairnet, in a film called *Gone with the Wind* and snoods dominating feminine hairstyles for the next five years. And it's more than that. It's John Wayne's ability to withstand pain or danger, telling a generation of American males how they are supposed to behave under circumstances of pain or danger.

DAVID PUTTNAM: American cinema formed what might be called my ethical understanding of the world.

WILLIAM FRIEDKIN: Everything, every piece of film I've ever exposed, is both an adventure and an education. And it's the greatest way of life imaginable. And it's such a great medium. You know, there's so much possible in it.

JOSEPH E. LEVINE: Shall we go home? Has anybody else got anything to say?

DAVID PICKER: The movies somehow always survive.

AFTERWORD

Reading and editing more than three thousand transcripts is a daunting task. We studied every Harold Lloyd Seminar, every oral history, every AFI-sponsored conference on film education, and were overwhelmed with the richness of our choices. We also had the opportunity to use Sam Wasson's 2022 interview with Michael Ovitz, as well as Jeanine Basinger's interviews and conversations with individuals such as Frank Capra, Raoul Walsh, Richard Schickel, and others. Our selection process—and the inevitable cuts and eliminations—was very, very difficult. There were so many choices! On the other hand, there were heartbreaking absences: no interview with John Ford or Cary Grant, Ida Lupino or Harry Belafonte, Joan Crawford or Lena Horne, John Calley or Lew Wasserman, just to name a few. In the end, we realized that those and other absentees actually *were* represented, because this book is a long and open conversation among (and about) almost everyone who worked in Hollywood. We drew from all our sources, cleaned up the language where necessary, eliminated conversational digressions, and edited for clarity, structure, and transition. We sought to preserve the original sound and spirit of all voices. Their language and choice of pronouns is theirs. This book is a labor of love, and as we worked, our respect for the working world of Hollywood— those much-maligned individuals who have given us our American movie heritage—grew even larger and deeper.

ACKNOWLEDGMENTS

Bob Gazzale, who said yes and we love him for it.

Thank you to the AFI for giving us full access to their copyrighted material.

Our agent, David Halpern, who took care of us. Our editor, Noah Eaker, who was undaunted by the enormity of the challenge.

Also at HarperCollins: Edie Astley, Katherine Beitner, Milan Bozic, Mary Gaule, and Nancy Singer.

At the Robbins Office: Kathy Robbins, Rick Pappas, and Janet Oshiro.

AFI librarian Emily Wittenberg, who found what we needed. Rob Jahrling, who was an enormous help.

For their counsel, our friends Leonard Maltin, Brandon Millan, Ben Model, and Lou Valentino.

And all those who conducted the interviews used in this book and the interviewees themselves. Without them, this history of the real Hollywood could never exist.

ABOUT THE AUTHORS

JEANINE BASINGER, "one of the most acclaimed film historians of her generation" (*New York Times*), is the author of twelve books on film, an award-winning teacher, a trustee of the American Film Institute and the National Board of Review, and serves as an advisor to Martin Scorsese's the Story of Movies project. A pioneer in the field of university film studies, she is also the founder of Wesleyan University's Cinema Studies Department. She lives in Connecticut and South Dakota.

A former student of Basinger's at Wesleyan, SAM WASSON is "one of the great chroniclers of Hollywood lore" (*New York Times*). He is the author of seven books on film, including the *New York Times* bestsellers *Fifth Avenue, 5 A.M.: Audrey Hepburn, Breakfast at Tiffany's, and the Dawn of the Modern Woman*; *The Big Goodbye*; and *Fosse*. He lives in Los Angeles.